NIJINSKY

AND

The Last Years of NIJINSKY

BY

ROMOLA NIJINSKY

SIMON AND SCHUSTER
New York

PUBLISHED BY SIMON AND SCHUSTER

A DIVISION OF GULF & WESTERN CORPORATION

SIMON & SCHUSTER BUILDING

ROCKEFELLER CENTER

1230 AVENUE OF THE AMERICAS

NEW YORK, NEW YORK 10020

SIMON AND SCHUSTER AND COLOPHON ARE TRADEMARKS OF SIMON & SCHUSTER

MANUFACTURED IN THE UNITED STATES OF AMERICA

1 2 3 4 5 6 7 8 9 10

LIBRARY OF CONGRESS CATALOGING IN PUBLICATION DATA

NIJINSKY, ROMOLA DE PULSZKY.

NIJINSKY AND THE LAST YEARS OF NIJINSKY.

REPRINT OF THE AUTHOR'S 2 WORKS, ORIGINALLY
PUBLISHED IN 1934 AND 1952, RESPECTIVELY, BOTH BY
SIMON AND SCHUSTER, NEW YORK.

INCLUDES INDEXES.

1. NIJINSKY, WASLAW, 1890–1950. 2. BALLET
DANCERS—RUSSIA—BIOGRAPHY. I. NIJINSKY, ROMOLA
DE PULSZKY. THE LAST YEARS OF NIJINSKY. 1980.

II. TITLE.

GV1785.N6N623   792.8'092'4 [B]   80–13520

ISBN 0–671–41123–3

Publisher's Note

In the train of two recent major events, the fabulous sale of Nijinsky's unexpurgated diary at the Sotheby Parke Bernet galleries in London and the release of the movie about Nijinsky, (with the expectation of still another to come) Simon and Schuster is herewith re-issuing, in one volume, the two famous books about the universally acclaimed greatest of all male ballet dancers. Both were written by Romola Nijinsky, his wife, and were best sellers years ago (*Nijinsky* in 1934 and *The Last Years of Nijinsky* in 1952) but have since gone out of print. This new volume contains facsimiles of both of those two original books; hence, each book has a different typeface and contains its own separate index. The index for *Nijinsky* appears on page 435 of that volume and, of course, the index for *The Last Years of Nijinsky* is found at the end of this book on page 447 of that volume.

PORTRAIT OF NIJINSKY BY SARGENT

Nijinsky

BY

ROMOLA NIJINSKY

HIS WIFE

FOREWORD BY PAUL CLAUDEL

NEW YORK
SIMON AND SCHUSTER
MCMXXXIV

Designed by Robert Josephy

With the exception of the name of Diaghileff
all Russian names have been spelled with a
"V" ending rather than with a double "F".

To the Memory of

FREDERICA DEZENTJE
WITHOUT WHOSE AFFECTION AND FRIENDSHIP
THIS BOOK COULD NOT HAVE BEEN WRITTEN

1

ACKNOWLEDGMENTS

I WISH to thank Madame Karsavina, Messieurs Legat, Fokine, Bolm, and Professor Roerich, for much valuable information and kind help. Also Mr. Lincoln Kirstein, the editor of *Hound and Horn*, for his immense labour and patient researches into the history of ballet, and Mr. Roger Dodge for the loan of so many photographs from his collection.

Finally, I would like to thank Mr. Arnold L. Haskell, the well-known English *balletomane* and critic, and Mr. Warren Zambra for their practical help in preparing this book.

ROMOLA NIJINSKY

Contents

CONTENTS

Illustrations

Foreword

RIO DE JANEIRO *is the only big city of my acquaintance that has not succeeded in turning out Nature. You are plunged in the sea, the mountains, the virgin forest that tumbles down into your gardens from all sides, intrudes its mangoas and palm-trees into the houses, escorts the tramlines with its clear waters, leaves on the rotten gateways of the negro laundries patches of bougainville and spiced greenery. The popular quarter itself dances and canters all the way down to its meeting with the ocean, over the hills that are the last stirrings of the mountain. And from wherever you may be, from the hotel terraces or the windows of drawing-rooms, you have only to raise your head to see all kinds of peaks and strange horns wrapped in the dark mantle of the forest, Tijuca, Gavea, Campo dos Antes, Corcovado, and the Profile of Louis XVI. Always behind you stands waiting something immense and black, something fresh and brilliant, and with one bound you are in it.*

It was there that on the stage of a theatre for me undistinguishable—through a mass of unimportant plasterwork—from an esplanade of the forest, I saw for the first and last time, Nijinsky. We had already reached the third year of the war; he himself had just escaped from a concentration camp, and for me, the acute accents of the little orchestra which under Ansermet's baton was addressing the backcloth through the curtain wave mingled simultaneously on that strange antarctic shore, with the noise of the ocean flinging its prodigious fireworks against the breakwater of

xiii

Beira Mar, and that of the ever present cannonade over there. I was like someone who is about to enter a ballroom from the outside, throws his cigar one way, and casts a final glance the other way towards the horizon where a dreadful moon is spreading its blaze behind a curtain of poisoned vapours. The storm had thrown up between Capocabana and the Sugarloaf the gaily-painted vessel of the Russian Ballets, and I was invited to take my ticket like those one-time emigrants going to applaud some exile from the Royal Opera on a chance stage of Coblenz or Spa.

Nijinsky appeared.

I had never had much taste for the conventional art of ballet such as it is practised, sometimes with an idiotic perfection, in more than one State Theatre, or by the sinister Pavlova—any more than for the prowess of singers and violinists. Beauty is a thing that responds rarely to a search. It is natural that sham artists, irritated at the capricious and divine generosity of inspiration, should try to replace it with superstitious execution of a mere formula, and by that frenzied labour to which the mocking lips of the Latin Janus have attached the epithet improbus. But the crown of France is not won by breaking stones, and merit will never merit grace. So I was one of those who have never prized any other dance than that of the East, in which the feet rarely leave the ground, and which is either a discourse whose phrases, starting from the central twine of muscles and entrails and addressing by means of the body that revolves all the points of a circumference, spread themselves out through the joints right to the extremity of the phalanges, the slow manifestation or, on the contrary, the instantaneous discharges of a complete movement—or else the untiring answer of the apparition to a verse a hundred times caught up and repeated by the flute and the drum.

Nijinsky brought with him something else; the feet have at last quitted the ground. He brought the leap, that is to say, the victory of breath over weight. Just as the singer or the actor, by the movement of his arms, merely increases the swelling of his chest that is being lifted up filled with air, so the dancer's inspiration, and that urge of our desire towards life are strong enough to detach him from the earth, all it remains is a springboard triumphantly trodden by his feet. It is the possession of the body by the spirit, and the utilisation of the animal by the soul—again, and again, and once again shoot up, great Bird, to your encounter with that sublime defeat. He falls again, as a king comes down, and once more he darts away up like an eagle, and like an arrow snapping from the crossbow of its own accord. For a second the soul carries the body, this vestment becomes a flame, and matter has passed. He traverses the stage like lightning and hardly has turned away, when he is back on us like the thunderbolt. It is the great human Creature in its lyric state, interrupting our savage dance like a god. He paints our passions on the canvas of eternity, he takes up each of our most vulgarized movements, as a Virgil does with our words and our images, and transposes them into the blessed world of intelligence, of power, and of the upper air. Even in "Scheherezade" when the negro, doubled up like a spring, runs over, or rather measures—with those ten electric points at the end of those arms no longer arms, but at once lips, a greedy tongue, and a spirit —a body ideal round the half-visible real body of the beautiful woman, the gesture, potentially lubric, takes on an unspeakable dignity and grandeur.

And that "Après-midi d'un Faune" ah what loveliness, what joy, what a poignant melancholy. It took place both in Sicily and on that abandoned terrace in the middle of the virgin forest that my friend Milhaud knows well, near a great overflowing basin be-

neath a wall of green stones, and the flaming moon among the leaves like the cymbals in every gap of the orchestra.

Once Nijinsky consented to accompany me to the Legation, and I could see him at close quarters. He walked as tigers do, it was not the transference of an inert mass from one position of balance to another, but the supple alliance with weight, like a wing on the air, of all that machine of muscles and nerves, of a body that is not trunk or statue, but the complete organ of power and movement. There was no gesture so small—the one, for example, when he turned his chin towards us, when the little head swung round suddenly on that long neck—that Nijinsky did not execute with glory, with a vivacity both ferocious and suave, with overwhelming authority. Even at rest, he seemed to be imperceptibly dancing, like those sensitive vehicles that used to be called "eight springs." There was a green half-light in the dining room, and the sun of midday with the intermittent cry of cicadas reached us dulled by the mango trees, there was a green shade on the cloth between the fruit-dishes and the silver service, a gleam of emerald played in the glass salad-bowl among the fragments of ice. And Nijinsky spoke to us of the great work he had completed during his years of internment in Hungary. He had found a way to write down and annotate dance as they do music. It was true. The book exists, and Madame Nijinsky tells me that it is being translated.

And now over the divine dancer's face there is a black veil. He is somewhere in Switzerland and I am at Los Angeles and Madame Nijinsky is sitting beside me in the hall of this hotel and showing me strange drawings. They are human faces and the great Sylph's own portrait drawn with trajectories that cut across one another. At the meeting-place and heart of circular forces and algebraical whirlwinds rises a head made of interfering lines. It is as if the man was made, limbs and face, of a knot of movements distributed and re-

xvi

covered round him by the dancer; function of a number, intoxi-
cated center, realisation of a soul in the explosion of a spark.

Greeting there where you are, Nijinsky, God be with your
darkened soul. Over the forbidden threshold where those two inter-
twined sisters, admiration and pity, meditate, and remember,
prayer can still find a way. . . .

PAUL CLAUDEL

Washington, March 27, 1927

Translated by Lord Derwent

PART ONE

Chapter One

MY FIRST ENCOUNTER
WITH
THE RUSSIAN BALLET

EARLY in the spring of 1912 I was invited to attend the first performance of the Imperial Russian Ballet in Budapest. The city was in a great state of excitement. Fantastic tales of the glamorous, exotic beauty, and of the attainment of great heights of artistic achievement, had preceded this unique company, which was a part of the Imperial Theatre of St. Petersburg.

I recalled that in my childhood I had once seen a performance by former dancers of the same Imperial Ballet, and above all I remembered the imperceptible smoothness and fragile elegance of the *prima ballerina* Preobrajenskaya, as delicate as a Meissen figurine. For her partners she had the two dashing Legat brothers, Russia's foremost dancers, complete technicians of their time. So now I expected to see an equally enchanting performance.

The brilliant audience which gathered in the Municipal Opera House to welcome the Russian artists, who had already taken Paris and all Western Europe by storm, was formed of the *élite* of the then prosperous Hungarian capital. The people of Budapest were rich, critical, and intelligent. With all the pride of a small capital they maintained a running competition with Vienna. They expected a great deal. Budapest was willing to be

3

shown, but it insisted on the most capriciously high standards. As soon as the orchestra struck up the first few bars of the overture, everyone felt that the strange, powerful, alluring music was the composition of a great master. And then, as one ballet followed the other, we were transported from the tall red temple of Egyptian stone to the cruel luxury of a Persian harem and to the endless barren Tartar steppes. A magic hand lavished upon us the inexhaustible variety of gorgeous colours. It was a riot of hitherto unknown colours: purples, greens, of unthinkable depth. Oranges, all enveloped in the golden barbaric art of Byzantium. The very soul of each country and period was revealed. The exquisite art of the dancers was indescribable. The audience sat awe-struck and breathless.

The impressions of that first ballet performance were so overwhelming, it was difficult to grasp and appreciate the greatness of the individual dancers themselves. Even the smallest rôle was portrayed by an artist who was a star in his own right. This was the policy of this astonishing company. The fact that an equal number of male dancers shared with the women important and dominating parts in the performance was also most unusual at this time. We soon understood how this remarkable company had been able to resurrect the long-lost art of the ballet, and raise it to hitherto unknown heights, wherever they had appeared before.

On leaving the theatre, I learned that the brightest star of the company had not been able to appear this evening because of a slight indisposition. I determined to attend all their performances. The next evening found me again at the theatre. The programme was composed of *Cléopâtre*, Schumann's *Carnaval*, and *Prince Igor*. Once again the audience was a brilliant one. Seeing *Cléopâtre* a second time, I was better able to appreciate the perfection of Astafieva, Fedorova, and Bolm's dancing. The scenery used for

Schumann's *Carnaval* was a heavy velvet curtain of royal blue, painted with beautiful garlands of roses. The costumes were of the lovely Biedermeier period. The audience instantly grasped its light-hearted gaiety. The scene changed. Pierrot, Papillon, and Pantalon flirted and swept across the stage, like so many little whirlwinds. Suddenly a slim, lithe, cat-like Harlequin took the stage. Although his face was hidden by a painted mask, the expression and beauty of his body made us all realise that we were in the presence of genius. An electric shock passed through the entire audience. Intoxicated, entranced, gasping for breath, we followed this superhuman being, the very spirit of Harlequin incarnate; mischievous, lovable. The power, the featherweight lightness, the steel-like strength, the suppleness of his movements, the incredible gift of rising and remaining in the air and descending in twice as slow a time as it took to rise—contrary to all laws of gravitation—the execution of the most difficult pirouettes and *tours en l'air* with an amazing nonchalance and apparently no effort whatever, proved that this extraordinary phenomenon was the very soul of the dance. With complete abandon the audience rose to its feet as one man, shouted, wept, showered the stage with flowers, gloves, fans, programmes, pêle-mêle in their wild enthusiasm. *This magnificent vision was Nijinsky.* My one desire, from that moment on, was to know more about the extraordinary manifestation of art embodied in this entire company, and the individuals who had succeeded in creating it.

It was not very difficult for me to carry out my plan. My mother, Emilia Markus, was the foremost dramatic actress of Hungary. She kept open house, and it was customary for eminent foreigners to visit her home and pay their respects. I immediately got in touch with some music critics and a group of advanced painters and sculptors to obtain an introduction to some member of the

Russian Ballet. I succeeded in discovering that one of my compatriots was a friend of Adolf Bolm, the Russian character dancer. He took me back stage and presented me. Bolm was not only a powerful dancer, but very sociable, extremely cultured, well-read, and musical. He was the son of the concert master of the Imperial orchestra. We entertained him, showed him Budapest, and through him I made the acquaintance of many members of the company with whom he seemed to be very popular. I could find no opportunity to meet Nijinsky, nor was I certain whether or not I wished to know him. His genius swept me off my feet, but at the same time I had an uncanny feeling of apprehension. Bolm spoke of him in the highest terms, almost as a priest might speak of divinity.

The company was composed of sixty-five members. Each dancer was a graduate of the Imperial Dancing School of either St. Petersburg or Moscow. The school of the former city was considered the better. I learned from Bolm that Russia's first landscape painters and portraitists had turned their attention to scenic design for the Imperial Russian Ballet. The music, too, was the work of their greatest composers, Liadov, Glinka, Moussorgsky, Borodin, Rimsky-Korsakov.

After a week of triumphant success, the Imperial Ballet journeyed westward on their tour, carrying with them the heart of another conquered city. How I longed to be with these people always, and to follow them all over the world! The opportunity to see them again was given to me three months later in Paris.

The annual performances of the Russian Ballet in Paris were in the nature of festivals. It was here that they presented their new programmes. In each new creation they surpassed themselves. They had increased the measure of their artistic accomplishments to such heights that it seemed impossible to go any farther. And yet again and again they poured forth yet more beauty and more beauty. This revolution swept along with it painters, poets, writers, sculptors, architects, the reigning kings of fashion, and its effects were felt even in the political world.

During the following months I abandoned my training for the theatre with the celebrated French actress Réjane, and, carried away by a greater ambition, I worked diligently to become a dancer.

Around Christmas, when the Ballet visited Budapest a second time, I was at home for the holidays. I spent most of my time with Bolm, and made friends with others in the company, especially with their teacher, Enrico Cecchetti. He was Italian by birth. He loved to call himself "the King of the pirouettes," and he never tired of talking of the time, some fifty odd years ago, when he was the Don Juan of Rome and the Idol of the Italian capital. He would pose with great pride whenever he told tales of his youth. "For thirty years I have been teacher and coach of the *greatest* and *best* dancing school in all the *world:* the Imperial School of Dancing in St. Petersburg," he would assert with great eloquence and true Italian fervour. The *Maestro* (as everyone called him) was not only the perfect teacher, but also the jealous guardian of the pure, classical traditions of the Ballet. Among his pupils he counted such dancers as Pavlova, Karsavina, Mordkin, Bolm, and Nijinsky. I soon discovered I could win his heart through flattery. I had a genuine admiration for him and a very real affection, but I had to use him in order to achieve my purpose— to become permanently attached to the Ballet.

During their stay in Budapest, I was present at every performance, at every rehearsal, and, by very special permission, at the classes of the *Maestro*. These classes were compulsory for each member of the company. The first thing every morning, wherever they happened to be, was a class with Maestro Cecchetti, just as though these artists were still students at the academy in St. Petersburg.

It was a strange sight to see these Russians in their high patent leather boots and fur caps going along the gloomy corridors of the Royal Opera House, which was their home during this second visit. On their arrival, the monotonous, dull routine of the musty old building was instantly changed into a vibrant, pulsating, feverish activity. One of their own famous conductors, Pierre Monteux or Inglebrecht, immediately took possession of the orchestra. It was astonishing how contagious was their spirit. Whoever came into personal contact with them—musicians, electricians, stagehands, dressmakers, hairdressers—all displayed unsuspected gifts in their respective fields, as though working under a spell.

While a rehearsal was in progress on the stage, in the dimly lighted auditorium, in the midst of a group of men, stood a figure of medium height; his hat drawn down over his ears, his coat collar turned up. Simultaneously he gave orders to the chief electrician, conferred with the conductor of the orchestra, was interviewed by three reporters, and discussed business matters with the administrative secretary. This man seemed to be a real authority in every branch of the organisation. His mere presence made one feel that he was not only a versatile and gifted director, but also a *grand seigneur*. Everyone obeyed him blindly. This man was Diaghileff—Sergei Pavlovitch Diaghileff. He was the master magician of the Russian Ballet.

At rehearsals I always hid in some dark corner of the theatre, fearing that if I attracted attention I might be sent away. On this occasion I happened to be sitting in the back of the house with a newspaperwoman, who had come to watch rehearsals. She raved on and on about Nijinsky. Impatiently I interrupted her pæans by saying, "If you really know this 'wonder' so well, then please introduce me to him at once." We went over to the group of men where Nijinsky was conversing with Diaghileff. It was an exciting moment. One would never have thought that this unassuming young man, with his Tartar face and the appearance of a Japanese student in his badly fitting European clothes, was the same being as the marvellous apparition the whole world had learned to admire. The introduction actually occurred. In the ensuing conversation there was a bit of confusion, which was greatly aided by the diversity of languages spoken. Nijinsky misunderstood my identity, and thought I was the *prima ballerina* of the Hungarian Opera, whose name had been brought into the conversation at that moment. As time went on and I grew to know more and more about Nijinsky, I learned that it was probably due to that error on his part that he greeted me with so charming and respectful a bow. For many, many times after that first introduction I was introduced to him, and never was there more than a polite, fleeting acknowledgment and never by any chance did he recognise me.

Meanwhile, at my mother's home, we entertained the Russian artists lavishly. They had all been our guests except Diaghileff and Nijinsky, who were unapproachable. Bolm never left my side. As usual, he was my source of information, and from him I knew all the inside stories of the company. We spoke a great deal of Nijinsky, and of the young girl who bore such a close resemblance to him—his sister, Bronislava. She possessed the dreamlike quality and the lightness of Pavlova, together with the overpowering acting ability of her brother. To see the two of them dancing together was an unforgettable experience. Then there was the glamorous Matilde Kshessinskaya—favourite of the Tsar, the whole Imperial Court, and idol of the intellectual and artistic world of St. Petersburg. She was continually surrounded by a special bodyguard. The strangest and most contradictory rumours were abroad concerning this lovely woman and great dancer. She had a magnificent country estate, a palace in town where she maintained a court like a Grand Duchess. Her receptions were unequalled in luxury. Even in comparison with the wealth of the times, her priceless collection of jewels caused comment. Whenever she appeared on the stage, she wore real diamonds and emeralds, as large as walnuts. Although she was a member of the most exclusive Court in the world, this magnificent woman was very generous and tender-hearted to everyone. She had an open purse as well as an open heart, and no one who came to her for help went away unrequited. According to gossip, in his bachelordom the Tsar of all the Russias was ignorant of all but a strictly celibate life. The wise Court chose the glorious and distinguished Kshessinskaya to convert His Majesty. She succeeded splendidly, we are told; slightly better than the Court would have wished. But those who were instrumental in staging this love-affair always knew how to correct the pranks of fate. So on one cold, wintry morning the motor-car of the Imperial favourite skidded, and, due to this unfortunate accident, the expected royal baby never saw the light. In later years Kshessinskaya's name was linked with that of the Grand Duke Vladimir, the powerful Commander-in-Chief of the entire Russian Army. The wagging tongues maliciously quoted that the gold borrowed from France to buy new cannon went into the coffers of the *ballerina.* Her influence at Court and in theatrical circles was omnipotent. No one dared contradict her, not even Count Fredericks, the Court Minister and most intimate friend of the Tsar. Kshessinskaya was at home in all the intrigues of high politics too. But she did not want to be left out of the tours of the Imperial Ballet abroad. She quickly understood that the tours were not undertaken purely from artistic impulses, and that they

10

had a far-reaching political significance, and served to bring a friendlier relationship between foreign countries and Russia much more quickly than any diplomatic stratagems. Even Diaghileff, the absolute ruler in the company, treated Kshessinskaya with distinction, except in artistic matters, where he never loosened his iron grip.

These exuberant personalities were something entirely new to us. The better we came to know them, the more evident it became that it was impossible to get to know them at all. Contrary to all European theatrical customs, their private affairs never interfered with the rigid discipline of their work. Everyone was fascinated by them. Even the serenity of the old, jovial porter at the stage door was disturbed. This enormous, lumbering old fellow, who was called "Tiny" by everyone, had, for forty-five years, guarded his post at the stage door, quietly smoking his pipe, totally unconcerned by what was going on inside the Opera, impervious to the famous artists and unusual personalities that passed him at the door. He came at a certain hour, left at a certain hour, smoked his pipe, and remained in his shell. He was *blasé*. But these Russians did something to him. No matter how many hours earlier than his appointed time he arrived, he was always too late, and the dancers were working at high speed. Finally it became a race with the inevitable. He never won. While other artists turned around in their beds, the *Maestro* had already shouted himself hoarse in his classes. From eight in the morning until two in the afternoon the *Maestro* exercised his pupils in separate groups. Those who had not worked late the evening before were in his first class, as well as those whom he thought less perfect in technique. He grouped his pupils according to artistic capacity. Thus he kept the later period, from twelve to two, for his star pupils—Karsavina, Kshessinskaya, Nijinsky. Simultaneously

11

rehearsals were in progress on the stage from ten in the morning until the late hours in the afternoon. It was a mystery when the dancers could find time to rest or sleep. *Maestro*, greatly flattered by my constant presence in his classes, encouraged my dreams to become a dancer, in spite of the fact that I was already seventeen years of age. He thought that with great perseverance he could yet make something of me, and I sat day after day respectfully watching him teach. Bolm wanted to teach me too, but, realising that it was practically impossible for me to join them, he advised my mother to send me to the Wiesenthal sisters in Vienna. They were members of the Imperial Opera at Vienna, who, under the influence of Isadora Duncan, had become concert dancers. The thought of having to study with them was very distasteful to me. I was interested in the Russians, and especially in Nijinsky. I used to watch him closely at dinner. He listened to the gypsy music and seemed to observe the people with an aloof, distant air. His half-closed eyes gave an extraordinary, fascinating expression to his face. His features were decidedly Mongolian, and the almond-shaped eyes were a dark brown, although on the stage they seemed a dark blue or green. He was of medium height and very muscular, but on the stage he seemed tall and slender. Even his physical being seemed to change according to the part he danced. The fact that he never greeted me on passing my table infuriated me, and one day I boldly ran after him in the corridors of the Opera and asked him for his autograph. He stopped and gave it to me with a charming smile, but from the way he looked at me I knew that he didn't recognise me. I wondered why. Occasionally I caught his eyes resting on me, but as soon as I looked at him he quickly turned his glance elsewhere.

I was determined to find some way by which I would be able to stay with them. *Maestro*, who by that time was my sworn ally, advised me to speak to Diaghileff, but somehow I was afraid of him. I really wanted to ask Nijinsky to help me, but Bolm said, quite casually, that even members of the Ballet could not approach him. He was always followed by Vassily, his valet and Diaghileff's faithful slave; never spoke to any one of them except at, and about, their work. And I had heard enough gossip to know that Diaghileff kept an impenetrable Chinese wall around Nijinsky. I could not understand this strange air of isolation around Nijinsky, but I realised one thing very clearly: that I would have to proceed with the utmost caution. Nobody noticed my adoration for Nijinsky. I learned later that the company thought that, apart from my artistic admiration for the Russian Ballet, I was interested in Bolm. I was very fond of him as a friend and admired him as a great artist. It remained for *Maestro* to notice, even before I myself was aware of it, that I was in love with Nijinsky. For one morning he arrived at *Maestro's* class earlier than usual. I knew that I would have to leave the rehearsal hall, and got up to go. As I passed the *Maestro*, he whispered, "Beware, Nijinsky is like a sun that pours forth light but never warmth." His prophetic words came back to me in later years.

They left for Vienna, and I followed them. For weeks every ticket had been sold in advance. The same excitement prevailed in Vienna as in Budapest. The Court, society, the world of art, and the great public eagerly awaited their arrival.

They immediately took possession of the Opera House, with its own orchestra and staff, just as in Budapest, and one would never have known the charming, nonchalant Viennese of the week before. Now, intoxicated by the Russian Ballet, they worked like slaves.

To enter the Opera House during rehearsals, even for a member not actually working on the stage at the time, was impossible,

13

according to the very strict (military) regulations. But why was my godfather head of the Imperial Family's archives and the confidant of Franz Joseph? To help me. And why was my brother-in-law the first Wagnerian star of his day? To serve me, of course. So, therefore, I set them to work and obtained a special permit to allow me to come and go as I pleased.

The opening was a command performance. Even the Emperor, who was already very old and led a retired life, made an unusual exception and appeared. The seventy-five most important members of the reigning house of Hapsburg fought bitterly between themselves for places in the three archducal boxes. Even the *loges* of the Imperial suite were crowded with eager Hapsburgs, and the ladies- and gentlemen-in-waiting had to content themselves with whatever orchestra stalls they could get.

The performances were made even more astonishing because there was now added to the brilliance of stars like Kshessinskaya and Kyasht, the presence of Thamar Karsavina. The judgment of Paris that she was the equal of the divine Pavlova was fully justified.

The Press everywhere was unanimously at their feet. Only one critic, Ludwig Karpath, the influential Hungarian musical critic, dared lift an opposing voice. A real intellectual, intimately connected with the Wagner dynasty, he had a fighting spirit, and the profound conviction that, for the healthy development of art, opposition was always essential. He could not bear to have the Russian Ballet's supremacy pass absolutely unquestioned, more for its sake than any carping notions of his own.

Nothing could escape the attention of Diaghileff. Yet, unapproachable as he was, and offended as he might have been, he granted Karpath an interview as soon as he asked for it.

Hard as it was for Karpath to ask for a meeting with Diaghileff after his attack, he did it only for my sake. The large, corpulent man could never forget that I had once rendered him a small favour in Marienbad years ago. I had seen his childish terror of the darkness, and I offered to accompany him through the forests at night to his hotel, some distance away. My whole destiny was changed through this small incident.

I was neither awed nor embarrassed when we went to see Diaghileff. I was determined to obtain my point, and, when my mind was definitely set, nothing and nobody mattered.

Diaghileff received us in the middle of the afternoon, in an empty public reception-room of the Hôtel Bristol. As soon as he entered we felt his dominating personality. We expected a cold, a resentful reception. But Diaghileff, who with every gesture and word expressed at the same time the superiority of an emperor and an irresistible charm, confused both Karpath and myself by the warm interest he took in our requests. He made us feel absolutely that nothing interested him more than my intention to become a dancer. With conscious magic he led the conversation around, so that, without Karpath noticing it at all, he made me speak, against my will; apparently a young society girl had come to the great artistic organiser with a request. In reality, two powerful enemies had crossed swords for the first time. Diaghileff held the thing I most wanted—Nijinsky. And he sensed at once, with his fine instincts, however subconsciously, the approaching danger. I just as quickly realised that he wished to read my mind. Karpath was completely unaware of the fine covert duel that was being fought between and behind words, and mostly in thought. And by this time Karpath was entirely lost in admiration for Diaghileff.

"I think Bolm is wrong in advising you to go to the Wiesenthals." One thought seemed to follow the other, aloud. "The ideal thing for you would be to become a pupil of the Imperial Dancing

School in St. Petersburg. But of course it is not feasible, even with the greatest possible pull for you are not a Russian, and you are long past the required age." He paused. "I think the best thing for you to do would be to take private lessons from Fokine in St. Petersburg."

With apparent joy I jumped at the idea.

"I would love it." I misled him deliberately. "It has always been my dream to go to Russia."

He then asked my impressions of the different ballets and the artists of his company.

My answers must have been correct. He smiled approvingly. During all this time I felt that gradually I was falling under his spell. I tried to fight against his almost hypnotic power. With a desperate effort I began to rave about Bolm as a man, not as an artist, like any little "flapper" would. And then Diaghileff, with unexpected strategy, turned and asked, "What about Nijinsky?"

Without hesitation I answered, "Oh, Nijinsky is a genius. As an artist he is incomparable. But somehow Bolm is more human to me"—and I continued my extravagances about Bolm. By this time he was convinced of my good faith, and then said the fatal words:

"I will speak to Maestro Cecchetti. He has taught all our greatest artists. I am sure he will take you as a special, private pupil. This way you will have not only a marvellous teacher, but also the possibility of travelling with us and closely studying our work."

I thanked him gratefully, and so our interview ended. I had won my first battle. I could scarcely believe I had succeeded in fooling such an inconceivably clever man as Diaghileff.

The same evening, when I went back stage, *Maestro* greeted

16

me from afar with enthusiastic gestures and loud shouts of Italian joy.

"Sergei Pavlovitch has decided that you should study with me. I am overjoyed, *bambina*. I will make you work frightfully hard, *cara mia*. But you will see in a few years what a dancer I will make of you." He embraced me and kissed me on both cheeks. He always liked to kiss young girls; when he was enthusiastic and excited he would rub his small fleshy hands, and in high spirits he always talked about his youth, when all the women in Rome were in love with him. After a few details of past love-affairs, we finally settled when and how I would start to study. I was to join them on the 4th of February in London.

When I left the Opera House, I did not walk; I flew to my brother-in-law and my sister to tell them of my good news. Eric was won over entirely by the Russians. And he was very difficult to convince, being himself a great artist; but after the first night not only did he go to every performance, but he watched the rehearsals as well. He had never seen so great and finished an artist as Nijinsky work so hard every day. When I told him my good luck, he heartily congratulated me, and said it was a rare chance, and that it was the opinion of the ballet-master of the Hof-Oper that from the point of view of classic Italian ballet the technique of the Russians was so perfect that not even the Italians outdid them, after hundreds of years of tradition. It was the quintessence of the classic school.

After a few days the Russians left Vienna. This time I bade them good-bye happily. I knew now that I belonged to the Ballet.

17

Chapter Two

THE CHILDHOOD
OF
VASLAV NIJINSKY

On the 4th of February, 1913, I began to work enthusiastically under Maestro Cecchetti in London, where I joined the Russian Ballet. From that moment my whole life was consecrated to its art; but the centre of my interest was Nijinsky, his past, present, his personality, and his genius.

Apparently I knew him, although he never noticed and invariably failed to recognise me. I did my utmost to approach and learn more of him. At first I saw and thought of him only as the rest of the world did, as a great artist and a prodigious dancer. Only much later did his extraordinary personality become clear to me. Nijinsky was essentially a seeker after truth, a kind, sweet soul, a philosopher, and a helper of mankind. His aim was to comfort, to perceive, to uplift and bring joy to humanity. He considered that his amazing talent was merely a gift of God, with which he had been entrusted to accomplish his purpose.

Already at school he had been called the "eighth wonder of the world," on account of his incredible gift for dancing.

He had attained the highest point in the art of the dance that a human being ever reached. His personal inheritance, the race from which he descended, his childhood and early

18

training, the soul and tradition of the country where he passed his youth, all were instrumental in fashioning the ultimate artist.

He was born in the City of Four Hundred Churches, Kiev, in South Russia, on the 28th of February, 1890, according to the Russian calendar.

He was christened Vaslav, and baptised some months later in Warsaw in the Roman Catholic faith, which was his mother's. His mother, wishing to save him from future military service in the Russian troops of the army, had him christened in the Polish capital, so she could obtain a certificate from there. She even went so far as to give a false date—1889—as the year of baby Vaslav's birth, because children born in that year were privileged in the order of their military service.

Vaslav's parents were both of Polish origin. His father, Thomas Nijinsky, a handsome, dark, temperamental, high-strung, and ambitious young man, was already a dancer of the fourth generation in a family in which the art of dancing and technique was handed down from father to son, as in the dancing dynasty of Vestris and Petipa.

Thomas Nijinsky lived and danced in Russia, where he was both famous and popular, but on account of his Polish descent, and because he did not graduate from the Imperial Schools, he could never obtain his greatest desire, which was to become a member of the Imperial Theatre. This was the tragedy of his life. Thomas Nijinsky was a perfect classical dancer, a master technician, and, according to Vaslav, surpassed even him in technique. He was an excellent acrobat, had a superb *ballon*, and was splendid also in character parts. Thomas had his own troupe, and danced with them all through Russia, and even ventured as far as Paris in the late 'eighties, for the International Exhibition, to

19

perform at the Olympia. This was the first time a Russian dancer had appeared in the Western metropolis.

While touring the Polish provinces of Russia, he met one day, in Warsaw, Eleanora Bereda, a student of the Warsaw School of Dancing. She was a beautiful, delicate girl, with blue eyes, golden hair, and a perfect body. She had a sweet, placid nature, and was the daughter of a well-to-do, religious, cultured, but conservative gentry family. On her mother's side her ancestors came from the Transylvanian nobility. Her father, a wealthy Polish landowner, led the life of a country gentleman, and, after gambling away everything he owned, shot himself. Her mother died of grief shortly after, and the orphans were taken to an uncle in Warsaw. This uncle, the president of the Polish State railways, took complete charge of the children and wished to bring them up according to his ideas. Eleanora, being the oldest, mothered her brothers and sister, and everything went well until one day Eleanora suddenly declared her overwhelming desire to become a dancer. This conservative and deeply religious family was scandalised at the thought of having one of their kin on the stage. But Eleanora would not abandon her idea, so she was disinherited. She struggled along, and without any help from her family developed into the most exquisite type of character dancer.

Thomas Nijinsky fell violently in love with her. His fierce, passionate love-making frightened the quiet girl, and, though she was flattered by the courting of the famous dancer, she was not in love with him. He would never have succeeded in his persistence had he not terrified her by threatening to kill himself if she refused him. Panic-stricken, the young girl finally consented.

The first few years of their married life were fairly happy. She was a sensitive and affectionate woman, a dreamer. After a little while she sensed that this violent, impetuous man was not

20

only a gifted dancer, but possessed an artistic spirit and an enchanting personality. Eleanora became deeply attached to him.

Thomas, not being a member of any theatre, had no permanent residence. So, wandering from city to city, they had to exercise their beloved art and earn their livelihood as best they could. The Nijinskys, with their troupe, crossed all the Russias, from the Baltic to the Black Sea, from Poland to the Caucasus, from Siberia to Turkestan.

One day, while travelling in the Caucasian wilderness on the Grusinsky road, the military highway which leads to Persia, an accident befell them which cast the shadow of a later tragedy on the little family. It happened between Tiflis and Vladikavkas, somewhere in a small mountain village in the midst of great forests, where they had stopped for the night. The troupe's wagon halted by an inn, where there was a stable, a tavern, and rooms for travellers. During the night, after they had retired, the inn was attacked and raided by bandits. Their savagery, cruelty, and the suddenness of their onslaught had a terrifying effect on the young expectant mother. Eleanora lost her power of speech for three days.

Her first baby, a boy, was born soon after. He was named Stanislav. The sturdy, muscular, fair-haired little baby resembled his mother. Already, in his infancy, he showed an unmistakable predisposition for music and dancing. A year later Vaslav was born. He was the image of his father. He had a dark complexion and big brown eyes. His mother danced on the very evening of his birth, an hour before the baby's arrival. So he was a real child of the stage. From the moment of his birth he was engaged in the service of the art whose priest he was to become.

Eleanora, who was very religious, took the children to church whenever the family went. Those churches, with their big, bulbous, glittering towers, the deep, sonorous chimes and mellow bells, the gloomy scent of incense, the colourful painted walls, the golden icons, and the richly robed, jewelled, long-bearded popes, made a profound impression on the already vivid imagination of the baby, Vaslav.

Endless travelling was their life. There were interminable coach rides through immense fields of wheat, of golden corn, vast plains, endless steppes, dusty roads, highways deep in mud, mountains, valleys. Summer and autumn merged into snowy winter, and still the troupe moved like a small dark ribbon in a borderless land, covered with deep snow, under a grey, monotonous, leaden Russian winter sky. In rain or sunshine, day and night, night and day, the troupe moved on. Under the blazing summer sun, in the snow storms and bitter blizzards of hard winters this heroic little group of artists slowly fought its way through the most hidden and forgotten corners of European and Asiatic Russia. So little Vaslav learned to know and love Russia.

There was no end of interesting variety for the children of the Nijinsky family. They very seldom stayed in any place longer than a month. They moved on from city to city, through villages, where at the entrance a toll-gate was invariably thrown open by scrutinising, furry Cossacks or uniformed guards, to whom passes had always to be shown and money paid.

Then came their temporary home, always an inn or some hostelry, bleak rooms with paraffin lamps that usually smoked terribly, and big porcelain stoves on which the children loved to sit or sleep amid the smell of vodka and the sweet hum of the samovar.

From the moment of its arrival in a new place the troupe was busy day and night. They had to be artists, stage hands, all at once. First the scenery was unloaded, then costumes and properties and personal belongings. Then came rehearsals with the local musicians, who were not, as a rule, accustomed to accompany ballet-dancers, sometimes culminating in fights and tears. Eleanora tried to keep the children close to her, in the dressing-room or behind the scenery. She thought it was safer for them. But the boys ran out in the streets, played about the theatres, whenever they became tired of watching their parents. To the children, the elders when dancing suddenly became knights and princesses, nymphs and fauns. The children could not distinguish between reality and fairy-tale, for the ballets they saw seemed more real to them than life itself.

They ate and slept in the theatre, in some corner of the stage, or on the laps of their parents in the mail coaches. Sometimes they passed nights with *moujiks* in their carved wooden huts, when no inns could be found. During their travels they saw marvellous countries and cities, many tribes, many different customs, costumes, dances, and songs. The songs and dances of all Russia became their nursery rhymes. And in this infinitely colourful, varied environment little Stanislav and Vaslav grew up. A little girl, Bronislava, was added to the family circle.

Vaslav could only faintly remember the events of this period. As he said himself, "My mother could probably recall when I cut my first tooth, but hardly the time when I began to dance." However, he did recollect distinctly when he appeared in public for the first time—at the age of three. His father composed a *pas de trois* for the child prodigy, a sailor dance, which little Vaslav executed with his brother and tiny sister. He was intensely proud of this little sailor dance.

Thomas soon discovered that among his gifted children Vaslav had the greatest talent, and began to instruct him. In these early dancing lessons Thomas taught him the most elementary steps

23

and the five positions. Vaslav enjoyed these lessons immensely; and always begged his father to show him new steps whenever he had the time. His father did not believe in too rigorous a training for a child so young. From this time on the children often appeared in the ballets.

Thomas Nijinsky's passion for his wife faded. While travelling in Central Russia he met a young dancer, a Jewess. Soon afterwards he had a violent love-affair with the girl. Eleanora, full of affection and devotion to her husband, noticed his unfaithfulness, but she could do nothing but bear her sorrow in silence. The girl joined their troupe and they went on dancing from one place to another.

Eleanora had engaged a *nana* for her three children, and one day, in Warsaw, where Thomas at the time was *maître de ballet*, when she had to go to a rehearsal she left the children under her care. An organ-grinder stopped under the window. Stanislav, climbing up to the sill, leaned out curiously, lost his balance, and with a scream of terror fell out of the third floor. His fall was stopped by the railing of the balcony on the first floor. His father heard the cry, the confusion of voices, the shrieks of the *nana*, and, rushing out on the street, saw his eldest son in the perilous position. He rushed up and rescued him from death. But the shock and the concussion of the brain which the child must have suffered had sad consequences. His development halted. This strong, physically healthy little fellow never advanced any further mentally.

Eleanora imagined also that the shock she had received when the bandits attacked them in the Caucasus was partly responsible for Stanislav's mental illness. She was heartbroken, and Thomas, deeply grieved, tried every doctor he could find, in every city where they performed, in the hopes of finding some cure. When the boy became worse, he was taken to a specialist in St. Petersburg in order that he might secure the best treatment that the capital could afford, and to do this the family settled there permanently. The tragedy which had befallen the little family, instead of bringing the parents together, further estranged them. Thomas was increasingly irritated that in spite of his success he could not enter the Imperial Theatre. The continual silence and sadness of his wife depressed him, and the gap between them widened. The final break came when his mistress was with child, and he asked his wife to divorce him so that he could marry the girl. It is a peculiar strain in Russian men that they feel it a duty, if a woman bears them a child, to marry her and legitimise the child, in spite of the tremendous difficulties that the Orthodox Church puts in the way of divorce. Eleanora, a devoted Catholic, could not and would not divorce him. She refused once and for all, and Thomas, exasperated, left his family.

An accident in which he broke his leg prevented him for a long time from dancing and hindered him from providing for both his families, though for a few years he supported them as best he could. The small amounts he used to send his wife arrived more and more irregularly, and finally they stopped altogether.

Eleanora, bereaved, stood in the world alone with three small children. One of them was seriously ill, needing constant care. She had now no income except the occasional meagre salary she earned by giving dancing lessons, or here and there by an infrequent appearance. Stanislav's accident made it clear to her that she could not leave her children alone in the care of *nana*; to pursue the career of a dancer, which demanded constant practising, rehearsing, and concentrated interest, became impossible. The only alternative was to find some occupation which would allow her to stay with her family. As a young girl she ran away from her family to become a dancer. Now she decided to sacrifice her dancing for the sake of her children.

She rented a flat and opened a *pension*. By letting rooms and

25

cooking for her boarders she earned a modest living for herself and her children. She did all the manual work herself, but in spite of it she could barely succeed in getting along. Vaslav was always around his mother, never leaving her side, a real mother's boy, helping her in the kitchen and wherever he could in her daily work. He watched over the place when she went in the morning to the markets. Vaslav was her only assistant, as Stanislav was sick and Bronia a baby.

But this housework had its joys, too, for the little boy. The final clearance of the dishes in which mother cooked was always left to him. Vaslav, who was very fond of sweets, greatly enjoyed cleaning out the kettles in which she previously had prepared the different icings and chocolate creams. He became a connoisseur of cooking himself.

Her good cooking soon made the place popular, but Eleanora, incorrigibly good-hearted, could never insist when one of her guests failed to pay her. During these early years Vaslav was accustomed to being her defender, opening doors watchfully, arguing with tradesmen creditors, looking over the bills that were delivered and which Eleanora was often unable to pay. They were always forced to economise to the last extremity. Small Vaslav made an early acquaintance with the sad and difficult side of life, and his mother confided her troubles in him.

Summer came. The heat in the city was unbearable. Eleanora decided to send the children to the country, but, with little money, she boarded them with peasants, paying almost nothing.

An entirely new life opened for Vaslav. All day long he was free to play hide-and-seek in the fine, fresh hay, or walk with a band of boys in wide poppy-fields, or bathe in the little brook near the village. The children loved to stage cock-fights, but on one occasion Vaslav was attacked by one of the angry fowls. The rooster

26

cut his forehead wide open with its beak. The child, bleeding, ran home crying, where the kind peasant woman wiped away the tears and cured the wound. But the mark on his forehead remained for ever.

It was the busiest time of the year for the peasants: the harvest season. They rose before dawn to go out into the dew-wet fields to cut wheat, rye, oats, and millet, put it on big crosses, and to pray for clear dry weather. When the corn was high, the children ran delightedly through the stiff green plants, like an army of soldiers at attention. In the evenings, groups of workers, coming home from the fields, sang enchantingly the beautiful folksongs in three or four repeating tunes. The boys followed behind, trying to imitate their carriage, their walk, and their songs. The long twilight fused into the high starlit nights when the harvesters returned to their village. In these surroundings Vaslav learned the appreciation of simple lives, their joys and values, their sorrows and hardships, the inevitability of death. Here for the first time Vaslav came into close contact with the omnipotence of Nature. He worked in the fields with the *moujiks*. At first it seemed easy enough, but he soon found out that work in the fields was not merely fun, but hard and tiresome labour. The young boy's sensitive soul understood under what burden the peasants had to toil, how miserable was their fate in famine if bad weather killed their crops. This boy, the son of trouping parents, who in their constant travels could never set root in a single spot, found now the tie which bound him to his country, his race, his tradition. When the summer passed, and Vaslav returned to the city, he carried in his heart an eternal love for Russian soil.

No matter how hard she worked, Eleanora could never make a sufficient living. The children grew and needed some education. So she went even so far as to humiliate herself by asking help from her husband. Thomas met the situation with an embittered spirit. His artistic ambitions were unfulfilled. His accident had made his long years of work, his assiduous studies, his successful past, seem futile. In this mood he advised his wife that, everything taken into consideration, it would be much wiser for the children not to follow in their parents' footsteps. He suggested to Eleanora that the best thing to do would be to apprentice both boys to some tradesman—for instance, to a watchmaker. He argued that a watchmaker who knew his work could. always make an honest living and have a more or less secure existence, compared to the life that might fall to the lot of even the greatest dancer. No, his sons should not go through this suffering.

For Eleanora, his decision was a terrible blow. She was, after all, deserted by her husband; she had given up her beloved art for the sake and future of her children. All for what? To make trades-men of them. Nevertheless, on the advice of the doctors, she gave Stanislav a trial in a watchmaker's shop. First the child seemed interested, but after a few weeks he became restless, irritated, and had to give it up. Eleanora and the physician now realised that Stanislav would never be able to do even manual work.

To take the burden of Vaslav's education from her shoulders, and to fulfil her long-cherished dream, she took the seven-year-old boy, at the beginning of the autumn, to the Imperial School of Dancing. She presented him to qualify for the required exam-ination. Although the board of examiners found that the little boy was remarkably fit, and showed a marked disposition for dancing, nevertheless they refused his entrance on account of his youth. They told his mother to bring him back two years later.

The next years passed in a continuous effort to make a living. The only brightness on their horizon was the possibility of Vaslav's entering the Imperial School.

Chapter Three

THE IMPERIAL SCHOOL
OF DANCING

AT LAST the day arrived when Vaslav could enter the Imperial School of Dancing. The Imperial School and Theatres were a familiar topic in the Nijinsky household. How often had the children heard that their father could never dance amid these splendours, merely because he had had his dancing education in Warsaw. It was the dream of every child who was ambitious to become a dancer to be a pupil of the Imperial School. Tales were told about the difficulty of being admitted into the school, its discipline, the incessant study, its luxurious surroundings, the Court performances, the feasts, with the great Grand Dukes and even the Emperor himself.

Russians have always loved dancing, as the mural paintings representing scenes of dancing, dating from 1071, on the Cathedral of Santa Sofia in Kiev, and in the Pitchersky Cathedral prove. The Greek Orthodox Church has always violently condemned dancing, but in spite of their steady opposition, lasting throughout the ages, the love for dancing flourished among the *moujiks* as well as in Court.

In the seventeenth century, ballet was introduced to this barbaric, semi-Oriental country by the Tsar Alexis Mihailovitch, the second Romanov ruler, at his wedding festivities. He was the first

29

to create a permanent theatre and ballet. Foreign ballet-masters were engaged, and soon produced native instructors. The successors of Alexis Mihailovitch followed in his footsteps in sponsoring the art of dancing.

Peter the Great took a personal interest in it by composing ballets and by dancing in them himself and ordering his Court by ukase to do the same. With the help of his prisoners, the Swedish officers, he taught his Court. The first serious attempt to organise a school of dancing had been started in 1735 by the Tsarina Anna Ivanovna on the request of Christian Wellman, the teacher of gymnastics at the Imperial Cadet School. He was permitted to take twelve poor boys and girls and train them as professionals. The Tsarina was so pleased with the results that she took all the expenses of their education and maintenance upon the State and allowed them one of her palaces. The first director was Landet, a French ballet-master, and the children were supervised by the widow of a Court coachman. This was the humble beginning of the famous Imperial School of Dancing. But the great task of civilising this immense empire was carried out by Catherine the Great. She reorganised the school in 1779 on the model of the Imperial Cadet Academy, from which the *Corps des Pages*, the Imperial bodyguard, was formed. She built the first stone theatres and opened them to the great public.

Tsar Paul united the Imperial School with the Smolny Institute, which was the most exclusive school of the empire, and, as it was a convent, the clergy opposed the union, but in vain.

At this time, Charles Louis Didelot, the French ballet-master, was invited. We can consider him the father of the Russian ballet. He was the one who emphasised the importance of systematic training, and of the true dramatic spirit: "A true dancer must be also a good actor and a poet at heart." He was strict, almost a fanatic, but, thanks to him, the school produced outstanding dancers and the ballet took the prominent place in Russian art which it never lost until the Revolution. He was for twenty-eight years the director of the Imperial School, a favourite of the Tsar, and, thanks to him, the century-long opposition of the time had to cease. He was the first to invite foreign *ballerinas* to dance at the Mariinsky Theatre, and so St. Petersburg became acquainted with the art of Taglioni, Elssler, and others. His successors tried to keep up this spirit, and ten years later the French dancer Marius Petipa succeeded him. Petipa, whose inventive genius was inexhaustible during the sixty years he was member of the Imperial Theatre, composed sixty ballets, reconstructed seventeen, and supplied thirty-seven operas with ballets. Petipa not only created a rich repertory for the Mariinsky Theatre, but also developed and enlarged the vocabulary of the dance by innumerable new steps.

The tales which were circulated about the Imperial School were founded on truth. The exclusiveness of the institute, and its close contact with the Court, gave it a halo. As the *Corps des Pages*, the pupils of the school were part of the Imperial household, and belonged to a privileged world.

In this superb school of art the dancing was taught by the best masters for eight years. Based on military principles, the school was run with an iron discipline that was never slackened. The supreme head of the school was the director of the Imperial Theatres.

The moment a child was admitted, the parents virtually relinquished all rights, and the pupil was formally "adopted" by the Tsar.

A rigorous physical examination made by doctors and the ballet-masters decided which of the children could be taken for a two years' probation, during which time they still lived at home but were otherwise supplied with everything by the Imperial School. Usually several hundreds applied, but only six to ten were taken. If they proved to have adequate disposition during the two years, they were taken permanently into the school, and at graduation became automatically members of the Mariinsky Theatre.

The Imperial School was installed in a huge early baroque palace between the Nevsky Prospekt and the Fontanka River, in the middle of the most exclusive district of St. Petersburg, on Theatre Street. It was simply furnished, but this palace of the eighteenth century, with its panelled walls, huge rooms, big crystal chandeliers, exhaled an atmosphere of luxury.

The school had its own chapel, with big choir and yellow and white marble pillars, where divine service was held on Sundays and holy days; its own infirmary, with doctor and nurses in constant attendance, where the children had to undergo an examination every Saturday during the eight years; and its own theatre, where the annual examination took place, and which they shared with the pupils of the dramatic school. Their dormitory was spacious—big enough for forty, and only occupied by twenty-five. Each pupil had his own numbered cubicle, over which his own icon was hung. One of the five governors, who had the supervision of the pupils, slept at the end of the dormitory. They had a special bathing establishment on the premises, where every Friday the boys received "Russian baths," and a chiropodist attended to their feet, which were nursed with almost religious care.

At the preliminary examination on the 20th of August, 1900, when Vaslav was presented, he was chosen with five others from among a hundred and fifty boys. He was very shy and timid, and could hardly answer the examiners, so much the luxurious surroundings impressed him. But Nicolai Legat, the famous solo dancer, who was among the examiners, noticed his extraordinary thighs and well-developed body, and insisted that he should be taken.

Vaslav was provided with the regular trousseau, and never had he known such luxury: six changes of underwear; three uniforms, a black for every day, dark blue for the holidays, grey linen for the summer; two overcoats, the one for the winter with heavy astrachan collar; patent leather boots, and pumps for home. The uniforms were like those of the Cadet School, with high velvet collar, on which a silver lyre, the insignia of the school, was embroidered. Their caps were like those of the Army, with the Imperial Eagles on them. Vaslav was extremely proud when for the first time he could parade in his new clothes. But perhaps the greatest joy was when he received his dancing kit and shoes. Vaslav was meticulously neat, and took great care of his wearing apparel. He always looked clean and well groomed.

For Vaslav, the change was tremendous. He had hardly ever been away from home and his mother's care, and the classes seemed very difficult to him, as the pupils had also to study the regular subjects of an ordinary school. In all subjects unrelated to art, except mathematics and geometry, Vaslav was not good. From the first moment he entered the school his five classmates began to tease him, mocking at his Mongolian features and almond-shaped eyes, and gave him the nickname "Kitajec" (Chinaman). This nickname hurt Vaslav, as the Russo-Japanese War did not make the Mongols popular in Russia. In everything Vaslav shared the life of the other pupils, except in food, as in the first two years he had to bring some from home. His mother was not able to supply him with the same delicacies as the others. But Vaslav did not know the feeling of envy; he always offered to share the little presents he received from his teachers or elder pupils with the others.

One person alone was able to pierce the wall of Vaslav's reserve—his master, Nicolai Legat. He was not only an extraordinary dancer, but a fine teacher with a charming, gay personality and great understanding. From the first second he laid eyes upon Vaslav he knew that he had found something in him which could be developed, under proper conditions, into great art. Vaslav loved to study with him. Those lessons seemed like holidays. As soon as he entered the dancing-room he seemed to throw off his shyness and enter his natural atmosphere. With worshipping admiration and blind obedience, he executed with infinite ease the steps Legat with great patience showed to his pupils. Out of these lessons a mutual sympathy grew which lasted ever after. And Vaslav told me later that he owed all to Legat's untiring tutoring. Even his fellow pupils were entranced as soon as Vaslav began to dance, and very soon the rumour was spread in the Imperial School that a new star was rising. Only Vaslav seemed ignorant of the fact.

After the two years of probation were over, in 1902, Vaslav was permanently admitted to the Imperial School. Now he became a boarder. At first he missed his mother tremendously, but now the serious study of art had begun. From the first year on, the pupils were used in the ballets and operas at the Mariinsky Theatre as walkers-on, or in small parts. The boys loved to go to the theatre, to which they were taken under the supervision of the governor on duty, in special landaus belonging to the Imperial stables. The pupils had their own dressing-room on the fifth floor of the Mariinsky Theatre, where they were supposed to stay while not busy on the stage, but Vaslav always found a way to escape and to hide himself in the wings to watch his ideal, Chaliapine. It was he who made a lasting impression on young Vaslav's imagination, and whom he ardently desired to follow. He watched his every movement and studied his make-up, and very soon was able to make up with such amazing virtuosity that his teachers were surprised. It was in *Aïda*, as one of the negro boys, that he first stepped on the stage of the Mariinsky Theatre. Often he took part also in the operas, and, as he was extremely musical, soon knew them by heart. He was cast as Gottfried, Prince of Brabant, Elsa's brother, in *Lohengrin*, and was very proud of his first solo part.

Vaslav, like his parents, was brought up in the Roman Catholic faith, and was profoundly religious, but somehow already, at this age, he could find God's presence everywhere, and, as the majority of the pupils were of Greek Orthodox faith, he attended their services in the school chapel, which he loved for its golden altar and huge yellow marble pillars. Father Vassily, the pope of the school, had always a kind word when Vaslav bowed before him, in spite of his different faith. And Vaslav admired his dignified carriage and his glittering gold cross.

Vaslav adapted himself well to the daily routine. At 7.30 the bell was rung by the usher, and the pupils had to get up. This was a difficult moment for Vaslav, as he loved to sleep, and tried to snatch a few more moments of extra rest. Then they went to the wash-house, which was a feature of the school. Round the walls were placed the lockers of each boy, and in the middle of the room there was a large circular copper basin, to which a fountain supplied the tepid water. Within fifteen minutes, they had to pass the governor, waiting for them at the door of the dining-room, which was opposite to the dormitory. Here the boys had to give up their handkerchiefs every morning, to be exchanged for clean ones. Before starting breakfast, one of the older boys said grace.

A simple Russian breakfast of coffee, tea, rolls, and butter was served. The children were allowed to eat as much as they wanted, and the nourishment of the school was as good as that of the Imperial family, who often sent them delicacies from their estates.

After breakfast they formed a crocodile, and accompanied by a governor, went for a walk until nine o'clock, either on the Nevsky Prospekt or to the Kasansky Sobol. The well-mannered, uniformed children were known and liked among the inhabitants of the capital.

Then, upon their return, lessons followed. Vaslav quickly became a good piano player, and in his free hours played in their rest-room for his class-mates.

At ten the dancing classes began, and lasted daily until noon. The school had several large dancing-rooms, where the floor was sloped like that of the stage and made of soft pinewood.

The boys came attired in their regular dancing costumes to the classroom: black trousers, white shirts. Those who excelled in their dancing were allowed to water the floor.

At noon, a light luncheon was served, and, after, the children had one hour's rest. From one to five they devoted their time once more to the regular subjects.

Then a large dinner followed, of several courses, after which they rested or played games. The most popular was the Russian national ball game called *lapda*, in which Vaslav excelled; as he did in fencing. Other forms of sport were at the time strictly forbidden, as they might develop the muscles in a different way than that required for dancing.

They would have ballroom lessons with the girls, and during those classes innocent flirtations naturally started, and, as all communication was strictly forbidden, the children used to hide their *billets doux* in secret places, such as under the leg of the piano.

If discovered, they were punished, and dessert was withheld. All the boys had their platonic sweethearts except Vaslav, who already at the time had only one real love—that for the dance.

Among all the lessons except that of the classical dance Vaslav loved best that of pantomime. It was taught by the great mime Guerdt himself, who admired Vaslav's ability, and proudly told his colleagues at the Dramatic Theatre: "Russia's coming great actor is a pupil of the dancing school, the little Nijinsky."

In the classes for "make-up" Vaslav was greatly interested. In a large room which was fitted out like a theatrical dressing-room, with adequate red and green lighting effects, mirrors and tables, the pupils had to study the anatomy of their faces, the effects of the colour and lines, and how to create a characteristic make-up.

Vaslav was indeed a strange child. He did not mix with the other frolicking pupils unless expressly called by them, as by this time he had become used to being ignored by his class-mates, who were jealous of him. Silently he meditated in a corner or invented some prank. He was mischievous by nature, and whenever there was fun he was the schemer, and on such occasions his suggestions were gladly accepted. In fact, he was always involved as ringleader in all the pranks which arose. He painted the chair of the professor of mathematics with ink; he distributed sneezing-powder in the class. Only at the dancing lessons they could not drag him into any insubordination. Those lessons and the stage were sacred to him. In his studies he was slow, and the teachers, who did not quite understand his psychology, thought him lazy; for this he was often deprived of sweets or of his vacation. Vaslav patiently submitted, and passed the hours locked up in the room specially kept for this "detention." The walls were covered by the photos of ballet-masters and great dancers of past centuries, and Vaslav was greatly absorbed in studying their gestures and costumes, and did not realise that he was actually punished.

The superintendent of the school often complained to Vaslav's mother about his laziness, and she pleaded with him, with tears, to be more diligent. Her boarding-house was not prospering; she lived in constant poverty and need of money. She was forced to pawn her most cherished belongings. Slowly everything she owned found its way to the pawn-shop, and never to return. And, when everything seemed to be at its worst, an unexpected blow staggered the poor woman; Vaslav was suspended from school as punishment for his latest trick.

One day, when the boys had to go to the theatre, they took along in the bus their toy bow and arrow. Vaslav was an excellent shot, and, aiming through the window, unfortunately hit the tutor in the eye, who, infuriated, asked for the culprit. Vaslav stood up and confessed the crime, and his expulsion followed. His mother wept bitter tears; her most beautiful dream shattered, her hopes crushed, the immediate need to feed another hungry mouth was a real catastrophe for her. The transition from the luxurious comfort of the school to the bourgeois flat, smelling of cooking, from the life without worries to one of want, deeply impressed the sensitive Vaslav. He met the neighbours with a sense of humiliation and shame. They all knew he was expelled from school. Vaslav noticed that among them was a too conspicuously dressed woman, smelling of cheap scent, laden with vulgar laces and ostrich feathers, who visited them constantly, especially at meal-times. She drank Eleanora's tea, ate her food, and gossiped, gossiped continuously.

The days were filled with constant fear of creditors, and the possibility of being turned out of the flat. One day Eleanora had to meet an unavoidable debt; she needed five roubles. But she had nobody to ask except the friendly neighbour. She had to make a terrible effort to go through the ordeal to ask for this loan. Vaslav was in the room when she explained the pressing situation. The woman listened with attention and interest, like an understanding soul, but, when Eleanora finally brought her request, she sighed, began to cry how sorry she was, and refused. With words of consolation, she sailed out of the flat. Eleanora burst out crying as the door closed behind her. So they would be without any food for the children! Vaslav huddled in a corner, watched the scene motionless. Now he realised his mother's situation, her sorrow, and he made up his mind to work and study, to make a great effort to become a great dancer, so that soon he could be of help to her.

The disciplinary measure was rescinded, and Vaslav returned to the school. From that day on he kept his promise to himself and studied assiduously. Soon he excelled his classmates and became the pride of his masters. Two years after Vaslav's admission, Bronia became a pupil of the school.

However thrilling the participation in the performances at the Mariinsky, it could not be compared to the Court performances. Everybody, from the *maître de ballet* to the footmen, was agitated on such occasions. The children were told not to forget the rigid etiquette of the Imperial Court. As they were taken over in their carriage, they were deeply impressed by the fact that soon they would be face to face with the Tsar of all the Russias, their master, their "Little Father." The palace gates were thrown open; the guards saluted; inside more soldiers, Kammerjunkers.

As they entered the ballroom they were for a second blinded by the splendour of it, filled with the members of the diplomatic corps with their satin ribbons, smothered under the jewelled

39

orders, the gold of their uniforms reflecting in the crystal lights. The children were nervous at the sight of the audience, their Majesties, their Highnesses, and their "suite." But, as soon as the first bars of the music were played, all went smoothly. When they danced, they were in their own atmosphere. After the performance, the Tsar and Tsarina spoke graciously to them, gave them presents, and served cake. Those who danced exceptionally well received a distinction in the form of some jewellery, and one evening Vaslav, as he moved up to kiss the hand of the Tsar, after finishing his solo, was presented by the Court Chamberlain with the gold watch with the initials of Nicholas II. This was the highest sign of His Majesty's pleasure to a pupil of the Imperial School.

It was much less terrifying to dance in the palace of the Grand Duke, where there was no royal restraint, and after their dance they were allowed to sit on the laps of their Imperial Highnesses and play with their glittering jewels and decorations.

Vaslav's talent developed with astonishing rapidity during these years. His fame was thoroughly established in the school, and his inherent natural gifts exceeded those of anyone in the annals of its history. Vaslav was full of energy and ambition to perfect himself; he was never satisfied, and as he felt that pirouettes did not come to him quite as easily as jumps, he decided to practise them until he reached the highest grade. But this untiring ambition almost caused his death. One day in the classroom, where dancing was forbidden, waiting for the teacher, Vaslav began to pirouette and to make *tours en l'air*. He was so engrossed in his practising that he did not pay sufficient attention to the benches. He landed with full force against one, and injured his abdomen dangerously. For three months he lay between life and death, flat on his back in a hospital, but his rugged constitution finally pulled him through. After a long enforced rest, Vaslav resumed his study, and progressed with unfaltering certainty to his ultimate brilliance of technique. Outside events rarely penetrated the walls of the school. In calm seclusion, well protected, these hothouse plants developed undisturbed. After the lost war with Japan, however, revolution swept over Russia. On the 9th of January, 1905, Vaslav was quietly walking with his school books under his arm towards his mother's apartments when suddenly he was confronted with a tidal wave of swarming people, who were running like furies to the Winter Palace. The demonstration was led by Father Gapon. Vaslav was carried away with the mob, which pressed around him with terrific force. He tried to get out, but struggled in vain against this flood of humanity. When the rushing crowd came close to the palace, a squadron of mounted Cossacks, armed with their terrible knouts charged. The wild onrush stopped suddenly; stones and bricks flew in the air. The snorting, plunging horses dashed into the mob. The knouts fell on heads and backs like a hailstorm. Women screamed, men shouted, children cried. Vaslav tried to shield himself with his books, and, bending down, he suddenly felt a terrific pain, and the running of his own warm blood over his face. With wild strength one of the Cossacks had cut him on his forehead. The deep gash left a scar, next to the one the rooster had inflicted. This scar always reminded him of that dreadful scene, the merciless attack of the Cossacks on the weaponless, starving people who were asking for bread. Vaslav became ever after that brotherly towards his fellow men, and began to understand the suffering of the masses.

Late in January the strikes of the terrible year of revolution came to a head. The national revolt had been violent, but little report of it managed to creep into the fastness of the Imperial Dancing School. Even the Mariinsky Ballet Company, usually so loyal to the Court, which supported and protected them, had been

41

infected by the contagion of unrest that was everywhere in the air. Fokine, Pavlova, and Karsavina presented certain claims for the improvement and maintenance of the standards of the company in October of 1905, and with great gallantry and courage attempted to stop a performance of Tchaikovsky's *La Dame de Pique* as a sympathetic strike.

The revolt failed. The republic proclaimed at the mass meeting of the 16th of October fell. The three great dancers, deserted by the majority of their colleagues, who refused to strike and signed a declaration of loyalty, awaited dismissal and arrest.

In the school there was an unknown atmosphere of tension. The corridors were quiet. The governors seemed preoccupied. The older boys were worried and even the little ones knew that an aching suspense paralysed the nation. A revolution was momentarily expected. But, in spite of it, the lessons, the practice, the rehearsals, continued. Only one morning Serge Legat, Nicolai's brother, did not appear. Nor did he ever teach again.

Serge Legat had somehow signed the declaration of recantation, against his will. Already in a highly strung state of mind from a desperately unhappy love-affair with Marie Petipa, the great *maître de ballet's* daughter, he was plunged into the abyss of grief and shame at what he considered to be the betrayal of his friends. Perhaps Vaslav did not know then that he had raved all night: "Marie, which is lesser in the eyes of God, that I should take your life or mine?" He did not learn until much later that they had found him in the morning with his throat slit by a razor.

Vaslav went on studying, practising ceaselessly. His progress was amazing, and he was cast in quite important solo parts, the first time in the ballet *Paquita*, when he danced the mazurka. It was a great moment for the young pupil to be rehearsed by the great Petipa himself with the members of the Mariinsky Theatre,

42

as if he were their equal. More parts followed . . . and then, in 1906, Obouchov, who was now Vaslav's teacher, reported that he could teach him nothing more, as he surpassed his masters in their art.

His success was such that the director of the school offered to make him a regular member of the Mariinsky Theatre two years before graduation. It was an unheard-of event, without any precedent in the history of the school. Vaslav was extremely proud and exuberantly happy, but he begged to be allowed to finish his classes and to graduate at the regular time. So for two more years he remained, at his own request, at the school. But the Mariinsky Theatre made a lot of use of his talents, and gave him in 1907 the important part of the Marquis in *Pavillon d'Armide*. The graduation performance usually took place in the Mariinsky Theatre, and on that night the house, with its blue velvet curtains and upholstering, its gilt plaster and heavy pyramids of hanging crystal, was filled with the *élite* of St. Petersburg society. Mozart's *Don Juan* ballet was chosen for the occasion, and Vaslav had the distinction of appearing on the same bill with such artists as Obouchov and Legat. His partner was Ludmilla Schollar.

Vaslav's success was immediate and overwhelming, his happiness great. His fellow pupils, the artists of the Mariinsky, surrounded him, congratulating, and he could only smile with tears in his eyes when Petipa patted him on his shoulder. Then his idol Chaliapine arrived and embraced him. Turning towards Petipa, he said, "Did I not tell you years ago that he would be the pride of Russia?" And then, kissing Vaslav on both cheeks, continued, "Slavuska, just go on dancing like you did to-night."

In a few days he had to leave the Imperial School, which had been his home for eight long years, where he could devote all his time and energy to his beloved art. As usual, the last days were passed in fêting the graduate. As the last day arrived, Vaslav went from room to room saying farewell to those familiar places. Finally he went to the chapel and knelt before a golden icon, the image of the Saviour, thanking Him for his blessings throughout those years of study, and praying ardently for His divine protection in the coming years, so that he should become not only the glory of the Mariinsky, but a true servant of God.

Chapter Four

NIJINSKY
AND THE
MARIINSKY THEATRE

In MAY 1908 Vaslav graduated with distinction from the Imperial School and automatically became a member of the Mariinsky Theatre, whose pride he already was.

The Imperial Opera House of St. Petersburg, officially known as the Mariinsky Theatre, was named in honour of the Tsarina Maria Feodorovna. Like the other Imperial theatres of St. Petersburg and Moscow, it belonged to the Tsar, and was supported by him under an annual subsidy of two million gold roubles. It was under the supervision of a Minister of the Court, who was directly responsible to the ruler for the management of the Imperial theatres and schools.

About one hundred and eighty dancers in all, male and female, including soloists and *prima ballerinas*, comprised the *corps de ballet*. All had to be graduates either from the St. Petersburg or Moscow Imperial School. Upon graduation a dancer became first merely a member of the *corps de ballet*, later a *coryphée*, a *sujet*, then a *prima ballerina*, and, highest of all, a *prima ballerina assoluta*, or, if a man, *soloist to the Tsar*.

All the dancers had to proceed, if possible, through this grading, and parts were assigned according to ability. Their term of service extended, from graduation, for twenty years, after which, even if they were at the height of their careers, they had to retire on a small pension for life. This rule was only broken in exceptional cases. If the dancers were of unusual merit, they were retained as teachers in the Imperial School. The Mariinsky and the school were intimately connected. The same iron rule dominated both. The time for rehearsals, the order of a performance, were published in an official notice hung on a board in the theatre every Monday morning, and the more important members were notified by a letter and printed schedule.

Into this institution, with its glorious traditions, Vaslav entered at the age of seventeen. The *balletomanes*, who had recognised his extraordinary talent and predicted for him a great future, hailed his *entrée*. He made his début in the ballet of Mozart's opera, *Don Juan*. It was an unforgettable moment in both Vaslav's and Eleanora Bereda's lives.

He was rapidly given more important parts, and danced regularly now, as her partner, with the *prima ballerina assoluta* Matilde Kshessinskaya, as well as with the *prima ballerinas* Preobrajenskaya, Pavlova, and Karsavina. Greater and greater parts were given to him. The expert public of St. Petersburg sat spellbound before this slim, light child who floated, hardly touching the ground, and who executed the most technically difficult steps without any effort. They saw in him the reincarnation of the classical style of Noverre, the leaps of Vestris, the ethereal qualities of Taglioni, and the fire of Camargo. Even Petipa, who had seen the great dancers of the last century, was amazed that so many gifts had been showered on one human being. And soon Vaslav was called *"Le Vestris du Nord."*

His days were spent in exercises at the Mariinsky Theatre, rehearsals, performances, and lessons with Maestro Cecchetti.

The old Italian's idea of a good dancer was more a human machine, with sinews hard as wires, muscles like steel springs, the heart an inexhaustible pump, rather than a human body which might tire. But Vaslav never failed to learn from him, and his supreme standard of technical perfection was the greatest incentive for an artist of Nijinsky's calibre.

But in spite of this he found time for himself. He was passionately fond of literature, and read thoroughly. His great favourites were Shakespeare, Ibsen, Chekhov, but above all Tolstoi, who cast a spell over him. They were similar in their essential nature, not only in their love of mankind and of the soil and soul of Russia, but in their conception of art to lift humanity and serve God. On free evenings he often went to the opera, especially to hear Moussorgsky and Wagner.

In spite of the fact that Vaslav was acknowledged by his teachers, fellow artists, and the public, and was aware of his own talent and capacity, he yet felt there was something unattained, something lacking in his art. The perfection of his technique did not satisfy him. It had been developed for many centuries, so that now it shone brilliant as a diamond. But it was not enough to transpose music into terms of the dance. Dancing had an independent function, which it had as yet never fulfilled. He applied this technique, of which he was a master, and its musical accompaniment, not as a pretext for display or as parallel accents, but as a dominating entity.

Petipa's compositions represent an epoch in the plastic art. The *romantic school* of the ballet was a mixture of the classical tradition, of absolute technical virtuosity, combined with pantomime. The ballets of Petipa were on a spectacular scale, but whatever story they embodied was merely a transparent pretext for a consecutive series of dances calculated to display the great-

47

est technique. As perfect as they were of their type, Vaslav realised that they already belonged to the past. Michel Fokine was responsible for the new phase in the evolution of the ballet, but, due to the traditions of the Mariinsky Theatre, Fokine could not realise all his reformatory ideas otherwise than gradually. The genius and determination of Petipa brought the ballet to a peak of virtuosity. Now Fokine wanted to use this as an instrument, and not as an end in itself. His earliest compositions, *Acis and Galatea, La Vigne* and *Eunice,* set in a Grecian background, were transitory works. Fokine was bringing to an actual flame the ideas which flickered in the creations of Isadora Duncan, dilettante of genius, who visited St. Petersburg for the first time in 1905. She had been enthusiastically received, and created a furore with a part of the public at least. Her chief aim was to bring back dancing to its most primitive form, *la danse antique.* Her idea of the primitive was acquired from the figures on Greek vases of the Great Period. The liberation which she proclaimed had been fermenting for some time, and it was independently and triumphantly realised by the mastery of Fokine, who with his great technical training could afford to be as free as he wished.

Only in nineteenth-century Russia did the ballet advance from the gymnastics of its classical formulæ and keep up the traditions of the classical dance. The genius of Marius Petipa, the creator of the Russian romantic school and a great figure in the history of dancing, kept to the old forms, but introduced a wider use of pantomime, and he created many ballets with national dances embroidered into the scheme. The abstract movements of the dancing and the pantomime were connected by the *pas d'action,* where the dramatic situation dictated the gestures and movements. The *corps de ballet* was now used for plastic groups and treated as something more than decoration.

The ideas of Fokine were the logical consequence of the strength of the *romantic school*. As Petipa was a monumental figure, so was Fokine. His contribution was profound, but, like an artist, he understood that in dancing, as in the other arts, development does not lie in the annihilation of former achievement, but rather it is its retention for use in newer forms and further development. For this reason recurrent dilettante protestants against the classic line, from Heinrich Heine to Isadora Duncan, have failed, where Fokine succeeded.

Fokine succeeded in his great advance because he had in his power all the controlled possibilities of the human body. He expressed the formalisation, the essence, of human emotion through the forms of the classical dance, but he broke away from the academic form of Petipa in that he used the whole body and broke the rigidity of movement. He used the hands, the arms, the torso, where before only the legs moved. The groups of dancers were now arrayed asymmetrically. The subject danced is no longer a pretext, but the foundation upon which the whole ballet is built. The music used is in a more intimate relationship to the dance than ever before. The step from Petipa to Fokine in the dance is wider than the step from Mozart to Wagner.

Vaslav spent a great deal of time in museums and picture galleries, especially the Hermitage. He was a great admirer of Holbein and Dürer, but most of all he was drawn to the Italians of the Renaissance. He studied their masterpieces carefully, particularly Leonardo, Raphael, and Michelangelo. He realised that harmony and beauty of movement were of supreme importance, and that technique existed only to enable the artists to express their conceptions more perfectly. From that day on Vaslav put this lesson into his dancing. The amount of pirouettes and *entre chats* were no longer so important to him as the harmony of movement, even if it required less bravura. The effect on his dancing was subtle and compelling, and the audience was conscious of the change, even if they could not define it.

Vaslav used to take long walks by the side of the canals in the evening, when he was free. The fog enveloped the houses, the walls of the bridges, in a luminous haze; a mysterious twilight, hooded from the sun, a time for calm meditation. The idea of the Preaching Monk, which he recalled from his early childhood, returned to him from time to time. To follow a pure, ascetic life, to teach the masses, to seek truth, were all singularly fascinating to him. But each time his overwhelming love for the dance conquered.

Shortly after Vaslav had left the school his mother moved into a larger apartment, in a more select neighbourhood. This was more expensive and far above their means, but they had to live up to the standard of a member of the Imperial Theatre. Vaslav had lived magnificently for eight years at the Tsar's expense. It was a change to have graduated from the school, where everything conceivable had been provided without thought of money, and now to have to live and support brother and sister on sixty roubles a month. Clothing and food and labour, however, were comparatively inexpensive at this time in Russia. Eleanora engaged a servant. The apartment was cosy and meticulous. Vaslav inherited from his mother her neatness, sense of order, cleanliness. He always looked tidy and well groomed, even after several hours of strenuous exercises.

Eleanora Bereda was an excellent cook, and prepared all of Vaslav's food herself. She adored him as her favourite child, and this was reciprocated by Vaslav. Even in later years, when they were parted from each other, no matter how exhausted he was, he would send her a note every day, though he disliked writing and never wrote to anyone else.

Saturdays and in the summer months Bronia returned home from the Imperial School. In these times Vaslav continued the lessons he began to give her in former years. So, almost unconsciously, she absorbed his creative spirit, his ideas, his sense of form.

The only shadow over their tranquil lives was the incurable illness of Stanislav. His mother kept him at home, nursing and watching the boy, who, though most of the time passive and obedient, was mentally undeveloped. His blank face would light up with joy whenever Vaslav danced a little for him in the apartment. Stanislav was extremely good-looking, like his mother, with fair hair and blue eyes, slightly taller than Vaslav, for whom he had a real adoration. Anything that Vaslav suggested to him he would do, and when he became excitable a word from Vaslav would quiet him.

During one of the holidays, when they were all at home, dining, Stanislav became excited. They tried to calm him as usual, but they failed, and when Eleanora sternly commanded him to behave himself he hurled a knife at her. Vaslav, with his incredible swiftness, grasped his hand in time and mastered him.

But after this scene they decided to carry out the advice of the doctors, who knew Stanislav might at any moment become dangerous, and confine him in an asylum. A cruel moment for all of them! Vaslav took all the necessary steps to have his brother placed in the best State institution they could afford, and afterwards on every Sunday, accompanied by his mother, visited Stanislav, bringing little presents for him and his nurses.

Vaslav took every tragedy in his life placidly, with a seeming

51

outward indifference. Inwardly he felt it more deeply than the others, with an almost Oriental fatalism.

Vaslav did not go to the cafés and music-halls with the other boys. His life was wholly divided between his mother and his art. At the Mariinsky he was liked, always quiet, polite, and reserved, and his colleagues as well as his superiors respected him in spite of his youth. The *prima ballerinas* not only liked him as a superb partner, but because he had agreeable manners and was easy to work with. Even the male dancers had a kind word to say for him, and he was universally liked, without malice or envy, with only one exception—Anna Pavlova, who at the time had already achieved the grade of *prima ballerina*. She was an exquisite dancer, with a matchless technique which almost attained the perfection of Kshessinskaya. The fact that she was able to revive the long-gone charm of Taglioni gave her an outstanding position at the Mariinsky Theatre. One evening, after completing a *pas de deux* with Vaslav, noticing that his shouted name recalled him oftener before the curtain than her, she fainted back stage in an uncontrollable fit of jealousy and resentment. Vaslav, ignorant of envy, pitied her.

The generous Kshessinkaya, always anxious to help, entertained lavishly in her hospitable house, where Vaslav met Prince X. He was a well-bred aristocrat, with delightful manners and decadent tastes. He surrounded himself with the most attractive young men of the fashionable regiments and the *Corps des Pages*, and lived in a surfeited atmosphere of semi-degenerate indulgence. X took a great liking to Vaslav as soon as they were introduced, and constantly invited him to his palace. He was seventeen years old, and for the first time he saw *life*. Now that he was a part of these receptions and not merely a decorative ornament, there was a fascination in walking up a flight of heavily carpeted stairs, passed on by one footman to another, until one was announced into the big bright room blazing with lights. Yet amid all the laughter and complete abandon there was never a woman to be seen. They would go to the fashionable restaurants, like Medved or Cubat, to social gatherings, and everywhere gaiety reigned, champagne and gold flowed—Vaslav never drank, but his nature, full of mischievous charm, made him, even in these male gatherings, an agreeable companion and not a spoil-sport. A sentimental intimacy between X and his friends was taken for granted. The young men were closer to each other than mere friends. Nothing that he saw seemed particularly unnatural or abnormal to Vaslav. Before, he had known only school. Now, this must be the way the rest of the world chose to behave.

Eleanora did not oppose these sorties. She thought that after the isolation of school the time had come for Vaslav to know life. Of course, neither she nor Vaslav in their innocence understood the meaning of X's affection.

During Carnival there was the great *bal masqué* at the Mariinsky, where the *élite* of St. Petersburg appeared. It was the event of the season. Everybody was costumed and wore masks. Vaslav was requested by X and his friends to wear a lady's costume of the eighteenth century. Considering this a prank, he put on a dress of that period, with all the jewellery and laces, and with great ability he mimed a lady of the Rococo. He looked as if he had walked out of a Watteau, assuming the very air of the eighteenth century. Nobody could have told that this charming masquerader was not really a girl. For Vaslav this was all only a part to play, but not to the others, and only later was he shocked into regretting his perfection and his innocence.

X one evening offered at another of his innumerable parties

53

an unusual attraction by inviting a group of the loveliest Vengerkas [1] of St. Petersburg to amuse his young friends, if any of them should happen to take a fancy to such an unfamiliar mode of distraction.

Vaslav was frightened by the intrusive manners of these women, but respecting womanhood deeply, even in these caricatures, and not wishing to offend them, he humoured them in their desires. He never had any false fear of sensuality, and his dancing often showed a deep intuition of the passionate. But he who until now had had no association with women was, after this first experience, profoundly hurt in his soul. He shrank even from the memory of this evening.

Vaslav's fame grew greater from day to day, and his father, who had all these years been separated from them, touring Russia with one ballet company after another, began to hear of his son's achievement. One day he expressed the desire to see him. At first, Eleanora, with a heart full of bitterness, tried to prevent the meeting. But Vaslav tenderly persuaded her to grant Thomas's wish. He loved his mother deeply, and naturally resented his father's behaviour towards her, but, after all, he, the son, had no right to judge. So, after considerable coaxing, she let him go.

It was at the time of the summer vacation, and Thomas Nijinsky was in Kazan. It was momentous for Vaslav to make the acquaintance of his father, whom he could only vaguely remember. As he had only a little money to spend, he did not travel all the way from St. Petersburg to the interior by train, but went as much of the way as he could by steamboat down the Volga to reach Kazan. He had not left the capital, except for brief excursions, since he

[1] In Russian, Vengerka means a Hungarian woman, but, since almost all prostitutes in Russia were Hungarian, the word became synonymous with cocotte.

was six years old. His early childhood journeys all over the empire were as unreal as dreams.

Now the vast stretches of country unfolded themselves before him endlessly, and for hours he stood at the rail of the boat watching the flow of the majestic river, the ever-changing panorama of its banks, cities, villages, with the bulbous golden church towers between the poplars, the white shining loneliness of isolated monasteries, and the roll and shimmering wave of the cornfields.

So, slowly, Vaslav approached his father, whose loss may well have caused the tragedy of his life. It was a great moment for both of them when they finally met. Vaslav, at this time, was physically almost the image of his father, and Thomas Nijinsky saw himself completely in the dark, lithe, youth, who had fulfilled his own most cherished hopes. Perhaps as an artist he felt an unconscious pang of jealousy, but at the same time he was exuberantly proud of his famous son. His conscience was burdened with his neglect and injustice, as he faced the boy who had become the provider and protector of his family. But Vaslav had no word, no gesture of reproach. He smiled his irresistible, charming smile, expressed his respect for his father, and his gratitude for the talents he had transmitted to him. For Vaslav knew then that the amazing power of being able to jump so high, to float in the air, and to descend more slowly than to rise, he inherited from his father.

The few days they spent together in Kazan were very happy. They became great friends as Vaslav told his father all about himself, the work at the Mariinsky, his ideas, and his life. They danced for each other. Thomas was literally speechless when he realised that Vaslav's dancing revealed what was the hopeless dream of most dancers, the quality of genius. As a parting gift

Thomas gave his son a pair of cuff-links. Vaslav always wore and treasured highly these inexpensive gold buttons set with some semi-precious stones from the Urals—his father's only present to him. Thomas promised to come the following winter to St. Petersburg to see him dance at the Mariinsky, but fate decided otherwise, and they never saw each other again.

Chapter Five

THE RUSSIAN
RENAISSANCE

IN THE winter following this trip Vaslav met the person who played the most important part in his life, both as an artist and as a man—Diaghileff.

Sergei Pavlovitch Diaghileff was widely known among the artistic and intellectual circles of the Imperial Theatres, and in the social and political life of St. Petersburg. Ever since he first appeared on the horizon he had started a powerful irresistible artistic movement. Sergei Pavlovitch was the son of Paul de Diaghileff, a general in the Russian Army, who belonged to the nobility, and was a great amateur of music and the owner of large distilleries. Sergei Pavlovitch was born on the 19th of March, 1872, in Nijni Novgorod, where his father was stationed at that time. His mother was a musician with an agreeable voice, and often sang for charity. Sergei Pavlovitch was brought up very carefully on his father's estate among the gentry of the land, and later in Perm. His mother and aunt and the ever-faithful *nana* guarded him. Discipline, and the motto *Noblesse oblige,* were the chief factors of his childhood. His parents kept open house in their large home in Perm, and it was run as a kind of local Medicean palace, with great luxury and real Russian hospitality. Sergei Pavlovitch attended the gymnasium at Perm, with little interest

57

in his school work after the excitement of the evenings at his parents' home. He was surrounded by a military aristocracy, with the constant factor of serfs in obedience.

Sergei Pavlovitch was an extremely gifted and clever boy, and soon became the pride of the *lycée* of Perm, but had a very patronising attitude towards his classmates and even professors, as he knew the importance of his own family and how anxious they were to be invited into the Diaghileff mansion. So Seroja, as he was called, instead of using his brilliant mind, simply took his school years easily by copying his classmates' work and bossing them. His tendency to enchant, and then make use of the talents of others, could already be noticed; also the streak of cruelty in his nature if anybody dared to resist his wish. He expected everybody to serve him blindly. He had the real nature of the Russian autocrat. He could make anybody suffer without even wincing and then walk away with a smile. At home he was cherished and spoiled. He had elegant clothes and was carefully groomed— more like a little prince than a son of the gentry.

His aunt exerted a very great influence on Sergei Pavlovitch's life. This remarkable woman, who, excelled in the handicrafts in which all Russian women are gifted, organised the first art schools for the peasants on her estates.

Sergei Pavlovitch's father wished him to become a soldier like himself, but his aunt gave him the strength and the encouragement to choose for himself another career.

Diaghileff, even at a very early age, was a dandy. His charming, extremely personal manners elegantly suited him, and when he talked he gestured with one hand and snapped the fingers of the other, a trick learned from some grown-up whom he admired.

Sergei Pavlovitch came to St. Petersburg to finish his education at the Mai School. It was the first time he had been to the capital, but he soon felt he had lived there all his life. His manners were not of the provinces, but of the world. His uncle, the Minister of the Interior, gave him the immediate *entrée* into Court society. Letters of introduction brought him in contact with Walter Nouvel, a young man of good family and of his own age, with musical interests, who was the centre of a small circle of painters and writers, and far more to his liking than the official society. Nouvel introduced him to Alexandre Benois, a young painter of French descent, who later became his close friend and adviser. A worldwide authority on the eighteenth century and a great connoisseur of painting, he was later to design so many of the famous settings for the Ballet Russe. Already considered by official circles as the most suitable head of the Imperial Museum of Art, the Hermitage, his fame was well established. Nouvel, Benois, Filosovov, Diaghileff's cousin, and other young artists and students of art soon became very good friends and were constantly together, hearing the latest music, seeing the latest paintings, and discussing the latest ideas from Paris. They formed, indeed, as he later called them, a *laboratoire artistique*, and, without the others being conscious of it, Diaghileff came to assume very quickly, in his delightful, gracious way, the leadership of the little circle, and to direct and control their artistic destiny with a guidance as insinuating as it was strong and directed. It was Benois who knew painting, who knew the museums as if they belonged to him, and he gave to Diaghileff the rich accumulation of his taste and information whenever the impulse or the opportunity offered itself.

Diaghileff attended the University of St. Petersburg. He was a brilliant student, but his private fortune obviated the necessity of any profession. His inherited love of music impelled him to take courses in harmony at the Conservatory of Music under Rimsky-Korsakov, and he became a real virtuoso of the piano, and since he had an agreeable baritone voice, of which he was inordinately proud, he studied singing. He tried every means to determine for himself some definite artistic vocation. In the second year of his studies he went so far as to compose a fragment of an opera in the manner of Moussorgsky, whom he passionately admired, and whom he felt he had, in a way, discovered. But when it was given an audition to the circle of friends, Filosovov, Benois, and Nouvel told him frankly that it was pastiche. That they were correct in their judgment is supported by the words of his teacher, Rimsky-Korsakov, who some three years later, at his graduation, said: "Do whatever you want, Seroja, but promise me never to become a composer." And so Sergei Pavlovitch abandoned any idea of becoming a musician, yet he understood music and had a clear musical judgment. The painters said he was always a dilettante in the plastic arts, but in music he knew his ground, just as it was said of Disraeli that the writers called him a good statesman, and the statesmen a good writer.

Diaghileff quickly assumed the exquisite life of the capital. His less sophisticated new friends were scarcely used to the scale of his life. He behaved as a *boyard* in his little court of friends, encouraging, condemning, putting one unsuspected talent next to an unknown gift, planning and making himself known in the right places. Perhaps Diaghileff's most individual power was in being able to pursue an idea, to slave for it, to accomplish it after terrific labour, and then suddenly to turn on it, profane and degrade it. In personal relationships he was always dependent on mastery. It must be he who was the direct inspirer, the power that set creation in motion.

At this time Diaghileff encountered a young Jew, shy, proud, sensitive, and extremely gifted. He had a wonderful talent for stage decoration, and Sergei Pavlovitch, with a suggestion here, a word of admonition, drew him into the circle. He was a Jew, to be sure, but he was also something of a genius, and his name was Leon Bakst. At the time of his meeting with Diaghileff he was already well known in his own right, a *protégé* of the Grand Duke Vladimir, through whose influence he had been commissioned by the Government to make paintings for the Ministère de la Marine. He had graduated from the École des Beaux Arts of St. Petersburg and he had returned from studying in Paris with the Finn painter, Edelfeld. His real master, however, was Vroubl, from whom Bakst took his colours, his wild palette, and made a bold innovation by introducing them to the stage. It was Vroubl's idea to abandon the *constructed* scenery, and to treat the whole stage, not as an artificial reality, but as a living picture. Bakst was a member of the School of St. Petersburg, as others have been members of the Tuscan, the Roman, or the Venetian School. It was in opposition to the School of Moscow, which was less refined, less Western, than the painting of the capital.

Diaghileff would defend and praise Bakst, and, when his success seemed too assured, he would apply the needles of distrust: "Oh, yes, I think Leo does enchanting things—such colour, such taste, and so delightfully *démodé*." Maybe he would merely infer that Bakst had always been a good decorator, even when he'd first discovered him, but that there were others with equal talent.

Diaghileff was clothed in a worldliness which it was impossible for him to discard. He, Nouvel, Bakst, and Benois often drove out to Tsarskoe-Selo for picnic excursions. They would embark on a hot summer day from the sweltering city, the carriages full of hampers of food and wine. They would pass through the broad alleys of Orienbaum, Nouvel whistling a tune from last night's opera, Benois on the lookout for a château at the end of a little lake, a bit of Marly-le-Roi set in Peterhof. And when they arrived and spread the cloth out on the grass, Diaghileff could only smile a little weakly, helpless in the open air, wishing for the proper table and chairs, white linen and wine buckets, to which he was accustomed.

At this time Diaghileff, finished with his study of law and music, started on his first trip to the West. But for Diaghileff this tour was not, as with other young men, only a finishing school. For him it was the first taste of what could be done in the wide world, of what *he* could do.

The great excitement of the *fin de siècle*, *l'art pour l'art*, was at its height, and at Dieppe in 1894 he met Jacques Émile Blanche, the portrait painter, and the young Englishman whose contributions to the *Yellow Book* made the name of Aubrey Beardsley famous. The watering-place, populated half by English artists and society, half by Flemish and French people on a holiday, had its casino and *plage*, and here the young Russian, more French than the French, promenaded, and watched and listened. There others were amused and impressed by his facile manners, his dandy's air, masking, under the Western veneer, the unquenchable, smouldering fire of the unaccountable Slav. His Russian friends nicknamed him Chinchilla, from the single white strand in his hair.

When they asked him little questions about Russia, he answered with a mysterious hesitancy. He would never deny or affirm the flattering rumours that always seemed to follow him. Perhaps he was indeed the illegitimate son of a Romanov; perhaps not. Who could tell? He soon became an accomplished boulevardier, and loved Paris with a comprehensive passion, and an intensity only possible in an adopted Parisian.

With a grand gesture he commissioned Blanche to paint portraits of his cousins, and returned to the Court Society of St. Petersburg determined not to practise law, or go into Government service, but rather to organise young Russian artists into a more self-conscious group, in opposition to the Academic School, which sent exhibitions of their historical canvases all over the empire, and hence were known as *peripatetics*. Diaghileff had seen the Impressionists in Paris, and realised that there was a rich vein of Russian fantasy that could be drawn upon.

He began to go back and forth regularly from St. Petersburg to Moscow, bringing the artists of one city into contact with his friends of the other. In the capital he kept permanent table at the Hôtel de Europe for the pleasure of his circle, Bakst, Nouvel, Benois; Roerich, the painter and Thibetan scholar; Maliavin; the great designer Golovin; the critic Ossovsky; Prince Argoutinsky-Dolgorukoi, a cultivated amateur; and General Brezobrazov, the leader of the Mariinsky *balletomanes,* an old soldier who made a study of ballet technique and who knew the shapes of the legs of each *ballerina* far better than his strategy or ballistics.

Although Sergei Pavlovitch had little understanding for the charm and beauty of women, he always found time to lavish attentions upon the important social leaders of art and society. His charming manners were irresistible, and his power grew by seducing with his enchanting smile the omnipotent ladies of St. Petersburg. He always found time to turn up at the right place for tea, to kiss the hands that held the most possibility of power, to say a few amusing words, and to leave for the palace before they'd hardly known he'd come or gone. He was laying his foundations sensibly.

In Moscow he had a similarly representative and powerful group of friends on whom he could depend. There was the Court painter Serov, and Korovin, the stage designer; there was the chief critic of the Moscow Press, Kashkin, and, by no means least, two rich merchants, Ostrukov, and the caviar and fish magnate Sava

Mamontov, who supported Chaliapine and built handsome theatres from which started the Arts Theatre of Stanislavsky. The movements which Diaghileff inspired, and the theatres of Stanislavsky, were the two greatest single facts of the Russian Renaissance, developing out of the art and tradition of the Imperial Theatres.

Inspired by his impressions which he received on his trip to the West, Diaghileff organised the first exhibition of contemporary French and English painters at the private galleries of the Musée Stieglitz, and in 1897 made his official début as an "organiser" in the world of art. The official critics flattered it with their most violent disapproval. Society, however, on whom Diaghileff leaned always the most heavily for his support, began to come in considerable numbers and made it a social success.

But the attacks of the critics by no means discouraged Diaghileff, and the following year he arranged at the same small museum a show of Russian painters, young and old—Benois, Maliavin, Vroubl, Repin, Serov, Somov, Korovin, and Levitan.

The name of Sergei Diaghileff began to be mentioned more and more frequently in the circles which moved around the activities of the artistic interests at the Imperial Court. It was arranged that this young aristocrat, who was already Kammerjunker, should somehow be attached in a semi-official capacity to Prince Sergei Volkonsky, the new intendant of the Imperial Theatres, and advise him on special novelties in connection with the staging of opera and ballet.

Diaghileff was also entrusted with editing the official *Annual of the Imperial Theatres*, a traditional survey which covered the entire yearly activities of the five theatres in Moscow and St. Petersburg. It had formerly consisted merely of programmes, notes, and photographs, plainly bound in dark brown buckram stamped in gold. Now, unasked, Diaghileff enlarged its format to a quarto, had it beautifully printed and lavishly illustrated with many photographs, scenic and costume designs, costing something over thirty thousand roubles, which effectively exhausted the moneys of the survey.

His activities at the Imperial Theatre by no means took up all his time or fulfilled his ambition. Now, in 1898, with the financial aid of Princess Tenishev and Mamontov, he founded the magazine of art and letters, *Mir Isskoustvo* (*the World of Art*), upon which he spent most of his own fortune. This journal was exceptionally brilliant both in its presentation of material and its list of contributors. He invited the best-known painters to illustrate it.

Diaghileff had been restricted enough under official discipline to know what unconditional freedom meant to an artist or a writer, and he gave absolute liberty to the people whose work he commissioned. It included not only his familiar circle of painters and musicians, but also such writers as Dostoievsky, Merejkovsky, Turgenev, Chekhov, and Leo Tolstoi.

Sergei Pavlovitch had the courage—or, as many people considered it, the effrontery—to question the æsthetics of Leo Tolstoi in an exciting literary controversy which brought him a great number of new readers. He was so convinced of his opinions that he actually went down to Yasnya Poliana in an effort to argue with the old patriarch. Tolstoi, as can be imagined, hated the dilettante from St. Petersburg, who must have seemed to him the personification of everything he most opposed.

In the fine arts the magazine became the semi-official organ which particularly defended and furthered the work of those artists who expressed fantasy or archaism such as, Nicolai Roerich's Scythian researches, Benois's revival of the eighteenth-century baroque of Potsdam and Versailles, and Bakst's Orientalism. They were all of them passionately united against the hard,

65

generally accepted naturalists. The best of the young painters soon left their easels and began to design and paint stage scenery, a most valuable and popular method of propaganda for the newer spirit.

Now Diaghileff began to organise exhibitions under the auspices of the *Mir Isskoustvo*, and in 1889 he imported from Paris a great show of the Impressionists. This was his first real contact with the French galleries and patrons. The extraordinary success of this exhibition was of historic importance for the future of Russian painting and for the stage design of the world.

Diaghileff did not co-operate very well with Volkonsky at the Imperial Theatres. He saw no reason why his friends, who were, after all, the best painters in Russia, should not be commissioned to do scenery, and for this reason he independently asked Benois to design Delibes's ballet *Sylvia* in an entirely new production, which was a deliberate break with nineteenth-century perspectived scenery. *Sylvia* was never permitted to be shown. Diaghileff hated the petrified bureaucracy that encumbered the management, and he was not particularly tactful in his expression of it. Finally Volkonsky, in 1901, irritated beyond measure, asked him to resign. Diaghileff refused and was summarily discharged under the preposterous Article III of the Imperial code, by which the discharged servant is never again permitted to enter Government service.

To the stupefaction of everyone, not more than a week later Taniev, an important official, nominated Diaghileff for another position at the Ministère de la Cour, although the Tsar always disliked him personally, and told his cousin, the Minister of Commerce, that he'd "one day play him a dirty trick." All this time he kept up his editorial activities on *Mir Isskoustvo*, he constantly visited the studios of new artists and new writers, and attended every concert of modern music. With Nouvel, who was always

SERGEI DE DIAGHILEFF
(SACHA)

LE PAVILLON D'ARMIDE   (*Nijinsky and Pavlova*)

absorbed in music, he helped in 1901 to found the Society for Evenings of Contemporary Music, and presented for their initial Russian performances the French moderns of the day.

Mir Isskoustvo, the shows of painting, the evenings of music, led to a great deal of talk in the capital. Diaghileff, who was conceded by the artists at first as a charming, helpful Mæcenas, but a dilettante, very soon showed that he was anything but that. He had the uncanny gift of discovering talent in absolutely unknown young people. And he was always untiring and ready to sacrifice all personal advantages to secure opportunities for them. Now, in his tastefully furnished, elegant apartment in the Zamiatin Peroulok, he kept open house, and it became a custom for the progressive artists to come in at night after the theatre or concert. In these informal gatherings around Diaghileff's hospitable table was founded that nucleus of the artistic movement which so profoundly affected the art of the twentieth century.

Watchful for every possible development of art he penetrated into the remotest provinces in an effort to secure the best paintings, which he knew hung, unknown to connoisseurs and collectors, on the walls of old country estates, for a retrospective exhibition of native Russian art. Wrapped up in a greatcoat lined with nutria, he was driven over the long country roads to the big mansions of governors of the provincial districts, who were so impressed by his official air that they thought he might be a *chinovnik*, an envoy of the Tsar, on a secret mission. From rooms where the plaster was falling from the ceiling, from attics and old closets where the paintings hung loose in their frames, and from cellars where the damp had mildewed the canvas, he brought together a great collection of historical material, which made a great impression when they were well hung in the old Tauride Palace in 1903. Nobody had realised that this kind of traditional painting was so rich in

Russia. The result of the trip was a magnificent iconography of Russia of the first historical importance, which he later offered to the Government as a permanent collection, an idea which was turned down, and in the later disturbances many country estates were burned and the pictures forever lost.

On his return he had said, "The era of summing up the past has arrived. . . . I am deeply convinced we are living at a great historical moment. The time has come for a new culture, to be raised by ourselves, but one that will eventually thrust us in our turn aside." So strong was the influence of this national exhibition that a group of painters actually started a *Patiomkin tendency* of intense Slavic inspiration, named after Catherine's great Minister who tried to maintain the Russian Empire as an organic, indigenous whole.

Mamontov, who had supported *Mir Isskoustvo* in 1904, had, however, suffered great financial losses. Diaghileff, who loved the magazine, made every effort to save it. He had spent a great part of his own capital to continue its publication, but its expense was crippling, and he was forced to discontinue publication.

About the year 1906 Diaghileff started to interest his French friends in securing an invitation from the Salon d'Automne to have Russian painters exhibit in Paris. It meant a great deal of diplomacy through the Foreign Offices of France and Russia, and in the official circles of the French artists. But Diaghileff was a master in pulling all the necessary strings, and he never failed to obtain what he wanted. Fortunately, his artistic integrity was such that neither personal ambition nor advantage could tempt him. This was Diaghileff's greatest virtue.

For the first time Paris saw at this exhibition the work of Russian painters and sculptors. Every school of Russian painting was represented, from the earliest icons to the fantasies of the most advanced Impressionists. Leon Samoilovitch Bakst was commissioned to redecorate the Salon d'Automne, which he did charmingly, with an arrangement of lattice-work like a winter garden. Bakst had designed ceiling decorations for great houses in Paris and Moscow. The Grand Duke Vladimir, through Diaghileff's secret urging, commissioned decorations for ballets at the Hermitage Theatre, and he had designed the scenery and costumes for the classical season of the *Hippolytus* and the *Œdipus* at the Alexandrinsky Theatre. He was himself a member of the Salon d'Automne, and for his services to French art was decorated with the Legion of Honour. The patrons included the Grand Duchess Maria Pavlovna, a great patroness of Russian painters and wife of the Grand Duke Vladimir, and the Comtesse de Greffuhle. The success of this exhibition was colossal. Diaghileff's star rose higher and higher in the sky of artistic Europe.

Encouraged by his reception of the year before, he organised in Paris in 1907 a series of five *Concerts Historiques* of Russian music. As usual, Diaghileff secured the patronage of many eminent people. The programmes were composed of music from Glinka to Scriabine, from Borodin to Balikierev, Moussorgsky and Rimsky. Before these auditions Russian music meant only two names to the French: Tchaikovsky and Rubenstein. Scriabine and Rachmaninov appeared as pianists, and his *chefs d'orchestre* included Nikisch, Rimsky-Korsakov, Glazounov, and Chevillard. The success of the orchestral season surpassed even the exhibition of painting. Diaghileff's ambition became greater. Now he wanted to show the Russian operas, and again he succeeded. In 1908 he brought Russian opera to Paris, presenting for the first time *Boris Goudounov* and *Ivan the Terrible,* with Chaliapine, Smirnov, Lipkovska, and Baklanov, from the Imperial Opera, to a dumbfounded Western world. Benois was made artistic director.

Diaghileff, the amiable dilettante, had become the invincible magician. He was highly praised by the Imperial family, the Court, the Society of Paris and St. Petersburg; and the artists considered his judgment infallible. His position was now impregnable. Then the innumerable intrigues against him began. Everybody in an artistic position of importance imagined that he would be displaced by him. The curator of the Imperial Museums, the director of the Hermitage, the intendant of the Imperial Theatres, all formed a secret alliance, which was readily joined by those whose mediocre talents had been ignored by Diaghileff. The head of this Anti-Diaghileff League was General Teliakovsky, the new intendant of the Imperial Theatres, who had followed Volkonsky. He was an inoffensive man and a satisfactory director, who even introduced reforms at the Imperial Theatres by encouraging Russian painters and musicians. But he was by nature unimaginative. Teliakovsky, cunningly, had his spies at Diaghileff's gatherings, and as soon as they heard of an idea he quickly tried to realise it. Teliakovsky was too weak to hold such an important position, and he tried to humour everybody, from the Court Ministers to the public, the critics, the singers, or *prima ballerinas,* the Grand Dukes, and above all the mighty Kshessinskaya, which was difficult enough, as each had contradictory aims and objects.

Vaslav had heard of Diaghileff's artistic gatherings. He knew many members of the Mariinsky Theatre who frequented them. He had even met Diaghileff, *en passant,* during a performance. One day Bakst asked Vaslav to accompany him to one of these reunions. From that day on started the collaboration, which gave so much to art, and created the deep affection of these two remarkable men. Although Diaghileff was twenty years older than Vaslav, he immediately found the way through the boy's reserve, and won his friendship, which, in spite of all misunderstandings and quarrels, Vaslav unalterably kept for him. Diaghileff was at once attracted by his strong, resilient body, by the subtle, elusive combination of a boy's bearing with a feminine softness, and by the steady, glowing power which was the chief force of his character. As Vaslav later told me, "Among all the people I have ever known, Diaghileff, of course, meant the most to me. He was a genius, the greatest organiser, discoverer, and developer of talents, with the soul of an artist and a *grand seigneur*, the only man with universal talent that I could compare to Leonardo da Vinci." And in a way Vaslav was right. Diaghileff was a real man of the Renaissance. He was not a musician, yet he sang a little and played the piano well; he was no artist, yet he drew a little; he was no dancer, yet he knew dancing in its most perfected style. In short, he knew enough of everything to make his authority respected in each field, and he had the added alchemy of perception, of suggestion, which drew out of everyone his greatest possible energies. He was, in the best sense of the word, a dilettante, but the dilettante raised to the *n*th power, the dilettante all-powerful, the dilettante whose career was the furtherance of other more intense talents. Not only in Russia at this time, but later in France, Italy, Spain, the artist benefited by Diaghileff's wonderful gift of right advice. Ravel, Picasso, Marinetti, Derain, Gontcharowa, Albeniz, and an endless number of others were revealed through him to the public and themselves.

Vaslav loved to attend the evening gatherings, where he soon felt quite at home, and very soon these revered artists who were present not only had discussions with, but came to listen to, this inspired youth. Diaghileff's affection for Vaslav was profound, and he soon felt that he was not only a prodigious dancer, but a seeker after new forms and new ideas. Diaghileff now spent a great deal of time with Vaslav, and he took him to visit the studios of painters, to the Hermitage, to private collections, and to concerts. He advised him on the choice of reading and in all other matters. His influence over Nijinsky by no means pleased Teliakovsky's group, and malicious gossip began to be circulated about these inseparable friends. But nobody could dissolve the bond between them. They were united in a common aim—to raise Russian art to the highest peak. Diaghileff's was the guiding hand, by which Vaslav could develop and reach his ultimate height as an artist, a dancer, and a creator.

Vaslav was naturally greatly interested in all Diaghileff's undertakings, and he was overjoyed at his success. One day, in the early winter of 1909, he came to him with a proposition. "Sergei Pavlovitch, why not form a troupe from the Ballet of the Mariinsky Theatre and take it to Paris? Don't you want to show the world what we dancers can do?" For a moment Diaghileff was taken aback, then he began to think. Vaslav was perfectly right. Western Europe had great music, great painters, great theatres. But Russia was the only country to possess in this century a great ballet and great dancers. Diaghileff was convinced, and so the Russian Ballet was born to Western Europe.

But to take it to Paris was another matter, and almost impossible to carry out on account of the insurmountable obstacles. There were the immemorial traditions of the Mariinsky to break down, permissions to obtain from the Tsar, and the endless routine of referring requests from one office to another, the question of precedent and official assent, and there was, finally, the essential subsidy to be granted by the Imperial Government.

But Diaghileff was not the man whom obstacles could frighten. On the contrary, the greater they were the more he was determined to overcome them, and so he started at once with his marvellous ability to organise and to attack the several roads which led to the possible realisation of his ambitious scheme. His influence at Court, through his uncle and the intimate friends of his father, was already at work. The Grand Dukes he knew well, also Count Fredericks. And the critics, Rimsky-Korsakov, Serov, who was the portraitist of the Imperial family, and last, but not least, Kshessinskaya, the favourite, all made their utmost efforts to further his wishes. Before Teliakovsky and his group could realise what was happening, Diaghileff had obtained the order of the Tsar to take the Ballet to Western Europe. The Foreign Office instructed the Ambassador in France, Isvolsky, to offer him every available help. At this time the alliance between Russia and France was pending, and Count Fredericks made a special point of the fact that a visit of the Russian Ballet to France would strengthen the diplomatic and political relationship between the two countries. He placed at Diaghileff's disposal a subsidy large enough to cover the expenses of the project, and the Hermitage Theatre was put at their disposal for rehearsals.

Benois, Bakst, Prince V. N. Argoutinsky-Dolgorukoi, an expert in the antique, N. N. Tcherepnin, the composer and conductor of the Mariinsky orchestra, General Brezobrazov and Valerian Svetlov, two *balletomanes* and critics of dancing, met constantly, an unofficial committee, in Diaghileff's flat, with its walls hung with unfinished drawings from *Mir Isskoustvo*, and piles of music all over the shelves, and over their tea they discussed what they would do. They agreed that they wanted above all to show Russian ballets. There was *Konick Gorbunchok*, a Petipa creation of the mid-nineteenth century, with a Russian libretto and music by Pugni. Without a word, Diaghileff strolled over to the piano and started to play the banal, empty measures. *Konick* was never mentioned again. They thought of the *Sleeping Beauty*. It was a perfect example of Russian *mise en scène* of the classical period, with a won-

73

derful chance to show off the dancers' technical virtuosity, and the pretty Tchaikovsky music. But it had a Perrault story, and, besides, the French called Tchaikovsky the Russian Massenet. There was *Giselle*, the historic rôle of Taglioni, and Bakst insisted on the inclusion of the old ballets with white *tutus*. Pavlova would be a perfect *Giselle*. But it was too long, and perhaps Paris knew it too well.

There was the *Swan Lake*. That would be better. It was definitely old-fashioned, but it was a masterpiece of Petipa. Benois would paint a new curtain for it and design the new dresses. What else? Fokine's *Pavillon d'Armide*. It was in a way still in the old tradition a *ballet d'action*, but with a very great difference. There were *ensembles*, variations, *pas de deux*, but a solid consecutive action of mimed interludes that held the dramatic narrative together. The story was no longer a mere pretext for dances.

Fokine had first heard the score of *Pavillon d'Armide* at a concert, when its composer, Nicolai Nicolaivitch Tcherepnin, was conducting a suite, transcribed from his ballet. Afterwards he asked to be introduced to the musician, and told him how much he liked it; could he use it for a ballet? Tcherepnin said he would be delighted, that indeed it had been commissioned as a ballet for the Mariinsky, that Benois had designed all the costumes and scenery, but somehow, much to their great disappointment, it had never been produced. At first Fokine produced only the part of the Tapestry coming to life, in a special performance at the Imperial Dancing School. It turned out so well that the young choreographer was asked to do it in its entirety at the Mariinsky in November of 1907.

One of Teliakovsky's *aides* had a personal grudge against Benois which threatened the very existence of the new ballet. When it was finally staged, against great difficulties, it was by no means an official success. But old Petipa, now retired, sent a card of congratulations on the night of the first performance to the man who was to be his successor. Fokine gave his old teacher, Guerdt, the leading part of the Viscomte de Beaugency as a compliment, and at first Vaslav only danced in a *pas de trois*.

To demonstrate something of Russian national dances, Diaghileff decided to use the second act scenery of Glinka's *Rousslan and Ludmilla*, for which Korovin had painted a great mediæval hall as a setting for a *divertissement*, to be called *Festin*.

While Diaghileff was arranging the programme, assigning the designs for scenery, selecting the music, the group of artists set out with feverish enthusiasm to perfect the chosen repertoire. He invited Tcherepnin and Cooper, the two eminent conductors of the Mariinsky Theatre, to join them. Then Diaghileff selected the dancers. The first one to be asked was the *prima ballerina assoluta*, Matilde Kshessinskaya. Then he invited from the Mariinsky company as well Thamar Karsavina—who held the same rank of *prima ballerina* as Anna Pavlova—Sofia Fedorova, Baldina, and Smirnova, fine classical dancers, and the male soloists, Mihail Fokine, Adolph Bolm, Monakov, Bulgakov, Kshessinsky, Matilde's brother, and Vaslav Nijinsky. Diaghileff used his free hand lavishly. He would select the best dancers of all the Imperial Theatres, not only from St. Petersburg. So he invited from the Bolshoi Theatre in Moscow, Mihail Mordkin and Theodor Koslov, and the *prima ballerina* Koralli.

Everything was proceeding smoothly. Every possible aid had been given to him, when suddenly an incident occurred which threatened the very life of the undertaking. The mighty Kshessinskaya did not like Diaghileff's idea of giving prominent rôles to Koralli. She told him so. Diaghileff in turn made it clear to her that he would not tolerate anyone interfering with his functions.

Kshessinskaya felt insulted, and immediately went to the Grand Duke Vladimir, the Tsar's uncle, her very intimate friend at that time. A few weeks before their planned departure the authorities withdrew the subsidy from Diaghileff's troupe.

It was a terrific blow, but as the authorisation to use the dancers was not withdrawn, Diaghileff acted quickly to accomplish his plans and rented a small theatre on the Ekaterinsky Canal and continued his rehearsals there. He immediately got in touch with his influential friends in Paris, and they arranged to subscribe enough money to pay for the rent of the Châtelet Theatre. Gabriel Astruc, the French impresario, managed the business and interested Sir Basil Zaharov, while the Comtesse de Greffuhle, Robert Brussel, Boni de Castelane, Polignac, and Misia Edwards sponsored the enterprise.

Finally, the great day of departure arrived, and when the troupe boarded the Paris-bound express the platform was full of well-wishers. Vaslav's mother came down to see him off. Many of the noblemen who had estates in France were accompanying the Ballet. The train left the St. Petersburg station with a flutter of waving hands behind, bearing unsuspected to the great audiences of the West the most powerful Russian invasion the modern world had known.

Chapter Six

THE FIRST
PARIS SEASON

IN RUSSIA the spring had hardly touched the trees, and the long train rolled along through vast winter-killed fields and an occasional town. This was the first time Vaslav had left Russia. As the train rushed through Germany he was fascinated by the sense of order and routine shown by the well-kept roads that ran parallel to the tracks, the canals, the neat clean towns, all the methodical arrangements of signals, conductors, and guards.

The windows of the cars were filled all the time by the faces of the young Slavs, staring out at the unfamiliar neatness of the trim East German towns. Absorbing with their eyes the fleeting landscape, they talked endlessly in their soft Russian tongue of the reception they might expect in Paris, of the merits of the French dancers.

With every minute that brought the train closer to Paris, Vaslav's curiosity and excitement rose. Suddenly, faint as in a dream, upon its hill stood Sacré Cœur, and the towers and blurred rooftops of Paris came into focus. "You see, Slavushka," pointed Chaliapine, "that is Montmartre, and there, where my finger points, you can faintly see, towards the left, the Tour Eiffel. Yes, that's it." The long journey was actually over. This was Paris at last.

"Gare du Nord." A few more minutes and the train stopped.

Under the great dome of the station the platform was full of waiting Russians who came to welcome the Imperial Ballet. Vaslav and the rest of the dancers were completely bewildered by the noise and excitement, the eternal shouting of the blue-shirted porters in a strange language.

Vaslav wanted to drink in every small detail of this most famous city in the world. He turned left and right to catch sight of the line of the atticked roofs, the full boulevards and avenues, their names as familiar as his own from the history, novels, plays, and the newspapers he had read. It was the first day of May. Fragrant spring air charged the atmosphere of the city with delicious electricity, which cannot be found anywhere but in Paris. As the coach rolled along the avenue, they passed by the grand façade of the Opéra, its flight of steps, the Carpeaux dancers, the columned balcony arcade, and above, the dome, crowned by a lyre. Here the traditions of the antique French dance were still maintained, here the words of Noverre were living precepts, and the name of Gætan Appolon Balthazar Vestris was still alive.

Not far along the Avenue de l'Opéra they stopped at a small, unpretentious hotel, the Hôtel de Hollande, which no longer exists. After a short rest, they went straight to the Châtelet Theatre, where they were to give their performance and where Vaslav exercised under Maestro Cecchetti.

The Châtelet, owned by the City of Paris, was a huge, old-fashioned house, consecrated to spectacles of old-fashioned popular appeal, *Around the World in Eighty Days*, with great scenic effects, fires on the stage, storms, and hurricanes. When Vaslav was shown into the huge auditorium, it was dark and dusty. He said it looked like a lake without water. Neither Vaslav nor the rest of the company saw anything of Paris for the next few weeks, except the buildings that bordered their drive from their hotels to the Châtelet. The constant rehearsals worked them up to fever pitch. The Russian conductors, Tcherepnin and Cooper, took charge of the famous Colonne orchestra, and endless rehearsals were necessary to acquaint the French wood-wind and brass with the amazing new sonorities, which at first seemed almost incomprehensible to them.

Maestro Cecchetti was stricter than ever, and, in spite of the fact that the dancers had innumerable rehearsals with and without the orchestra, he never allowed them to miss a lesson. His classroom was filled with admiring French and Italian dancers, and friends of his who marvelled at the wonderful discipline and technique of his *pupils* of the perfection class.

The shabby old Châtelet was being rapidly transformed.

Diaghileff invaded the musty hall with an army of carpenters, decorators, and electricians. They had to construct an entirely new floor on the stage—of pine, the elasticity of which is most suitable for dancing—which covered over the orchestra pit and eliminated the first rows of stalls. The columns and balustrades were recovered in new velvet, and green potted plants were placed in the corridors. Diaghileff had brought a complete technical staff with him and the mechanic, Valtz from Moscow, supervised the traps and elaborate changes of scenery required in *Armide*. Everything proceeded rapidly. He was here, there, and everywhere, behind the scenes, in the lobby, in the orchestra, advising and supervising.

Astruc, the indefatigable impresario, had asked young Jean Cocteau to write and illustrate a booklet announcing the coming marvels. Auguste Rodin, Odilon Redon, Marcel Proust, Jean-Louis Vaudoyer, Reynaldo Hahn, Gerard d'Houville, la Comtesse de Noailles, Jacques-Émile Blanche, Robert Brussel, José Maria Sert, by their talk, threw the artistic and literary circles of Paris into a ferment of anticipation.

And in this tower of Babel Vaslav, as often as Fokine could spare him, exercised without allowing himself to be disturbed, unaware even of his surroundings. Whenever there was a free moment amid the din, Vaslav escaped from the glaring, shifting lights, the crashing chords, the calls of the stage-hands and the electricians' signals, into a dark, quiet corner of the big stage, where, unobserved, for two or three minutes he could repeat an *entre-chat royal*,[1] or a *grand fouetté à la seconde*.

Vassily, Diaghileff's faithful valet, once a servant on his father's estate, who had found himself in trouble and been pardoned through Sergei Pavlovitch's good offices, watched over Vaslav like a nurse, keeping the curious at a distance. Vassily was a real Russian *moujik*, crop-headed, with a heavy beard. Erect and sinister, almost always silent, without a trace of servility, he knew how to command respect by his dark presence. He seemed to know everything that was going on without ever being told, and he would have committed murder for Diaghileff without a tremor. Like a shadow, he was omnipresent, hovering over Vaslav except when Diaghileff appeared. Then he would vanish, only to be mysteriously at hand whenever his master needed him. He was in charge of the small dancing-shoes which were especially made for Vaslav by Nicolini of Milan. They were of soft kid glove-leather, and he used from two to three pairs each ballet, for his feet when dancing swelled and split the thin hide. Vassily always stood in readiness with half a dozen pairs of shoes and a flat surface where Vaslav could scuff the soles with powdered rosin.

The preparations were so intense that no time could be spared even for meals. Therefore Diaghileff ordered food to be brought over from Larue's famous restaurant. Larue had once been the

---

[1] The *entre-chat* is a step of crossing the feet in mid-air a number of times. *Entre-chat dix* (ten times) has only been performed in modern times by Nijinsky.

Tsar's chef, and he loyally maintained that French and Russian cooking could not be surpassed. The platters of caviar, the heaps of blini, the tureens of bortsch, carried over from Larue's by the waiters, in the restaurant's silver service, were set around on up-turned boxes of props and costumes, and the dancers ate on the stage, barely taking a bite between steps.

Finally the great day of the *première* arrived, and, as before a great storm, there was a torpid calm.

Paris has seldom seen such an audience as came into the revivi-fied Châtelet on the evening of the 17th of May, 1909.

Pavillon d'Armide, Festin, and *Prince Igor* were on the pro-gramme. The bells in the corridor rang, the house lights started to dim. People left off talking to each other. A few late-comers rushed in, amid half-breathed apologies. Tcherepnin appeared from un-der the stage, stepped upon the podium, his baton acknowledging the perfunctory applause. A tap on the music-rack, and he began the opening strains of his own *Pavillon d'Armide.*

Vaslav had absolutely no idea what was going on on the other side of the asbestos curtain. As usual, he had arrived at the theatre with Vassily around seven o'clock and had gone straight to his dressing-room, changed into his practice costume, and gone on the stage to exercise for an hour. This he had done invariably all his life before each performance. After this, he went in to make up.

Nobody was ever allowed to enter his dressing-room, and it was an unusual event if even Diaghileff was permitted. The great-est possible order was maintained there, for Vaslav was scrupu-lously neat. His costumes were already hung up and prepared, his dancing-shoes lined up in one row on the floor. On his dressing-table, in military precision, was set out his make-up—sticks of Leichner grease paint, from the darkest to the lightest.

His make-up took him almost half an hour, and he did it with

81

enormous care. Indeed, only Chaliapine knew as well as he did how to make up. Often, when inventing a new character, Vaslav would ask the professional advice of Bakst or Benois. When he was finished with this the hairdresser came in and affixed his wig and head-dress with glue, so that no leaps could dislodge it. Then clever Maria Stepanovna, the wardrobe mistress, entered to inspect his costume and see if anything needed a needle and thread. In many of his rôles, notably in *Spectre de la Rose* and *Faune*, he had literally to be sewn into his clothes.

All this happened in silence. Vaslav, from the moment he had entered his dressing-room, had no other thought than his part. He was already in its mood, and disliked anyone to speak to him.

Bakst and Benois, with Diaghileff, had the artists pass in review before them on the stage, to see if they had been made up and costumed as they had been instructed. For each ballet they had to conform to the wishes of the designer, and no variation was tolerated. The chief stage manager was responsible for seeing that they did not wear rings or other personal jewellery, or anything not indicated for the costumes, and especially no pins. These rulings were strictly upheld.

This was the first time that Paris was prepared to watch a whole evening of ballet divorced from opera or spoken dramatic interludes.

Fokine had created Vaslav's dances with a great display of technique. They were stylised into the essence of behaviour at the Sun King's Court. The mimed action was fluent, stately, and human. From what Vaslav told me later, the instant he began to dance his first variation a murmur went through the public which almost terrified him. The audience burst into an unceasing storm of applause after his first *tour en l'air*. He sensed the complete abandon of the public in response to his performance. When he leaped off the stage, there were resounding cries for *"Encore, bis, bis, bis"*; but the rules of the ballet rigidly forbade any artist appearing except when his part called for him.

The *entr'acte* was applauded wildly through, without a stop in the bravos. Robert de Montesquieu, with his white gloves and gold-handled cane, waved again and again over the audience. Paris was stupefied and transported.

The uproar was terrific; the critics were almost hysterical. They crowded the stage in a mad, breathless excitement. But Vaslav did not know of all this, as he was changing in his dressing-room.

He took off the necklace which Benois had designed for him, little realising that he had set a fashion. At first the jewelled collar had rested low on the top of his satin coat. Thinking the line was bad, he raised it, so that it formed a choker around his neck. Cartier was quick to perceive the innovation, and the great ladies of Paris and London for the next two seasons wore collars of black moiré and diamonds, pearls and brilliants, *à l'Armide*.

From the parterres of Versailles to the steppes of Central Asia! The prelude of the Polovetsian dances from Borodin's *Prince Igor* swarmed over the violins, and the stage revealed the round hide tents of a Tartar encampment, with Roerich's gold and smoky russet sky. Lines of women in baggy trousers circled, trailing dusky veils. Fokine's wonderful choreography was the perfect equivalent, in its asymmetrical cadences, of the counterpoint of chorus and orchestra.

Le Festin was an arrangement calculated to show the entire troupe in national dances, orchestrated from the work of several composers. It opened with the march from Rimsky-Korsakov's *Coq d'Or*; then dances from *Lesghinka* by Glinka, *The Golden Fish* by Tchaikovsky, a Glazounov czardas, a Moussorgsky hopak, a Glinka mazurka, a Tchaikovsky trepak, a *pas classique hongrois* by Glazounov, and a stirring finale taken from Tchaikovsky's Second Symphony. Vaslav danced a *pas de quatre* with Adolf Bolm, Mordkin, and Koslov, which created a furore of enthusiasm.

Only at the end of the performance, when Diaghileff opened the door to the stage, the "sanctuary," to his friends, the *élite* of Society, the artistic circles of Paris, did Vaslav realise that something quite unusual was going on. He was surrounded by an increasing crowd of marvellously bejewelled ladies, men—everybody asking questions which he could not understand, as he did not know a single word of French. Nouvel and Gunsburg did their best to answer for him. Overwhelmed by all the questions, the flattering hands, the terrific rush and enthusiasm of people who wanted to meet him, shake his hands, touch him, even look at his shoes, he became violently embarrassed and fled into his dressing-room. Vassily guarded the door. Diaghileff went on to a big party with his friends and sponsors, but Vaslav begged to be excused, and, completely bewildered, drove back through the lamp-lit streets to the hotel, leaving the streets crowded with the enthusiastic audience, loath to go home.

As he hated to get up early, Sergei Pavlovitch breakfasted in bed, receiving the reports of his secretaries, dictating his correspondence, reading the telegrams of congratulations. Diaghileff had the blinds always drawn, and the electric lights burning brightly, even if it were midday, like an old Marquise afraid of the daylight. He spoke on several telephones at once, and worked untiringly with his technical staff and his friends, with rarely a free moment, as he had not only to supervise everything to the smallest detail in connection with the Ballet, but he also had pressing social obligations; patrons and patronesses to call upon, respects to pay to the Grand Duke, and the thousand small attentions whereby he maintained the large circle of his supporters.

Vaslav, the morning after the *première*, dressed as usual and wanted to go down to the Châtelet to practise, but while he was putting on his suit his door was forced open, in spite of the ever-watchful Vassily, and an excited band of strange, gesticulating men stormed the room. At first Vaslav thought: "My God, even in France it is like Russia. The police are searching the suite for political reasons." But not at all. They were only reporters and photographers, who tried desperately to explain to Vaslav that he was indeed the sensation of Paris, that the cultivated audience of the town already named him *Le Dieu de la Danse*, and that by this time he was world-famous.

Soon Diaghileff, Bakst, and the rest came over from their rooms and rescued him, explaining the whole story, after which he docilely posed for the cameras. Vaslav was exuberantly happy that the reception in Paris had been so immediate and so warm, that they understood and loved his art so well.

Diaghileff and the dancers were fêted wherever they chose to appear. However, Vaslav very rarely accompanied them, as he disliked to alter the routine of his day the very slightest.

In the morning, after a few cups of tea, he would go down to the theatre for a lesson with Maestro Cecchetti. A rehearsal with Fokine was followed by a late lunch around four o'clock with Diaghileff at Larue's, where Bakst, Benois, Gunsburg, and the more intimate of the *balletomanes* always gathered. Their crowd enlarged from day to day, for every one of the friends brought friends of his—French and English musicians, painters and actors, Gunsburg, his international banker friends, and Nouvel, his statesmen and diplomats. In this way Vaslav met everyone of importance in the international world—constantly observing, but keeping silent.

After lunch he went for a drive in the Bois, usually with Nouvel or Bakst, up under the great lindens and horse chestnuts, past the lake with the children sailing their toy boats, past the parasols and gay tables of Armenonville, and back slowly, with the long shadow of the Arc de Triomphe behind them, to the hotel, where Vaslav's *masseur* rubbed and relaxed his muscles for an hour, and then he went to sleep for another hour in a darkened room. At half past six he was awakened by Vassily, and they would leave for the Châtelet and the evening's performance.

The other novelties of the season were *Cléopâtre, Les Sylphides*, and *Les Orientales.*

While *Pavillon* showed unmistakable signs of the new spirit, and demonstrated Fokine's real power, it did not include the sensational innovations of *Cléopâtre. Une Nuit de Cléopâtre* had been originally prepared for the Mariinsky stage, after the well-known story of Théophile Gautier, where the Queen seeks a night's lover who is willing to die at dawn. Fokine, who could only accomplish a little of what he wanted on the stage of the Imperial Theatre, was constantly asked to produce ballets for charity, where he had absolute freedom to do as he wished and the pick of the ballet company. So for a single charity performance he re-studied *Cléopâtre*, rifling the Imperial costume wardrobes for new costumes. Spears formerly held in Petipa's old *Fille du Pharaon*, a helmet or a shield from *Aïda*, a few dresses from *Eunice*, combined with a little paint and thread, looked admirable. Arensky's music he had re-orchestrated, introduced bits of Liadov, Glazounov, Rimsky-Korsakov and Tcherepnin, and made out of the ballet an actual danced tragedy—not a pantomime, but a drama where words were gestures and the chorus group movements. Instead of the faces of the dancers being set in rigid smiles, they actually moved, gave expression to desire and grief.

For Diaghileff, Bakst now designed entirely new costumes and a huge architectural scene. The magnificent setting, with its splendid colouring, brought the atmosphere of Egypt, with a perfect understanding of the mood—an Egypt realistic, fantastic, that immediately acted on the audience like a light, delightful narcotic. The music carried them further into the Egyptian mood, and when the dancers appeared the audience was completely prepared to receive the impression which the artists wanted to create. Between great red gods which framed a high hall was a court of a temple. At the back, through other columns, was a glimpse of the glistening Nile.

Vaslav, a young soldier, and Karsavina, a slave-girl, a veil carried between them, enter the temple in a dance which is a *pas de deux*, not of conventional supported adagio, but love. The Queen was carried in on a palanquin which could have been a painted mummy-case. Set on the floor, her wrappings were whirled off her by slaves. A black panther of a man crouched under her divan, aching to kill the young warrior who came out of the temple shadows to her with helpless attraction. Cleopatra's part was mimed, not danced, in a semi-stylised manner—not rigid, but reminiscent of the hieroglyphics.

Ida Rubinstein's beauty and magnificent body fitted this part perfectly. The little slave-girl, which was danced by Karsavina, alternating with Fokina, carried the action to the point where Nijinksy made his entrance with infinite verve and *élan*. There was a dark rout of negroes, a swaying dance of heavy Jewesses with swinging ornaments, and finally a wild bacchanal of Greek captives in an ecstasy of Dionysian frenzy, led by Karsavina and Pavlova —here only a dance in a ballet, but whose substance Pavlova lived on for years later in her Bacchanal.

The freedom of the use of the whole body, the actual flesh seen through slashed silk trousers, the breasts tossing under their gold nets, the hair loose, the great leaps of the Ethiopians, the intense drama and the quickening *tempo* to the climax, was an achievement which is a chapter heading to any history of dancing in our time.

The evening began with *Les Sylphides* (in which Vaslav danced with Pavlova and Karsavina), the enchanting evocation of Taglioni's classic style which Fokine had designed as a monument of formal choreography to music by Chopin. Benois had given the dancers long Victorian *tutus* and frail white diamanté wings and set it all against a mournful, romantic scene of a deserted, ruined holy place. Vaslav's conception of this part was to impersonate Chopin. Therefore he brought out the very essence of Slavonic languor and softness.

In his blond wig, the curls down to his shoulders, in white tights, *crêpe de Chine* shirt, and black velvet *gilet*, Vaslav danced like a body without weight, so that whenever he came down one had the feeling he was already on his way up—like a rubber ball, the harder bounced, the higher it rises. He floated, literally floated, and for a second stopped in the air. His unbelievable capacity of almost flying stupefied the audience and his *entre-chat dix* was another miracle. No one could achieve more than six *entre-chats*, or on rare occasions, eight.

From front stage to back stage he covered the whole distance in the air at a single bound, and left them gasping. Never stopping for a second—for even in his pauses he re-echoed the preceding movement—he made the audience feel as if this preceding movement and the one to come were fused in a thrilling whole. Vaslav never stopped to make a preparation before executing a leap, however difficult it might be, as the other dancers did. He explained to me later that dancing should be as simple as one breath taken after another, and, though every step is a separate action, it must seem to be the natural and harmonious consequence of all previous action. Thus his dancing had an unending, constant weaving rhythm, which gave to the spectators an inexpressibly wonderful sense of beauty.

His *entre-chat royal* caused a furore among the dancers and ballet experts. But his technique was so perfectly understood that he never made it felt.

Vaslav had a perfectly proportioned body. He weighed almost one hundred and thirty pounds. His legs were so muscular that the hard cords stood out on his thighs like bows. With his unusually powerful arms, controlled by the highest technique, he could pick up and lift his partners with such ease that it seemed as if he only held a doll of straw. He did not, like the other male dancers, support the girl with both hands on her hip, but with one single arm he raised her straight from his side.

His hands, when not in a *danse de style*, when the costume and manner were not dictated by its nature, were always held with the fingers close together, in a simple natural way. He told me that one must always watch children if one wishes to learn the proper way of using hands beautifully, because children are always unself-conscious. One never sees a baby extending its little finger when raising its hand. Everything in his dance was worked out to the minutest detail.

When the last ballet of the evening had been danced, the audience stood up and applauded in swelling, ecstatic thunder. The curtain went up again and again, but the performers, according to their rules and traditions, never took a separate bow, but received their ovation in the position in which the curtain found them. Vaslav always made his bow in keeping with the style and mood of the particular ballet in which he happened to be dancing.

While Diaghileff was embracing Karsavina or congratulating

Bolm, amid the hubbub of excitement as the artists and spectators mingled to discuss their impressions and the stage hands busily removed the scenery, Vaslav imperturbably continued dancing in order not to come abruptly to a full stop, just as a horse is trotted up and down with decreasing momentum after a race gradually to calm its quivering muscles. Then he hurried off the stage, brushing by the other excited dancers, past Diaghileff, into his dressing-room.

The day's routine usually ended in a big dinner, but very often a group of them went to the Café de la Paix. Sometimes they played an interesting game to amuse themselves, each one guessing the profession or occupation of a chosen passer-by. Bakst gained his impression by the face and head; Benois from his clothes, shoes, the colour of his cravat; Vaslav from the stranger's bodily movements; and Diaghileff from a general impression. To verify the guesses, Bakst was sent after the stranger to ask him!

Every morning Diaghileff showed Vaslav the sheaf of newspaper and magazine criticisms, which he collected with considerable care. The eulogies naturally pleased Vaslav, but they never went to his head. He always remained the simple, modest boy he was. But there was one criticism of which he was enormously proud. This was the quotation by a journalist of a criticism of the great Vestris, the idol of France, by Beaumarchais, the author of *La Mariage de Figaro*, now referring to Vaslav: *"Il faisait oublier le comble de l'art par la plus ingénieuse négligence."*

The Russian Opera was performed at the Châtelet, on alternate nights with the Ballet, *Boris Godounov, Ivan the Terrible,* and *Prince Igor.* Chaliapine, Smirnov, Kastorsky, Chernov, Lipkovska, Petrenko, Zbrouevska, were the stars of the company, which had its own superbly trained choruses. The effect on the audience and musicians of Paris was only second to the profound impression of the Ballet. Vaslav, like a child absorbed, watched Chaliapine every time he sang, either from the auditorium or behind the scenes, and afterwards he would frequently join Diaghileff and the rest for supper. Chaliapine, who called Nijinsky "Slavushka," had a Chinese servant who adored Vaslav and always let him into the master's dressing-room.

Vaslav was always fascinated by Bakst's constant sketching, on menus, marble-topped tables, napkins, or scraps of paper. He started himself to draw, at first a little timidly, until Bakst told him he had a real talent for it undeveloped. But Diaghileff would not hear of his doing this. "Let him alone, Levoushka," he would say; "don't distract him. He's got enough to do as it is, with his dancing." Bakst and Diaghileff, accompanied by their Parisian friends well acquainted with the peculiar specialties of Paris, would make occasional sorties on the town, late, after supper, but Vaslav was always left behind safe in the hotel, with Vassily to watch over him. But they never treated him like a child, nor patronised him in the manner of older men. They respected his opinions and his presence and adored his gifts. The ballet company was proud of him in a curious, detached way, for they only saw him when he worked on the stage with them.

Vaslav had very little idea of the sophistication of the capital. He arrived in Paris with only a blue and a brown suit, besides his costumes. Brought up on clean tap-water, he drank out of the faucet in France and came down with a terrible attack of typhoid fever, so that he was unable to finish the season. Sergei Pavlovitch had no faith in French doctors, and he was fortunate in being able to call in Dr. Botkin, the Tsar's personal physician, who happened to be in Paris at the time. Botkin was just able to pull him through, but Vaslav had been terribly sick. When he had made a thorough physical examination, Botkin went to Diaghileff and told him there was something curious about Vaslav's glands. "Sergei, take care of him—there's something about it I don't like." But no one gave it any attention at the time, and Vaslav was soon on the road to recovery.

The Paris season was over. The troupe packed up, made arrangements for shipping scenery, trunks, and costumes, and anticipated the still greater honours and welcome which awaited them in St. Petersburg, the triumph accorded to the return of a victorious army.

Diaghileff decided to go on a well-earned vacation with Vaslav and Bakst to Karlsbad.

Vaslav enjoyed Karlsbad, with its hills, excursions into the pine forests, and the little Russian church. The place reminded him of Narzan, in the Caucasus, which was a similarly smart Russian resort. They had pleasant rooms with balconies looking down from a hill-top. Vaslav didn't take the cure. He did absolutely no work for two months, no exercises, only massage. After two or three weeks of rest they went down to Venice.

The beautiful trip through the Tyrol and over the Italian Alps pleased Vaslav, and he was up early and would not move away from his window till bedtime. They stopped at the old Hôtel des Bains at the Lido, and as soon as they were settled Benois took Vaslav all over the city, into every church, palace, museum, and private collection he knew, explaining the paintings and architecture, and Vaslav in his turn took them down to the beach for a swim. He was an excellent swimmer, and could do all manner of tricks, including pirouettes, under the water. With Benois, they dragged Bakst into the Adriatic, enjoying tremendously his terror of the sea. Diaghileff never went near the sea. His hatred of water nearly amounted to a phobia, and in his suite at the Lido the curtains were always drawn on the windows that gave out on the lagoons.

They had a marvellous time in Venice, sightseeing and swimming all day, and talking with new friends all night. Shortly after their arrival a large circle of new acquaintances was formed around them. D'Annunzio had known Diaghileff, and joined them whenever he could. The first time the poet met Vaslav he was already far gone in his royal mania, and turned to him, saying, "Pray dance me something." As soon as he understood the imperative quality of the remark Vaslav was quite angry, and answered quickly, *"Please write me something."*

But after the first meeting he became friendly and congenial, and there was no hitch in their friendship.

Isadora Duncan was also in Venice, and Vaslav met her for the first time at a crowded party in the palace of the great Italian beauty and queen of Roman society, the Marchesa Casati; the beautiful eccentric, who had made her début in Rome by driving into a ballroom in a chariot drawn by lions, with a live snake as her main costume.

Isadora Duncan did everything she could to be with Diaghileff, because she hoped he would engage her to play parts similar to those mimed by Ida Rubinstein. But Diaghileff, with his consummate tact, always avoided every possible encounter in which she might force him into any definite answer. Not only did he avoid meeting her personally, but also refused to express an open opinion of her style of dancing. He was indeed relieved that Vaslav could speak nothing but Russian, because the latter would have told her or anyone bluntly what he thought of Duncan. Vaslav was only silent because he never understood the questions, and they were never translated to him.

Isadora Duncan did not conceal from anyone her desire to

sleep with every famous man she met, since she wanted to have children by them, to help propagate another artistic generation. Naturally she asked Vaslav to create with her a dancer, and when Diaghileff, very much amused, translated her invitation to him, he merely smiled.

They knew Duncan had no basic knowledge of the technique of the dance, and, although she produced something entirely new in our time, her execution betrayed her secret and her weakness. She was an amateur. It went so far, in their unshakable opinion, that whenever they saw something bad, poor in execution or taste in dancing or opera, whereas they had formerly dismissed it by saying *"C'est du Munich,"* they now said *"C'est du Duncan."*

They enjoyed the parties and the gay company, but they mostly loved to sit by themselves on the Piazza San Marco, in front of the Confiserie of Floriani, eating *gelati*. In the evening the piazza was full of people listening to the band concerts, and Vaslav, watching the wheeling pigeons and the different types of passing Italians (officers gracefully corseted with slender effeminate waistlines, capes swishing in the breeze, black eyes snapping brilliantly; swarthy skinned women gesticulating) composed their criss-cross movements into dances. Perhaps it was here that he first thought of composing choreography himself.

At the end of August they had to return to Russia, as Vaslav's leave was up. With regret they left Venice, but they were proud and happy on their triumphant return to St. Petersburg.

Chapter Seven

THE FRIENDSHIP
OF SERGEI DE DIAGHILEFF
AND VASLAV NIJINSKY

THE NEWS of the Ballet's tremendous success and Nijinsky's personal triumph in Paris had of course preceded them. St. Petersburg received the conquerors with open arms; the papers were full of them, and they could really say about the Paris season, *"Veni, vidi, vici."* At the station Vaslav was met by his mother and his sister Bronia. Eleanora Bereda could scarcely believe that it was her Vatza of whom she had read so much, and she kept sobbing and laughing at once, and talking to him all the time. The first days passed in feverish excitement. There was so much she had to be told about Vaslav's success, about the trip, about Paris and Venice.

When the rehearsals began, Vaslav reported at once at the Mariinsky. Baron Fredericks expressed to him the satisfaction of the Court and himself, congratulating him on his success and thanking him for the service he had rendered Russia through his dancing. His colleagues received him with cheers, but soon his life came again under the iron discipline and rules of the Imperial Theatre, with its exclusive and expert audiences, whose tickets had actually been handed down from generation to generation.

This was Vaslav's third season at the Mariinsky since his

graduation. More and more parts were assigned to him after the Parisian success. Up to now he had appeared most frequently in *Juan*, with Trefilova and Pavlova as his partners, in which he had already danced in 1907, a year before his graduation. Then there was *Armide*, of course; *Une Nuit d'Egypte*—known to Paris as *Cléopâtre*—*The Talisman*, and *Giselle*.

Giselle was a famous French ballet, after a poem of Theophile Gautier's, with music by Adam. The choreography was arranged by Koralli, and it was performed for the first time on the 28th of June, 1841. It was Carlotta Grisi's most famous rôle, and ever since it has been the most exacting and desirable of the classical dancer's parts—almost a Hamlet of the ballet. It was a perfect vehicle for Pavlova. She danced a young village girl who, betrayed by a Prince in disguise, goes mad and commits suicide. Anna Pavlova was magnificent in this exhausting tragic *pas seul*, a heroic Ophelia of the dance, a wonderful example of technical virtuosity combined with an overwhelming dramatic intensity. It was her favourite part.

In the famous second scene, when we see her grave, and the Prince scattering blossoms on it, kneeling and offering prayers for her resurrection, Pavlova emerges from the damp ground like a ghost of frightening beauty as she subtly casts off the veils of death and floats about the stage like a creature without bodily weight, to dance her *pas de deux* with the Prince.

Pavlova's performance was perfect, and she had a proprietary interest in the ballet. She resented so much the more Vaslav's phenomenal success as the young Prince. That a male dancer should be applauded, called for again and again and showered with flowers like a *prima ballerina assoluta*, was an unheard-of event.

Vaslav thought very highly of the art of Anna Pavlova. He

CARNAVAL
(DE MEYER)

Left: SCHEHEREZADE
(DE MEYER)

Right: PETROUCHKA
(ELLIOTT & FRY, LTD.
AND P. & A. PHOTO)

found her technique matchless, her attitudes and arabesques extremely beautiful, and he loved to dance with her. Her lightness and exquisite frailty appealed to him. He enjoyed dancing with her at the Mariinsky, where she fulfilled herself as a lyric poet of the ballet, and, although intensifying her emotion and establishing her swooning style, she could not overdo it there, controlled by the iron discipline and tradition of the Mariinsky, as she later did with her own independent troupe.

Vaslav felt that the quality of their dancing came from the same source, and that in his flying movements, at least Pavlova could give the impression by her lightness that they complemented each other. Their dances together in *Les Sylphides* were of a consummate sympathy beyond description.

Diaghileff, after his return, was fêted as never before. The subsidy withdrawn the previous year was now almost forced upon him. Kshessinskaya invited him often to her palace, and made it quite clear that she wished to be included in the next tour. Diaghileff had been officially approached to bring the Ballet back to Paris the next spring, not to the Châtelet, but to the Opéra itself. His evening meetings were resumed again, and during this winter the unforgettable ballets of *Carnaval* and *Scheherazade* were created.

Fokine, who always seemed doomed to create his best work outside of the Mariinsky, had been asked to design dances for a ball. The magazine *Satyricon* had arranged an evening party in the Sala Pavlovna, a large public ballroom. The editor Kornfeldt, and his friend the poet Patiomkin, told Fokine that they were calling the party *Carnaval*. Fokine immediately thought of Schumann's enchanting early piano pieces. They translated characteristic bits of Schumann's life and letters to him, as he spoke no German, and he absorbed the atmosphere of the period. Who would do the decorations and costumes? Fokine suggested Bakst, of course. Kornfeldt said he would be perfect, but too expensive. Fokine persuaded him to do it for half his usual fee, and gave him part of his own pay, for which Bakst presented him with a painting. Bakst was enchanted with the idea, and immediately saw costumes of the time of Schumann, the Austrian Biedermeier period of eighty years before. Fokine had only three days for rehearsals, and was forced to practise in a ballroom where the carpenters were pounding all over the floor, preparing the wall decorations.

Diaghileff was right in his judgment about *Carnaval,* and, when he finally presented it, not a single movement had been changed. Schumann must have visualised movement, composing this piece. It needed great courage to transcribe music written for piano for full orchestra. It was almost sacrilegious and unmusical, and Diaghileff, who was a fine musician, knew this. But if it were done, it must be done, as in the case of *Les Sylphides,* by eminent musicians who would understand the subtlety of Schumann. Diaghileff chose Glazounov for this extremely delicate and difficult task. The score of *Carnaval* proves that Diaghileff was right to entrust the orchestration to him, for he rendered it perfectly. And in spite of the fact that both Liadov and Tcherepnin also collaborated, the final effect was as harmonious as if it had been orchestrated by a single person.

Carnaval is the frame in which these personages appear before us: the sad, heartbroken Pierrot, always teased, always seeking a sweetheart; Papillon, the gay young girl who flirts and plays with Pierrot, who takes her so seriously; Florestan and Eusebius, the one the romantic, the other the stormy, temperamental side of Schumann's own nature; Pantalon, the ancient *beau,* chasing eternally after Columbine; Harlequin, the mischievous; and all the young men and girls laughing, dancing, teasing, flirting. The music and the dance simultaneously express the same idea. In *Carnaval*, as in *Les Sylphides*, movement is for the first time given its due place. Fokine re-created in his choreography the period of Alt Wien. *Carnaval* is a perfect gem among Fokine's ballets. It is harmonious from beginning to end. The Valse Noble, danced by eight couples, remains the masterpiece of the waltz.

Bakst, to whom the scenery and costumes were entrusted, very cleverly chose a curtain as background. This is now a banal form of scenery, for every dancer uses it at recitals, but it was Bakst's innovation. He chose a heavy velvet of royal blue, with a deep and warm hue. On the bottom were painted heavy garlands of leaves and vivid pink bouquets of roses, which contrasted marvellously with the darkness of the velvet. At each side of the back of the stage was a ridiculous and enchanting red and green striped Biedermeier sofa.

The men, in tail-coats of different colours and tall black velvet top hats, lace jabots and white gloves, looked irresistible. The girls swung great panniered skirts of steel-blue taffeta, and wore small velvet bonnets and white kid gloves. They all carried black velvet masks, which they held before their eyes and put on only when they danced. Pierrot appeared in his loose, familiar dress and his endless, huge, white, tragic, helpless sleeves and big ruff of black tulle, and Columbine in her white full taffeta skirt, with garlands of cherries painted on it by Bakst himself, and, in her hair, Karsavina, who created this part, wore also a wreath of cherries. There is Chiarina (Fokina), the coquette, who danced, in a dress sewn with small tassels, with two other girls. Their *pas de trois*, all magnificently performed on points, was one of the most perfect and seductive creations Fokine has ever done. And above all there was Harlequin, mischievous, sly, half cat, half spoiled child, in his white *crêpe de Chine* blouse and huge black neatly tied bow, with his skin tights painted in red, green, and white octagons by Bakst. This needed the skill of a master, because it was extremely difficult to paint the pattern on the leg so that the muscles would not distort it, but the costume was so perfect that every ripple of Nijinsky's leg showed as if the markings were transparent.

The whole ballet completely proved the logical brilliance of Fokine's invention and the soundness of the theories, which, though he had set them down in a famous letter to the Mariinsky management, were still ignored by them. In five clearly stated principles he had laid down the laws of modern ballet-dancing:

"It is impossible to form combinations of ready-made steps; one must create an expression to fit the subject at hand.

"Dancing and mimetic gesture have no meaning unless they describe the dramatic action, and gestures can never be used as mere *divertissement*.

"Conventional gesture can only be used when the style of the ballet demands it. Gestures of the hand alone must be replaced by gestures of the whole body.

"Groups and *ensemble* dances must be used expressively as a whole and not merely as a symmetrical decorative background for the soloists.

"And, finally, there must be an unbroken alliance between dancing and the other arts of music and painting. Special ballet music is not required. Music of nearly any fluency can be accepted."

Fokine's originality was manifested in more ways than one. His brother was one of the first automobile merchants in Russia, and Fokine was naturally interested in his success. The other dancers were vastly amused at an artist's connection with business. Diaghileff himself never attempted to correct or influence him, and relied implicitly on his taste and ideas. But, when he was designing the brilliant dances for *Prince Igor*, Benois and General Brezobrazov, a little shocked at their violence, approached him with shy, tentative suggestions. They could only ask him to "change it; well, just change—how shall we say it?—a little." They didn't know exactly how to change it, but felt that a difference would help. Fokine flatly refused. He said he knew what he was doing and he would do it. It has not taken history to tell him how right he was.

Sergei Pavlovitch did correct him, once. At a rehearsal of the mimed part of *Coq d'Or*, Fokine had a character grasp his hand to his side at a reference in the song to his liver. From the back of the house came Diaghileff's authoritative voice, "The other side, Michel; the liver's on the other side."

Diaghileff, ever on the look-out for new dancers to present, made frequent trips to Moscow, where he was well known, and acquired Katherina Geltzer and Alexander Volinine, first dancers of the Imperial Opera there.

Among the new dancers from St. Petersburg, Diaghileff decided to take along Fokina, the wife of the *maître de ballet*. Biber, Puni, Poliakova, Doubrovska, Loupokhova, and Loupokhova II, who later became famous as Lydia Lopokova. They were all graduates of the Imperial School, fine dancers, and of course a valuable addition to the troupe.

The only one who had not so graduated was Ida Rubinstein, who was to accompany them on the tour to create the mimed rôle of Scheherazade, after her success as Cleopatra. During the whole winter she worked arduously with her master Fokine. To Kshessinskaya was assigned the important part of Armide. *Giselle*, although already in the Mariinsky's classic repertory, was remounted by Diaghileff as the perfect part for Pavlova. But this year she pre-

101

ferred to tour by herself in Denmark and Sweden, where the ballet has always been kept on a high standard. After the first season, impresarios flooded the stars with separate offers. But most of them realised that the Russian Ballet as a whole was an unparalleled organisation whose great strength lay in its unity, that their art could be developed in this way to its highest point and their individual talents shine best in this frame. Pavlova was blinded. She was a magnificent dancer, but she loved personal success more than the perfection of her art in its entirety. This was the fundamental difference between Pavlova and Karsavina. The latter always sacrificed her private ends to that of dancing. Pavlova could have performed a real service to her chosen art by educating the masses who loved her, instead of following their undeveloped taste. Her scenery and staging in the first years were mediocre, and with her music she made similar concessions to public taste. Later on she realised that in spite of her own marvellous performance she would not be accepted unless she raised the quality of her production. Then she asked Fokine to compose dances for her, and Bakst and Benois designed a few *décors* and costumes.

Pavlova as an interpretative dancer ranks with the greatest. She has her niche safe beside La Sallée, Camargo, Grisi, and Taglioni, but she never was, in the full sense, fair to herself. Diaghileff and his colleagues regretted immensely her defection from their company, but they never forgave her for her prostitution of her own gifts and of their great art.

Vaslav and Diaghileff, whenever they happened to have a free evening among the constant duties of the Mariinsky and the feverish preparations for the next Western season, used to go to theatres and concerts. Ibsen and Maeterlinck were constantly shown, and the plays of Maeterlinck appealed immensely to Vaslav. The dreamy, semi-mystical, illusory sense of reality struck a re-echoing note in his own nature, and he read many of his books as well. He always wanted to make a ballet of *Pélléas and Mélisande*.

One evening they went to a concert given by members of the composition class at the Conservatory of Music. On the programme was the first hearing of a short symphonic poem called *Feu d'Artifice*. Its author was a young man of twenty-six, the son of a celebrated singer at the Imperial Theatre—Feodor Stravinsky. After the performance Diaghileff called on the young Igor, whose father he had known and admired, and, to Stravinsky's utter amazement, commissioned him to write a ballet expressly for his company.

For a long time Fokine had had the idea of a distinctly Russian story for dancing, founded on native legends. Fokine told the story of the *Fire Bird* to Benois, over innumerable glasses of tea, and with every glass he added another embellishment, and every time he repeated the tale he put in another incident. Benois was enthusiastic, and they went so far as to tell Diaghileff and asked who would be a good one to compose the music. Liadov's name was mentioned. "What," cried Fokine, "and wait ten years!" Nevertheless, the commission was awarded to Liadov and three months passed. Then Benois met him on the street and asked him how the ballet was progressing. "Marvellously," said Liadov. "I've already bought my ruled paper." Benois' face fell, and the musician, like a character out of Dostoievsky, added, "You know I want to do it. But I'm so lazy, I can't promise."

Diaghileff thought at once of Igor Stravinsky, and the conferences between him, Benois, and Fokine commenced.

Fokine heard Stravinsky's *Feu d'Artifice* and saw flames in the music. The musicians made all manner of fun of what they considered his "unnecessary" orchestration, and he was touched by, and grateful for, Fokine's congratulations. They worked very closely together, phrase by phrase. Stravinsky brought him a beautiful cantilena on the entrance of the Tsarevitch into the garden of the girls with the golden apples. But Fokine disapproved. "No, no," he said. "You bring him in like a tenor. Break the phrase where he merely shows his head on his first intrusion. Then make the curious swish of the garden's magic noises return. And then, when he shows his head again, bring in the full swing of the melody."

Fokine made the choreography extremely fantastic. The steps are as rich in variation, as light and weird, as the story itself, especially in the solo dances of the *Fire Bird*, which constantly imitate the movements of a feathered creature.

Golovin's scenery of a garden, with the castle of Kotschei in the background, surrounded by trees, is wonderful as in a dream, stylised, but so convincingly unearthly, so sensuous, that one is in another world. The costumes were based on native Russian dress: fur-edged coats, stiff with gold and jewels, and high, embroidered leather boots.

Stravinsky was wild with enthusiasm to compose the music. By commissioning him Diaghileff proved his uncanny gift of the divining-rod again, which sensed talent wherever it lay latent. Just as with Vaslav, he gave Stravinsky an immediate opportunity to unfold his art. He knew at once that he had disclosed perhaps the foremost genius of contemporary music, and for this service alone Diaghileff deserves our lasting gratitude.

Stravinsky threw himself whole-heartedly into the composition, and he had little enough time in which to complete it. He was extremely eager, but, in spite of the awe he had for Diaghileff and the respect held for his elders like Benois and Bakst, he treated them all as his equals. He was already very decided and wilful in his opinions, and in many ways a difficult character. He not only wished his authority acknowledged in his own field of music, but he wanted similar prestige in all the domains of art. Stravinsky had an extremely strong personality, self-conscious and sure of his own worth. But Diaghileff was a wizard, and knew how to subdue this young man without his ever noticing it, and Stravinsky became one of his most ardent followers and defenders. He was extremely ambitious, and naturally understood the tremendous aid it would mean to him to be associated with Sergei Pavlovitch's artistic group.

Vaslav and Igor soon became friends. He had a limitless admiration for Stravinsky's gifts, and his boldness, his direct innovation of new harmonies, his courageous use of dissonance, found an echo in Vaslav's mind. The two of them were the youngest of Diaghileff's collaborators, so they naturally found themselves somewhat together. But Vaslav in a way was more unworldly in the manner in which he lived, and felt that his art was a medium to be used to ennoble humanity. Stravinsky was blunter; he understood the material life, and he was interested in his personal success. His music, his reputation, were important, but his creations are in the largest scale of achievement of our time. And every important work of his, from the *Fire Bird*, through *Petrouchka*, *Sacre du Printemps*, the unproduced *Liturgie*, to *Pulcinella*, *Apollon Musagète*, *Renard*, the operas *Rossignol* and *Mavra*, and the oratorio *Œdipus Rex*, were first given by Diaghileff.

Vaslav's attachment to Sergei Pavlovitch grew stronger and stronger. They were in complete harmony in their ideas about art. Vaslav more than willingly allowed himself to be moulded like soft wax in Diaghileff's hands. He was the ideal pupil, following his master without resistance up to the point where he no longer needed him, where he had outgrown him. Vaslav's affection for Diaghileff was of a profound order. He implicitly believed in him—his manner of living, his notions of life. He let himself be completely guided by him. Diaghileff, in his turn, cherished and spoiled him in every way he knew, trying to attach him more and more all the time. Diaghileff's boundless admiration for Nijinsky the dancer was even overshadowed by his passionate love for Vaslav himself. They were inseparable. The moments, in a similar mutual relationship, of dissatisfaction and *ennui* which come to others, never came to them, as they were so intensely interested in the same work. To make Sergei Pavlovitch happy was no sacrifice to Vaslav. And Diaghileff crushed any idea of resistance, which might have come up in the young man's mind, by the familiar tales of the Greeks, of Michelangelo and Leonardo, whose creative lives depended on the same intimacy as their own.

The relationship between them was so real that it was therefore universally taken for granted. Diaghileff and Nijinsky were one in private life, and nobody would even have dreamed of inviting one anywhere without the other. Diaghileff's artistic group had always known and accepted his outlook on life. Bakst was the only one who, because of his passion for womanhood, tried the hopeless task of reforming Diaghileff. But Diaghileff was merely amused or annoyed when he listened to Leo Samuelvitch's dithyrambics about women as with words and drawings he undertook to prove to Diaghileff the beauty of those whom he forever shut out of his life.

Diaghileff tried to convince Bakst that there can be no real artist who has not the characteristics of both sexes; that almost all great geniuses in the past were homosexual, or at least bisexual. Normal love, according to Sergei Pavlovitch, was merely a necessity to continue the race—an urge of nature, an animal action deprived of all beauty, and degrading to those who longed for spiritual and æsthetic pleasure; but that love between the same sex, even if the persons involved are quite ordinary, because of the very similarity of their natures and the absence of a presupposed difference, is creative and artistic. Yet Diaghileff was by no means entirely a sensualist. There was a strong æsthetic pleasure in his affection for Vaslav, who always in his art and in his life was able to radiate beauty, to heighten emotion to the point of ecstasy —like tightening the string of an instrument more and more to the moment of snapping, and instead of the expected break, to sweep the other into infinite bliss.

The nearest thing approaching a misunderstanding between them was about his sister Bronia. Diaghileff did not want to include her in the company. She had graduated from the Imperial School with honours, and had already obtained important parts at the Mariinsky. She had in her dancing the same quality as Vaslav: a marvellous technique, a great range of performance, chiselled down to perfection, as well as unusual strength and lightness. In her was combined something of the ethereal charm of a Pavlova, the technique of a Kshessinskaya, a great dramatic gift, and an inherent, overwhelming temperament. Bronia was not only a *ballerina*, but a brilliant actress, and she had all the requirements for a distinguished character dancer.

Diaghileff saw in her the material for quite a remarkable dancer, something new and unusual; but he objected steadfastly that the public always wanted *ballerinas* with sweet and pretty faces, and they would not accept the novelty of her dances unless she was pretty. Bronia had a fascinating face and a beautiful body, but she had nothing remotely resembling a conventionally sweet and pretty face. Vaslav, who loved her, was hurt by Diaghileff's attitude. She took lessons from him privately and learned a lot by it. There was a perfect understanding and co-operation between them during these years. She was proud of her famous brother, knew what a genius he was, and that she could only im-

107

prove her own talents by observing his. They lived with Eleanora in their comfortable apartment. Vaslav was very sensitive to cold, and had influenza every winter, and it disturbed his mother increasingly, as she felt that the climate of St. Petersburg was dangerous for him.

In the early spring they commenced to rehearse the ballets they already knew and the new creations for the Paris season. This year, as last, a great retinue was ready to accompany them West. *Pavillon d'Armide, Prince Igor, Le Festin, Les Sylphides,* and *The Fire Bird, Carnaval, Giselle,* and *Scheherazade,* made up the repertory.

They left for Paris with even more excitement than before. As usual, Nouvel and the other intimates of Diaghileff came along. Vaslav told me he felt like a small child before an examination. This time they were avidly awaited in Paris. The Press and the public welcomed them like old friends. The performances were sold out weeks in advance. They were met at the station by hundreds of people eager to make plans for parties and ways to entertain them. Diaghileff said, "Please, please let them alone. We came to work, not to amuse ourselves."

The season at the Opéra was to open in May and last through June. Vaslav was thrilled to perform in the atmosphere where his idols, Noverre and Vestris, had danced. As before, the practices, rehearsals, and lessons from Cecchetti continued unabated. There was no time for anything but the most rigorous preparations. But Paris was familiar now, and there was no sense of strangeness, no tension of insecurity as to how the French audience would receive them. Only now they had to dance better than ever to maintain the supreme impression of the initial season.

Diaghileff engaged Pierné, the conductor of the Lamoureaux concerts and the foremost conductor of France at that time.

Then came the first performance of *Scheherazade*. This was Bakst's unquestionable masterpiece. Nowhere did he so completely express his creative ideas as in this ballet. He surpassed anything even he had yet done in the incredible luxury of his colour. The scenery had no flats or practicable projections. It was all painted on the vivid walls and ceiling of the harem in motives of green and violet blue, rising from a shrill pink carpet. A voluptuous sensation was suggested by the mixing of these sensuous colours. The effect on the public was the arousing of an immediate excitement. The front of the stage was draped in a gigantic curtain, its folds of varying greens, on which designs of blue and circular patterns of pink were sprayed. Colour had never before been so riotously used. In the blue background were three immense doors of silver, bronze, blue, gold. Huge Arabian lamps swayed from the ceiling squares, and heaps of enormous cushions sprawled all over the stage. The costumes of *Scheherazade* were in the most perfect Persian style. Here again Bakst's profound knowledge of Oriental art manifested itself.

The story by Bakst and Fokine was inspired by the tales of the *Thousand and One Nights*, and the music of Rimsky-Korsakov's greatest symphonic poem admirably suited the action of the story. Rimsky-Korsakov had been a naval officer, and much of it describes the sea, but here the second movement is omitted, as the *tempo* is too slow to be danced, and it would make the ballet too long.

Rubinstein, tall, with movements of a great plastic beauty, was admirable as Scheherazade. Her gestures were a combination of dignity and sensuality, and expressed the essential languors of a woman who demanded sexual satisfaction. The slave, danced by Vaslav, brought out the animal side of human nature—physical love. When all the rest of the harem and the slaves sink exhausted after their love-making, Zobeide leans on the Golden Door, queenly high, like an obelisk, awaiting the expectant joy in silence. A pause, and suddenly a superb, golden animal jumps up to an incredible height from a crouch and with one movement he possesses her. His jump is as a tiger's, once caged, now free for his victim. He bounds with her on to the divan, for the maddest, fiercest activity of love. Nijinsky was inexpressibly, voluptuously wild, a cat caressing, a tiger devouring, now at her feet, now at her breasts and mouth, stroking and exciting her. He would swing himself, hesitating, from side to side, as a feverish animal might do, staring at this pale, marvellous woman whom he so desired with every nerve and muscle in his body quivering. Whenever the slaves sank, the golden slave soared up, a self-hypnotised Dervish, spurring the others by his amazing *tours en l'air*, dominating the orgy.

When the Shah returns, he is the first to see him. One moment of petrifying fear, then with a leap he is gone. But he is chased back, flashes through the stage clad in gold tissue, his jewels sparkling. Struck by the soldier's sword, his head just touches the floor, then his whole body shoots into the air, legs uppermost, silvery, glistening, like a fish tossed on to the sand, the nerves and muscles shudder all through his frame, and the golden slave lies dead, on his face.

Nijinsky idealised, even in his make-up, the slave, the negro. He was painted a wonderful deep prune colour, with a silvery sheen against which were drawn up his golden trousers, a luscious contrast of colour and texture.

Scheherazade was a triumph for Bakst, the *Fire Bird* for Stravinsky, and *Carnaval* for Fokine, and, whenever he danced any of the three, a personal triumph for Nijinsky.

To see Nijinsky, perhaps to meet him, to touch him, was the

highest wish of hundreds of Society women. And they devised all sorts of subterfuges to gain their ends, which were mostly wrecked by the vigilance of Vassily. On one occasion he was so mobbed he had to seek refuge in a shop. Only when Diaghileff himself personally brought somebody to meet Vaslav were his duties relaxed.

Vaslav did not mind his isolation. In fact, he never noticed it. He never knew Diaghileff consciously submitted him to the most rigorous seclusion. His mind was too occupied, his time was too filled by his dancing and the constant companionship of Sergei Pavlovitch. The intimate circle of Benois, Bakst, Stravinsky, and Nouvel, whom he saw from day to day, completely satisfied him.

Of course, he was often with Fokine, who had always taken a very active part in the creation of the stories, and their mutual work at the theatre brought them constantly together. Vaslav had the deepest gratitude and admiration for Fokine's genius. Fokine's liberation of the ballet from its rigid classical tradition found its most ardent and revolutionary exponent in Nijinsky. At last, in Fokine's choreography, he could dance with the whole body and express ideas with every possibility of the anatomy. Vaslav had interpreted Petipa's creations to the entire satisfaction of that strict master. All technical difficulties were surmounted by his nonchalant ease. But through the medium Fokine gave to Vaslav he was able to develop his talent, and his latent wish to dance with his complete soul, using every part of his body.

In each part—as an Egyptian slave, as a Russian peasant, as Harlequin, as Chopin's living memory—he had the chance to give a complete and separate impersonation. He was so different in each part that he was almost unrecognisable. Where the essential Nijinsky existed was a constant mystery. His face, his skin, even his height, seemed to change in each ballet. Even the colour of his eyes shifted from greenish-blue in *Les Sylphides* to dark hazel in *Scheherazade* and *Cléopâtre*. Perhaps the stage lights had something to do with it, but it also must have been due to his expression and the way he framed his eyes.

In *Carnaval* it was the mischievous Harlequin, teasing, insolent, sharp and light as steel; in *Les Sylphides*, the very ghost of the romantic poets suffering from the eternal *mal du siècle*, floating through the air in an inexhaustible rhythm; in *Cléopâtre*, clinging to the ground in fear and adoration of a great queen, but forgetful of everything but her body when she takes him. Egypt incarnate arose through Vaslav, a living, moving fresco from a Theban temple.

In each different ballet there was only constant his one unmistakable signature, his genius. But one always forgot Nijinsky as a person when he danced. We were put in the true mood of the part. As soon as he appeared on the stage an electric tremor was transmitted to the public, hypnotised by his purity and his perfection. The eyes of the audience followed him from one side of the stage to the other, as if they were helpless, in a trance.

To him, dancing was, of course, more natural than speaking, and he was never so much himself, or so happy and free, as when he was dancing. The moment he stepped on the stage, nothing existed for him except his part. He was never aware of his public, and exulted in the sheer, free joy of movement. But he never tried to stand out and crush the other dancers, or give more importance to his own rôle than the *maître de ballet* had intended. He was always entirely harmonious and restrained himself, the more to blend in with the *ensemble*. Yet his work was so paramount that, without obliterating the others, he was nevertheless a sun shining stronger among them. As soon as he was on the stage, somehow the other dancers were electrified to their utmost capacities. He brought out of them a reflection of his own harmony and beauty, and it was constantly said that the same ballet had never the same intensity when Vaslav was not dancing.

Since he never danced for the sake of applause, and was so sure of himself, he was never subject to stage fright. I once said to him what a great pity it was he could never watch himself dance. He said, "You are mistaken. I always see myself dancing. I can visualise myself so thoroughly that I know exactly what I look like, just as if I sat in the midst of the audience." Unlike many other trained ballet-dancers, he never watched himself in a mirror to correct his faults, but he had an instinct of muscular control and needed no sight to tell him where he failed.

His triumphs never changed him, and he was modest, kind, and reserved. Diaghileff let him meet a number of the French artists who regularly attended the performances—Debussy, Ravel, Guitry, Bourdelle, Blanche, "Sarah," Faure, and Saint-Saëns—and they were always surprised on first meeting this silent, self-effacing boy who only smiled at them.

He always excused himself, through Diaghileff, from the continual round of receptions, luncheons, and dinners. But he made exceptions in the case of Debussy, with whom he loved to dine, and with Jacques Émile Blanche, who had an enchanting house at Passy, where he painted Vaslav extremely well in his Siamese costume of *Les Orientales*.

He also saw much of Jean de Reské. There he could at last communicate with words. Reské was like a father to Vaslav. He was Polish, and so was Vaslav's mother, and he always claimed him as a compatriot. But Vaslav loved Russia with every fibre of his being, and always insisted on his Russian citizenship. De Reské was a great patriot, and his aristocratic birth, his fame and wealth, assured him an important position in Parisian life. But as often as not Vaslav was alone with him and Diaghileff *en famille*.

De Reské saw to it that certain of his chosen friends should meet Vaslav, and he also gave a chance to the creative artists who wanted so much to know him.

At this time an important group of young men, the lions of the *jeunesse dorée* of Paris, attached themselves to Diaghileff, and they followed him all over Paris, like a court in attendance. Their leaders were Maurice Rostand and Jean Cocteau. Later on others joined them, and they kept constantly in touch with all the movements of the *avant garde*. Reynaldo Hahn gave Vaslav an autograph of Vestris, and of all the presents with which he was deluged he cherished this most.

Poiret, who had just opened his new home on the Rue Faubourg St. Honoré in an old palace, gave a fantastic party in honour of the Russian Ballet, with incredible lighting effects and luminous fountains, and even the sands in the garden paths were coloured *à la Bakst.*

Madame de Euphrussy repeated her wonderful *Sylphides* fête of the year before, where the dancers shimmered in the pale moonlight of her midnight gardens. Madame Misia Edwards, the wife of the editor of *Le Matin,* often entertained them. She was a Polish woman and had a great *train de maison.* She was a backer of Diaghileff's, and partly responsible for the assurance of his subsidy.

Another person who was an enormous help to Diaghileff was the Comtesse de Greffuhle. She had tremendous political influence, and was always a staunch and resourceful friend of his. All the others were petted and spoiled, Rubinstein and Benois among the artists, and Bakst among the great ladies and gentlemen of the world of society, happiest when he was in the smartest house. Perhaps he felt this was some compensation for his early difficulties, due to his Jewish descent but surely he was too great an

artist to need such a public acknowledgment. Diaghileff did everything he could to put his collaborators in the limelight, saw to it
they were displayed properly off stage as on.

So, in great work and in the social life of parties and balls, the
season of 1910 passed, with performances every Tuesday, Thursday, and Saturday. Everyone was overjoyed that their second year
proved even more brilliant than the first.

This year there was an international exhibition in Brussels,
and the Russian Ballet had been officially invited to appear at the
Théâtre de la Monnaie, the opera house of the Belgian capital.
After Paris, only a few rehearsals were necessary to accustom
themselves to the new stage and the new orchestra. They were their
usual terrific sensation, and the Court attended each performance,
while Vaslav and the rest were presented to King Albert and his
Queen. Here the Ballet separated, most of it returning to Russia
for the vacation.

Vaslav and Sergei Pavlovitch once more left for Karlsbad and
the Lido.

Chapter Eight

NIJINSKY'S BREAK
WITH THE
MARIINSKY THEATRE

In the early autumn of 1910 Nijinsky and Diaghileff returned from the Lido to St. Petersburg. During their six weeks' vacation, Sergei Pavlovitch took the cure in Karlsbad, and Vaslav had complete relaxation. Many plans for the next season were formulated.

Diaghileff's position in St. Petersburg was impregnable. Perhaps now the Intendant Teliakovsky had some justification for fearing him. Diaghileff's ideas were accepted and sought. The Court, the Press, and the artistic world considered his opinions infallible, and it would have been only natural that some great official position should be offered him. After the increased success of the last Paris season, his fifth year of continuous activity in the liaison of French and Russian arts, all manner of rumours went around as to his eventual appointment. He would be nominated as the next intendant of the Imperial Theatre. He would become director of the Hermitage and control the State Museums of Art and Archæology.

As the officials of the Mariinsky felt it necessary to be covertly suspicious or jealous of the ballets Diaghileff's group was creating, there was no possibility of Russia seeing them danced as Paris had, free from the hindrance of traditional restraint.

So the Duke of Aldenburg invited Sergei Pavlovitch to present *Festin, Igor, Scheherazade,* and *Cléopâtre,* just as he had at the Châtelet and the Opéra, but now here in the great Narodni Dom. The capital was naturally eager and enthusiastic, but, unluckily, the big People's Palace was burnt down and all their plans had to be cancelled.

Diaghileff enjoyed being home. Somehow in Russia the organisation, the arrangements, even the creation, seemed to progress more easily. At his evening gatherings, they commenced to formulate the next Paris programme: *Petrouchka, Sadko, Narcisse,* and *Spectre de la Rose.* It was decided to produce the Submarine Ballet from Rimsky-Korsakov's opera *Sadko.* Anisfeld designed the undersea *décors.* He had previously been of invaluable service in the actual execution of all Bakst's designs. Bakst merely made the *maquettes* and the sketches for the scenery. But the carrying out of his *décors,* which were so greatly admired throughout the world, was done by Anisfeld. He made a bold innovation, which revolutionised the manner of scenic painting, by spreading the canvas out on the floor and splashing pots of paint in the proper places, instead of a precise indication with the brush and ruler. His free methods had a great deal to do with the loose richness of the scenery, which was as brilliantly realised as a fine painter's canvas.

Diaghileff also wished a ballet expressly written for the new season, in the classic style, in which both Bakst and Fokine excelled. Bakst had been to Greece in 1905 with his friend, the painter Serov, and memories of the Pheidian period were swarming in his head, bursting for re-creation. Nicolai Tcherepnin, the eminent conductor of the Mariinsky Orchestra, was composing the orchestral score.

Narcisse, Sadko, and *Petrouchka* did not seem wholly sufficient

117

as novelties for the new season, and they were all long spectacular ballets. Diaghileff thought that a short piece was needed to complete the programme—something of the order of the *Princesse Enchantée, a pas de deux,* which Vaslav and Karsavina could dance together. An evening's bill was usually composed of one long and two short ballets, Vaslav taking part in two only. *Les Orientales* had been dropped from the repertoire as too old-fashioned, so Diaghileff remembered the suggestion made in Paris the year before of *Le Spectre de la Rose.* Jean-Louis Vaudoyer, the poet, one of the young men in his Parisian suite, had quoted to him Théophile Gautier's lines:

> *Je suis le spectre de la rose*
> *Que tu portais hier au bal.* . . .

The poem, *Loin du Bal,* could be transcribed into an exquisite ballet.

Petrouchka was based on a well-known native folk legend and adapted by Benois, the great connoisseur of Russian folk-lore. Benois was opposing an intense Slavic nationalism to Bakst's internationalism. He was with Stravinsky creating a Russian Ballet for Russians to dance. It was to be more native than *Igor* and less remote. Both Benois and Fokine had seen street-fairs in their childhood, with puppet shows, hung with familiar dancing dolls—the Magician, the Ballerina, the Moor and Petrouchka, Russia's own Pierrot, her Tyl, her Puck—with the attendant hand-organs and trained bears, and ancients from the Caucasus with long beards and strange fur clothes.

All these ideas were developed at Diaghileff's gatherings, and one artist made suggestions to the other—an idea, a touch, a plan —and it was so complete a collaboration that it was impossible to know where the work of one began and the other ended. The creation of this atmosphere of unjealous mutual composition was Diaghileff's great achievement.

Vaslav meanwhile lived with his mother, who was only too happy to have him back home again. She was so bewildered by the way things seemed to happen. She had always felt that her Vatza was going to be a great dancer, but she could hardly connect the overwhelming reports of him with the son she knew. The ballets which had been created for the tour had not as yet been given at the Mariinsky, and Eleanora could only see him in the old repertoire. She adored him, and she said it was like going to church on Sunday to watch him dance as the glory of the Imperial Theatre. When she saw him in *Cléopâtre* and *Les Sylphides,* even though they were hard for her to understand, she nevertheless realised the beauty and exquisite quality of Vaslav's performance, and that he not only danced but acted.

Her boy had created something which she had seen only once before, in Russia's pride and national idol, Chaliapine. Just as she knew instinctively that if one subtracted the voice and orchestration of Boris, Chaliapine's presence on the stage would still be sublime, so she felt that even if Vaslav did not dance, but merely walked or moved across the stage, it would still be the expression of great art.

Stanislav's illness had always been the greatest worry and misfortune of her life, and she could never get over it. Bronia, as a girl, was close to her, but her violent energy almost frightened her mother. Vaslav was always patient, and he gave her all the tenderness and affection for which she longed. And these days were very happy ones for Eleanora. In spite of his work he had considerable time to spend with her, and to spoil her, and he would always go with her whenever she wanted to visit Stanislav.

Vaslav's success continued uninterrupted at the Mariinsky until the fatal evening of his performance in *Giselle*, after which he tendered his resignation. There have been many contradictory rumours about this episode, and there were at least three actual contributory causes for the incident. According to some witnesses, the Grand Duchesses Olga and Tatiana, daughters of the Tsar, were present, and their escort was shocked at Vaslav's costume. Another more persistent explanation was that the Dowager Empress Maria Feodorovna, who was occupying the Imperial box that night, felt that Nijinsky was not sufficiently clad, and passed her displeasure on to her suite. Word was brought to the intendant of the Imperial Theatres, and Vaslav's resignation was requested. But Maria Feodorovna, in later years, on a visit to her sister, Queen Alexandra, in London, was asked by the Marchioness of Ripon, Vaslav's devoted friend, if the story were true. She denied it, and said that she had never made any remark whatever about his costume; she was not even aware of the reason for Vaslav's quitting Mariinsky and attributed it all to a malicious Court intrigue of which she had no knowledge at the time. She was proud that Russia possessed such a dancer, and she personally asked Lady Ripon to tell this to Nijinsky and say how sorry she was for the whole affair.

Giselle, which had always been in the repertory of the Mariinsky, was now presented with the costumes, scenery, and arrangement that Diaghileff had used in Paris. Vaslav's costume, designed by Benois, consisted of close-fitting white silk tights with a black velvet *gilet*, which was the same as he had appeared in at the Opéra. The small slip that male athletes and dancers use had not been included by Benois. According to the regulations of the Mariinsky, all dancers of the company were obliged to wear it to hide their forms. Vaslav, whose only idea was to appear as the artistic personification of Benois's designs, discarded the archaic

120

garment. Although he had obtained permission to do this from one stage manager, Director Kroupensky appeared on the stage and made severe remarks to him about the indecency of his costume, which revealed his form too markedly, and demanded that Vaslav change it immediately. This was just a few minutes before the curtain was raised. There was no time to change the costume, and it was impossible to make their Majesties and the public wait. In any case, Nijinsky did not feel himself at liberty to take off the costume assigned to him by the designer, who was in the audience, unaware of the fatal incident.

Princess Galitzina, an eye-witness, who happened to be sitting in a directorial box, has told me that as soon as Vaslav appeared thus dressed, Teliakovsky jumped to his feet, dashed into the small ante-chamber where he had a desk with bells connected to the back-stage offices, and summoned the stage manager. He was in a frightful temper, and ordered Vaslav to change at once. Vaslav refused. It was the costume which Paris had approved, and he saw no reason now to appear differently. He finished the second act of the ballet as he had commenced. After the performance, Teliakovsky demanded his presence in his box, and, furious, suspended him for a time from the Imperial Theatre as a punishment. This had never before happened in the annals of the Imperial Ballet, and aroused a terrific storm of protest. The papers were full of it. St. Petersburg and Moscow were in commotion.

Of course, Bakst, Benois, and all the friends took Nijinsky's part. The blow hit Vaslav, but it was obviously meant for Diaghileff, who accepted the challenge and persuaded Vaslav, greatly incensed at the preposterous suspension, to send in his resignation from the Imperial Theatre before any official action was taken. After a good deal of discussion, and after Diaghileff had definitely promised to form a permanent organisation where all their artistic dreams could be freely realised, Vaslav agreed to resign.

The Mariinsky was completely taken aback. They had never dreamed of such a contingency. Vaslav had graduated with honours from the Imperial School. His artistic career was assured. He was soloist to the Tsar, the pride of Russia, and a lifelong member of the Mariinsky Company. That he should voluntarily leave was unthinkable. They would not allow Vaslav to resign. They needed him, and, besides, an unheard-of precedent might be created. Also, they had begun to hear of Diaghileff's new plans. So they made offers to him which culminated in a proposal of the highest salary ever paid, even to such singers as Chaliapine, with similar privileges to appear in foreign tours, and his performances at home limited to his desires. It was an unusual proposition for a dancer, but Diaghileff made it possible for him to refuse.

And when he passed the Russian frontier at Eydtkuhnen in the spring of 1911, without realising it, he left Russia forever. Had he known, he would never have left it permanently. He believed in, and loved beyond anything, Russia, and wanted to be a part of it.

Eleanora was deeply worried about Vaslav, and did not at all approve of his leaving the Mariinsky. She knew Diaghileff, and respected him a great deal. He was always extremely attentive and courteous to her, but somehow they were so very far apart, and she always felt shy when she saw him. But she could hardly set her opinion against his will. Vaslav wrote her from abroad daily.

It was no simple task that Diaghileff had set himself in raising and supporting a permanent company. More than once the difficulties seemed absolutely insurmountable. The Russian painters, musicians, and technicians could go on working for him. Fokine could go on creating choreography even if he had his duties at the Mariinsky. But could he acquire enough dancers who would be free from the Imperial Theatre for his European seasons? He began to make offers, higher salaries than had ever been paid before; the smallest was a thousand francs a month all the year round.

The great possibilities, the glamour attached to Diaghileff's previous success, tempted many. A number of the Mariinsky Company were quickly engaged. He also picked good dancers from Moscow and Warsaw. Bolm came along. He was an ardent follower of the new movement, and resigned from the Imperial Theatre to join Diaghileff permanently, and he soon became an important pillar of the organisation. Sofia Feodorova, the fine mime Astafieva, Bronia, of course, and others, also joined permanently. Diaghileff achieved a real *tour de force* in getting Kshessinskaya and Karsavina, the greatest *ballerinas* of the Mariinsky, early in the spring. They agreed to make flying trips from Paris to St. Petersburg whenever they had to appear.

The whole winter passed in preparation for the tour; the models for the scenery, the costume designs, were completed before they left for Monte Carlo. As soon as the theatre-managers in Western Europe heard that the Ballet was free to give performances in other months besides June and July, they were flooded with offers. Diaghileff decided that they would appear in Rome for the International Exhibition, then Berlin, Paris, and perhaps London. It was the year of King George's coronation. And, in spite of all the adjustments of personal difficulties, of wounded vanities here, of petty jealousies there, of the threats of a lack of financial support, and all the complications of transportation of a big company by train, with scenery and carloads of luggage, all across Europe, they arrived safely in Monte Carlo.

Here Sergei Pavlovitch intended to take a rest and to prepare the whole programme in peace. He had also in mind, to gain as backing for his company, the high patronage of the hereditary Prince of Monaco, so as to be attached to the Monte Carlo Opera House. They stayed this season at the Monte Carlo Palace Hotel, quite close to the Casino, and usually Sergei Pavlovitch took his meals on the balcony of the Hôtel de Paris. Here he held his round table conferences and very soon became the centre of the artistic and intellectual world, as wherever he went. Stravinsky came all the way from Russia particularly to discuss the score of *Petrouchka*, which was originally intended as four piano pieces, only for concert production. Vaslav and Diaghileff were both enthusiastic over the music, and they were full of ideas about the choreography. Stravinsky had finished the piano score before they left and was now rearranging it for full orchestra.

As usual, the mornings were spent in practising, but very soon Vaslav complained that he was not used to working without a coach, that practising alone required an unnecessary moral effort, and that he unconsciously slipped into lapses of laziness. He insisted on having Cecchetti, and so Diaghileff immediately started to pull wires in an effort to secure him. This was by no means an easy task, as not only was *Maestro* attached to the Imperial School, but he also had a school of his own, full of promising pupils. But Diaghileff finally succeeded in winning him over, and *Maestro* resigned from the Imperial School, leaving his own in the charge of his wife, and arrived in Monte Carlo, sighing, cursing, "*Corpo di Bacco*, I can't have peace anywhere. Vaslav Fomitch, you don't need me. Where is the rehearsal room, anyway?"

And so they began to practise in the Palais de Soleil, a disused theatre. Diaghileff took occasional trips to Paris, and had long conferences with Gabriel Astruc and Marinelli, his French impresarios, and Eric Wollheim, who was to manage the affairs for his first London season.

It was at this time that Nijinsky met the Marchioness of Ripon. The Marchioness was an extremely interesting and delightful woman, who was not only one of the most prominent leaders of London Society of her time, but also a great patron of the arts. She had organised many special performances in her London house, as well as in her beautiful country place at Coombe Court, where she received the leading artists of the world. Through her intimate friendship with King Edward and Queen Alexandra she had been able to give a great deal of aid to her friends. She was an extraordinary personality, kind, helpful, conscious of all the small weaknesses of the society in which she moved. She went back and forth from Paris to Monte Carlo, and Sergei Pavlovitch grew more and more dependent on her.

In March of 1911 the Russian Ballet appeared for the first time in Rome, at the Teatro Costanza. The Russians were extremely nervous about their Italian reception. There had been a century-old rivalry between the Italian and the Russian schools of dancing, and there was a definitely organised party of opposition which arrived *en masse* at the *première*. All Maestro Cecchetti's friends had come to the rehearsals.

When an old Italian ballet-master had visited *Maestro* in St. Petersburg, he said: "Yes, your Russians are marvellous, but they have the mannerisms of ducks." He meant that from the Italian point of view their limbs were not flexible enough. For Cecchetti had realised, almost as soon as he had come to Russia, that there was something about the bony structure of the Russians which was different from the more supple Latins, and he based his style on the limitations and possibilities of his new pupils. With that in mind he answered his old friend: "We may dance like ducks. It is of no importance. You dance like frogs!"

On the first night, with the opposition grimly entrenched in the orchestra stalls, the company was pardonably anxious. And when the dancing started the whole audience broke into loud whistling. The hearts of the dancers dropped. It seemed a complete failure, their first. They did not know then that whistling was the Roman mode of applause.

Sergei Pavlovitch used to take Vaslav and Karsavina off sight-seeing. He wanted to show them the Coliseum in sunlight and in moonlight, the Catacombs, the Campagna, the Vatican, San Pietro. Cecchetti was almost apoplectic. Sight-seeing was all very well for Diaghileff. He didn't have to dance. For dancers it was a rank waste of time. They should stick to the perfecting of their pirouettes and leave antiquity to their old age.

Scriabine, the composer, was also in Rome, giving concerts and piano recitals, with the simultaneous projection of rays of light from an early colour organ; there was Marinetti and the first excitement of his Futurist Manifestos, and they would all investigate the biggest and the smallest and the best restaurants for chianti and spaghetti, and soon learned to wind the limp strands around their forks like natives.

Fokine was busily rehearsing *Petrouchka* in a big hall underneath the stage of the Teatro Costanza. The others had to be shown their dances in detail by the *maître de ballet*, but Nijinsky was so familiar with the vocabulary of the dance that he merely had to be told, and the steps indicated by Fokine's fingers: "Here you do two pirouttes *à la seconde*, then a *tour en l'air*, then a *fouetté* to the right, *pas de bourrée* back, and finish the phrase with an arabesque." Vaslav could retain the directions in his memory, and rehearse whole sequences in his mind. Fokine and Vaslav enjoyed working together, because the one could actually see the designs the other had invented at the very moment of conception.

Unlike playwrights who can write speeches for actors once and for all, and unlike composers who can transcribe in a legible notation for their performers, choreographers not only had to compose ballets, but teach the arrangement of the composition, every time a new ballet is composed, because, although there were several systems of choreographic notation, practically all of them were unintelligible.

Petrouchka was perhaps Fokine's greatest masterpiece, although he didn't realise at the time, and *Petrouchka* was Vaslav's favourite part. It grew on him as he became more and more used to it; and the longer he danced it the more monumental was his conception. The superb rôle of the marionette called for an unusually gifted dancer to interpret the gay, pathetic, and extremely difficult steps, but Vaslav amplified the crazy doll into the symbol of the spirit of the Russian people, oppressed by autocracy, but resurgent and unconquerable after all its abuse and frustration.

Pavillon d'Armide was still, to all intents and purposes, a *ballet d'action*. *Scheherazade* was a brilliant excuse for dancing, *Carnaval* a series of exquisitely tender dance scenes; but *Petrouchka* was the first danced drama of our day, and it has parallels, in its combination of music and dancing, with the intention, if not the realisation, of Wagner's music dramas, with their synthesis of action and orchestration.

Petrouchka was twenty-five years ahead of *Scheherazade*, which had been a striking innovation of the year before. *Petrouchka* and Nijinsky's choreography of *L'Après-midi d'un Faune* are the greatest steps in the development of ballet since Marius Petipa.

The choreography was extremely complex. The action in the street scene, with its entrances of coachmen and nursemaids,

127

gypsies and mendicants, soldiers and *moujiks*, were not merely round dances, but interlocking patterns of continuous action, against which the tragedy of the Moor, the Magician, the Ballerina, and the Marionette is mimed.

Nijinsky grasped at once the infinite possibilities of the marionette with the living soul.

As the Magician touched the three hanging puppets they came to life. Nijinsky's Petrouchka made one convulsive movement like dead matter suddenly charged with electricity. This *pas de trois*, danced in a mad *tempo*, is the quintessence of choreographic technique, and, while the face of Petrouchka is blank, his scintillating feet execute steps of incredible virtuosity.

Petrouchka, poor, roughly handled doll, suffers from the Magician, who personifies Autocracy, from the unfaithfulness of the Ballerina whom he loves, and from the maltreatment of his rival, the Moor. Alone in his room, Petrouchka kneels, then whirls round, trying to break through the walls. A series of pirouettes and gestures of the arms is all the movement. But Nijinsky succeeded in rendering so convincingly the sorrows of the ill-treated captive, his utter despair, his jealousy, his longing for liberty, and his resentfulness towards his gaoler, that Sarah Bernhardt, on witnessing the performance, said, *"J'ai peur, j'ai peur, car je vois l'acteur le plus grand du monde."*

When Ellen Terry saw it in England she became Nijinsky's fervent admirer.

When Sergei Pavlovitch had been working in St. Petersburg, there was his own circle of artists and musicians at his beck and call. He could spend as many easy evenings as he wanted over as many leisurely glasses of tea as they could drink, discussing what they would do next season in Paris. But now, actually travelling in Western Europe, everything was different. In Rome he had

L'APRÈS MIDI D'UN FAUNE
(DE MEYER)

LE SPECTRE DE LA ROSE   (*Karsavina and Nijinsky*)

to be planning for three weeks ahead in Berlin. In Berlin, there was Paris, not two weeks off. And in Paris there was a packed two months, followed immediately by London. There was not only the worry of arrangements, but the multiple difficulties of securing guarantees.

Stravinsky would dash in, worried and upset because his child had come down with measles and he could not finish *Petrouchka*. Fokine would object that Fokina had not been given the parts she wanted. Suddenly a wire would be brought in from St. Petersburg: Karsavina was not free till next Thursday, and if she arrived in Berlin at 8.30, could they make *Cléopâtre* the last ballet of the performance? If Kshessinskaya was given a bigger part than Kyasht, which would be angrier? Where in God's name were those shoes ordered for Vaslav Fomitch ten days ago? Have they made sure that the width of the stage in Berlin will fit the scenery for *Scheherazade?* Will Sergei Pavlovitch please speak to M. Bakst himself this time, and make sure? We know what happened last time. Will the lights be correct? Do we get new reflectors? Could Monteux have the next orchestra ready in time, adequately rehearsed for the special *tempi* the ballets demanded? It was a terrific strain on Sergei Pavlovitch, but he had his staff of secretaries, *aides*, and assistants, who would execute his wishes and commands in the constant turmoil and confusion of the tours. There was Drobetsky, a charming Austro-Pole from Lemberg. He was married to the dancer Sofia Pflanz, and he spoke Russian, Polish, French, German, and English with ease. He was thin and nervous, with a blond, droopy moustache, and was the centre of the Polish group of the Ballet company. Both the Russians and the Poles had their separate social lives, away from the scenes of the ballet, where they would play cards or dominoes, or go sightseeing, or generally amuse themselves at restaurants and cafés.

Drobetsky made most of the salary payments and bought railway tickets. Sergei Pavlovitch drove him nearly crazy. He would never tell him what he had personally arranged, and poor Drobetsky might do all the work over again before he discovered that Diaghileff had already seen to it. The Press would arrive to get information. Diaghileff might refuse to see them, but he would be furious with Drobetsky if he presumed to give any interviews himself.

Then there was a certain courier. He had been an anarchist living in London and he was never allowed to return to Russia. He was hard, direct, and extremely efficient—the advance agent— and could go through any necessary dirty business coolly and never speak of it again. He was a kind of secret agent or spy of Diaghileff's, but, though no gentleman, he was by no account mean or untrustworthy.

Tsauschovsky was the chief electrician and prop man. He had charge of all transportation of scenery and properties and was a superb technician. He had a flat nose, spoke excellent French, and eventually died from an extreme preoccupation with women.

Dmitri Kamuchov had red hair and a beard like a Greek Orthodox pope. He was suave, and spoke all the European languages. He was a kind of maid-of-all-work, good-looking, with excellent manners, and slightly common. And there was Grigoriev, a thin Slav, the typical bureaucratic employee. It was then his job to come in and knock: "M. Nijinsky, Madame Karsavina has just finished her first variation."

A superb wig-maker, who constructed all the elaborate head-dresses for the ballet by himself, always accompanied them. And of course there was Maria Stepanovna, the wardrobe mistress, who was on hand when Bakst was designing his costumes, and who was always consulted on their actual making. It was she who went along with him to choose materials, because, once a dress was made, it had to be reduplicated time and again during the season. The stiff white tarlatan *tutus*, for example, used in *Les Sylphides*, were thrown away as spoiled after each performance. The tights for the dancers were made by Châtelet of Paris, and every so often great crates of ballet-shoes would arrive from Nicolini in Milan. Nijinsky's shoes were now made of special kid by Georges of London.

Diaghileff's chancellor of the exchequer and treasurer of the Russian Ballet was Baron Dmitri Gunsburg, a Russian Jew of a famous banking house. Part of his large family lived in Vienna. They were only less important than the Rothschilds. Gunsburg was blond, with a pale moustache, extremely well dressed and cosmopolitan, the soul of kindness and a delightfully gay and entertaining man. He liked women a great deal, and could never understand Diaghileff's intolerance of them. He would flirt politely with the girls of the Ballet, but he would never become in the least intimate with them, treating them rather as an owner of bloodstock would feel towards his famous stables. At *premières* he would always send Karsavina great bouquets, and Vaslav a watch or cuff-links or a pin. He was devoted to Vaslav. Gunsburg was slightly terrified of Sergei Pavlovitch, who would say, "Dmitri, let me have thirty [or forty or fifty] thousand francs, will you? There's a good fellow." He financed everything with his own cash, and it was his pleasure to do so. He always had to have quantities of ready cash, but he loved to travel with the Ballet, in the heart of the excitement, and it gave him a unique position at home, backing the Ballet as he did. He would occasionally return to St. Petersburg to attend to his family and his business affairs, and he was always greeted as the brilliant financier who preferred to follow in the train of art than pile up more gold. He was shot by the Bolsheviks in the early days of the revolution.

In Berlin they presented the Ballet at the Theater des Westens, which was at some distance from the heart of the city.

Kaiser Wilhelm announced he would be present at the *première* but through his Court Chamberlain he ordered that the dancers should appear in tights in *Cléopâtre,* for the benefit of the priggish Prussian Court audience. Diaghileff flatly refused to have the dancers do any such thing. "Either he will look at us as we are, or we shall not give the performance." But, in spite of this rebuff, the Emperor came with his suite, and was so delighted with the Russians that he had the dancers presented to him afterwards.

Vaslav was oblivious to most of this. It meant little or nothing when the gossip was repeated to him later. He met hardly anybody because he was so preoccupied with *Petrouchka,* with Stravinsky and Fokine. Besides, the public of Berlin was not the same to him as the Parisian audience which he loved. But he and Diaghileff were delightfully entertained by the great Herr Doktor Bode of the Kaiser Friedrich's Museum, who showed them the magnificent examples of Italian painting and sculpture which he was collecting for Germany.

Diaghileff, who cordially hated the ubiquitous Prussian efficiency, indulged in the snobbism of pretending to speak only French, although he knew German perfectly well, and he did little to endear himself to the German people, either to the artists or to the *Junkers,* and they had their unconscious and probably unsuspected revenge.

Vassily usually sent their wash out every week. When it was brought back, he sometimes paid cash for it and sometimes did not. It was often forgotten as too small an item to be considered. But in Berlin, instead of sending a bill, which might eventually have been honoured, the laundry sent a warrant officer with a summons. Vaslav was told that the police were raiding their trunks and they were to be arrested as Russian spies. He decided all Germans were secret agents in disguise, and was in a constant state of nerves at what he took to be their unfriendliness.

The little choreographic poem called *Spectre de la Rose,* which was inspired by Théophile Gautier's poetry, became a gem among Fokine's compositions. Merely intended as a *divertissement* to fill out the programme, and hurriedly composed, it was so exquisite that it became a classic.

A young girl returning from her first ball leans against the French window of her room and dreamingly recalls all the pleasant impressions of the evening. She thinks of her ideal, and slowly kisses the rose he gave her, which she was wearing in her bodice. Intoxicated by the spring air, the scent of the rose, she falls asleep on a near-by chair. Suddenly the soul of the rose, an intangible, dreamlike apparition, emerges from the moonlit window, in a single leap behind the dreaming girl, as if blown by a soft caressing wind. Is it the scent of the rose, or the echo of a promising love? We do not know. A slender sexless being, ethereal, soft, enfolding, stands before us. Not a flower, not a human being. Both. You cannot tell whether it is a youth or a maiden, a dream, or a wish, something unobtainable—something we can only sense. Slender and beautiful, like an unfolding rose, the warm smoothness of the velvety purple petals, sensuous and pure at the same time. With infinite tenderness a full moment it stands at the sill of the window. *Le Spectre de la Rose.* Then in its glorious lightness it whirls through space. It is not dancing, nor yet a dream. We feel everything pure, lovely, beautiful. Here reality and vision meet.

With one single leap he crosses the entire stage, bringing us the fulfilment of our dreams; the scent of a blossoming garden on a June night, moonlight, mysterious but so infinitely restful. There he is floating, floating enchantingly. Suddenly he stands behind the girl and awakens her to a dazed, semi-conscious state, where she finds her wishes, her dreams, her love itself, in beauty. He carries her through the ether, enchanting, caressing, loving, offering her with a chaste gesture the essence of love, and revives in her all the happy moments of her inmost feelings at her first ball, and, when she glides softly into the chair, falls at her feet to prove its tender submission. Then, with one incredibly light leap, he rises high in the air and once more dances around her, re-echoing the beauty in its supreme conception. The girl, soft, trusting, slumbers, but the spirit of the rose can only be held for one second against our heart. After conquering the space in which he floats he is again behind the girl as at the beginning. With one soft kiss he gives her a part of the unattainable and then forever leaps into the infinite.

That was the *Spectre de la Rose* that Nijinsky gave to us: the romantic poem of Gautier, the perfect classical *pas de deux* of Fokine, with the soul breathed into it by Nijinsky. This charming variation, this lovely Biedermeier picture of Bakst's, became a very prayer. As Vaslav was told, *Spectre de la Rose* made one want to cry from bliss. He told me, "I wanted to express beauty, purity, love—above all, love in its divine sense. Art, love, nature, are only an infinitesimal part of God's spirit. I wanted to recapture it and to give it to the public so that they may know He is omnipresent. If they felt it, then I was reflecting Him." So he did to all of us who were fortunate enough to see him. We knew that we had not only witnessed an artistic performance, but the communion of an initiate with divinity.

Bakst created the chamber of a young girl, high, fresh, white, and blue. Under a great muslin curtain is her alcoved bed, near to it her embroidery frame; against one wall a pink cretonned couch, a white table, and on it a white bowl of roses. At both sides and at the back huge French windows open to the gardens of night.

Bakst wanted to hang a cage with two canaries in it by a ribbon from the centre of the window. But Nijinsky asked, "How will I ever get in?" Every time the cage was taken down and hung somewhere else, Bakst would replace it, almost in tears.

Nijinsky's famous last leap in *Spectre*, in which he crossed the whole stage, from the front to the back, in a single bound, was an astonishing *tour de force*. He became almost annoyed with this part, which he had loved so much in the beginning, as everyone constantly associated him with this leap. That's why he used to say, *"Je ne suis pas un sauteur; je suis un artiste."* After the first performance, Marinelli, the London impresario, asked Vassily to show him Vaslav's shoes, to see whether or not they had rubber soles. Many others inspected the stage for traps or other mechanical contrivances. When he made his entrance back stage, Cocteau and the others watched him carefully, almost as if to find out if he were hiding charms in his shoes to aid him.

At the *première*, Jean-Louis Vaudoyer, the poet who had had the original idea for the ballet, came up to Fokine, its choreographer, almost in tears, from gratitude. He said Fokine had created a perfect thing. It was more Gautier than the poem itself; it was a triumph. Fokine was a genius. Fokine tried to stop him, deprecated his own part, reminded him that after all he had also something to do with it. "Nothing," cried Vaudoyer; "all I did was to introduce Théophile Gautier to Michel Fokine."

At the performances the wings were so crowded with spectators waiting for the final leap that electricians and stage hands would storm at people of great importance, friends of Diaghileff or Astruc, who had been magnetised by the phenomenon. Finally a special prohibitive ruling had to be made because the work of the technicians was seriously impeded.

I did not see *Spectre* back stage until London. I was surprised when I was asked to get out of the way. Four men—Nijinsky's *masseur*, Mr. Williams; the chief property man; Michel, and Vassily—held their eight hands together, crossed, to form a net, and against this I was astonished to see Nijinsky land. As he stood there panting under the hissing Klieg lights, Williams massaged his heart and Vassily applied wet cold towels under his distended nostrils.

Bakst's original design for the costume was done on Nijinsky himself. He sketched it on the shirt Nijinsky was wearing. Bakst had painted samples of silk pongee, in rose, rose lavender, dark reds, and various pinks, and these were given to Maria Stepanovna to have bolts of the material dyed. Bakst cut the forms of the rose-petals himself. Some had to be tight, others loose, and he instructed her just how to sew them on so that the costume was created anew each time Nijinsky danced. It consisted of a close-fitting, fine silk elastic jersey, into which Nijinsky was sewn, covering his entire body, except part of his breast and arms, where bracelets of silk rose-petals bound his biceps. This jersey was stitched with rose-leaves, which Bakst would colour as they were needed. Some were ragged, as from a dying flower; others were stiff and firm; while still others curled even from his thighs. And after every performance Maria Stepanovna would refresh them with her curling-iron. On his head he wore a close-fitting helmet of rose-leaves, and the whole effect was an extremely close blending of different reds, rose-violet, pink, and purple, shading one into another, which is the essential indefinable tint of the rose.

Nijinsky's make-up was conceived to personify a rose. His face was like that of a celestial insect, his eyebrows suggesting some beautiful beetle which one might expect to find closest to the heart of a rose, and his mouth was like rose petals.

The costume seemed always to disintegrate mysteriously after each time it was used. It was sent up, with the others, to be refurbished, yet somehow or other it was always shorn of many of its petals. This happened again and again. No one could explain it. Maria Stepanovna, intrigued by the affair, made a special investigation on her own account. She found out that Vassily had built himself a house out of the petals of the rose, which he would clip off the costume to sell as souvenirs to the sentimental ladies of Paris, who stormed him with their secret requests. Zenon, Drobetsky, and the rest of the staff called it the "Château du Spectre de la Rose," and told Vassily that he had Vaslav Fomitch to thank for making him a capitalist.

Narcisse, on the other hand, was not an unqualified success, although there were many enchanting features in it. Vaslav, because of his plastic movements, looked like a living Pheidian marble. He wore an ash-blond wig, secured by an apple-green ribbon, and a white classic chiton, gathered tightly over one shoulder. His sister, Bronia, as the chief bacchante, was the epitome of Dionysian ecstasy; with a superb daring she allowed herself the ugliness of abandon, the corruption of satiety. The whole ballet was white and green, except for the costumes of the shepherds and the bacchantes. Karsavina, as Echo, had a delicious piece of choreography, repeating on the third plane of the stage Nijinsky's gestures on the first. Diaghileff advised her not to trip lightly like a graceful nymph. "I see rather a monumental figure —a tragic mask: Niobe."

A dance of frogs, of forest denizens, green goblins and toady sprites opened the ballet, in a throw-back to the old days of the Mariinsky, and almost smacked of vaudeville. Fokine's arrange-

137

ment was late Greek, lush, a little vulgar. Vaslav said to Sergei Pavlovitch: "This must be Greece of the decadence." He felt the best periods must have been more precise, with sharper edges, more angular and architectural.

When Nijinsky, as Narcissus, finally falls into the pool to kiss his own reflection, and goes down a trap-door, Bakst at first insisted that a large papier mâché narcissus be shoved up. But Vaslav protested so much that it was finally abandoned.

The dancers were not supposed to eat or drink before a performance. But Vaslav, to moisten his lips and throat during a dance, would rinse his mouth with water and orange-juice and spit it out. Cecchetti flew into a violent rage if he caught anybody swallowing a mouthful, and took great delight in telling the story of a dancer who drank black coffee before a performance, and died of heart failure.

When Diaghileff tired of the elaborate food of Larue's or Foyot's, he would take Vaslav, Bakst, Benois, and Stravinsky to the Restaurant Viand in the Rue Donau. It was a tiny place with a single door off the pavement, and two tables on the *rez de chaussée*. Madame Viand was a good French *bourgeoise;* who went herself to *les halles* every morning and picked out the food she would cook. At home, she sat at the *caisse*, with a little stair going up behind her to the two or three private rooms, observing everyone who came and went with the minutest scrutiny. Monsieur Viand was an energetic if patronising host. He always knew beforehand, and for years afterwards, exactly what M. Bakst or M. Nijinsky liked to eat, and one could never order independently, since he insisted he knew far better than they. He always said he was the man actually behind the Russian Ballet, because if they didn't eat food they could digest, they couldn't dance. But he was terrified of Madame. She was a remarkable woman, providing superb *merlan, éperlans*

138

frites, and excellent Vouvray, and Sergei Pavlovitch always asked her advice and opinion on the affairs of the Ballet and its effect on the people of Paris.

Lady Ripon made a great many of the initial and most influential arrangements for Diaghileff's first season at Covent Garden, and Eric Wollheim, a clever and honest impresario, administered all the actual business. Sergei Pavlovitch always demanded a cash guarantee of forty thousand gold francs a night, so that he could be assured of losing only a minimum amount, and Sir Joseph Beecham backed the performances.

Lady Ripon knew how to handle Diaghileff better than most women. She loved Vaslav like a son, and gave him much solid and lasting counsel. At first he couldn't speak to her at all, but from the beginning he had a profound affection for her. She also liked Sergei Pavlovitch and admired him, of course, but she knew very well just how to make him keep his distance from her affection for Vaslav. She was Nijinsky's first real friend, apart from Diaghileff. She had plans for him. She wanted him to marry, and later, when he did, she was one of the very few who continued to stand by him. She felt he should be released from the powerful influence of Diaghileff.

The English audiences had been accustomed to good dancing. They had taken to themselves Adeline Genée, a fine classical *ballerina*, whom they adored. They had seen Anna Pavlova in variety, as well as the enchanting Karsavina, with her own small troupe. They had read the extravagant praise lavished on the Russian Ballet by the French press, and with their characteristic scepticism put it all down to the usual Parisian enthusiasm at the *dernier cri*. Nevertheless, this time there was an added note of conviction in the Continental praise, and there were not a few Englishmen who had actually seen the Russians at the Châtelet,

the Opéra, at Monte Carlo even, so there was more than a mere
rumour that marvels awaited London.

It was the year of the coronation of King George the Fifth
and Queen Mary. And for the coronation a gala performance was
to be given before a Covent Garden filled with people who sym-
bolised the last great aristocracy of the world. The programmes
were to be printed in gold on sheets of white silk.

That foreign artists were commanded to appear at a special
coronation performance was very unusual, and the Russians felt
a great honour had been bestowed upon them. The Queen Mother
of England, Alexandra, was the sister of Maria Feodorovna,
Dowager Empress of Russia, and a great friend of Lady Ripon,
who had much to do with the actual arrangements of the occasion.
The command performance took place in Covent Garden on the
26th of June, 1911. The programme included excerpts from three
operas—*Aïda* with Destinn, *Romeo and Juliet* with Melba, *Barber
of Seville* with Tetrazzini and McCormack—and our *Pavillon
d'Armide* with Nijinsky, Karsavina, Bolm, Cecchetti, Nijinskaya;
Tcherepnin conducting the Ballet. Everybody was nervous. It was
an unusual experience to dance in so full a blaze. Thousands of
lights illuminated the theatre, thousands of opera-glasses darted at
them. They could not help being distracted by the audience, the
most fantastic ever seen. The whole theatre, decorated with roses,
formed a beautiful garden, peopled with gorgeous uniforms and
the exotic splendour of the Oriental costumes of the representation
of India, Persia, and the Far East. The royal box scintillated with
diamonds. The artists all felt that they danced badly.

Chaliapine sang part of his most famous rôle, *Boris Godounov*.
Just before he was to go on, one of the chorus from the Imperial
Opera in St. Petersburg caused a disturbance (as in a similar inci-
dent occurring three years later) saying that the great bass had

struck him, and the entire choir refused to appear. Nothing could persuade them to change their minds. They stubbornly would not go on. Meanwhile the new King and Queen of England waited in the royal box, banked with pink roses. Finally Diaghileff, in utter desperation, by an almost super-human force of will, ordered the performance to continue, and by threats of group expulsion from the Imperial Theatres forced them to sing.

After the performance the dancers were terribly depressed and disgusted, for nobody from the Court appeared to congratulate or thank them, as was usual in Russia, and they did not even receive a souvenir programme. They had been quite spoiled in Russia, always receiving personal praise from the Emperor and Empress, and costly presents as souvenirs. Diaghileff swore, and then set out to get a souvenir programme for Vaslav.

But, everything considered, the Russian Ballet was a great success in London. The English public was more quiet, courteous, and reserved in its appreciation than the French. Vaslav always felt that in England he could really relax. And the loyalty of the English audience could be depended upon. He knew that if he came back to London at the age of sixty-five, unable to turn a single pirouette, they would still applaud him for what he had been.

Lady Ripon acted as their social manager. She advised them to change their headquarters to the Savoy, which was à la mode. She told Diaghileff which invitations to accept and which to decline. And she arranged enchanting week-ends for them at the great English country houses.

Another most charming Society hostess became one of Nijinsky's good friends, and wished to have as close a relationship with him as Lady Ripon. She would come to call every morning at the hotel, with her arms full of cut tulips, jonquils, and fresh roses, and look at him adoringly. She was very sweet, and

141

amused him very much. He was extremely fond of her, and she tried to arrange little parties to entertain him. She was sure he was bored, because, speaking no English and little French, he was usually silent. So she asked Harry Melville, the great London dandy of his day, to amuse him. Melville talked delightfully, like a fine French *raconteur*. Nijinsky listened attentively, and after a long silence ventured only: *"Little Tich, c'est un très grand artist."* The talk went on and on, and then silence, and again Nijinsky's simple question, comment, and answer: *"Little Tich, c'est un très grand artist. N'est ce pas?"*

In London it was so much easier than in Paris. Lady Ripon would simply say: "I must have Vatza for the week-end," and she would take him on the private days to Hampton Court or Windsor, and leave him to wander in the gardens for a whole afternoon; or to Arundel Castle, England's greatest Catholic house, the Duke of Norfolk's seat.

Chapter Nine

NIJINSKY
AS
CHOREOGRAPHER

EVER SINCE his departure from the Mariinsky, Nijinsky's life had passed in ceaseless work, dancing the old repertoire and the numerous novelties across the Continent, on many stages, in many countries. It was a strenuous, difficult life, with constant journeying, new theatres, new orchestras, fresh audiences, which might easily destroy the health of an artist as well as his creative impulse.

But on Nijinsky it had a different effect. His intuitive conception of his art, his associative ideas, were only strengthened as he crossed Europe from one place to another, coming in close contact not only with the artistic past, but also with the living creations of these countries. He silently observed, admired, and criticised what he saw, and lived it. He selected the different lively impressions, strained them through his essential taste, retaining a great deal and throwing off the surplus.

And during these years, when he triumphed all over Europe, and to all appearances was utterly absorbed in his dancing with the Russian Ballet, a tremendous change took place in him. He was developing from the graceful, technically perfect dancer of the classical ballet, which achieved its brilliance through grace, lightness, and fluent line of beauty, to the contemplative revolutionary who wanted to throw over the very attributes which made him famous. In the early part of 1912, Nijinsky, the interpretative artist, became the creative.

In St. Petersburg it had already been noticed that there was a different quality in his dancing from anyone else's. But this was perhaps due more to the supremacy of his technique and the adaptability of his body. In his Parisian creation one could see more clearly the change which was taking place in him. He had danced the rôles in Fokine's ballets with consummate perfection, not only as Fokine wished and dreamed, but over and above this he gave a personality, a particular soul, to each part, which even amazed its choreographer, who recognised that this indeed was the very character itself. Here Nijinsky first showed his creative power, and in the summer of 1911, in Karlsbad, he formulated his initial ideas on *L'Après-midi d'un Faune.*

Petrouchka, his favourite part, gave him his initial opportunity to show his faculty as an actor. The whole conception of this ballet was nearer to Nijinsky's own ideas. While he was dancing it, he felt full of a swelling energy, a latent strength released, a sense of his own individual capacity for origination, which gave to the part an unusual intensity. Nijinsky was overtaken by an irresistible urge to create.

Nijinsky felt that the real liberation of ballet had not yet taken place. Duncan and Fokine had sensed it, but had failed to carry it out to the full. Both were fundamentally founded on grace and the circular movement, Duncan without technique, Fokine in its full possession. Why did they fail? Duncan wished to throw over everything, good or bad, that had ever been done before. Fokine brought a new impulse into the older conception, made a step forward, but both missed the essential truth. Dance is the art of producing and combining movement. It has not only to express a dramatic action or an emotion, but the movements of the dancer must be each penetrated by the living idea. The idea underlying, as in all art, must be the basis also of the art of movement. There Nijinsky made a very definite distinction between movement and the dance, which is a combination of movements. It was clear to him that the first and most important thing is to express an idea through movement, as a writer through words, as a musician through notes on a scale. It is so clear, so simple, that one can hardly understand why no one, from Noverre to Fokine, discovered this truth before, and as the dancer of the twentieth century he did not find an adequate vehicle of self-expression in the technique of the past, just as the accepted stage language of pantomime was useless to him in comparison with his personal method of conveying his meanings.

The "antique," the "mediæval," the "classic," and the "romantic" were different schools to Nijinsky.

His conception of the art of dancing was limitless, its variety of modes infinite. He took his first radical step by attacking the idea which was closest to most of us, by rejecting grace, charm, fluency, and the whole classical technique. He created a new technique and demonstrated that the classical steps, such as *entre-chats*, pirouettes *tours en l'air*, could also be made by eliminating the whole school based on the five positions. Any imaginable movement is good in dancing if it suits the idea which is its subject, but it has to be based on some formulated technique.

Nijinsky, therefore, treated movement literally, as the poet the word. He eliminated, consequently, the floating, sinuous gestures, the half-gestures, and every unnecessary move. He allowed only definitely rhythmic and absolutely essential steps, as in verse one uses only the words needed to express the idea, without rhetoric or embroidery for its own sake. He established a prosody of move-

145

ment—one single movement for a single action. He shows this first clearly in *Faune*, as in all his ensuing creations. He uses immobility consciously for the first time in the history of dancing, for he knew that immobility could accentuate action often better than action itself, just as an interval of silence can be more effective than a sound. He introduced a new theory in the facts of plastic expression, which until now he had only sensed and imagined but had never revealed, for he realised fully that dancing is not an art of fixed principles but an art which has as its progressive purpose the expression of human personality and ideas.

Nijinsky revolutionised dancing by bringing it to its fundamental principles in the use of straight lines and angles, but only as an opposition to the serpentine and the spiral, on which all former dancing was conceived. The straight line was by no means his ultimate aim. It was merely a form of expression he voluntarily chose to liberate movement, by proving that any line or angle and every form can be good in its proper place. His great innovation lay in that he created an utterly new technique, which is no less important than the previous ones of the older schools. In *L'Après-midi d'un Faune*, as in the *Sacre du Printemps*, the movements are based on this technique. The feet are no longer turned out, toe to heel, heel to toe, as in the classical five positions, but all those movements of the body and the five positions are reversed. He showed that what might first be thought to be ugliness and primitivism can be as perfect a form of expression as the far too easily accepted beauty and charm. He took crude movements on purpose, to change our conception fundamentally. Every movement can be made in the art; all movements are possible if they are in harmony with the basic truth of the conception, even in their most violent and dissonant gestures.

Duncan, like Fokine, understood Greece as the gracious billowy curves of the Parthenon friezes. Nijinsky, with his *Faune*, took an utterly different view. It is the severity of Attic carving, the simplicity and faith of the pre-Pheidian sculptors against the charm and elegance of Praxiteles, significant character against grace. For Nijinsky, the conception of art is to express the most one can with as few simple, monumental gestures as possible; Pheidias and Michelangelo against Praxiteles and Giovanni da Bologna. The nineteenth-century *maîtres de ballet* were strongly influenced by the Græco-Roman remains, and they entrusted the dramatic part of their ballets into the hands of pantomimists, who acted without dancing, while the *ballerinas* danced without acting. They concentrated on the perfection of their vocabulary of steps, regardless of the idea of the drama or period, *décor* or costume.

Praxiteles, in his stone, concentrated on elegance, grace, beauty, equally regardless of whether or not his subject was divine, human, or demon. Nijinsky always rebelled against this grace of form for the mere sake of grace. To express a literary and a moral idea was his aim, and therefore he brought acting and dancing together through the medium of movement.

Before him, all the stories of ballets through the centuries were placed in settings which explained the dancing. The Court festivals of the Petipa ballets, *Sleeping Beauty*, *Swan Lake*, later *Armide*, the harem of *Scheherazade*, the bacchanals in *Cléopâtre*, the flirtation of *Carnaval*, all explain that dancing is logical under the circumstances.

Nijinsky for the first time used and treated dancing as an absolute medium, without excuse or explanation, in *L'Après-midi d'un Faune*. The tennis game of *Jeux*, the activity and death of *Tyl Eulenspiegel*, do not call for dancing as a form, and, in spite of this, the drama, with its climax, was expressed clearly through the medium of the dance.

These ideas on the art of choreography were very clear and definite in Nijinsky's mind. They had been developing during the years of his travels, but he did not speak of them, even to Sergei Pavlovitch, who until now had been unaware of Nijinsky's desire to compose. *L'Après-midi d'un Faune* was thought of first while they stayed at the Villa Schæffler in Karlsbad during the summer of 1911.

Nijinsky took for his subject a simple incident from ordinary life which happens to every human being: the initial awakening of emotional and sexual instincts and their reaction. The day-dreams, the longings, of a modern schoolboy are similar to the half-voiced desires of those primitive creatures, the ancestors of man, part animal, part male human being. A young boy lies half asleep on a hot, suffocating afternoon; the surroundings weigh in upon him, and he has unconscious, imperative desires for which he cannot account but which he wishes to satisfy. Some girls appear, and he tries to caress them. As soon as he becomes more insistent, they take fright and run away. He has himself no idea what has happened. He is hurt and disappointed. An object lost by one of the girls is found by him. He smells its scent, and the person who lost it suddenly appears before him in his imagination. He kisses it, and, by holding it close to him, the associations of the object satisfy the desires of his dream. An everyday incident of fetichism.

This subject Nijinsky took and placed in the period of ar-chaic Greece, connected in his mind with the firm adolescence of art. The little dramatic action in this plastic choreographic poem is expressed through the absolute medium of movement. Should we produce the *Faune* without music, it would be a complete har-monious whole. It requires no accessories. It is explicit in itself.

That he chose this subject to present his ideas and methods in choreographic art can be explained by the fact that he himself at this period went through the first impulses, not only of creation, but of his mature emotional life. Until now he was not awakened. He had been the obedient pupil, then the dancer, always completely and absolutely concentrated on the dictates of his art. All his emotional experiences of everyday life he unconsciously passed through and absorbed into his art. Until now he was an instrument of choreography, essentially and completely (as Pavlova was all her life), but now life and his instincts claimed their due. The experience with X. was superficial. It gave Nijinsky a different outlook on people, on nature. Those with Diaghileff were merely a proof of his devotion and admiration for Sergei Pavlovitch, a gratitude expressed in the way it most pleased Diaghileff. He was always seeking to discover the truth in art and life. In these early years of their friendship Nijinsky was convinced that Sergei Pavlovitch's attitude to life and love was the right one. In artistic questions he was in a position to argue and defend his own opinions, but in life he gave the older man the lead.

Now, for the first time, he felt that perhaps there was something else somewhere, something else different, of which Sergei Pavlovitch was not aware, and could never comprehend. His fallibility began to dawn on Nijinsky. His own impulses were too strong for personal restriction, and had to find some outlet. Naturally, with Nijinsky they found their way through creative expression, and he conceived the idea of *Faune*.

He had thought much about these problems for months and months. Already, when *Narcisse* was produced, he mentioned to Diaghileff that the Dionysian Greece of Fokine was by no means the best period, and rather a decadent one at that. As the idea of *Daphnis and Chloe* came up, he said to Sergei Pavlovitch, "I have in mind a choreographic poem, not a ballet, which I would like to

149

do. My idea of Greece is utterly different from Bakst's and Fokine's." Diaghileff was interested and amused. "Why, Vatza, why not work on it?"

"I have done so," said Nijinsky, "and the whole *œuvre* is already quite clear. Of course, I should like to have the music composed for it."

Diaghileff became enthusiastic, and encouraged Nijinsky, but he wanted to have it produced as soon as possible, in the next season. They began to consider the composers from whom they could draw, so that one could be commissioned to do the music. Sergei Pavlovitch wanted to know all about his plans for *Faune*, but Nijinsky insisted that he would show him only at the rehearsals, because otherwise he would not understand what he was trying to do. So Diaghileff began to go through the literature of music after Nijinsky explained to him his ideas of Greece. Hours and hours they spent at the piano, but they totally failed to find what they wanted. Finally there was Debussy's *L'Après-midi d'un Faune*. Nijinsky was enchanted. Yes, the feeling, the atmosphere, was exactly what he wished, but the music was too circular, too soft for the movement he had conceived. In everything, except its lack of angularity, it was the very thing he wanted, so finally, *faute de mieux*, he decided to use it, realising that the musical movement would not be the same as his own plastic expression. The piece was composed in 1891, after the Eclogue of Mallarmé, so naturally it could not echo the ideas that Nijinsky wanted twenty years later. But the underlying feeling was the same. The criticism that the choreography and the music were in angular and circular opposition, later voiced in the press, was correct, and known from the first by Nijinsky. But no existing piece was more suitable, and there seemed no time to call in a composer. Sergei Pavlovitch went over to see Debussy, whom he had known ever since the musician's visit years before to Russia, and Debussy was delighted that a work of his should be used, and gladly gave his permission.

The coronation season was over. The troupe split up, departed, and went on their vacations back to Russia. Diaghileff had had many conferences during the season with Bakst and Fokine, to whom he wished to entrust the novelties which were contemplated for the coming season. The company by this time was firmly established, and it was sufficient to send Nouvel or Drobetsky to Russia and Poland to make offers for Diaghileff for new members of the Ballet.

Fokine, until now, had been absolute *maître de ballet*. The ballets, apart from the ones of his own designing, were all of the classical period. Diaghileff, in the coming season, was making two distinct innovations—the introduction of Nijinsky as a choreographer, and a foreign, a French, composer in the person of Debussy. Also a Jean Cocteau–Madrazo–Reynaldo Hahn ballet was contemplated—the East Indian legend of the Blue God. Maurice Ravel was composing the music for *Daphnis and Chloe*. The single Russian novelty in sight was *Tamara*, after the poem of Lermontov, for which Balakierev had written a symphonic poem many years before. Bakst adapted the poem for the ballet, designed the marvellous costumes and scenery, and, of course, Fokine the choreography. Fokine was not aware that Nijinsky was intending to compose on his own. Except for Diaghileff and himself, nobody knew. Sergei Pavlovitch thought it would be better to wait, and break the news to Fokine when he came back from Russia with his new creations. Diaghileff knew that he would be extremely upset when he heard that his supremacy as a composer would be challenged. Up to now, for a century, a country, a company, had had only one *maître de ballet*. It was natural, therefore, that the change should displease Fokine, who was at the height of his

151

artistic career at this very moment, particularly with his individual temperament. But Sergei Pavlovitch was fearless when he had an idea, and he took it on himself to break the news. Finally he would understand and, being a great artist, he would in time see the necessity of different composers for the development of their art. The greater difficulty would be to appease Fokina, whose influence on Fokine was great. Fokina had a prominent part in the ballet, and she was a very excellent dancer of her type. But many of the misunderstandings which arose could be accounted, according to Diaghileff, to Fokina's influence.

The creation of *Dieu Bleu* and *Daphnis* necessitated Diaghileff's constant presence in Paris, and he decided to spend a greater part of the summer there. This idea was welcome to Nijinsky, as he wished to compose and finish *Faune* before they started the autumn tour, for which Diaghileff had already signed contracts for Germany, Austria-Hungary, and Monte Carlo, as usual, before going to Paris.

To retain the troupe was not possible, and Nijinsky did not even consider it necessary for the early rehearsals, but he needed one artist on whom to compose, and Diaghileff requested a dancer of the company, Alexander Gavrilov, to give up his vacation and remain in Paris.

Gavrilov was young and enthusiastic. Shortly after he had been graduated from the Imperial School in 1910, he had left the Mariinsky to join Diaghileff. He had heard so much of them, and as soon as he met Diaghileff, Fokine, and Vaslav, the combination of their talents opened utterly new vistas on dancing for him. He was glad to stay. It was a hideously hot summer, Nijinsky took Gavrilov down to the café in the basement of the Châtelet, and over a couple of bocks explained with great excitement just what he wanted him to do.

Every day, at the top of the dusty old Châtelet, in the rehearsal room, they worked on *Faune*. The only other person there was the pianist. Not even Diaghileff was admitted. Here Nijinsky composed, with Gavrilov as his material, as a sculptor works his clay. Each fragment was worked out and indicated by Nijinsky, then expressed by Gavrilov. Nijinsky would demonstrate, Gavrilov imitate, and very often whole phrases were rejected, or completely changed in movement. Every single day for two months they worked in the heat and dullness of a Paris summer.

Occasionally in the evening they took a drive around the lake in the Bois, or dined at the Château de Madrid, or went to little hidden places in the forests of Saint Cloud and Meudon, and sometimes they visited Maurice Ravel at Montfort.

The late summer finally arrived, and Nijinsky, with Diaghileff, departed for their beloved Lido, to spend three solid weeks in freedom and relaxation. *Faune* was completely ready. Now, at last, Nijinsky had peace of mind. He realised, though, that to teach the troupe his new creation would be sure to present extreme difficulties, as it demanded an utterly new technique.

The days slipped by, and in the first week of October they joined the troupe, which had gathered under Grigoriev in Dresden. Most of them had come back from Russia, and were full of news about what was going on at home, and how envied they were by their fellow dancers.

Bronia arrived. She had spent the summer with her mother in St. Petersburg. Eleanora was well, and happy about the success of her children, but she was longing for Vaslav. Alone in the capital she led a quiet life, for the first time without financial worries, and with leisure. Vaslav at once made arrangements for his mother to come, and thought the best place for her to join them would be

153

Monte Carlo. Eleanora would love the Riviera, and there he would have more time to be with her.

They had before them a long list of engagements—Dresden, Leipzig, Prague, Vienna, Budapest, before going in March to Monte Carlo. Maestro Cecchetti arrived, sunburned and in high spirits after the summer spent in Italy, and he was greeted with the usual enthusiasm, and had to listen to all the vacation stories of each member, to which he lent an ever willing ear.

One day, during a rehearsal in Leipzig, word came that Thomas Nijinsky had died suddenly of pneumonia in Kharkov. Nijinsky had not lived near his father for many years, but it was a distinct shock to him. He had always hoped that some day they could be more together. He took the news calmly, the troupe, as they heard of it, coming to him to show their sympathy. Nijinsky was sitting in the dimly lighted auditorium watching the rehearsal as Bolm, having some free moments, came down and expressed his regrets over the sad tidings. Nijinsky thanked him, looked up, and smiled. Bolm was amazed at this, and decided he must be heartless. Only years later, when Vaslav's long illness began, we learned that this peculiar outward expression, a smile at sad news, or weeping at joy, may indicate the exact reverse of the true psychological reaction.

This year the Berlin performances took place at the Kroll Opera House. They were held in a festival atmosphere, and Berlin turned out, friendly and appreciative. The Kaiser himself was their principal patron. The director of the Imperial Berlin Museums told Sergei Pavlovitch that on one occasion, when some matters connected with the Museum were discussed at a Cabinet Council, the Kaiser held forth on dancing, and actually showed the assembled Ministers some of the steps in his favourite ballet. He then proceeded to say:

"Gentlemen, there is more beauty in this Russian Ballet than in all our Museums from the cellar to the roof."

And the Kaiser gave strict orders that the directors of all the Imperial Museums should come and see the Ballet.

Karsavina made flying visits from St. Petersburg, and this tour was carried out chiefly without Kshessinskaya. Bronia travelled with the other girl dancers, and received the same treatment as they did. She seemed to be happy and satisfied. Vaslav did not want to give her an exceptional position, in order not to destroy the discipline of the troupe, and thought that when the time came for her to be a *prima ballerina assoluta*, she would get the privileges which were due to her rank.

But some of the remarks of the other dancers began to impress Bronislava Fominichina's mind. Why did not Vaslav Fomitch travel with her? Why did she not stay in the same Palace hotels as her brother? Why did she not accompany her brother and Sergei Pavlovitch at their different receptions? Whenever other members of the troupe were asked, not only Karsavina and Vaslav, but of course Bronia was taken along.

Whether or not she realised at this time the exact nature of the friendship between Nijinsky and Sergei Pavlovitch is hard to say. She must have known Diaghileff's admiration and jealous guardianship over Vaslav Fomitch. All this time Vaslav was trying to persuade Diaghileff to give her the parts she deserved through her talent. Diaghileff had opposed her as long as the ballets called for sweet and pretty *ballerinas*, but, now that *Petrouchka* and other creations came up, where art, and not the idea of a pretty face, was important, Bronia began to be cast as an understudy for Karsavina, with whose parts she was alternated, with great success. Naturally she had more the spirit for these parts in the new creations than anybody else, and in *Faune*, Vaslav intended to give her an important rôle.

Artistically speaking, Bronia was satisfied, but of course the suggestion of her colleagues annoyed her. And several times she made peevish, girlish remarks to her brother about her disappointment at not living and travelling with him. Vaslav Fomitch tried to explain that it was a personal matter that made him share his life with Sergei Pavlovitch and not with her. He could not tell his own sister of the relationship which made him stay with Diaghileff.

The reception in Prague was an exceptional outburst of enthusiasm. The Russians were fêted as nowhere else before. In this great popular success not only their transcendent art, but the fact that they were Russians, played an important part. Prague, the capital of the province of Bohemia, belonged to the Austro-Hungarian monarchy, and the greeting of the Ballet was in the nature of a political demonstration from the populace—that as Czechs they belonged to the Slav race and were a sister nation to Russia. The applause was so wild that they even broke the orchestra stalls and threw all kinds of objects on the stage in their mad acknowledgment.

At last the Ballet arrived in Vienna. The quiet, distinguished routine of this Imperial capital, the ordinary way of life of the common people, the streets crowded with uniformed officers, booted and spurred, the hussars with their dolmans, the Imperial equipages with whiskered footmen on the box, the broad Khärtner Ring and the beautiful buildings, all manifested the splendour of the reigning house and the richness of the nation. Everything and everybody seemed prosperous, gay, and light-hearted. In many ways Vienna reminded Vaslav of St. Petersburg and the broad Russian way of life, even to the big baroque palaces and the atmosphere of regal ordered patronage. Nijinsky loved the huge, majestic Opera, with its ideal stage, the spacious rehearsal rooms where everything was perfect for dancing. He felt quite at home here, for it was very much like the Mariinsky in its surrounding atmosphere and the way in which it was run.

The Viennese ballet-master, as well as the *corps de ballet*, received the Russian visitors with sympathetic friendliness, which, after the first rehearsal they watched, turned into incredible admiration. And the Ballet itself, with its Italian *maestro*, who was a strict upholder of the traditional Italian school, was the first to proclaim the supremacy of the Russian dancers and the genius of Nijinsky. He used to take his own artists to watch him and show how hard and faultlessly, with what unbelievable energy, he practised, never stopping, even after having attained human perfection.

Cecchetti was radiant. At last he felt at home, and the praise of his Viennese colleagues, who were in constant attendance, delighted him. The rehearsals were of an easy nature, as the stage and the orchestra were equally perfect, and Monteux, who was an ideal conductor for ballet, clucking to the wood-winds as if they were horses, since he spoke little German, made them understand exactly what he wished to obtain. And, then, nearly all of the Viennese spoke perfect French.

Sergei Pavlovitch chose the earlier novelties to show Vienna for the first time: *Swan Lake, Armide, Cléopâtre, Scheherazade, Les Sylphides, Carnaval,* and *Spectre* were given. The Press, as well as the public, were unanimously at their feet. The stage was laden with flowers, and the applause tumultuous, in spite of the fact that the Court, with its strict Spanish etiquette, and even the aged Emperor, who broke eleven years of mourning for his wife, appeared constantly. Archduke Raïner, the eighty-year-old doyen of the House of Hapsburg, never missed a performance. He was wheeled into his box, and followed every step and every gesture like the keen *balletomane* he was, and always led the applause. In the intermission one could look up at the Imperial *loges* and see young King Alfonso, on a visit to his cousins, trying to imitate the *entre-chats* and pirouettes he had just seen. *Spectre de la Rose*, with its Alt Wien *décor*, was such a success that the audience applauded until Nijinsky and Karsavina had to encore the whole ballet.

Diaghileff had many friends in Vienna, among them E. Sachs, a cultured old gentleman who made occasional trips to Russia, and spent a great deal of time in different European capitals. He was a charming *viveur*, with the same tastes as Diaghileff, and he lived in an old palace in the Seilern Statte, which breathed an exquisite air of art and a *mondain* life. One of the real "old school," he was a perfect host, an enchanting *causeur* surrounded by a highly intellectual group, and he was famous for his collection of objects relating to old Vienna and had wonderful prints and engravings. He also had an extremely interesting dancer's library, with souvenirs of Camargo, Vestris, and Elssler among his treasures. There were the slippers of one, the Spanish comb of another, the manuscripts of Noverre. Nijinsky loved to pass his late afternoons in the quiet palace, among these mementos which meant so much to him.

Baron Dmitri Gunsburg plunged readily into society, as a branch of his family lived here and had a high place in banking circles. Sergei Pavlovitch declared that Gunsburg had really begun to develop into a *maître de plaisir* of the Russian Ballet, and so he had, with his gaiety, humour, and pleasantness. They fêted him like a *prima donna*, and he thoroughly enjoyed it. He tried his best to drag Diaghileff and Nijinsky with him, but he did not succeed very often. He represented the Russian Ballet in a marvellous way socially, and paid flying visits to Diaghileff's suite to sign the cheques that backed their enterprise, hardly glancing at the figures.

Diaghileff was guaranteed, even in the smallest city, eight thousand gold francs a night, but he never made less than fifteen or twenty thousand. The yearly income of the Russian Ballet was about two million gold francs, as the houses were invariably sold out weeks ahead of the time they arrived, with the prices three times as high as usual. In spite of this, if Sergei Pavlovitch made two million he always spent three, and Gunsburg, without a question, paid up the difference. It pleased him to do so. It was a privilege, after all, to outplay Deutsch de la Meurth, the Aga Khan, and Sir Basil Zaharov, who were also helping Diaghileff. Sergei Pavlovitch often teased Gunsburg, saying: "Dmitri, you are like an aging cocotte, always on the go, always looking fit, and we, the Russian Ballet, are your *amant de cœur*."

Nijinsky liked Gunsburg. He was gay and amusing in his whirlwind apparitions. He had always something entertaining to say and always knew the latest about everything that was worth while in the world of art and politics, and he was a faithful reporter. He had a real friendship for Nijinsky, whom he admired deeply, and often wished he could take him along without Sergei Pavlovitch's constant escort. But he was a man of the world and tried to take things as they were.

Nijinsky spent hours in the Albertina, fascinated by the drawings of Leonardo and Holbein. He visited the Lichtenstein, the Akademie, and the Kunsthistorisches, and was really thankful that the orchestra made it possible to have fewer rehearsals, to allow him more time than was usual for himself. They stayed at the old Hôtel Bristol and made occasional visits to Sacher's, where Frau Sacher, the grand old lady of Vienna, the friend of Emperors, the protector of the young aristocrats and artists, the wise matchmaker and angel of peace in political intrigue as well as in love-affairs, held her court. Frau Anna Sacher was a great character, and her fame resounded even in St. Petersburg, where she was known to be one of the sights of Vienna. She was, of course, present at the performance, and welcomed Nijinsky and Diaghileff to her world-famous restaurant. "Why, he is merely a boy, this miracle," she would say in her charming Viennese accent, *"Ja, wir haben auch einmahl eine Elssler gehabt, unser Johann, ja, der hat mahl uns unter die Füsse gespielt, wir lieben tanzen, aber so was wie Sie no das ha'ma noch nie g'sehen."*

Karsavina had to return to St. Petersburg, and Kshessinskaya accompanied them to Budapest, where the next appearance of the Ballet was scheduled in the first days of March. Nijinsky contracted a very bad cold as soon as he arrived in the Hungarian capital, and he had to stay in bed, unable to appear at the first two performances, as he was too feverish. Already, in Vienna, he had danced with a high temperature. At the Hôtel Hungaria, in his rooms overlooking the Danube, he was resting and thinking that soon his *Faune* would be produced. He hoped people would understand it. It was a new path in choreography, extremely advanced, but it could not fail to find a response. He was becoming tired of the eternal success, and people staring at him as a prodigy, when he was so much more than that. He was feeling and thinking deeply. He wanted to show there was more in life than the momentary satisfaction of a craving towards beauty. His leaps, his lightness, his ease, his grace—could not they see, could not they understand, that he had a message for them, deeper than the pleasure he brought to their lives? Dancing, as beautiful as it is, passes, dies with the disappearance of the interpreter. Did Vestris or Taglioni leave anything after them but a magical memory? A mere dancer only lives on in these ways. But he wanted to show his public the

VASLAV NIJINSKY   (1913)
(ELLIOTT & FRY, LTD.)

L'APRÈS MIDI D'UN FAUNE

meaning of life, the way lasting happiness could be obtained. Success, wealth, were passing. The real, the intangible good was helping and loving unselfishly. He danced for these ideas, and in such a manner to best express them, and this was the secret of his miraculous performance.

Sergei Pavlovitch came back late to the Hungaria, after the performance, and took his meals on a table near Nijinsky's bed. They heard the fascinating music of the gypsy orchestra playing constantly in the restaurant below. Vaguely it brought back to Vaslav Fomitch memories of his childhood, his trips into the Caucasus and near the flowing Volga.

Kshessinskaya was often with them and nursed Vaslav. Her own golden samovar, with its accessories, was moved near his bed, and she prepared tea in the Russian way. "Foreign people don't know how to make it, anyhow," she declared. She had been received as a queen by the public of Vienna and Budapest, the fame of her talent, her beauty, and her close connection with the Russian Court preceding her. Kshessinskaya surrounded Vaslav with her exquisite feminine manner, and he, who was always attentively cared for by Diaghileff, somehow felt an inexpressibly soothing presence. Sergei Pavlovitch was highly amused by Kshessinskaya's attentions, but he knew it was merely a friendly gesture. She was so pleased Vaslav had obtained success abroad, and wanted simply to show her devotion. And she really intended to gain some influence over Vaslav to balance that of Diaghileff, if this was possible, as she was anxious to have Nijinsky return to the Mariinsky, if only for a few months in the year. She was a wise and diplomatic person, and Vaslav passed the afternoons chatting happily with her, just as any boy of twenty would do. Kshessinskaya travelled with her own retinue and lived in the royal manner. Diaghileff often teased her, and one evening at dinner he remarked:

"Oh, Matildoshka; yes. You are superb. You deserve all your success, even to the two Grand Dukes at your feet."

"But, Sergei Pavlovitch," she answered quickly, "I have two feet."

The troupe was enchanted with their stay in Budapest. The whole city was wild about them, and the Press could not say enough. They were received with flowers, gifts, and cheering, while the students at the University unharnessed their carriage horses and pulled the artists home themselves. Nijinsky flew from the demonstrations, but he was glad they were so popular. At the rehearsals the Russians could not rave enough over the Hungarian hospitality, the beauty of their women, the wonderful gypsy music, and the thousands and thousands of cafés where the inhabitants of the city seemed to pass their lives, discussing politics. Bolm was busily praising the manners, the parties, the society, and of course Gunsburg was so taken up that he swore to Diaghileff that unless he took a rest after Vienna and Budapest he would collapse. Luckily Monte Carlo seemed to promise some relaxation. But not for Diaghileff, who knew that Fokine would arrive for the rehearsals of the novelties, and he would have to be told about *Faune*, and not for Nijinsky, who had to produce *Faune* in Monte Carlo. Even Vassily disappeared from time to time and murmured on his return to Diaghileff that the Vengerkas deserved their names, as no one could compete with them in making love.

A few days after their arrival at Monte Carlo, Eleanora Bereda Nijinskaya came. She was greatly excited at leaving Russia for the first time and by the wonderful luxury of her journey all the way from St. Petersburg, on which she had been escorted by one of Diaghileff's secretaries. Vaslav and Bronia were waiting for her at the little station near the Casino, and drove her to the hotel, where she was to stay with them. The first time the family was reunited she was so happy that she could only cry and cry. Diaghileff and Vaslav took her about, showed her Monte Carlo and the Grande Corniche. The performances began, and every evening she attended faithfully. Everybody tried to be of help and show her around, but she preferred Drobetsky's escort, as he was Polish, and therefore they could understand each other so well.

Vaslav devised everything he possibly could to make his mother's stay happy, and never had Eleanora realised before in what triumph this company worked and how luxuriously they lived. But she had a profound respect for the Mariinsky as an institution, and, while she was pleased with their success abroad, in her heart she regretted that Vatza had left, and she did not believe that any good came out of this wandering gypsy life, which she had led when she had first married Thomas Nijinsky. She was sure everything would have been different if he had only had a permanent place as a member of the Imperial Theatre.

Diaghileff and his circle surrounded her with the utmost respect and attention, but she felt really at ease only when she could drive around with her Vatza and Bronia alone. She preferred this far more than all the stately dinners at the Hôtel de Paris. But soon Monte Carlo affected even Eleanora. After all, she was still a comparatively young woman, and one day she declared to Vaslav Fomitch that she had decided to go shopping. So they went over to Nice, and boxes and boxes of dresses and hats followed her back as if she had been a young bride. And she appeared every day in a different silk or taffeta dress, and with bonnets tumbling with ostrich feathers. Vaslav did not dare to venture to say anything about the newly chosen clothes, for fear of spoiling her pleasure.

Eleanora saw the novelties of the Russian Ballet and was at once won over. *Spectre* became her favourite, and, although she was distinctly of the old classical school, she had a quick, clear perception in artistic matters and felt the new era had come to stay and was right in itself. She was delighted to be with her old friend Enrico Cecchetti, whom she had practically always known, since he had been *maître de ballet* for a time in Warsaw. They used to sit on the terrace, almost like a loving couple, under the palm-trees, and in the afternoons they could be found at the Café de Paris, sipping their orangeade. There Eleanora sweetly tried to convince *Maestro* of the interest of the new ballets, of *Petrouchka's* great qualities. But *Maestro* defended the old style. So they had endless discussions on the subject, but *Maestro* held to his fortress relentlessly, and would not concede an inch of his cherished tradition.

The rehearsals for *Faune* began, so as to be ready by the time Fokine was expected, and also to give him ample time to rehearse his own three ballets, *Dieu Bleu*, *Daphnis*, and *Tamara*.

For *Faune*, seven girls were chosen, their heights playing a certain importance in the choice, as they had approximately to be the same, as it was composed on one plane as in a bas-relief. The part of the chief Nymph was given to Nelidova. She was the tallest of them all, and so formed the centre of the frieze. Bronia was to be the Nymph who confronts the *Faune* and runs away in a panic, a small but very difficult part of which she gave an extremely remarkable presentation.

From the very first rehearsal, Nijinsky explained to the troupe that they would have to try to forget their technique of the five positions and to take utterly natural ones. Almost as if they were children, he showed them the first steps. In *Faune* there is no dancing in the old sense of the word. It is a consecutive series of movements. All is executed in profile; that is to say, the legs are in profile as well as the head, and the hands show either the palms or their flat backs. The torso is held opposite, hips turned out toward the spectator, as one sees in archaic Greek or Egyptian sculpture. This position seemed to cause the artists extreme difficulty. They simply could not move. So after two rehearsals, each of half a day, Nijinsky found that he had first to teach them to walk, and thus slowly build up his new technique. This took them almost three months. *Faune* had one hundred and twenty rehearsals, of which at least ninety were taken up training the dancers in the method. *Faune* does not consist of any complicated form of steps or movements. The dancers always walk backwards or forwards in profile, on the heel, with very slightly, almost imperceptibly, bended knees. In the beginning this presented an almost insurmountable obstacle. The dancers would always fall back either into one of the five positions, or into their ordinary way of walking, and at this time Nijinsky found out that very few women really know how to walk, that our civilisation has formed an artificial way of walking which was influenced partly by the *Grand Siècle*. Women have the tendency to put the tip of the toe to the ground first, to give the impression of grace and lightness, instead of first putting the heel down, which gives firmness and natural rhythm to the body. This is the way one should walk, and he taught his artists to do this. This experiment of Nijinsky's actually proved that the so-called "modern" or "natural" method of dancing needs a training as long as, if not longer than, the classical school requires.

Nijinsky spent his whole day rehearsing with the seven dancers. The performances in Monte Carlo commenced in the usual way, and he only went from the rehearsal-room to his dressing-room for the evening's ballets, and back to bed. Fortunately, they did not dance every day. Eleanora had to return to St. Petersburg, and Vaslav hoped to be able to go back to Russia after the London season and spend the summer with her, as he was homesick.

Now at last Bakst and Diaghileff were admitted. Sergei Pavlovitch was at once enthusiastic. At last the art of choreography had achieved a new form. Both he and Bakst immediately understood its tremendous importance. The door was at last opened on a new vista and the possibility of a new school, distinctly separated from the classical; in fact, the dance of the twentieth century from which the real modern form could develop.

For the other members of the troupe, the stay in Monte Carlo passed agreeably. The performances did not follow each other as rapidly as in the cities, and in the daytime, when they were free, they could amuse themselves out of doors enjoying the sunshine and gaiety of the Riviera. Among the many persons who were seen a great deal with the Ballet was the Aga Khan. He never failed to send beautiful flowers and presents to the stars, as well as to the other dancers of the *corps de ballet*. Once he presented Karsavina with a string of pearls, and she, furious at what she considered a proposal, stormed to Diaghileff. "Not at all, Tamarochka," he said; "accept them as you would a bouquet from anyone else. It is only his compliment to your art."

The Aga Khan used to sit in the afternoon at Rumpelmayer's, before him a mountain of toast, easily resting his feet on a table, and entertaining the members of the Ballet, as well as for supper at the Café de Paris afterwards. Nijinsky liked him, and was greatly amused by his suite and the two attendants, day and night, faithfully before his door, seated cross-legged on the floor. The Aga Khan extended an invitation to Diaghileff, Nijinsky, and Karsavina to come to India. But how could they, as much as Nijinsky would have liked it? They would never have the time between seasons.

Finally their stay in Monte Carlo was over, and the time approached to go on to Paris, where the rehearsals with Fokine were supposed to take place for *Dieu Bleu, Tamara,* and *Daphnis and Chloe.* There were two new parts for Nijinsky. He told Sergei Pavlovitch that the rehearsals for *Faune* were well advanced, but in spite of this he would have to keep them up until the very day of the *première.*

The season was to take place at the Châtelet. Nijinsky and Diaghileff stayed as usual at the Hôtel Crillon. Fokine was already there, and began to rehearse at once. Diaghileff asked him over to the hotel, and told him in a casual way that a new choreographic poem was going to be introduced by Nijinsky, and the work was almost finished. Fokine seemed to take the news fairly calmly.

Fokine's three ballets, including *Tamara,* were on a grand scale, and needed the whole troupe. First *Dieu Bleu,* and then *Tamara,* was rehearsed, with Adolf Bolm and Karsavina creating the chief parts in the latter. The essentially Russian music of Borodin is well known, the sinister choreography, as well as the tall, curious scenery, were suited to it, having all the cruelty and native colour that the mediæval Caucasian Queen's Court required.

The season began in the middle of May, and the first novelty was the *Blue God,* which received a lukewarm reception, except for the personal success of the performers. *Spectre, Fire Bird, Petrouchka, Prince Igor,* were also on the programme. *Tamara* was more enthusiastically received, but somehow Fokine felt that his constant faithful muse had deserted him. He began to complain about the lack of time he had for rehearsals, as *Daphnis and Chloe* was still in rehearsal. He asked Diaghileff for more rehearsals, but Diaghileff refused, saying that the troupe was already so much overstrained that they could not stand any more rehearsing. Three days before the *première* Sergei Pavlovitch suggested that they abandon *Daphnis* entirely. Fokine begged for the three days, although he knew six or eight rehearsals were imperative. The

167

choreography was extremely complex, particularly in the last scene, where groups of dancers rush in and out, and finally move to a reassembled climax. *Daphnis* had to be rehearsed even on the day of its first performance. Fokine was irritated and nervous. He had the feeling that his position as a *maître de ballet* was being undermined. He heard more news about *Faune*. Rumours were on foot that something utterly new was in formation. Nijinsky, as always, complied to all that Fokine requested of him, and gave an exquisite performance of a Greek youth in *Daphnis*. But, in spite of this, the ballet itself failed to obtain a permanent success in the repertoire. Not one of the three novelties choreographically attained the standard of *Carnaval* or *Spectre*.

Diaghileff saw that Fokine's mood was not all that could be desired, and also he was aware that part of his irritation was directed against Nijinsky. He could easily have tried to explain matters, and create a friendly atmosphere, with his great diplomacy, but Sergei Pavlovitch had more than one strange twist in his character. He never wanted his collaborators to get on well. On the contrary, if any ill will developed, he rather stimulated it. He wanted blind obedience and loyalty to himself and to no one else, and, if the others should hate each other, it fitted marvellously into his schemes. If the creative powers of the Russian Ballet could be friends one day, perhaps they would feel they no longer had need of Sergei Pavlovitch. Fokine had become too dominant. Diaghileff never liked this, and, in all his artistic career, as soon as an artist attained a supreme position, he tried to pull him down. Because there must be only one reigning power, and that should be Sergei Pavlovitch Diaghileff. Yes, certainly he was interested in bringing forward a new *maître de ballet* to further a new school of choreography, but the other motive was always there behind. He made Bakst, and dropped Roerich and Benois for him. He raised Stravinsky and played him off against Prokoviev. He launched Massine and changed him for Dolin, Lifar, and others. And thus Bakst was cast away for Larionov.

Diaghileff did not keep his artists with him, giving chances for all of them. Once they were discovered and really developed, he threw them away as a used glove. Again and again, during the twenty years of the reign of Diaghileff, there is in the troupe one dancer, one ballet-master, one composer, one painter, in a supreme position, and then out he goes. It was never the case that they had outlived themselves, or their art was *passé*, as Sergei Pavlovitch would always explain their disgrace to the public. Stravinsky, Benois, and Fokine are still great masters. Each of the artists who had been collaborators, or who were discovered by him, could have gone on for the glory and development of the Russian Ballet, but Diaghileff unfortunately, as he was a great constructor, so was he also a supreme destroyer. The Russian Ballet had had more and more of a success, and, since they had left the Mariinsky, Sergei Pavlovitch had begun to lose his head. He started to have *la manie de grandeur*. He liked to call the troupe the "Russian Ballet of Diaghileff." At first he played with the idea. Then he began to believe it himself, that he was its creator. He forgot that his dancers were members of the Mariinsky, that they were graduates of the Imperial School. He forgot that his guard of scenery painters, his composers, his choreographers, were the product of Russia and its art, with centuries of tradition behind them. Diaghileff, the discoverer and organiser of genius, thought that he, like God, had created in his image every single artist of this company. Few of the artists sensed this at the time. Nijinsky began to notice it, and Benois, who had known Sergei Pavlovitch so well, must have. Later each one was to make this discovery of Sergei Pavlovitch's character; and in many ways this caused the downfall of the Russian Ballet in later years, when it really became *Les Ballets Russes de Sergei de Diaghileff.*

Fokine thought that a lack of time for the rehearsals of *Daphnis* was caused on purpose by Nijinsky. Everything that went wrong at this time he interpreted in this way. Nijinsky, seeing Fokine's irritation against him, was inwardly hurt. He did not do anything to displease him. On the contrary, he felt Fokine, who had been his *maître de ballet*, should have welcomed and encouraged him, as a younger artist, in his development. They were working for the same ideal: the art of the dance. The atmosphere was charged with electricity. This misunderstanding, the expectations for *Faune*, keyed up the nerves of all the artists. The final rehearsals arrived with the full orchestra, and its members were dumbfounded. And they agreed among themselves that the most outstanding creation they had ever witnessed was *Faune*.

Chapter Ten

L'APRÈS-MIDI
D'UN FAUNE

BAKST had his scenery hung, but Nijinsky, who had only seen the models, was displeased. They had rather lively discussions. Nijinsky said, "Bad enough that the music is not the same as the movement. Now the scenery fails to form a harmonious part." But Bakst himself was enchanted with the scenery, and Diaghileff also thought it very good.

At last the day of the first performance arrived, the 29th of May, 1912. Perhaps for the first time in his life, Nijinsky was nervous. Would the public understand? Would they affirm that his ideas were right? This day was one of the most important in his life.

The dancers were instructed by Bakst in making themselves up. They had very whitish-pink eyes, like those of a pigeon. He painted them first himself. They wore no tights, and had nothing under their pleated gauze tunics, which were cream colour and painted by him with the motif of Greek keys, some in light blue, others in apple-green. They were barefoot, with their soles and their toe-nails pinked as well. They all wore tightly fitting wigs wound from cords painted in gold, their formal locks falling on to their breasts. The girls really gave the impression of Greek

171

statues in a frieze. Bakst took infinite pains to make them so, and the effect was exquisite.

Nijinsky, as the Faun, wore closely fitting tights which came up to his neck and around the arms. They were painted by Bakst in a coffee colour with big brown spots, which were disposed in such a manner, continuing on to the bare arms and hands, as to give the impression of the skin of a Faun itself, and the difference between flesh and costume could not be discovered. Around his loins he wore a garland of small evergreens, which ended behind in a small tail. His head was covered with the same kind of a gold cord tight wig as the Nymphs', and he had, as well, two little flat curling horns. He was the very image of an adolescent Faun, a young being half animal, half human. In the costume, as in Nijinsky's expression, one could not define where the human ended and the animal began.

His facial make-up utterly changed the apparent structure of his face. He underlined the obliquity of his eyes, and this brought out and gave a slumberous expression. His mouth, chiselled by nature, he made heavier. Here also was an infinite languor and a bestial line. His face, with its high cheekbones, lent itself admirably to the transformation. His ears he elongated with flesh-coloured wax and made them pointed like a horse's. He did not imitate; he merely brought out the impression of a clever animal who might almost be human.

Even Diaghileff and Bakst had caught the nervous excitement of this evening. Sergei Pavlovitch was fidgeting backwards and forwards from the auditorium to the stage, where Bakst commanded the electricians, as he found last-minute improvements. The whole troupe was assembled in the overcrowded wings—Karsavina, Kyasht, Lopokova, Bolm, all of them.

A similar excitement reigned in the auditorium. Paris, all

Paris, had gathered. They had heard of a new ballet—a new ballet by Nijinsky. The programme said music by Debussy, *L'Après-midi d'un Faune*, which was inspired by their own Mallarmé's exquisite Eclogue.[1] How would this young Russian interpret Greece in the creation of two eminent French artists? What would his conception be? Yes, they expected something utterly different from Fokine's ballets, but nobody supposed that a new form of art would be presented. On one of the programmes they read:

"On devrait danser *L'Après-midi d'un Faune*, au milieu d'un paysage avec des arbres en zinc." Phrase dite de Stéphane Mallarmé.

". . . Ce n'est pas *L'Après-midi d'un Faune* de Stéphane Mallarmé; c'est sur le prelude musical à cette épisode panique, une courte scène, qui la précède:

Un Faune sommeille
des nymphes le dupent
une echarpe oubliée satistfait son rêve
le rideau baisse pour que le poème commence dans toutes les mémoires."

The audience sat motionless during the twelve minutes of this choreographic poem. They were so taken aback, so surprised, that they gave no sign whatsoever. But as soon as the curtain fell the most incredible uproar occurred. Like a storm, the approval and disapproval broke loose, giving out an incredible noise. Nobody could even hear the voice of his neighbour. Wild applause, shouting took place in one of the most exciting receptions in the history of the theatre. Rodin, sitting in a box close to the stage, stood up and cried, "Bravo! Bravo!" Others whistled. Calls of *"Bis! Bis!"* *"Épatant,"* *"Ridicule,"* *"Inoui,"* *"Superbe,"* alternated, and the roar of applause grew and grew. The fight in the audience con-

[1] During this season a French gentleman complimented Nijinsky on his expression of Mallarmé's *L'Après-midi d'un Faune* in movement. Surprised, he had to admit that he had never heard of the poem. So two artists' ideas met through the medium of Debussy's music.

tinued. They discussed loudly their impressions, and argued. One could clearly see how intellectual Paris was divided into two distinct camps, pro and contra *Faune*. But the approving part of the public won.

The curtain was raised and a second time *L'Après-midi d'un Faune* was performed. After this, the applause became frenetic.

Sergei Pavlovitch ran to Nijinsky's dressing-room, where already Bakst and the others were assembled. "It was a success." "No, they do not grasp it." "*Mais oui*, they feel that something stupendous has taken place." And each one reported their personal impressions of the public reaction. Friends of Diaghileff and Nijinsky, *balletomanes*, poured in. Vassily could not keep up his barricade, and Nijinsky was surrounded, praised, and consoled by those who thought the audience had not accorded *Faune* its merited acceptance. It was indescribable chaos. Nobody was certain what had happened, who had won; was it a success or not? Exactly as after a decisive if hard-fought battle, one does not at first know who has gained the victory.

Rodin came up, and with tears in his eyes took Nijinsky in his arms. "The fulfilment of my dreams. You brought it to life. Thanks." Certainly he was understood, Nijinsky felt now, at least by those who really mattered.

Sergei Pavlovitch, next morning, as usual after a *création*, read the criticism. He saw at once that *Faune* had received nearly unanimous notices in the Press, but that a real controversy over a new æsthetic form had sprung up. The whole Press unanimously acknowledged that a revolution in choreography had taken place. And so the Press went on in praising, discussing, this new form of art which so unexpectedly was presented to them.

The *Figaro*, one of the most important newspapers of France, did not include any criticism, but, instead, its editor, M. Gaston

Calmette, well-known in political life, and as the owner of the paper, ran the following attack in an editorial on his front page on the 30th May, 1912.

A FAUX PAS

Our readers will not find, in its accustomed place under "Theatre," the criticism of my worthy collaborator, Robert Brussel, upon the first performance of *L'Après-midi d'un Faune*, choreographic scene by Nijinsky, directed and danced by that astonishing artist.

I have eliminated that review.

There is no necessity for me to judge Debussy's music, which, besides, does not in itself constitute a novelty, as it is nearly ten years old, and my incompetence is too complete upon the transcriptions of these subtleties for me to be able to discuss with the eminent critics, or the younger amateurs who tax a masterpiece with the reading of "Prelude, Interlude, and Paraphrase Finale," transposed by a dancer upon the work of Mallarmé.

But I am persuaded that all the readers of *Figaro* who were at the Châtelet yesterday will not object if I protest against the most extraordinary exhibition with which they presumed to serve us as a profound production, perfumed with a precious art and a harmonious lyricism.

Those who speak of art and poetry apropos of this spectacle make fun of us. It is neither a gracious eclogue nor a profound production. We have had a faun, incontinent, with vile movements of erotic bestiality and gestures of heavy shamelessness. That is all. And the merited boos were accorded the too-expressive pantomime of the body of an ill-made beast, hideous, from the front, even more hideous in profile.

These animal realities the true public will never accept.

M. Nijinsky, little accustomed to such a reception, badly prepared likewise for such a rôle, took his revenge a quarter of an hour afterwards with the exquisite interpretation of the *Spectre de la Rose*, so prettily written by M. J. L. Vaudoyer.

Sergei Pavlovitch, reading the *Figaro*, for the first moment was greatly shocked. It was such an incredible action, such an unheard-of attack: Calmette of all people, to come out in defence of the morality of Paris! All of Diaghileff's fighting spirit was aroused; after all, important as Calmette was, he was no authority on art, but his opinions meant much to the public at large, and he thought, and then decided to challenge him. Diaghileff's friends, and the *balletomanes*, as well as the personal admirers of the Russian Ballet, came to the Crillon at once. They all had discussed what would be the right thing to do by the time Nijinsky, who had taken a well-deserved rest, awoke from his late sleep and came in to Sergei Pavlovitch's rooms. All sides of the question were considered. Followers and newspaper-men called up, came to the hotel, and tried to talk to Diaghileff or to see Nijinsky, to know what they thought of the Calmette attack. Members of the Russian Embassy came in and explained that they were convinced that Calmette had made this attack, merely using *Faune* as a pretext, because in reality he wished to attack the policy of the French Foreign Office, Poincaré, and the Russian Ambassador, Isvolsky, who were trying to strengthen the Franco-Russian alliance and friendship. The *Figaro*, and the political group which the paper was representing, pursued a different attitude in politics, and, in attacking the Russian Ballet, the strongest propaganda for Russia in France, they attacked the *rapprochement* with the country itself.

News came that the prefect of police of the city of Paris had been requested to stop the next performance of *Faune* as an obscene spectacle. The news went through Paris like a hurricane, and threw the whole city into a great state of excitement; and in the *salons* and clubs, the newspaper offices, as in the corridors of the Chamber of Deputies, anyone and everyone was ready to jump at anything which was said for or against *Faune*. Just as the audience on the evening before, so now all Paris was divided into two camps. Of course, with Calmette and his party taking the side of the anti-*Faunists*, it made them extremely strong.

In an incredible agitation, rumours were repeated and grew. The *Gaulois* appeared with an article stating that an apology was due to the public. The anti-*Faunists* seemed to gain ground. What was to be done in this purely artistic matter which now rocked the whole public? Nothing was settled by Diaghileff as to what course the Russians should take. Nothing was definite by evening, except that they learned that Calmette had obtained from the police an injunction to prevent the further performance of *Faune*. Inquiries were immediately made, and Diaghileff was informed that the last gesture of Nijinsky, the Faun lying on the veil, was the one to which the police objected. Sergei Pavlovitch and the others devised a subterfuge. They requested Nijinsky to change this last move-ment, but he refused, saying that he could not see any offence to the public morals in his conception. Nevertheless, for one or two performances the end of the ballet was slightly modified, but with-out any appreciable difference.

Next morning brought a great surprise to all the Russians as well as to the Paris public. An article, in answer to Calmette, appeared on the front editorial page of *Le Matin*, a paper as im-portant as *Figaro*, signed by no less a person than Auguste Rodin. He said:

During the last twenty years, dancing seems to have set for itself its task of making us love the beauty of the body, movement, and gesture. First there came to us from the other side of the Atlantic the famous Loie Fuller, who has been justly called the rejuvenator of dancing. Then came Isadora Duncan, teacher of an old art in a new form, and to-day we see Nijinsky, who possesses at the same time talent and training. The intelli-gence of his art is so rich and so varied that it approaches genius.

In dancing, as well as in sculpture and painting, flight and progress had been smothered by routine laziness and inability to rejuvenate. We admire Loie Fuller, Isadora Duncan, and Nijinsky, because they have recovered once more the freedom of instinct and discovered again the soul of tradition, founded on respect and love of nature. This is the reason why they are able to express all the emotions of the human soul.

The last of them, Nijinsky, possesses the distinct advantage of physical perfection, harmony of proportions, and a most extraordinary power to bend his body so as to interpret the most diverse sentiments. The sad mime in *Petrouchka* seems, in the last bound of *Spectre de la Rose,* to fly into the infinite space, but in no part is Nijinsky as marvellous and admirable as in *L'Après-midi d'un Faune.* No jumps, no bounds, nothing but attitudes and gestures of a half-conscious animal creature. He stretches himself, bends, stoops, crouches, straightens himself up, goes forward and retreats, with movement now slow, now jerky, nervous, angular: his eyes spy, his arms extend, his hands open and close, his head turns away and turns back. The harmony between his mimicry and his plasticity is perfect. His whole body expresses what his mind dictates. He possesses the beauty of the antique frescoes and statues; he is the ideal model for whom every painter and sculptor has longed.

You would think Nijinsky were a statue when he lies full length on the rock, with one leg bent, and with the flute at his lips, as the curtain rises, and nothing could be more soul-stirring than his movement when, at the close of the act, he throws himself down and passionately kisses the discarded veil.

I wish that every artist who truly loves his art might see this perfect personification of the ideals of the beauty of the old Greeks.

This acknowledgment of Nijinsky's composition, coming as a public tribute from the greatest of modern sculptors, aroused one can imagine what feelings in Calmette and those critics who condemned *Faune.* To say anything further against *Faune* was impossible. But Calmette did not want to be ridiculed, and therefore immediately attacked Rodin.

I admire Rodin deeply as one of our most illustrious and able sculptors, but I must decline to accept his judgment on the question of theatrical morality. I have only to recall that, in defiance of common propriety, he exhibits in the former chapel of Sacré Cœur, and in the deserted chambers of the excellent nuns at the Hôtel Biron, a series of objectionable drawings and cynical sketches, which depict with greater brutality and in further detail the shameless attitudes of the *Faune,* who was justly hissed at the Châtelet. And, now that I am speaking my mind, I may say that the morbid mimicry represented by the dancer on the stage the other evening moves me to less indignation than the spectacle offered every day by Rodin in the ancient convent of Sacré Cœur to regiments of hysterical women admirers and self-satisfied snobs. It is inconceivable that the State—in other words, the French tax-payer—should have purchased the Hôtel Biron for 5,000,000 francs simply to allow the richest of our sculptors to live there. Here is a real scandal, and it is the business of the Government to put a stop to it.

A world-wide controversy exploded. A storm of protest was hurled at Calmette. The admirers of Rodin were up in arms. M. Pierre Mortier, editor of *Gil Blas*, sprang to the defence of Rodin, pointed out that the *Faune* was the *leitmotiv* of his art, and declared that instead of expelling Rodin, as Calmette had suggested, the State should maintain him in the Hôtel Biron for life, and convert it into a Rodin Museum, providing he could leave his work to France; which was in fact done later.

A campaign to support Rodin was started, in which the names of the most eminent figures of France in the artistic, literary, and political world were enlisted: The ex-president Loubet, Raymond Poincaré, the Premier, Leon Bourgeois, Clemenceau, Aristide Briand, Barthou, Hanotaux, Anatole France, Mistral, Jules Lemaître, Monet, Besnard, Maurice Barrès, Octave Mirabeau, Paul Doumer, Jacques Émile Blanche, Rafaeli, Zuloaga, Catulle Mendès, Marie Cazin, Judith Claudel, and many others. Then the rest of the Paris public tried to get in to a performance of *Faune,* to judge for themselves what this question was that had stirred the intellectual world to its depths. It was a real *tour de force*, however, to get in, as all the tickets for the Russian season had been sold weeks before, and every conceivable influence and political pull was called into play to obtain places in the Châtelet.

Then *Figaro* published a huge Forain caricature showing Rodin, in his studio at the courtyard of the Hôtel Biron. A model enters with a dress over her arm:

"Oh, Master, where can I put my clothes when I pose?"

Rodin: "Just there, in the chapel."

179

This was carefully designed to arouse the clerical animosity of the Faubourgs, and a fresh list of adherents swarmed to Rodin's side. The new petition was signed by Isvolsky, the Russian Ambassador; the Senators Dubost, d'Estournelles, de Constant, Gaston Menier; MM. Edmond Haraucourt, Pierre de Nolhac, and Mmes. Alphonse Daudet, Lucie Félix-Faure. Forain, the cartoonist, was attacked by the critic Louis Vauxcelles for his lack of æsthetic self-respect in demeaning himself to draw the caricature in the first place. A Government commission was asked to report, which was favoured both by the President of the Republic and the Prime Minister.

Rodin was asked to defend himself, but he merely said in a statement:

"I have no time to waste on answering M. Calmette's attack on me. I admire Nijinsky's work and consider him a marvel of harmony. He is a dancer of genius. I wish so noble an effort as *Faune* would be understood in its entirety, and that all artists could come for instruction and communion in this spectacle of beauty."

Le Figaro, Le Gaulois, La Liberté, the anti-*Faunist* papers, were silenced. The police appeared and witnessed the performance, but they inclined before the public opinion and *Faune* was not forbidden.

Finally there was a definite triumph for the pro-*Faunists*. Diaghileff was delighted. He realised that Calmette had rendered him a greater service than anybody else before. For from Paris to Constantinople, from London to St. Petersburg, from Berlin to New York, *Faune* was discussed. In later years Diaghileff found it convenient to create a furore of controversy by having his creations attacked, but there was never again the world-wide publicity that was spontaneously accorded *Faune*.

But Sergei Pavlovitch had not time even to gasp a breath, after this turmoil, before another arose. Fokine, through the extraordinary success and violence of *Faune*, seemed to drop into oblivion. Nijinsky was now hailed as the great modern choreographer, the innovator of a new school. *Daphnis and Chloe* was the last novelty of the season, and also a ballet with a Greek background. It was difficult for it to come after *Faune*. But, even in spite of *Faune*, the ballet would not have been a great success. The critics in the Press, as well as the public, said of it: "Its composition is weak, and the choreography is confused and less characteristic than we are used to see at the Ballet Russe."

Of course, Fokine was greatly upset and blamed Diaghileff, and above all Nijinsky, for the failure of his novelties this season. So, by the time *Daphnis* was performed, the idea which for some time had been ripening in Fokine's mind became a determination. He would leave the Russian Ballet. He had been closely associated with it. He was one of the great monumental pillars on which the structure of it was built. The Ballet without Fokine, at that time, was inconceivable. Here in this troupe Fokine had had his first unchecked liberty. Here he had received the inspiration and collaboration to unfold his admirable talent. And here among them he had developed into one of the greatest choreographers of all time.

But nobody tried to displace the false ideas of Fokine, or to salve his hurt pride. In fact, those who should have done so only excited him the more against Nijinsky. And so, finally, after the performance of *Daphnis and Chloe*, Michel Fokine sent in his resignation to Diaghileff. He wished to sever all ties with the Ballet if other choreographers were with them. To this Diaghileff could not and would not accede.

Fokine, who, after Petipa's retirement, was attached to the Mariinsky, but could not obtain the position as an official *maître de ballet,* and was only able to compose on his own for charity performances, now, after his stupendous success abroad with the Russian Ballet, was at last nominated as first ballet-master of the Mariinsky Theatre.

The rumours that Fokine was about to leave quickly spread through the company. But they refused to believe it. Years ago, in the second Paris season, he had already threatened to do this. But that time it was for an infraction of one of his rules. It was understood that no part of the ballets or dances could be encored. Neither could any artist acknowledge applause during the performance. One night, in *Cléopâtre,* somehow the Bacchanal was encored. Fokine was so upset that he immediately left the theatre with the intention of never returning. But Diaghileff, who agreed with him in this ruling, severely punished the stage manager who had made the mistake, and brought Fokine back next day.

This time they hoped it would be the same, but Fokine meant it seriously, and, as soon as they knew this, they decided to take formal leave of him. The company offered him a loving-cup, with flowers, and it was supposed that the principals of the company, Nijinsky and Karsavina, should present it. But Diaghileff told Nijinsky not to do this, as Fokine, according to Sergei Pavlovitch, did not even want to see him. So Nijinsky, hurt by this unjust animosity, kept to his dressing-room while the farewell took place on the stage.

Fokine was saddened deeply by his absence, and with tears in his eyes said good-bye to the other members of the Ballet. If Sergei Pavlovitch had permitted Nijinsky to appear, perhaps a reconciliation would have taken place, instead of this wilfully engineered misunderstanding, and the fate of the Russian Ballet would have been utterly different.

Chapter Eleven

"JEUX"
AND
"SACRE DU PRINTEMPS"

THE HECTIC season of 1912 in Paris was coming to an end. The novelties, the controversies, were hardly over, and the social obligations and prospective artistic plans filled the time and the mind of Sergei Pavlovitch. Nijinsky could not very well free himself of them either. There was a veritable onslaught upon him from painters and sculptors. He had been painted, sketched, sculpted, by innumerable artists all over the world. In the past, Blanche, Bakst, Lepape, Serov, Dethomas, and many others captured his traits and motions, but they had to steal the moments when Nijinsky was free —a gesture, an attitude back stage, or in the rehearsal-room. Now Rodin came forward, among many others, to sculpt Nijinsky. And it was arranged that after the morning practice he should go to Rodin's Meudon *atelier* for the sitting.

The shopping tours also began. Nijinsky was extremely neat and meticulous but simple in his dress. He possessed a small wardrobe, and never had more than two suits at one time. He spent most of his day in practice costume at the theatre. This was the one luxury in which he indulged himself. Tremlett, the fashionable shirtmaker of Paris and London, made his dancing shirts after a special design, in delicate, lovely *crêpe de Chine* of pastel shades.

183

He had hundreds of pairs of dancing-shoes. During one of his drives through Paris he discovered, at a small *boutique* on the Rue Caumartin, some quaint braided kid sandals which he bought and wore at rehearsals, when not dancing, and this started the vogue for Deauville sandals that became so fashionable.

After the *première* of *Dieu Bleu*, Cocteau, one of the authors, offered Nijinsky a gold pencil with a sapphire cabochon which Vaslav always wore. Nijinsky had a real passion for sapphires, and Sergei Pavlovitch, knowing this, offered him at each Parisian visit a sapphire ring from Cartier. Vaslav was claimed to possess the finest sapphires, and he was soon named "Le Roi du Saphir." Now the advice of Gunsburg was needed, and he was delighted to go on these errands accompanying Nijinsky as an arbiter of fashion. Tremlett was given a large order for underwear, and dressing-gowns, in which Nijinsky looked very well, as he did in pyjamas; but he looked very awkward in street clothes, which did not suit his well-proportioned body. He had broad shoulders and a slender waist—sixty-three centimetres, not more than that of the Venus de Milo. It was decided that the order for his suits would be given to Davies, the famous London tailor who worked for the Prince of Wales. At Thonet a beautiful fitted case was ordered, and Nijinsky presented himself with the flattest of watches from Benson. He was as happy and proud as a child with it. Ever since the Tsar had given him that watch many years ago, when as a pupil he had danced for him at the Imperial School performances, the watch that ended at the pawnshop, he had never possessed another one.

In the evenings Nijinsky loved to go for supper to the Château de Madrid or the Pré Catelan. There, on the green lawn, it was peaceful, and in the fragrant acacia-scented air he felt restful. They were often accompanied by Debussy, who was delighted with the sensation that *Faune* created. He was enthusiastic with the idea of collaborating with Nijinsky on a new composition. With Diaghileff as their interpreter, the proposition was discussed, and one evening, dining on the terrace of the Pré Catelan, under the arc-lights that cast rings of shadows through the fans of the horse-chestnut leaves on the table-cloth, he noticed the flight of the moths attracted by the lights circling round and round; and there he conceived *Jeux*. He told Debussy that he imagined an incident in modern life, athletics and the spirit of modern youth, *"les jeux de sport, les jeux de l'amour."* The story was supposed to be enacted near a tennis-lawn at dusk after the game. It was to be the essence of flirtation, the modern form of love. Half felt, half accomplished gestures, emotions playing physically at the game of tennis, emotionally at flirtation—a love-affair between a young boy and two girls both separately and simultaneously—the eternal triangle under an utterly new aspect. This was the basis of so many of the modern ballets conceived years later by Massine, Nijinskaya, Balanchine, and others.

Nijinsky was always interested in sport, and always watched it enviously. He would have loved to take part, but as a pupil of the Imperial School he was strictly forbidden every sport except swimming, for sports developed muscles unsuitable for dancing. Even too much walking is not good for dancers.

Nijinsky began his sittings with Rodin. Usually Sergei Pavlovitch took him up to the studio, sometimes he motored to Meudon alone, and Diaghileff came to fetch him. The latter was much occupied, and Rodin wanted to be alone while sculpting. First he made many sketches, passionately interested in drawing all the muscles of his model. Nijinsky posed in the nude. Finally Rodin decided on a pose which was very similar to that of Michelangelo's *David*, the torso reposing on the right leg, while the left was slightly inclined, the head turned three-quarters to the right, the right arm

185

raised, and the hand turned towards the head. Nijinsky patiently posed hours and hours for the master. When tired, Rodin would make him sit down and would show him all his sketches, and, as they could not speak together, drew what he wanted to explain, and Nijinsky indicated by movements. Their code might have been very complicated for others, but they understood each other perfectly. The sittings were divided by lunch, at which time both model and master rested. Rodin loved simple food but was a great lover and expert of wine. At his luncheons the most excellent wines of France, and especially the Bourgogne, which he preferred to all others, were served.

Sergei Pavlovitch was rather alarmed by the intimacy which developed so quickly between the aged sculptor and the young dancer. Rodin was an artist. There were so many things that they did not need even to say to each other, for they knew them instinctively. There was a unity between Rodin and Nijinsky from which, for this very reason, he was excluded. And he knew it. Sergei Pavlovitch became jealous, but he controlled himself.

Fêtes and entertainments succeeded one another; those of Mme. Euphrussy, of the Maharajah of Kapurthala, Mme. Edwards, the Embassies. And everywhere the presence of Karsavina, Nijinsky, and the Russians was demanded. Those receptions were of great splendour and elegance, each trying to outdo the other. But the Aga Khan was the one who carried away the prize. During the London season that same year, at his garden party he had Nijinsky and Karsavina dance a Variation, in honour of Their Majesties and his other guests. Diaghileff asked, for Nijinsky alone, fifteen thousand gold francs for four minutes of dancing. At the last performance at the Châtelet, at which many foreign personalities were present, Richard Strauss, who for a long time had wished to collaborate with the Russian Ballet, was in the audience. He went

186

back stage to see Nijinsky with his wife Paula, who was a very capable and energetic woman. She was very firm with Sergei Pavlovitch too and, entering Nijinsky's dressing-room, she clasped him in her arms, kissing him on both cheeks and patting heavily the shoulder of the *Spectre de la Rose,* almost crushing him as well as the petals of his costume. Rostand and the others, greatly amused, witnessed the scene. The enthusiasm of the public at this farewell performance was such that they had to encore the whole *Spectre.* Karsavina made a charming little speech to the public in the name of the whole company, and she who shared the succcess was literally bombarded with flowers.

The statue of Nijinsky was unfortunately never finished, for Diaghileff found continual excuses to prevent the sittings. His jealousy had now become uncontrollable. One day he arrived at the *atelier* sooner than expected. It was a heavy, storm-laden, suffocating afternoon, as only Paris can have in July. Sergei Pavlovitch went through the house and found both artists in Rodin's sanctuary, Nijinsky sleeping peacefully on the couch, covered by a shawl, and Rodin also asleep at his feet. The intense heat, the hours of posing, the heavy wine, had fatigued the aged sculptor as well as Nijinsky, who was not used to drinking. Diaghileff did not wake them. He left without being noticed, and only confided in Bakst. The incident was never mentioned, but he energetically hindered any further sittings, and because of this he undoubtedly robbed the world of a masterpiece.

Nijinsky had had practically no time since they left Monte Carlo to see his sister alone. Bronia was very successful this season. The part in *Faune* had increased her popularity. In the troupe she was greatly liked as a gay and good comrade. But her brother did not know that she had quite a lot of attention paid to her at this time by a young dancer of the troupe. Her fame grew; and being the sister of Nijinsky created some sort of halo about her. Some of the dancers secretly thought that a close relationship with the Nijinsky family might be helpful, and then Bronislava was kind, good-hearted, and charming. So many little flirtations began, from which the serious one was with the promising dancer Kotche-tovsky. He asked Bronia in marriage, and she consented. The news greatly surprised Nijinsky. Somehow he had believed that she was as utterly wrapped up in her art as he himself, and the announcement, therefore, came as a disappointment. From now on Bronia would have some other interest in life besides dancing. He almost felt he was losing a comrade. He did not hide this feeling, but expressed it to Bronia, who bitterly reproached him with the fact that she could not be constantly with him, so she might as well get married. The marriage was celebrated very quietly in the Russian Church in London in the presence of Sergei Pavlovitch and Nijinsky, who gave her away.

The London season passed in its usual festive manner. Lady Ripon gave a garden party at Coombe Court, and in her theatre there Nijinsky and Karsavina danced. Queen Alexandra and the Empress Maria Feodorovna were present, both of whom expressed their admiration for the two artists. Queen Alexandra mentioned to Nijinsky that every time she attended a performance and *Spectre de la Rose* was on the programme, she changed from her box to an orchestra seat in the middle of the auditorium so that she could get a full view of his dancing and the final leap.

Sargent was a close friend of Lady Ripon's. She commissioned him to make portraits of her two favourites; Nijinsky in the costume of the *Pavillon d'Armide*.

Nijinsky came to many of these parties after the performances. He was silent, smiling, and extremely shy and boyish. Compliments coming from the public rather embarrassed him. He had wonderful manners, thanks to his innate charm and the strict training of the Imperial School, whose pupils were brought up in the spirit of the *Corps des Pages*. Then, also, Diaghileff had an excellent influence over him in this respect, as he was an *homme du monde jusqu' au bout des ongles*. Nijinsky wandered unnoticed through the *salons*, or eating quietly at a little table. His great favourites were Lady Morrell and her husband and the Bradley Martins, Americans who played an important part in London social life. Old Mrs. Bradley Martin was like a grandmother to him, spoiling, petting him, having him to private lunch, just the two of them. Nijinsky was presented with a gold and tortoiseshell manicure set by her, so that he would think of her daily. He spent many quiet hours at the town house of the Morrells. He was taken to tea on the terrace of the Houses of Parliament, and enjoyed immensely the atmosphere reigning there. One day, at a lunch at Lady Cunard's, where many were present, Nijinsky, who had already begun to pick up a few words in English, said, "Lady Morrell is so tall, so beautiful, like a giraffe." Diaghileff felt rather uncomfortable and tried to explain, but Nijinsky insisted, "No, no, giraffe is beautiful, long, gracious; she looks like it." And Lady Morrell understood the compliment.

The cosmopolitan society of the *grand monde* needed a fresh thrill, and Mr. Marquet, the owner of the Casino of Monte Carlo, launched a new resort. He wanted to do everything to make the place a success. Fabulous hotels were built, a racecourse as good as Longchamp was laid out. Smart shops, casinos, a lovely indoor swimming-pool near the beach, all in Pompeian style, and even grass was planted in place of the sand beach. Deauville had its opening. Marquet secured a few appearances of the Russian Ballet at the Casino. A very high price was guaranteed, and Diaghileff signed this contract. Nijinsky objected very much. He thought the

Russian Ballet should stick to its tradition to perform only in opera-houses.

Nijinsky again had to give up the idea of returning to St. Petersburg that summer, for it would be nearly over by the time they could leave Deauville. Sergei Pavlovitch gave two months' vacation to the troupe. But he had many plans to decide and to settle with Nijinsky. Since they had left St. Petersburg in the early spring of 1911 they had never been separated for more than one or two days. Sergei Pavlovitch, who had a deep reverence for Vaslav Fomitch's genius as a dancer, and equally admired his developing qualities as a choreographic composer, held him under his influence in everything except choreographic art. Here Diaghileff recognised that he himself was the dilettante and Nijinsky the master. But he did not want to relinquish an inch of his influence in other matters. Until now he had had a comparatively easy task. At the beginning of their friendship Nijinsky was merely a boy, eager to learn, to listen, and to be guided. Diaghileff brought him in contact with artists, painters, musicians whom he valued, and whose influence on the development of his art was of the utmost importance. The atmosphere Sergei Pavlovitch created was the right one to bring his talents into bloom. In a way Sergei Pavlovitch was a barricade which separated him from real life and therefore gave him the freedom to live completely for his art. Sergei Pavlovitch, of course, continued to maintain the seclusion of Nijinsky when they left Russia. The continual travelling brought Nijinsky in contact with innumerable people who wanted to be his friends. He made friends, but in a few days' time he had to leave, and so any continuous relationship was made impossible. Whenever Nijinsky made an effort to learn a language, Sergei Pavlovitch discouraged him. "Why lose time on this? You have more important things to do." The more Nijinsky could be kept isolated from the world, and the longer, the more it pleased Diaghileff, who was desperately attached to him. His friends of the past had left him; some had married on account of social obligations. Never did he find in anybody the personification of his life dream as completely as he did in Nijinsky. This had to be a life-long friendship that nothing could break. Of course, Diaghileff knew the rumours that went around in St. Petersburg. It was inevitable that they should be repeated by "some good friend" to Eleanora. She was always the one who wished and prayed for Vaslav's return to the Mariinsky. Now the Dowager Empress declared openly that Nijinsky's return was required at the Imperial Theatre. If Vaslav Fomitch visited his mother's home, he would live there at her house. She would try to ask him to remain. Diaghileff knew Nijinsky would neither leave the Russian Ballet nor himself. He was too devoted to both, but perhaps he would appear a few times at the Mariinsky every season and form a tie outside of Diaghileff's sphere. No, this could not be permitted. As long as Eleanora could see her son only under his supervision she could not gain her point. Nijinsky himself felt that continuous travelling was too exhausting for all of them, and told Diaghileff that serious artistic work could only be accomplished if they had somewhere a permanent home where at least a few months could be spent. Bakst now maintained a home in Paris. Benois and Fokine were still in St. Petersburg. Karsavina was attached to the Mariinsky, and came to join them only for a few months. Stravinsky, on account of his wife and children, lived on the Lake of Geneva. But Diaghileff would not listen. He again arranged for a long German tour, including Berlin, Vienna, Budapest, a London season in February, then the annual season of Monte Carlo and Paris, and London again. An interminable succession of appearances. He was approached several times with very tempting offers from North and South America. But he said, "No, too far away. We have plenty to do in Europe."

The one deciding factor which Sergei Pavlovitch used to keep Nijinsky near him during the time of the vacation was that work had to be done on the intended new creation, *Sacre du Printemps*. Years ago young Stravinsky had, while composing *Fire Bird*, conceived a theme. It was too brutal and strong in its manner to be used in the more magical, delicate *Fire Bird*. This theme suggested to Stravinsky more than prehistoric Russia. The theme at that time was cast aside. Roerich, the great man on archaic Russia, always hoped Diaghileff would produce an essentially Russian Ballet which would represent, not a period or a mood of the Russian race, like *Igor*, *Fire Bird*, or *Petrouchka*, but the very essence of the soul of the Russians, a sort of national *épopée*. So Roerich dreamed of the rituals of ancient times. After *Faune*, the creative urge of Nijinsky became more pronounced, and, now that Fokine had left the troupe, Diaghileff encouraged him in every way to compose. He needed Nijinsky more than ever, but Nijinsky felt that creation should come spontaneously. Luckily for Diaghileff and the Ballet, he was now occupied with a new idea, which grew and clarified itself in his mind from day to day, to create a choreographic tableau where his ideas, his school of dancing, could be developed in full. To do this he had to take an archaic period, a primitive emotion. He wished to return to the creative moment, and chose the primitive period of Russia, the worshipping of nature and its rites. He told his idea to Diaghileff, who exclaimed excitedly, "How strange! Roerich's secret desire." So he brought the three together, and the wish of Nijinsky that a ballet should not be composed on existing music, scenery, or story could now be carried out. Here really the librettist, musician, scenic artist, and the *maître de ballet* were obeying one and the same inspiration, and so their composition was started simultaneously. This complicated ballet needed infinite time. Nijinsky warned Diaghileff that he would require a great number of rehearsals as he developed the technique, and that the steps would be extremely difficult to execute.

With *Jeux* and *Sacre* in mind he had every moment occupied, and he worked intensely during this whole year, Stravinsky working in Clarens and making many trips to meet them.

Diaghileff required a third novelty, and secured another *maître de ballet*, Romanov of Moscow, to whom he gave Florent Schmitt's *Tragédie la Salomé* as a ballet for Karsavina. Soudeikine, the young Muscovite painter, was commissioned to do the scenery. Monteux and Inglebrecht were retained as conductor and assistant conductor respectively. Nijinsky found that Monteux had developed into an ideal conductor for ballet. He was musically very well qualified, but during the last year he had improved immensely his choreographic sense. Without changing the *tempi*, which would have been unmusical, he had the kind of sense to know how to conduct for dancing. *Petrouchka* and *Faune* were played all over Germany during the tour of the winter of 1911-12. The Russian Ballet again visited Leipzig, Berlin, Dresden, and Vienna, and here the public without any reservation praised the new school of dancing. Nijinsky had to be ready by the early spring when they arrived in Monte Carlo for the rehearsals. Therefore in Berlin he made only one exception—to visit Dr. Bode, who was a great admirer of his and who wanted to present him with a wonderful copy of a frieze of the fragments of the Parthenon at the Kaiser Friedrich Museum. He arranged a reception where artistic and intellectual Berlin wished to pay tribute to *L'Après-midi d'un Faune.*

This year Karsavina had great difficulty in obtaining leave from the Mariinsky, for Teliakovsky did all in his power to cross Diaghileff's plans. Kyasht, who was a graduate of the same class as Karsavina, whose good friend she was, danced her rôles after Vienna, as Karsavina had to return to St. Petersburg. Piltz, who developed into an excellent dancer, received more important parts than in the past. She was very lovely.

The tour of the Russian Ballet proceeded smoothly and successfully, in comparative peace. Monteux and Inglebrecht, on account of the score of *Petrouchka*, which presented difficulties, demanded that the orchestras be reinforced. The number of rehearsals were insufficient and the performance of this ballet for this very reason had to be abandoned during the second Budapest season, where the company arrived around Christmas of 1912.

Vienna also extended a most gracious reception to the Ballet, which on its second visit there caused almost a musical revolution. For Vienna undoubtedly is the most music-loving city, and has so high a standard that its orchestras at that time were the best in the world. The symphonic orchestra, the Philharmonic, is that of the Hofoper. With much ease and great artistry they had played until then, with few rehearsals, whatever score Diaghileff put before them. It was not the case now. As soon as Monteux gave them *Petrouchka*, they began to rehearse it with signs of disapproval, which augmented at each repetition. Monteux had great animosity to overcome. He tried to soothe them in the best way he could, but the orchestra, which was slightly influenced by the Anti-Slavic propaganda in the Press, on account of the Balkan War, was not so easily calmed. Diaghileff, who knew what was going on, resented that art and politics were being mixed up. So one day he made a remark about this which the orchestra ignored. Even at the last rehearsal they played *Petrouchka* with such mistakes that Diaghileff was annoyed. He thought it was done on purpose, and he remarked in French to one of his friends listening to the music, *"Quelle cochonnerie la façon dont-ils jouent?"* One can well imagine how shocked the orchestra was upon hearing this. They immediately put their instruments down and left the auditorium. A strike of the *Hof-Oper* orchestra was an unheard-of thing in Vienna. Each member was an eminent artist or teacher of the Conservatory of Music. The intendant as well as the director tried to quiet them, but not until late in the afternoon was the affair settled, when Diaghileff apologised.

This whole visit to Vienna did not seem lucky for Diaghileff. Karsavina wired that she was not quite sure if she could perform in Monte Carlo. And lately Nijinsky, who was now down with influenza, seemed irritable. He insisted on having his room to himself, saying that otherwise he could not sleep; that he was so absorbed in *Sacre* that everything and everybody disturbed him. It was unmistakable that he meant Sergei Pavlovitch, for nobody else gained admittance into their suite. He went so far as to keep to his rooms for three days, requesting Diaghileff not to come unless he was asked for, and for three days he was not asked for. Nijinsky was developing rapidly as a creative artist, as a real man. He felt he must be alone to think. There were so many things he wanted to understand about himself. He was devoted to Diaghileff as much as ever. He felt that their friendship and understanding were perfect, but lately he had become annoyed whenever Sergei Pavlovitch wished for actual proofs of his devotion. Diaghileff seemed in a way to humour him, and tried to give him all possible attention, but he sensed that there was something else behind this. One night, when Vaslav Fomitch was feverish, he wanted to have some oranges, but in Austria in early winter and at night it was impossible to get any. When the Hôtel Bristol failed to procure

195

some and Vassily came home empty-handed, Diaghileff himself
went out at three o'clock in the morning to try all the restaurants
and cafés. Finally, in desperation, he awakened Sachs and, both
joining forces, knocked at the Sacher. The omnipotent *maître
d'hôtel* was called, and of course gave them the precious fruit,
which both of them triumphantly brought to Vaslav Fomitch at
dawn.

The complete score of *Sacre* was now in their hands, and
Vaslav Fomitch worked at it note by note. He went over it carefully with the pianist and visualised the dances before him as he
played. The groups of ancestors, those different tribes and the
adolescents, the young girls joining hands, tramping down the
ground to try to plant the seed deeper and deeper in the earth,
so that when spring came, life-giving plants might bloom forth
triumphantly. But how annoying that amid those mental pictures
the face of that young dancer from Budapest should emerge.
Vaslav Fomitch wondered, "Why do I remember her features?"
That silent figure dressed mostly in black velvet, who sat mod-
estly in the corner of the stage watching the dancing, who appeared
at every corner like a shadow, somebody who loved dancing as
much as he did.

Diaghileff took every pretext to talk to Vaslav Fomitch, who
was more silent than ever these days, and in Vienna one late
afternoon he asked: "Vatza, there is a young girl from the aristocracy of Hungary. She wants to study dancing with Cecchetti.
Shall I take her along? It would be quite an interesting experiment, and would enhance the prestige of the troupe. Later others
might join."

"No, I do not think it is right to take dilettanti with us."

"But she has an artistic background; her mother is the greatest
dramatic artist in Hungary."

Nijinsky hesitated a moment, then said, "All right, give her a chance."

Neither Nijinsky nor Diaghileff ever suspected that at this time they were being constantly watched by my "associates"— at the Hofoper by Mr. Schweiner, the dresser. Usually if any foreign male celebrity came to the Viennese Opera House, Schweiner dressed him. And he knew everybody, from Reské to Caruso. He was an amusing Austrian with an intense sense of humour, who always identified himself with his charges. In the afternoon at the café he often used to say, "To-day we are singing *Tristan* or *Don José*," and he proudly departed. Schweiner felt like a king robbed of his throne, and looked upon Vassily with contempt. But he was useful in securing little bits of information. At the Hôtel Bristol my friend Dagmar Schmedes was invaluable. Not known either to Diaghileff or to Nijinsky, she bluntly followed them to the restaurant, everywhere in the hotel, and one day, as if she was making a mistake, even entered the room of Nijinsky, who was just dressing, and was rather surprised at this interruption.

It was in London, in February, that Bronia came up one afternoon to the Savoy to see her brother. She broke the news to him that she would not be able to dance the part he was composing in *Sacre*, as she would have to cease dancing shortly. She was expecting a child. Nijinsky could hardly believe it. Who could have expected this of Bronia, the ideal dancer, who had all the qualities he dreamed of in art? The terrifically difficult dances of this part, the chief girl's part, nobody could do but Bronia, who not only possessed the marvellous classical technique, but also to an amazing degree the new technique which Nijinsky created in *Faune*. It was a blow to the creator, and he could think of nothing else but that at the time. An ideal woman dancer should never

197

marry, for having children was a terrific handicap for her. Nijinsky was greatly upset, and told this to Bronia, who burst into tears and left the hotel. They did not speak to each other after this incident for several weeks. She was also hurt that the promotion Kotchetovsky hoped to get to assistant stage manager did not come, Kremenev being nominated instead.

Back in Monte Carlo once again, the rehearsals took place on the Casino stage, while *Maestro* held his classes as usual at the Palais de Soleil. It contained a spacious stage and a nice terrace where one could lie in the sun. Diaghileff and Nijinsky did not live either at the Monte Carlo Palace nor at the Hôtel de Paris, but at the Hôtel Riviera Palace—a new hotel just opened on the top of the hill. It took about thirty minutes to get there by automobile. But the view was heavenly, and it gave absolute privacy, which was what Nijinsky was seeking at this time. Karsavina, always attractive, smartly dressed, with her interesting dark figure, used to take walks along the terraces with the Aga Khan and the other friends of Paris, London, and St. Petersburg. Everybody seemed to be on the Riviera this year. All the other dancers, when they had a moment free from *Sacre*, went to the Café de Paris or rested under the palm-trees on the banks of the Place du Casino. It was a free, open, out-of-door life. Sometimes one could see Nijinsky arriving in the autobus from the "Olympus," as we called the place where the Riviera Palace was built.

Often in the evening I used to walk around the Place du Casino and watch Nijinsky sitting with Chaliapine or Diaghileff at the Hôtel de Paris, having supper on the terrace. I lay down on the bench under those blooming magnolia-trees and watched them for hours and hours.

Jeux is perhaps of all Nijinsky's ballets the least known and understood. Unjustly so, for it is another cornerstone in the evo-

198

lution of the modern school of dancing which Nijinsky started. From all remote traditional surroundings, from tales of poetical content, with one leap Nijinsky carried the ballet into the midst of modern life. The musician expresses his epoch. The author writes about the very century in which he lives. Only the choreographer took refuge always in past ages. In *Jeux* three young moderns live, feel, and play, through the absolute medium of dancing, the very essence and emotions of the twentieth century. This contemporary tennis ballet challenged to its deepest root the until now accepted traditions of choreography. The dances were of plastic lyricism, athletic and youthful, for Nijinsky was an adept of youth. In *Jeux* the individuals are young, in *Sacre* the society, and in *Faune* the earth itself. The scores as well as the dances are interludes; all wonder, hesitation, and with no knowledge of the end. The dances presented a parallel to emotional experiences, yet without imitating the actions of real life. For Nijinsky said, "Art is not an imitation of nature, but it is the image of nature obtained through artificial means." The choreographic movements in *Jeux* were stylised, and were on the same principle as *Faune*, only in this new work the frieze was alive and moved in space, the gestures were split up so that it would give the impression of many small movements consecutively following each other as they logically developed, and through this it gave the impression, as some called it, of a *ballet cinematographique*. Each limb made a different movement and followed a different rhythm. Here Nijinsky gave a clear demonstration of the ideas that Dalcroze advocated and which could not be carried out to the full in his school. Again a new idea was lost, for the pupils were not professionals and did not have adequate training, as in the case of Duncan. *Jeux*, according to many, was a triumph of angularity, and introduced post-impressionism to the Russian Ballet. Nijinsky wished to give the expression of lightness, and for this reason he wanted to do all his dances on the point. This had never been done by a male dancer. *Maestro* was greatly amazed, therefore, when Nijinsky asked him to coach him. He thought it would be impossible, but within three months Nijinsky mastered this difficulty. However, it was not applied to *Jeux*, because, after consideration, Nijinsky decided that it would be contrary to the ballet's athletic conception.

In *Jeux* the scene is in a garden near a tennis lawn, the game just concluded, and dusk falling. Electric lanterns shine among the summer foliage, and a lost ball rolls across the stage. A young man appears, searching for the ball. He is joined by two young girls. At once the search is forgotten and they flirt, first the youth with one girl, and then a change of partners, but this does not suit the other. While the young man hesitates, the two girls console each other and begin a flirtation between themselves. The young man decides, rather than lose either, to take them both. From somewhere another tennis ball is thrown across the garden, and with a sudden scared glance they look around and run off merrily. In emotional feeling Nijinsky made a step forward. In *Faune* it was the awakening of love in a youthful being. Here in *Jeux* the feeling is modern too. Love becomes, not the fundamental driving force of life, but merely a game, as it is in the twentieth century. The object (here the excuse of finding the ball) is easily abandoned and flirtation begins, but this is also quite as easily given up when the idea of the former activity is recalled. He sees here love as nothing more than an emotion, a pastime, which doesn't even require consummation, which can be found among three as well as among the same sex.

Bakst created a charming setting of vivid greens and blues and purples. The music of Debussy was youthful and fresh, but with a number of passages of a more robust nature than he had previously used.

The costumes this time were not designed by a scenic painter but by the fashionable leading couturier of Paris, Paquin. Nijinsky wore a white tennis shirt and flannel tennis trousers, buttoned tight below the knee. The two girls, danced by Karsavina and Schollar, wore white flannel skirts and pullovers.

Nijinsky was supple, athletic, and acrobatic in his part. The critics said: "We admire Nijinsky and the faith of this young artist, who in the very moment of his greatest triumphs abandons those prodigious dances in which he is unique in the world, and which bring him a safe success, for his conscientious and tenacious research, for strict charm of the sculptural lines and the beauty of attitudes. It seems that very intimate and sensitive bonds exist between the intelligent efforts of this dancer-genius and the art moderns, whose aim is not to reproduce with servility the aspects of nature, but to find an idealistic and personal transposition."

Jeux had a fairly warm reception, but no doubt the meaning escaped the great public. It was a great mistake of Diaghileff, and perhaps the first proof of coming shortsightedness in artistic matters, that he did not rather produce *Jeux* at another time. It was too refined, too delicate to be followed by the primitive, dynamic *Sacre*, which was awaited with great excitement. It was the first collaboration of the two moderns, Stravinsky and Nijinsky. The one with *Petrouchka*, the other with *Faune*, had convinced Paris that they were the epoch-making geniuses of their respective arts. And much was expected of their joint collaboration, when it was known that for the first time music and choreography were created simultaneously.

On the 29th of May, 1913, at the Champs Élysées Theatre, the *Sacre du Printemps* was performed for the first time, on the very

201

anniversary of the *première* of *Faune*, for Diaghileff was superstitious. I wondered what the reaction of the brilliant, excited audience would be. I knew the music of *Sacre*, and had seen bits of the dancing from back stage during the last rehearsals, where I hid behind Karsavina and Schollar, and had been escorted by Dmitri Gunsburg, and Grigoriev threw furious looks at me, but I just looked through him as if he were of air. With Gunsburg beside me he could do nothing. I thought the public might fidget, but none of us in the company expected what followed. The first bars of the overture were listened to amid murmurs, and very soon the audience began to behave itself, not as the dignified audience of Paris, but as a bunch of naughty, ill-mannered children.

One of the witnesses, Carl VanVechten, wrote about this memorable evening: "A certain part of the audience was thrilled by what it considered to be a blasphemous attempt to destroy music as an art, and, swept away with wrath, began, very soon after the rise of the curtain, to make cat-calls and to offer audible suggestions as to how the performance should proceed. The orchestra played unheard except occasionally, when a slight lull occurred. The young man seated behind me in the box stood up during the course of the ballet to enable himself to see more clearly. The intense excitement under which he was labouring betrayed itself presently when he began to beat rhythmically on the top of my head with his fists. My emotion was so great that I did not feel the blows for some time."

Yes, indeed, the excitement, the shouting, was extreme. People whistled, insulted the performers and the composer, shouted, laughed. Monteux threw desperate glances towards Diaghileff, who sat in Astruc's box and made signs to him to keep on playing. Astruc in this indescribable noise ordered the lights turned on, and the fights and controversy did not remain in the domain of sound, but actually culminated in bodily conflict. One beautifully dressed lady in an orchestra box stood up and slapped the face of a young man who was hissing in the next box. Her escort rose, and cards were exchanged between the men. A duel followed next day. Another Society lady spat in the face of one of the demonstrators. La Princesse de P. left her box, saying "I am sixty years old, but this is the first time anyone has dared to make a fool of me." At this moment Diaghileff, who was standing livid in his box, shouted, "*Je vous en prie, laissez achever le spectacle.*" And a temporary quieting-down followed, but only temporary. As soon as the first tableau was finished the fight was resumed. I was deafened by this indescribable noise, and rushed back stage as fast as I could. There it was as bad as in the auditorium. The dancers were trembling, almost crying; they did not even return to their dressing-rooms.

The second tableau began, but it was still impossible to hear the music. I could not return to my stall, and as the excitement was so great among the artists watching in the wings I could not reach the stage door. I was pushed more and more forward in the left wing. Grigoriev, Kremenev, were powerless to clear this part of the stage. Opposite me there was a similar mob in the back of the scenery, and Vassily had to fight a way through for Nijinsky. He was in his practice costume. His face was as white as his *crêpe de Chine* dancing shirt. He was beating the rhythm with both fists shouting, "*Ras, dwa, tri*" to the artists. The music could not be heard even on the stage, and the only thing which guided the dancers was Nijinsky's conducting from the wings. His face was quivering with emotion. I felt sorry for him, for he knew that this ballet was a great creation. The only moment of relaxation came when the dance of the Chosen Maiden began. It was of such indescribable force, had such beauty, that in its conviction of sacrifice it disarmed even the chaotic audience. They forgot to fight. This dance, which is perhaps the most strenuous one in the whole literature of choreography, was superbly executed by Mlle. Piltz.

The story of the *Sacre du Printemps* is already contained in its title. It is the adoration of nature in its most primitive and powerful form.

Winter death reigns. Vegetation is in decay. It is the weakening of nature's impulse to fertility. But the everlasting, omnipotent, inherent power of growth breaks through, and spring comes.

Choreographically this ballet is the highest and purest composition of modern dance which has been created up to now. The movements express fear, joy, and religious ecstasy. They are first purely ritual movements of a primitive kind. The dancers shiver, tremble, and vibrate at the entrance of the seer. Later come emotional values in the movements of the dance of the Chosen Maiden. Her leaps, her jerks, are the ultra-modern descendant of the pirouettes and *entre-chats* of the classical school, and their choreographic value is the same. Nijinsky contradicts the classical position by making all steps and gestures turn inward. The choreography was the most amazing and correct visualisation of the score. Each rhythm was danced, the counterpoints were built up choreographically in the groups. It is through rhythm, and rhythm only, that the dance identifies itself with the music. The rhythmical counterpoint is employed in the choral movements. When the orchestra plays a trill on the flutes, movements thin out, and so do the dancers. Then the tune begins on wood-winds two octaves apart, and on the stage two groups of three dancers each detach themselves from the lines and dance, corresponding to the tune. The mouse-like shuffling of the sorceress, the rapid steps of the young men, correspond to the musical expression of the movement as the intricate rhythms of the joyful dance of the Chosen Maiden. At the end of the first tableau great circles (women dressed in scarlet) run wildly, while shifting masses within are ceaselessly splitting up into tiny groups revolving on eccentric axes. It is in this direction that the development of ballet is infinite. Even the costume colours were reflected in the music. With *Faune,* Nijinsky led us near to nature in the archaic, mythological period. In *Sacre* he took us far back to the awakening of nature itself and to the instinctively found rituals of the primitive man. No doubt in *Sacre* Nijinsky most clearly expressed his creed. Both choreographically and musically it was far ahead of its time. The dancers as well as the orchestra, and especially Monteux and Mlle. Piltz, accomplished a gigantic task. Even to-day, to dance or conduct *Sacre* is difficult, but in those days it was almost a superhuman effort.

Everybody at the end of the performance was exhausted. The month's long work on the composition, the endless rehearsals, and finally this riot——. Once more Vassily's guard broke down and Nijinsky's dressing-room was stormed, Diaghileff, surrounded by his friends and the *balletomanes,* explaining, discussing. Nijinsky took the whole affair more quietly now that it was over, and, nobody needing his energy and encouragement, he could let himself go. Stravinsky was in a frenzy. But they all agreed and knew that their creation was good, and that it would be one day accepted. They were so excited that they could not go and have supper right away, so somebody suggested a drive *au tour du lac.* And Diaghileff, with Nijinsky, Stravinsky, and Cocteau, drove around in the Bois to quiet down, and only toward the morning did they return home.

Chapter Twelve

NIJINSKY'S MARRIAGE

WHENEVER we moved from one city to the other *Maestro* gave me two or three days' vacation. I always travelled alone with Anna and not with the company, as we used better and faster trains. We always tried to get the train on which Nijinsky and Diaghileff were travelling, but until now we had failed. Anna, as usual, had to do the intelligence service to find all details about Nijinsky's trip to London. I did not quite trust her information, so that my joy was so much greater, boarding the midday express train at the Gare du Nord, when I saw Vassily ordering Michel around with the luggage, buying illustrated papers, and handing them through the open window of the train's corridor to Nouvel. Nijinsky was on the platform talking to Drobetsky. Anna had done well; our places were reserved in the compartment next to that of Nijinsky's. I quickly hid myself so that Diaghileff should not notice me. Finally the train pulled out and everybody settled down. I was desperately trying to read the illustrated paper, but could not understand anything, as my thoughts were constantly in the other compartment. I sent Anna out, who came back with the report that "le Petit," as we called Nijinsky between us, was reading quietly. She also went over to the dining-car to find out when they were going to have their lunch, at the first or second *série*, and to try to obtain accommodation if possible at the same table. But she failed. We could not even get to the same service. I was furious. Finally I could not resist, Diaghileff or no Diaghileff. What was the good of travelling by the same train if I could not see him? So out I went. Cautiously smoking a cigarette in the corridor, I passed the window of Nijinsky's compartment. He was with Nouvel, reading and talking. I wondered where Diaghileff was, but, throwing all caution aside, I remained. Nijinsky looked exceedingly smart in a greyish-green travelling-suit, with light grey cap, suède gloves, unbuttoned, on his hands. He did not notice me; at least, I thought he did not. After a while he stood up, came out, bowed, and passed before me. I did not know what to do from gladness, and ran breathlessly into my *coupé*. *"Anna, Anna, 'le Petit' vient de passer et de me saluer!"* I was triumphant. Again for two months I could live on the memory of this incident. What I did not suspect was what all this journey held in store for me. Five minutes later I was again in the corridor, seemingly smoking and admiring the landscape we passed by. I sat on a *strapontin* and gazed out, turning my back to Nijinsky's *coupé*. I don't know how long I was looking out, but suddenly I felt the same peculiar electric shock as when I saw him entering the stage, and turned slowly round and looked into Nijinsky's fascinating, Oriental face. He smiled, looking curiously like my pet Siamese cat that had given me the first impulse to follow him all around the world. His eyes were more oblique than ever, but I noticed they were not green, as they had seemed on the stage, but soft brown, like velvet. He stood near me, overtowering me as I sat there. He took hold with one hand of the copper railing of the window and put one foot on the radiator. I could not help looking down. His foot looked so elegant in his yellow shoes; there was something so fascinating about it that I could not take my eyes off it. Nijinsky smiled, followed my gaze. Then, trying to divert my attention, in his broken French he said: *"Mademoiselle, vous connaissez Londres. Content voyager?"* I answered with a torrent of French all about London—my school years there, England, its charm. He did not understand a word, but listened indulgently. Then I realised that I was holding a monologue, and stopped abruptly, so embarrassed that I could not move, and my eyes followed each movement he made—how he arranged his glove; it was so enchanting. I must have seemed impossibly stupid to him. He gazed silently out. I followed his eyes, how long I do not know. I was spellbound. Then suddenly Nouvel called him—and I became frightened, but Nijinsky not in the least; softly, naturally, he opened the door, talked to him without any nervousness, as I had expected, and went in. I fell into my compartment half fainting. I was so excited that on arrival in Calais I could not say a word to Anna. Nijinsky, followed by Nouvel, without bothering about anything, went on the boat. I could not see Diaghileff anywhere. We left Paris in glorious weather; by the time we arrived in Calais it seemed clouded and grey and a high wind was blowing. Anxiously the passengers asked the porters and sailors what kind of crossing we could expect, and they reassured us. Within five minutes after we sailed the boat seemed to leap to the sky and fall into a bottomless precipice. The passengers who had proudly sat and arranged themselves on their deck-chairs, with covers, pipes, candies, and books, hurriedly disappeared below. Within half an hour all state-rooms were engaged and the deck deserted. I too felt deadly sick. The whole boat seemed to go round with me. I did not know what to do, it was so suffocating. So courageously I tried the advice of one of the sailors to go on the deck. As soon as I arrived, the wind almost blew me down the stairway. I fought against it and made the round of the deck. Not a soul; everything deserted. I wondered what had happened to "le Petit." There he was, leaning against the railing with his back to the sea, laughing and chatting with Nouvel, who lay flat, opposite him, in a deck-chair, all rolled up in covers like a mummy, with a greenish-blue complexion, so hidden by shawls that only the tip of his nose could be seen. I immediately decided that though I die I would stay. With all my will-power I stood there smiling, in the howling wind which blew my veil, my skirt. A sailor pulled up a chair in the sheltered side near Nouvel, tucked me in covers, and I bravely smiled at Nijinsky. He seemed to be greatly amused. Nouvel crawled more and more under the covers, closed his eyes, and became mute. Nijinsky began to talk to me in Russian, with a few French words. Now it was my turn to listen and not to understand, but his expression, his mimicry, were so expressive that I hardly noticed that our conversation was merely pantomime. I forgot the stormy sea. It seemed like a minute and we were already in Dover.

Poor Anna had been terribly sick. "Never again." "But, Anna, I found a marvellous cure against sea-sickness; to flirt." And she actually doubted my word when I told her I flirted "*avec 'le Petit.*'" But where was Diaghileff, where was Vassily? I don't know. I suppose too sick to come on deck to keep their vigil. For once I had succeeded. As we pulled up at the station in London I saw Diaghileff, smartly dressed as always, standing there with a group of distinguished-looking men waving their straw hats to Nijinsky. He jumped alertly off the train and was immediately surrounded and whirled away to a motor-car. As I passed by, to my great amazement he took off his hat and waved good-bye. Diaghileff turned around and looked at me. I was surprised at Nijinsky's courage.

Back at work again, Cecchetti was very pleased with me. I practised even at home, until he forbade me to overwork myself. I lived in a very smart but small hotel in Mayfair behind St.

James's Palace. I knew London well, and had a wonderful time with my English relatives, who took me around, visited the picture galleries, and took me for beautiful drives in the park. As often as I could I asked them to take me to lunch and dinner at the Savoy. Nijinsky and Diaghileff, as usual, were staying there; their head-quarters were at the grill-room around three o'clock. There, near the open fireplace, Diaghileff had his reserved table, where he held his court.

The London programme was practically the same as in Paris. The favourite ballets, *Sylphides, Spectre, Igor,* of course, were repeated, as well as the same novelties. *Dieu Bleu, Salomé, Jeux,* and *Sacre* were given. The *Dieu Bleu* and *Salomé* had a polite but not over-enthusiastic reception. In the first Nijinsky, in the latter Karsavina, achieved great personal success. *Jeux* puzzled the audience immensely. They were greatly interested to see for the first time sports done on the stage, it was so novel. But somehow the extreme *finesse* of the underlying subject and the stylisation of the movement escaped their understanding. They expected a real game of tennis played by Nijinsky, Karsavina, and Schollar. The critics complained the tennis-ball was too big. But they never realised that the tennis was merely a suggestion to bring to choreographic art the atmosphere of sport and the modern athletic spirit, and poor Bakst had to make the ball bigger to make it visible. He was dealing with art and theatrical effect.

There were also lengthy comments in the papers about Nijinsky's tennis trousers, because they were not made according to the classical pattern. The *première* of *Sacre* was of course the chief event of the season. Many of the public had already seen it in Paris. The critics were discussing *Sacre* in the foyers during the *entr'actes* of the other performances. One could feel they were greatly impressed, and finally tremendous applause broke out.

Part of the audience did not take part in it. But everyone felt that they had heard and seen something quite unusual and far-reaching, only they could not quite comprehend it yet, and their reaction was of expectation of what this new creation would lead to. They responded intellectually and not emotionally, as had Paris.

One paper wrote: "*Sacre* is nature worshipped with arbitrary gestures. So the music, as the dance, is the pure rhythm. Nijinsky starts the dancing revolution." Another said: "Nijinsky in this ballet is freeing the dance from its perennial taint of mere conventional prettiness." One of the leading papers stated: "The audience felt that the authors went too far, that they have ridiculed the ideals of beauty. Yet it may be suggested that the audience was wrong and that Mr. Nijinsky and Mr. Stravinsky are probably right, that in a few years we shall have learned that there are other things in music and ballet than sweetness and sensuous beauty, just as there are other things in painting than domestic subjects." So London understood after all.

As often as I could I went on the stage before the start of the performance. Sometimes I was lucky to find "le Petit" practising. He did not turn his head quite so abruptly away when I looked at him. Sometimes I noticed a shadow of a smile. During the *entr'actes* he always disappeared in his dressing-room. And after the performance, as usual, he was surrounded by his friends and the adoring audience. Outside the theatre big crowds always waited, not gesticulating, shouting, as in Paris, trying to touch or to kiss Nijinsky or Karsavina, but politely murmuring, "Bravo! Bravo!" Nijinsky and Diaghileff, with their friends, had a late supper at the Savoy retaurant. Nijinsky sat there like a prince. He had something so refined about his disappearance, and a dinner jacket suited him. He so often had a distant observing look in his half-closed oblique eyes which I adored, and which was fascinating beyond all

211

else. He seemed now almost to take it for granted that I was here, there, and everywhere where he appeared in public. He must have wondered how I managed it. I was really glad now that I had spent so much on my clothes in Paris. As I always went with some friends, it must have seemed natural to Diaghileff that I was present. He realised that I moved in the same society as he himself.

Nijinsky was simply adored by his English friends. They loved his simplicity, his naturalness, his enjoyment of all the fun, and he tried to take part in their sports.

Maestro also liked London. He had so many friends, Italians, artists, and *ballerinas* of the old school. When he was free he made his usual rounds of the different ballet schools to see Adeline Genée dancing at the Coliseum, Astafieva in her school, Pavlova and her troupe at the Palace. Then also the nice Italian restaurants were to his taste. The only rather upsetting moment was when Madame Cecchetti announced her arrival from St. Petersburg. She was carrying on *Maestro's* school in St. Petersburg during his absence. She was a splendid teacher, an energetic, kind, but self-willed woman. She knew what she wanted, and *Maestro* was rather henpecked. The nice flirtations with the young dancers had to have an end; no more taking them out for supper. But *Maestro*, being a great pedagogue, and believing in discipline, never took out his own pupils or members of the Russian Ballet.

He was overjoyed, and showed us proudly, on his birthday, the presents he received, and especially his cane with its heavy gold knob, given him by Nijinsky. He used it always now, correcting us with it, and we wished there were less gold on it. I was luckily told in time about the approaching birthday, and gave *Maestro* a golden purse filled with sovereigns. This present pleased him immensely, and it proved later on to be a diplomatic move on my part. One morning, while I was practising, Nijinsky and Karsavina arrived for their lesson. This had been advanced for some engagement they had later on, so we were dismissed. I took a long time to change my dress. As there was no other exit, I knew I would have a chance to see them. As I passed, Nijinsky and Karsavina were doing their *grand battement* already in the centre of the hall. *Maestro*, who had no corrections to make, watched with the eyes of a hawk to detect at least some little mistake. "Tamaroschka, please, just a little bit higher your arms" (they were perfect). "Vaslav Fomitch, *glissade, entrechats cinq, pas de basque-double, cabriole en arabesque, pirouettes, quatre tours en l'air*," and invented the most unbelievably difficult combination of steps, yet with the precision of a clock immediately the obedient pupil executed them. It was a real joy to watch this lesson. The exercises *à la barre* then in the centre were executed without stops, in perfect unison. The following adagios, allegros, whatever step came to the mind of *Maestro*, were promptly done. Both at the same time. Or he took Nijinsky separately. While he was making pirouettes, or *tours en l'air*, Karsavina practised her points quietly in a corner. *Maestro* made a point of making them do all exercises and steps strictly according to the classical tradition. And invariably before each lesson he started his little speech. "Tamara Platonova, Vaslav Fomitch, you may be celebrated, great artists, but here in my class you are my pupils, nothing but my pupils. Please forget here all your crazy modern movements, all that Fokine, Nijinsky nonsense. Please, *ras, dwa, tri, chetiri* . . ." I was speechless. The two obeyed him far more than we ever did.

Karsavina wore some worn pink or white *tutus* with a deep décolleté blouse of the same colour. She brought her own darned ballet-shoes in her hand, shoes which had seen many days. She became rather disarrayed at the end of the lesson. Nijinsky, as usual, wore his black, close-fitting dancing trousers, blue, green or white beautifully made *crêpe de Chine* shirt (like the one in *Sylphides*), and white or cream *chevreau* ballet-slippers. Often he himself took the watering can from *Maestro* and sprinkled the floor, while *Maestro*, with devilish joy, criticised the ballets of the evening before, showing that this or that step was made with a millimetre of error; that in spite of all the success their dancing was all rubbish, and the good old days of Petipa were the real ones. He could hardly even forgive the existence of *Spectre* or *Sylphides*. His love stopped at *Swan Lake* and *Giselle*.

He never got tired of complaining of the music. "Very soon, Gaspada, I will not be able to go on the stage, to listen to that sick-cat music of Stravinsky and those crazy French composers."

Vassily was not admitted to these lessons, to my great joy. *Maestro* was omnipotent at his classes. All Vassily could do was to wait in the dressing-room. Diaghileff only appeared sometimes at the end to fetch Nijinsky.

I learned that a new ballet, *Joseph and Potiphar*, was contemplated by Nijinsky, and the principal part was for him. Diaghileff commissioned Richard Strauss to compose the music for it. Ever since the Russian Ballet appeared in Berlin and Vienna, Strauss had expressed his wish to compose a ballet for them. This plan was discussed several times among them. Strauss wanted very much that his customary collaborators, Count Kessler, and the Austrian poet, Hugo von Hofmansthal, should write the story. So they finally agreed. The story of Madame de Potiphar was chosen with the help of Diaghileff; Bakst, who was consulted, conceived the idea of transposing the whole period for the scenery and settings in the time of Paolo Veronese. With its luxurious possibilities, it was more appealing to him, and he saw much more variety in this style to be developed than in the biblical period. The part of the innocent, shy, but religious youth, Joseph, suited Nijinsky's appearance and temperament. Diaghileff signed a contract with Strauss for a hundred thousand gold marks for the musical rights of this ballet. An unheard-of price, and an unheard-of thing for Diaghileff to sign a contract. The artists worked merely on a verbal agreement. The lowest salary, a thousand francs a month and second-class travelling assured, was paid to the *corps de ballet*. They used to get their salaries every month from the stage manager, Grigoriev, or the secretary, Mr. Drobetsky, or, as it happened quite often, they gave the troupe something on account, with the apologies of Sergei Pavlovitch. He had had to pay out so much for scenery, musical rights, etc. Next month the default amount would be replaced, and so on. Only Karsavina got her sixty thousand francs for two months paid punctually, for she was still a member of the Mariinsky, and Diaghileff did not wish her to tell at home that he was not prompt in payment. As for Nijinsky, his salary only existed in theory, for Sergei Pavlovitch, very soon after Nijinsky had left the Mariinsky Theatre, had asked him to lend the money he earned for the enterprise. *"Vatza, j'ai besoin, je dois payer les nouveaux décors, ou Stravinsky ne veut pas travailler sans être payé tout de suite. Ce qu'il est mercenaire. Je prends ton salaire pour les prochains mois."* And so Nijinsky's salary, during those years of enormous financial success, wandered into the *caisse* of the Russian Ballet and was spent for its upkeep. That Nijinsky worked harder than any of them, that the whole structure of the organisation rested upon him, never entered the head of Diaghileff. Neither that, if Stravinsky insisted on being paid, it was not only for mercenary reasons, but because he had a delicate wife and small children. Nijinsky never reminded Diaghileff, who, except for the modest sum Nijinsky sent for his mother and brother, never gave him any money.

215

There were rumours of a South American tour. I could not believe it. After all this effort, now to be separated from the Ballet! What could be done? I interviewed *Maestro*. "Is there any truth in these rumours?" *Maestro* confirmed them. They were supposed to leave on the 15th of August, after a brief vacation of two weeks, for the Argentine and Brazil. These countries had often invited the Russian Ballet, but they never could fit this trip in with their plans. This year, finally, Diaghileff was able to accept a most profitable contract, and the troupe had to sacrifice its annual vacation.

The soloists were not very enthusiastic, especially Karsavina, and it needed a lot of pleading on Diaghileff's part to induce them. All of them were deadly afraid of the long ocean trip of twenty-one days. The crossing on the Channel was bad enough. So many of them declared that for nothing in the world would they go in that *pays du nègre*. Diaghileff was worried. Monteux refused also to go, so he engaged René Baton, the capable conductor of the Pasdeloup Orchestra in Paris, to replace him. I too was worried. How could I go? I still had a part of the money left which had been advanced to me by Mr. K., the banker, but how to induce the Ballet to take me, my family to let me go? My chance came through the refusal of many of the dancers to go. Drobetsky was commissioned to go to Warsaw and to bring back from there a few talented young dancers. *Maestro* was also requested to find some. And there I reaped what I had sown with my birthday present to *Maestro*. He declared to Sergei Pavlovitch that it would be quite a gain to engage me, and that also Hilda Munnings and Hilda Bewicke were sufficiently advanced to enter the troupe. So we were engaged. Honestly I was not yet entitled to be a member of the troupe. I wired home. A few days later my mother and stepfather arrived in London. They were pleased at last that after all the studies I had achieved something constructive. My mother must have already seen me as a *prima ballerina*. They attended my lessons, which *Maestro* gave in private. He became purple in his efforts to make me dance properly. My parents, in ecstasy, rushed up to the Savoy to make an appointment with Diaghileff. Diaghileff did not appear next day, but instead Drobetsky came and excused Diaghileff, who was too busy to see us. We waited for more than an hour in the lovely yellow reading-room of the Savoy near the lobby, and I was alternately gazing in the fireplace and watching the lobby to see if I could get a glimpse of Nijinsky passing by. How many times I had been watching there for him!

Everything was settled. I was to be taken on a trial tour. If I proved that I could dance they would engage me in the autumn as a regular member, with a salary. At present they would only pay my fare—second class, as for all the other members. My parents consented. I was to buy a first-class ticket for myself, and Anna would use my ticket, for I had to have a *garde de dame* on this journey. Drobetsky promised to look after me with his wife; so later did Baron Gunsburg, who had met my mother through mutual friends.

At one of the last performances in London I was in the balcony, from where I had an excellent view of the stage. *Sylphides* was being danced. By this time I had become not only familiar with the music, which was comparatively easy for me, but I knew practically all the steps of most of the ballets. Nijinsky in *Sylphides* was a dream. I could see it again and again and discover new beauties. This evening he danced the mazurka; suddenly a prayer came to my mind which repeated itself silently: "Thank you, my Lord, that you have permitted me to live in this century, to see Nijinsky dance." As a child I had always regretted not having lived in the Cinquecento, not to know the great artists of the Renaissance, and now my wish in a different way was granted.

At the end of the season Anna and I, after completing all preparations for the South American tour, finally went to an enchanting little village in Sussex. I used to lie in the green grass and gaze at the sky and the majestic old oak-trees, and dream about the ballet and my impressions of Nijinsky. That feeling of apprehension about him I had lost. On the contrary, now he fascinated me. I could not resist the desire to be near him. It is true he was only absorbed in one thing—his art. Society, success, wealth, fame, and flirtations did not seem to mean anything to him. He was surrounded by an impenetrable wall built around him by Diaghileff and by his own reserve. But hadn't I pierced this wall just an infinitesimal bit? It is true we all heard that he had no interest in us women. I knew it. But didn't I catch, in spite of this, here and there a smile, a glance which he threw to me? Where others failed, why shouldn't I succeed? We were both of a different race, nation, could not speak each other's language—a world of difference separated us. He was a world-famous artist, I merely one of the millions of society girls. Every logical argument was against me, but I had in me something more, the invincible desire to awaken Nijinsky's interest. And if ever his genius should be perpetuated, I wanted to be the medium of this transmission. I passed these two weeks determinedly concentrating upon my wish.

On the 15th of August we left for Southampton. Not speaking Russian, I was lonely. I had never been in daily contact with the troupe and they had already formed little groups on the train. On arrival at Southampton the immensity of the boat impressed me. I had never been on an ocean liner before. The Royal Mail Steamship Company's *Avon* was quite the latest novelty in ocean service.

We were soon on the high seas. I went down to lunch, and found my place at Drobetsky's table. So he kept his word, which he had given to my parents. His wife and Bolm were seated there, and a charming young French Argentinian, M. Chavez, who had some great dressmaking establishment in Buenos Aires. Some of the artists were sitting at other tables. Baron Gunsburg, with his friend Mme. Oblokova, a charming divorcée of St. Petersburg society, was occupying a table with Piltz and Kovalevska.

René Baton and his wife were at the captain's table. Mr. Baton was a great stout man, like a kind, big bear, with a long beard. His wife was typically French, talked with great volubility, and, as I heard, was a capable singer.

After lunch I rushed to see the passenger-list, which was posted on a board. I could not see Nijinsky and Diaghileff anywhere. My God, if they had not come! Was it possible? And I already under way to South America. I heard that Karsavina would join us in Buenos Aires, that she was travelling with her husband on an Italian boat, which was faster. I trembled. If Nijinsky were to go also on that boat! I spent two solid hours trying to find out, and faced the possibility of disembarking at Cherbourg, where we were due at five in the afternoon. But on reading the passenger-list my heart gave one great jump. "Deck A, Cabin No. 60, Mr. Sergei de Daghileff. Cabin No. 61, Mr. Vaslav Nijinsky."

At once I became gay and happy and raced all through the ship, looking at the passengers, making friends with the stewards and stewardesses, with the sailors, barmen, and began to flirt with the officers. Quite exhausted by all this, I went to my cabin to rest. Anna had already arranged it, and it looked almost like home; photos, flowers in silver vases, cushions, and silk covers, all over the place. And near my bed a picture of the "Miraculous Jesus of Prague." I fell asleep, and only awoke around tea-time. On my way to the dining-room I met Drobetsky, who was rushing with Grigoriev and Kremenev, Michel, his wife, and a few of the dancers towards the lower decks. "What is the hurry? Aren't you coming to tea?" "Sorry, I can't; we are going to receive Nijinsky who is boarding the ship here in Cherbourg." What a relief! I could have kissed Drobetsky for it. I joined the group. We went on Deck D, where the staircase had been lowered to take up the passengers. As we looked down on the approaching tug, we saw, among a group of French passengers, some dancers of the troupe standing with Nijinsky, and close behind him the gloomy Vassily. "Le Petit" was in a very elegant travelling-suit and coat and a smart round travelling-hat which became quite the fashion. He was looking up to us, saying in Russian, *"Kak bolsh'oi parahod."* As he came up the gang-plank, everybody rushed to him and asked questions. *"Vaslav Fomitch slava Bogou sh'to wie zdes. Kak pojivaete."* He smiled, took off his hat—*"Spasiba gaspada ochen harashow"*—and disappeared with quick steps into the lift. I pirouetted away in my happiness. At last Nijinsky was safe on board. All was well, and I had twenty-one days before me. Fate was kind. My cabin was also on A Deck, on the very same corridor as Nijinsky's, some distance away, but I could quite well supervise his door. In my great satisfaction and joy I had completely forgotten Diaghileff. Where was he? But I had no chance to find out until dinner, when Drobetsky told us that he was not coming to South America. It was said officially that he was kept back in Europe by unexpected business, but he told us in confidence that Diaghileff could not overcome his terrible fear of an ocean trip and went for a rest to the Lido. Baron Gunsburg was officially in charge of the company. He also was co-director, but only in name until then.

We all soon settled down to the agreeable routine of deck life. My deck-chair was on the north side, near those of the Gunsburgs and Drobetskys. I spent a great part of my days with Oblokova,

Kovalevska, and Piltz. Oblokova was already in the forties but extremely well preserved and smartly dressed. She had beautiful jewels, and her greatest pleasure was match-making or arranging little love-affairs. In the morning I used to pace around the deck for one or two hours either in Gunsburg's or Bolm's company. I soon noticed that a sudden friendship had sprung up between Nijinsky and the Batons. They took hold of him the very first morning on deck. I overheard the conversation. With deep respect Baton was praising Nijinsky's art, and Mme. Baton joined him in an unending flow of words. But Nijinsky shook his head.

"No, no, moi pas comprend, moi parle petit nègre."

At this Baton flung his arms around Nijinsky, kissed him on both cheeks, so it could be heard on the whole boat, and declared, shouting, *"Quel enfant adorable, quel simplicité, c'est moi qui serai votre nana pendant le voyage."* And Baton was true to his word. No real nurse could have looked after a child with more attention and devotion than he and his wife had for Nijinsky on the trip. The day after we left Cherbourg the members of the company who were travelling second class got permission to visit us. Thereafter they came over quite often.

Lisbon was the last European port where we called, the last chance where Diaghileff could still join us, as I heard that he might. I dreaded this, and prayed steadily that he should not. By this time I was on friendly terms with most of the passengers and seemed to be quite a favourite.

We formed a little group to visit the Royal Castle at Cintra, the Gunsburgs, my old flirt Kovalevska, Piltz, and Bolm, all attired for the *escale* loaded with photographic cameras, binoculars, and hats as if we were already in the tropics. We got into small boats and were taken to the shore. We had the whole day before us. I could not see Nijinsky. One day lost for me. We took carriages and drove all around this quaint old Southern city. It was frightfully dusty—even the palm trees looked grey—but it had some beautiful palaces and cathedrals. We had a queer, spicy lunch with a lot of Portuguese red wine, and departed to Cintra in high spirits.

This palace and its gardens were really enchanting. We enjoyed it, and after spending a small fortune on postcards and small souvenirs, returned to the port. The launches were waiting for us, and we were rapidly transported. I could have cried with disappointment, seeing Nijinsky in the next boat with Chavez and the Batons. Next time I resolved to be with him.

After breakfast I usually came on deck and found Nijinsky in his deck-chair reading or studying some designs. He seldom looked up and never greeted me. I was furious. Why, what had happened? After all, in London he melted just a tiny bit. Now he ignored my existence again. My God, how hopeless! The day Nijinsky came on board I said to Anna, "Now here is my chance. Twenty-one days of ocean and sky—no Diaghileff. He can't escape. By the time we arrive I will have a flirtation with 'le Petit.' *Ce que femme veut Dieu le veut.*"

Anna smiled unbelievingly, and every evening, without a word, she tore off one day from the calendar, looking at me. I was quite annoyed by this, but never said anything to her. We were all on deck until lunch, after which many read or went to sleep.

I soon discovered that Nijinsky spent his time differently. On Deck C, in a small hall where the staircase led to the dining-room, was a piano. Here, around three, René Baton played Bach preludes, fugues, and Nijinsky was composing. At first I sat very timidly on the top of the staircase, and was requested to leave by the chief steward. A day later I came back. This time René Baton politely asked me to go. Nijinsky seemed sunk in the notes. I could have boxed his ears. Always indifferent! It was exasperating. Suddenly he looked up and pantomimed to Baton that I could stay. So I was officially installed on the step. Every afternoon I was the first to be there, and I appeared unfailingly. It was remarkable to watch him compose.

Baton played on the piano and Nijinsky stood beside him. Sometimes he closed his eyes and gave the impression that he did it to concentrate more on a whole choreographic theme. Or with his fingers he danced a full variation, which he composed while Baton played the piece; or he stopped him suddenly, made him play the same bar several times. All the time, as he stood there, one could feel that he was dancing constantly the steps he invented. And so a whole ballet was created before my wondering eyes. Occasionally he searched with Baton for hours for a suitable chaconne, or prelude. He stopped Baton often, saying, *"Crois, plus vite"*; and Baton laughed. "How true. I made a mistake. It is supposed to be faster." Nijinsky, as I was told later on by musicians, was extraordinarily musical, and he felt the very essence of the music. Baton told me Nijinsky was composing a new ballet on the music of Bach, to be as pure dancing as his music is pure sound. He wanted to lay down the harmony and the fundamental truth of the movement. It was supposed to be put in the period of Louis XIV, but without a story, as it should be purely choreographic. Always when Baton failed to make himself understood, Gunsburg was summoned as interpreter. Very soon I tried to make myself liked by them. As I had been educated in Paris, and spoke French like a native, I won Mme. Baton's heart easily. But I liked them both. They were kind, good-hearted people. Among all these Russians we formed the little Western European colony. Of course, nobody knew that I was admitted to observe these hours of composition. I often wondered why I was permitted.

The days passed very quickly in this gay, peaceful atmosphere.

We neared Madeira Island, and had another day of *escale*. This time I tried to form a group with the Batons and Chavez. The latter joined us, but the Batons told me they were going with Nijinsky and they did not invite me to join them. I was upset. So we went—the Drobetskys, Chavez, Bolm, Kovalevska, and myself.

It was a clear, beautiful day, the island was enchanting, but nothing pleased me. At the landing all the sailors and fishermen in their colourful native costumes were shouting, offering coral necklaces, souvenirs, laces, and their services to guide us. We took the funicular up to the hotel on top of the hill, from where one could see the whole island, and far out on the sea. We had late lunch, and chattered and smoked. I noticed that it was beginning to get dark, but everybody said it was the mist of the sea. So I kept to myself what I thought. We were supposed to go down on small wooden sledges which were checked by long ropes held by several men, so they would not glide too rapidly into the chasm. As they were all enjoying pleasantly their coffees and liqueurs, suddenly we heard the boat's signal. It was supposed to be given an hour before leaving, and there we were, at a distance that under the most favourable circumstances we could not cover in less than two hours. What should we do? They all jumped. Drobetsky running for information into the hotel, the old German-Argentine discussing with the sledge-keepers how quickly they could get us down to the village, Chavez, trying to calm us, saying the captain would wait for a time, and that, after all, Madeira had good hotels and was not a bad place to stay. But Kovalevska screamed, "What will I do without my clothes?" And Oblokova readily acquiesced to that. Bolm almost cried, saying, "*Tamara* and *Igor* won't be possible without him." Drobetsky came back in despair. Gunsburg was nervously clasping his hands. Finally our old friend decided.

"Let us try to make it. The next boat will pass in three weeks. We cannot afford to be left behind." I could have cried with disappointment. To be left in Madeira—to see Nijinsky go! So we started on the ghastly glide down the hill at a dizzy speed.

Mme. Pflanz was screaming as we literally flew down. Again we heard the signal. We could not even speak, thinking only of arriving in time. Finally we reached the bottom of the hill and saw the port in the distance. Arriving in the village, we jumped out of the sledges and began to run towards the landing-place. The last launch was gone; the third signal was given; the funnels were smoking. We screamed at the top of our voices. Energetically our old friend rented the best boat and soon six men were rowing us towards the *Avon*. Somebody must have noticed that we were missing. Luckily we had Gunsburg with us. They must have looked for him. A motor-boat was sent out and at last we knew that we would be picked up. It was a terrific excitement as we boarded the boat, and at dinner they could not speak of anything else but our adventure.

Nijinsky used to come on deck every morning around eleven. He was always very smartly dressed in a light-coloured suit or white flannel trousers and dark blue coat. I often wondered what he was doing so late; sleeping probably. One morning, as I could not sleep, I walked around the upper deck. It was a clear breezy day, about eight o'clock. On the north side of the boat I saw a crowd watching attentively. What could it be? Nobody plays tennis or deck games at such an unearthly hour. The crowd was around a space which was kept apart by ropes tied from the railing and the life-boats up to the wall of the funnel-house. In the middle of this space, in the sunshine and the refreshing breeze, Nijinsky practised. So that was the way he spent his mornings? It had never occurred to me. The passengers who loved a brisk walk in the morning, and the sporty Englishmen who had seen and admired the Ballet in London, were looking on, with exclamations of approval and admiration.

It was interesting to watch how much those sports-loving men could understand and appreciate the tremendous work which was needed to make a perfect dancer. To watch Nijinsky practise was a special pleasure. All movements were perfect, without hesitation, with an assurance that gave one the feeling that the dance for him was like breathing for any other human being. Each attitude so like sculpture, that I could well understand why Rodin had said that "each pose was a living Michelangelo, Donatello, Giovanni da Bologna." Vassily "the inevitable" stood near the watering-can and rosin-box with a bath-towel. The audience seemed to annoy him, but Nijinsky did not mind. He was smiling. He seemed to be so much gayer and rested than I had ever seen him before. Once or twice he even gave explanations about his steps to the Englishmen, who discussed each motion from their athletic point of view. Mr. Williams, Nijinsky's private *masseur*, stood in their midst. The sailors hidden near the life-boat, the officer in the crowd, and even those on duty on the bridge, peeped from time to time. I wondered if the boat would not stop soon if they went on in this way. For an hour and a half every morning he practised under the same conditions. Of course, I was present; I even sacrificed my morning sleep. When he finished he slipped his dark green silk dressing-gown over his practice costume and disappeared, accompanied by Mr. Williams and Vassily, in the lift. It did not take me long to make the acquaintance of Mr. Williams.

I had suddenly developed an interest in athletics. For hours I listened about the boxers and their matches, the Henley regattas, the training for them, about the athletic club where he was chief *masseur;* the difference between the Swedish school and the medical massage—I became almost an expert—also about the family of Mr. Williams, his four sisters who were nursery governesses on the Continent, his parents, and his native village. But in return for my enthusiastic listening I learned to know the whole musculature of Nijinsky, which Williams knew and loved, each muscle separately. Because Nijinsky was so perfectly built, he gave up his steady position in London to travel with him all around the world, only to give him an hour's massage each day. He could talk for hours about dancing—only anatomically, of course. After one hour of this soothing massage he was exhausted, he who could massage the strongest boxer for several hours easily, but Nijinsky's muscles were of iron.

I walked around the deck from eleven to seven, always when Nijinsky was in his deck-chair. My *Beaux* alternately had to escort me. Every time I passed "le Petit" I either greeted him or talked louder or laughed so that he should look up and see me. I was determined not to give him any peace until he noticed me. I got tired of being introduced all over again, always to be forgotten and ignored the next second. What miles I walked around that deck, I who hated so much this kind of exercise! Every evening Anna slowly, silently, triumphantly, tore off another slip of the calendar. In the evenings we had dances and entertainments. The weather was perfect. Baron Gunsburg, now that we were further south, appeared in a white dinner-jacket. He looked like a bar-tender to us, but one of the Englishmen explained that this was the regulation kit in the tropics, and was worn by all smart officers. Of course, it was the very thing for Gunsburg to do. But he looked well in it. Only around his waist he had wrapped the most wild, Bakstian shawl, purple green, orange!

Bolm by this time knew everybody worth while on the boat. He was amusing and sociable, perhaps too quickly familiar, but

227

well liked, and he shared the position of *maître de plaisir* with
Gunsburg. We used to take long walks around the deck after
dinner. Often Kovalevska, with whom I became very friendly,
joined us.

Nijinsky sometimes passed near us with Baton or Chavez, but
never was aware of us; was it only pretence? One morning
Kovalevska came with a flushed face and talked to Piltz like a
torrent. Finally they told me what had happened. Grigoriev had
ordered all members of the troupe to practise every morning on
deck. We had to have a class. It was, as we found out, Nijinsky's
idea. He thought twenty-one days would be too long for the
troupe to be without training if they had to dance afterwards.
I was panic-stricken. I was used to *Maestro,* and was shy and
afraid of the others; he knew my shortcomings and could help
me out. Somehow I always hoped that a miracle would happen and
I would be a good dancer by the time we arrived in South America.
I confessed my fright to Kovalevska, and she proposed to show me
all the parts I was supposed to have, so that I should know the
steps before rehearsals. Often she came to my cabin or I went to
hers, and we had breakfast together. We looked at each other's
wardrobe and clothes, her beautiful jewellery, the photos; we discussed lengthily all gossip and happenings.

She was perfectly beautiful, with the face of a Madonna, and
had great success as a woman in Paris and London, yet she remained unspoiled. We started to practise next morning. It was
not as easy as it looked. The boat seemed to glide on the water,
which was like ultramarine oil, but the moment we began our
pliés or *battements* we lost our balance. How could Nijinsky do it?
It was ten times as difficult as usual. I wished for a storm so that
he could feel how difficult it was for us to practice on the boat.
But next morning, when a terrific sirocco blew up, he was dancing

with as perfect ease as ever. The days passed in practice, enjoyment, flirtation and laziness. Anna went on tearing the calendar's
slips. Nijinsky was keeping his daily routine: practice in the morning, study, reading in his deck-chair until lunch, then composition
with Baton, which I faithfully attended. Now I knew from Baton
that the Bach ballet was to be transposed for organ and big orchestra, and the clavichord would not be used. He chose Benois to design the scenery as the most familiar with this period. Nijinsky
had visited Richard Strauss previously with Diaghileff at Baden-
Baden, and later in Garmisch, where he had a villa. Strauss played
a part of the score of *Potiphar* for them. Nijinsky was greatly
disappointed by the music, as it was not at all what he had expected
from Strauss after *Salomé* and *Elektra*. He thought it a very feeble
composition, and told Diaghileff he did not want to compose the
choreography. Diaghileff tried to persuade him, but Nijinsky could
not be influenced, not even by Diaghileff, if he felt a thing was
wrong from an artistic point of view.

Baron Gunsburg flew on deck after lunch one day saying they
had just decided there would be a costume ball that evening. Of
course, the members of the Ballet must have the most amusing
costumes. The hairdresser of the ship had costumes for hire, but
we decided they were unworthy of our company. Also they were
quickly taken by the other passengers. Oblokova suggested everybody should make up his own costume. A mad rush began. Every
one of us raced from one another's cabin backwards and forwards.
Everyone made his costume in secret. They advised me to have a
Hungarian gypsy costume. The second class was invited. After
running around for hours to get together all I needed, with Anna's
help I tried it on, but did not like it. I immediately went over to
Oblokova. She was pleased with it. Maria Stepanovna and our
hairdresser were as busy as on the day of a dress rehearsal. Guns-

burg came after me, advising: "Romola Carlovna, I have thought it over, I have a brilliant idea for a costume for you. It would be so original. You are so slim, you look almost like a boy. Hide your hair and put on these pyjamas of mine." And he passed a pair of lovely tailored apple-green pyjamas to me. "Great! But don't tell anybody," he said.

When I was all dressed—or, that is to say, undressed—1 showed myself to Gunsburg, who approved it. As the time came to go to dinner, somehow I felt something was wrong. I looked at myself in the mirror. It looked all right. But an inexplicable feeling kept me back. I changed and put on a lovely evening dress from Callot Sœurs, dressed my hair, and half an hour later I descended to dinner. They all shouted at me, "Where have you been? Where is your costume? What happened?" I only shook my head and, going down the staircase, I met Nijinsky's eyes. He looked up at me, and I noticed a sigh of relief. The two of us, and of course the officers, were the only ones not in costume: Oblokova as an odalisque, Gunsburg as a marquis, Bolm as Nebuchadnezzar, and so on. Of course, all the prizes went to the members of the Ballet.

The ball was gay, and lasted until late in the morning. Most of us had breakfast in costume. Nijinsky disappeared around one o'clock, after having watched the merry-making.

The following day we were all sleepy, but had to be at Gunsburg's "Equator Party" at 12.30 p.m. As we passed "the line" we were baptised with champagne by those who had already crossed this latitude.

One evening as we paced around the deck, Chavez turned to me saying: "That is all very well, Mlle. de Pulszky. I understand your admiration for the ballet, for Nijinsky's art; for all of us on the stage he is the *Dieu de la danse;* but in life he is a human being, a charming young man in fact. Why are you afraid of him?"

"I am not," I replied furiously.

"Then come on. I will present you to him."

"I don't want to."

"Now, come on, don't be silly. You admire him. He is captivating. He won't harm you. We are great pals, in spite of the fact that we can't speak to each other very much."

"I refuse. I won't go. I am sick of it. I have been presented to him over and over again, and he does not even know I exist. Let me alone." By this time Chavez had dragged me to the other side of the deck.

It was a beautiful moonlit night; the ocean looked superb. In the main lobby they were dancing some tango, and the lights of the hall threw their shadows on the dimly lighted deck. It was practically empty. A few men smoked in their deck-chairs, and couples were in the dark corners, flirting, whispering.

Nijinsky was half leaning against the railing, in "smoking," holding a small black fan which was ornamented with one gold painted rose. He was rapidly fanning himself. He looked so strange. His eyes were half closed and oh! so slanted. He conversed in a soft, melodious voice with Kovalevska in Polish. I was trembling as Chavez said, *"Monsieur Nijinsky, permettez moi de vous présenter Mlle. de Pulszky."* He did not move; his eyes just closed with an imperceptible *nuance* and he slightly inclined his head. Kovalevska at once began to explain to him who I was and all about my love of dancing. Nijinsky listened without saying a word. Chavez insisted, *"N'ayez pas peur,"* and repeated to Nijinsky what he told me before about him. I felt that both Kovalevska and Chavez were expecting me to say something. But suddenly every thought deserted me. I felt a chaos of emotion, saw nothing and nobody any more except the dark, graceful silhouette of Nijinsky and his fascinating eyes. I suddenly heard myself speaking. *"Je veux vous remercier que vous avez élevé la danse à la hauteur des autres arts."* Kovalevska translated. He did not move. Suddenly he looked at the small ring I wore. I followed his gaze, and, pulling it off my finger, I passed it to him, explaining: "My father brought it from Egypt; it is a talisman supposed to bring luck. My mother gave it to me as I left with the Russian Ballet." It was a green-gold serpent whose head was crushed by a scarab. It had a strange design. Nijinsky held it for one moment and then put it on my finger, saying in Polish, "It will bring you happiness, surely." We all four of us began to walk around the deck. Suddenly Nijinsky stopped, looked into the phosphorescent waves. They were more luminous to-night than I had ever seen them before. I saw he was fascinated by the motion of the sea. He looked and looked. For a long time we watched in silence. Then I began to talk in French, choosing the easiest words about dance, music, and Wagner, whose work I idolised: *Lohengrin, Valkyrie, Tristan,* Bayreuth, and my childhood days, which I had spent with my sister and brother-in-law at the Wahnfried at the rehearsals in the Festspielhaus. I don't know if he understood a word of what I said, but he seemed to listen attentively. I had to talk to hide my nervousness, my confusion. Then Chavez called us.

They were pacing up and down the deck. "Come, come and look at the new constellations, the stars which cannot be seen on the northern hemisphere." We looked up and saw in all its brilliant splendour the Southern Cross.

The great part of this night, as usual, I spent in kneeling before the picture of the Petit Jesus de Prague, praying for His miraculous intervention. Hours and hours, with a fanatic concentration, I implored, almost forcing the "divine child" to grant my wish. At first my request was personal—to make Nijinsky interested in me. Now that for the first time I began to feel, to see, the superhuman intelligence working for me, now it was, "Make Nijinsky happy some way, somehow; save him from the way of life he is leading with Diaghileff." Unacknowledged even to myself, I wanted to reform him for myself, but cunningly I thought I might deceive God with my unselfish prayer, taking it for granted that the Almighty Himself had an orthodox attitude towards sexual relationship, and would condemn a form of it which He Himself created.

We were nearing the South American continent. The next day we saw from the distance a brown line; it was the coast of Brazil. We were all happy and almost wishing that this trip should never end. I was in high spirits, of course, but great was my amazement when Nijinsky the following day, except for a polite bow, ignored me as much as before. Once I managed to get in the lift in the morning in which he was also going to practise. I thought that perhaps he would now look at me, as my coral silk dancing costume and ballet-shoes suited me well, and were quite becoming, but not even a glance. I walked and walked around the deck almost to exhaustion. Nijinsky was taking lessons from an Englishman on how to light and smoke a pipe. It must have been fun, for they were all laughing a lot. As I knew, he never even smoked a cigarette. But I was more furious than ever. I passed the days with my usual set and never even referred to "le Petit's" existence. I was peeved, and decided to ignore him.

Kovalevska proved a patient, kind teacher. I had already learned from her the parts from *Igor, Scheherazade, Cléopâtre,* that I was supposed to dance. We were learning *Sylphides,* but she was not quite sure, neither was Grigoriev, if I would be cast in it. It depended upon what Nijinsky would think. I felt that I would rather die than dance before him. That whole appearance on the stage seemed to be a hazy night-mare, and I put even the idea itself away from me. If only *Maestro* would come along! But instead of that he was eating spaghetti in Milan.

During the trip we had many balls, as did the second class. This night after dinner, as we were chatting on deck, we heard weird, enchanting Spanish music. One of the dancers came over from the second class and called us. "Come on, they have a ball in the steerage. They are dancing boleros and fandangos, tarantellas and real tango." We all went. The steerage was full of Italian and Spanish peasants called "swallows," going over to the Argentine for the harvest. On the deck they danced, they played their music on cisharmonicas, singing among them. All around, the curious spectators looked on. Their dances were enchanting. "Le Petit" was there with the Batons. The latter explained with words and hands the rhythm, the eight pitches of a single note of the Spanish Tsigane music. Nijinsky seemed to have extreme pleasure watching these genuine dancers of folk-lore, and he applauded. Gunsburg found that they had a decidedly far better time in the third class than we had.

Returning, I managed to come close to Nijinsky. Exasperated by his last days' indifference, and encouraged by the champagne we had at dinner, I pulled myself together, and, taking Kovalevska by her hand, I asked her to translate with infinite excitement and determination. I said, "Vaslav Fomitch, you have forgotten last year at the Monte Carlo Palace Hotel, the little pillow your mother sent to you, on which you always slept and which I heard you cherished so much. I have it. May I send it back to you?"

Nijinsky gave me one long look and, mounting up the stairs, said to Kovalevska, "Tell her please to keep it."

I could have choked him.

Only a day more and we were due in Rio de Janeiro, the

234

dream city with the most beautiful harbour in the world. Our friends and fellow passengers could not praise its site sufficiently. And then five more days—and Buenos Aires, the end of our trip, and of all our delightful intimacy and the possibility for me to be so informally near Nijinsky. I had failed; I was beaten. I could not even reply to Anna when, the previous evening, tearing the calendar slip off, she said calmly, "The sixteenth day. Really, Miss Romola, I wouldn't run after a hay-cart which refuses to give a lift," quoting an old Hungarian proverb.

As we were sitting in the bar before lunch, the Batons, Kovalevska, Piltz, and the others, Gunsburg came up. "Romola, please come. I have to talk to you." I became quite upset. My God, what had I done? Did I dance too badly? Did Kremenev or Grigoriev report me? I could not think. The others teased me. I followed Gunsburg silently on deck. There he stopped, and with a terribly formal face he said, "Romola Carlovna, as Nijinsky cannot speak to you himself, he has requested me to ask you in marriage." We looked at each other, and then I burst out: "No, really, Dmitri Nikolaivitch, it's awful. How can you?"; and, blushing, half crying, I ran as fast as I could down to my cabin, where I locked myself up for the rest of the day.

So they all made fun of me. This terrible joke. They had noticed what I was up to. I felt like a fool. I could never face them again. But what was I to do? To stay in the cabin until Buenos Aires and then to return home to Budapest directly? Yes, that was the only possibility, without even seeing them again. But Nijinsky I could not leave. Never to see him dance! Certainly he would be greatly angered if he knew about Gunsburg's incredible joke.

I stayed in my cabin. They knocked at my door, the page-boy saying, "Please won't you come up for tea?" Kovalevska asked admittance, inquiring if I was sick. I did not even let Anna in, saying I had a terrible headache, didn't want to be disturbed and was trying to sleep. How much did they know?

After dinner a nice note came from Gunsburg: "Dear Romola Carlovna,—I am so sorry you are not feeling quite well. Why did you run away? If you are unable to come on deck, please let me know your answer. I must say something to Nijinsky. I can't keep him waiting like this." I wondered. The note fell out of my hand, and it seemed to me that on the face of my miraculous Jesus of Prague a smile lingered.

Quickly I put on an evening dress and summoned Anna. She fixed my hair, and I sent her up to find out where they all were. She reported: The Batons were with some French people in the drawing-room; Gunsburg, Bolm, and my set were all in the bar, where pools were held. Nijinsky she could not see anywhere. I was relieved. Probably he had retired already. It was past eleven o'clock, so I went on deck and walked around. Unexpectedly, from nowhere Nijinsky emerged and said: *"Mademoiselle, voulez-vous, vous et moi?"* and pantomimed, indicating on the fourth finger of the left hand a ring. I nodded and, waving with both hands, said, *"Oui, oui, oui."*

Very gently taking my hand, without a word he led me up to the upper deck. This was deserted. He pulled two deck-chairs under the captain's bridge, and there we sat in silence, hearing the rhythmically recurring steps of the officers on duty, the sound of the waves, following the line of the smoke which rose from the funnels, a dark ribbon against the clear night sky, which was covered by milliards of stars. I could feel the soothing, unceasing throb of the boat, and my own wildly beating heart. Everything was so peaceful in this tepid tropic night. I knew Nijinsky felt as I did. And as this white boat sailed placidly, with an inward, hidden tremor, in the vastness of the infinite ocean, towards its destination, so did we towards our fate.

Next morning as I woke I lay motionless. Was this all only a dream, or was it really true? Could it be possible that I was engaged to be married to Nijinsky? The stewardess, followed by Anna, brought in my breakfast tray. Soon somebody knocked, and Kovalevska, fully dressed, whirled into the cabin, flung her arms around me, kissed me in the Russian fashion. "Ah, Romola Carlovna, I am so happy, so happy! This is indeed wonderful news. I congratulate you with all my heart. Unbelievable. But somehow I always knew Vaslav Fomitch is not as people say." And suddenly, as if she would have caught herself on something, she stopped. "I mean, I am glad for both of you."

"How did you know it?"

"Well, I just received a note from Vaslav Fomitch asking me to tell you that he wishes to take us both on land to see Rio, and to get the engagement-ring. He invited me to escort you both as chaperon and in the capacity of an official interpreter." And so she pirouetted around. "I am as glad as if it were my own day of betrothal. Oh, to see the faces of the others when they hear! Now hurry up. Take your bath. Dress quickly. We are supposed to meet Vaslav Fomitch on the quay at eleven. And we must not miss the view of the entrance to the port."

As we arrived on deck, everybody was there viewing the panorama which was unfolding itself before our enchanted eyes. We steamed slowly up the bay. The bay of Rio. Against the deep azure sky in blinding sunshine, all enveloped in a golden glamour, stands out the circular range of palm-covered mountains like a cascade, following an inexhaustible torrent of plants, trees, flowers; in the middle of the bay the mighty Peak of the Pão de Asucar, the mountain directly and proudly rising from the sea in the shape

237

of a loaf of sugar, with the blue-white waves splashing all around, playing, caressing. The houses became more distinct, white, lovely marble buildings, graceful against the deep green background. A huge, beautiful, natural amphitheatre encircled us. We could only look and look, and we ran from one side of the boat to the other, exclaiming at each turn: *"C'est presque mieux que du Bakst."*

Here we drew alongside the well-constructed quay, and very quickly we could disembark. Everybody was so occupied with the beauty of the spot that I could escape with Kovalevska without being noticed and meet Nijinsky at the quay. We jumped into a car and drove through the lovely broad streets, through a wide avenue full of shops, bordered with slender palm-trees which stood hundreds of metres high, like a long line of soldiers. At the end stood the lovely theatre. Kovalevska and Nijinsky spoke all the time I sat between them, and I felt like a schoolgirl out on a Sunday treat.

We stopped before a jewellery shop, and they both asked for rings. Heavy wide golden marriage-rings were shown. Probably they were after the taste of the fat Spanish and Portuguese women. Nijinsky did not like them. I was glad, because their weight had inspired me with awe. Finally he selected two rather flat, dull gold bands, and wrote on a piece of paper the names and dates which he wished to have engraved.

We changed our horse-car for an automobile, and drove up to one of the mountains called Sylvestre, the most heavenly place on earth. Here, in the middle of the virgin forest on the top, was a hotel, the smart place of the town in the early spring. The first people we saw at the place were the Drobetskys and our friends the Anglo-Argentine couple. They were just finishing lunch and were ready to go for a drive in the jungle which surrounded the hotel. They were rather surprised to see our trio.

We were very gay during our lunch. It was the first time I ever sat with Nijinsky at a table. We decided to drive through the dense forests, with their towering, orchid-laden trees, amidst flowers, millions and millions, quaint, unwholesome-looking, but sensual blooms, in all kinds of shades—violent reds, greens, blues. The mountain-tops rose above here and there. We were lost, plunged into this ocean of foliage. The air was tepid and caressing, and suddenly, by certain turns of the narrow road, a stream of icy-cold current hit us for a second. It was all like a dream, this drive, all the time sitting between Kovalevska and Nijinsky. Until dusk we drove, and then, on our way back to the steamer, Nijinsky called for the marriage-rings. As he jumped into the carriage, I noticed the engraving on the ring: "Vaslav-Romola 1/9/1913." He put it on my finger. Kovalevska congratulated us again and kissed us both.

Later in the evening, as the boat steamed out slowly from the bay of Rio, I went on deck. It was almost deserted. Everybody was dressing for dinner when Chavez came up excitedly. "Ah, is it true what I have just heard? What a day! This marvellous city, and the two great bits of news: The *Imperator* on fire, and Nijinsky engaged. I do not know whom I should congratulate, myself or you. You see, I was right. He is the *Dieu de la danse*, but off the stage he is a human being. I am so glad, but so glad."

Coming down to dinner, I went straight to my table as usual, to the Drobetskys' but, as I wanted to sit down, the Batons waved frantically, Vaslav smiled, and Gunsburg came over to fetch me, and they made me sit from then on by Nijinsky. The whole dining-room noticed the change, and the members of the Ballet who were present whispered to each other nervously.

As we went on deck, Bolm met me on the stairs and pulled me aside. "Romola Carlovna, I have heard—I can't believe it—what is this talk about you and Nijinsky? I never imagined. Why, you did not seem to be interested in him. What happened?"

"Well, well, I don't always say what I think and feel."

"But, after all, to get married—to a man you don't know—a perfect stranger—a person you can't even talk to."

"But I know Nijinsky. I have seen him dancing many, many times. I know his genius, his nature, everything."

"You are a child. You know him as an artist, not as a man. He is a very kind young man, a charming colleague, but I have to warn you he is utterly heartless."

"Why do you think that?"

And then Bolm told me that two years before, during a rehearsal, the news came of the death of Thomas Nijinsky. Bolm apparently went up to Nijinsky and expressed his condolences. Nijinsky only replied with a smile and a low "Thank you." Imagine anybody smiling at this kind of news—must be a heartless person.

"Not necessarily," I replied. "No, no, I am sure he has a kind heart. Anybody who dances as he does must be so. And I don't care."

"Romola, I have to warn you. I know your parents. I have received the hospitality of your family. It is my duty. Nijinsky's friendship with Diaghileff, you may not understand, is more than merely a friendship, you see. He can't possibly be interested in you, and it will ruin your life."

I faced him now and very determinedly said: "I thank you. I know you mean well, but I am going to marry him in spite of everything, even if you are right. I'd rather be unhappy serving Nijinsky's genius than be happy without him." Bolm bowed very low and left me.

Finally I joined the others, the captain coming towards us,

regretting not having known the news sooner so he could get loads of flowers in Rio, begging to have a wedding on board where he could officiate. Gunsburg was all for the idea. A marriage on a steamer. Oblokova was just like a mother, worried how we could get a decent trousseau in South America. "My God, if we were only in Paris."

Mme. Baton rushed up complaining, "*Pour l'amour de Dieu,* some of you come on and rescue René. One of the girls is having hysterics because Nijinsky is to marry somebody else, and with all the men on board she had to faint in my husband's arms."

The control between the first and second class was broken through and the whole troupe rushed across to verify the news. I was surrounded and asked questions and questions, everybody glad and excited. They almost crushed Nijinsky.

So the evening passed. We were all exhausted by the excitement of the last days. On my way down to my cabin, Nijinsky accompanied me. At the door he stopped. I was rather surprised. I was nervous, as I was not sure, and confused about what might happen. I knew so much about love theoretically, ever since I was nine years old, from the world of literature; from Boccaccio to Shakespeare, from Sappho to Casanova; but I was a stupid girl. Our education in Hungary was peculiar. We were brought up in the idea of polygamy for men always and in all circumstances, and liberty for a girl as soon as she had an engagement-ring. But I did not know Russian men, and especially the type of Nijinsky, who had a profound respect for womanhood and admitted the sensuality only of consecrated deep affection. He smiled and kissed my hand—I could not help admiring his movements—and he left me. I pressed my hands against my madly beating heart and felt faint, and was not quite sure if I should be flattered or offended. Perhaps, after all, Bolm was right.

241

Next morning, as Anna came in, I just said very casually, "Anna, I am glad to say you will have less to do from now on. You need not count the days, tearing off your calendar slip. *The hay-cart is willing to give me a lift.* I am going to marry Nijinsky." The whole day passed in wild preparations for the engagement dinner which the captain was offering us that evening. Before lunch Nijinsky and Gunsburg emerged from the radio-room. After obtaining the captain's permission, they were able to dispatch a radio to Budapest to my mother. That time the radio was only for emergency and official messages—S.O.S. The cable was a beautifully worded *demande en mariage* inspired by Nijinsky and set into literary French by Gunsburg, who was very proud of it. Gunsburg was so busy he felt his importance. Now he not only had to represent Diaghileff, but also to arrange everything for the wedding.

The dinner was a gala affair, the dining-room beautifully decorated with tropical plants, an exquisite dinner served, and champagne in the real Russian fashion. Everybody was toasting happily, wishing us luck, until Mme. Piltz gave a distracted look at her husband, held her handkerchief, and flew out of the place. Then the boat seemed to lie on its side; a couple of others became white and disappeared. Some of the guests heroically gulped their champagne, and then the *Avon* made a *tour en l'air.* There was general consternation. We had entered St. Catherine Bay, which is known, with its undercurrents, as the worst in the world, even in peaceful weather.

Our engagement, and the fact that we were nearing the end of the journey, upset the daily routine of the boat. Everybody began to make preparations. We passed Santos and Montevideo and entered the La Plata River. My radio officer congratulated me with a pained smile. Grigoriev, who regally accepted my greetings before, almost went to the floor, curtseying to me. I never saw anyone in my life transformed so suddenly from a slave to an autocrat. Since Diaghileff was no longer with us, he had become haughty and made himself dreadfully important. The three strange-looking men dressed in white, who according to Chavez were *des marchands de femme*, never approached me now as before. And the nuns and monks due for the Argentine gave me a beatific smile. Late in the evening we saw a range of brilliant lights on the horizon. It was Buenos Aires. Waiting to arrive, Nijinsky stood with me at the railing and said: "*Ya ne hatchou mariage parahode, hatchou véritable terre église.*" ("I don't want a marriage on ship-board. I want a real church wedding.")

We went to stay at the Majestic Hotel, the Batons, Gunsburg, Kovalevska, Nijinsky, and myself. He had a big suite on the first floor. I had my room on the third. The next few days passed in a frantic way. The usual work of the troupe was supposed to start on Monday. We arrived on Saturday night. Sunday we went sight-seeing with the Batons. The city was very interesting, the lovely park called Palermo, with its rare plants and trees, and the Penguins Aigrettes walking on the grass. Mme. Baton and I were chasing them, as we wanted badly to pull a few feathers out of them. Chavez was our guide. Buenos Aires was a mixture of Paris, Madrid, and Brussels, lovely, luxurious palaces, buildings, trees, and vegetation. We met Nijinsky later on. He had already investigated the Teatro Colon, the opera-house, and its stage. Karsavina, whom we met at dinner, and to whom I was introduced, was quite excited about the news of our engagement. She was charming, lovely, a real *grande dame*.

Gunsburg was running around to the Embassy, church, and city hall, to arrange for the marriage.

I was called to the first rehearsal on Monday, and cast in a

243

number of ballets by Grigoriev. The theatre was enormous, the largest opera-house in the world—a wonderfully built stage, and the dressing-rooms, with their bathrooms, were the last word in comfort.

Nijinsky was practising, and sent over a message that he wished me to keep on my dancing costume as he intended to give me a lesson. I was petrified. I tried to escape but could not. Trembling, I went up, almost crying, and began my exercises *à la barre*. I looked at him. A strange person stood before me. There was no recognition in his face: the impersonal look of a master towards his pupil, I ceased to be his *fiancée*. I was just a dancer. I expected shouts and cursing, "*à la Maestro*," but instead found infinite patience. And as I made a wrong step or position he showed me the way to do it, and I found it easy and succeeded in executing the required steps. He always stopped me when I wanted to force any movement.

Rehearsals, practising, drives in Palermo. Every afternoon Nijinsky came up to my room at the time of the siesta. It was full of flowers, and it seemed so strange to see him there; and the little Jesus of Prague on the table was mocking.

Gunsburg arrived every hour with some fresh news and new complications. I was an Austrian subject; Nijinsky, a Russian. We had no papers. I was under age.

Cables to Hungary, to Russia, were dispatched. I think this was the first time that the Embassies in Argentina had anything to do. Oblokova ran around for dresses and presents. Finally, the following Tuesday, Gunsburg whirled us off to a church. He declared that we had to go to confession, as Nijinsky and myself were both Roman Catholics and we could not be married in church unless we did so.

The Iglesia St. Miguel was the church in Buenos Aires where

all smart marriages took place, so of course our *mondaine* Baron
made the arrangements there. We were taken to that place for confession. Nijinsky disappeared with the priest and very soon he
was released from the confessional. No wonder, as the priest
could not speak a word of Russian or Polish.

I followed. I always disliked confessions, as I could rarely
regret my sins and never liked to promise things which I was pretty
sure not to keep. But I went through with it and it was not so bad
after all. The priest made a point of it that I should promise him
to prevent Nijinsky from dancing *Scheherazade*, so that the performance of this "immoral ballet" should be made impossible. I
told him I would do my best. Then we were dragged into a nice
cool parlour, where three priests were waiting for us, to make us
sign a document that all our children would be brought up as Catholics. The priest to whom I had confessed was very good-looking
and I liked his black eyes, so I asked Gunsburg to arrange that he
should marry us. But this was impossible, as he was too young, and
the bishop wanted to hold the ceremony himself; but they promised
me that he would assist.

Four days after our arrival Gunsburg finally completed all the
necessary arrangements. The marriage ceremony was set for
Wednesday, the 10th of September. As everybody was excited and
nervous, running from one room to the other, racing out to hairdressers and shops, I got hold of Mrs. Baton and we had a lovely
walk and talk in the city. At one o'clock I was taken down to the
city hall by Oblokova and Gunsburg. There were assembled already a few intimates, the Drobetskys, Kovalevska, Chavez, the
Batons, with Nijinsky and the Russian and Austro-Hungarian
ministers, the staff of the legations, and the representatives of the
Press.

A squat Spaniard came out with a huge ribbon across his chest in the Argentine colours. He looked terribly formal, and stood before us. On the desk full of flowers stood a crucifix on a dark green blotter, which was covered with a huge parchment document on which a lady was floating, holding a band on which our names and the date were printed in huge red letters. It was the smartest certificate of marriage, in full accordance with Argentine taste. Then this kind old gentleman asked questions in Spanish. Baton pulled out a notebook and gave dates and names in French, which were immediately translated to the Mayor by the official interpreter. The two ministers confirmed it in Spanish. Then Vaslav was questioned and answered in Russian. I talked in Hungarian and French. Finally the Mayor made a speech in Spanish, to which we listened very attentively. We were made to sign the document which was to make us man and wife.

.   .   .   .

During the whole wedding breakfast toasts were proposed and we were congratulated. They all seemed happy and Karsavina was constantly smiling at us.

I hoped to spend the afternoon quietly, but failed. Anna, who was very superstitious, could not agree to my plan of wearing a pale blue dress at the marriage ceremony. She considered it unlucky, and went to complain to Mme. Oblokova. Mme. Baton and she dragged me to all the dressmakers of Buenos Aires in search of a white dress. Finally, after hours of seeking, we succeeded in buying a lovely pale cream coloured wedding-dress. But our difficulties were not at an end; white shoes, orange blossoms, and a veil had to be found. With the help of Maria Stepanovna, late in the afternoon finally everything was ready. Everything except the orange blossoms, which could not be obtained and were unknown at all the flower shops. By the time I arrived at the hotel to dress, Anna was frantic and Baron Gunsburg almost in tears. It was nearly seven o'clock, the time fixed for the ceremony, and the others were already waiting for us at the church. I was flung into my dress and whirled away by the Baron.

At the entrance of the Iglesia St. Miguel, M. and Mme. Baton, Nijinsky, and the others of the wedding party were waiting for us. I was taken up the aisle to the strains of the wedding march from *Lohengrin*. I felt guilty at being late, and noticed a disappointed look on Nijinsky's face, who seemed to be anxiously waiting, so I did not look around. The ceremony was long. The clergy, greatly ornate, officiated. The flowers were lovely; everything seemed to be so hazy and strange: the priests, the escort, the guests, even the bridegroom. Was it true or only a dream? Could it be really possible that in a few moments, before God and men, I was to be given in marriage to the *Spectre de la Rose?* I glanced at him. He was very serious and solemn. To him it seemed a sacred moment. The ceremony, which was said in Latin and Spanish, was of course incomprehensible to me. I was rather nervous. Would I know when to say "Yes"? I was strangely fascinated by the heavily gilded wings of the baroque angels. The altar was the most atrocious sculpture one could imagine, and I could not take my eyes off it. But everything went well. The questions were asked of us in French, and we both answered clearly and audibly. Nijinsky produced the wedding-rings at the right moment. The good-looking black-eyed priest smiled at me encouragingly. During the whole long, fatiguing ceremony the only sentence which I could understand, and always later remember, was when the priest asked me in Spanish: "*Will you always stay by him in happiness as well as in misfortune, in health and sickness, forever?*" And I promised.

So he blessed us, and as we turned we faced the others.

Some of those present were laughing happily; others were in tears and rushed up to us. We were kissed, congratulated, by the clergy, the artists, and the society of Buenos Aires who were present at this unusual wedding. I was almost crushed in the embrace of fat, old, but charming fashionable Argentine ladies. They were beaming with smiles and all wished us happiness.

As we drove back to the hotel, Nijinsky and I were very silent. A few moments before the carriage drove up to the entrance, Nijinsky took my hand and, kissing it, placed a beautiful yellow-pink pearl engagement-ring on my finger.

On the very evening of my wedding, which had taken place in accordance with the Argentine customs, we held our dress rehearsal at the Teatro Colon. I had been extremely upset the whole day, more on account of the rehearsal than my wedding. I was supposed to dance in *Scheherazade* and had stage fright.

As I arrived on the stage, the girls all rushed up to me, congratulated me again, and admired my beautiful ring. Somebody remarked that pearls were unlucky, but I had always wanted one. The ballet began, and everything seemed to go fairly well until the moment when we had to make our entrance. We had a *pas de trois* to dance before Zobeide (the Sultana) and her golden slave (Nijinsky). The idea that he would see me dance froze my blood, and I do not know how I made my entrance. I danced and danced, and when the others stopped I went on dancing, and in their abrupt pause fell headlong on the stage, but I remained on the floor and the audience did not notice anything.

The dress rehearsal was apparently successful, but this did not lessen my nervousness. The ordeals of the day were not over.

I had to go home to face Nijinsky—my husband.

Ever since the evening, a year and a half ago, when I had seen this marvellous vision for the first time I was drawn to him with an irresistible feeling. I hoped, prayed, willed for this miracle to share his life, and now that it had become true I was frightened, desperately frightened.

What was going to happen? What was marriage, anyhow? I had nobody to turn to or to ask; I was alone in a strange land.

Anna very thoughtfully ordered a cold supper for us, in my little drawing-room, which awaited us upon our return to the hotel. Nijinsky came upstairs with me. We ate in silence. Anna retired as soon as she saw that everything was in order. I was getting more and more nervous, being left alone with Nijinsky. But he only smiled, and served me attentively. We were both so embarrassed that we could not even express ourselves in pantomime. And when, after supper, Nijinsky kissed my hand and left me, I was so relieved that I almost cried from thankfulness.

My début was better than I had dared to hope, and I was relieved when I was cast in the *Swan Lake* with Bolm. He made it easy for me, as during our dances he spoke to me on the stage and made me forget my stage fright. One evening in *Swan Lake* Nijinsky danced the part of the Prince. I was cast in the part of the Princess, his *fiancée*. I arrived gaily at the wings and gave him my hand, so that he could lead me on to the stage. As soon as we were seated on our throne and Karsavina began to dance her Variations I turned to Nijinsky, wanting to chat with him as I always did with Bolm in the same ballet. But, to my utter amazement, he gave me a strange look of complete lack of recognition. He was no longer my husband, but the Prince himself. The stage, his work, his art, were sacred to him; this understanding flashed to me. He lived his part, and everything else for him ceased to exist.

Many times at Buenos Aires this was proved to me. Of course, I thought that now that we were married I could come and go to his dressing-room; but to my great amazement, when I went in he

249

very gently caressed my hand and asked me to leave. Sometimes I met him back stage before he made his entrance, and more and more I saw that he had become his part. Once he passed me before the performance of *Faune*, and already, going from his dressing-room on to the stage, he walked in the same way as in the ballet. This was not a pose; he already had placed himself in the very mood of his part. His greatness, his genius, revealed themselves to me. I felt that there was an indescribable distance between us.

My amazement grew, for at home he was gay, laughing, mischievous, like a boy always trying to play some prank. We could not speak to each other yet—only a few sentences—and the Baron had to translate. The morning after my wedding we went to practise at the theatre as usual. Everybody smiled in a way which rather annoyed me. I also resented their inquisitive questions. I wondered what they would have said if they knew that Nijinsky had not returned to my apartment the previous evening, and that there had been no necessity for my placing all the movable furniture in front of my door, which I had so carefully locked.

Every morning I received a large bouquet of white roses from him. This was handed to Anna by Vassily with a furious look. Then we went to the theatre to practise separately, and finally I received my lessons. How happy I was to have them. I myself felt the immense improvement I made under Nijinsky's tutoring. The most difficult steps became easy if I carefully imitated his movements. The sense of harmony in the movement was the chief factor. He insisted on this more than on acrobatics. But when I did the exercises he made me do them correctly, according to the rules. We repeated not only those of the classical school, but also the ones established by Nijinsky himself, which are of infinite variety. Exercises for the arms, hands, even fingers, shoulders, and the head. In the afternoons we used to take long drives in the park.

Especially we enjoyed the Zoological Gardens, which are extremely interesting, with all the tropical birds and animals. Nijinsky would watch their movements for a long time, and made me notice everything lovely around us. It seemed to me that life began to have a new meaning. Suddenly I realised that so much beauty surrounds us which, before, I had failed to observe.

The whole day seemed to me like a holiday; I could be constantly with Nijinsky: at his meals, out driving, at home. I often watched him as we walked along the path near the lake at Palermo. He seemed to float. Every movement of his was soft and powerful, like those of a tiger, with an indescribable elasticity.

By this time I had moved down on to the first floor to Nijinsky's apartment, at his own request, which was made to me through Baron Gunsburg. This "suite" was composed of five rooms. The centre of the apartment was a large drawing-room, where we used to take our meals. On both sides the adjoining chambers were turned into living-rooms, and each of us had a bedroom at the opposite end of the apartment.

On our return from the performances Nijinsky used to write to his mother; he never forgot to do so. He seemed to be gay and happy and very proud when he spoke of me, and said, *"Maia Jena"* (which means "my wife"). I felt myself quite important. My fear of Nijinsky began to vanish. The charm of his personality, the tenderness of his whole being, radiated so much goodness, such beauty, that the evening he chose to remain I felt I was making an offering on the altar of happiness.

PART TWO

Chapter Thirteen

THE BREAK
WITH
SERGEI DE DIAGHILEFF

THE FOLLOWING weeks passed in infinite happiness. Nijinsky danced more wonderfully than ever, and the serious meditative look which he always used to have off stage gave place very often now to one of mischievous gaiety. Sometimes he seemed to me like a child who has received his first grown-up suit. To Nijinsky, marriage meant tremendously much, as I found out later. He became himself at last. His genius had always bloomed irresistibly, but now Nijinsky himself grew up and became a man. Always, since his childhood, he had been seeking the truth in art and life—the meaning of it. Now he found that love in marriage was the way. His profound affection for Diaghileff did not change but he was sure now that Diaghileff was mistaken in his ideas of love and in thinking he could turn him, Nijinsky, into a puppet.

Nijinsky was honesty itself. He came one day and told me, after having learned the words for hours from the Baron, his past relationship with Sergei Pavlovitch. He wrote a long letter to Diaghileff, explaining the reason which had made him marry, and assuring him that unalterably he would remain his true friend and serve the cause of the Russian Ballet.

Vaslav, as I now called him, told me that Diaghileff would

understand; he was such a wonderful person that, even if he was unable to love in this way, he would approve. Vaslav had unlimited faith in Sergei Pavlovitch. I wondered. But surely he must know better than I!

Late one evening, when we were alone, Vaslav came and sat on my bed and handed me a note translated by the Baron:

"I have a brother, Stanislav. He is insane. You have to know it."

For a second I was numbed and frightened. As I looked up, Vaslav had an impassible drawn expression. I threw my arms around him.

Vaslav wrote to his mother about our happiness.

At this time I was cast in the part of a nymph in *Faune*, and was intensely proud, especially as Vaslav was very pleased. I learned in eight rehearsals what had taken other dancers one hundred and twenty. And it was really difficult; we could not follow the music by the measure of the dance as in the other ballets—we had to count uninterruptedly, otherwise we would have been unable to keep the right rhythm.

I had requested Vaslav not to come to watch at *Prince Igor* as he intended. This was the first ballet in which I danced and he did not take part. I saw an expression of extreme amazement in his face; but, "I have to watch, to see that everything goes well. I am not watching you alone, but all the artists," was translated to me. And, as I saw him in the wings, I ran off the stage panic-stricken! As punishment I was suspended for a week. At first I could not comprehend why Vaslav had punished me, but always and always I could see that he separated the artist and the person, and treated each as they deserved.

For two days I was disagreeable. He failed to understand my

NIJINSKY AND HIS FAMILY

FESTIN

reason. Finally, one afternoon, in my broken Russian, I asked him what he thought of my dancing. He told me frankly I had great dispositions for it, but, as I began late, I lacked the technique and could never become a perfect dancer. "But you could dance very beautifully certain dances which I will compose for you." So then I understood that anybody who is not trained as a child can only obtain a limited way of expression in the art of dancing. "Will I never be able to dance like Pavlova, like Karsavina?" I cried. "No, never," he told me. Then and there I decided that I would give up my career as a dancer. Vaslav tried to persuade me not to do it, but I decided I would study with him but never appear in public. To serve his genius was far more important than my own ambition.

The first impulse which made me follow the Russian Ballet, or, in reality, Nijinsky, was the wish that his genius should be perpetuated through me. This intense desire never left me since a spring morning in 1912, when I awoke, and on the wall opposite my bed the sunrays through the shadow of the leaves of the acacias danced so beautifully and gracefully, and I saw before me Nijinsky. But now that we were married, which fact I never dared to hope or dream of before, I became so enraptured in him that I did not wish to have a child. First of all I consulted Mme. Oblokova, but she only shook her head and laughed. Mme. Baton read me a strict sermon, and said how marvellous it must be to become a mother. Then I went to the Baron, who faithfully translated my request, and Vaslav said: "For five years we shall live for art and our love, but the supreme happiness and the fulfilment of life and marriage is to have a child, and, after that time, when we will be in our permanent home, we shall have one." I agreed.

We continued our tour. In Rio we stopped at the beautiful hill-top hotel in Sylvestre. Vaslav and I were never tired of driving in those glorious forests to admire the flowers and butterflies, which were huge and in all imaginable lovely colours, deep turquoise blue, emerald green, orange. Even the sparrows in this country were beautiful. The woods were full of small but inoffensive monkeys, which gaily jumped around—to Vaslav's intense pleasure. One morning he found one in our bathroom.

I was very much afraid of the snakes; they were abundant in the forests, and I was told by the servants at the hotel that they frequently glided into the rooms. Anna lived in constant terror of them, and also in a constant state of war with Vassily. The latter performed his duties near Vaslav as faithfully as ever, but completely ignored both myself and Anna. I did not pay any attention to this impertinence, but Anna deeply mistrusted him. She claimed that only for the sake of Vaslav Fomitch our lives were spared. She was sure that otherwise it would be the greatest joy for Vassily to poison us. Sometimes, when I caught Vassily's glance, I myself was not sure whether Anna was not right. He certainly hated us. I learned also that he was the only one who did not come to our marriage service.

Already, in Montevideo, I sometimes felt faint; here I took an intense dislike to food, especially to coffee; I could not even bear the smell of it; and in Brazil everything seemed to smell of coffee. Vaslav became worried about my paleness, the artists smiled, Drobetsky extended his congratulations, and the doctor on whom I called confirmed that I was going to have a child.

Vaslav seemed to be pleased and proud.

Early in November the tour ended in Rio. The homeward journey seemed ghastly to me. I was laid up in my cabin, constantly sea-sick. I used to cry to the English doctor, who tried everything in his power to help me. Vaslav became a little nervous, seeing that

I felt depressed. But to have a child was such a blow to me now that I wanted to live only for him.

Vaslav consoled me, and said the baby was going to be a wonderful dancer, and called him, in memory of South America, "Le Petit Nègre."

His days were passed in composing, Baton playing for him. I noticed only once a weariness come over him.

Now we could speak pidgin French and Russian, and used to carry on quite a conversation. I began to rave about all the Callot dresses, Reboux hats and Cartier jewels, and of all the *mondain* life I was going to lead in the future. I was brought up to believe that this was what marriage meant, and Vaslav, to whom all this was strange, perhaps, for a second, felt a little tired of it all; he had yet to teach me. But he smiled and said: "I am only an artist, not a prince, but anything I can have is yours. If these things make you happy, I will give them to you." But I sensed that he did not approve of my point of view, and this irritated me. Vaslav's idea was to spend a few days in Paris, where we were supposed to meet Sergei Pavlovitch. Then to go to St. Petersburg, where he wanted me to meet his mother and sister and to know my new home. We decided on the way we would stop a few days in Budapest, where Vaslav wanted to pay his respects to my mother. This did not overjoy me, as I was anxious to get to Russia. We left the troupe at Cadiz, where we took the Sud-Express for Paris. While we passed the frontier, at Hendaye, we were sitting in the dining saloon having dinner when Vaslav suddenly became livid, jumped up, and left. I went after him, and found him in our compartment—having fainted. I tried to summon a doctor immediately, but there was not one on the train. The *chef du train* brought some ice and smelling-salts; and as Vaslav came to himself he complained of intense headache, which he had often when on a long train journey. From that time I gave up smoking, as he could not stand even the smell of cigarettes. At the Imperial Schools they were not allowed to smoke.

Our stay in Paris, which we had intended to spend quietly, became a series of entertainments. The papers announced our arrival, and the Russian nobility present gave one reception after the other in our honour. They all wanted to show me the hospitality of my newly adopted country. I was spoiled and entertained. Lovely presents and exquisite jewellery were showered upon us. The newly built Trianon Palace Hotel in Versailles was turned into a *féerique décor* for the reception which Prince H. gave for us.

On our way to Budapest, my sister met us in Vienna. At last Vaslav hoped to arrive in a peaceful family circle, but he was painfully surprised. On our arrival in Budapest, instead of the loving embrace of a mother, a crowd of reporters, camera-men, and photographers awaited us. My mother entertained largely, and we were dragged from one reception to the other, stared at like strange animals from the jungle, and questioned. I knew Vaslav was disappointed, but he never said anything, and politely went wherever my mother wished us to go.

All this time, I had made up my mind not to have a child. I spoke to my mother about it, and she agreed with me. She was still a very young and lovely woman, married a second time, and, as a leading actress, she knew that the fact of becoming a grandmother would be widely advertised to her own disadvantage by her women colleagues. Our house physician was called in, and he explained to me that, as I used to be rather a delicate child myself, it would endanger my life to become a mother. An intervention, therefore, was imperative, and every arrangement was speedily made for this.

Vaslav was rather sad, but only ventured to say he would like to consult another authority. The night before I was supposed to enter the sanatorium I became suddenly terrified, and explained to Vaslav that I would rather risk dying than allow an operation to take place. An immense relief and pleasure was expressed in his face. He kissed me gently, and whispered: "Thank God. What He has given, nobody has the right to destroy." Later, when we could speak to each other, he told me that every human being has the right to decide in these questions of life and death, and he did not feel the right to interfere or prevent me as long as I was firmly decided not to become a mother, but he was infinitely thankful to God that he made me understand in time.

We decided to spend Christmas in St. Petersburg. Vaslav was immensely happy to return to his mother and country. He tried to explain how good she was, and also told me what a devoted sister and friend I was going to find in Bronia, for whom his attachment was deep. Two days before our departure, in the evening, a telegram was handed to Vaslav. As he read it, he gazed for a long time, and seemed not to comprehend it. After a long while, he gave it to me. It was in French, and ran as follows: "Your services with the Russian Ballet are no more required. Don't join us. Sergei de Diaghileff."

I was petrified. Vaslav, the glory, the greatest dancer, the pillar of the Ballet, outcast, dismissed, as a servant, from the creation of art for which he was responsible, because of his marriage. This was Diaghileff's revenge.

Now, for the first time, it dawned on me that perhaps I had made a mistake; I had destroyed, where I had wanted to be helpful. But as I burst out crying, Vaslav smiled with great gentleness, and said: "*Pas triste, c'est erreur et si c'est vrai! moi artiste peut travailler seul.*"

261

The news of Vaslav's dismissal was known in a few days throughout the world. Offers were showered upon him, from impresarios, theatres, with incredibly high salaries. But Vaslav refused. The agents came personally to Budapest to win him over. The fee rose higher and higher, but Vaslav shook his head, and asked the secretary of the Russian Consulate, who was constantly with us: "Please tell them I cannot do anything inartistic. I must first have the right ballets, artists to appear with me. I must think, create, and, under no circumstances will I appear in a vaudeville house. I cannot be unfaithful to my art."

No money could tempt him.

Monsieur Rouché, the director of the Paris Opéra, offered him one hundred thousand gold francs a year if he would consent to become *maître de ballet* and *premier danseur*, appearing twenty times a year. But when Vaslav saw the material that the Opéra offered, he was obliged to refuse.

He had always done everything to heighten the art of dancing, and this he was determined still to do in the future. The impresarios became discouraged, my family was furious; my stepfather, who had an excellent business head, was distracted to see such a fortune cast quietly away. I understood Vaslav and agreed with him, feeling unhappy that he had to go through this trial for my sake. But whenever I brought up the subject he immediately stopped me. My stepfather tried to explain to him that he would have to earn money for me, and for his future child, which I thought very tactless of him, as Vaslav married me without any dowry. Vaslav calmly smiled, and, with a pitying look, told him: "I know. I have also a mother and an insane brother to look after, but I have some little savings, they will not be in need. I will dance, but in the right way." He was so harassed by everybody that we left for Vienna.

But we did not find peace there either. The son of a famous London impresario personally followed us everywhere, with an exceedingly high offer from Alfred Butt, the owner of the Palace Theatre in London. Vaslav believed that this place was not a variety theatre, but one of the most distinguished houses in London, equal to Covent Garden or Drury Lane, where he had appeared before; and Alfred Butt gave him full liberty to form his own company and programme. So Vaslav signed a contract for eight weeks for the following spring. Everybody seemed at peace except Vaslav and myself. Bronia wrote him that she as well as her husband Kotchetovsky had resigned from the Ballet, and were at Vaslav's disposal. Vaslav asked them to come to Paris and talk everything over.

Vaslav planned to form a company of thirty-two dancers, and to compose ballets. From the old repertoire he was requested to give the *Spectre de la Rose,* and two classical ballets, *The Princess Enchantée* and possibly *Les Sylphides.*

He had to have scenery and costumes designed, and new music composed, and all this meant tremendous work and time. But Vaslav undertook this courageously. His first visit was to Bakst, to whom he wanted to entrust the scenery. We drove up to the Boulevard Malesherbes, where he had his studio. I remained in the carriage, as I did not wish to disturb their meeting. After a very long time, perhaps two hours, Vaslav came down. I saw tears in his eyes, which he tried to hide, but he had to tell me the result of his conversation with Bakst. He flatly refused to work for Vaslav. He told him that he personally could understand Vaslav's feelings, but had to withdraw from all artistic associations with him in the future, as Diaghileff insisted on this. He also felt it his duty to tell Vaslav the truth, that his dismissal from the Ballet was not the end, it was the beginning, of a state of war which Diaghileff had declared against Nijinsky. And he repeated Sergei Pavlovitch's own words: *"As high as Nijinsky stands now, as low am I going to thrust him."*

After long debates with Bronia and Kotchetovsky, it was decided that they would go back to Russia to choose and engage the dancers, and bring them back to Paris. Anisfeld the painter was summoned; he accepted the offer, and began to design the *maquettes* for scenery and costumes which were of extreme beauty. Vaslav personally supervised everything; even the execution of the costumes at Mme. Muelle's, who always worked for the Russian Ballet. Among the musicians, he invited Ravel, who proved to be of great loyalty and kindness. He was a charming young man, always a little extravagantly dressed, but full of gaiety. Untiringly he played for Vaslav, helped him in the choice of music, went to the music publishers to obtain the rights, and orchestrated the new ballets in an exquisite manner. The superhuman effort on Vaslav's part seemed to promise a programme of great artistic value.

But I knew that this was not the work Vaslav wished to do. He wanted to create a ballet of pure abstract dancing more on the line of *Sacre* or the Bach ballet. To compose something similar to the pre-*Faune* time was against his conviction. But now he was forced to create a frame in which he could appear, a new medium through which he could express and further new ideas.

And I knew he suffered from this forced task, but he never complained or referred to it.

Vaslav tested dancers in Vienna and Paris, but, as much as he wished, he could not engage any of them, as they lacked either the artistic understanding or could only dance with their legs. Bronia returned with a well-chosen company, mostly graduates from the Imperial Schools, who were dissatisfied with things in Russia and revolted at the news of Diaghileff's scheme. They were engaged for the period of one year.

The rehearsals began. Vaslav worked practically day and night. Now all administrative and organising tasks rested on his shoulders. He had hardly any time to eat or sleep. I became worried. Bronia was untiring too. She spoke only Russian and Polish, but I soon noticed that she did not like me; she seemed to resent everything that happened and blame it on me. I was the intruder in the Russian Ballet, in the family. She isolated herself behind a screen of ice which I could never penetrate. At Larue's, or at Viel's, I used to await them for lunch sometimes until four or five o'clock in the afternoon. But they worked and danced all the time.

Finally the day came when we had to leave for London. The Press received Vaslav with enthusiasm. Lady Morrell was standing at the door of our suite at the Savoy, her arms full of spring flowers, to welcome us. Lady Ripon came in the afternoon, and assured us how happy she was about our marriage, and that we could count upon her in every way. She told me that it was always her wish that Vaslav should marry, and that she had tried in the past to introduce him to suitable young ladies! But as long as he himself had chosen, she could only approve, and offered to become the godmother of our future child.

The next two weeks passed in feverish preparation. Zenon offered his services to Vaslav and was accepted; he proved to be of real service. The theatre was sold out. But we seemed to be pursued by bad luck, or, more truly, by Diaghileff. First a police injunction was brought forbidding Bronia to appear, as Diaghileff claimed in the court that he had not accepted her resignation. Endless proceedings were taken to allow Bronia to dance, and to prove that she had not broken her contract.

Vaslav was greatly upset several times, which did not improve matters. The first day, he was requested to come personally to Alfred Butt's office and pay him his respects. Vaslav could not make out what they wanted of him. Brought up at the Imperial School, a member of the Mariinsky Theatre, he was taught to pay respect to only one person in the world, the Tsar. Everybody else, even the grand-dukes came to bow before the artists. Alfred Butt, whom he had never met before, was, for him, the owner of several theatres, a business man, and, as much as he was ready to call on him as a private person, he refused on principle to call as an artist on a theatrical manager.

Of course, this gesture of his was misunderstood, and caused a lot of trouble. Then a very regrettable incident occurred. Vaslav was practising quietly alone on the empty stage of the Palace Theatre, when a stage hand passed, and, not noticing him and seeing me, before I realised it, patted my cheeks with an impertinent suggestion. Vaslav jumped at him and knocked him down. Of course the man screamed, and a fight began. I was dumbfounded, I had never seen Vaslav like that.

All these incidents put him in an extremely nervous condition. Once, at a rehearsal, Bronia was not feeling very well, and, although she did not say anything to Vaslav about it, she did not dance quite so well as usual. Vaslav criticised her and she burst out crying and left the stage. As soon as Vaslav had entered his dressing-room, he was followed by Kotchetovsky, who insulted him, and spat, like a Russian *moujik*, at the floor before him. Vaslav did not answer, he only became a shade paler.

His sensitive soul was hurt; he was attacked from every side, and why? Now I understood why Diaghileff had isolated him from the world. Perhaps he was right after all. At the dress rehearsal, Vaslav realised that he had been misled, that the Palace Theatre was a variety theatre, a very smart one, but nevertheless it was a vaudeville house. He could not break his word given to the public, or let down the thirty-two artists who had faith in him; but to lower the artistic standard of the Ballet was equally impossible.

He had to go through the ordeal which the appearance at the Palace meant to him. What no money could make him do, he accepted for the sake of loyalty to his fellow artists and respect for his public.

The day of the opening, Mr. Williams told me that Vaslav seemed to be very feverish, but he went to the theatre. The public received him with enthusiasm, but I was blinded with tears to see Vaslav dance, in his exquisite programme, after a clown's number, and before a popular cabaret singer's act.

The second day brought a fresh attack; now Fokine, who had returned to the Russian Ballet, was persuaded by Diaghileff to bring an injunction to prevent the *Spectre de la Rose* from being given. Again he was used as a tool in Diaghileff's powerful hand, who convinced him that he had had to leave the Ballet before on account of Nijinsky.

By now Vaslav was unable to stand on his feet, and, alarmed, I 'phoned to Lady Ripon, who called in Sir Alfred Fripp and Sir Bruce Porter. I had given Vaslav some aspirin, as I knew, from home, it was good for fever. But Sir Alfred told me that I almost killed him, as he had an athlete's heart and was in an extremely dangerous condition. He was very, very sick. He tried to go and dance, but could not. Sir Alfred went personally to the management of the Palace Theatre and explained. They said, of course, that they understood, and we assumed, no doubt without warrant, that the clause in the contract, which stated that in the case of his not appearing for three consecutive nights he broke the contract, would not be enforced. But we were mistaken and, after three days, they declared that Vaslav had broken his contract. This was a very serious matter. Vaslav had spent about two thousand pounds on scenery, costumes, authors' rights, orchestration, and transport of the artists from Russia; and, in addition, guaranteed to pay thirty-two artists during the year. All this was based on the contract with the Palace Theatre, which now was suddenly ended. On the advice of our friends I called in Sir George Lewis, and requested him to make an arrangement with the Theatre so that no loss should occur to either party. Vaslav was willing to go through with the agreement, but the negotiations broke down. It is possible that the management of the Palace realised that Nijinsky did not make the concessions to the taste of the variety theatre's public as Pavlova did—and, after all, they paid him five times as much.

Vaslav was ill for two months. Sir Alfred Fripp assured me that, as strong as he looked, he was not the type of man who could stand so much excitement and worry. "Let him dance and rest, but no organising—no administrative work." Vaslav had realised this always—that an artist should live only for his art—but now we had a new problem. Sir George Lewis made an arrangement with the company; the artists themselves went to him, and said they were satisfied with the salary they had received during the rehearsal period and the week which had been paid to them for the three days they had danced, and they asked only their fares back to Russia, releasing Nijinsky from their one year's contract. It seemed fair to us all, but Vaslav refused. He said: "They trusted me. It is not their fault that I became sick, that my contract was broken. I signed to pay them for a year, and I will do it." So his savings from the Paris bank were withdrawn, and Vaslav paid all the thirty-two artists in full.

I now insisted that Vaslav should rest, and live only to restore his health. I could induce him to do this as I was approaching the time of the birth of my baby, and Vaslav was willing to stay with me constantly. We took long walks in Richmond Park, and used to picnic in the beautiful Surrey country-side.

Vaslav said that the last weeks before a child is born the mother should spend in privacy—"To me it is lovely, and sacred to all men who love their wives, but no stranger should witness this transformation." So we went to the Semmering.

At this time, Vaslav received an invitation from Madrid to dance for the King and Queen of Spain at the wedding reception of Kermit Roosevelt, which was to be given at the American Embassy. He did not want to leave me, but a Command Performance was hard to refuse. The salary offered was three thousand dollars for one dance. We needed the money now that the savings were gone. My stepfather was willing to accompany Vaslav on the trip, and they left for Madrid. I received every day a short note, written in Russian, of which I was proud, as I knew Vaslav never wrote to anybody. He addressed me as "Femmka," or "Roma."

In Madrid, Vaslav was received with the warmth and appreciation to which he was accustomed. King Alfonso as well as the Queen led the others to make him feel at home. I heard from witnesses that the dance on the stage, which was placed in the beautiful gardens, was unforgettable.

On the return journey, Vaslav decided to stop in Paris, and to be present at the first performance of the Russian Ballet, and the *première* of *Joseph and Potiphar*. Vaslav wanted to show the world that he was not afraid of Diaghileff, that he did not regret his marriage, even if his former friends tried to ruin him for it. The intimates of Sergei Pavlovitch, of course, knew the reason of the break. What they did not know was that Diaghileff dismissed Nijinsky of his own accord, and without consulting anybody. He gave vague excuses to his friends: "Nijinsky is greatly changed, under

the influence of his wife. She wishes to be the leading *ballerina*.
Sacre was too modern, we ought to have more of the Fokine ballets,
and he won't return unless Nijinsky is out of the troupe." Nobody
knew exactly what had happened. The Comtesse de Greffuhle, Lady
Cunard, and others were too tactful to ask Diaghileff. Many rumours were in circulation. The suite of the Russian Ballet backed
Diaghileff, as well as all the men who led lives like Sergei Pavlovitch; and they proved to be extremely powerful, strong, unforgiv-
ing enemies. In all classes and positions they were everywhere
against those whom they considered unfaithful to their ideal; like
a steel wall they stretched across the world. But could Vaslav help
it that he had found himself, and changed?

We learned that Richard Strauss was extremely disappointed
that Nijinsky would not dance in his ballet. The *première* of *Joseph
and Potiphar*, then called the *Legend of Joseph*, was a world-wide
artistic event. A German composer's work would be performed at
the Opéra, where that year the performances were scheduled. The
French Government also decided to accord the Cross of the Légion
d'Honneur to Richard Strauss. It was almost a political event.

But Diaghileff tried to console Strauss and his co-authors,
Count Kessler and Hofmansthal, and to convince them that the
ballet would have the same artistic standard as all former productions. Bakst was replaced by José Maria Sert. The idea to place
the scenery at the time of Paolo Veronese was kept, and proved a
success. The whole Ballet was produced with old Venetian splendour, and Diaghileff lavished all the money he could obtain from
his backers upon this season. It was the most expensive the Russian Ballet had ever given. The part of Potiphar's wife was given
to Kusnitzova the singer, who was a beautiful woman. Joseph's
part caused Diaghileff a lot of worry. He went personally to Russia
the preceding winter, to invite Fokine, and to find a dancer whom

he could star. Some of his old collaborators had the courage to tell him that he was mistaken in letting his private emotions interfere with artistic creations and matters, but it was of no avail. Diaghileff was dominated by only one idea, to ruin Nijinsky, nothing else mattered.

Diaghileff engaged a young dancer, from one of the Moscovite private dancing schools, by the name of Leonide Miassine, later changed to Massine. He was a good-looking boy with dark eyes. At their arrival he gave him over to *Maestro's* care, with the request: "Teach him all you can, and make him dance like Nijinsky."

But in spite of all the expense, luxurious scenery, lavished on this season, of all the exciting novelties offered by Diaghileff, the season proved to be a disappointment. Never were the bill-boards more carefully designed, never had Diaghileff appeared so faithfully at all social occasions, never before had he entertained the Press. He did all this now. Yet *Joseph and Potiphar* failed. It represented an enormous effort, but it lacked the spontaneous impulse of true artistic creation. *Midas* did not receive a good reception either. *Papillon*, a weak copy of *Carnaval*, failed. The only success of the season was Rimsky-Korsakov's opera, *Coq d'Or*, which was produced as a ballet. At the rehearsals, when Diaghileff saw the old-fashioned movements of the singers, he suddenly got a genial idea, which was to place them as a chorus all round the stage from where they sang, and their parts were played by the dancers. It proved to be of extreme artistic interest, and had the great success it deserved. The triumphant success of the two, until now, unknown young Russian painters, Larionov, and, especially, Goncharova, the designer of the scenery and costumes for the *Coq d'Or*, saved the season. Both were from the Moscow School. Larionov was a Russian futurist, Goncharova was already well known

271

through her original and beautiful illustrations of fairy-tales for children's books. Her work had a freshness of design, a new range of colour, so much virility and imagination that with one stroke she was placed equal to Bakst.

Vaslav was enchanted by her talent and work. Also the *Rossignol,* an early opera of Stravinsky, was completed especially for this year, and produced exquisitely. Benois designed the scenery as a *chinoiserie.* Diaghileff tried everything with which to tempt the public; all kinds of rarities to make them forget the absence of Nijinsky, but he failed. Everywhere, everybody was asking, complaining, missing him.

At the *première* of *Joseph and Potiphar,* Vaslav attended in an orchestra stall, and very few of those present knew that the deeply regretted favourite was sitting in the audience. In the intermission, Vaslav went to Mme. Edwards's box, which was full of the Diaghileff suite. A frozen silence greeted him. Mme. Edwards tried to keep up the conversation. Then Cocteau, and some other young men present, laughingly turned to Vaslav and remarked: "This year, your creation is a child. The *Spectre de la Rose* chooses the part of a father. How utterly disgusting is birth." Vaslav was hurt, and stood up and answered: "The entrance of the *Spectre de la Rose's* child will be quite as beautiful as his own entrance, which you always admired." He bowed and left them.

No, never would they understand each other.

And now he realised that he, as a man, as a nature, had never really been understood in this fashionable, cosmopolitan society.

Upon Vaslav's return to Vienna, we made all the necessary preparations to receive our baby. We had engaged a suite in the sanatorium, a wet nurse was chosen for the child as well as a nurse for me. The professor awaited our telephone call and we were breaking our heads for a name for *Le Petit Nègre.* There was never any doubt that we would have a son. We both intensely wished for it, and it simply could not be otherwise. I wanted to call him Boris or Loris. Vaslav suggested Wladislav, and we decided on this.

The days passed, we visited all the lovely places of the Wiener Wald, but there was no sign of Wladislav. Finally we got tired of waiting. Even my brother-in-law Erik Schmedes, who liked Vaslav immensely, and was with us all the time, declared that this was an unheard-of breach of etiquette! Everybody in Vienna was waiting for the event.

Richard Strauss's new opera *Elektra* was having its *première* at the Opera House, and the intendant of the Hoftheater, Prince Montenuovo, knowing that Vaslav was in the city, sent us an invitation to attend, and had offered us a box, with the remark: "If this modern music won't hasten the baby's arrival, then nothing will!"

The opera was extremely interesting, and Vaslav liked it. Afterwards we dined gaily at the famous Opera Restaurant. Prince Montenuovo's prophetic words proved true. *Elektra* was too much for the baby, and next day, the 19th of June, our child was born.

Kyra Vaslavovna Nijinsky was a girl, and I was very unhappy about it. Vaslav did not show his disappointment. He waited with my sister next door to the operating-room, and, as the nurse announced to him, "It is only a girl, but a nice one," for one second he lost his self-control, and threw his gloves on the floor. But he never said anything about this to me. On the contrary, he tried to console me and praise the loveliness of the baby. Her hair was curled and black, like a *petit nègre*, but she had beautiful green eyes, as strangely fascinating, as oblique as Vaslav's very own. At least one of my wishes had been granted. She was extremely muscular and the more she grew the more she resembled Vaslav.

From the very first second the child was shown to Vaslav the adoration which he always had for his daughter began. I think

273

that, after his art, she was the most precious thing to him. Vaslav had always a great reverence and understanding of children.

Vaslav superintended the trousseau of the baby. He could not admire enough every movement and gesture of the child. She was placed in a lovely white basket which he had near to him in the garden, where I was carried.

Vaslav's happiness in the baby seemed so limitless that I forgot every difficulty of the past month. My mother, at my own request, was not called in time, as I did not want her to be present. She blamed Vaslav for this, and as soon as she arrived attempted to get hold of the child. I was extremely upset, especially as I remembered that a few months back she was the one who endeavoured to persuade me not to have it. Vaslav defended my mother when I complained but asked her not to interfere. My stepfather raised his hands against Vaslav. I jumped out of my bed, which brought on serious complications. My mother was requested not to visit us any more. This painful incident proved to me that my family and ourselves could never get along.

Congratulations poured in from all over the world. Then an official invitation from the Production Committee of the Russian Ballet Performances in London arrived, with a special request from Lady Ripon. For the Marchioness proved to be the most loyal friend Nijinsky ever had. She had used her tremendous influence, and declared to Diaghileff that unless Nijinsky danced with them there would be no season of the Russian Ballet in London.

So Diaghileff had to consent.

Lady Ripon insisted in her letter that Vaslav should travel to London at once, whatever his decision. We all wished Vaslav to go and dance, and he was willing to forget Sergei Pavlovitch's unjust behaviour. So Nijinsky left to join the Ballet, and take part in the London performances.

I was still laid up, and he went alone. Lady Ripon and Baron Gunsburg were awaiting him, and told him he was to dance *Faune*, and *Spectre*, and some other parts. Three performances in all. They hoped that with Vaslav once back everything would be arranged satisfactorily. He was overjoyed. He wanted to be a part of his beloved Ballet. He wanted to be a true friend to Sergei Pavlovitch. But the latter avoided him. Vaslav did not meet him, and as he went to the theatre accompanied by Drobetsky, who always remained loyal to him, he realised at once that the kind scheme of the Marchioness could not succeed. The company completely ignored Nijinsky. They did not speak to him; they did not even bow. Of course this was all done under the instructions of Sergei Pavlovitch. He was forced to call and tolerate Nijinsky, but he wished to show that he had not forgiven.

Vaslav went through the rehearsal and returned to the Savoy. He wrote a letter to Lady Ripon thanking her for the great effort she had made, but explained to her that as long as Diaghileff kept to his present attitude an artistic collaboration between them was impossible.

He left on the next train for Vienna, as he was afraid that if he saw the Marchioness again he would have to give in to her entreaties.

Chapter Fourteen

PRISONERS
OF WAR

On sunday, the 28th of June, 1914, I was resting in my bed in the Loew Sanatorium in Vienna. Through the open windows came the scent of the acacia-trees and roses in bloom. I could see Kyra in the garden in her little snow-white basket, guarded by the nurses. Everything seemed to be peaceful, and I thought fate had been very kind to me. The little *Jesus of Prague* had granted my wish. I was the wife of Nijinsky, and the baby might have inherited his wonderful gifts. So, after all, I had served him. Vaslav was on his way to London. He would dance again with the Ballet. Diaghileff would be a friend. Great ballets would be composed, and we would all be so happy.

Suddenly a loud, ceaseless ringing of the church bells broke out. For a long time I listened, then later Kyra was brought up, supper served, and everything made ready for the night's rest. The church bells still tolled on. Nobody knew the reason why. The assistant doctor came to make his round. As usual, he sat down to chat with me and to smoke a cigarette. I knew that he was off duty in the afternoon and had intended to go to the races. He trembled as he lit my cigarette. "Well, doctor, did you win? What is new in town?"

The face of the light-hearted, flirtatious Viennese assistant quivered, as he said: "His Imperial Highness, the Archduke Franz Ferdinand, and his wife, the Duchess of Hohenberg, were shot this afternoon at Sarajevo, by a Serbian subject."

So this was the reason for the ringing of the church bells.

Among the many visitors I received, my godfather, His Excellency Thallocy, came often. Thanks to his intimate connection with the Imperial Family, he was well informed. He said it was a blessing for the monarchy that Franz Ferdinand was out of the way, but that Serbia must receive an exemplary punishment—not only the murderer, but the whole nation, as it was a political crime and they were all responsible. In a few days Vaslav returned, and I had forgotten all about this incident.

We decided to return to St. Petersburg as soon as I was allowed to travel. We constantly received letters and wires from the Marchioness of Ripon requesting us to return immediately to London, all three of us. We thought, of course, it was to allow Vaslav to take part in the season of the Ballet.

But as she insisted that we should come, Vaslav asked Professor Halban, who declared that he could take no responsibility for me if I undertook so long a journey. So we made up our minds to take his advice and stay in Vienna until the end of July, and then, with a week's stop in Budapest, to allow a rest for Kyra and myself, to proceed to Russia.

We arrived in Budapest on a hot summer day—the 23rd of July. A dreadful storm broke out—almost a hurricane—that broke all the windows at my mother's villa, and the big bell of the St. Stephan Basilica fell.

"Some misfortune is going to happen," one of my mother's peasant maids declared.

Next day I saw in the papers that an ultimatum had been sent to Serbia.

277

The following evening Vaslav and my mother decided to go to the circus; Vaslav had loved clowns ever since his childhood. I felt tired and stayed at home. Late in the afternoon great crowds formed in the streets, all covered with garlands of flowers, singing and dancing. Strangers kissed each other; it was like a national fête. My family returned, also in a great state of excitement. I could hardly get the news out of them. Vaslav could not insist enough how amusing the clowns were, how lovely the dancing of the peasants was in the streets. The reason of this hysterical rejoicing, which I finally learned from my stepfather—it had escaped Vaslav, who did not understand the language—was that at last war was declared.

We spent the following days quietly with Kyra in my mother's garden, but, even so, we could feel the intense excitement of the city. Ceaselessly regiments of soldiers marched by, covered with flowers, singing, accompanied on the roadside by their laughing and frantically waving women relatives.

Vaslav was always a pacifist, and condemned war and all recourse to force. Politics had no interest for him. He claimed that all misunderstandings and quarrels could be settled if we only had the strong wish for it and would grant others the same right to happiness as we claim for ourselves.

We went to the city to make our reservation on the Nord Express, but, to our utter amazement, we learned that the frontier towards the east was closed. We immediately proceeded to the Russian Consulate. It seemed deserted. We rang the bell, and after a very long time it was answered by a footman, who showed us through a long range of rooms. The carpets having been taken up, the marvellously polished floors were now visible; the furniture, covered with white linen, made the place look uninhabited.

Nowhere was there a sound. In the Consul's drawing-room

278

everything was tidied and covered with paper. Only the two great portraits hanging opposite each other on the wall and smiling— that of the Tsar and the Tsarina—seemed unaltered. Somehow I had the feeling that no harm could happen to Vaslav as long as they seemed so quiet.

Excellency Priklonsky, the Consul-General, rushed in with out-stretched hands and began to talk excitedly in torrents of Russian, of which I understood very little. It seemed that he had packed everything, as he could not get any sensible instructions from the Embassy in Vienna. There they did not know, either, what was happening. They had orders apparently to prevent war. "It is true that the frontiers are closed. The Embassy will probably leave in case of an ultimatum." But he himself did not know if he could go with the diplomatic train, for he had to stay as long as he was not officially recalled. He advised us to stay quietly where we were for the next few days, as everywhere trains were full of troops and it would not be possible to travel with the baby. But we could count upon him to let us know in time, and he would do everything in his power to take us with the diplomatic train to Sweden, from where we could easily reach Russia in case of war, which of course was unthinkable.

But the unthinkable happened, and, before we could realise it, the whole world was aflame. And the marching of the troops went ceaselessly, endlessly on.

Vaslav stood sighing before the window, "All these young men marching to their deaths, and for what?"

I was amazed. Why did he think of those utter strangers? What did it matter? Why didn't he think of all the worries and complications this new state of affairs might bring to him? Every day I made a new discovery. Vaslav was thoughtful, modest, not in the least conceited, and so embarrassed if anybody complimented him. All his thoughts were for the happiness and welfare of other people, not only his family, his friends, but perfect strangers. I have never known anybody like him.

From morning till evening I tried to find a way whereby we could leave Hungary, but there was no escape; all railway lines were in the hands of the military authorities. Finally my uncle, Garibaldi de Pulszky, president of an important private railway company, came to my rescue and promised to smuggle us out through the south to Italy. Our great difficulty was Kyra, only six weeks old. She had a wet nurse, as I could not nurse her. Anybody would recognise us with her. Then there was the danger of travelling with such a small baby in the terrific heat, in countries at war. Vaslav was worried, but I felt I had to find a way to bring him to his friends and country.

The following morning a shy-looking man came to the house. He was in civilian clothes and almost apologetic. One could see at once that he was carrying out an order to which he was not used, and it seemed to embarrass him. He spoke to me in Hungarian and asked us to follow him to the Prefecture of Police. My heart stood still. What did they want from us? Why? He refused to answer. Vaslav smiled wearily and tried to quiet me. "It's nothing; don't worry; let us go."

In half an hour we stood before the chief of the detective bureau. In fluent French he said: "Mr. and Mrs. Nijinsky, in the name of the military authorities I am obliged to arrest you and your daughter Kyra as enemy subjects. All three of you have to remain wherever you will be allotted on our territory until the termination of the hostilities, as prisoners of war."

Prisoner of war! Prisoner of war! Prisoner of war! I could

not understand. Impossible! And I spoke to the chief in Hungarian. "But certainly you must be mistaken. What has my husband to do with the war? He is not in the army; he never has been. He was exempt from military service as soloist to the Tsar. He is the greatest artist of the dance. Surely this must be a mistake? A cultured nation like Hungary cannot treat Nijinsky this way."

But he repeated, "I am sorry; it seems unjust, but war is war. You are Russians. We are at war with your country."

"But do not be silly; there must be a way. The relatives of people in high positions all stay at home, they do not go to the front. So there must be a possibility for me, with relatives near the Emperor at Court, to have my husband released. My uncle is Minister of the Foreign Office."

"Try it; perhaps you will succeed, but I must carry out my instructions."

We were shown into the next office, where three red slips were handed to us. Each had a number on it and bore our names: Vaslav Nijinsky, Romola Nijinsky, Kyra Nijinsky. In French we were told that we were to stay at my mother's house, confined until further orders. We must report every week to the police and avoid passing barracks, fortifications, or any buildings of a military nature. All correspondence must cease, of course. We were supposed to pay all expenses.

Silently we returned home. Vaslav's face was expressionless. I was deeply depressed and revolted. So not only had he to leave the Russian Ballet, now he had lost even his freedom on account of our marriage.

But Vaslav had faith, and turned all his attention to Kyra. The world seemed to cease to exist for him. From morning till late evening he accompanied the baby everywhere, and watched over her sleep. At our arrival we found the rooms in the tower of my mother's villa arranged as a nursery, and here he made his refuge.

I had not given up my attempts, and went to my aunt, Polixena de Pulszky. She was an extremely influential person politically, with a brilliant mind, and had the leading political and artistic *salon* in the country at that time. We thought and plotted together in every way, and she insisted, and succeeded in making my Uncle Garibaldi send us the necessary authorisations for the railways for the Italian frontier. But, on the day we were supposed to leave, my old governess, Miss Hegedus, who had chaperoned me the first time I saw the Ballet, came with the message from my uncle to warn us that it was too late; the authorities had learned of our intention; we would be arrested and punished; it was safer to stay. So we had to abandon all idea of escape.

Every day the papers announced a new victory of the German and Austro-Hungarian Army. It seemed that by Christmas everything would be all over and we would be free. Kyra developed beautifully, and we spent all our time with her or walking in the woods near my mother's house.

All this time Vaslav had great difficulties in practising. He could not obtain permission to exercise in a theatre or school. The rooms in my mother's house were not big enough. During the summer months he exercised on the big terrace, but this was paved with stone and was too hard for dancing.

One day we were again summoned to the police for some kind of registration. A young bureaucrat, feeling extremely important in his new uniform, questioned us. When I gave him my maiden name, he looked up. "What! Romola de Pulszky, the grand-daughter of the great Francis de Pulszky, the first founder of Hungarian democracy, the friend of Kossuth? But you are Hungarian."

"No," I answered, "I am the grand-daughter of Francis de Pulszky, but I am the wife of Nijinsky and a Russian now."

"You should divorce," he said.

"I thought you were here to fill in the slips for the prisoners, not to give advice." And I turned my back on him.

Next day the papers were full of the incident. They called me a "traitor." According to them, I had denied my country and claimed to be Russian. Many of my acquaintances did not greet me any more. One very patriotic young poet, who used to rave about Vaslav, spat on the ground before us as we passed in the street. I could have choked him. But Vaslav impassibly walked on and said, "Don't take it to heart; be sorry for them that they do not understand better. They are not bad, only misled." But I could not take Vaslav's attitude.

My mother was furious. She made me understand how disagreeable, in fact, it was to have Russians in her house; how impossible it was for her, the first actress of Hungary to have a son-in-law who was Russian. It was harmful to her career, as well as to my stepfather's, who was at that time in the Press department of the Prime Minister Count Tisza, and of course anxious to advance.

So intrigues began to make me divorce Vaslav, naturally without success, but the constant nagging was painful. I now knew not only how unwelcome Vaslav was in my mother's house, but that he was despised, and he, with his fine instincts, began to feel it too. We were not allowed to leave the house and more and more we withdrew from everybody into Kyra's room. But soon my mother penetrated even there, and began to give orders concerning the upbringing of the child which were in opposition to Vaslav's ideas and mine. We wanted the child to be at peace, to have meals at regular hours. My mother ordered her to be fed any moment she cried and to have her carried in the nurse's arms day and night. This naturally gave cause for new scenes.

My mother changed her tactics. One day an official of the city came, to whom she had promised that Vaslav would dance for the Hungarian soldiers at a benefit concert. Vaslav refused to do it. "I am a prisoner. I cannot dance for those who are killing my countrymen, even though I consider all mankind my brothers. If I danced for the wounded, it could only be if half the proceeds were given for the Russians." With this the proposition was dropped.

The servants, seeing my mother's attitude, refused to serve us. Soon we had to do most of the things ourselves, but this we did not mind. We received our food very irregularly, sometimes lunch at four or five in the afternoon, and I saw that Vaslav felt faint.

My stepfather never failed to tell us the contents of the bulletins, and with great triumph declared: "To-day we have taken twenty thousand Russians," or "To-day the whole Preobrajensky regiment and seventy thousand men perished in the Lakes of Mazuri." Vaslav became livid and left the house. I went in search of him. He came back after hours of walking in the woods alone. He suffered intensely through the knowledge that thousands of people were daily killing each other, and he could not help, he could not prevent it. He was unable even to exercise his art and to give joy through this. He was beaten in his ideals of humanity, of charity, and of friendship. Then Diaghileff had failed him. Everything sacred seemed to tumble.

Sometimes in the evening we went to my Aunt Poly's house. We had to use the servants' staircase going up to her apartment, to prevent difficulties for her, but, once there, we felt at home. She treated Vaslav as the artist, not the enemy. They all made cigarettes for the Red Cross, and we helped. Their broad-minded intellectual conversation was the only distraction Vaslav had during those long and weary months.

The year 1915 began, and the victories of the Central Powers became rarer. My stepfather had little occasion now to boast, but this did not ease our position. We were completely isolated from the outside world. Vaslav and myself had to suffice for each other. I knew that he was happy in his marriage, and that he never blamed me for anything that had happened to him since. And in this winter, when we were completely left to each other, in spite of the circumstances we were perfectly happy.

Kyra's nurse became gloomier and gloomier. Her *fiancé* was sent to the front. She had expected to marry him and to take her own baby to herself in the spring, but the war frustrated her plans.

As the spring began we prolonged our walks, and through Vaslav I learned to love nature. Each flower, each tree, had a meaning for him; he could find an expression of beauty in them, which he made me understand. Our funds at this time diminished rapidly, our letter of credit on a Paris bank, of course, no longer being honoured. We had to use our ready cash, which at this time was low.

One day the Chief of Police noticed that we arrived rather exhausted when we had to report to him. We told him we had no more money for carfare and were worried about the nurse's wages. He advised us to go to the American Consul, who had taken over the interest of the civil Russian prisoners. Our sole income was an allowance of 30s. a month for the three of us.

Then a sudden stroke of luck happened. My chief occupation was to pack and unpack our trunks. Somehow it seemed to me we would soon be able to leave. In brushing Vaslav's dinner-jacket, I found in the inner pocket several hundred francs in gold. This meant a fortune to us, as we got a high rate of exchange.

During the winter we read together the works of Tolstoi, Chekhov, Pushkin, and the marvellous treasures of the Russian literature unfolded before me. Not only its style, but the deep meaning of its contents, were revealed by Vaslav. How well he could explain in *The Resurrection* the feeling of Prince Nekloudov, the altruistic love of Maslova. And these were Vaslav's people, who felt and thought and loved unselfishly like he did. I understood him. But I could not help feeling, as we read Dostoievsky's *La Maison des Morts*, that I had brought a similar fate on Nijinsky. His days passed in complete isolation from the world and of all artistic manifestation. When I spoke about it, he bravely replied, "Others are dying, suffering far more. I have my art in my soul; nothing and nobody can take it away. Happiness is in us; we take it with us wherever we go."

Naturally, in a way Vaslav was glad of the Russian victories, but we knew that German troops were called to the help of the Austrians. We knew also that, in case Budapest was attacked, German and Austrian officers would be lodged in my mother's house, and how could Vaslav alone, as a prisoner, defend me from the attentions of the officers, which were unavoidable?

Lately Kyra had been very restless. We could not find out why, then suddenly one morning I discovered the reason. The nurse gave her almost no milk. I asked her why. She impertinently declared, "I found out that your child is a Russian, so she had better starve. My *fiancé* is fighting the Russians. I am not going to nourish her any more." I burst out crying. What should I do to find another wet nurse, who would perhaps be bad for the baby? Where, how could I do this? I began to plead with her. Vaslav came in and found out the cause of my sorrow. Quietly he told the nurse to go, and said to me, "Don't worry; I will take care of her."

And he kept his word. He went to the city to a children's physician and returned with him, carrying under his arm a book about the upbringing and care of babies and a sterilising apparatus. With infinite care he sterilised and prepared the bottles, and from that noon on he fed Kyra himself.

Vaslav carved small wooden toys for her and painted them. They were in brilliant colours, but he was always careful to use inoffensive paint; he seemed to think of everything. He repainted the whole nursery and its furniture. Instead of a white hospital room, it became an enchanted habitation of a Russian fairy-tale.

My cousin Lily de Markus, a virtuoso, a pupil of the famous Sauer, played the piano brilliantly. She had a good heart and realised what it must mean to Vaslav to live this life without art. So she offered to play for him every day. And immediately the ideas regarding a new composition took form in his mind. He had for quite a while thought of creating a ballet of the mediæval age. The angularity of the movements and dances of this period lent themselves admirably to express Vaslav's ideas. He danced before me a few parts of his new ballet, and they reminded me of the attitude of statues on the purest Gothic cathedral. Naturally he would have loved to have the music composed for the ballet, but this was impossible at the time. So German music was the kind to be considered, as the Gothic composition of the ballet required it. So my cousin Lily played all the modern Germans. As she played Strauss's tone-poem, *Tyl Eulenspiegel,* Vaslav became enthusiastic. He saw the ballet at once. It was the very thing that he wanted.

Again he wished to use masses, not altogether as in *Sacre,* but in groups and by making twenty people do the same movement as if they were one. Where and when this ballet could be produced was a mystery, but we did not think of it. Vaslav was a changed person. He became mischievous again, and I saw his face light up with joy.

Sometimes he danced for us the gypsy dances of Russia. He would suddenly be transformed into a wild, fierce, savage girl, trembling all over from the tips of his fingers to his toes, shaking his shoulders as if they were independent of the rest of his body. And then he would imitate the different *ballerinas* of the Mariinsky. We often begged him to show us how Kshessinskaya danced. But we loved it most when he showed us how the peasant women flirt whilst dancing. He had an inimitable way of throwing inviting glances, and undulating in such a lascivious manner as to stir up the senses of the spectator almost to frenzy.

For many months I watched him designing and counting, drawing with infinite care; sometimes very late at night, I awoke from my sleep and Vaslav was still bowed over his writing-desk. My mother complained he used too much electricity.

I became interested in this work, which seemed like geometry, like mathematics, and which was neither. Vaslav was pleased by my sudden manifested interest, and explained to me that he was attempting to find a system through which dances and all human movements could be written down. He said that for centuries noted *maîtres de ballet* and dancers had tried to find a solution to this problem, but had never succeeded in a satisfactory way. "Music can be noted; so can words; but unfortunately dancing cannot. And so the most precious compositions get lost and are forgotten."

Also he explained to me that the music and the art of movement were very similar, and obeyed the same laws. The difference was that they came to our mind in different ways, the one orally, the other visually, but in fact their theory of harmony was founded on the same principles. He developed the theory of the dance. Every day, as a test, to see if it would be practical for general use, he taught me the system of notation.

The Russian Army retreated and the war seemed endless. My

mother became more irritable with Vaslav, and for everything that went wrong in or round the house, he was blamed, first secretly, then openly. The automatic boiler of the hot-water system broke. "Mr. Nijinsky must have spoiled it," said the valet. My mother forbade him to take a bath or use hot water.

In the ante-chambers the walls became mouldy; small mushrooms grew there, which ruined the velvet wall-covers and the parquet floor. "Mr. Nijinsky brought the mould in with the child's plaid from the garden and infected the place," they declared.

And then one day my mother's pet cat disappeared. It was a fat, old, ordinary cat. My cousin, who lived at the next villa, was a great hunter; he had excellently trained dogs, and those dogs took a great dislike to my mother's cat and chased her whenever they could. My mother, as she returned from the city, received the news that the cat could not be found. She flew into a rage. "It is Vaslav; he must have killed the cat." Vaslav's eyes closed; his face was immobile. He looked very much like a Tibetan lama. Everybody was in an uproar; they all searched for the cat. "There she is, darling Mima," said the valet, and pointed to a linden-tree, in which the cat blissfully browsed, and my cousin's dog was lying in wait at the bottom of the tree watching her.

But this did not make any difference to my mother. She turned to Vaslav, convulsed with rage, and screamed:

"You hateful man, you damned Russian, you! You are the one who did it. I wish you were out of my house forever, you silly acrobat, you circus dancer!"

Already, at the start of her cursing, Vaslav turned round, and in a second mounted the two storeys up to Kyra's room—to peace, to his child, away out of all this hatred.

But my mother's powerful voice followed him: "You cursed one, you hateful one!"

I could not comprehend my mother. Why was she so unjust? Why did she hate Vaslav so? He was always kind, respectful to her, and came, at first, with the reverence and love of a son.

Even now, when I complained, he said, "It is your mother; you have no right to judge."

But I could not stand this any longer. Next day I went to our Chief of Police and begged him to send us to a concentration camp.

"I will see what can be done," he said. "But Nijinsky is a civil prisoner; he can't be sent to a concentration camp. It is against the international regulations, which cannot be offended.".

What, what to do?

I did a bold thing. I asked Vaslav to let me go to Vienna. I wanted to consult Professor Halban. He was rather anxious on account of the risk I was taking. Should I be discovered, they would arrest and punish me. But I was born a Hungarian. It was my native country and language. There was no reason why they should discover me. Vienna was four hours away by train. I could easily make the journey in a day and return the same night. Vaslav could spend the day at my Aunt Poly's, who did not like my mother and had ceased all relationship with her at the death of my father years ago. So at home they would not notice that I was away.

I carried out my plan successfully. I boarded the train and at noon I arrived in Vienna. So far so good. But the difficult task now began. I had to see my godfather, His Excellency Thallocy, who at that time was one of the five members of the War Council residing at the War Office. How to get in without being noticed? But I had to take the risk. At the entrance, a soldier with bayonet questioned me. I said, "I am the god-daughter of Excellency Thallocy, and have to see him urgently." I was shown into an inner office.

An officer looked me over, and I asked him to take in a note to my godfather asking him to receive me.

Within a few minutes he came out himself. He pulled a serious, strict face, but as soon as we were left alone he said "You Russian subject, I am going to arrest you and send you to gaol. The idea of penetrating to the War Office, when our respective troops are fighting at Przemyšl!" Then he kissed me and patted me on my shoulders and said, "In spite of it all, I like your bravery and your loyalty to your husband. That is how it should be; that is the way Hungarian women have been through all ages.

"No, to send you to the concentration camp is impossible, but we might transfer you to a place in Bohemia, where Russians are liked. These Czechs were always for the Allies. Or we can exchange you to Russia against some other prisoners. I will see what I can do.

"Of course, I know your mother; she is a great woman, lovely; I was very much in love with her in my youth. A very, very great actress, but as a mother-in-law—brrrrrr! I can just imagine. But, you stupid child, can't you understand? Don't you know human psychology? Your mother, the great artist, was chained to Hungary all her life. Her success never passed the frontiers, because she played in Hungarian. Your husband's art is universal. He is known and admired everywhere. Your mother is jealous, perhaps unconsciously. But she could control herself. In fact, I am going to reprimand her personally on my next visit to Budapest. She has no right to mistreat our prisoner, and one of our most precious ones." He smiled mischievously. "You do not know how many crowned heads and representatives of neutral countries have approached us. But as long as he is so valuable to them and to Russia, we are going to ask a great price for him."

And then I learned that they were bargaining with Russia,

through the International Red Cross Offices, for the exchange of Vaslav against five high officers of the Austrian Army—generals, colonels, and a major.

He told me to return to Budapest and wait quietly, and gave me a pass, so that I should not get into trouble on my return journey.

The few hours I still had left I spent at my brother-in-law's. He knew from his own experience my mother's temperament and the family situation, and was very, very sad about our life. Erik Schmedes was a Dane, and through his legation he promised to send news of us to my mother-in-law in St. Petersburg, and try to get some answer. Which promises he kept.

I did not bring any change to our situation, but I brought hope.

Now Kyra began to take her first steps, and Vaslav was enchanted. Also she began to utter *"Tataka,"* which meant, in her special Russian, "Father." Vaslav worshipped her, and Kyra seemed also to reciprocate this feeling; nobody else interested the child except him. So his constant, unfailing care day and night, his patience, were rewarded. Vaslav could play with Kyra for hours. He threw her in the air, to Kyra's delight, rolled with her in the grass, and they pulled the carved coloured duck together.

She used to jump in her bed, arching her body. "You see, she will be a dancer; she is dancing already." But Vaslav's great joy came one morning when Kyra, sitting in his arms, began to move her arms and head in perfect rhythm to the tune of the street-organ. "She is my little Camargo."

The weeks passed, and then a new ray of hope came, in the form of a letter from the Marchioness of Ripon, which was smuggled through by a Spanish friend who came on a special mission to Austria-Hungary.

She wrote with great affection: how she tried to warn us, when she thought there was danger of war, how unhappy she was that her dear Vatza had to go through this trying experience. But she was working for our release; we would be liberated; all her friends were trying to help. She asked news of "my little *ballerina*," as she called Kyra, and told us all about her hospital, and the sadness the war brought to all of us. "Never will I be able to laugh again after seeing all this human misery, and in these hopeless days the memory of your dancing is the only beautiful thing. It was worth while living to have seen it," wrote Lady Ripon.

Vaslav avoided my mother, and they hardly spoke to each other. Now she came with a new proposition. She advised Vaslav to change his citizenship, to become Hungarian, Polish, or anything. But Vaslav refused. "I was born a Russian; I can give thanks to my country, which made me an artist, and I will remain Russian."

One day, when we had to report, we were reproached with teaching Kyra only Russian, and forbidding her to learn Hungarian. But I said, "She is only sixteen months old. Of course she will be learning Russian, but she is too small to speak any language yet." But I wondered who had denounced us.

During this winter my mother was supposed to play the part of Zaza in Victorien Sardou's drama. She came to Vaslav and asked him to show her how to make up for this particular part. Vaslav asked her to describe the character. He then made her up as a very refined woman would look in middle age—still beautiful, but faded. The make-up was extremely suitable and artistic. But my mother thought Vaslav intended to be unkind. "Well, you don't make me look like a young woman," she said. "But you are supposed to be a *demi-mondaine* round the fifties, you told me; that is what I tried to portray," he replied.

This incident again aroused her antagonism, which I hoped had quieted down, but I was mistaken.

My Aunt Poly, to whom I had spoken about the attempt to exchange us for some Austro-Hungarian officers, thought of her own son, who was a physician in the Army and a prisoner now at one of the concentration camps at the Lake Baikal. She decided to see my uncle, Baron Burrian, Minister of Foreign Affairs in Vienna, to obtain his help so that this exchange should be made.

Vaslav must have missed very much the possibility of dancing. Practising alone could not be satisfactory to him. Often he took hold of me and we waltzed together, humming the tunes of the lovely waltz in Tchaikovsky's *Eugène Onegin*. Vaslav did not waltz the same way as we did, but very smoothly and with the correct beating of the three steps, as it was danced in the time of the real Viennese waltz, 1830.

During those long months of our internement, when we were thrown utterly on each other's company, we gained a knowledge of each other's character which under different circumstances would have hardly been possible.

Vaslav inspired and influenced me, in my feelings and outlook on life and art. He opened to me an unlimited vista of humanity, and gave me constantly new ideas from the undrainable richness of his thoughts.

In our great isolation we talked over many subjects. I asked Vaslav about his parents, his childhood, and the years in the Imperial School. He told me all about it—this school where he was so happy. Then he recounted to me those years with Sergei Pavlovitch, their friendship, and the great love he had for him. "I will never regret anything I have done, for I believe that all experience in life, if made with the aim to find the truth, is uplifting. No, I do not regret my relations with Sergei Pavlovitch, even if ethics condemn it." Then he related how, on the boat going to South America, he first felt he was after all mistaken in love, and the overwhelming desire took hold of him to go to Siberia, and to live the life of a preaching monk. But dancing—dancing—to give that up was so difficult. "And then I saw you; in fact, I noticed you on that wintry day in Budapest when you were sitting in your black velvet dress in a corner, watching with such adoration the exercises of the artist at the rehearsal. I saw you worshipped my art. This struck me—'A spoilt girl of Society and she possesses a soul.' Later, when Sergei Pavlovitch told me he intended to take you with the troupe, I advised him to do so. Then I began to watch you, and on the boat the day you spoke to me about my little pillow from my mother—of Wagner and his music—I decided to marry."

"But how dangerous. I might have been a flirt, a coquette, anything; you did not even know my name."

"Yes, I knew everything. I knew, in that first moment, we were meant for each other."

He explained to me, "You are so very young. At present you feel I am the whole world for you. We married; this is a sacred bond, but only if we make it sacred. This is only possible if we are always frank with each other. Every human being has the right over himself at any time. You promised to love me, to be truthful. But how can anybody promise to keep up an emotion? If you meet somebody you love more, you must come and tell me. I will do everything, if the person is worthy, to obtain your happiness. Do not think that you are not free because you married."

Our marriage was so completely happy that I often had a feeling of anxiety that something would happen. Vaslav was a playmate for Kyra, a child when he was with her. For me he was a real companion, a friend, a brother, a husband, a lover. He could understand all my moods, my thoughts and desires, and he took an interest in everything with which I was occupied. I found that no friends of mine could share my feelings as he did. He was able to place himself in the soul of a woman. He treated me with great reverence and natural gaiety. I had unconsciously the feeling that I lived with an extraordinary being, a genius, but he never made this felt. He was the simple and natural young man. One could almost forget that he was Nijinsky. In love as in art, Vaslav was a master.

One late winter evening, when we returned from one of our long walks, my mother, who had an attack of 'flu and was laid up, called me into her room. She spoke on all kinds of indifferent topics. I recounted how we had taken a long walk in the hills, and remarked to my stepfather, "Well, if those poor old wires in the cornfields are the fortifications, Budapest will not resist long."

Next morning, while I was still in bed, a detective came to fetch us. We reported to the police. Vaslav and I were immediately separated at the entrance, led into different rooms, and questioned. For hours I was put under cross-examination; so was Vaslav. I could not make out at what they were driving.

The chief told me. "I understand that for months your husband was working on some kind of a plan. It is a military one. Do you know of it? It must be some code. Our attention was called to it by patriotic people."

"Ridiculous! My husband is working on the system of notation of the human movements. Ever since the time of Louis XIV dancers have been searching for it. It is true that he spends the greater part of his day, till late in the night, on this work. But it has no more to do with war or military schemes than the canals of Mars."

"This matter is very serious," he replied. "There is evidence against you that you try to make a Russian of your daughter. A manuscript was found in Nijinsky's desk which looks like mathematics, but it is not geometry and it is not music, so what can it be?"

"The system of notation of the dance."

"Well, unless Mr. Nijinsky is able to prove this, you will be separated from each other; he will be sent to some fortress and come before a court martial. We are at war."

I began to tremble. I knew that Vaslav was the most pacific creature, that he was the most honest being, that he could never, never do anything of this sort. But everybody seemed to be in an abnormal state of mind; a real war-psychosis was raging.

Experts of music and mathematics were called in, and Vaslav explained to them his system. It took several days of investigation, and then those men congratulated him on his epoch-making creation.

The next time we reported, I insisted on knowing from our chief who had denounced us. "I cannot say; it is an official secret. But it was really a ridiculous thing to do. It also put us in a rather awkward position, but we had to investigate the matter once it was brought to our notice. Of course, we were told Nijinsky was working on a military plan."

"But who—who could have insinuated anything of the sort?"

"Well, well, over-anxious, blinded persons, who are perhaps rather nervous about their own position. Family misunderstandings often cause remarkable events."

I understood he referred to my parents. "Did it come from home? Please, please say."

He bowed his head and said, "Don't ask me, but I wish you could be sent to some other place of internement."

Years later, when the terrible tragedy happened and I came

297

back with my sick husband, I met this chief, and he said, "I wonder if that regrettable incident during the war is not greatly responsible for this horrible drama."

One autumn day a Hungarian theatrical impresario came up to see us, telling us that he had just returned from Switzerland, where he had received word that Diaghileff was trying to communicate with Vaslav. He intended to go with the Ballet to America, and Vaslav must come. To America! It seemed so fantastic, and a message from Diaghileff did not seem genuine to us either.

I received a post-card from my godfather quoting an old proverb: "Now as long as you have hoisted the bell in the church tower, go and ring it." I could not make out what it meant until an order came from the police that as we were to be transferred to Karlsbad, in Bohemia, we should get ready. Never have I packed everything so quickly before in readiness for a departure. We reported to the police. As the prefect bade us farewell, he said, "I do hope we have not been too hard. I tried to do my best. Sometimes we are obliged to carry out instructions which we do not approve ourselves. You have my full sympathy." And then, turning to Vaslav, he said, "You should interrupt your journey in Vienna and see her doctor." He looked me in the eyes and almost suggested, "You feel very sick, don't you?" I replied, "Yes." "All right, I will report this to the authorities." We understood he showed us the way to liberty.

Chapter Fifteen

"LENT"
TO AMERICA

WE ARRIVED in Vienna early in January 1916, without money and still war prisoners—and for how long? But in spite of all this we felt relieved. In Karlsbad, even if we were going to be interned, we would be among Slavs.

At the station, we looked at each other; we had to go to the police, but we must leave Kyra somewhere. She was tired out from the railway trip. So we called on my brother-in-law, Schmedes. He was very popular in Vienna—he was their very own Tristan and Lohengrin—and now he was treated doubly with respect; not only was he "Kammersanger of the Hofoper," but also a neutral subject. He came with us to the police.

"Here, Excellency, I am introducing to you a prisoner, my brother-in-law, Nijinsky."

"I am so pleased, but enchanted. What luck! Would you give me your autograph? Oh, the *Spectre de la Rose*, how divine; and the *Princesse Enchantée*—I really do not know which I prefer. What a joy it has been to see you dance! If only this unfortunate war would be over! What a handicap for art, which can only develop in a monarchy, in peace and prosperity! Oh, I see—your papers. Of course, of course—interned. Well, well, we here in Vienna know how to differentiate, we can make distinction. The

299

law is all right, but we have to know how to apply it; a great
artist is at home everywhere." He was humming to himself the
Gralserzahlung. "By the by, dear Schmedes, do you take the
breath just before *'bin Lohengrin genannt,'* or before *'Mein Vater
Parsifal tragt seine Krone?'* " And he rang one of the numerous
bells on his desk. A very elegant young man appeared in a
cut-away.

"Mr. Nijinsky, allow me to introduce to you my secretary,
Count Ludwig X. Count, we have the honour to have as a guest
in our city the world's greatest dancer; he will remain here some
time, as Madame Nijinsky is not feeling well. You can always let
me know, Mr. Nijinsky, when you want to go to Karlsbad—perhaps next summer; that is the best season there; don't bother to
come here to report, and do go and see the revival (new *einstudier-
ung*) of *Die Meistersinger.* I really think it is an excellent performance. I love your Walter Stolzing, Schmedes.

"Any time you wish to communicate with your family, just
ring up the Count, he will take care of it, we can send the letter
through the International Section of the Red Cross. Sorry to in-
convenience you in this way."

Indeed this was a most unexpected reception. But where and
how were we going to live? At the American Consulate in Budapest, before we left Vienna, we were given some American identification papers, specially issued for Russian prisoners, which
allowed us to travel. The Consul told us that in Austria the Spanish
Embassy looked after the Russian prisoners, so we knew we had
to report there.

Vaslav went up to Mr. Wolff, the proprietor of the Hôtel
Bristol, and asked him if we could have a room for a few days,
and told him that we had no money to pay. Mr. Wolff laughed,

"But Mr. Nijinsky, you honoured my hotel in the past, of course you are welcome. I will give instructions that one of the suites be prepared—a bedroom, a room for the baby, a living-room, and bath. You are to make yourself at home, order anything you wish, stay a year—two—as long as the damn war lasts! You pay me when the war is over."

As we reported next day at the Spanish Embassy, the first secretary of the Ambassador received us, and told us how pleased they were that we arrived in Vienna.

"In fact, you know, we have transmitted several demands to His Majesty the Emperor Francis Joseph for your release. His very Apostolic Majesty, King Alfonso of Spain, intervened just a few days ago on your behalf, after the attempt of the Danish and the *pourparlers* for an exchange from the Russian side failed. Believe me, Mr. Nijinsky, we did our best, but the Austrian conditions were ridiculous. Five high officers of the *Generalstab*, among them General Kuzmanek, the defender of the fallen fortress Przemyšl, for a civil prisoner, were unacceptable. As much as Russia wanted to have you, on military principle, they could not consent.

"His Holiness the Pope asked for your liberation also—you are a Catholic and an artist. Of course, after this, it will be impossible for them to refuse."

Later we found out that the Marchioness of Ripon and the Comtesse de Greffuhle tried every way for our release, and called the attention of Queen Alexandra and the Dowager Empress Maria Feodorovna to Nijinsky's fate.

When Vaslav told him about our financial distress, he laughed. "But we shall give you money, on your letter of credit on Paris, or the amount you wish without it, naturally."

It seemed we were dreaming. Vaslav just caught me as we arrived home, and we waltzed and waltzed until I fell breathlessly into the chair.

M. Gregor, director of the Hofoper, told us we could go any day to the Opera, and gave us a pass.

"Where are you going to practise?"

"At home, in my room," said Vaslav.

"Oh, no, we cannot allow that." Next morning he wrote to us that unfortunately he could not let Vaslav practise, on account of the war, at the Hofoper, but that the stage at the Theatre an der Wien was, at any time during the day, at Vaslav's disposal—the lovely old-fashioned theatre, with an ideal stage for dancing, where once Fanny Elssler celebrated her greatest triumph.

At this time, Vaslav was composing the *Mephisto Valse*. It caught the romantic, the languorous Slavic chord of his soul, and showed how romanticism could be expressed with strength, virility, exuberance. Vaslav took an imaginary episode of Dr. Faust's life: Faust, accompanied by Mephisto, in search of love, enters a roadside tavern, attracted by the sound of music. Dusk is falling. A group of villagers are gambling round a table; the landlord following the game with interest and is flattering an elderly, fat, rich merchant, who is eyeing the greedy landlord's beautiful golden-haired daughter. The village bag-pipers are playing. A servant unceasingly replenishes the foaming tankards.

A young peasant, suitor of the landlord's daughter, clumsily begins to dance with her, but the father stops them at once. Faust and Mephisto enter. The landlord rushes up to the distinguished, richly dressed cavaliers.

Mephisto, with a quick glance, sums everybody up, and takes his stand behind the rich merchant. Immediately the calm and jovial atmosphere changes. They become frantic with desire . . . to win . . . to win. . . .

The proprietor's daughter comes in with drinks, and stands spellbound before Faust. Her suitor has begun to gamble with money lent him by Mephisto. Mephisto suddenly seizes the violin and begins to play. The village men and maidens openly abandon themselves to love-making, the girls no longer repel but seek the lecherous advances of the men, and the landlord's daughter until now resisting, begins to dance for Faust. As the frenzy reaches its climax the singing of a lark is heard in the starlit woods—through the open door. Mephisto, still playing, approaches the door, and pair after pair disappear. Finally, with complete consent, the landlord's daughter throws herself into Faust's arms, and he triumphantly dances with her out into the woods—towards love.

The whole story was told as a choreographic poem, in gestures of the period, which Vaslav translated in a brilliant series of classical dances—as he understood the classical school and could make use of it. It was a living Dürer—full of fire, brilliant, flaming, from the moment Mephisto appeared. The "variation" of the maiden was a sequence of *entre-chats, tours en l'air*, jumps, all toe dancing, but in an exquisitely mediæval way. In spite of its languid romanticism, of its amorous feeling, it was strong and plastic, with clearly defined gestures, and it had the neatness and sparkling of a beautifully cut glittering diamond—and it was in complete harmony with Liszt's music.

Vaslav danced for me the parts of the forty-five dancers in his simple practice costume. He rendered the characters of the old fat landlord, the lecherous rich merchant, the awkward heavy *fiancé*, the servant, Mephisto, Faust, the guests, the girls. I forgot that it was one person dancing and not a whole troupe. And he danced,

303

with infinite lightness and brilliancy, the part of the maiden. Never, never, have I seen among all the great *prima ballerinas* anybody so tender, so maidenly, so light, so harmonious, so perfect in their attitudes, and so matchlessly equal on their toes.

Vaslav just laughed. He thought it was a success if I had so utterly forgotten the absence of the troupe.

He visited the private collections, escorted by friends. The Hofmuseums and the Albertina, were a source of joy to him. So were the concerts at which we assisted, and the performances at the Opera.

My brother-in-law, brought up in the strictest traditions of Bayreuth, where he sang at the festivals—taught by the great Cosima herself—listened to Vaslav's conception of how Tristan, Lohengrin, and Tannhäuser should be acted.

Vaslav played these parts for us, and Erik agreed that they were in the spirit of Wagner. After those discussions, he changed in many ways. His performance gained in beauty and originality, and especially in correctness of style and gesture.

For Vaslav, Wagner was not only a great musician but also a great *maître de ballet.* His operas were full of choreographic composition, as Vaslav pointed out to us. The arrival of the guests at Wartburg, in the second act of *Tannhäuser,* that of the pilgrims in the third, the Gralsritter scene in *Parsifal,* the march of Elsa, before her wedding, from her Kemenate to the Cathedral, are purely choreographic and of great beauty.

Vaslav liked the idea of composing the dances for *Parsifal, Tannhäuser,* and *Die Meistersinger,* and hoped that after the war he would be able to do this for the festival at Bayreuth.

At this time Kokoscha, the Viennese painter, made a drawing of Vaslav. Vaslav often assisted the ballet rehearsals, and when they were practising.

Vaslav was requested by my sister to watch the dancing of the daughter of a friend of hers, Mme L., who was herself interested in art and did a lot for artists. She had put one of her villas at Schonberg's disposal. Her daughter wanted to become a dancer, and we went to see her. Vaslav believed in an early training, not later than twelve or thirteen years if possible—after that age, the muscles, the tendons, are too far developed to get the necessary flexibility. The daughter was sixteen already, and danced, but did not know how. This in itself would not have mattered; all Vaslav was looking for was disposition, but I could see from his face that she did not have any.

Vaslav was gentle and kind-hearted. He always tried to encourage and help, but on the question of dancing he was adamant, was just, but told the truth.

"My advice is: you should not waste your energy, your time, your money on studying, you have no talent whatsoever for the dance." I felt sorry for the girl. She looked crushed and hopeless.

Going home, I reproached Vaslav: "But how could you be so cruel, why did you not leave some hope?"

"Because there isn't any; that girl will never dance, and it would be far more cruel to let her live with an unattainable desire, when she would only waste her life. We must show, for the sake of the art of dancing, that dilettantism is a great danger. Those who love dancing, but have neither the ability nor early nor adequate training, why can they not just learn for themselves enough to appreciate fully the ballets? So many music-loving people play their instruments at home; but why do they show before the public their pitiful performances? I wonder if any audience would stand for a piano recital, full of mistakes or improvisations, glorifying the 'modern school,' saying Beethoven is old-fashioned and impossible. That is what all these so-called 'modern schools' of danc-

305

ing and its representatives are doing to our art, which needs,
more than any other, the public's true understanding. Then began
the fashion so prevalent to-day for any untrained person to set up
as a teacher of dancing."

So many have taken a few lessons of rhythmic gymnastics or
have been on a cruise in the Orient in search of a few native movements, and on the strength of this have declared that the "classic
school" was old-fashioned. "Mushroom dancers" was the term
Vaslav used for them.

Rumour reached us that Richard Strauss had heard we were
interned in Austria-Hungary, and had requested the German Ambassador in Vienna to try to release us.

A few weeks later, when he came to Vienna, we met him.
Vaslav was keen on asking his consent to produce *Tyl Eulenspiegel*
as a ballet. Strauss was overjoyed when he heard that Vaslav had
already adapted it. He whole-heartedly accorded his permission,
and even offered to make changes, if necessary, in the musical
score. But Vaslav replied that he would not want a bar to be
altered, he found the symphony so perfect and so suitable.

Mephisto Valse was ready. Vaslav began to work on an idea he
had had for a long time—to create a Japanese ballet. He was
interested in the Orient and knew all their dances, though how he
did was a mystery to me. He loved Hokusai and the ancient periods
of the Far East. But how different was his idea of all those dances
from the ones we had witnessed in the different recitals and opera
houses! Vaslav's Japanese dances, monumental in the extreme,
were a series of poses, few movements and distorted like a Lao-
coön group; pauses, then a slight inclination of the head, a lower-
ing of the eyelids, an unbelievable turn of the wrist, the fluttering
fingers. The Japan of Nijinsky was that of the Samurai—powerful, grim, tragic, and full of tradition.

Unfortunately this ballet was never completed.

Mme. L. took us to visit Schonberg. It was a wet and dreary afternoon when we went to the villa in Hietzing where he lived. Vaslav felt great sympathy for him, and was interested to hear some of his new compositions. He had heard *Pierrot Lunaire* two years previously, whilst in Berlin, and wondered how Schonberg would develop.

Schonberg and his wife received us very warmly. Schonberg and Vaslav soon forgot our presence and exchanged their ideas.

Schonberg painted at the time "curious and mystic pictures," which certainly had a strange appeal.

A very heated discussion broke out between Schonberg and Vaslav. The first claimed that in music no training is needed, as anybody who has talent could compose or play the piano without certain study. Vaslav tried to apply the question to dancing, and finally they decided they were mistaken and training in both arts was essential.

My godfather told us, at lunch one day, whilst he served us *bortsch* and *koulibiaka* (as good as can be made at St. Petersburg), that we were quite often discussed at the sittings of the *Kreigsuberwachungs-Amt*.

"Then, my dear Vaslav, you seem to be a very rare and precious person to the 'Holy Russian Eumpire,' and to our distinguished enemies the Allies. We have received more requests for your release than history has ever known for a war prisoner. I must say that, in spite of the fact that you are a Moscovite, I like you, and, though I am no judge of dancing, I do feel that you not only dance with your feet but with your brains and soul. This is the reason that I defend your interests at those sittings—not because my very charming and foolish god-child ran after you to the Antipodes and made you marry her. After all, to be a bachelor

307

is the only sensible way of living. Anyhow, to those very eminent colleagues of mine the name of Nijinsky is like the red cloth to a bull. I am sure we will have a new demand for your release at the next sitting, but who will make it? It is a puzzle to me since all the crowned heads and neutrals have already intervened on your behalf!"

His prophecy, in fact, became true, and from a most unexpected corner.

Early one morning the telephone rang. I did not answer it quickly or over-enthusiastically, as I thought it was very stupid of my sister to ring us at such an unearthly hour. But as I listened to the call I became mute and could hardly answer.

"Vaslav, we have to dress and go at once to the American Ambassador, Mr. Painfield; he has some very urgent news for you."

We went; it was the Ambassador who received us. "Dear Mr. Nijinsky, I am so glad your release has been sanctioned. On instructions from home, I have requested your release, and I received, yesterday, a favourable answer from the Foreign Office. You are free, and can at once proceed to America."

The news was so sudden that Vaslav could not answer, neither could I.

To be free at last; it seemed unbelievable to us. Mr. Painfield smiled, but he understood that we were overcome.

He then told us that the Russian Ballet was going to New York, that, in fact, they were already there; that Mr. Otto H. Kahn, the chairman of the board of directors of the Metropolitan Opera House, had requested Mr. Lansing, head of the State Department, to arrange that the Austrians should release Nijinsky. After great difficulties, the Austrians had agreed to lend Nijinsky to the United

States for an indefinite period, with the understanding that he should go "on parole."

First they wanted an official guarantee that Nijinsky would be prevented from returning to Russia, but they had trusted the faith of the Ambassador, who promised that Nijinsky would obey the conditions.

Our great joy was short-lived. The secretary reported to the Ambassador, in our presence, that the Foreign Office had made one reservation: that Kyra and I should be retained as hostages. Mr. Painfield thought this a very strict measure, and Vaslav refused to go to America while that condition remained.

"I will not leave my wife and child, as happy as I would be to go and dance in America. That would be impossible."

Mr. Painfield became very anxious that Vaslav should go, and promised to interview Baron Burrian, the Minister of Foreign Affairs, at once.

My well informed Aunt Poly went to see Baron Burrian, to make a desperate effort that Vaslav should only be exchanged against my cousin Feri; but though she failed, the American Ambassador, being more influential of course, soon advised Vaslav that all three of us were free.

We received instructions to leave next evening for Berne, Switzerland, where a representative of the Metropolitan Opera House would await and conduct us to New York as quickly as possible—Vaslav being anxiously expected there.

Our journey to Berne passed in comparative comfort. We were given a first-class compartment, and the two detectives who accompanied us to the frontier were occupying the next one. The train was full of officers returning to the front. Some windows were broken, and the steam heating left much to be desired. The velvet upholstering of the seats was ragged and stained, as were the carpets. It was evident that the railway carriages had seen better days and were in great need of repair.

On one side of the carriage I made a bed for Kyra, and arranged her as comfortably as I could, and the other side I prepared for Vaslav. Travelling was always hard for him. He could not stand being locked up in such a small place for many hours, and the motion of the train seemed to affect him, also he suffered from violent pains in his head.

I could not sleep; the change from our past mode of living to liberty was so tremendous, and the painful incident, which we had had on the last day, troubled me. My mother came to Vienna, as soon as she heard we were released, with flowers to congratulate us. After all it seemed that we were not entirely forgotten by the world. Nijinsky once more became to my family a celebrity. I could not forgive, and Vaslav, for the first time since I have known him, showed that he could be hard. When my mother approached him, he turned away, and, with a strange look, said to the person standing near him, "Who is this lady who wishes to talk to me?"

Ceaselessly through the night, trains passed us, full of soldiers going to the Italian front. I was sorry for those exhausted, haggard, and pale-looking men who were crowded into the baggage-cars and were taken to death. They looked dirty and hungry, and did not sing now like they did in those August days of 1914 when they were covered with flowers.

At the small mountain station of Feldkirch, the frontier, we descended, and, having reported with our papers at the military office, we were instructed to go to the village and stay there until we were notified that we could leave. I was inquisitive to know how long it would be before we received this notification, on account of the child, but the authorities were unable to enlighten me.

Our luggage was taken from us by the authorities, to be inspected, and we were told that no papers or books, in any form, could be taken with us. The snow-covered Alps glittering in the brilliant sunshine surrounded Feldkirch with its neat Tyrolean houses, nestled among the dark pine trees on the flank of the mountain. We were shown to a hostelry called Posthotel. Our lovely big room was so cosy, with the window where the bright sunshine poured in; the big porcelain stove was fully loaded, and threw out a great heat; the furniture was made of light wood, and the clean beds, with their enormous old-fashioned eider-downs, delightful.

"How much like Russia," exclaimed Vaslav. He became a real child; the whole day he was pulling Kyra on a sleigh, or sliding down with her from the mountain-side—to their mutual joy.

At last we were free again! Once a day we used to go down to the station and inquire when we would be allowed to leave Feldkirch, but always the officer on duty shook his head and said, "I do not know."

We were approached by several people at the inn, who tried to talk about the war. Vaslav told them he could not speak German, and avoided all conversation.

One day, as we were lunching, a middle-aged woman, in deep mourning, was seated at our table. She began to speak to me, but I hardly answered. We seemed to meet her wherever we went, and one evening, while we were having tea, she joined us without invitation, bursting out crying, telling me that her husband was killed in the war, and venomously declared that the Austrians had willingly provoked the war; that it was an injustice to humanity to slaughter people. She tried to see our reaction, by engaging me in conversation, for she knew she could not succeed in interesting Vaslav. He slightly closed his eyes, and I understood he wanted to

311

let me know something was amiss. I excused myself, without answering the widow's question, and said good night.

We found out next day from our chambermaid that the widow was employed by the military authorities; she was an *agent provocateur*.

One day, at noon, one of the detectives burst into the room: "Within fifteen minutes you have to be at the station!" I threw everything into the suit-cases. Vaslav put Kyra on the sleigh, and pulled her, galloping, to the station. Upon arrival, we were shown into different rooms; Kyra and myself were completely undressed, and our skin tested to see if there was any secret writing on it. I had to undergo a medical examination to prove that nothing was hidden on me. I was livid with rage, but did not dare to say anything. Finally we were put on the train.

I cannot describe the emotion we felt as we passed the little bridge dividing the Austrian Empire from Switzerland—and freedom.

Our stay in Switzerland was short, but full of excitement.

In Berne, where we were received by the Russian Legation our hotel windows faced the Eiger, the Monch, the Jungfrau, the glorious panorama of the Berner Oberland. It appeared to us like heaven; wanting to fête it, we ordered a big lunch. Cream, butter, chocolate, sugar, all in profusion, we did not dare to touch. It first seemed unreal—then we fell on it. Vaslav stopped us very wisely; even so, Kyra and myself were upset for days by these unusual delicacies. Next morning, the Russian Minister, Baccharat, presented us with a diplomatic passport, according to instructions received from St. Petersburg. It was a very imposing-looking document, with big seals and a coat of arms, which said, in French and in Russian: *"Au nom de Sa Majesté Nicolas II, Empereur et Autocrate de tout les Russes, je vous prie de laisser passer, accorder protection et tous les facilités à mon sujet Vaslav Fomitch Nijinsky, sa femme, et son enfant."*

In the evening there was a dinner in our honour at the Legation. Already, when we had visited the Legation in the morning, several members of the Embassy had been introduced to us, among them General X, the military attaché. Everybody received me with every kindness, and treated me as their countrywoman. Not for a second could I feel that they considered me an enemy; I was the wife of Nijinsky.

Vaslav said to me, "Do not speak of our past experiences, and of what is going on in Austria-Hungary; we must be fair to everyone."

I could not forget the way some people treated him in Budapest; I could not forget those past hopeless months, the unjust accusations against Vaslav.

At dinner the military attaché was seated next to me. He very cleverly turned the conversation on conditions in Hungary, the food, the clothing, what the people said and thought, and the journey near the Italian front. I was tempted almost to tell the truth; after all I had not promised not to do so, and they certainly had made Vaslav suffer; but again Vaslav imperceptibly closed his eyes. I bowed my head, and replied, "I am sorry, we were so isolated I do not know anything," and thought of the piece of uneatable bread, hard as stone, I still had in my suit-case. The attaché would have loved to see it, and to be able to judge the food conditions in Austria-Hungary, but I obeyed Vaslav, who was always just and correct, even to his enemies.

Here for the first time we heard what was going on in the world and in Russia. Vaslav became pensive and said that this unfortunate war in which so many millions were losing their lives was the beginning of a new phase of social order. They would all

313

lose, victorious and vanquished. Human nature was alone to blame for the war. Never would we have peace unless it was understood that we are all equal, all entitled to live under human conditions, all here to help to better mankind. The system itself should not matter so much as the aim: Love, Kindness, Charity and Understanding. Nobody should know need. This war would not end at the cessation of hostilities.

I listened intently, to Vaslav's prophetic words.

Two days later, in Lausanne, we met Mr. Russell, the representative of the Metropolitan Opera House. He came to escort us to New York. We were a little surprised, as Vaslav had not received any direct invitation from America, and we did not completely understand all that was going on, but Mr. Russell explained.

The Metropolitan Opera House wished to present the Russian Ballet to the American public in its original splendour. Diaghileff signed a contract, which, financially, was extremely satisfactory, and the Opera House requested him to bring the original Ballet, with all its stars, Karsavina, Nijinsky, Fokine, and Bolm, to the States. When Diaghileff signed the contract, he knew that if he could succeed to reassemble the troupe, whose members were largely dispersed in the Allied countries, the stars, with the exception of Bolm, he would not be able to bring along. He trusted that, once in New York, the management of the Metropolitan Opera House would accept whomever he brought over.

As Diaghileff knew, Fokine was in military service in Russia, Karsavina was expecting a baby, and Vaslav was a prisoner of war. He went to New York, and simply told the Metropolitan that he was sorry, but this was *force majeure* and he could not help it. The Metropolitan was naturally surprised, and explained to Diaghileff that it was impossible to perform under the conditions;

they had promised the American public the original cast, and it was impossible to cheat them.

Diaghileff told his intimate friends that, after all, he had come to America to make money, and even if the performance was not as perfect as that rendered in London and Paris it would be still far better than anything ever seen in America. This indeed, coming from Diaghileff, was an amazing statement.

Vaslav told Russell that in the ordinary course he did not think he would have been able to dance in the Russian Ballet after all that had happened between them before the declaration of the war, but, as long as the United States had worked for his liberation, he was at their disposal, and was ready to dance before the American public.

In Lausanne, we received word from Sir George Lewis that the lawsuit he had opened against the Russian Ballet to recover the half-million gold francs, which the Ballet owed to Vaslav as unpaid salary, had been won in the English courts, but, as Diaghileff was not a resident in any country, there would probably be great difficulty in collecting it.

At this time, Stravinsky lived at Morges, near the Lac Leman, with his family—a short distance from Lausanne. As soon as he heard of our arrival, he came over and took possession of Vaslav. I only knew him by sight—now I made his acquaintance. He was dressed like a dandy, with the most indescribable taste. He thought it was very chic, and there was something touching in his *naïveté* and conceit. He seemed extremely sure of himself, and was fully convinced of his genius, which he undoubtedly had, but the way he spoke of it seemed rather childish, and, at the same time, charming. One would have thought a man as great as he would have been more dignified. When he came to see Vaslav he was extremely courteous to me. He spoke to Vaslav for hours of his plans, his

315

compositions, the ideas of Diaghileff, his injustices; the torrent of his words never seemed to stop. He tried to assure himself he was independent of him: "I am a composer, and sooner or later people will realise the value of my music. Of course, Sergei Pavlovitch is a great help, and especially now that the war is on. In Russia, anyhow, it is impossible to be played, when one has modern ideas. He can't crush me. His enmity against you I fully disapprove, but we must be just; he suffered terribly when he heard that you had married—he never imagined this possible. He received a cable, I understand, from Vassily Ivanovitch, at the time you had your wedding ceremony. Sergei Pavlovitch received it in London at the Savoy Hotel, where he was staying at the time, and we learned that he became livid and fainted. It must have been terribly hard on him. We could all understand this, but what was one to do? It was one of these insoluble conflicts. All these personal feelings have no right to hinder the development of art." After all, Nijinsky, Stravinsky represented the modern art in Russia. Diaghileff was an equally important factor in a different way. Why should small matters like money and love-affairs stand in the way? I felt so crushed. What did I have to do among those men—those gifted initiates of God? After all, Stravinsky, Vaslav were young and we were all full of hopes.

Stravinsky immediately made friends with Kyra. He was a father, and rather an expert on handling children. We went around Lausanne to the different cafés with Stravinsky as our guide. Vaslav was like a boy of seven; at last he was with a friend, a fellow artist, somebody to whom he could speak the same language, somebody who understood him fully and completely.

Stravinsky asked us to come and see him at his home at Morges. We went to his house, which was near the lake and faced the Mont Blanc, but in spite of this it was Russia. The arrangement of the rooms, the furniture—a simply furnished villa, but somehow Stravinsky and his wife had transformed it into a place near Moscva; the walls were hung with drawings by his eldest son, who had already proved himself a possessor of talent. The wife was a real Russian woman, a devoted wife and mother; in her great simplicity there was the strength of one who devoted herself— her life and personality—to the genius of another. She was the ideal wife for a great artist.

We enjoyed the home life, and the peaceful atmosphere of the Stravinsky family.

Madame Stravinsky was a real artist in handicraft. She embroidered, knitted, and painted beautifully. I always tried to please Vaslav by emulating these Russian women, but with little success.

Igor began to tell us about the new quintet he was composing for wind instruments only, and also of *Mavra* and the contemplated ballet *Noces*.

A very heated discussion developed between him and Vaslav. Stravinsky was bitterly attacking Beethoven, Bach, and all those composers who some years before he so respected and now were just "the Boches." It seemed almost incredible. The Russian School, ever since the "big five," declared war on the German School of music and its traditions. Since Moussorgsky, they had wanted to affirm their native conception, and had allowed themselves to be influenced by the French point of view.

It seemed terrible that Stravinsky should let himself be blinded by the fact that Russia was at war with Germany—that the war should make any difference to his opinion. I was sure he could not feel as he spoke, deep down in his heart. It was—it must have been—just a protest. Vaslav could perhaps understand him when he raged against Richard Strauss and Wagner, but Bach—to drag him off his pedestal was too much.

317

"Why should we take any regards towards those Boches, when my own publishers in Germany are not publishing me at present? God knows if they will go on distributing the compositions of Tchaikovsky and Rubinstein."

"Of course, I do not agree with you concerning *Faune*, the music is spiral and the choreography is angular."

"You are right—absolutely—but Sergei Pavlovitch and I could not find anything else at the moment," replied Vaslav. "It is inartistic from the musical point of view, as much as I admire *Faune*, which in itself is a masterpiece."

One evening he came to us in a frightful temper. This time, Diaghileff had played him a really dirty trick. It was arranged that as soon as Sergei Pavlovitch arrived in New York, he should arrange that an official invitation should be extended to Stravinsky, who was to go and conduct his own ballets at the Metropolitan. This would be an appropriate occasion to present himself to the American public. But, as soon as in New York, Sergei Pavlovitch forgot his promise. Naturally Stravinsky was hurt at this lack of attention. He insisted that if Vaslav was a real friend, he would make it a condition to go to America only if Stravinsky was asked also. I thought this was rather stretching the bounds of friendship. Stravinsky talked, raged, and cried; he paced up and down the room cursing Diaghileff.

"He thinks he is the Russian Ballet himself. Our success went to his head. What would he be without us, without Bakst, Benois, you and myself? Vaslav, I count upon you." The two departed to the post office, filled with the decision to counteract this new outrage. Luckily they could not write in English, and I was summoned to help them out; the rather violently worded cable to Otto H. Kahn I was able to translate into a politely worded request.

The hoped-for invitation for Stravinsky did not arrive, and we had to leave for Paris.

As we pulled in at the station of Pontarlier, Russell asked me not to say that I was Hungarian born. I had the Russian diplomatic passport, which did not show my original nationality—the Russians had given this, as a courtesy to Vaslav.

Russell and I passed a most disagreeable quarter of an hour. Vaslav was not aware of this; an official interpreter was present, a Frenchman, who spoke fluent Russian, but he was so busy talking to Vaslav, and so interested to see somebody who had escaped the Austrians, that he did not pay any attention to me.

Russell gave the necessary explanations, after which we were shown into a wooden waiting-room. On the French side, near a small iron stove, were soldiers, covered with big shawls, trying to keep warm. They gave us the best seats and covers for Kyra and myself. As soon as they learned we were released prisoners of war, they began to serve us with boiling red wine, which they prepared on their stove, and which went down excellently in the bitter cold February night.

When in Paris at last, we could stay only one day, as our boat was due to leave next evening from Bordeaux. The Préfet de Police had to countersign our French visa. Everything had been attended to. The Comtesse de Greffuhle very kindly made all necessary arrangements in advance, so that after the official visit we were able to make a tour of the leading dressmakers and millinery establishments.

Nobody would have recognised us twenty-four hours later as we went to the Quai d'Orsay to catch the train. We were elegantly dressed, and followed by sixteen trunks, loaded with flowers, and accompanied by our maid and nurse and escort, Mr. Russell. Many old friends and admirers of Vaslav turned out to say good-bye to us.

On the train, we met the future wife of Bolm—a charming woman whom I had met several years before in Vienna. She was to join Bolm in America. Bolm had cabled to us, and we had promised to bring her safely over.

In the luxurious train, we had to pull down the curtains to ward off the spying eyes of the German aviators. All trains leaving the capital had to obey this regulation; it gave us a rather creepy feeling.

On reaching Bordeaux, we boarded the *Rochambeau*, a French liner, which even at that time, well deserved overhauling. Our crossing lasted almost two weeks, and was very stormy the whole time. Vaslav was constantly with the doctor of the steamer, Louis Moret, who was the celebrated etcher, and, on account of the war, was in the service of the shipping line.

They discussed, at length, Vaslav's theory of notation, and he corrected the few anatomical errors that existed. We both wondered what awaited us in that distant land. Would it bring at last, peace and understanding with Diaghileff? Would it mean artistic and personal liberty for Vaslav?

One morning, while walking on the deck, we saw the first sea-gulls circling over the mast, and we were told we had passed the nearest point to the American mainland, that of the Nantucket Lightship.

Chapter Sixteen

THE
NEW YORK SEASON

GREAT excitement reigned over the whole boat as we steamed slowly towards "quarantine." Some magic place, it seemed to us, as everybody on board for the last twenty-four hours spoke of it with awe. The captain, proud to have brought us safely all over the Atlantic to American waters, gave his last orders on the bridge. The few Americans on board had proudly told us about all the marvels we might expect; that immense fortunes could be made overnight in the land of unlimited possibilities, where everybody had liberty and could make a living if they only wanted to work, where no class distinctions hampered advancement, where idealism and humanitarianism were still guiding forces.

Nervously they rushed from one side of the boat to the other to get the first glimpse of the pilot ship.

A small boat appeared and accosted us, and the pilot came on board. A few minutes later a larger steam launch came alongside. Officials in uniform boarded, the first being the doctor, who immediately was taken by the arm by Dr. Louis Moret and they disappeared behind an immense sheaf of papers. He was followed by rather stout-looking officials, the immigration officials, who had a very serene look. Right after them came an agitated, gesticulating group of men carrying cameras. Mr. Russell hurriedly pulled

321

Vaslav into his cabin. "Those are the reporters and camera-men. Wait here until I take you along to the immigration authorities first; we can see them later."

In a very short time they had searched through the whole boat, from the bridge to the hold, and had found out everything that had happened since we had left the French shores. I have never seen such wizardry as the work of those reporters. Vaslav was discovered within a second, in spite of Russell's scheming. And they made friends then and there. Vaslav liked their natural good-humour and *naïveté*. They were here to report about him; they were all earning a living; each one wanted something exclusive—and Vaslav tried to satisfy them. They patted his shoulders, grasped Kyra, spoke a few words in Russian to her, got hold of Vaslav's legs to feel his muscles, and chewed gum. Vaslav became extremely interested in this, and one of them right away volunteered to show him how to do it. Then they took us all up to the upper deck and photographed us from every angle. Vaslav only smiled and said a few words. Russell looked crushed under the torrent of questions he tried to answer. "Mr. Nijinsky, what do you think about the war, and will it last long?" "Who is greater, Karsavina or Pavlova?" "Have you heard about Rasputin?" "Is he really the power behind the throne?" "How many teeth has little Kyra?" "How do you spell it?" "Do you prefer American women to French?" "Your opinion about the submarine warfare?" "Is Picasso a cubist or futurist?" "What is your favourite sport, and rôle?"—and so on, until the chief steward came up to tell us that the immigration officers were ready for us.

Once past the authorities, the reporters took hold of us again, but this time to reward us for our docile submission to their former interviews, and we were taken to the upper deck to witness

one of the most enchanting and stupendous sights of the world—
the skyline of New York.

Vaslav lost his head completely as, from the heavy yellow,
grey mist, suddenly slender, tall buildings rose to the sky like a
city of minarets and campaniles.

To the great pleasure of the reporters, Vaslav in his enthusiasm
began to jump, and we had to laugh as those newspapermen called
out, "Hallo, Mr. Nijinsky, you just stay here. Do not fly away, for
God's sake."

As we walked down the gang-plank we saw a group waiting for
us with flowers: the representatives of the Metropolitan, some
former school-friends of mine, members of the Russian Ballet, and,
in the front, Diaghileff. I walked down first, and he bowed very
low and, kissing my hand, offered me a beautiful bouquet of
American Beauties. Vaslav, carrying Kyra, followed me closely.
Sergei Pavlovitch kissed him on both cheeks, according to the
Russian custom, and Vaslav, with a quick gesture, placed Kyra
in his arms. He looked embarrassed, and handed the child to the
next person standing near to him. Drobetsky was smiling like the
full moon. Massine was introduced, then Sergei Pavlovitch walked
away with Vaslav, and I prayed that this might prove a real pact
of friendship.

Vaslav seemed to like the stimulating rush of New York and
the quickness of the elevators, especially those called "express."
I think, if he had had time, he would have ridden in them the
whole day long. He immediately saw how much easier and more
practical the arrangements were here than in Europe.

As soon as we entered our apartment the telephone bell rang
uninterruptedly. Maria Stepanovna arrived for fittings—ballet-
shoes were brought—photographers came—flowers in profusion

arrived from well-known people, then unknown to us. Then the secretary of Mr. Otto H. Kahn came to take us to his office.

After polite phrases were exchanged, Mr. Kahn recommended the sights we must see. Vaslav thanked him for the American intervention on our behalf. I thought the moment had come for me to explain the situation: that Vaslav would readily dance at the Opera, but not with Diaghileff, as long as he did not pay the amount he owed Vaslav for his past salary. And I explained that Sir George Lewis was unable to collect the money, as Diaghileff always very cleverly evaded payment. Kahn, being a business man, was understanding, and asked me to send him over the judgment, so that they could see what could be arranged, and also said that they were willing to make a private contract with Vaslav.

We tried to forget the disagreeable fact that Diaghileff owed Vaslav half a million francs, for which we would be obliged to fight. Vaslav would have preferred to drop the matter altogether, but, thinking of his family, he felt he could not do it, and left the whole case in my hands. I could not deal with the situation alone. Years before I had met a young girl, Madeleine, in Karlsbad, and we had become very friendly. She welcomed me now at the docks, and said her uncle's office would take care of our legal matters. He was one of the most eminent lawyers of the United States, and had a charming wife with whom I used to go to Bayreuth as a girl, Mrs. Minnie Untermeyer. Madeline took us down to the office in the Equitable building, which was quite an experience for Vaslav: a subway station in the building, hairdresser, soda fountain, drug store, where we could eat. With Madeline he went all over the building, whilst her brother, Mr. Untermeyer's young nephew, Laurence Steinhardt, and myself, discussed the matter.

Laurence was to represent Vaslav in business. This was the first important case which was entrusted to him by his uncle's office. He was a very agreeable, good-looking young man, with a brilliant mind, and was extremely quick to grasp a difficult situation. In a short time he was quite at home in the complicated mediæval intrigues of the Russian Ballet, and within three days he settled the case in which many eminent lawyers in Europe had failed during three years. The fight was not easy, as Diaghileff, King's Bench Division's judgment or not, did not want to recognise that he was indebted, and, when he finally did, he refused to pay.

Vaslav was ready to dance for nothing for the New York public. The Metropolitan was ready to boycott him if he did. Some kind of black-listing and theatrical trust arrangement was explained to us—that if Vaslav did not dance at the Opera, he would be forbidden to appear anywhere in America. After three days, during which we had ample time to visit all the marvels of New York, Steinhardt arrived with a contract with the Metropolitan for eleven performances, and the arrangement that every week Diaghileff had to pay a part of his debt to Vaslav through the Metropolitan, from the amount he was supposed to receive after the troupe's expenses and salaries had been paid.

Vaslav's first impression and sympathy for America strengthened with every day. He always believed in youth, and here, in this country, youth was given the opportunity which it lacked in Europe. "Here one need not be a long-bearded professor to be in an important position and to achieve something," remarked Vaslav.

The Russian Ballet arrived in January and had performed at the Century Theatre, leased by the Metropolitan for this purpose, as in their own building the regular opera company was performing its annual season. The arrival of the Ballet was greatly heralded. It was not such a triumphal success as in Europe because Diaghileff failed to bring the stars. Now the opera season was at an end, and the Ballet was to perform at the Opera House itself for three weeks. The Director of the Opera, Mr. Gatti-Casazza, and his nearest associates were displeased with Mr. Kahn's newest importation, the Russian Ballet.

The golden days of the Metropolitan when Caruso, Tetrazzini, Reské sang were followed by a very important phase of German influence under the dictatorship of Conried, who introduced German music and world-famous German singers to the States. Then Gatti was engaged, and everything became Italian. He reigned over the Metropolitan for years without any interference, and, thanks to the glorious voice of Caruso, who made every season a success, he could get away with mediocre performances. Gatti settled down for a lifetime, and the arrival of the Russian Ballet meant new influence—Russian operas, singers, and the much-feared Diaghileff. The same dreaded idea came to their minds as to Teliakovsky's; would not Diaghileff, with his great knowledge and culture, make a very suitable director for the Metropolitan?

So the Italian clique got busy to prevent this, and the first step was to see that the Ballet should not become an undisputed success.

Vaslav did not have the attitude towards the public in general that many other European artists had: "Anyhow, they will not know the difference." "On the contrary," he said, "maybe this public has not yet the artistic understanding and clear perception that ours has after centuries of long training."

We lived at Claridge's, where, thanks to Laurence and Madeleine Steinhardt, everything was arranged for us in a perfect way. She looked after Kyra and the nurse, and helped me to sort out the numerous invitations to open exhibitions, charity bazaars, receptions, meals, football and boxing matches, church meetings, and heaven knows what else. Thanks to their help, we accepted the right things; and I appeared in Vaslav's place when it was necessary, and the reporters received ready typewritten interviews. Everything was American and businesslike.

Rehearsals began, and the company behaved very politely to Vaslav; also great courtesy was shown to me, more even than in the old days. Diaghileff must have given his orders. Bolm arrived, and we were truly delighted to have him with us. He was one of the few who kept aloof from petty intrigue and who regretted Diaghileff's attitude towards Vaslav, just as he had regretted Fokine's leaving previously. Bolm was ever a good friend and a loyal colleague.

Vaslav's American début took place at the Metropolitan Opera House at a matinée on the 12th of April. The Diamond Horseshoe was present in full force, and the audience was as brilliant as in the great Paris galas. The programme consisted of *Prince Igor, Spectre de la Rose, Scheherazade* and *Petrouchka.* When Vaslav made his *entrée* in *Spectre,* the entire public rose and for a second he was embarrassed by this Royal reception, but they had reserved a still further surprise in the form of a shower of American Beauty rose-petals, and in a few seconds the whole stage was inches deep in scented leaves. Vaslav, standing in the midst of them, seemed to be the very spirit of the rose.

A few days after our arrival Diaghileff invited us very formally to lunch at Sherry's. He was alone, Massine having been left at the Ritz, where they were staying. Over our first cocktails he adopted a very *mondain* tone, but soon he dropped into Russian, and I could see that he was reproaching Vaslav and that his anger was rising. Vaslav answered him calmly, and turned the conversation into French: "Seroja, all matters of business are attended to by my wife, and must be discussed with her. I now have a family to support, but I am willing to do now, as in the past, my utmost for the Russian Ballet. I am the same; I have not changed

327

towards you. I am grateful for our past friendship, and it only depends upon you for us to be united again in our common aim. My wife is a part of me, and she understands this, and wants, as much as I do, to further the cause of the Russian Ballet. Please, please understand me."

But Sergei Pavlovitch was beyond forgiveness. I could see that he still loved Vaslav and deeply resented my existence. He began to reproach him for the lawsuit. "We never had a contract; there was never any question of money between us. What has happened to you, Vaslav?"

"But, Sergei Pavlovitch, you take money from the theatres, and make them pay in advance too. Be just," I told him.

"No, it will become impossible for me to run the Russian Ballet. Fokina wants to manage Fokine and dance all the leading rôles. You, madame, are mercenary. How do you expect the Russian Ballet to exist under such conditions?"

Then Vaslav began to speak to him about his new compositions, *Tyl* and *Mephisto*, but Diaghileff showed no interest. "It can't be worth much if it's German music." "But it's Richard Strauss, whose music you yourself produced a year and a half ago," I ventured. "Well, times have changed; the war is on and in any case Strauss, *c'est du cabotinage.*"

During the three weeks of the season, when I had to represent Vaslav at various functions we could not refuse, my time was one mad rush. There were not only the endless social obligations, but Kyra's daily routine, and it was essential always to be ready for some new complication with Sergei Pavlovitch, who worked with subtle determination on his scheme "to ruin Nijinsky." Every day some fresh surprise awaited us. First he circulated the rumour that Vaslav was a deserter. It so happened one evening that the

Russian Ambassador, Bakhmetev, was in my box, and, as Diaghileff came up to greet him, I at once brought up the subject.
"Excellency, I don't know if you are aware that Vaslav, through
our lawyer, has made inquiries about his present military position,
and that he has decided to return to Russia at once unless he is
fully authorised to stay here, as we understand that Sergei Pavlovitch says that things are not in order." Diaghileff excused himself
and pleaded a misunderstanding, but the Ambassador made it
clear that Vaslav was released on parole and "lent to the United
States." Mr. Kahn joined us and tried to quiet me, then Diaghileff said, "I give you my word of honour that it is all right."
"That does not suffice, Sergei Pavlovitch." "But my word will, I
hope," said Kahn. My affirmative reply made Diaghileff pale with
anger, but the episode was closed.

Diaghileff's next move was to spread the rumours that Vaslav
had gained in weight, that he had the manners of a *prima donna*,
that he was the Caruso of the Dance, old-fashioned. This hurt Vaslav, all the more as it came from Diaghileff.

At that time in Venice a great flood had taken place, rendering
many homeless, and it was decided by the members of society,
who knew and loved the Lido, to organise a benefit performance
of *tableaux vivants* after Italian Masters. Mrs. William K. Vanderbilt, Sr., a gracious, regal woman, who by her manner and
understanding reminded us of Lady Ripon, lent her house for the
occasion. I did not understand at the time that this exclusive mansion, usually closed to all save the four hundred, was on this
occasion open to all those who would pay two hundred and fifty
dollars or more for charity. Diaghileff passed me, and as usual
complimented me on my dress, a *chef d'œuvre* by Callot Sœurs;
but he was not fêted, and seemed bored. When Vaslav came to

change from his chosen costume, a Gondolier of Carpaccio, it was discovered that most of his underwear had disappeared, taken by some of the Society women as souvenirs!

When we arrived in New York we heard that the *Faune* was being danced in a very changed manner. Massine excused himself by saying that it was taught to him that way, and that it was not possible to remember it movement by movement. Vaslav offered to rehearse it, but Sergei Pavlovitch would not hear of it, so that finally Vaslav said that he preferred that under the circumstances it should not be produced at all. Diaghileff made a scene, but I reminded him that, as he did not own the rights of this ballet, the least he could do was to respect the author's wishes. All the time Vaslav still hoped that Diaghileff would change and that they could be friends once again. It could not be said, now almost three years after Vaslav's marriage, that Diaghileff was still reacting from shock and anger, yet his hatred was ferocious and his pursuit of Vaslav relentless.

One afternoon I noticed smoke coming out of the closet in our bedroom. Vaslav promptly gave the alarm, quietly took Kyra in his arms and made for the fire-escape, taking me by the hand. I hesitated, thinking that I might save the money, jewels, furs, and passports. Vaslav only laughed and pulled me away. "Leave those material things. You give them far more importance than they really have." Luckily it proved to be nothing. We were not so fortunate on a second occasion. On our return from the theatre one night, Vaslav noticed that Kyra was restless, and that her hands were bandaged. The nurse had to confess that she had spilled boiling soup on the child's hands. She was very badly hurt, and, though we summoned a doctor there and then, could only get real relief the next day when Miss Cottenet took us to Dr. Robert Abbé, the famous surgeon, who attended her for three months, and who became our very dear friend.

On his free evenings Vaslav loved to walk up and down Broadway. The brilliant lights, the stream of traffic, and the sky-signs interested him. He never tired of watching the procession of "types." The "movies," too, were always a great attraction for him, and he had implicit faith in their future. He believed that in time it would be possible to photograph dancing; but he also believed that special dances must be composed for motion-pictures. He said that even the acting must differ from that of the theatre. He and Diaghileff had often discussed the possibilities of motion-pictures, which Vaslav claimed as the future form of entertainment, which could eventually be developed into a fine art.

Sergei Pavlovitch saw in them merely a technical invention that was a cheap form of entertainment, and always refused to have the Ballet filmed. He was also upset that gramophone records had been made of some of the ballet music. All mechanical invention was distasteful to him. Once we went with friends to the Ziegfeld roof-garden. The programme was excellent; the girls beautiful and well disciplined. The noise of the new form of music was infernal, but Vaslav loved jazz. Ever since he had heard it for the first time in a night-club he realised that it was typical of our time, and would influence the future of music. He loved the rhythm, the saxophone and brass combined with the percussion, so unusual at the time.

We met the so-called Stanislavsky of America, David Belasco, who called Vaslav *l'homme oiseau*, and his son-in-law, Morris Gest, the impresario. Gest undoubtedly knew the ways of American production; he was very enthusiastic, but artistically left much to be desired. He came with the most incredible propositions, that

331

Vaslav should dance *Spectre* sixteen times a week—whether in a booth or a circus I cannot remember.

The Metropolitan was contemplating a new season of Russian Ballet for the following year. Mr. Kahn asked us to come and see him about it. He explained that he would like to arrange a coast-to-coast tour, and that even if a deficit were involved he did not mind, as he wished to educate the American public. He realised how disturbing was Diaghileff's presence, and asked Vaslav to become artistic director and to supervise the entire tour. The proposition surprised Vaslav, who did not wish to offend Diaghileff, who was anxious for a Metropolitan contract, vital to the very existence of the Russian Ballet. It was only when Kahn declared that the return of Diaghileff was not to be considered that Vaslav agreed. In fact, the Metropolitan rented the Russian Ballet from Diaghileff under the specific clause that during this time he was not to return to the United States. They hoped that in this way peace would reign on the tour, but how little they knew Diaghileff, and his ability to make his presence felt even at a distance.

As the heat-wave began in New York we moved up to the Majestic Hotel, on Caruso's advice. He had already initiated us into several of the mysteries of American life. Week-ends we spent with friends at Long Island, in houses whose luxury could only compete with Grand Ducal palaces. Vaslav loved especially the bathrooms attached to each bedroom, with their towels and bath-mats in the same vivid colours as the salts and scents. *"Très ballet russe!"*

A friend, M. Pali Strauss, took us one day to the Biltmore to see Maurice and Florence Walton. As soon as Maurice heard Vaslav had arrived he had a spot-light thrown on our table, and made a little speech, while Vaslav hid himself behind the table-cloth.

Strauss gave a luncheon in his apartment at Sherry's in honour of Duncan and Vaslav. The Kreislers were present, and the art critics of New York. During lunch, Duncan said to Vaslav, "You remember, Nijinsky, years ago in Venice I proposed to you that we should have a child together. What a dancer we could have created! The idea did not seem to appeal to you then; I see you are changed now; you are less intolerant towards us women." A frozen, embarrassed silence followed her words. Vaslav smilingly replied to her challenge: "I did not change. I love everybody, as Christ did." Later Duncan wanted to dance with Vaslav, but he was against improvisation and only accompanied her with a few gestures.

One Sunday, on one of our various excursions, dining at a little country inn where coloured people served, one of the waiters danced a cake-walk for us. He danced it wonderfully, and proudly declared that he could dance *Spectre* like the great Nijinsky. He was amazingly light and graceful. He was as pleased as a child when he heard that Vaslav was "the great Nijinsky."

The difficulties of the coming season were beginning. It was agreed that two novelties should be given, and *Tyl* and the *Mephisto Valse* were chosen. The Metropolitan wanted a star as *prima ballerina,* and representatives were sent to St. Petersburg, but it was doubtful who could come. We were in constant touch by cable with Benois and Soudeikine, as Vaslav wished for one of them to design the scenery, but neither would come on account of the war. Finally, Mr. Cottenet, a director of the Metropolitan and a patron of artists, came to Vaslav's rescue, taking him to Greenwich Village to see a young American painter, "Bobby" Jones, who might be able to undertake the work. He was a tall, shy man, but he inspired confidence in Vaslav, who agreed to give him a trial. He explained to Jones his ideas for choreography and design, and made him familiarise himself with the music.

By way of relaxation, Vaslav decided to buy a motor-car, and our choice fell on a Peerless. He learned to drive and in the mornings used to take Kyra out. At the time a terrible epidemic of infantile paralysis broke out, and our one idea was to get Kyra out of danger, so we left for Newport, where we had been invited. There again it was one long round of invitations, till we felt we could stand it no more, and then, when a few cases of the illness were reported on Rhode Island, even our hosts did not try to detain us any longer. We left by car for Boston. Next morning, to my great amazement, the chauffeur waved good-bye and jumped off the car. "What does this mean?" "I am going to drive," said Vaslav. I was aghast, because, while he could drive straight ahead quite well, he would back the car round with a fearful swing, and he knew nothing about the engine, which was essential then. I saw ourselves stranded in the open country. The first day passed comparatively calmly, though in a few small towns Vaslav drove on the wrong side, and was shouted at by the passers-by. He almost ran into a tramcar, but at the last moment pirouetted aside. I was so angry that I sat silent, but Kyra, alone in the back seat with all her dolls, was enjoying herself immensely. Once we entered the State of Maine the scenery became so lovely that I almost forgot to be angry. We passed the seashore, with its large beaches, the pine-woods with century-old sweet-smelling trees. It was not easy to travel with Kyra. The food was uneatable; coffee, ham and eggs the whole time. The ham was sugared, and we could not swallow it. We were offered a dreadful drink—ice cream soda—and once Vaslav was so brave that he even tried a drink called coca-cola, but this was his first and last venture. We had to change tires at least half a dozen times; we had trouble with the carbureter. Vaslav in an important and knowing manner opened the bonnet and disappeared from view. Then he lay under the car and made some mysterious repairs. He loved all mechanical inventions, and had an undoubted talent that way, but in this case I suspected he was better able to take the car to pieces than to put it together again. He had many little tricks of driving that I disliked intensely. He was never quite sure with which gear to take a hill, so he tried them all in turn and then, when the car refused to pull, he just let it slide backwards, to Kyra's immense joy. Our trip took us six days instead of three. Finally we arrived at Bar Harbour, one of the most beautiful places in the world, and, as the Cottenets and Dr. Abbé had houses there, we met with a great reception. In fact, we were very seldom at home. Vaslav would leave in the car early in the morning with Kyra, the nurse, and the painted duck. There was a beautiful marble theatre on the top of the hill among the pine-woods, with sliding doors. On the lawn was an open Greek amphitheatre, where performances would be given during the season by the world's greatest artists. Here Vaslav put Kyra on the lawn with her toys, slid the doors back, and practised for hours alone. Sometimes I came to watch unnoticed. Kyra often forgot her toys and watched "Tatakaboy, how he leaped and flyed." The higher he jumped, the more she shouted for joy. It was wonderful to see these two beings, who adored one another and forgot everything else as he danced for her and she tried to imitate. Then suddenly Vaslav jumped off the stage, got hold of Kyra in his arms, dancing across the lawn, till finally he threw himself on the grass and they rolled down the hill together.

Later in the day we would go to the swimming-pool, where Vaslav tried to teach me. He was such a wonderful swimmer that crowds used to watch him when he dived or swam under water so long that they thought he would never come up again. He pirouetted in the water and leaped like a fish. He also began to play tennis and was a constant winner, jumping high so quickly, with such a sense of speed and distance, that he was able to hit each ball, and make its return impossible. It was incredible to think that he had never played before.

Every Thursday afternoon there was a concert in the theatre, and as, owing to the war, most of the artists did not return to Europe, we outdid New York. Kreisler, Hofmann, Zimbalist, Godowsky, Bauer, and others performed. Each gave a recital, and sometimes they combined. Vaslav created special dances, one the cakewalk of Debussy, which he called *Le Nègre Blanc*. We often went over to see the other artists at North Seal Harbour. Harold Bauer played Scriabine a lot for Vaslav, who also, at the Schellings', took lessons in flirting from the "debs." Carlos Salzedo, the young French harpist, came over from Camden to visit us. He and Vaslav were great friends and planned future recitals, which, unfortunately, never materialised. They played pranks together, going down to the post-office and sending a business wire to Mr. Coppicus, one of the managers of the tour, whose name they spelt out, letter by letter, in French, to the bewildered clerk, and it certainly sounded very funny: Ci—o—pi—pi—

The Hofmanns also came to us, and he and Vaslav shared a taste in mechanics and would tinker with their cars. Hofmann would sometimes play for us and accompany Vaslav. He told us that since seeing Vaslav in *Sylphides* he played Chopin differently.

In Bar Harbour we had our first and last domestic fight. I had to visit the dentist, and, as he wanted to give me an injection, I slipped out of his chair and flew out of the house, leaving the surprised dentist and Vaslav alone. I was so scared that I took a car and went some sixty miles away, only returning at dawn. By that time all Bar Harbour was aroused and armed, looking for me in the woods and at the bottom of the lake. Vaslav was angry and scolded me, but I threw some pillows at him and we both laughed and made it up.

Then Jones arrived, escorted by Laurence Steinhardt. Vaslav found the designs for the costumes to his liking. They were different in colouring from the Russians', although equally brilliant, but it was obvious that Jones had felt their influence. The scenery designs were interesting, but not what Vaslav wanted, and they spent days together working at it. Vaslav suggested a drop curtain which would represent an open book and on its page an awkwardly designed owl, sitting with its claws on a mediæval hand-mirror. Tyl's *Eulenspiegel*. He conceived of a market-place with city hall and cathedral, exaggerated in their slant leaning towards one another, distorted as the life of those ages.

Meanwhile, with Steinhardt I went over the Metropolitan contract, which called for forty weeks, a transcontinental tour, and three weeks in New York. I was worried, as they wanted Vaslav to dance five times a week, which seemed too strenuous. We finally arrived at the solution that three times he should dance two ballets and on the other two evenings just one. Even then I was afraid that he would be overworked, with the travelling and all the artistic direction.

We had to leave for New York, as the company was due to arrive at the end of September, and the season was to open in two weeks' time. Vaslav had only this time at his disposal to teach two ballets as complicated as *Petrouchka*. How he would be able to do it I could not understand, but Diaghileff would not send the company over sooner, in order to economise rehearsal salaries. We were sad to leave this enchanting island, where for the first time in years Vaslav found relaxation and recreation.

Chapter Seventeen

THE
AMERICAN TOUR

IN THE old Grand Central Palace, one autumn morning, the troupe
of the Russian Ballet assembled in practice costume, waiting for
Vaslav.

Grigoriev, the general stage manager nominated by Diaghileff,
assisted by Kremeniev, Barocchi, Lopokova's husband, and Drobetsky, as secretaries, formed the general staff. They received
Vaslav in polite silence. He spoke a few words asking them to give
of their very best, as he was determined to do, to make the Ballet
a success in the new countries, in order to assure the very existence
of the Russian Ballet itself, which, Vaslav pointed out, must survive the war. The rehearsals began. There were quite a number of
new members sent over by Diaghileff instead of sixteen of the best
dancers, whom he retained in Italy, and some of the new ones were
of mediocre talent and capacity. The two *ballerinas* brought from
Russia did not yet deserve this title, as they had just graduated
and were still inexperienced. In one of the new dancers, Mlle.
Spessivsteva, he thought he had found very fine material. Her
dancing was very light and ethereal. She would be excellent in
Sylphides and in all classical ballets.

Vaslav had also to superintend the painting of the scenery in

338

Jones's studio and explain to him how the paint must be poured on the canvas according to the Russian style and not put on by brush.

By this time *Tyl Eulenspiegel* was cast, and Vaslav was doing the same for *Mephisto*. He had always dreamed of a dancer who would look and act like Chaliapine, but, as such an artist did not exist, he asked Bolm for this very important rôle. Bolm resented the fact that Vaslav was chosen as artistic director—at least we were told so—and did not show much enthusiasm to dance in this ballet.

The very first disagreeable surprise we had was that one morning, arriving at the rehearsal, there was only one dancer present as a strike delegate. They had discovered that in America "the strike" existed, and had promptly begun one. They said they were Russian citizens and refused to dance to German music. Mr. Herndon, representing the Metropolitan Opera, at once took the matter up and explained to them that, although strikes existed, there were also laws to prevent them. They were artists and not organised factory labour; that they had had no injustice done them and their contract required them to dance to all kinds of music, and they would be deported if they did not fulfil their obligations.

What they really wanted we did not know, but two valuable days were lost. Vaslav was saddened to see that the troupe was trying to cause trouble, but he plunged himself all the harder into work, so that the two new ballets should be produced in time. There were only twelve days before the opening at the Manhattan Opera House. *Tyl* is a ballet on a grand scale. The dances were technically difficult. Only two members showed great zeal, H. and a new member, Kostrovsky. The latter was a very able dancer, a silent man with calm manners, rather strange eyes looking very much like a Kalmuk. His wife was also a dancer, and if possible still quieter, and with a crushed, hunted look. This man, Kostrovsky, used to hold court during the intervals at the rehearsals; the greater part of the troupe sat around him at his feet, listening attentively whilst he made speeches. I asked Mrs. Spessivsteva, the old mother of our new *ballerina*, what all this meant. She explained that Kostrovsky was preaching; he was a disciple of Tolstoi; lived according to his ideas, tried to save the world, and in the meantime reform the Russian Ballet. "A harmless dreamer," said Drobetsky. "Crazy as a nut," declared the American administrative staff.

Kostrovsky took to Vaslav from the first moment, and showed an adoration which was not only for his art but for his nature. He followed Vaslav everywhere like a dog, eagerly looking for a smile. To the troupe he began to preach Nijinsky as a saint. "He is working for us, for our children; he is unselfish. Do not strike; you are harming yourselves. He can exist without us, but we cannot successfully without him." His words seemed to create a quieter atmosphere.

The dances of *Tyl* had fascinated the artists, and, in spite of the fact that they had made up their minds to be disagreeable, they could not resist its merits. Vaslav, who rehearsed them, had to supervise the costumes, the make-up, and he did each artist's himself, for in this ballet he not only wanted to bring the make-up in harmony with the costume, but also to be symbolic. Each character was supposed to be a personage from a mediæval tale. The candy merchant had to look like a "lollipop," and a very thin, tall dancer was chosen for the part. The baker's costume was designed like a *Baumkuchen*, one of the national sweets of old Germany, and so on.

But Vaslav had to be everything, *maître de ballet*, scenic artist, *régisseur*. He had to supervise all the work usually done by the composer, Diaghileff, Bakst, and Benois, to arrange the lighting, to instruct the administrative staff, and to arrange the programmes.

At the costume rehearsal, Vaslav, who had to be one moment on the stage, the other in the auditorium, kept on his rehearsal shoes with heels. One of the dancers constantly made mistakes, so Vaslav jumped on the stage and corrected him, but his shoes were slippery and he twisted his foot, with one painful gesture falling back and fainting. For one second we were all nailed to the floor. Had he broken his foot? If so, we did not want to know. Nobody dared to lift him.

One of the American stage hands picked him up and carried him to his dressing-room. A terrible rush began. Dispatches were sent out; messages, telephone calls. The artists stood silently in front of the door crying: "Nijinsky has broken his foot! How dreadful!" Bolm rushed up. In one moment, as from nowhere, everybody was there. As soon as he regained consciousness, he was taken by ambulance to Dr. Abbé's clinic to have an X-ray taken. Many of the artists came along in their practice kit and waited, until they heard Nijinsky had sprained his ankle, but would be unable to dance for at least six weeks.

The management was in despair, with so much money involved, the whole tour organised, theatres engaged all over the country. The cancelling of these dates would mean a tremendous financial loss to the Metropolitan, and one hundred and fifty people's salaries were at stake. "I must dance. I have to," said Vaslav. It was arranged that the rehearsals should go on, now that the troupe knew *Tyl*, but its opening should be postponed to the last week of the three weeks' season in New York. Dr. Abbé could not make any statement as to whether Vaslav would appear, but promised to let him dance on the tour. So they had to open without Vaslav. He worked in bed. Conferences were held about the programme, and all other questions settled. Vaslav was usually a very good patient; now, when he injured his foot, he was extremely difficult. Dr. Abbé insisted on having day and night nurses, so that his orders should be carried out, but Vaslav would not tolerate anybody near him except me and his *masseur*. Kostrovsky and H., who seemed to be the latter's disciple, came, and begged to be allowed to stay, and tried to keep him company. I was not convinced of H.'s religious and ascetic tendencies, as I remembered his past.

Among the many flowers which were sent to Vaslav, perhaps the loveliest basket was that of Anna Pavlova, who was dancing in New York. One morning she asked me personally to the telephone. As she inquired after Vaslav, she asked me: "Please tell me the truth; Vaslav Fomitch has broken his leg, hasn't he?"

"No, fortunately, though we thought so at first."

"Oh, really not?" And her voice dropped, as though she were disappointed. I did not say anything about it to Vaslav.

Then Vaslav was allowed to stand and make a few steps, but still bandaged. He was practically carried to the theatre to conduct the rehearsals of *Tyl*. The season opened, but the box office receipts proved that Vaslav's absence was keeping the public away. Dr. Abbé showed me the X-ray picture and explained the amazing fact that Vaslav's foot anatomically was not constructed like that of other human beings, but was a mixture of the construction of man and bird. "How do you explain this?" "Oh, it is atavism—fifth generation of dancers. The result not only of his training and constant practising, but of those of the ancestors. This is the secret of his amazing elevation; no wonder he can fly; he is a human bird." He asked me to give him the X-ray, which he wished to present to some medical museum.

Vaslav's foot was in fact remarkable. It was sturdy and very muscular; he could use his foot and toes as he could his hand. He could even grasp a bar or rope with his toes, like a bird on a perch. But his ankle was extremely thin, the bones very apparent, and the muscles seemed to quiver even when the foot itself was at rest. His legs, so muscular, but especially his ankles, looked like those of a fine, full-blooded racehorse. When he flexed his foot upwards, the distance was exactly the same from the ankle to the heel as from the toes to the ankle. Vaslav claimed that owing to this he was able to rise so easily.

Finally, Dr. Abbé consented that Vaslav should dance a few times in New York, but with a bandaged foot, and that all the steps which made his bodily weight rest on the right foot (which was the injured one) should be shifted over to the left. How extremely difficult this was only a dancer can realise.

A few days before the opening, Monteux suddenly discovered that he was French. Now he came out with the amazing statement that as the Allies were at war with Germany, he could not and would not conduct a work of Richard Strauss. He would rather break his contract. Again Mr. Herndon was patience itself, and the good-humoured Alfred Seligsberg, who had withstood many storms with tenors and conductors as adviser of the Metropolitan, tried to smooth the matter over, but with no avail. Monteux steadily refused.

"But you conduct *Carnaval*. Schumann was Austrian. Wasn't he an enemy?" ventured Dr. Seligsberg.

"But he is dead. Strauss is alive. A living Boche. No, never will I conduct his music."

This was extraordinary conduct, seeing that it had been on Vaslav's special request that Kahn had intervened with the authorities in France and obtained Monteux's exemption from military service. Kahn was furious, and ordered that another conductor should be summoned. This meant that during the entire coast-to-coast tour they had to engage a second conductor for the sake of one ballet.

Mephisto Valse had to be given up, anyhow, as Vaslav was unable to rehearse it, and Dr. Abbé simply forbade him this extra strain.

Tyl Eulenspiegel took the public by storm. The artists, the dancers themselves, raved about it. They declared that it was Nijinsky's finest piece of work. It was his first ballet since the break with Diaghileff, who was always anxious to make the world believe that the ballets "by" Nijinsky, Massine, and the other choreographers were really his own creations. But *Tyl Eulenspiegel* showed the world how little Sergei Pavlovitch had to do with the creation of a ballet. Vaslav was particularly pleased with the un-grudging approval of the musicians present for his greatest work. Hofmann, Zimbalist, Godowsky, and Bauer all congratulated him on a perfect interpretation of Strauss.

Tyl, the hero of mediæval Flemish folk-lore, was danced by Vaslav. He embodied what Tyl was—the spirit of humour of his race. Tyl is the prankish youth who encourages and helps the poor and torments the tyrant. Always gay, always illusive, nothing can subdue him. His love for the people is victorious, for, though he is put to death for helping his townsfolk, his spirit triumphantly lives on in the heart and mind of the Flemish race.

It is noon, the busiest hour of the great yearly market. The market-place is full. The peasants have brought their poultry, vege-tables, cattle, flowers; the merchants their silk, jewellery, sweet-meats, to tempt with bargains the strolling townsfolk. The market is the heart of the little mediæval town. The gloomy towering cathedral throws its shadow over the gathering. The town hall, where the very fate of those outside is decided, is unusually quiet. Here is the notary, drinking with a few friends who have already sold their wares; there the priest trying to sermonise to some children, who are far more interested in stealing sweets and fruit from the stalls. Now there passes the lady of the castle, whose servants bargain for some Oriental silks. So life goes on. The poor, with wide-open eyes, walk around to glimpse, at least, all this display of riches and food that they cannot have, and the gaunt beggars clamour for alms.

Now what has happened? A lithe youth, with a mischievous smile, has twisted them all up and tied them together in a huge roll of expensive cloth from one of the merchants' stalls. They are all bound together, the chatelaine, the judge, the beggar, the priest, the merchant, the peasant, all the nicely established and jealously guarded feudal caste system united in a prank of Tyl's. And now, with the tailor's big scissors, he cuts the cloth, and they all fall pell-mell apart. Indescribable confusion. Everything rolls on the ground. The townsfolk seize the rich materials; the beggars fill themselves with food to their hearts' content; the children snatch up the apples and tempting-looking sweets. Gold, food, bales of cloth and silk roll to the hands of the poor, thanks to Tyl, who has disappeared, while the rich merchants run to the town hall to complain.

But who is this awesome priest, preaching so beautifully and promising eternal bliss in the hereafter? The ladies, the learned, the poor, all follow him with reverence. The beggars venture to ask him for alms, but he, with his impassible, beatified face, tells them to accept his promises and wait, wait. Then suddenly he pulls out his empty pockets, throws his hood back, and with a shrug of his shoulders leaps away. Tyl—who even dares to make fun of the clergy. All the folk roar with laughter as the priests disappear into the town hall to denounce this new prank.

The cathedral doors are thrown wide open; the service is

ended. Among the worshippers, the beautiful chatelaine emerges with her suite. Rich dresses, golden chains, pearls; the townsfolk give them place with reverence. The trains of the three lovely ladies stretch right across the huge stage. As they emerge from the Cathedral, it is like the unfolding of a triptych. But, while two of them are diverted by sweets and merchandise offered to them, the third listens to the courting of a young cavalier in rich attire. She is conquered, forgets her high position, and kisses the cavalier; then all the children burst out laughing, for under the cavalier's cloak are not these the green tights of our Tyl? . . . Yes, he is fooling again. The horrified, outraged ladies hurriedly depart, while their retainers go to seek the magistrate.

Now here are the learned ones. Five professors of the University, sunk in their parchments, trying to solve some difficult mathematical or astrological problem. They don't know it is market-day; they don't care; every day is the same to them. They are only interested in their science; humanity can go to pieces while they solve their riddles. Then another professor appears, exactly like them, but he comes from a foreign country. They surround him, while he gives them an interesting explanation of his "thesis," each trying to apply it in his own manner. They get desperately confused, and when they gather again for further information the foreign professor laughs in their faces, and shows them the poor, shrinking in corners, and tells them it is more important to solve everyday problems than to seek abstract truth. It is Tyl again, attacking science now. Incorrigible, exasperating Tyl, making fun of every rank and of all authority. The professors disappear to denounce him in the town hall.

But the quietness of the deserted market-place at dusk does not last long. A gay song breaks the silence. Here is Tyl again, but this time not disguised. He runs from one street to the other, calling the poor frightened people from all over the town, and they, intoxicated by his courage and joyous spirit, forget their difficulties and miseries and dance round their Tyl, who is always their comforter. He inspires them with the idea that they could always be happy if they were brave enough to throw off once for all the iron discipline of the caste rule. After all, we are all equal, dances Tyl, and is carried shoulder-high to the town hall to dethrone the reigning authority. But they are surrounded by soldiers, thrown in a panic, and everybody tries to escape the severity of the magistrates. That terrible sound of the drums. Tyl is accused. He bravely replies with a laugh, but this is quickly crushed, and, wherever he turns, another accusing group faces him. The priests, the merchants, the lords and ladies, the professors: all ranks are united to extinguish the spirit of liberty of the people, their joy of living. Judgment is given, and at once poor Tyl, who still believes it is all only a joke, is hanged, and dies as he lived, with laughter on his lips.

Once more the market-place is active, for now the people gather and lament their cowardice in not daring to defend Tyl. Now their only protector is lost for ever. But no. . . . Who is that springing up from among the group of moaning women? It is our Tyl, our Tyl. His spirit lives on forever to cheer those who need it.

Tyl was indeed the most perfect of Nijinsky's choreography. It was sheer dancing from beginning to end. Critics who asserted that Nijinsky's methods were too sculptural, and could not therefore be applied to flowing movements, were silenced. *Tyl* was as much "dancing" as *Carnaval*. Only each gesture, each dance, expressed a thought according to Nijinsky's fundamental idea. He did not share the theory that movement should be for its own sake,

347

later laid down and followed by Bronislava Nijinsky when she became *maître de ballet*, or that it should merely express a mood or a feeling or simply the music, as Fokine and the others maintained.

On the 30th of October we began the transcontinental tour. The troupe consisted of about one hundred and twenty people: fifty-five dancers, fifty-two musicians, and the technical and general staff. The Press agents went ahead. The train was run in two sections. The baggage-cars, with the scenery and lighting apparatus, went on with the technical staff, to give them time to unload and set up in the theatre before our arrival, as in many of the forty cities we visited the artists only arrived an hour or so before the show was due to begin. Everything had to be ready. There was the difficulty of setting up scenery on stages of different sizes. Often the orchestra pit was so small that we had to sacrifice the first few rows of stalls.

On the Russian Ballet Special everything was arranged as pleasantly as possible for everybody. Sleepers, diners, observation cars, on which we lived for five months. The chef made whatever we asked for, even Russian dishes. Our drawing-room had been very nicely fitted up, and we soon made ourselves at home. Only the nights proved disagreeable, for the beds in American sleepers are along the windows, so that there is always a draught. Also they were much too narrow and short for Vaslav, who was used to sleeping in a large bed, where he could stretch himself. He usually slept in every angle of the bed, and mostly across it. If the bed was not a double one, he often fell on the floor. He needed space, in sleeping as much as dancing. When the stay in a city was very short, the company could remain on the train. But we always tried to go to a hotel, even if only for a few hours, so that Vaslav could be able to rest in a real bed and get some fresh air.

348

Vaslav and I went to Mr. Herndon's compartment every morning to discuss whatever needed attention. Different towns asked for different ballets.

Interviews for the Press had to be prepared. They were made out on the train and handed to the reporters on arrival. Alterations had frequently to be made in the cast, owing to illness.

When we arrived in Boston, Vaslav was upset from the very first day of our arrival. The reporters told him that again the rumour was around about his being a deserter, and it was also printed in one of the papers. We tried to find out who had done this mischief. We had many friends in Boston, and were much entertained, but Vaslav enjoyed most the evenings in the company of Sargent, who at the time was painting the library in the city, and George Copeland, the pianist, who played Debussy for him.

About the end of November we arrived in Washington, where we gave three performances. President Wilson and the whole Diplomatic Corps were present, and Vaslav went up to render thanks officially for their help in securing his release from Austria. Also we were magnificently entertained by the different Embassies. Our days passed in a social whirl which we could not very well avoid. We tried during the whole trip to keep away from social obligations as much as we could, but this was difficult, for in each town the Mayor, the leading clubs, the Elks and other prominent people, all wanted to entertain us. But the travelling was so hard on everybody that we were glad to rest as often as possible.

On our arrival at Atlanta, Vaslav received an official summons to appear within ten days at St. Petersburg before the military authorities. Vaslav could not understand it, as he was exempt for good, but thought it might be some new regulation. Of course, he wanted to leave at once for Russia, but to be in St. Petersburg within ten days would have been impossible. Laurence explained to us over the telephone that the Metropolitan would not let Vaslav go until his contract was fulfilled. The other difficulty was that he was still a war prisoner to Austria, only lent to the States on the understanding that he would stay in neutral countries during the war and not take arms against the Central Powers. He was really in a dilemma. It was arranged with Mr. Herndon that Vaslav should return immediately to Washington escorted by one of the secretaries, and take up the matter with the Russian Embassy. So he did. Before he left he rehearsed the *Spectre* with his understudy, Gavrilov. Vaslav was supposed to rejoin us in New Orleans.

I stayed with the troupe, and as usual went to the theatre. I was amazed to see on the programme that Vaslav's name was still on as dancing the *Spectre de la Rose*. I went to the management and asked them why it was not changed. They told me that so many people would have returned their seats if they had known that Vaslav was not dancing, that to avoid the loss they did not make this change, and as Vaslav was obliged to leave they were sure he would not object. I did not feel that under the circumstances I had the right to interfere. The lady next to whom I was sitting was in ecstasy over the *Spectre*. "Oh, the great Nijinsky! How marvellous!" Such is the power of suggestion. But later she remarked: "I can't see that he leaps so very high."

By this time many friendships had been made in the company. The musicians and the great part of the technical staff played cards and dominoes. The dancers read a lot. Vaslav bought them a very large library. Kostrovsky was the chief librarian, and he continued his lectures on Tolstoi. We were very often with the Herndons. Mrs. Herndon was a very lovely woman and a very agreeable companion. The Fradkins were newly married and he was very gay. Vaslav was amused by him, and we became very friendly.

350

Fred Fradkin was a first prize winner from the Paris conservatoire, and had been chosen as concert master for our orchestra. He was a very promising virtuoso.

Old Mrs. Spessivsteva, who was teaching me Russian, was a character straight out of a Chekhov play. We laughed ourselves sick when she began to show us what she was like when she was a young member of the ballet and flirted with the officers at Moscow. She baptised our troupe the "Circus of Sergei de Diaghileff." She was the first to know of everything that happened, and under the seal of great secrecy she went around and told it to everybody. But she was a kind-hearted old woman, and used to serve tea to all the troupe in her compartment. She carried her own samovar, but, as she almost set the train on fire, she was requested to get the boiling water from the dining-car. Of course, she found, and we agreed, that the tea was not the same as when she boiled the water herself.

New Orleans proved to have a great charm. With its quaint old streets and buildings, it impressed us as a Southern French town. The lovely Opera House in which we performed was beautiful, very old and in exquisite taste. Here we first saw palm-trees and all the surprising Southern vegetation. We visited Antoine's, the famous French restaurant, and we did not regret it. The lunch he served us, the wine and his famous *omelette surprise*, were as good as those of Larue. We were told that the "high spots" of this town were the brothels, so we decided with the Fradkins that we would go and see them. But Vaslav refused. He thought it very much against his principles, and his respect for womanhood, but I insisted; I had never been to such a place and was curious to go. I told Vaslav I would go anyhow. He warned me I would be very much disgusted. I told him he could not know, as he never had been in any. So we went. What amazed us most was to see all the mixtures of different races. Vaslav had no racial prejudices, and was always kind and considerate to people, whatever race they were. He talked with them and offered them drinks. They were all amazed to see that otherwise he had no interest.

As we left we met a number of our dancers, and, to my amazement, one of the preachers among them.

During the trip some differences arose between Monteux and Fradkin. We heard it was chiefly due to the difference in the exchange of the French francs as, owing to the exchange, he received less than his own concert master. Frequently Fradkin was unjustly rebuked during rehearsals. Vaslav always tried to make peace, but did not succeed. As he could not very well interfere between the conductor and the concert master, he showed his respect for Fradkin by taking his violin out of his hand and carrying it himself after Fradkin to the restaurant where Monteux and others were already seated.

We had a lot of trouble in the South, as we were requested not to make up as negroes, and to perform *Scheherazade* as it was composed was unthinkable in any of these cities. So we left it out of the programme. Then in some cities the women's clubs objected to the bare legs and wanted tights on. Of course, we did not give in on this point. We were usually met at the station by a committee of the most prominent people, the Chamber of Commerce, then the reporters. Vaslav, who never cared for publicity, was usually exhausted by meeting strangers.

To escape the usual reception, Vaslav and Fradkin decided one day on the train to change parts, and at Tulsa, Oklahoma, they carried out the plan. We were received by a Committee of Freemasons. As the hotels were very primitive, they kindly invited the

SIAMESE DANCE—LES ORIENTALES

NARCISSE

company to stay in their houses instead of the train. Vaslav got off the train after Fradkin and carried his violin. Fradkin answered the advancing reporters as they were sent on to our group by Herndon. "This is Mr. Fradkin, the concert master," Fradkin introduced Vaslav to them. "Where is Nijinsky?" "I am," replied Fradkin. As he was rather stout, there was a wondering expression on the faces of the newspaper men. It was a great surprise when Fradkin's kind, fat face smiled at the reader in the evening papers. The dancers were aghast until we explained what happened. But this was not the only joke Vaslav and Fradkin played. Before our arrival in one city we gave the management, as usual, the name of the hotel where we wanted to stay. We went there, but did not like it, and as we were to stay only the day we decided to return to the train and spend the day driving in a motorcar. Great was the consternation of the staff when they looked for Vaslav in the afternoon and were told that he had left.

But they were not the only ones who made trouble. Revalles was presented by a Boston admirer with an alligator, and she took it along with her; she used to keep it in her washstand at night, and on her neck during the day. Mme Spessivsteva senior and myself were frankly afraid, but so were the negro porters and one day they refused to serve her in the diner unless she took the alligator back to her compartment. Finally all the porters decided to go on strike, as they said it was unlucky to have it on the train, and in the end she was asked by the management to give it away, which she did to some zoo.

One day real trouble broke out. Mr. Herndon used to arrive at the station about twenty minutes to two (our departure from each city was set at 2 a.m.) so that he could see that everybody was there and all in order. When he arrived he saw the musicians

collected in the waiting-room. They refused to leave. Their spokes-
man, Fradkin, explained to him that as the orchestra were entitled
to a first-class Pullman berth according to their contract, they would
not accept a second-class car. One of their Pullmans had had to
go to the repair shop and a new second-class car was switched on
for the time being. But they were all union men and would not
hear of it. Herndon told them it was impossible to get a first-class
car that night, and that he was going to leave on schedule. He went
to the engineer and told him to start at two, but slowly. The whis-
tle blew, the train started, and the musicians with a mad dash
scrambled on board.

During the trip very often different members came to our
drawing-room to talk, or we met them at the observation car.
Kostrovsky and H. came up to Vaslav first with questions to ask
regarding the new books to be bought, then for some other instructions. Then Kostrovsky remained always longer and longer in our
compartment, first reading to Vaslav, then talking for hours and
hours. I knew, of course, that it was a pleasure for Vaslav to be
amongst his countrymen and speak Russian. But I would rather
have seen him with Bolm, or others of the Imperial School graduates, than with those *moujiks*—not on account of their origin, but
because of an instinctive distrust I had of them.

As we boarded the train at Kansas City we saw some Indians
sitting in a great central lobby. The Fradkins were with us, and
we went up and talked to them. They had clear-cut features; some
of them were very beautiful but all had a distinguished look. They
spoke nicely and showed us their babies on their backs; then they
asked where we came from, and Vaslav explained, adding a few
words about his dancing; they immediately praised their own
dances; and then they noticed Fradkin's Stradivarius, which he

354

always carried in his hand. "Is that your baby?" "No, I haven't a baby." "Are you married?" The old Indian shook his head, then he turned to Vaslav. "And you?" Vaslav began to tell him all about Kyra's perfection. "Where is she?" "In New York." "No good; child should be with her parents," said the old man. And Vaslav agreed with them.

From there we went to Des Moines and then to Omaha. By this time we were so tired that we decided to take rooms in a hotel just for a few hours. We left the luggage on the train. Fradkin did the booking, as always. We went in and immediately ran a bath. While Vaslav was in the bath, somebody energetically knocked on the door. I opened, and a man told me he was a sheriff and wanted to arrest us, as he declared we were renting rooms for an immoral purpose. I ran to the Fradkins, who violently explained that we were married. But this did not help. They wanted proof— certificates and what not. I went to fetch Drobetsky who was at hand, and finally, I think, Herndon came and we were allowed to proceed with our baths.

The evenings when Vaslav did not dance he used to watch the performance from the wings or the auditorium. *Scheherazade* was played, and I, who had seen it so many times, was surprised to see the outstanding miming of the old Eunuch. I had never noticed it before. Since Cecchetti was not with the troupe, one of the other soloists danced it. I was so intrigued that I went back stage and found that the unknown artist who played the Eunuch that night was Vaslav. He had jumped in in the place of the usual dancer, who was suddenly taken ill.

Vaslav decided that every part should be understudied, and the understudies should once in a while dance their parts in a small town. Until now only Vaslav and Karsavina were "rested" in cases

355

when the programme called for three ballets in which they were supposed to dance, but never did except on special occasions, in Paris or in London, when Bolm had replaced Vaslav; Nijinskaya or Kyasht, Karsavina. No regular system had ever been applied to understudying. But Vaslav thought that through such a system it might be possible to develop a new generation of dancers. So he cast each starring part; Gavrilov, H., Kremeniev, all received instructions among the men, and, among the women, Hilda Munnings, Nemchinova, and others. Directly Diaghileff heard about it he protested, but later he must have been glad enough that Vaslav had given those members of the *corps de ballet* a chance. How else could he have starred Nemchinova or Sokolova in the years to come? Some of the soloists immediately complained to Kahn.

By the time we arrived in Denver trouble was definitely brewing on this account, and a part of the troupe again went on strike. Vaslav told them that his mind was made up and that he would cast the one he thought most suitable for the part. The ones who were thus passed over again sent a threatening letter to Vaslav that they would treat him "as the choir served Chaliapine in London." That meant a fight to a finish. Vaslav was quite unmoved, and as we passed those hostile dancers at the end of the performance he just raised his hat and said, *"Das vedania, Gaspada,"* and they gave way like sheep and let us go by.

One day we went to Pike's Peak by car. Vaslav had invited Kostrovsky and his wife and H. Kostrovsky preached all the way, while H. maintained a slightly hostile attitude towards me. I wondered how he dared; it wasn't till later that I understood.

We left Denver after the performance and headed for Salt Lake City. The country we had to cross was lovely, and everything lay in a deep snow. The whole country, especially the mountains, seemed to be asleep.

At our first performance in Salt Lake City the prominent people were introduced to me, as was usual wherever we went. Among them was the head of the Mormons, a very strict and distinguished-looking elderly gentleman. I returned his call in the next interval. To my confusion, four ladies in his box were introduced to me as "the prophet's many wives"—Mrs. X. the first, Mrs. X. the second, and so on. The first invited us to visit their place the following day. As soon as the interval was over I rushed back stage and told the dancers about the incident. They all thought I was joking. The next morning we actually did go over, and were guided by the prophet's second wife all through their museum, library, and schools, finishing with their great hall, which has remarkable acoustics. She explained to us how the work is divided between the wives. One acts as secretary to the husband, another looks after the children of all, the third does all the housekeeping. I ventured to ask if they were not jealous of each other. "No," she said. "Why should we be? We all have our interests, and we share in the affection of our husband." I thought it was quite a sensible institution, and most suitable for artists, since their wives have a real job. If they only aim at helping their husbands and protecting their interests, there is little enough time left for household duties or children.

We left as usual at two in the morning. Next day was Christmas Eve, which we had to spend on the train, as we were going on to Los Angeles. Mr. Herndon showed us very nice attention in arranging an empty baggage-car for an informal dance. Some of the orchestra played and a buffet supper was served, with hot grog and punch. After dinner I had a Christmas-tree in our compartment, hung with the presents for the company. They were all invited to come in, but they had to do so in turns, as the drawing-room, of course, was too small to hold so many people at once.

Great was our amazement the next morning at breakfast when

357

we looked out of the dining-room car window. Instead of the snow-capped mountains, a sea of orange-groves was all around us, deep green studded with golden fruit. Vaslav was so tired of hotels that we decided to split an apartment with the Fradkins and "keep house." Fred immediately wired for one while we were still some way from the city, and at our arrival it was ready! Inside another half hour a Japanese cook was engaged, and he cooked a wonderful dinner for us. Vaslav played all the time with the bedsteads, which he found he could pull out from the wall and swing up vertically out of the way. The Japanese cook taught us how to make tea, and we applauded him for his artful way of cooking rice. Vaslav had never been in the kitchen since his childhood, but he found his way there to watch the Japanese. The cook's movements amused him. Vaslav danced a Japanese dance for him, and the cook said, "Gentleman lived long time in Japan!" which was complimentary but untrue.

To amuse the Fradkins, Vaslav did all kinds of acrobatic tricks; he rolled, threw himself about, and jumped in the most incredible way. Fradkin asked why he did not use all this in a ballet, but Vaslav said he just did it to show that for a dancer to be an absolute master of his body he must be an acrobat, but that acrobatics was not an art in itself and that was why he did not apply it.

We visited the Spanish missions, and of course were invited to see the studios in Hollywood. To the latter place we had to cross about twelve miles of waste land by motor. Hollywood itself was then a few wooden shacks, and one or two studios among the pepper-trees. Chaplin was very enthusiastic about the ballet. He never missed a performance, and tried hard to get the ballet to stay another week, but this was impossible, as our tour was settled. The first night when we heard that he was in the audience all our company was excited. We all admired him. He came back stage in the interval and was taken to Vaslav's dressing-room. Vaslav always thought Chaplin was the genius of the cinema, a wonderful mime. They immediately became friends. Chaplin then went on to the stage and was introduced to the troupe. They all applauded, and Chaplin returned the compliment by walking up and down in his own special way and doing a few tricks. The company enjoyed it so much that they did not want to let him go, and the interval lasted twice as long as usual. The public became impatient, but, when they heard what the reason of the delay was, took it good-humouredly. On Chaplin's invitation we went to visit his studio. He was making *Easy Street* at that time, and we were all photographed in the set. He said how much he would like to make a film with Vaslav, but at that time he did not feel he could stay in California.

Vaslav was approached to buy land in Hollywood, but I unfortunately dissuaded him. Wherever we performed he received offers to buy all kinds of things—oil well shares, cattle, mines, and so on.

I was very glad that during the last week Vaslav was constantly with us. The Fradkins and Herndons had a good influence on him. I noticed that he was gay and natural with them. But as soon as Kostrovsky and H. got hold of him, he reacted like a sensitive plant and folded himself up. He became silent, meditative, almost gloomy, more so than I had ever seen him before, even in our most difficult days of the break with Diaghileff or during our interment in Hungary. I could not follow their conversation in Russian, as it became very abstract philosophy, but I could make out enough to see that Kostrovsky was like a parrot repeating Tolstoi and the teaching of Christ. Vaslav was impressionable and was open to any ideal of charity or love of mankind. When it came from him spontaneously I welcomed it, for I knew it was a part of the unselfish nature of his genius. But now that I noticed they were trying to accentuate it and provoke it, I was rather resentful. We all saw it: the Fradkins, the Herndons, myself. But the reason it was done was not clear. "To be with Nijinsky makes them feel important," said some of the dancers. "H. always runs after Diaghileff, Massine, and now Nijinsky for personal advancement," said the others. I thought myself the reason was that Kostrovsky was a fanatic; one could see it at once. He was genuine; he lived according to his ideas and made his family miserable while he was trying to make the world happy. Kostrovsky and H. stayed in our compartment sometimes the whole night through. Vaslav was exhausted, and needed rest after the performance, but they went on preaching to him. With the stubbornness of mules and the slow understanding of *moujiks* they pretended not to understand my hints and requests to leave him in peace. Then I openly tried to keep them away from Vaslav, but they were like leeches; it was impossible to get rid of them.

Barocchi, Lopokova's Italian husband and for that reason Diaghileff's new secretary, a strange-looking man with a long, heavy beard, of which he was very proud, was nicknamed by the troupe "Bluebeard." We did not see him after Denver, as he was hiding on account of the "misfortune," as he called the incident that happened to him in that city. He went to a barber's shop and dozed off in the chair. The barber shaved off his precious beard, and when he awoke and found his beard gone he fainted and for days did not want to show himself to anybody. He was a very strange person, somnambulist, and some claimed he had clairvoyant powers.

In San Francisco, Vaslav discovered a second-hand flying-machine which looked more like an abandoned sewing-machine than anything else. For $2.50 a ride was promised. Vaslav was at once all for a trip. We tried to keep him back, but he had set his heart on it, and, before we had time to realise it, was circling above us. Even with an expert pilot and in a first-class machine, at that time flying was a great risk, but there in these conditions it was tempting the gods. I prayed all the time until the machine was sighted and Vaslav stood by me again. I was really angry with him this time. He was enthusiastic and pleased, and explained that it was one of the most glorious, exhilarating feelings one could imagine, and that from the air the world was extremely beautiful.

The day of our arrival was New Year's Eve, and we spent the evening together in the hotel, and, as New Year's Eve celebrations always have a touch of the mystic, we asked Barocchi to tell us our fortunes. He could read palms very well, and did so; when he arrived at me, he promised a long life and good health, but said, "Within five years you will be separated from Vaslav Fomitch. I see a divorce, but not exactly." I laughed—"Ridiculous and impossible"—but felt rather uncanny. Then he looked at Vaslav's palm and, as though he had received a blow, staggered back and covered Vaslav's hands with his own. "I don't know, I can't say . . . sorry, it is strange . . ."

"Am I going to die? Come on, say it."

"No, no, certainly not, but . . . but this is worse . . . worse."

"He is hedging," we thought, and turned away from him, little thinking that Barocchi saw correctly.

We stayed two weeks in San Francisco, but for the second week we lived in Oakland, where we discovered a nice quiet hotel. We were much entertained by society here, and visited all the surroundings. Also we were invited to Berkeley University. The grounds were lovely, but very different from Yale. It was a great pleasure ten years later when I revisited the University, to see an exhibition of paintings and to hear from the teachers that Vaslav's visit and dancing had made a lasting impression and had deeply influenced the art students.

One evening in San Francisco the conductor was suddenly taken ill during the performance of *Tyl*, but the situation was saved by the piccolo-player, who stood up and directed the orchestra, following Nijinsky's steps.

Never since we married had there been the slightest misunderstanding between us. Vaslav's ever-present genius was overwhelming, but he was so natural, so kind, that whatever question came up, whatever complication arose, I knew and felt that I could always come to him and find understanding, comfort, and affection, even if it was a matter to his personal disadvantage. Lately I had begun to feel a change in Vaslav, so subtle that one could only sense it. He was the same and yet I felt that there was a new nuance in his attitude towards everything, even to his art. What had happened? I felt alarmed. I could not confide in anyone. So I sat down and wrote a letter to Bronia in Russia: that Vaslav, who could not be influenced by anybody, not even by Sergei Pavlovitch, seemed strangely hypnotised by the sermons of Kostrovsky and H. It seemed not only to affect his mental attitude towards life, but also his health, which began to worry me. Unfortunately, Bronia never received this letter. Kostrovsky, following Tolstoi, was of course a vegetarian, and very soon induced Vaslav to become one. This was most inadvisable. Vaslav, with his constant strenuous work, was told by his doctors to eat light but very nourishing foods, and especially those which gave strength to his muscles in a concentrated form. Meat was a chief part of his diet. Now that he did not even eat eggs, of course he was greatly weakened.

In Vancouver I received a letter from my uncle Gari, who asked me to extend some financial help to my kinsman, who had been sent to the Argentine some time before and whom on account of the war he could not now reach. Vaslav gladly instructed his bank to pay him an allowance regularly. After Vancouver, during the whole of January, we performed in the Western States, Seattle, Tacoma, Spokane, St. Paul, Minneapolis, Milwaukee, and the whole trip seemed to us a nightmare. I hardly saw Vaslav. When he was not dancing he was closeted day and night with Kostrovsky and H.; he hardly slept or ate, and they went on with their reformatory ideas. To have chosen Vaslav for this I thought outrageous. The salvation of the troupe was entirely forgotten by these self-constituted prophets. His rest, his nourishment, taken away, Vaslav became strangely irritated and weak. I felt that something had to be done.

I spoke to Vaslav very frankly, and told him that with all my love and admiration for him I could not agree to his new idea that he should give up dancing and become a peasant farmer or live the life of a *moujik* in Russia. I could understand that he was exhausted by the caravan life which the Russian Ballet had led since his separation from the Mariinsky. That he was right that art needed peace, and that creative work could only be achieved in a quiet atmosphere; that he was not a being who could exercise his art for commercial purposes. I was ready to go to Russia, to any place with him, but I could not believe that he wanted to throw away what he loved most—dancing; that it could not be his own

363

conviction, that he was under some spell. Vaslav became thoughtful.

At the time of our arrival in Chicago I declared that on account of this interference with our life I would return to New York and stay with Kyra, and if he had really decided to live the life of Tolstoi I would return alone to Europe. He could keep Kyra if he wanted, as I could never adjust myself to that life. Vaslav took me to the station, and he looked so sad and so humble that I could not help telling him that whenever he needed me he had only to call and I would always come.

For another six weeks the company went on touring Michigan, Ohio, Indiana, Tennessee. Vaslav used to send wires all the time and call me up. I felt he was rather lonely, but I wanted to make him see that he had to choose between the gloomy pair and me.

Laurence agreed that I had made the right move in frightening him thus. Nijinsky was far too sensitive to be left the prey of such adventurers, whatever their aim was. The company was tired out by the time they arrived in Chicago, and Vaslav was disappointed because everywhere the audience had raved about his leaps and his pirouettes but had no real understanding.

In New York my time was passed with Kyra, who had improved greatly and was now very lovely. She resembled Vaslav more and more. I was also very busy with all my social obligations.

At that time we heard the first rumours of the possibility of the U.S.A. entering the war on the side of the Allies.

I wondered what our status would be in case of war. I was informed that Vaslav could stay in America or perform in a neutral country during the hostilities.

On the 24th of February the transcontinental tour ended in Albany. I went to the station to meet Vaslav.

Vaslav called me up at long distance from Cleveland to ask my advice, as he had received a cable from Diaghileff asking him to come to Spain as soon as the American tour was finished and to take part in the Russian Ballet's performances there and in South America later in the autumn. I told Vaslav not to promise anything until he had consulted Laurence. I was surprised to hear of Sergei Pavlovitch's invitation. During the whole winter he was in Italy with Massine and the sixteen dancers whom he had retained. With them he formed a second company, and told his intimates that it was the "modern one" with which in the future he would create artistic ballets. The other one was going to be the money-making organisation. I noticed a change in Vaslav. He began to wear his silk shirts again, his rings, which under Kostrovsky's influence he had discarded. At lunch he ate the same dishes as we did.

The season was over; the troupe was returning very soon to Europe. We also had to make our plans. Vaslav, much as he liked the States, declared that it was not the atmosphere in which to create, and travelling constantly annihilated all artistic inspiration. He wanted to settle down and do some creative work. But where? To Russia we could not return. He took it for granted that I would go with him. I knew that in everyday life he was rather lost. His upbringing in the Imperial School isolated him from the routine of ordinary existence as much as the years spent in Diaghileff's company, where everything was done for him. I often noticed that to buy a ticket or to rent a room seemed a task for him. How would he be able to manage to obtain a visa while travelling? I felt as though I were abandoning a child. I said to him, "Vaslav, until the war is over, I will stay with you whatever happens." The hope in Vaslav flared up again that an understanding could be after all reached with Sergei Pavlovitch. Undoubtedly he missed his friendship and the Sergei Pavlovitch of the days gone by.

Laurence and Vaslav discussed future plans, and decided that Vaslav should go to Europe, either to take a rest in Spain or Switzerland or, if a suitable contract could be arranged, to go with the Ballet to South America. A tentative contract was drawn up. Vaslav told us that on Kostrovsky's and H.'s request he wired to Diaghileff: *"En principe j'accepte discuterons projets en Espagne."* Neither of us three knew at that time that Spain is the only country in the world where, according to law, a cable is a binding contract. But Diaghileff, who was in Spain, knew. He could not send the troupe to America without Vaslav, as the Teatro Colon in Buenos Aires, after the happenings in New York, insisted that a signed contract from Nijinsky should be shown to them before they concluded their agreement with Diaghileff.

Vaslav made me presents of most exquisite jewellery and furs. During the last few days, when we had completed all our arrangements for a departure, we went up to Laurence's office to make our wills. The submarine warfare was raging, and we were told that this would be advisable under the circumstances. Then and there I learned that Vaslav had given me everything he earned in America and disposed only of the things he owned in Europe. I refused, but Vaslav was determined. "You have to; you cannot work; anything might happen to me, then you will be left with Kyra. I can always take care of myself; I can dance."

The day of our departure arrived; we left on the same ship as the company. A great crowd of our friends accompanied us to the steamer. We felt rather depressed. We had found a hospitable country which became a second home, and now we had to leave it. We stood together waving, and as the skyline of New York slowly faded in the mist I began to cry hysterically. Vaslav turned toward the open sea, trying to hide his tears. We felt that safety and liberty were vanishing together with the last faint outline of the North American coast.

Chapter Eighteen

SPAIN
AND
SOUTH AMERICA

THE STEAMER on which we sailed for Spain was in "*perfecto estado hygienico*" according to a shiny brass plate on the upper deck, but whoever made this bold statement must have been blessed with an extremely vivid imagination. It was a veritable museum piece, known to have been abandoned under water for at least sixteen years, and as insecure as a shell on the waves. The whole place was infested by well-nourished rats, and it was quite impossible to put one's feet on the floor. After one night, I simply refused to go to the cabin, and installed myself on deck, in a chair, for the thirteen days of the trip. It was bitterly cold and stormy during the whole voyage. Vaslav stoically accepted the situation and slept a few hours in the cabin, but mostly he kept vigil over Kyra.

We intended to spend our two months' holiday in Spain, so that Vaslav could talk his new offer over with Diaghileff, and work in peace on the system of notation, but, at the time of our arrival, Diaghileff was in Paris.

Vaslav had danced in Madrid before, and the friends he had made then constantly invited us out. We became very friendly with the Duc and Duquesa de Durcal, who were related to the King. Within a few days, Vaslav received an invitation to visit the Royal

Palaces when he pleased. The Royal Theatre was put at his disposal, and he at once began to practise there.

We thought Madrid would be a real southern city, warm and
brilliant with sunshine, but it proved at this time of the year extremely cold, with biting wind. Our first few weeks passed very
pleasantly with new friends, work, and visits to cathedrals and
museums. Vaslav loved Goya. He never tired of looking at his
work, especially of *Los Caprichos,* and we went over to Toledo
to visit the places where he lived and worked.

In the evenings, we were usually taken to the theatres and cafés
to see real gypsy dancers. The austere movements of the men
dancers appealed forcibly to Vaslav, and very soon he used these
movements himself in dancing.

Spring came, everything was bathed in sunshine. We used to
sit and read together in the Prado while Kyra played among the
irises. Our reading was mostly Oscar Wilde's poetry and the work
of Selma Lagerlöff and Sir Rabindranath Tagore. The latter had
got hold of Vaslav's imagination, and I was glad, because this
philosophical poetry counter-balanced the fanatical teachings of
Tolstoi which seemed to have had such a destructive effect on Vaslav's peace of mind during the past winter. We had entirely forgotten the inconveniences of our recent trip, until one afternoon when
I opened one of the closets and found it full of mice. I began to
cry, seeing the damage they had done to my dresses.

"I give you furs, jewellery," said Vaslav gently, "and anything you wish, but can't you see how silly it is to attach importance
to them? And have you ever thought how cruel it is to kill those
animals? And how dangerous for the pearl-divers and for the
miners who provide your jewellery—they also have children, and
yet they must endanger themselves daily for the adornment of
women."

So, after all, Tolstoi was still preying on his mind.

One morning, I picked up the paper, and saw: "The abdication of the Tsar in Mohilew." The Russian Ambassador could tell us no more than was in the papers. To us, in Spain, the revolution gave the impression that it was going to be an extremely peaceful one.

Soothed by the beautiful surroundings, Vaslav worked very hard on perfecting his System of Notation. Undoubtedly he now hoped that at last the reconciliation with Sergei Pavlovitch would really take place. He also discussed with me the possibility of a return to his own country.

"I am sure the revolution is not going to make any changes in the artistic life of Russia. We love art and we will always work for its sake, and of course they must ask Sergei Pavlovitch to be Director of the Mariinsky now."

He wanted to discuss his own plans with Diaghileff. Vaslav intended to dance until he was thirty-five years of age, and then to devote himself to composition. Also he wished to found a school where he would teach his own ideas, and, attached to this, an artistic laboratory, where composers, *maîtres de ballet* and artists, regardless of nationalities, could work out their ideas. Another of his plans was to arrange a yearly festival where some of the performances would be entirely free. The festival theatre was to be built in the Russian style, carved in wood and painted, like some of the private theatres that have already been designed by great artists for wealthy people in Russia. Vaslav hoped to earn sufficient money during his dancing career to realise this project.

The day of his return from Paris, Sergei Pavlovitch burst into the lobby of the Ritz and embraced Vaslav passionately. *"Vatza, daragoi moi, kak tui pajivayesh."*

The greeting was as affectionate as if they had parted only a few hours ago, and no misunderstanding had ever occurred. It was the Sergei Pavlovitch of the old days. They sat down in a corner and began to talk. Hours and hours passed, and it seemed that the old friendship was restored. From that day on we were practically all the time with Diaghileff. The contract for South America was just brushed aside, and Sergei Pavlovitch simply said: "We open in Madrid at the Theatre Royal, and then we will give some performances in Barcelona. Massine has composed new ballets. I want you, Vatza, to look at them and give me your opinion. Have you composed anything new? I want you to do so."

Recent events in Russia were also discussed at great length, and Vaslav explained to Diaghileff his plans for the school and festival theatre. But Diaghileff objected: "Why think of the future of ballet? That is not our task. Dance and compose for our company, and leave the future generation to look after itself. I do not wish to return to Russia; I have worked too long abroad—the artists at home would ask what I wanted there. They would say that I wanted to take advantage of the newly acquired possibilities of the liberty for which they had had to fight. They would say, '*Je suis vieux jeux, vieux régime.*' I could not survive in the new Russia. I prefer to stay in Europe."

But Vaslav did not yet give up the idea of gaining Diaghileff for his plan. "We can't go travelling about the world forever like a caravan of gypsies; we shall never be able to create real artistic work that way. We belong to Russia; we must go home and work there and make a trip to the West once in a while."

Diaghileff's little circle, here as elsewhere, was formed of the *élite* of the advanced guard. He brought Picasso, who was very little known at that time, to us one day. He was reticent and very Spanish looking, and when he began to explain anything, he became full of excitement, and used to draw on the table-cloth, the

371

menu cards, and on the top of Sergei Pavlovitch's ivory walking-stick. Diaghileff was to me as a fatherly friend, protective and kind, at this time. Vaslav triumphantly said, *"Tu vois femmka je t'ai toujours dit qu'il sera notre ami."* And Vaslav told me again how Diaghileff had helped a former great friend when he got into difficulties, years after his marriage, and his wife sought Sergei Pavlovitch's aid.

Vaslav was so happy that he would have done anything to please Diaghileff, and the matter of the contract was not brought up. "Sergei Pavlovitch is the same as ever; there is no need of discussion; he will be fair to me—let us give him a chance to prove it."

Every day, Diaghileff thought of some place of interest to take us to. He was very friendly to me during those days in Madrid. His amazing hypnotic power did not seem to have lessened with the years; while listening to him at dinner once, when we were watching the ladies dancing at the Palace Hotel, I could understand how he subtly suggested his ideas about women to his youthful followers. For as he criticised the lines of the women's bodies, I myself, too, could see only the ugliness of them.

One evening we went to a theatre where Pastora Imperio was giving a recital. To us the name did not mean anything. We were told that she was a gypsy singer from Cadiz, that her fame extended to the Latin-American countries. She was the idol of Spain. As she appeared on the stage, behind the simple curtain, she did not make a great impression. We saw only a rather faded, stout southern woman, but the moment she began to sing, accompanying herself with movement and castanets, we forgot that she had no voice, that she was middle-aged and fat. With a few gestures she offered the history and the soul of Spain. Vaslav and Stravinsky, as well as Diaghileff, could not keep quiet on their seats, and, like three school-children, applauded, laughed, and cried, according to the mood this ageless marvel dictated.

The performances in Madrid began. Vaslav danced his usual parts. With great interest, he watched the new ballets of Massine. Vaslav always welcomed with enthusiasm the advent of a new artist if he brought something to art. Feelings of jealousy or envy were quite foreign to him. For him, Massine was a young artist with ambition, and his only wish was to help and applaud him, when he deserved it. The fact that Diaghileff used Massine as a tool to ruin him, did not in the least alter Vaslav's attitude towards Massine. Just the contrary. He said, "I do hope that Massine will fulfil all that Sergei Pavlovitch hopes from him as a dancer and as a choreographer. I only wish there were many more choreographers." Unlike the other *maîtres de ballet*, he was solely interested in the advancement of dancing; the personal question never entered his mind.

His enthusiasm for *Les Femmes de Bonne Humeur* was very great. He was glad to find that Massine had undoubted talent for composition. He discussed this ballet with Diaghileff, making a few remarks about certain things he would have done otherwise. Sergei Pavlovitch immediately said, "Of course, *tu sais*, Vatza, I found him as a private pupil in Moscow, when I had to have a youth for the part of Joseph. He has had very little experience as a dancer. He never thought of composition until I guided him. Naturally, it was a tremendous task for me to put this ballet on, as I had to explain to him all the steps and gestures, which he then showed the troupe." In one word, Sergei Pavlovitch claimed to have composed all the ballets instead of Massine—as in the past he had tried to do with Vaslav. We already knew, of course, this weakness of Diaghileff, which in later years developed tremendously, but, just as Vaslav had done, Massine also composed ballets after he separated from the Diaghileff company.

Parade did not please Vaslav. "Serge, this production is an essay, not fit to be shown to the public yet. You were trying to do something here which was not even clear to Massine himself. It comes out of a desire to be modern, but it is not felt, it is an artificially constructed choreography."

"But, *mon cher*, we must do something new for Paris every year. We can't be less modern than Marinetti. Futurism, cubism, is the last word. I do not want to let the position of an artistic leader slip away from me."

Vaslav simply could not see this strained point of view. There were many other questions now on which they could not agree. Vaslav was no more a pupil, he had become sure of his own views; he strongly urged that motion pictures should be taken of the ballets as documentary evidence for future productions, though of course not for public show. But Diaghileff brushed this suggestion aside in the same easy way as the plans of the school and the system of notation. "Vatza, why think of the future generation, of the future of the dance? Let them take care of themselves, just let us occupy ourselves with the present."

Now that the performances had begun, we had less time to go out with our friends, but I insisted that we should not give them up entirely, for I did not want Vaslav to isolate himself from the rest of the world and live only with Diaghileff and the Russian Ballet. I could not trust them after all that had happened in the past. As soon as they returned from their holiday, Kostrovsky and H. practically installed themselves in our apartment, day and night. They hung around Vaslav after rehearsals. H. seemed to forget his courting and Kostrovsky his wife. The latter stood, with his shining, fanatical eyes, in the middle of the drawing-room, talking, talking, while H. pretended to listen with awe. Every second sentence was a quotation from Tolstoi, and Vaslav listened attentively. Either purposely or because he was unfortunately not only fanatical but also unintelligent, Kostrovsky mixed up the teachings of Tolstoi. He preached that art is not justifiable for its own sake, but must have as its end the spiritual development of the individual. He wanted to convince Vaslav that he should work for the Russian Ballet as long as it needed him, and then retire to the land, like Tolstoi.

I began to resent the growing influence of these two self-appointed "teachers." They not only tried to influence Vaslav in his attitude towards Diaghileff and religion, but in his private life, his diet, his choice of friends, and lately his relationship with me. This indeed seemed to fill the cup. One evening, in a dark corner near the stage, I saw Diaghileff conversing very excitedly with H., not as an officer with his subordinate, but like two accomplices. The truth flashed through my brain; what I feared, what I had not dared to admit until then, was suddenly clear. It was all a carefully laid plot to estrange Vaslav from me and restore him to Sergei Pavlovitch's clutches.

I had to use my influence to counteract this scheme, and tried to surround Vaslav with people who meant well for him. I accepted invitations, and even encouraged the Duchess of X.'s advances to Vaslav. I almost threw them together, because, unconsciously, I felt that two loving women could achieve more than one in holding back an idealist from falling into the abyss of utter day-dreaming to which these fanatics were dragging him. Sergei Pavlovitch knew Vaslav's character; he realised that only through altruism could he

375

estrange him from marriage, normal life, and art, and make Vaslav give up dancing forever in order to cultivate the earth, like a peasant.

The idea of becoming a preaching monk which he had in his youth, the wish to retreat from the world to the isolation of a Siberian monastery which he had had on the boat going to South America before our marriage, haunted him. On that voyage he was in conflict with himself. He understood that Diaghileff was an invaluable adviser in art, that Diaghileff's very being was necessary for his own existence, but he also fully realised that their relationship was a mistake, that love for him must come through a woman.

But now that Vaslav was fully aware of himself, not only as an artist but as a man, why, why did he want to renounce all that love, life, and art could offer, and return to the soil?

I sensed now that Sergei Pavlovitch would rather annihilate Vaslav completely if he could not own him both as an artist and as a man.

We discussed what was to be done with Kyra in case Vaslav went to South America. To send her to my mother-in-law in Russia, in the middle of the revolution, was quite out of the question. We had decided to send her, with a trustworthy nurse, to a well-known children's sanatorium in Switzerland, but, at Kostrovsky's and H.'s instigation, Vaslav now said: "The child has the first claim on a mother's care." But I firmly put my foot down: "The child that needs my care is you, Vaslav, and I go with you."

I tried to provide as many distractions as possible for Vaslav, and we often passed the day with the Duchess of X., who was so obviously madly in love with Vaslav that he objected to going out alone with her, as I suggested. One day, we motored out to the Escorial; a dreary trip through barren desert, but at the last turn of the road we could not restrain an exclamation, for suddenly the grand austere building arose out of nothing, like a mirage, and dominated the whole horizon. The strict, imposing lines of the structure were overwhelming. Vaslav, rooted in admiration, said, "Spain. Religious fanaticism expressed in granite."

As he stood there, so small, so confident in the dazzling sunlight, before entering the gloomy pitiless home of the Inquisition, I wondered how it was that he did not see how the "teachers" were trying, through religious fanaticism, to seize his soul and destroy him.

The Duchess of X., being related to the King, was able to show us everything. After the rooms of Charles V, the crypt seemed almost cheerful.

At lunch, on the terrace, Vaslav seemed to have regained his mischievous ways. He said to me, "Please, *femmka*, do not leave me so much alone with her." He was too discreet to give her away, but too honest not to put me on my guard.

The King with his Court attended almost every performance and was expressive in his admiration. He often came to the rehearsals, and the Duchess of X. told us that in private he attempted to imitate Vaslav's leaps. One evening, he came so late that we could not keep the public waiting any longer. Alfonso said to his aide-de-camp, "Please ask Nijinsky to excuse us for the delay, and tell him: *Je viens d'accoucher d'un nouveau gouvernement.*"

Our intimate life was ideally happy. Sometimes the strangest feeling would come over me, and I felt that the women of mythology may have felt as I did when a God came to love them. There was the exhilarating and inexpressible feeling that Vaslav was more than a human being. The ecstasy that he could create in love as in art had a purifying quality, and yet there was something intangible in his being that one could never reach.

Now Vaslav began to wonder if cohabitation were only justified in case a child is born as the result. Before he had considered the state of my delicate health and the responsibilities of parentage, but now he suggested that either an ascetic life or a child every year was the right way. I immediately understood that this must be Kostrovsky's idea, in order to get me out of the way. One night, when they were discussing this subject, I declared open war.

It was three in the morning. I had listened for hours, seeing how cunningly they were trying to destroy our happiness, and at last, on the verge of tears, I exclaimed, "Why don't you leave my husband alone? You don't dare to talk about his art, because you know that on that subject you cannot influence him. You are not his friends, but his enemies. If you want to create happiness, do so first in your own homes. Your wife, Kostrovsky, is miserable, your children without shoes, because you give your money away to strangers; and you H., if you want advancement, why not ask for it frankly? Vaslav Fomitch would help you. I forbid you both to interfere in our married life. Leave us, this place belongs to Vaslav and me."

Vaslav had never seen me like this before, and for a moment he was taken aback, but then said, "Please *femmka*, they are my friends; do not try to withhold our hospitality."

Kostrovsky and H. sat waiting, with impertinent provoking faces, to see how things would develop, but I turned round; "Vaslav, you have to choose between the diabolical influence of these people and me. If within half an hour these people are still here, I shall leave you."

I waited in the other room, and Vaslav came in to try and persuade me that they were both of good faith, but my determination was unshaken, and, as they were still there when the time was up, I went out into the night.

Next morning, Vaslav found me in the Prado and begged me

to return, saying, "It shall be as you wish." From that day on, Kostrovsky and H. never entered our home any more; but in the theatre they still seized opportunities to get at Vaslav.

We now left for Barcelona, where the Russian Ballet was to perform for the first time, and lodged in the same hotel as Sergei Pavlovitch. The Duchess of X. followed us, and I was rather glad, for I felt she was an ally. Drobetsky, who was ever our staunch friend, informed me that my suspicions that Diaghileff was working through Kostrovsky and H. were not unfounded, and that some trouble was looming. So I thought it was time as ask if Vaslav's salary was to be paid, or did they expect him to dance for nothing as in the past?

One morning we did a lovely motor trip to Montserrat, accompanied by the Kostrovskys and H. Four thousand feet high, Montserrat has a very architectural effect, and the oddest granite cliffs, which take on the forms of curious human figures. Rising suddenly from a plateau, abundant with vineyards and luxurious southern vegetation, it is almost unapproachable, only a narrow path, flanked by perpendicular rocks and bottomless precipices, leads up to the summit. This mountain is supposed to be Parsifal's "Montesalvate." The higher one gets, the lovelier the view is, and on the summit there is a monastery, which Vaslav visited with Kostrovsky and H. alone, we women not being admitted. At lunch at the little inn, Kostrovsky, having ordered a vegetarian lunch, reproved Vaslav for ordering meat, but Vaslav said, "I approve of the idea of vegetarianism, but I cannot, unfortunately, carry it out; as long as I dance, I need solid nourishment." Kostrovsky said, "Then give up dancing."

The evenings we spent with the Duchess of X., who was by this time desperately in love, and wanted to become Vaslav's mistress. Jealousy never entered into my head, and I was even rather pleased when Vaslav returned later than usual one night, but this escapade had quite a different effect upon him than I had expected. He was mournful, and told me frankly:

"*Femmka*, I am sorry for what I did. It was unfair to her, as I am not in love, and the added experience, that perhaps you wanted me to have, is unworthy of us."

Lunching one day with Diaghileff, the latter began to talk about our South American trip, but Vaslav said, "I am not sure I will go, Sergei Pavlovitch. I need a rest, and do not like the idea of being separated from my child in war-time. South America will not be a creative trip artistically."

Diaghileff, with a freezing smile, returned, "But you have to go, you are under contract."

"Have to?" said Vaslav. "I have no contract."

"You cabled me from America agreeing in principle. That is a contract."

"But I also cabled that we would discuss the matter in Spain."

"That is beside the point. In this country, a cable is a binding contract"—and S. P. laughed—"I will force you to go."

In the afternoon, Vaslav notified Sergei Pavlovitch that, as no contract existed, he would take no further part in the Russian Ballet, and we left for the station. But as we boarded the Madrid express, two men touched Vaslav's arm: "M. and Mme. Nijinsky, will you please follow us, you are under arrest." We were aghast.

"On whose authority?" I ventured.

"On that of His Excellency the Marquess of Z., Governor of Catalonia, in the name of the King."

We were escorted to the police station, where, with the aid of several interpreters, they explained that we had been arrested at the behest of Diaghileff—as Vaslav was breaking his contract. If he did not dance that night, he would be put in gaol. Vaslav was pale, but determined: "Very well, put me there! I have no contract. In any case, I can't dance now; I'm too upset." He sat down.

"M. Nijinsky, please promise to dance, then I will not have to imprison you."

"No, I won't; I can't."

"Show us the contract which Diaghileff pretends to have, and then Nijinsky will dance," I said. "Anyhow, you have no right to arrest me; I am a Russian citizen, and not a member of the Russian Ballet. I will complain at the Embassy at once if you do not let me go immediately."

The prefect became rather uneasy, but, very much against his wish, released me. Followed by a detective, I dashed to the telephone, called up the Duc de Durcal in Madrid, who informed the authorities there of what was going on. Within an hour an order arrived from Madrid for our immediate release, and Señor Cambo, the eminent Spanish lawyer, arrived to take up our case with Diaghileff.

The Barcelona authorities now realised that they had made a dreadful blunder, and were full of excuses. It was too late to catch the train, so we returned to the hotel, where Drobetsky and the Spanish director were awaiting us. The director cried out at once: "The public are disappointed, they are returning their tickets by hundreds. It's you they want to see dance. I am ruined, because I have to pay Diaghileff whatever happens, and now I have not made a peso. My last season was a failure, too."

Vaslav was sorry for him. "For your sake, I will dance to-night. Tell the public, please, why I am late."

Next day, Cambo discussed the situation with us. Spain was the only country in which a cable was a binding contract. So Vaslav was bound to go to South America. He regretted now that

381

he had not listened more carefully to Laurence Steinhardt's shrewd advice, and that he had not shown him the cable drafted, word for word, by Kostrovsky and H. But Cambo assured us that Diaghileff would have to grant Vaslav the terms he asked. So he drew up a contract, that Vaslav was willing to go to South America, and that his salary was to be the same as in the U.S.A., payable, in gold dollars, one hour before the curtain rose at every performance. I insisted on such a clause. I did not want any lawsuits later on. If this clause was not fulfilled, the contract became void. It was originated by Fanny Elssler after she had been cheated many times by dishonest impresarios. Vaslav agreed to appear in all parts first danced by himself. The penalty for breaking the contract was twenty thousand dollars. Cambo and I went to Diaghileff with the contract. He received us in his drawing-room, with his usual tactics, sitting with his back to the window, and letting others talk while he listened. The contract was so cleverly drawn up that, while it fulfilled all his stipulations, there was no possibility of any trick being played on Vaslav. While Diaghileff's signature was being affixed, my mind went back to that meeting at the Bristol Hotel, years ago—how very different, and yet how very alike, the situation was.

Shortly afterwards, the Governor called on us, in gala uniform, with white gloves, and a huge bouquet. He came to apologise for the arrest, over which he seemed to be extremely worried, and asked Vaslav to put in a good word for him at Court by saying that he was not to blame for the incident.

We now returned to Madrid for a few days, and from there Kyra was sent to Lausanne.

Diaghileff and Massine and sixteen dancers departed for Italy, and we left with the troupe in the middle of July for South America. This time the troupe was in the hands of Grigoriev.

Vaslav seemed worn out by the excitement of the last few days, especially by the blow that had clearly unmasked Diaghileff's attitude; now he knew that an understanding was forever impossible.

On the journey, Michel said how sorry he was that Sergei Pavlovitch and Vaslav could not agree. "I wanted to, I did everything, I am heartbroken about it," replied Vaslav.

In Cadiz, we seemed to be shadowed all the time; perhaps they were afraid that we would not embark.

We sailed on the *Reina Victoria Eugenia*. This boat was the last word in luxury, but it did not have the home-like feel of the *Avon*. However, we soon settled down, and Vaslav became very busy teaching his system of notation to Kostrovsky and H., and discussing it with Cecchetti.

Maestro was rather depressed on this voyage. He did not like the atmosphere of strife that had reigned lately in the Russian Ballet, and disapproved of Diaghileff's action. He shook his head, and asked me, referring to his warning in Budapest long ago, "Well, is the sun giving you any warmth?"

"*Maestro*, I am perfectly happy, so is Vaslav too, in our marriage; our only sorrow is Sergei Pavlovitch's attitude."

"Yes, yes, I know. I was in London when the news of your marriage arrived. The cable was delivered to Diaghileff at the Savoy. He went livid in the face and fainted. It must have been a cruel blow. These Russians are a strange lot. For thirty-five years I have taught and studied them. They are my friends, I love them, but there is something about them that we Europeans can never, never penetrate. I do hope unhappiness won't come to you through your marriage. I warned you at the beginning. Sergei Pavlovitch should not mix up love and art; it's a very great mistake. And you, Bambina, should have stuck to your lessons; I worked so

383

hard with you, and you were a very promising pupil. But I am tired now, and I won't travel any more. This is my last trip."

Instead of Monteux, we had a new conductor, Ansermet, whom Diaghileff had discovered some time before in Lausanne. He did not seem to us nearly so good as Monteux. Once more the troupe seemed to be split in two camps, for and against Vaslav. The new conductor seemed to side with the last, who were led by G., and Kremeniev. We paid as little attention to them as possible, and kept away from the troupe as much as we could, spending a lot of our time with Andre, Brulé, and Regina Badet. Brulé called Vaslav, *"Le Dieu de la danse"*—which was what he was always known as in France.

Among the many passengers who tried to approach us was a young Chilean, a typical gigolo, extremely well bred and dressed. He was a nephew of some Spanish marquess, from whom he eventually inherited the title and fortune. At that time, however, he was completely broke, and, we all thought, on the look-out for an heiress. There was a slight cut of the adventurer in him, but he was amusing, played bridge excellently, and danced the tango divinely. Vaslav never allowed me to dance modern ball-room dances; he greatly disliked the then fashionable fox-trot, grizzly bear, etc.—"It is not like a waltz or even Boston; *c'est frotter le plancher"*—but he liked tango, and was interested to learn it from the Chilean Georges C. Vaslav danced it with indescribable elegance and smoothness. The lessons, of course, made us quite friendly with C. He tried to make love to me, and Vaslav seemed quite amused. He appeared absolutely devoted to Vaslav, and followed him about like a dog. "I wish I could be of service to him, as a friend or as a secretary. Do let me help you with your correspondence." But I did not; there was something about him which made me cautious—he was too eager.

Madame Kostrovsky seemed more distressed than ever, and one day she called Vaslav for help, and Vaslav then confided to me that Kostrovsky often had bad fits, falling unconscious to the floor. Vaslav was worried about him, and decided to consult a specialist on our arrival.

In Rio we were greeted by a group of friends and the staff of the Russian Embassy. We immediately went up to Sylvestre, to the hotel where we had stayed four years previously. Our little circle was composed of the Diplomatic coterie and some of the Brazilian families. We saw a lot of Edwin Morgan, the U.S.A. Ambassador, and Napoleo G., the music publisher, who introduced us to the native music, with which Vaslav was pleased to make some acquaintance.

The pleasantness of our life among these Brazilian friends was reversed the moment we entered the theatre. With the exception of Drobetsky, the management of the troupe did everything to make life difficult for Vaslav and to antagonise him. Vaslav, who adored his art, now almost dreaded the hour he had to go to the theatre. He went through his exercises, and through performances, more silently than ever. *Maestro* spent a lot of time with him, and one could see that with the golden heart of a real artist and colleague, he was trying to counteract the painful atmosphere created by the others.

One night, Vaslav woke me up, *"Femmka,* do you know that *Faune* is on the programme the day after to-morrow, and they did not even ask me?"

"It can't be possible."

"I told them it wasn't fair, as they don't own the rights, but they just shrugged their shoulders. But, *femmka,* I just won't allow them to do it."

"But, how can you prevent it, Vaslav?"

"Just wait," and he laughed in his mischievous, irresistible way.

Early next morning, Vaslav departed, with Napoleo and his other friends, on a mysterious errand, and at lunch-time they all came back triumphantly smiling at me. I could not make out what they were up to.

At this time Vaslav had a lot of trouble with the conductor. Vaslav was very strict about not changing *tempi*. He had a very orthodox conception of the interpretation of the classics. He always held that, in drama, music, and the dance, the author's idea must be adhered to absolutely. With Beecham, Monteux, Baton, and the others there never was any trouble. It was different now. Discipline in the ballet had greatly slackened, and if a dancer had some difficulty with a certain step, he or she just asked the conductor to change the *tempi*. Of this, Vaslav frankly expressed his disapproval. That evening the performance seemed to go very smoothly. The *entr'acte*, during which I admired the colourful audience, seemed to me unusually long. *Faune* was the next ballet on the programme. The public became restless; I wondered what could have happened. Vaslav's friends were smiling like conspirators. I went back stage; everything was ready, the scene lit, Vaslav in position waiting for the curtain to rise. But at one side of the stage there was a gesticulating group. The impresario, Grigoriev, Kremeniev, pacing up and down in a frenzy, Drobetsky trying to hide a smile. The impresario was talking to two police officials. What had happened? They told me: "Nijinsky, the author of *Faune*, has brought an injunction to prevent the presentation of *Faune*, as it does not legally belong to the Russian Ballet."

Nijinsky, the dancer, however, stood waiting to begin his part in the *Faune* according to the terms of his contract. "But, Nijinsky the author, and Nijinsky the dancer, are the same person," said one of the ballet. "Sorry; have you anything in writing to prove that you have the author's permission to perform it—yes or no?" And *Faune* had to be cancelled. Vaslav admitted that it was a trick on his part, but he thought it rather an innocent one after what he had had to endure the previous year from Sergei Pavlovitch and his sycophantic staff.

Our most pleasant recollection was meeting the great poet Paul Claudel, at that time French Ambassador in Brazil. He invited us to the Embassy to lunch, and introduced Vaslav to the promising young musician Darius Milhaud; one of the "group of six." Milhaud and Claudel were then composing a ballet, *L'homme et son désir*, and they wanted Vaslav to do the choreography. Vaslav was pleased with the idea.

Often Claudel took us motoring; he knew the most enchanting places. It was a great change and relief to be with persons like him, and to get away from the stifling atmosphere of the Ballet. Claudel, who had lived in the Far East, made Vaslav intimately acquainted with Oriental art.

The heat was overwhelming. The only thing that made the performances tolerable for the artists was the refrigerator system, with which the theatre was equipped. We accepted with alacrity the Russian Ambassador Tscherbatckoi's invitation to visit him at his summer residence in Petropolis, in the hills behind Rio, where we were welcomed with real Russian hospitality.

On our return to Rio, we had disturbing news by the mail from Europe. Kyra was well, but the head doctor of the sanatorium in Lausanne complained that he was in great difficulty because my mother had arrived from Hungary and, with the support of the Austro-Hungarian Consul, had claimed the child. We immediately cabled instructions, through the Russian Consulate, to keep Kyra in Lausanne until our arrival.

Our next city on the schedule was São Paulo. We went on one of the Royal Mail Company's boats. Painted grey, even to the port-holes, it looked gloomy, but this was the necessity of the submarine war. We were told that after sunset we were not allowed on deck, or to light lamps or cigarettes. At the stern of the boat there was a cannon. We laughed at the sight of it, but not for long. One day a ship was sighted on the horizon, and we all rushed to see it, for it was a rarity to meet ships on the high seas in those days of the war. The ship came rapidly towards us. An officer explained to Vaslav that, according to the international regulations of war, ships have to approach each other close enough to prove that they are friendly. This one suddenly turned round, put up a smoke-screen, and became invisible. The officers rushed to the gun, and the women shrieked. I ran up to the radio officer. Vaslav came after and tried to quiet me. I cried, "I have had enough of all this; please Vaslav, let us go to Switzerland and have peace."

"Yes, yes, we will."

Calmette, the head of the Research Institute in São Paulo, brother of Calmette of the *Figaro*, who had caused so much fracas at the first performance of *Faune*, showed us round his extremely interesting place, where serums against snake-bites and insects are prepared.

Claudel was at São Paulo, and we spent most of our time with him.

Already in Rio, I had received a letter from my kinsman B., who was then living in Buenos Aires, to welcome us to South America. He requested me to send him a photograph of Vaslav, which I did.

Montevideo was our next stop. This time it proved full of great social activities. The Embassies entertained us, and we became very friendly with Jules Lefaivre, the French Minister. Mitchell

Innes, the English Minister, invited us to a lunch, where we met several members of the Pavlova Company, who were then dancing in Montevideo.

On this tour, I used to sit in Vaslav's dressing-room, with a watch in my hand, waiting for Vaslav's salary—one hour before the beginning of the performance; and poor Drobetsky had to explore all the banks to find enough gold *à la Elssler*. In Montevideo he was unable to find it, and Vaslav again danced for nothing.

My kinsman B. now arrived from Buenos Aires. He had been sent by the family to the Argentine, in disgrace, a few years before the war. He was a brilliant lawyer, and had a real genius for politics, an incredible memory and knowledge; but unfortunately he lavished his talents on unworthy objects. His passion was to expose people's private lives. He knew the law so well that he could always get away with his attacks, on leading politicians, officers of the general staff, and society women, in a paper he edited himself. Even his own family was not exempt from his attacks. However, he got into real trouble when he exposed a high Hungarian general, and was then exiled to the Argentine. At the request of my uncle Gari, Vaslav had given him some financial help. He failed to make a good impression on Vaslav, who, however, gave him the several thousand pesos he asked for. Later in the night, he came back, saying that the money had been stolen from him, and asked for some more!

Vaslav and I took Kostrovsky to a specialist here, who told me, as I was the only one to speak Spanish, that Kostrovsky had epilepsy, was incurable, dangerously insane, and should be repatriated to Russia.

Four years had elapsed since we were in Buenos Aires. It was almost like coming home—this city where we had first known happiness. Great improvements had been made in the city. We were met at the docks by old friends, among them Señor Quintana, the son of the ex-President, and, in the group that welcomed us, we also found the Chilean C. who had taught us the tango on the boat.

Our apartment was in the New Plaza Hotel. Mr. Gavuzzi received us, saying, "Your secretary is in your drawing-room, with the gentlemen of the Press."

"But there must be a mistake," answered Vaslav. "I have no secretary."

When we were shown in, we saw the reporters drinking cocktails and holding printed sheets in their hands.

"What is this?"

"It is Mr. Nijinsky's interview."

Vaslav and I looked at each other speechless. Don de B., as my kinsman liked to call himself, had prepared and distributed this "interview" himself. The reporters also showed us some photographs, apparently autographed by Vaslav, and we recognised these as copies of the one I had sent privately to my kinsman!

Quintana took us all round, to the Races, and to the Jockey Club, where we met Sir Reginald Tower, the British Ambassador, with whom we became very friendly.

C. and my kinsman became very friendly. The latter asked me to come and see his home, and there he showed me his beautifully arranged dossiers of all the important people of the Argentine; every peccadillo, every love-affair, was recorded. "But what is the idea? Why do you waste your time in this way?" He replied, "You do not understand. To become a great politician, one has to know all the weaknesses of the leaders of society."

I now began to receive curious letters from acquaintances in

Europe, asking me if any of their letters to me had been stolen, and repeating rumours that were being spread about liaisons that Vaslav and I were supposed to have had with various people. I could not make it out. One day, my kinsman came in rather excitedly, saying that he needed a considerable amount of money at once to prevent a newspaper attack that was being organised against Vaslav by one of the Russian Ballet. I did not mention it to Vaslav, but gave B. the money. One morning later, to my amazement, I saw an article of political content in one of the papers, with my own name as the author of it. The article calmly divided up the Austro-Hungarian Empire! I rang up Quintana, and he undertook at once to deny my authorship of it.

Lately, too, B. had insinuated that there was an *affaire* between Vaslav and C. I laughed in his face. I knew Vaslav too well—he would have been the first to tell me. B. also wanted to take us to indecent motion-pictures, but Vaslav refused to go, and said: "*Femmka*, I would rather not see B. in our home. We can help him financially of course."

So we were not "at home" any more when he called. But he was too cunning, and, by making love to my elderly Spanish maid, and promising her a position with an arch-duchess in Vienna, he not only got her to allow him into our apartments during our absence, but also to give him our correspondence. All this, however, we only found out later.

The anniversary of our wedding arrived. The priest who married us gave a lunch in our honour, and Vaslav surprised me with a beautiful bag of heavy gold, and a vanity-case set with sapphires.

Pavlova was dancing at this time in Buenos Aires. We met her in the grill-room one day, when she came over to our table, and talked to Vaslav very sweetly in Russian. I looked at her curiously, remembering her telephone call at the time of Vaslav's accident in the U.S.A.

Things with the Russian Ballet did not go smoothly. But Vaslav went on with his work, seemingly not noticing their attitude. Curious things began to happen in the theatre—Vaslav stepped on a rusty nail. "How did it happen to be on the stage?" I asked. "By accident." Then, one evening while Vaslav was practising, a heavy iron counter-weight fell down from the grid. Vaslav instinctively jumped away, and only his quickness saved his life. An investigation was ordered: "An accident." I began to wonder about these happenings, and mentioned them to Quintana. He shared my opinion. In Vaslav's contract, there was a clause that he had to pay twenty thousand dollars if he did not fulfil the terms. Some people may have wanted to assist the hand of fate. So Quintana, who was a prominent lawyer, arranged with the authorities for detectives to keep watch on Vaslav—they used to come back stage.

One day, a menacing mob surrounded our hotel owing to strong anti-German feeling and Gavuzzi, the manager, came complaining to me that my kinsman had attacked him in the papers, saying that he was an illegitimate son of the Kaiser, and a spy. He thought this was probably because he had given orders that B. was not to be admitted to the hotel, after a scene which had almost cost my kinsman his life and myself my freedom.

One day, when Vaslav entered his room, he found B. waiting. He insisted on speaking to him, and rapidly began to tell Vaslav that I was his mistress, and had also been C.'s mistress. When I first heard B.'s voice, I went to enter the room, to stop him tiring Vaslav with his talk, but, when I heard the atrocious lies about myself, I was nailed to the floor. Suddenly I remembered how, one day, my kinsman had complained of the heat, and undressed and put on Vaslav's dressing-gown. He then laid down on the couch, and invited me to come and sit by him. But I refused, and asked him to dress and leave. I never thought then that he had any hidden motive for his behaviour, but now I understood the whole frame-up. As he could not get all the money he wanted out of me by loans, he was now resorting to other methods. I seized a revolver, and opened the door slowly. Vaslav was standing there motionless, pale, but very quiet. "Please leave this place at once; my wife is above all your calumnies, and whatever she pleases to do is right"; and, luckily for B., as Vaslav spoke I was surrounded by the manager and staff of the hotel, who put my kinsman into the street.

But B. was relentless. The next thing he did was to attack Vaslav, by accusing him of spying for Austria-Hungary, in the very paper which he had told me was going to print an attack on Vaslav by some member of the Russian Ballet. Quintana immediately brought a libel action, and B. was ordered to admit that the whole thing was a lie. It turned out that he already had a very bad record with the police, as he was known to have gone to the English, French, and German Embassies and offered his services to them all simultaneously. Someone at one of the Embassies told us how he had outlined to them his plan for starting a revolution in Hungary, and undermining the Army, if the Allies would supply him with funds. He was told however that revolutions are made on the spot, not thousands of miles away.

All this time Vaslav behaved with extraordinary calm. But in his strained, pale face, I noticed the same expression as at the time of our interment in Hungary. We both ardently desired peace. It was sad to see that Vaslav had to be watched by detectives to assure his safety among his own colleagues. The troupe recognised that Vaslav only lived for his art, and was not satisfied with anything short of perfection. They said, "One could never find a truer artist," but thought that he was stubborn, as he expected very exact execution. They misunderstood his extreme reserve, and thought him snobbish. They called him "Dumb-bell," because he was so silent. The members of the Mariinsky Theatre were different, they loved Vaslav truly. I prayed for the end of the season.

Vaslav was dancing *Scheherazade*. He had made changes in his make-up, which was now a deep hue of silvery grey. Watching him, I forgot all our troubles. Once, at the *finale*, when he made his final jump, when he is chased by the soldier who hits him on the head, the audience rose with a scream, and I did too, although I had already seen *Scheherazade* more than a hundred times. In that final jump, Vaslav, with the briefest touch of his head on the floor, flung himself into the air by the action of his neck-muscles, quivered, and fell. I ran back stage, but there was Vaslav practising *entre-chats!* So convincing had his execution been that we all thought he was hurt.

But what I had been dreading all the time finally happened. Since the detectives were officially admitted to the theatre, and supervised the stage, curiously enough no more accidents occurred. I shall never forget the astonished faces of the management of the Russian Ballet when they asked, as they thought, some loafing strangers to leave, and were shown the detectives' badges. One evening when *Petrouchka* was given, during the last scene, when Petrouchka shows himself to the magician from the top of the Puppet Theatre, the thing happened. Suddenly the whole structure began to shake, as in an earthquake, and Vaslav pitched forward. He did not lose his presence of mind, and endeavoured to leap clear. From that height he would undoubtedly have injured his leg on landing, but Cecchetti, risking his own safety, sprang forward and caught Vaslav in his arms.

The investigation proved that the scenery had never been fastened. The signal had been given to begin the ballet before the stage hand could fasten it firmly enough.

In spite of all the attacks that were made on him, even now Vaslav did not complain. He merely said, "Do not blame them. They do not realise what they are doing. *Il n'y a pas des hommes méchants, seulement des hommes bêtes.*"

Our friends in Montevideo asked us to visit them again at the end of the Argentine season, which we did, and, at the request of the French and English Ambassadors, Vaslav gave an extra performance for the wounded soldiers of the Allies, Arthur Rubinstein accompanying him on the piano. The public went wild with enthusiasm at this performance, but, as I followed Vaslav's floating movements on the stage in his mazurka in *Sylphides*, little did I think that I had seen him dance for the last time in the theatre.

We returned to Buenos Aires for a few days, to arrange our departure for Europe, deciding to leave on a different boat from the troupe. But Vaslav insisted on going down to the docks to say good-bye to the artists. "They are not responsible for the actions of Diaghileff and his staff."

As we waved good-bye to the slowly moving boat from the quay of the Rio de la Plata, we knew that we had said farewell forever to the Russian Ballet.

Chapter Nineteen

HOME
IN ST. MORITZ

Our Argentine friends escorted us to the dock, and Quintana promised to look after the lawsuit against Diaghileff, as the Russian Ballet had broken their contract at the very last moment by refusing to pay our passage back to Europe. Sir Reginald Tower assured us that he did not pay the slightest attention to B.'s calumnies, and that, whatever happened during the journey home, we were to remain calm. As we steamed out of Buenos Aires, it was rumoured that the Allies were looking for German spies who were supposed to be on board, under false names. Three days passed quietly. Then one evening, as I was dressing for dinner, the boat slowed down and suddenly stopped. I turned quickly to Vaslav, but he reassured me. "Don't be alarmed; it is nothing. Probably only the English cruiser we were told would stop the boat." I looked out of the port-hole. The sun was setting, and in front of its blood-red disc the shape of a swift, dark cruiser was rapidly looming upon the horizon. We went on deck. I was trembling. Some English officers came aboard. The passengers were asked to go down to the baggage-room and open their trunks. An officer went into every cabin and looked round. When he came to ours, he saluted, asked our names, and left. The search went on for three hours. I became frantic. "Vaslav, they will arrest me, take me off the boat."

"But what for, *femmka?*"

"Because I was born Hungarian."

"Now, *femmka, tu es bête.* The English are sensible people; they will not do anything to you."

Everybody was questioned; only we seemed to be left out. I rushed down to my cabin and seized the picture of the little Jesus of Prague, the one that had given Vaslav to me years before. It had always been my icon, but the prayer on the back was printed in German, so in a panic I tore it in two and threw it into the sea. As the picture floated on the waves, I could see the small head of the miraculous Jesus turned upwards, looking at me. I uttered a scream. I wanted to get it back, but it was already sinking slowly, and I had the uncanny presentiment that my happiness was sinking with it. Soon afterwards the investigating officers departed, and we resumed our journey in peace.

The homeward journey was uneventful. The only excitements were the radio reports of the war bulletin. Vaslav rested in his deck-chair practically the whole day, correcting the second revision of his system of notation. I would usually bring him a cup of beef tea and the news. One day I told him that the power in Russia had been seized by the local soviets, and Lenin and Trotsky, repatriated three days ago, had formed a Government. Vaslav was not even quite sure who they were, and remarked that it was strange that they should put somebody in power who had always lived away from Russia. We neither of us knew what this really meant for our country and the world.

On the voyage we were more reserved than ever, and did not make any acquaintances, as we had been warned by our friends in Rio of a certain Mr. R., a Belgian, who was on the boat.

In fact, this gentleman tried in every way to approach us. He was generally in the bar, or playing cards, and his wife was beautifully dressed. We were told that he was a partner in the firm of Lacloche, the best jewellery store in Buenos Aires.

On our arrival in Europe we took the Sud Express and went right through Spain. At the French frontier we had to change. It took a long time to pass the passport office. We did not like to push, and in consequence missed the connection, just seeing Mr. R. waving to us to hurry; our sleepers were in the same car as his. What were we to do? There was no other express train for two days, so we decided to put up at the local hotel and looked round for our hand-luggage. The porter who had it was supposed to wait for us on the platform, but he was nowhere to be found. Nobody knew where our luggage was, and after a frantic search we were told he had gone off duty and returned to his home on the other side of the frontier. I burst out crying, "My jewels!" and rushed to the station-master. He was no help at all. It was impossible to re-cross the frontier. The station was searched in vain. I spent a gloomy day crying for my pearls and lovely rubies, sapphires, all the bracelets, rings, which Vaslav had given me— all gone.

Next day the porter returned to duty and told us that he had put our luggage in our compartment on the express, assuming we would catch the train. "You fool!" I could not help exclaiming.

"*Tu vois, femmka,*" said Vaslav, "*tu aurais dû porter la boite à bijoux dans tes mains. En tous les cas ces choses matérielles ne sont pas importantes. Penses aux gens qui perdent leurs maris, leurs enfants, à la guerre.*"

But all this could not console me. The station-master thought the *chef de train* would put the luggage out at the next station, but I thought myself that it had been stolen by the porter.

However, we took the next slow train for Paris and inquired at each station. After a terrible journey of forty hours, in a compartment full of soldiers returning from leave, we finally arrived in Paris. No sign of our luggage. But Vaslav just said, *"Femmka, c'est perdu; n'y penses plus.* You see, you would not be worried if you did not care for that sort of thing."

But I was more worried than ever when, on trying to trace Mr. R., I found that Lacloche in Paris had no connection with the firm of the same name in Buenos Aires. All my suspicions were now turned to Mr. R. and, as it proved, correctly, only—he had not stolen the luggage, but merely deposited it safely at the office of the Wagons Lits to await our arrival in Paris!

Vaslav was full of joy as we neared Lausanne. He almost ran to the sanatorium where Kyra was. She was sitting on her bed and seemed almost as big as the teddy-bear Vaslav had given her before leaving Spain. She looked more like Vaslav than ever. He clasped her in his arms and danced round the room. Kyra screamed with joy. It was remarkable how the child changed the moment Vaslav entered the room. It seemed almost as though they had been one person split apart, and constantly wishing to be reunited. Sometimes I almost felt as if I were intruding on them. They were both essentially and fundamentally Russian—something we Europeans can never, never penetrate. They so easily adapted themselves to different circumstances, to joy, to sorrow, to luxury, to hardship.

After our bitter experiences, we realised that all association with Diaghileff and his company was over forever. Their ideas and those of Vaslav were now far apart. Diaghileff wished to go on producing sensational cubist and futurist ballets at all costs, while, much as Vaslav believed in acrobatics as an accessory to dancing, he did not see it as a final end, and did not wish the future of the ballet to follow the path of the music-hall. He greatly admired such dancers as Mitty and Tilio, but could not see them in the ballet atmosphere. He advocated that ballet-dancers should be trained as acrobats in order to give them greater power over their bodies. Diaghileff was only interested in the present, whereas Vaslav was also interested in the future.

We decided to settle down quietly somewhere, where he could compose until the end of the war. Vaslav dreamed of a return to Russia, to make his home there, to create the school, the theatre, and the artistic laboratory that he so desired. Also, he thought of having a *pied-à-terre* in Paris, so that he could keep in touch with Western ideas; and, anyhow, he adored Paris. He had already designed our future home in Russia with a special apartment for Kyra, all painted by Russian artists, with small furniture and everything in proportion for the child-mind. Now he asked me to find a suitable place to await the end of the war. We were tired of hotels, and so I finally decided on St. Moritz Dorf, that I had loved ever since I was a girl. I could never forget those gigantic Alps, with the bracing air, the dark pine-trees, and the magical sun shining on the snow. It was so like Russia that Vaslav would surely love it. "But I hate mountains. They hide the view. I want to see far, far away. I do not want to be shut in," said Vaslav. "Come and see it before you decide," I said.

So early in December 1917 we went to St. Moritz. The place was deserted, and, as I had anticipated, Vaslav was enchanted. We soon found a charming villa high up on the hill on the road to Chanterella. Quickly I engaged a staff and put everything in order. When the villa was first heated we stood together awestruck in the clear sunshine, facing the Alp Giop, watching the smoke escaping

A DRAWING BY NIJINSKY   (1919)

WATERCOLOUR BY NIJINSKY   (1922)

from the chimney of our first home. We could now live together, undisturbed, for the first time since our marriage.

The very first night in St. Moritz I was awakened by a terrifying noise like the roaring of guns. We were not very far from the Austro-Italian front, and in the mountains the echo of the guns might easily have reached us. Then the roaring became clearer, and I felt my bed shake. "Vaslav, what is this?"

"Some new arrival at the hotel; they are pulling the trunks about on the top floor."

But at the moment that Vaslav switched on the light our beds were pushed over to the other side of the room by some powerful unknown force. The lamp swung about, the pictures fell off the walls, and the bottles and things fell off the table, while the ground seemed to float about under us. "Be calm," said Vaslav. "It is nothing, only an earthquake." There was another strong shock. "For God's sake come on, Vaslav"; and nervously I put a slipper on one foot, a snow-boot on the other, threw a fur round me, and made for the staircase, forgetting this time jewellery and everything else. "Vaslav, come, come!" But he quietly began to dress.

Everyone was in front of the hotel, sitting in the snow with chattering teeth, more from fright than from the cold. "Let us go into the lobby, *femmka.*" The telephonist was trying to get in touch with Zürich. "In Samadan it is quite bad . . . the Rosegthal seems to be the centre. . . . Milan is all right. . . . Seventeen shocks already."

Vaslav was quietly watching the crooked tower. "It will be such a pity if it collapses." Luckily very little damage was done.

Next day Vaslav left for Lausanne to fetch Kyra and the nurse. I was rather nervous, as he could not speak German, and was completely lost when he had to attend to the necessities of everyday life. To book a room in a hotel and to buy a railway

401

ticket were experiences unknown to him. Vaslav was very proud, and was full of adventurous feeling starting out on his first trip alone.

Our house looked like a real home, with all our personal belongings. The entrance was full of ski and toboggans, as I had decided to take part in all the winter sports. The house overlooked St. Moritz, and the lake lay at our feet. Opposite was the beautiful Roseg Alp and the Piz Margna that sheltered us from the eastern winds, and snow glittering, snow everywhere, seven feet deep, that promised us a glorious winter. Vaslav and Kyra arrived, and in a few days we had fallen into our daily routine. I wanted to attend to everything for Vaslav, but he refused. "A man should not be served by his wife, *femmka*." The wardrobe of an old maid could not have been more perfectly in order and more spotlessly clean than Vaslav kept his things.

The balcony on the ground floor was cleared. There, every morning, for two hours, Vaslav did his exercises, with Kyra looking on and patiently watching Tatakaboy dance, and when he leaped she used to cheer and clap her hands, then often Vaslav, forgetting his iron discipline, caught her in his arms and waltzed round singing, *"Votre amabilité, maia Kotyik, maia Funtyiki."*

When shopping in the village, I used to signal the latest war news up to him practising on the balcony. There was a bulletin posted every noon in the middle of the village, and we had arranged a code of signals with my arms.

This winter was a very happy one. We were constantly together undisturbed, and went for long walks all over the Engadine. I used to practise on the Dimson skeleton run; it was my favourite sport. Vaslav was simply worshipped by the servants. If he met the cook on the way up to the Villa, he carried the parcels. If the coal was too heavy to put on the fire, he helped the maid, and he even flirted with the old laundress, bought her chianti, and chatted to her of her native Italy. He would play with all the children of the village. Sometimes we used to meet at Hanselmann's for an *apéritif* before lunch, where everybody goes during the season. Hanselmann, an Austrian by origin, the well-known *confiseur* of St. Moritz, quite a personality, played a leading part in the life of the place. He became a staunch friend of "Monsieur Nijinsky." Vaslav appreciated his *Käse-stängel*, gave him recipes for *Koulibjak*, and sometimes discussed the political situation with him at length.

We often went, too, to Dr. Bernhard's. His house was the last word in Engadine style, and was the meeting-place of many interesting Swiss and foreigners. Our neighbour, President Gartmann, also entertained us.

Kyra was developing well, and looked lovely trotting beside Vaslav in her teddy-bear suit. They used to lunge down the hill to Celerina at a breakneck speed. I was scared. "Nothing will happen to my *amabilité* as long as we are together," Vaslav used to say. The evenings we usually spent quietly at home reading.

Vaslav accompanied me when I went skating, and, though he did not take part in any of the winter sports, he gave me remarkable advice on technique and balance. His instinctive knowledge was amazing.

Then Vaslav discovered sleighs that he could drive himself, and twice a week we would go off in the morning, the three of us, either picnicking or stopping at some roadside inn for lunch. We explored the glaciers, passes, and lakes of the Bernina. With the coming of the season many of our friends arrived from Paris, and Vaslav seemed to be quite rested and soothed by the light-

403

hearted gaiety of his *entourage*. As a surprise for me, he invited my sister and my brother-in-law Schmedes. Erik was a kind soul, and Vaslav had not forgotten his loyalty.

The spring came, and with it the foreigners departed; we were left alone again with the natives, whose life was quite patriarchal. It seemed remote and five centuries back to us. The celebrated sports centre had become a very quiet Alpine village again. In the evening, at the Hôtel Post, the notary, the Mayor, and the doctor, would meet to discuss the welfare of their little community. Vaslav loved to listen to their debate; it reminded him so much of Russia. We were so much in love with St. Moritz that we did not wish to leave it even for a day.

The first timid crocuses pushed their way up and spring was officially here, but the torrents of melting snow kept us indoors more, and Vaslav resumed my lessons. He seemed lighter than ever; the number of his pirouettes and *entre-chats* was infinite, and, watching him make his *battements* and *pliés*, it sometimes seemed to me that he was lighter than the snow-flakes themselves. But his strength was of steel, and he bounded like india-rubber.

Once, while reading, I remarked to him how the people in each century seemed to resemble each other. "That is the result of costume," he replied, "for costume determines our movements." The idea was new to me, but, on thinking it over, I saw he was right. Vaslav was able, on seeing the lines and materials of a costume, to reconstruct the proper gestures of a period. He literally put bodies into the empty costumes of any historical period.

He was full of ideas for new ballets. He composed a delightful version of Debussy's *Chanson de Bilitis*. He said, "I want you to dance Bilitis. I have created it for you. It obeys the same basic choreographic laws as the *Faune*." It was in perfect harmony with the movement of the music, with all its delicate feeling and sweet perversity. This ballet was in two scenes, the first Bilitis and her shepherd, their love, their youth on the green islands of Greece; the second, Bilitis and her girl lover, who shares her sorrows, and her pleasures.

Vaslav's other creation was his own life put into a choreographic poem: a youth seeking truth through life, first as a pupil, open to all artistic suggestions, to all the beauty that life and love can offer; then his love for the woman, his mate, who finally carries him off. He set it in the period of the High Renaissance. The youth was a painter; his master one of the greatest artists of the period, a universal genius, just as Diaghileff seemed to him to be. He designed the scenery and costumes for it himself, modern, and yet correct to the period. "You know, *femmka,* the circle is the complete, the perfect movement. Everything is based on it—life, art, and most certainly our art. It is the perfect line." The whole system of notation was based on the circle, and so was this ballet. It was in accordance with Vaslav's previous methods, but, unlike *Faune* and *Sacre,* it was circular. The scenery was a design in curve, and even the proscenium opening was round. Vaslav worked out the whole design himself to the smallest detail, in blues, red, and gold, Raphaelistic in style.

Almost overnight our surroundings had changed. The frozen lake began to quiver, the slopes of the Alps, covered with fragrant flowers, had become a riot of colour, the pink alpen-roses, the sweet-smelling purple violets, and the cornflower blue gentians. The snow retreated to the summits of the peaks, which were now so familiar to us and had each its own meaning for Vaslav. We used to run up to the Alp Giop and throw ourselves down among the flowers. And, while lying there in the scented pasture, we spoke of many things. I told Vaslav about my parents' unhappy marriage, and blamed my mother, but he stopped me. "Don't be hard. You do not know the circumstances that made her act the way she did. We should never condemn anybody, nor have we the right to judge." I often complained about the difficult times we were having to go through during the war, but Vaslav said, "Do not look up to the more fortunate, look down to those worse off than yourself, and be thankful for your destiny."

I had been suffering slightly ever since Kyra's birth, and Vaslav urged me to go and consult a specialist in Berne. There it was decided that a minor operation should take place. I entered the sanatorium, and, when all was over, wired to Vaslav. He arrived by the next train, his arms full of roses, and spent two weeks near my bedside. In Berne he saw the Sakharoffs dancing. Next day, when I complained that I could not accompany him, he said, "You have not lost anything. It is merely attitudinising, not dancing at all. *C'est du Munich.*" I saw he was disappointed, as he was ever eager to see new talent to further his beloved art.

Autumn came, the air was crystalline, the colours graded from lightest topaz to sun-burned sepia. I was not yet quite strong, and Vaslav was anxious for me to rest. Vaslav took a great interest in the household, and, in the Russian patriarchal way, saw that the house was well provided with fuel for the winter. The wood was cut in our garden, and he used to help the men in their work. He also often visited the kitchen, to the great delight of the cook. He would lift the lids of the saucepans, and, if he happened to arrive when a cake was being baked, he usually cleaned out the bowl, just as in his childhood.

I used to give Kyra's Swiss nursery governess a day off to see her husband, an employee at the Palace Hotel. One day she was called down to him urgently, and did not return for two days. When she came back, she told me of the great misfortune that had ruined her life. Her husband had suddenly become insane.

406

He was to be sent to an asylum, and she must return to her parents. She told me of the heart-rending scene when she had seen him put into a strait-jacket. "But, Marie, didn't you notice anything before?" "No, he was always quite normal, only lately at night he used to walk round his room for hours and hours." Later, I told Vaslav that we should have to look for a new governess, and the reason why. He became strangely silent, and his face darkened. The new governess, a Swiss girl, brought up in England, had been for a long time in India, and in the evenings she would speak of her experience of fakirs and yogis. Vaslav became interested in the subject and began to study it.

This year the winter came early. When the snowing began, it went on for days and nights continuously. It was peaceful and warm; we seemed to be far away from the world, forgotten. The strange fascination of this isolated alpine village grew on us. In this sleepy whiteness, one morning the first news arrived from Bronia and *"Babouchka."* They were well and did not need anything. They had received the money sent by Vaslav, but when the November Revolution took place they had fled to Kiev. There was a letter enclosed to me saying that when the Bolsheviks seized power the gaols and asylums were thrown open, and poor Stanislav, left to himself, had been burnt to death. I had to break it to Vaslav; but how? I knew that he loved his brother. For days I was silent, but finally I plucked up courage and went to him. He was drawing at the time. *"Regarde, femmka, ça c'est notre Kouharka* and this is Marie." He showed me two lovely pastel portraits of the cook and the maid, transformed into Russian peasants, and a striking picture of Kyra. "This is Funtyiki; you think it looks like her?"

I hated to spoil his happiness. "Vaslav, I want to talk." He sat down in the arm-chair, and I on the edge. Petting and caressing him, I buried my face on his shoulder, and said quickly, "Stanislav is dead." A long silence, then Vaslav lifted my face and asked how it happened. I told him, and burst into tears. He looked at me smiling, but with a strange and deep quietness. "Do not cry; he was insane; it is better like this"; and he bowed his head. The same smile that he had had at his father's death came back again, and now I knew that Bolm had made a mistake, and that Vaslav was not heartless; on the contrary. But I felt it was strange—very strange.

Impresarios had heard of Vaslav's presence in Switzerland, and offers came pouring in, but I had to refuse them. One of them was bold enough to come to our home. I sent him off, but in the village he stopped Vaslav by asking for a match, and immediately began to make offers. Vaslav was so amused by the man's persistence that he asked him up to the house for tea, and promised that he would be given the first chance, when he was ready to dance again.

All this winter Vaslav was very busy composing and designing. His drawings were all based on the circle, and he developed an amazing technique of producing astonishing portraits out of a few circles.

During the long winter evenings, when it snowed and snowed ceaselessly, our little governess proposed that we should try some *séances*. We did, and it amused me, but Vaslav took everything more seriously the moment he became interested in any subject. We got some curious answers, which we wrote down and put away.

"What will happen to Hungary?" I asked.

"It will be a kingdom without a king."

"And Count Tisza?"

"He will be killed."

"And Russia?"

"Neither war nor peace. Twenty-two years of uncertainty, then a democratic confederate republic."

Many things were said about after death and the after life at these *séances*. I wondered if any of it was true.

"Of course, *femmka*, life goes on in another form. Birth and death are very similar. Both are part of a circle which goes on. We are an infinite part of God in the universe, and when we create something beautiful, we reflect Him."

Finally the day arrived when I could signal to Vaslav the unexpected news that an armistice had been declared. I ran up the stairs to the villa breathlessly to tell him the details, but he shook his head on reading the conditions. "Peace, peace. There can be no peace under those terms. War will go on, but in a hidden, different way."

We were now able to begin our excursions again. Going up to the Fexthal, we had to pass through Sils Maria, and I pointed out to him the house where Nietzsche lived and wrote his *Ecce Homo*. Vaslav liked this book. Lately he had been reading a lot of Maeterlinck's new words, *La Mort*, and meditated more than ever.

Vaslav's new ballet, a choreographic drama, was making great progress. It was to be a picture of sex life with the scene laid in a *maison tolérée*. The chief character was to be the owner, once a beautiful *cocotte*, now aged and paralysed as a result of her debauchery; but, though her body was a wreck, her spirit was indomitable in the traffic of love. She deals with all the wares of love: selling girls to boys, youth to age, woman to woman, man to man.

"But, Vaslav, how will you be able to express it?" He danced, and succeeded in transmitting the whole scale of sex life. "I want to show both the beauty and the destructive quality of love."

Speaking of his future plans, Vaslav said, "From next autumn on, if I cannot yet return to Russia, I will form my own company and live in Paris and dance." It was at this time, too, that Vaslav requested me to put down in writing his artistic ideas.

The winter season was beginning once more, and it promised to be a record one. The war was over at last. We decided to make our first Christmas in our own home and in peace-time a cheerful one, and we were convinced that after the sad, stormy years we were sailing at last towards a calm and happy future.

Chapter Twenty

MARRIAGE
AVEC DIEU

THE 24TH of December was passed in feverish preparations. The big pine-tree, which went right up to the ceiling, was brought into the drawing-room and placed near the open fireplace. We adorned it ourselves; it was a beautiful heavily laden tree, full of candies, toys, silver nuts and garlands, and on the top Vaslav himself placed a shining silver star—"The tree for Kyroschka." He looked it over with a critical glance. He wanted it to be very lovely, and so it was. We enjoyed preparing it. Vaslav had helped me to wrap up the presents neatly in silver paper; one for each of the household. Vaslav also remembered many children and sick people in the village, and we went round to take them their parcels.

Our Christmas Eve was a peaceful and happy one. Kyra's eyes opened wide when she saw the beautiful illuminated tree which Tatakaboy, as she called her father, lighted for her. Next morning I slept late, and was awakened by the maid, who came in trembling and white as a sheet. "Oh, madame, as I went into the drawing-room I found the Christmas-tree fallen on the floor. It means bad luck." I shivered. *"Femmka, c'est une bêtise;* it only means that it lost balance, was overladen on one side. I can't understand it; I made it so carefully." We went down to see it. There it lay on the floor, the silver nuts all round and the silver star broken in two.

411

We pulled it up, tied it, and I tried to forget the incident. During the last few weeks Vaslav had taken long solitary walks, which now became still longer; he seemed to be meditating. Sometimes I accompanied him, and we would walk silently through the woods, where only the murmur of the rushing glacier stream, deep covered under snow, broke the quietness.

Lately Vaslav had not asked me to dance for him as he did during the past summer and autumn, when he used to ask me to keep still for a few moments, and then to begin to dance, just trying to shut out all thought from my mind. At the beginning it surprised me; then I thought it would be a sort of improvisation, which Vaslav had always condemned as "inartistic." He assured me it was not. After a certain time I began to dance, strangely fascinated by Vaslav's oblique eyes, which he almost closed as if he wanted to shut out of himself everything else but my dancing. When I had finished, he said that I danced with a wonderful technique all the different parts of his newly composed ballet (I was not aware of it), the one he wanted Réjane to create. Each time I felt as if I were coming out of a trance, and got strangely irritable with the people around me.

I often asked how he was intending to develop the ballet, but Vaslav waved my question and sank back in one of his great silences.

I did not insist, as I felt he was creating ideas that I could not always follow. He had a vision for a century ahead which I did not possess. I remembered then how he could talk, always with authority, with scientists on their own ground, and that instinctively he was right. Professor Pichler, the great Hungarian mathematician, who was living at the time in Celerina, and used to come and see us quite often, was amazed that Vaslav not only understood, but was able to discuss his problems with him. Vas-

412

lav's keen interest in mechanics had not lessened either. After having invented a windscreen wiper for motor-cars, now he designed the then unknown eversharp pencil. *"Femmka,* send it to Laurence; he will get a patent for it." I did not take it seriously until years later somebody else made the discovery and put it on the market. Now Vaslav was trying to solve different mechanical problems and to simplify his system of notation. He used to work until late at night, and came to sleep only towards the dawn. One day, as I was lying in bed with a slight cold, Vaslav, taking tea with me, went to the window and gazed out on the lake, which was again immobile and silent. "Vaslav, what would you do if I happened to die?" "Work, dance, create, go on with life, and bring up Kyra." "Would you not marry again?" "No." He began to speak slowly, as if he was pondering every word. "Marriage, that is when we meet the one who represents to us the fulfilment of our ideals, the truth. It only happens once in life, to some people never. No, I would not marry."

"We are so happy, I am almost afraid sometimes something will happen," I said. "Yes, sometimes it must be hard to go on · with life if the one we love dies. But we have to go on. My grandfather was an awful gambler. He lost everything he owned and shot himself; it was very wrong of him. His wife died shortly after. It was a tragedy."

Lately Vaslav had been shopping. Cases of paints and pastels arrived. I thought it was more than was needed for a year, but Vaslav explained that owing to the war there was such a shortage that it was wiser to lay in a stock in time, which sounded very logical to me.

Sometimes I met Vaslav running on the road leading towards Chanterella, our favourite promenade. I did not approve of long-distance running in this altitude; I thought it would be too strenuous for him, so I made a remark. But he replied that the exercises did not provide sufficient movement for him, so that he had to find some others. He was now very silent. I tried to talk over different artistic subjects that I knew interested him, but he only gave me confused or evasive answers. But he was so much ahead in his ideas that it seemed only natural that I could not always follow. One Sunday we decided to sleigh over to Maloja. Kyra was glad and Vaslav was very gay that morning. As it took us about three hours to get there, Kyra and I got very hungry during the long drive. The road was extremely narrow during the winter, as it needed cleaning from the heavy snows and in certain parts there was always a space to await the sleighs coming from the opposite direction. Vaslav was as a rule a careful and excellent driver, but on this particular Sunday he did not wait, but simply drove on into the oncoming sleighs. We were in danger of turning over as the horses got frightened. The coachmen cursed, but this did not make any difference. Kyra screamed, and I begged Vaslav to be more careful, but the further we went the more fiercely he drove against the other sleighs. I had to clutch on to Kyra and to the sleigh to keep ourselves on. I was furious, and said so to Vaslav. He fixed me suddenly with a hard and metallic look which I had never seen before. As we arrived at the Maloja Inn I ordered a meal. We had to wait. Vaslav asked for some bread and butter and macaroni. "Ah, Tolstoi again," I thought, but did not say a word, and bit my lips. Kyra was anxiously awaiting her steak, and, as it was laid before her and she began to eat, Vaslav, with a quick gesture, snatched the plate away. She began to cry from disappointment. I exclaimed, "Now, Vaslav, please don't begin that Tolstoi-Kostrovsky nonsense again; you remember how weak you got by starving yourself on that vegetarian diet. I can't stop you doing it, but I won't allow you to interfere with Kyra. The child must eat

414

properly." I went with Kyra to the other room to have our solitary lunch. We drove home very quietly without a word.

Vaslav suddenly threw all his reserve to the winds, and declared gaily that he would take part in all the winter sports. We attended the ski-jumps, the bobsleigh and the skeleton races. We went riding and ski-ing. At the first lesson Vaslav asked our teacher to show him how to brake to stop, and the same morning he made telemarks. "Well, well, the gentleman only needs a few corrections," said the teacher, as Vaslav sailed down the slopes. "He is of course a practised skier." "What do you mean? It is the first time he has had ski on." "Remarkable, such perfect balance; he bends his knees just perfectly, with the elasticity of a practised skier. You are fooling me." But I was not surprised that Vaslav was so good; his wonderful training helped him in all sports.

I was pleased that he had become interested in sports. We went to lunches and dinners with our friends from Spain and England who were here once more, and even attended the dances at the Palace Hotel. Vaslav took a liking to skeleton running, though I thought it was too dangerous a sport and told him so, but he was so proficient after a few hours' practice that I could not object. Skeleton running is done in a narrow ice-run built on the slopes of the Alps, with dangerous curves. The speed is terrific, as the skeleton is made out of steel and the person lies head downwards on the skeleton, which is guided by the displacing of the balance. Vaslav became brilliant in its execution. Very soon he asked me if I wanted to go down with him, lying as a dead weight on top of him. I loved it, and I had faith in Vaslav, but, even so, I had to shut my eyes when we went flying through the run. Sometimes he took Kyra down, and I could only stand and pray until they arrived safely in the valley.

Lately Vaslav had changed his manner in skeleton running,

and when he fell I was alarmed. "But what are you trying to do?" "Oh, one should do sport like art, not with the intellect, but spontaneously, without knowing how it springs from the emotion. This is the way to create, to live." I did not agree.

On our walks he sometimes stopped and stood for quite a long time, not answering my questions, he seemed so far away.

Our days passed in continuous social activity. Then one Thursday, the day when the governess and maid had their day off, I was making ready to take Kyra out for a walk when suddenly Vaslav came out of his room and looked at me very angrily. "How dare you make such a noise? I can't work." I looked up, surprised. His face, his manner were strange; he had never spoken to me like this. "I am sorry. I did not realise we were so loud." Vaslav got hold of me then by my shoulders and shook me violently. I clasped Kyra in my arms very close, then with one powerful movement Vaslav pushed me down the stairs. I lost my balance, and fell with the child, who began to scream. I stood up, more astounded than terrified. What was the matter with him? I was unaware of having done anything wrong. He was still standing there menacingly. I turned round, exclaiming, "You ought to be ashamed! You are behaving like a *moujik*." A very changed Vaslav we found when we came home, docile and kind as ever. I did not speak about the incident, either to him or to anybody else.

As the days passed, Vaslav was working more and more. He seemed to make a drawing in three minutes with a lightning speed. His study and rooms were literally covered with designs; no longer portraits or scenic or decorative subjects, but strange faces, eyes peering from every corner, red and black, like a bloodstained mortuary cover. They made me shudder. "What are those masks?" "Soldiers' faces. It is the war."

They were artistic creations, even though so frightening and morbid. Then other designs came; fanciful butterflies with faces which bore a resemblance to Vaslav's and big spiders with the face of Diaghileff.

"That is Sergei Pavlovitch, and these butterflies are we, the youth of Russia, caught in his net forever."

Then his mood changed and he began to write. "It will be my diary, my thoughts." But he refused to show me.

I shrugged my shoulders. Artists had such moods, and I remembered my mother's hysterical fits when things did not go as she wanted in the theatre.

I woke sometimes at night to find Vaslav staring at me. "I am glad you watch over me; I feel so strange, Vaslav, I don't know what I might not do. Please look after me. I have a feeling I might hurt somebody and I do not want to do it." Yes, I too felt a strange change. I could not form a judgment about anything any more. I did not know what was lovely and ugly. I had lost the faculty of distinction. I only knew than an uncanny feeling was taking hold of me, something that I felt was draining all my vital force, my will to live. "I must be getting neurasthenic; I probably need a rest." And I asked my house physician to recommend a neurologist to me, which he did. "There is nothing the matter with you, but here is the address you wish."

Then one day I really grew alarmed. It was Sunday. Vaslav went out early in the morning. I was supposed to meet him at noon. Before leaving the house, I went to the kitchen to give final instructions to the cook about lunch. Round the table were sitting the maid, the laundress, and the stoker. As I came in, they abruptly stopped their conversation and stood up. "Good morning," I greeted them gaily. They hardly replied, but looked at me with sad faces. "What has happened?"

They set their lips and became mute. "But what has happened?

417

Are you all dumb suddenly?" Then the young man, our stoker, made a few hesitating steps and quickly said, "Madame, forgive me; I may be wrong. We all love you both. You remember I told you that at home in my village at Sils Maria as a child I used to do errands for Mr. Nietzsche? I carried his rucksack when he went to the Alps to work. Madame, he acted and looked, before he was taken away, just like Mr. Nijinsky does now. Please forgive me." "What do you mean?" I shrieked, and then Kati, the laundress, excitedly said, "Mr. Nijinsky is walking in the village wearing a big golden cross over his necktie, and is stopping everybody in the streets asking them if they have been to mass and sending them to church. He just spoke to me." I thought they were all raving, but I flew down the staircase leading from the villa to the village, where I saw in fact Vaslav stopping the passers-by. I got hold of his hands. He seemed embarrassed at seeing me. "What are you doing? What is this new nonsense? Vaslav, won't you stop imitating that old lunatic Tolstoi? You are making yourself into a laughing-stock." He looked like a punished child, very sad. "But, *femmka,* I did not do anything wrong. I just asked if they had been to church." I pointed to Kyra's big golden Florentine cross. "And what is this?" "Well, if you don't like it——" and he took it off. "The world imitates me; all the foolish women copy my ballet costumes. They make their eyes seem oblique, and it becomes the mode, only because nature gave me high cheek-bones. Why can't I teach them something useful, lead them to remember God. Why can't I set the fashion, since I do set fashions, that they should seek the truth?" I was quiet. He was right. "But you have a funny way of expressing your ideas."

Then one day we went on an excursion and Vaslav again wore his cross over his sweater. On our way home he suddenly began to drive fiercely and the sleigh turned over. I really got angry, and walked home with Kyra. Of course, he was home ahead of us. When I entered the house, the servant who worshipped Vaslav opened the door and said, "Madame, I think Monsieur Nijinsky is ill, or perhaps very drunk, for he acts so queerly. His voice is hoarse and his eyes all hazy. I am frightened." "Don't be silly, Marie. He never drinks, you know. Artists have moods, but ring up the doctor and say I need him for Kyra, and put her to bed at once." I went to our bedroom. Vaslav lay fully dressed on the bed, with the cross on, his eyes closed. He seemed to be asleep. I turned cautiously towards the door, and then noticed that heavy tears were streaming down his face. *"Vatza, qu'est-ce que tu as? Vatza, ne sois pas fâché?"* "It is nothing; let me sleep; I have a dreadful headache." He had had many of those lately.

The doctor came. I took him to Kyra, and told him everything that had happened these last months. He agreed that we must pretend that Kyra had a chill and that he was attending her. Not to make the plan too conspicuous. I asked him to remain for tea, and Vaslav joined us. He showed none of his usual anxiety on hearing that Kyra was not well, but seemed indifferent.

I left them alone. Vaslav rather liked the doctor, who was not only excellent and up to date in his profession, but very musical. They had a long chat, and as I came in the doctor said, "I have just suggested to Mr. Nijinsky that you should both go somewhere in the lowlands—let us say Lausanne or Valmont—to get a real rest after all your travelling, in one of our sanatoria." Vaslav was gay and seemed rather relieved. I had no opportunity to speak to the doctor in private, but next morning he telephoned. "Mr. Nijinsky needs a rest; he has a slight case of hysteria, probably due to overwork. I would advise you to go into a sanatorium with him, and in the meanwhile I will get a nurse, so that we can have him under observation." In order not to cause him anxiety I decided to say that he was a *masseur*, as Vaslav had wanted to engage one and had already made inquiries. Next day a solid, tall, good-natured German, a native of Munich, arrived. He had been the head nurse for the last twenty years of the State asylum, and, as he was just on a vacation, he would combine business and pleasure and take over the case. He was presented to Vaslav as the *masseur*, and went up daily to give him massage. He was a remarkable actor, as nobody in the house or in the village suspected his identity. He was both amusing and clever. Vaslav gave me a long, understanding glance when I introduced him, but became very friendly, and they used to go off for long walks and drives together. His presence made Vaslav his old mischievous self again. He was full of fun, and played hide and seek happily with Kyra, and together they built snowmen in the garden. Vaslav suggested that I should invite my sister to visit us, and a week later she was on her way from Vienna.

One day at lunch Vaslav declared he had decided to give up dancing forever and to realise his ideal of going somewhere in Russia to farm.

I lost my temper. "Really, Vaslav, you should not always harp on this plan to give up your art; and, anyway, if you go, you go alone. I have had enough; I can't become a peasant. I was not born one. Even if I love you I will divorce you and marry some manufacturer." And in my bad temper I took off my marriage-ring, the heavy golden Brazilian circle, and ungraciously hurled it at Vaslav. He seemed very surprised. In the afternoon I received a huge bouquet of about five hundred carnations, with the ring in it.

My sister called me up from the first station near the border. I told her everything, almost in tears. With her arrival a whirl of entertaining began. Vaslav went everywhere—dances, dinners, races. He even began to give her dancing-lessons, and went down daily to shop for us, buying scent, shoes, and gifts in great quantities. I was rather annoyed, as he spent several thousand francs on things we did not really need.

One morning he arrived with a load of sweaters, in every colour of the rainbow. "But why so many?" "*Femmka*, the shades are so beautiful. Why not?"

Our Spanish friends and also the Duc and Duquesa de Durcal arrived, and we were invited to tea. The usual crowd was present discussing lightly the armistice, the new dressmaker Chanel, the revolution in Russia, and other events.

"And you, Nijinsky, what have you been doing this year? Did you compose? Are you going to dance soon?" Vaslav leaned back nonchalantly on the couch, drinking his tea. "Well, I composed two ballets, I prepared a new programme for the next Paris season, and lately I have played a part. You see, I am an artist; I have no troupe now, so I miss the stage. I thought it would be rather an interesting experiment to see how well I could act, and so for six weeks I played the part of a lunatic, and the whole village, my family, and even the physicians apparently believed it. I have a male nurse to watch me, in the disguise of a *masseur*." I was speechless. So it was an artistic experiment which had made us all suffer and driven me almost crazy!

The ladies got quite excited. "Nijinsky, what a delightful experiment! How ingenious, wonderful, great!" I could have boxed their ears. An elderly marquis came over to discuss the matter in detail, and there was general applause.

Only Durcal remarked, "I think, Nijinsky, it was rather a cruel experiment, very hard on your wife." "Well, I know she loves me, but I never realised she loved me so much." Vaslav had really changed. I knew that this chaffing and superficial manner was not his. It almost seemed that he was now acting the part of a *blasé*

421

mondain aristocrat, and making fun of the others present. Mr. S., the nurse, after ten days' stay, came to me. "Madame, I am a psychiatric nurse, and have been so for thirty-five years. I know more than the greatest professors, and I have had greater experience. I nurse the patients, I live with them, while the Herr Professors only drop in for a few moments and go away. You are wasting your money in keeping a nurse. Mr. Nijinsky is the sanest person in the whole of St. Moritz Dorf." He departed, and Vaslav, who was now quite a friend, took him down to the station and saw him off.

My sister and Vaslav got on very well together. He gave her a few lessons to teach her how to walk. Vaslav said that so few people knew how to balance their bodies correctly, and showed us exercises. "Don't walk on the point of your toes, but put the middle of your soles down first." All the alarming symptoms disappeared, and I became convinced that Vaslav had fooled us. He was, thank God, all right.

The impresarios kept on writing and trying to secure his promise to dance in the spring. Vaslav seriously considered beginning in Paris. "I won't give a programme ahead. I will just put on 'Nijinsky dances'; they will have confidence in me." Also we discussed at length how to arrange our new apartment in Paris. "I think later on, *femmka*, we will build a house here in St. Moritz. It is near to Paris, to London, to Rome. Ideal for Kyra and for us to have a rest." I was pleased at these projects. How happily did I rejoin Vaslav at Hanselmann's at noon. I was training that time for the skeleton races. The season was advancing, but promised to draw out as the weather was beautiful. Some of our Viennese friends were at St. Moritz, among them Mme. Asseo, the great pianist, a friend of my sister and brother-in-law. Vaslav told them he intended to give a dance recital for all his friends present in

St. Moritz. The rumour spread like wild-fire that Vaslav would dance again. He was looking for a suitable place, as all the ballrooms in the hotels had polished floors, but in the lovely Suvretta House, the hotel in the pine forest, which looks like an enchanted castle, Vaslav discovered, with the hospitable and charming owner of the place, Hans Bon, a ball-room where the floor was suitable. He arranged to have tea served after his recital there, and everything was prepared. "What are you going to dance, Vaslav?" "You will see, all new creations." "Where will you order the costumes?" "I will make them myself, with your little Italian dressmaker. She is clever." And he began to work with her. Hundreds of yards of gorgeous coloured silks, velvets, and lamés were brought to the house.

Our intense desire all these years was to have a son, but on account of the war we waited. Ever since Kyra became Kyra instead of Wladislav we were dreaming of Borislav, as our future son would be called. Vaslav one morning suddenly declared, "*Femmka*, do you know of anybody—a great physician—who is a genius like Lombroso?" "I can inquire, but for what?" "I want to talk to somebody who would understand me, with whom I could talk over many things. I want to have a son now, and I want him to be perfectly healthy, not only physically but mentally." I was rather astonished at hearing this.

I asked Vaslav to come with me and watch my skeleton running before the races, and to give me his advice. I was in splendid form. He came, and as I ascended the steep slope he ran towards me with an excited look. "No, no, *femmka*, it is not right." "But why? I arrived in record speed." "You do it with your intellect; it must come from the emotion, and not from the brain, as all creations of art, as life, as nature." His voice sounded so hoarse and so nervous that I gave him a side-look and did not answer. We went to Hanselmann's. Vaslav lapsed into a silence and fixed a gentleman opposite him with such a glassy and disapproving look that the poor man got embarrassed and left.

The day of the recital arrived. I was kept completely in the dark, for the first time, of what was going to be the programme, but I did not mind this. I was sure it would be lovely. Vaslav remarked a few days before, "I am going to show how dances are created. I will compose them there before the audience. I want the public to see the work. They always get everything ready-made. I want to show them the pangs of creation, the agony an artist has to go through when composing, so I will even make the costumes in front of them." He stood in the middle of the drawing-room and draped himself in yards of material. In a few seconds he was able to make amazing costumes of utterly different periods. The Italian dressmaker was kneeling down helping to roll the silks. "What a pleasure to work with Mr. Nijinsky." Around five, the hour fixed for the recital, we drove over to the Suvretta, Vaslav, the dressmaker, and I. Vaslav was silent, just as before going to the theatre. I knew this mood and respected it. Before arriving at the Suvretta, I ventured to ask, "Please tell me what Bertha Asseo must play for you." "I will tell her at the time. Do not speak. *Silence!*" he thundered at me. "This is my marriage with God." A slight uneasiness crept over me. Vaslav looked so menacing, so dark, in his fur-collared coat, with his Russian fur cap.

I went to receive our guests. About two hundred were already assembled in the ball-room. Many uninvited were also present; everybody who could only get admission. Bertha Asseo was already at the piano. We waited a few seconds. Vaslav entered in his practice kit, and, taking no notice of the public, went up to Bertha and said, "I will tell you what to play." I was standing near the piano. There was an air of great expectation. "I will show you

424

how we live, how we suffer, how we artists create." And he picked up a chair, sat down on it facing the audience, and stared at them, as if he wanted to read the thoughts of each. Everybody waited silently as if in church. They waited. The time passed. We must have been like this for about half an hour. The public behaved as if they were hypnotised by Vaslav. They sat completely motionless. I got rather nervous as I caught a glance of Dr. Bernhard, who was standing in the background, and his expression confirmed me in the belief that my suspicion was justified. Vaslav was again in one of his strange dark moods. Bertha began as a prelude the first few bars of *Sylphides,* then *Spectre.* She hoped to call Vaslav's attention to one of his dances. Perhaps then he would begin. I felt quite upset, and wanted to relieve the tension. I went over to Vaslav. "Please won't you begin? Dance *Sylphides.*" "How dare you disturb me! I am not a machine. I will dance when I feel like it." I fought desperately not to burst out crying. Never had Vaslav spoken to me this way, and before all these people! I could not bear it, and left the room. Mr. Asseo and my sister joined me. "What is happening? What is the matter with Nijinsky?" "I do not know. I want to take him home. What shall we do?" We went in again, but by this time Vaslav was dancing—gloriously but frighteningly. He took a few rolls of black and white velvet and made a big cross the length of the room. He stood at the head of it with open arms, a living cross himself. "Now I will dance you the war, with its suffering, with its destruction, with its death. The war which you did not prevent and so you are also responsible for." It was terrifying.

Vaslav's dancing was as brilliant, as wonderful as ever, but it was different. Sometimes it vaguely reminded me of that scene in *Petrouchka* when the puppet tries to escape his fate. He seemed to fill the room with horror-stricken suffering humanity. It was

425

tragic; his gestures were all monumental, and he entranced us so that we almost saw him floating over corpses. The public sat breathlessly horrified and so strangely fascinated. They seemed to be petrified. But we felt that Vaslav was like one of those overpowering creatures full of dominating strength, a tiger let out from the jungle who in any moment could destroy us. And he was dancing, dancing on. Whirling through space, taking his audience away with him to war, to destruction, facing suffering and horror, struggling with all his steel-like muscles, his agility, his lightning quickness, his ethereal being, to escape the inevitable end. It was the dance for life against death.

A thunderous applause greeted Vaslav when he stopped, and he seemed to come back from very far. He smiled and acknowledged the compliments; he chatted with the guests. They were overcome with this dancing that was something that none of us had ever witnessed before. The first moments of terror were forgotten. Only I remembered, and Dr. Bernhard. Mme Asseo, who played bravely through the recital, seemed to be quite exhausted from the nervous strain. We had tea together, and, as I was still trembling inwardly, she kindly patted me. "It must be very, very difficult to be married to a genius like Nijinsky. I almost wish you could be free to marry one of our nice, charming, inoffensive compatriots." Since that day I never felt the same again. What was happening to Vaslav? How could I help him? What could I do? My sister returned to Vienna, and, soon after, my parents announced their visit to Switzerland. I wished that Vaslav could have seen somebody great like Lombroso, a genius who could understand and help him. Now again he was feverishly writing his impressions in his diary every day. It was in Russian, and, as he wrote with tremendous speed, it was almost illegible, but I could distinguish that the sentences repeated themselves continuously and that the two names Diaghileff and God dominated the diary.

Vaslav spoke often of his son. So one day I gathered up my courage and said that I had found a man as great as Lombroso, Professor Bleuler, a leading psychiatrist. "Let us go and see him." In a few days' time my parents arrived, and we all four left for Zürich. I saw that Vaslav's face was drawn as we drove to the station. St. Moritz was emptying. The melting of the snow began, and our sleigh had to struggle across muddy patches.

Next day I went alone to see Professor Bleuler. Vaslav did not want to accompany me. Bleuler was an old man with an infinite understanding in his eyes. I spoke to him about Vaslav, myself, our marriage, and life for almost two hours. "Very, very interesting, all you tell me. I can assure you there is nothing the matter with you, my dear. Anyhow, we do not become insane; we are born it. I mean, the disposition is there. Genius, insanity, they are so near; normality and abnormality, there is almost no border between the two states. I should like to meet your husband; extremely interesting. If you spoke of any other man I might be worried, but the symptoms you describe in the case of an artist and a Russian do not in themselves prove any mental disturbances." I was relieved, and came home happily. I told Vaslav how nice Bleuler was and that he thought I was healthy and that we could now have a son, and that he would like to make his acquaintance. Vaslav agreed, "Of course, so would I; he seems interesting. I was quite sure everything was all right. After all, *femmka*, I was brought up in the Imperial School, and we were there under constant medical supervision. Since I left there, except for my typhoid I have never been seriously ill." In a happy mood, we went out shopping, and I noticed that Vaslav stopped before the window of a great departmental store where babies' layettes were exposed; he smiled, and I knew he was thinking of the son he so ardently desired.

Next day, about three in the afternoon, we drove across the bridge on the Lake of Zürich to the hilly side, where in a wood at a little distance the State asylum is built, a big, old-fashioned building with iron-barred windows. But the smiling porter and the flowers which surround the directorial building, where Professor Bleuler received, took away the disagreeable impression. We sat for a few moments and then the Professor came out. I introduced him to Vaslav, and they both disappeared in his study. Calmly I looked over the illustrated papers lying round: the *Illustration*, the latest numbers of the *Sketch* and *Graphic*. I was relieved that all this unnecessary anxiety was over; at last everything would be all right. We had had such a hard time these first six years of our marriage—the fight with Diaghileff, war prisoners, all the disillusion; but now at last the happy time would commence. The door opened within ten minutes, and the Professor showed out Vaslav smilingly. "All right. Splendid. Won't you step in for a second? I forgot to give you the promised prescription yesterday." I smiled at Vaslav as I passed him, following the Professor; what prescription I could not remember. As he closed the door of his study behind him, he said very firmly, "Now, my dear, be very brave. You have to take your child away; you have to get a divorce. Unfortunately, I am helpless. Your husband is incurably insane." I thought the sunray which passed through the window above the head of the Professor was curiously full of dust. Why did he have that huge green table in the middle of the room? And those inkstands were irritatingly round—a circle; oh, yes, the Circle. That awful, that merciless circle of misfortune. I was vaguely hearing him ask me to forgive him for being so hard. "I must seem to be brutal, but I have to be to be able to save you and your child—two lives. We physicians must try to save those whom we can; the others, unfortunately, we have to abandon to their cruel fate. I am an old man. I have sacrificed fifty years of my life to save them. I have searched and studied; I know the symptoms; I can diagnose it; but I don't know, I wish I could help, but do not forget, my child, that sometimes miracles happen."

I did not listen; I had to get out of there quickly. I felt the place was going round with me faster and faster in a circle. I dashed through the door to the room where Vaslav was waiting. He stood near the table looking absent-mindedly at the illustrated papers, pale, strangely sad, in his Russian fur coat with his Cossack cap. I stopped and looked; it seemed as though his face was growing longer under my gaze, and he slowly said, *"Femmka*, you are bringing me my death-warrant."

Epilogue

FOURTEEN years have elapsed since the day that Nijinsky's mind became shrouded in darkness, when he withdrew from this world. Fourteen years since he has been living in a world where his imaginary creations are real personalities to him, and we, the reality, are only dream-like apparitions.

He is day-dreaming unceasingly, but without the loss of his memory. He knows he is Nijinsky, and he knows his family and is aware of his surroundings. He is mute for days, for weeks, for months. He is docile, obedient, patient and indifferent, neat and as orderly as ever. His physicians and nurses adore him. His charm is still present. A lightning flash of his old mischievous self brightens up the monotony of his apparent indifference. An attention, a kind word, a compliment on his dancing, brings a smile. The music of *Petrouchka* or *Carnaval* lights up his face with joy. His memory seems to be strangely intact when a Fugue, a Prelude of Bach, a piece of Debussy's or Stravinsky's music is played to him, and if the music stops he goes on whistling correctly the bars that follow. Experiments made prove that Nijinsky still remembers. When one of his own parts is danced before him and a false step is made he corrects it; if a dancer slips, he jumps up to help. Otherwise, he has shut dancing, the most treasured thing for him, utterly out of his life. Only once in a while he leaps up and makes a *tour en l'air* or pirouette as if he had just a few moments before finished the *Spectre de la Rose*. To the layman he appears as a silent, quiet, indifferent man. The wild rumours that were spread of him are unfounded and false; Nijinsky never behaved

430

like an animal. In his insanity, as in his health, he is the same, kindly, human. He never attacks, only defends himself. His illness is one before which medical science is at a loss. It is a Schizophrenia—a disease probably due to the malfunctioning of the glands; one of which the origin is little known and the cure not at all; one which leaves the organism intact, and is known as a functional disease. Unfortunately it is not caused by a germ, such as paralysis as the result of syphilis, and therefore it is incurable.

The day when Professor Bleuler made his statement, the day when I decided to try to save him from the fate to which he was condemned, my frantic parents arrived in Zürich. The idea that Vaslav was pronounced insane made them lose their heads completely. As they were unsuccessful in persuading me to seek a divorce, they decided to take our lives in their hands. My mother took me out for a walk, and, while we were away—Vaslav being still in bed, waiting for his breakfast—the police ambulance, called in by my panic-stricken parents, came, and the Hôtel Baur en Ville was surrounded by the fire brigade to prevent Vaslav's jumping out of the window, should he attempt it. They knocked at his door. Vaslav, thinking it was the waiter, opened, and was immediately seized. They tried to carry him out in his pyjamas. Vaslav, as I learned from the manager, asked, "What have I done? What do you want of me? Where is my wife?" They insisted that he should come, and the doctor, seeing his quietness, asked the nurses to release him. Vaslav thanked him, and said, "Please let me dress, and I will follow you." When I came back at noon, I found his room deserted.

Desperately I ran to Professor Bleuler, who helped me to find him. He was in the State asylum among thirty other patients, but, by that time, Vaslav, owing to the shock, had had his first catatonic attack. Professor Bleuler deeply regretted this unfor-

431

tunate incident, which brought on the acute development of the illness, which, under different circumstances, might have remained stationary. On his advice, Vaslav was taken to the Sanatorium Bellevue Kreuzlingen, where he not only found admirable care but kind-hearted friends in Dr. Binswanger and his wife. After six months, during which his physicians and myself had every hope that he would get well, suddenly he began to get hallucinations, grew violent and worse, refusing all nourishment. I took him home to St. Moritz, and, under the supervision of two physicians and three nurses, we tried to give him the illusion of freedom and domestic life. During the next seven years I attempted to rebuild, on the ruins of our happiness, a tolerable existence in St. Moritz; later, in Vienna and Paris. The greatest specialists in Europe and America were called in. They all agreed it was a case of Schizophrenia.

Professors Bleuler, Wagner Jauregg, Kreplin, Ferenczy, Freud, Jung, were consulted. "Give him the best physical care, and quiet surroundings, under the care of a psychiatrist." "Let him dream his dreams," they all advised.

Then I turned to desperate means—fakirs, healers, Christian Science—but everything failed. We took him to the theatre, to see the Ballet, to Balieff's Chauve-Souris, to clubs where Cossacks danced, and, when he saw these, his expression changed, and for a few minutes he became his old self again. But there were weeks of great violence, and then he had to be taken to a sanatorium, to which I followed him, and unfortunately found out that in all other places except Kreuzlingen he was either neglected, badly nourished, or even occasionally ill-treated.

After tremendous difficulties, Lenin was asked, by a signed petition of the attending physicians, to let Bronia and Vaslav's mother leave Russia and join him. We hoped the shock of meeting

NIJINSKY WITH KARSAVINA AND DIAGHILEFF   (*Paris*, 1927)
(STUDIO LIPNITZKI)

them again might help. The request was refused, but my sister-in-law, who was finally advised of what had happened, managed to dance herself through to the border, and to come to us with Vaslav's mother. But Vaslav remained impassive at the sight of them. It is only when Kyra comes that he smiles and says, *"Attention à l'enfant."*

．　　．　　．　　．　　．　　．　　．　　．

The years have passed, and one day in Paris Diaghileff came to see him. *"Vatza, mais tu es paresseux. Viens, viens, j'ai besoin de toi; il faut que tu danses pour le Ballet Russe, pour moi."* Vaslav shook his head. *"Je ne peux pas car je suis fou."* Diaghileff turned away, and burst out crying, "It is my fault, what shall I do?"

The physicians were right. The home atmosphere did not soothe him. On the contrary, the effort to behave normally provoked periods of violence; and then I decided to take him back to the place where he felt happy—where he was well treated and cared for at the beginning of his illness—to the Bellevue in Kreuzlingen. He is there now . . . dreaming. . . . His hallucinations refer to the war. He still hears the guns which have long ceased to echo. He still sees soldiers dying around him.

When I come to him, he approaches me with an infinitely grateful look, as a wise dog to the master who looks after him.

Through these fourteen years I have tried to overcome immense difficulties, and to offer to Nijinsky what still can remain for him —care, and a home; remembering, in the worst moments of agony, the sentence I once uttered at Covent Garden, seeing him dance in *Sylphides: "Thank you, my God, that I have lived in this century to have seen Nijinsky dance,"* and the promise I gave him at our marriage—*to stand by him in happiness and misfortune.*

EPILOGUE

Through all the tragic years there have been only a few who have proved to be true friends of Nijinsky in disaster as well as in his days of glory. To those I want to convey my deepest gratitude in his name and in mine: to the late Paul Dupuy, to Mrs. William K. Vanderbilt, Sr., to Carlos Salzedo, to Robert Alfred Shaw, and to Tamara Karsavina. While waiting for the miracle which could restore Nijinsky to his art, to life, and to us, in spite of everything the loyalty of these few friends makes me believe that Vaslav, the seeker after truth, was right when he said, as he was taken away to Kreuzlingen for the first time, pointing to the sky, *"Femmka, courage, ne désespères pas, car il y a un Dieu."*

NEW YORK, THE HAGUE,
1932–1933.

THE END

Index

435

THE LAST YEARS OF
Nijinsky

BY HIS WIFE

ROMOLA NIJINSKY

Author of the Original Biography: NIJINSKY

19 52

SIMON AND SCHUSTER, NEW YORK

TO TWO DEVOTED FRIENDS
Violet Ormond
AND
Lt. Col. William P. Yarborough
AND TO MY GRANDSON
Vaslav Alexei Markevitch

Contents

Contents

Vaslav Nijinsky at 22, at the height of his career.

Water color painted by Nijinsky shortly before he became ill.

Part of the residence of the Nijinskys after World War II in Austria.

In 1939, Serge Lifar, the distinguished maître de ballet of the Paris Opera, visited Nijinsky in the asylum at Münsingen, where Nijinsky was undergoing shock treatment. The doctors in charge wished to see whether their patient would react to the dancing and the problems of dancing as presented by Lifar. The evidence, as shown in these pictures through the gestures and the facial expressions of Nijinsky, was considered very favorable at the time.

PHOTOS: JEAN MANZON

At one point during Serge Lifar's visit, Nijinsky himself executed a leap reminiscent of his great style in the past.

JEAN MANZON

A similar leap as executed in Nijinsky's great days in the ballet *Orientale*.

COLLECTION OF ROGER DODGE

Nijinsky at 58 in a hotel in Surrey, where, considerably recovered, he was planning an advanced institute for the study of the dance. UNESCO had expressed an interest in its support.

During the last year of his life, Nijinsky lived, with Madame Nijinsky, in a private home in Surrey. Here the great dancer is offering assistance to his wife, Romola Nijinsky, who had already embarked on her writing career. A few months later the great dancer died.

THE LAST YEARS OF

Nijinsky

Chapter 1

Prologue

VASLAV NIJINSKY, the greatest male dancer of all time, had a meteoric career which lasted in all just ten years and ended abruptly when he was declared insane in March, 1919, in Zurich. He was only twenty-nine when he was forced to discontinue his profession. The five years he danced in his native Russia and the five years abroad, in Europe and North and South America, were sufficient to establish him as among the immortals of the dance.

I have told the story of this career—its origin, its great ten years, and its ending—in my book, *Nijinsky,* published in 1934. But my husband continued to live, and I to live with him, till his death in London in April, 1950. It seems to me both necessary and desirable, for the sake of the history of art and genius, and to help preserve the memory of the greatest and kindest human being I have ever known, to tell the re-

mainder of his story. It is the story of twenty-seven
years of the twilight of a god—years of misery, often
of heartbreak, but years so inspired by the presence
of a great and kind spirit, whatever the state of his
mental health, that I never for a moment regretted
my decision to remain with my husband even when
the best medical advice assured me there was no
chance of recovery.

At first I thought only of adding a few extra chapters to the old book. But the story grew in length, and
my publishers agreed with me that it would be better
to make an independent book of those last years. This
seemed especially advisable as I could not be sure that
the present generation knew much about my great
husband. It is eighteen years since my first book was
published, and it is over thirty since anyone saw him
dance in public.

And so it becomes necessary to write a short pro-
logue in which I can explain to my younger readers
what went before—like the "synopsis of previous
chapters" that precedes later installments in a serial.
Only I cannot find it in my heart to retell that story
once more as I did before. It is there for anyone who
wants to read it today, and for me it is not a fire to be
raked over again. Instead I shall merely discuss, as a
layman, of course, the factors that may have led up to
his insanity. In any event, it is necessary to know these

facts in order to understand the events of the story I have to tell—the way Nijinsky behaved, and the way others, myself not least, reacted to him.

My own private belief, for what it is worth, is that Nijinsky's insanity was functional in origin. Full of crises as his history was, there are others who have survived equally violent lives without paying for them with their minds. Furthermore, Nijinsky had an older brother who suffered mental illness at a much earlier age and when he had a comparatively simple life; so there may have been some hereditary predisposition to mental illness in the family. I do not know the true answers; and sometimes I believe that the professional psychiatrists, particularly the analysts, who lay so much stress on environment and so comparatively little on physical inheritance, cannot be much surer than I am.

At any rate, it is clear that certain phases of Nijinsky's life were upsetting enough to encourage any disposition to mental illness he may have inherited, and these I must sketch for the reader. They are four in number. First, his childhood, during which he was thrown more than most children on the love of his mother; second, the unusually strict and somewhat unnatural training he had to undergo in the Imperial School of Dancing at St. Petersburg; third, his association with that oddly gifted and baleful man Sergei

Diaghileff; and last, the enforced stopping of his work through the First World War. Some people have suggested that the primary causes were overwork; others the fact that he married. I am sure that neither of these causes is the true one, and other factors, in any case, were much more important.

Vaslav's Childhood

Vaslav was born December 28, 1890, at Kiev. He was brought up in the environment of the ballet and absorbed its atmosphere in infancy. Both his parents were excellent dancers; and the nomadic life that he led with his family as they danced traveling through the provinces of Russia must have given him an early feeling of insecurity.

The little boy was extremely devoted to his father, Thomas, a dancer of extraordinary virtuosity, especially noted, as Vaslav was to be later on, for his unique elevation. Unfortunately, the beneficial association between father and son had to cease at the time it became apparent that Vaslav's older brother, Stanislav, would have his mind permanently impaired. This happened after Stanislav had a bad fall and needed to remain in St. Petersburg for treatment. Eleanora, the mother, remained with the two boys and little Bronislava, giving up her career, while the father continued to tour. Eventually the long absences of the father led to a permanent separation between the parents; and with Stanislav ill, Vaslav and Eleanora were entirely dependent on each other for love and for a feeling of security. Furthermore, the level of income soon brought poverty and hunger to the little family, for Eleanora could not earn much.

Vaslav's chief characteristics at the time were truthfulness, a strong religious feeling, and an affectionate candor. He was extremely modest and sensitive. There was even an awkwardness in his manner—a diffidence that disappeared as soon as he danced, just like a butterfly when it unshackles itself from its cocoon and takes to graceful flight. All his desire, and all his parents' hopes, were based on his becoming a great dancer.

Vaslav's Training

At the age of nine Vaslav was one of the six children, in a competition of one hundred and fifty, to be admitted to the Imperial School of Dancing at St. Petersburg by the board of examiners. The importance to the family of this triumph can perhaps best be understood by noting the fact that Thomas Nijinsky had never been able to dance at the great theatres of St. Petersburg and Moscow simply because, as a Pole, he had been unable to enter the Imperial

School. Only graduates of this institution could become members of these ballet companies. Now young Vaslav was auspiciously launched on a career in which everyone felt sure he must distinguish himself, especially as Nicolai Legat, the leading dancer of the Imperial Theatre and teacher at the School, had especially recommended Vaslav to the examiners because of the unusual development of his thigh muscles as well as his remarkable elevation. Furthermore, Vaslav had the unique ability from the very beginning to execute with absolute precision any movement shown by his masters. He astonished his teachers by his enormous leaps and the ease with which he rose in the air and seemed to remain at the highest point of elevation as though suspended in space. The staff of dancing masters soon became aware that they had a child prodigy in Vaslav.

This was all to the good. So was the fact that now Vaslav had no more lack of bread, which had recently been a constant source of anxiety. The Academy of Dancing was under the supervision of the Imperial Household, which provided in a luxurious way for the upkeep of the Academy and all the needs of the students. They were supplied with an elegant wardrobe of uniforms, fur-lined coats and caps, and outfits for every occasion. The food was the choicest. The best teachers and a medical staff were attached to the

Academy, and it was housed in one of the Imperial Palaces.

On the other hand, it must have been a severe psychological wrench. The Imperial School resembled a convent crossed with a splendidly run stable where full-bloods are bred to win the Derby. The children were shut off from the world and its atmosphere of practicality. Suddenly Vaslav had become a member of a vast, distinguished, and exclusive state organization with all its special privileges, but his family remained outside. On the special holidays when he was permitted to visit his mother's home, he was ashamed that he alone was the recipient of the imperial favors, while his family remained unaided in their perpetual state of want. Yet, as an adolescent child, there was nothing he could do about it. The reaction of the change from poverty to luxury for the child himself was overwhelming, and he became even more shy.

He did try to overcome his inhibitions, but he met with rebuffs from his fellows. Partly this was because of natural jealousy, for everyone recognized his stupendous aptitude for the dance. In their childish cruelty, they ridiculed him for his Mongolian features and nicknamed him "The Chinaman." He resented their looking down on his Polish descent, especially as his mother, an ardent patriot, had idealized her native country. As Vaslav sadly commented later, "Communal life united us students, but it did not bring us together."

Several events that occurred during his early school life also made profound impressions—and unhappy ones. He came brutally into contact with political violence when, one day, walking with his fellows, he was caught in a demonstration of poor people begging the Tsar for bread. The mounted Cossacks rode into the crowd, slashing at all with their knouts, and Vaslav was struck on the forehead by one of the iron-tipped lashes. Vaslav knew well the meaning of hunger and poverty and identified himself with these unfortunates.

Some time later, still at a very impressionable age, the dashing and very successful dancer Sergei Legat, who had been teaching Vaslav, committed suicide. In a fit of depression, possibly over theatre politics, possibly over the unfaithfulness of his mistress, he had slashed his throat.

When he was about fifteen, the boys one day were hurdling an iron music-stand in what Vaslav presumed to be a friendly competition. One of the boys, just before Vaslav's turn came, suddenly raised the bar deliberately. This unexpected change caused Vaslav to trip and in doing so he crashed over the iron stand, which fell across his abdomen, causing severe internal injuries and put him, dangerously ill, for several months into the hospital.

Finally, one day the boys were whiling away the time with a slingshot when, apparently, Vaslav inadvertently hit the school doctor in the eye. Vaslav was not sure it had been his missile that hit the doctor, but he was afraid that they would all be dismissed, so he accepted the blame. Fortunately, he was not dismissed but only suspended for two weeks.

In reporting this incident, Vaslav wrote in his *Diaries* (published in 1936) : "I felt deeply grieved and almost fainted. I was frightened for my mother. I knew how difficult it was for her to earn money and I realized what it would mean to her if I would be sent away from school." Then he tells what happened when he went home: "My mother and I cried together. She gave me a thrashing. I was not afraid of the beating, although she hit me hard. I knew she gave me the punishment because she thought this was the best way to improve me. I only felt love for my mother. Impregnated with the desire to become the support of my mother and sick brother, I made up my mind to succeed."

The Career and Diaghileff

So far as dancing went, Vaslav succeeded from the very first beyond the dreams of anyone. Even before he was graduated, at the age of eighteen, from the Imperial School, he was given solo roles at the Mariinsky Theatre with the Imperial Company. And when he was graduated, May 20, 1908, there was a happy reunion with his father, mother, and sister (but the brother Stanislav could not join since he was now permanently confined to an insane asylum). Vaslav was soon given the leading male role in the new ballet *Pavillon d'Armide* opposite the *prima ballerina assoluta* Madame Kshessinskaya. Alexandre Benois, the great scenic designer, wrote: "When Vaslav appeared on the stage, the effect surpassed anything we expected. From the moment Nijinsky sprang out from the wings, his feet hardly touched the floor. We felt the presence of genius. The artists, the dancers, the public were swept off their feet."

One might have thought that this sort of success (and it continued just as great throughout the ten years of his active career) would have brought a sense of security. On the contrary. He himself tells us: "At eighteen I graduated. I didn't know how to dress. I had been used to uniforms. I did not like civilian clothes. I did not know how to wear them. After I graduated, I felt freedom, but this freedom frightened me."

As a new member of the Mariinsky Theatre, his salary was sixty-five rubles a month, which was insufficient for one person, let alone supporting his family on the standard expected of members of the Theatre.

Furthermore, the young man's extraordinary success incited the jealousy of his colleagues. While he made every effort to gain the friendship of the artists and the *corps de ballet* (efforts that probably were as awkward as they were sincere), there were intrigues against him from the beginning. For example, Kroupensky, the manager, scheduled him for only four appearances in an eight-month season.

The one person who was benevolent was Madame Kshessinskaya, who insisted that he should appear as her partner in the private performances at the Imperial Court and who also tried to introduce Vaslav into St. Petersburg social life by inviting him to her luxurious palace.

It was, as I have related in my earlier book, in society that Vaslav first met Sergei Pavlovitch Diaghileff. The character and history of this savagely ambitious and hypocritically shrewd egoist have been written about frequently and at great length. It is sufficient here to note two things about him. The first is that his strongest bent was to create something new, something astonishing, and that he had the organizational and fund-raising ability to succeed. The second is that he was not only a leading member of a greatly talented group of creative artists, including Benois and Bakst and later Stravinsky and others, but he was also prominent in the clan of St. Petersburg degenerates who had the same especially perverted morals as Sergei Pavlovitch.

At this time, Diaghileff had already been dismissed by the Tsar's order from an administrative post for his intrigues. It was therefore only in society that he could meet Nijinsky. Whether his desire to meet the dancer was to further his artistic ambitions or was personal, it is hard to judge. Probably both elements entered. At any rate, one of Vaslav's classmates claims that Diaghileff paid one thousand rubles to one of the members of the *corps de ballet* to be introduced. Vaslav wrote this about their meeting: "He asked me to come to the Hotel Europe, where he lived. I disliked him for his self-assured voice, but went. . . . I trembled like a leaf. I hated him, but pretended because I knew that my mother and I would die of hunger otherwise. I understood Diaghileff at once and pretended to agree with him. One had to live and therefore it was all the same to me what sort of sacrifice I had to make."

Prologue

The story of how Diaghileff organized a troupe of the greatest Russian dancers and introduced them, in Paris, to the Western world has been frequently told both by myself and by others. One cannot—and does not want to—take credit from Sergei Pavlovitch for this achievement, so important in the history of art. Despite extreme difficulty in obtaining the permission of the Court Marshal's office, he did bring the ballet company of the Mariinsky Theatre to western Europe. The troupe included the greatest artists, well known and applauded throughout Russia: Kshessinskaya, Pavlova, Tamara Karsavina, Legat, Guerd, Obukov, and Nijinsky—all graduates of the Imperial School, all life members of the Mariinsky Theatre. The effect was stupendous. Suddenly a new world of beauty and perfection was revealed with unlimited vistas, stimulating the artistic imagination of the Western world. Undoubtedly, since the Renaissance in Italy, such an epoch-making event in the world of art has not taken place. And Diaghileff was its prime mover.

What is less well known (and what I did not know myself at the time I wrote my last book) is a comparatively minor event during that first trip, which occurred the very year of Vaslav's graduation from the Imperial School. For the purposes of my story, however, it is of major importance, and I shall let

Vaslav tell it in his own words, as he wrote it in his
diary:

"During the year of my debut, I contracted typhoid fever in Paris by drinking water from a jug,
because I was too poor and could not buy mineral
water. I drank without suspecting the danger. I went
to dance and felt a great weakness in my body. Diaghileff called Dr. Botkin, whom he knew well.
Sergei Botkin was one of the Tsar's doctors. I felt
feverish but was not afraid, not realizing what was
the matter with me. Botkin looked at me and understood what had happened. I got frightened when
Diaghileff and Botkin looked at each other. They understood without words, and so did I. I got frightened. Botkin called Diaghileff into the other room
after he looked at my breast and saw a rash. I got
frightened. I realized that I had typhoid fever. I had
had it in my youth. I lived at the Hotel de Hollande,
which has now been demolished. It was a poor hotel,
but on the little money I had, I could not live in a
better way. Diaghileff made me an offer to let me
live with him when I was lying ill with a high fever.
I agreed. Diaghileff realized my value. Therefore, he
was afraid that I would leave him. At that time I
wanted to run away. I was frightened with life. My
mother was also frightened and I had inherited this
fear from her. I wept and wept and I didn't know

what to do. I did not want to agree. Diaghileff was sitting on my bed and urged me to do so. I was frightened of him, frightened, and I agreed. I sobbed and I understood death. I could not run away as I had fever. I was thirsty and asked Diaghileff to give me an orange. He brought me one. I fell asleep with the orange in my hand. When I woke it was squashed, lying on the floor. I slept for a long time not understanding what was happening to me. I lost consciousness. I was afraid of Diaghileff, not of death."

Perhaps there was a symbolical significance in that squashed orange lying on the floor. At any rate, this was only one early move of Diaghileff's to secure complete domination over Nijinsky for himself. The most efficacious of many such moves occurred in St. Petersburg during the season of 1911 when Diaghileff, without Nijinsky's knowing it, ordered his costume for *Giselle* altered in such a way that the directors of the Mariinsky Theatre considered it indecent and reprimanded the dancer. On the urging and prompting of Diaghileff, Vaslav tendered his resignation from the Theatre—and thereafter, for some years, was almost completely dependent on Diaghileff for the development of his career. From this time forth Russia's greatest dancer was not permitted to appear on her greatest stages. Nijinsky was a wanderer in foreign lands, wholly dependent on Diaghileff.

Not that Vaslav failed to have great success under the direction of his mentor. Wherever the company toured, he was hailed as the greatest dancer of the times. He had all the roles he wanted, and he was able to contribute epoch-making developments to the art of choreography through the creation of such ballets as *The Afternoon of a Faun, Jeux,* and *Sacre du Printemps,* and others that developed a fresh technique on which subsequent choreographers have based other developments.

Nevertheless, Nijinsky's personal and emotional life remained unhappy and insecure on account of this relationship with Diaghileff. No one should know better than I, his wife for thirty-seven years, that Nijinsky was *not,* by nature, homosexual. In addition, there are many passages in his published diaries to substantiate this point. It should not, therefore, be difficult for any reader to understand the unhappy strain under which Vaslav lived, away from his own country and forced to depend on the whims and wishes of a strange, willful, brilliant mentor. Nor must it be forgotten that at the time Nijinsky was a shy youth in his early twenties, Diaghileff a mature, experienced man of the world.

The opportunity to escape from this moral thralldom came unexpectedly, and, quite innocently, I played an important part in it. I say "innocently" because at the time I, a well-educated but still immature young society girl, had no way of knowing the situation I have outlined above.

The Diaghileff company had arranged a tour of South America in the season of 1913, and Diaghileff himself, fearfully afraid of the ocean, remained in Europe. Meantime, in love at a distance with the great Nijinsky, whom I had hardly met at all, I managed to get for myself a very minor appointment as a member of the company. As I told in my earlier book, I used every means I could to attract the attention of the dancer on shipboard, apparently with no success whatsoever as we were artistically oceans apart, and there was no language we spoke in common. Nevertheless, completely to my surprise, Vaslav sent me, through another member of the company, a proposal of marriage shortly before we landed. It was one of those unbelievable things that you could not put into a work of fiction because the reader would consider it too unlikely. I myself did not believe it at first and thought that Vaslav was teasing me in a cruel and childish sort of way. But it was a proposal made in entirely good faith, and we were married in Buenos Aires on September 10, 1913.

Never for a moment did I regret that marriage, despite my parents' harsh disapproval; and never for a moment, I believe, did Vaslav regret it. But the effect on Diaghileff was disastrous. I am not going to tell once more the many fiendish ways in which from that point on he endeavored to ruin Vaslav's career, ways which at times even threatened our very lives.

After the fact of his marriage was established, my husband hoped that Diaghileff would be willing to accept his platonic friendship, the only kind he was able to offer Sergei Pavlovitch. But Vaslav did not really know Diaghileff.

Our plans were made; better to say Vaslav decided, I acquiesced. We were to go to Europe after finishing the South American tour, straight to St. Petersburg to Vaslav's family. He hoped to take a rest there and then rejoin Diaghileff and his company later.

Vaslav knew the story of Diaghileff's last Russian love affair. His last friend, who was his private secretary, Mr. M., had married and after a few weeks' quarrel, Diaghileff forgave him what he considered as "unloyal behavior." Vaslav was convinced that Diaghileff cherished and respected Nijinsky the artist, and seeing that Vaslav was ready to devote his talent to further his ballet company, he would get over our marriage.

On our way to Russia in the autumn of 1913, we stopped for a few days in Budapest to visit my family. It was here that Vaslav received Diaghileff's wire saying: "YOUR SERVICES ARE NOT RE-

QUIRED." That any director or manager would dare to dismiss an artist of Nijinsky's standing in such a brutal manner was unthinkable. I am sure that at first Vaslav did not even understand the utter cruelty and meanness of Diaghileff's act. That was his revenge for Vaslav's having the courage to live his own life.

The defection of Diaghileff was doubtless a severe psychological blow to Vaslav, but its practical importance we could not at the time estimate. Vaslav faced the responsibility which was his courageously and without complaint. He was the family provider. His mother, his insane brother, Stanislav, depended on him. I was expecting a baby. Now, suddenly, Vaslav was without a contract. Much against his wish and conviction, Vaslav accepted an engagement at the Palace Theatre in London, a music hall, where Pavlova had danced for the last few years.

I noticed how, inwardly, Vaslav suffered by being obliged to appear in such inartistic surroundings. He had to form a company, find the dancers, compose several new ballets, and teach these new creations and manage the whole troupe, which was far too heavy a burden for any artist. A small but excellent troupe was formed and brought from St. Petersburg to London.

During those months Diaghileff unceasingly, in every possible manner, tried to influence the Paris and London society, the press and the theatrical world against Nijinsky. The last blow came when he induced Fokine to bring an injunction against Vaslav's dancing the *Spectre de la Rose* at the Palace Theatre. Exhausted by the tremendous strain of organizing and managing the company, Vaslav became ill in London and had to take a long enforced rest.

Vaslav returned to me in Budapest as soon as he could. Shortly after the birth of our daughter we were summoned to London by the Marchioness of Ripon, who was almost a kind of dictator in the social and ballet world there, apparently in the hope of effecting a reconciliation with Diaghileff—an effort that had failed once before. But I was too weak to leave and my baby, Kyra, too small to undertake such a long trip. By the time we were ready to join her, war was declared and all three of us were interned.

The First World War—and Career's End

Vaslav's first serious depressions occurred during the two long years he lived in this confinement, a prisoner of war in Austria-Hungary. Let him describe the effect of this confinement in his own words:

"My life in Budapest during the war was sad. I lived for a long time in my mother-in-law's house. It was dull—I was bored. I was interned there. Rus-

sia was at war with Hungary. I was called a bar-
barian of Russian origin. I was sad. And while I lived
there I composed the theory of the dance. I worked
on some ballets, but I felt sad. I knew that everybody
disliked me. We quarreled about politics with my
wife's stepfather. I lived from one day to the other. I
wanted to forget myself and started to write down my
ballets by the new system of annotation, which I had
invented. It was a long job. It took me two months to
do, while to perform needed only ten minutes. I felt
miserable and depressed."

In 1916 the American Ambassador in Vienna succeeded in getting our release, and through Mr. Otto
H. Kahn, chairman of the board of directors of the
Metropolitan Opera Company, it was arranged that
Vaslav was to appear once more with Diaghileff's
company. Vaslav tried to co-operate in every way,
and he had a huge success in the American tour. Unfortunately, he agreed to accompany the company on
a Spanish tour, and here the Diaghileff machinations
began all over again. There were attacks on his prestige, his work, and even his bodily safety. These were
carried out by Diaghileff's lackeys and hirelings, who
spread the rumor that Vaslav was suffering from de-
lusions during this trip of 1917-18 and had a mania
of persecution—all of which was utterly untrue.

Vaslav never spoke of any of these attacks against

him. It was I who went to enlist legal and police help in order to protect Nijinsky from the machinations of Diaghileff's hirelings. Now, we both realized that, the world aflame with war, the only thing we could do was to retire to a neutral country and await in peace the end of the war. We settled in the glorious Engadine. Here, I hoped that by leading a calm life Vaslav would find repose in tranquil surroundings.

We had been married now for almost six years. In spite of all the adversities we had to endure, we were perfectly happy in our marriage. There was never a cross word exchanged between us; no quarrels; no misunderstandings. I know Vaslav never regretted having married—although he paid an enormous price. He lost the possibility to dance, to exercise his art for which he had been brought up—the very essence of his whole being, and all because he chose to take me for his companion, instead of sharing Diaghileff's unnatural desires.

Very often I watched Vaslav as he played with baby Kyra, whom he adored. They were like two children, full of gaiety and undisturbed serenity. We were young and healthy. We had hope for the future. The war would end and we would return to Russia. The Revolution there seemed to bring a great change. There would be no more intrigues, bureaucracies to bar the country's greatest dancer from returning to his home, the Mariinsky Theatre. Among Vaslav's family we would start a new life. Vaslav, once more, would be given back to the dance.

As time passed, disturbing news arrived from Russia. My mother-in-law had to escape from St. Petersburg. Then, a little later, we heard that Vaslav's brother, Stanislav, had perished. I had to break the tragic news to Vaslav. He bowed his head very low and murmured, "Stanislav was very ill. The doctors claimed him incurable. Maybe God knew best in releasing him." For days afterwards Vaslav hardly spoke, and for a long time I did not see him smile.

Early in March, 1919, in Zurich the great psychiatrist Professor Bleuler told me Vaslav was incurably insane and advised me to divorce him.

There had hardly been a sign before this of the impending disaster which shattered our lives. Now that the war was over, I hoped the dreadful shadow which the hostilities with all the suffering of mankind had cast on Vaslav's soul would be lifted—but it was too late. The loss of his career, of his native country, the disillusionment over Diaghileff, and the war broke his spirit.

He withdrew into himself, began to live in his fanciful dreams, lost contact with the world, and became mute. The physicians, my family, friends, strangers —all advised me to lock him up in an asylum and leave him to his fate. Nijinsky, the miraculous dancer, ceased to dance. The world had no more use for him. He was abandoned now, unable to defend himself.

The most appalling human misery is insanity, when a human being is unable to think coherently; when he is no longer capable of expressing a wish; when excruciating emotions and thoughts race ceaselessly through his mind without giving one moment of respite.

To be thrown into the hands of indifferent doctors who see only "the case" and not the forlorn soul; to be given over to attendants who treat the patients like criminals—that was to be my Vaslav's lot—never! I hardly realized at the time that my decision meant a battle against the medical faculty, the authorities, and the whole world. The task before me was almost superhuman. I looked at Vaslav sitting helplessly mute before me. I clutched my hands in prayer; I shut my eyes and saw in a flash Nijinsky as he was—of another essence than ourselves—surrounded with an invisible magic halo.

Chapter 2

Awakening

ALTHOUGH outwardly I accepted the verdict of the physicians that there was no hope of Vaslav's recovery, in my inmost heart I never believed in this pessimistic outlook. Wherever I went, I got in touch with eminent psychiatrists, research workers, and laboratories, hoping that one day, somewhere, perhaps I would find a treatment which would cure him.

Late in 1927, while on a lecture tour in the United States, I heard that at the Viennese State Hospital experiments were being made by Professor Poetzl and his assistants on hopeless cases of schizophrenia. I wrote to Professor Poetzl explaining Vaslav's case. In his answer he assured me that there was a slight chance that the research work they were conducting might be successful, but it was far too soon to say anything definite, and I should inquire some years later.

In 1936 some reports reached me that at the Poetzl

Clinic the newly tried insulin shock treatment had yielded good results even in old chronic cases. I got in touch with them and was informed that Dr. M. Sakel, a young Austrian doctor who had apparently invented the treatment, was the man to be called in. I wrote to him at once but his reply was rather reserved. He was unable to give any opinion until he had seen and examined the patient. I left the United States immediately for Kreuzlingen, where Vaslav was in a Swiss sanatorium, and asked Dr. Sakel to join me there. At my request, a consultation was called which included himself and three eminent Swiss doctors.

At first I had great difficulty in overcoming the resistance of my husband's guardians, appointed by the Swiss Government, and of the medical staff of the nursing home against undertaking such a daring new treatment, but on the strength of the advice of the three Swiss doctors I finally obtained the necessary consent. Professor Rohr, Dr. Hammerli Schindler, and Professor Müller found Vaslav's physical condition very good and felt that the risk ought to be taken. Dr. Sakel told me that if I did not try the treatment the chance of a recovery was nil, but if we took the risk we might succeed. If not, as the case was already chronic, at least an improvement might be achieved.

It was a very grave decision to make. I realized that

the treatment was a great strain on the heart and on the whole constitution, and every day would be like a major operation. Many of Diaghileff's and Vaslav's old friends thought it was better to leave him as he was. They were afraid that even if he recovered, having been out of touch with the world for twenty years, inactive and unable to exercise his profession, his country and his work lost to him, he might be an unhappy man. "Perhaps it would be better to leave him to his dream world," they said.

I was of a different opinion. I knew him so well, and I was sure that if he could recover his lucidity he would be able to find some form of activity which would give him happiness. I asked the three specialists what they would do in my case. They said that even if Vaslav could only recover his reason for one hour, it would be my duty to allow the treatment, so I gave my consent.

At my request, Dr. Sakel was willing to give the treatment personally. In August, 1938, at a sanatorium in Kreuzlingen, he started it. Every morning Vaslav was given insulin shock to provoke an epileptic fit which, for some unknown reason, sometimes cures schizophrenia.

During the hours in which Vaslav was lying in deep coma provoked by the insulin shock, I suffered indescribable anguish and wondered how I could stand the torment. But seemingly he stood the treatment well, and when he recovered consciousness he answered the questions put to him quite clearly and logically. This was already an improvement, as for years he had suffered from mutism. Dr. Sakel explained to me that this treatment itself was like opening the way to a pit, but the real work was to draw out his withdrawn inner self into the outer world and to build up the bridge with reality. The breaking down of his passive resistance and the unifying of his split personality must be done by someone who was very near and dear to him: his mother, his sister, or myself.

My mother-in-law and Diaghileff were dead. My sister-in-law, Bronia, to whom I sent a friend of ours, Prince Casimir Mirsky, to explain what was being attempted and that we needed her co-operation, seemingly did not understand my request, as she did not come. Therefore, I undertook the task myself.

Every afternoon I tried to interest Vaslav with small and simple matters, subjects which were related either to his art, his youth, or his hobbies. At first, it was an extremely thankless task. His tendency was to withdraw into himself, but I insisted and forced him to try to be active. One had to draw his attention to something and then sustain it. Sometimes it was only a rose in the garden I showed him and made him gather, or he would listen to the piano or watch a game of tennis. Later on, I took him out of the park for walks in the street and showed him the children, or dogs and cats, of which he was afraid, having been isolated from the world and confined in clinics.

It took us all by surprise when Professor Bleuler, the world-famous authority on schizophrenia, announced from Zurich that he would come and visit us. We had not seen him since the tragic days in 1919 when he had diagnosed Vaslav's illness. I knew that he had retired, as he was by this time over eighty years of age, and was no longer Director of the State Asylum in Zurich.

The medical staff was greatly impressed and honored by his proposed visit, and I was relieved at the thought of having his expert opinion on Vaslav's present treatment.

He arrived early in the morning and was present when the insulin shock was administered to Vaslav. Later in the day we were all invited to Dr. L. Binswanger's private house for a luncheon party. Dr. Binswanger, the head of the Sanatorium Bellevue, was once Bleuler's pupil, and naturally pleased to see his former master there. Dr. Sakel also joined us. It was then that Professor Bleuler turned towards us, saying:

"My dear Madame Nijinsky, many years ago I had the cruel task of informing you that your husband was incurably insane, according to medical science as it was in 1919. I am happy today that I am able to give you hope. This young colleague of mine," and he took Sakel's hand, "is able to help. He discovered a treatment for which I searched in vain for over forty years. I am proud of him—and of you— because you did not follow the advice I gave you so many years ago to divorce your husband. You stood by him during those years of mental dimness, you guided him through this terrible illness. Now I believe you will be rewarded; he will once more become himself."

I turned away to hide my tears. . . .

There had to be a pause of two months in the treatment for the sake of Vaslav's physical condition. Dr. Sakel had left for America, but he arranged that Professor Müller of Münsingen, the Director of the State Asylum of the Canton of Bern, should continue the treatment during his absence.

So early in December, 1938, I took Vaslav to Münsingen. At that time this was the best-equipped clinic in Europe for the insulin shock treatment, except the Poetzl Clinic in Vienna. For about three months we stayed there in that huge, gloomy state hospital.

In the mornings, Vaslav was under the care of the doctors; the rest of the day I looked after him fol-

lowing the instructions of Dr. Sakel. Here Vaslav
had far more freedom. Dr. Müller very wisely encouraged every attempt to lead him back to normal
life and make him dependent on himself. Upon Dr.
Müller's advice we made longer and longer visits to
Bern and to the Bernese Oberland.

The improvement was slow but steady and distinct. We now even ventured to take Vaslav to public
places like restaurants, concerts, and the theatre,
where we saw the performance of Trudi Schoop, the
Swiss character dancer.

As Vaslav showed a great interest, Dr. Müller decided that once the second series of insulin treatment
was finished we ought to go, escorted by an attendant,
to a small, quiet hotel in the mountains. Here he
hoped Vaslav would adjust himself even more to normal surroundings. This was originally Professor
Bleuler's theory, who always believed in re-education.

For nearly a year we lived in a small hotel in the
Bernese Oberland, once more in the high mountains.
Again Vaslav saw the seasons passing in the Alps
just as he once had in Saint-Moritz. The place was
similar but not the same.

Everything went even better than we had hoped,
and we seriously began to consider making a home
for ourselves in Switzerland.

The news about the improvement in Vaslav's con-

dition spread like wildfire, and the most startling rumors were circulated about him. Our telephone rang
constantly, and inquiries came from all over the
world. According to some, Vaslav was to appear in
London, Paris, and New York. According to others,
they had already witnessed his performances. Wires
arrived from friends and from people who during his
illness had neglected him completely.

We were suddenly overwhelmed with offers and
advice of all kinds. Colleagues wired advising against
an appearance, as if Vaslav did not know himself
what was the best thing to do concerning his dancing
—he who in 1913 had already stated many times that
at the age of thirty he would give up parts like
Spectre and *Sylphides,* and appear only in character
parts like *Petrouchka* and the *Faun* or similar new
creations of this type. He was the very person who
always said that a dancer's career must be between
the ages of eighteen and thirty-two, and after this
age he wanted to devote his talents to composing and
directing.

Laymen know so little about mental illness. They
either imagine that the patients are raving and dangerous, or they think that from one minute to the next
they should act as normally as if they had never been
ill. But what was the use of explaining?

However, we who knew how matters stood were

thankful for every fresh sign of lucidity and recovery. The rest we left to fate.

Vaslav began to act and behave quite normally. The insulin shock had decidedly freed him from hallucinations. Normality set in, and the only sign of his past illness was his great timidity and a tendency towards silence. He very much disliked anybody's trying to engage him in conversation and got rather excited if anybody tried to force him. But as even in his youth he was inclined to be silent, the doctor thought it was better not to worry him on this subject.

It was only natural that leading this almost idyllic existence, trying to reconstruct a new life among the ruins of our shattered one, we paid very little attention to the outside world and its happenings.

Sitting on our terrace one day, basking in the sunshine, we were admiring the wonderful, mighty peaks of the Alps facing us when our attendant came in with a paper. He seemed rather excited and said that the Germans had concluded a treaty with Russia. It was in August, 1939, if I remember right. The Swiss in the village seemed to be quite upset about it. As the days passed, some of the visitors packed up hurriedly and left for their native countries, and there was a certain panic which seemed ridiculous in these calm, majestic surroundings.

Vaslav rather enjoyed observing the people. As a

youth, he used to sit with Leon Bakst at the Café de la Paix watching the passers-by. Now we went every day at noon to the little bar in our hotel. There we sipped our orange juice, looking at the crowds drift in from their walks or the swimming pool before lunch. Beromünster, the Swiss radio station, broadcast the latest news at noon.

This day, I remember the chatter ceased and there was a deadly silence when it was announced that Germany had refused the proposal that they should not occupy Danzig. . . .

Then suddenly, as out of the blue, Vaslav spoke.

"So once more they claim *'Deutschland, Deutschland über alles.'* This is the beginning of the second act!"

Chapter 3

The Second World War

JUST AS twenty-five years before, the cataclysm broke loose on a late summer day. The incredible became reality. Early in the morning the radio announced, "The German Army is attacking Poland." We knew the Second World War had begun. . . .

Sitting near the radio listening in, I remembered the first war. It started with the murder of Archduke Francis Ferdinand, Austria-Hungary's heir apparent, and years later when it ended in a holocaust few people recalled the reason for which the powers had attacked each other so savagely. Now it was on account of Danzig that once more Europe was plunged into disaster. What would it lead to?

This time the events did not overtake me by surprise. I was not inexperienced and knew what it meant to be on a war-waging continent.

Circumstances seemed more hopeful this time. We were in a neutral land, and there was no reason to think that any trouble might arise in Switzerland. We were in a small mountain resort in the Bernese Oberland, a healthy and secure place. I decided to stay there.

The locality, as if by a magic stroke, emptied within a few hours; on the market place which was the terminus of the mail bus excited crowds tried to find a last seat on the departing coaches which took the passengers to the lowland and the nearest railway station. The streets were crowded; one could hear the news in Dutch, French, Rumanian, Swedish. Everybody was wondering if they would arrive safely in their respective countries, and if their native land would be involved in this new war. We all hoped that somehow at the last hour a miracle would take place and peace would be restored.

As the owner of our hotel decided that he would leave a part of his house open, I arranged with him that we would stay on there indefinitely.

At first we were able to lead the usual manner of our daily routine; but one morning in Switzerland, too, the general mobilization was ordered and our attendant had to depart. This was rather a calamity for me, as I alone could not nurse Vaslav and be in constant attendance upon him. As soon as the mobilization order for the attendant arrived, I called up Dr. Müller at Münsingen and asked him to send us a new attendant. He informed me that this was out of the question. He himself needed additional help, since many of his attendants were being called up for duty in the sanitary section of the army. He was trying to employ women nurses, too, in the men's wards, so he promised to find me a competent psychiatric woman nurse for Vaslav.

Vaslav did not need any physical care; he needed a companion when I was not present, a person who could act as a valet, who would help him dress and undress, to shave him and to serve his meals. But most of all he needed somebody with authority whom he respected and who would be able to impose his will and restrain him if necessary. I believed that an able nurse could easily do this, but I was mistaken. Vaslav immediately took an antagonistic attitude and did everything in his power to scare the life out of one nurse after the other. Being a superb actor and mime, he looked at them so frighteningly and with such powerful, gloomy expressions that they were convinced it was their very last moments and they did not dare to stay with him alone in the room or touch him. . . . So my hope of having some help vanished, and my naughty, mischievous Vaslav attained his aim; he simply wanted me to look after him day and night, he wanted to be alone with me and to be once more the boss in his own home.

This was a natural, healthy reaction which delighted his physicians and me, as it was a definite sign of great improvement. But it put a tremendous load on me, as the responsibility was overwhelming. I was to assure Vaslav's bodily safety; but also, I was answerable for his normal conduct towards society. What this means even when we are guardians of a normal being most people can imagine, but what it is when you have to look after a schizophrenic patient is quite another matter.

Dr. Müller, whom I consulted over the telephone, advised me to give up having nurses, who were only annoying Vaslav by their presence. He very reluctantly said that owing to the circumstances we would have to give up our program of leaving Vaslav at liberty for the present, as he doubted that I could stand the physical strain of being with him constantly without even a few moments of rest. He felt we could not do anything else but bring him back to the asylum until the war was over.

But I was determined not to give up and to try the impossible. So I gave notice to the nurse, who anyway was spending her days strolling in the mountains or reading novels in her room, and took up my duties alone as a nurse.

At first Vaslav was sweet and docile as ever. He obeyed and followed me, and when I shaved him every morning he sat like a little angel. . . . He helped me to tidy the closet and room before we left for our morning walks, he accompanied me when I went shopping, he held the wool when I was knitting, and it seemed it was plain sailing.

Dr. Müller was delighted and congratulated me. But we were too rash in our judgment. Vaslav probably felt life was too smooth and dull here at six thousand feet above sea level, and it was high time to have a little excitement. . . . As in his old school days at the Imperial School, he was speculating on how to play a prank. Well, this he did in an unexpected way. During one of our walks when we were climbing, he pushed me unexpectedly and with great strength so that I lost the ground under my feet and landed on the hay which was strewn over the slope. What would have happened to me if Vaslav had shoved me a few seconds earlier when we were walking along the precipice God only knows. Did he do it on purpose, or just by a sudden impulse? I wondered. I knew that Vaslav's character was gentleness itself; he was never deliberately unkind to anybody. But I knew also that the very peculiarity of schizophrenia was that the patient acted on sudden uncontrollable impulses. That was its very danger, and this was what I had to watch out for. Was it possible to control Vaslav or to influence him? I realized that to use force was out of the question. Even when in the beginning of his illness those primitive brutal doctors and nurses had put him in strait jackets and iron beds, it needed four male nurses and injections to overpower him. And with what results? He became a human wreck—bewildered, confused, martyrized. I was determined that as long as I lived, no matter what he did, this would never happen to him again.

I decided not to mention to anybody what had occurred and to watch even more carefully. I stood up laughingly and patted my skirt clean of the hay which stuck to it. Vaslav joined me in the giggling as I said, "Oh, how funny, Vatzinko," and energetically linked my arm into his. . . . He seemed taken aback. I felt that he was wondering how I had the impertinence not to be frightened of him. I understood now that he was trying to scare me. I knew perfectly well that I had to keep the upper hand or my game would be lost.

Many years ago Professor Bleuler had advised me, among other things, that "one should never lose nerve when a mental patient becomes agitated or violent; on the contrary, then one must show utter fearlessness." Even in an asylum where the room is arranged for these specific cases, with only a few light pieces of furniture, no breakable windows, and automatically closing doors, it is difficult to encounter the patient's attack. How far more complicated it is if this happens in the country, with strangers around, or in a hotel where every object might mean bodily harm to anybody around, as well as to the patient himself. Next day, when as usual I took the breakfast tray into Vatza's room, with one powerful drive he landed the tray on the floor. I was dripping with tea; the scrambled eggs and stewed fruit flew pell-mell on the furniture, carpet, and everywhere. Vaslav sat up in his bed looking at me triumphantly. I bent down to pick up the unbreakable plates and cups, which I was wise enough to serve the meals on, and to clean up. But Vatza was determined to make a real show and threw after me first a chair and then the marble cover of the little table next to his bed. When even this did not have the desired effect of making me panic-stricken and leave the battlefield to him, Vatza, with a foreboding expression full of approaching terror, menace, and danger, with tremendous might made one of his famous *grand jetés* and landed next to me, towering over me with threatening gestures.

As quick as lightning, I remembered Bleuler's warning again that "I was like somebody riding a full-blood race horse; whatever he did, however he jumped, one had to remain in the saddle." I had to avoid a scandal to save his liberty, in spite of his actions. . . .

At this moment, my Vaslav looked very much as Ivan the Terrible must have looked. I saw in his veiled, misty eyes that he was beyond hearing or understanding me; he was wild with emotion and anger. But I did not move, I stood steadfast looking steadily into his eyes with an energetic commanding expression. Vaslav gazed back; a few moments passed, it seemed eternity. . . . Then slowly, imperceptibly he backed away. It was only a fraction of an inch, but I noticed it; I had won. I knew it, and with great gentleness and firmness I walked towards him ordering, "Vatza, *pajalusta saditse*" ("Please sit down"), and he did so.

Like the scenery in a theatre, our surroundings changed from summer to make place for autumn, and the slopes of the Alps were covered by sunburnt grass. The foliage turned into every shade of gold and brown, the entire countryside was flaming, while the towering snow-covered peaks glittered in the sunshine. The place settled down to its out-of-season routine. Overnight the world-famous mountain resort became a small, forgotten Swiss village. The inhabitants, who during the summer and winter seasons were such shrewd merchants trading in souvenirs made of carved wood with painted gentians and alproses, Swiss embroidery, skis, and toboggans, were now interested only in getting the stables in order for the home-coming cattle which had spent the summer in the Alps, as was customary in Switzerland.

It was a great joy for Vaslav to wander around the fields and woods, to watch the returning cattle driven home by small children, who were running around picking the last autumn flowers, the lovely lilac crocuses, and to look at the peasants cutting and piling up the wood in neat order around their houses.

Everything was made ready for winter. We were undisturbed, and it was an ideal place for Vaslav to make his first contact with the real world. His mood became more stable and balanced, and there was no doubt about it that through the insulin shock treatment the hallucinations which had tormented him for years had slowly receded and made place for a state of serenity.

After the attempt he made to get the upper hand, he gently settled down and allowed me to guide him. Life would have been supremely happy if the war had not come. Although we were in a neutral country in a calm and secure place, I felt that we were on top of a volcano and that anything might happen to us here in the center of Europe. The surrounding countries were all involved.

For the last twenty years, I had gone to the United

States to lecture and work. It had become a second home for me, and I knew that among its hospitable people would be the right place for Vaslav to be, especially as Dr. Sakel was living and practicing there. When he had finished his treatment, it had been understood that within a year Vaslav should once more go to him.

As soon as war broke out, I asked my American lawyer to undertake the necessary steps to obtain for Vaslav a visitor's visa to the United States and permit him to stay for some time for medical treatment. I knew it would take some weeks to obtain this, since Vaslav had suffered from mental illness and the visa needed special permission. But I was full of hopes and began to mention to Vaslav that we would soon go to America. He became interested in the project, and like a child who has received a long-coveted present at Christmas, his eyes opened and he smilingly said, "America . . . we go to America."

Weeks passed, and towards Christmas our daughter Kyra announced that she would come up with her little son Vaslav Markevitch-Nijinsky to spend the holidays with us. Little Vaslav, whom we also called Funtyiki, was a child of good disposition although he had a strong will. It was a great day when I could go to fetch them at the next railway station, which was about an hour-and-a-half sleigh ride from our home.

We formed a happy little family during those winter months. . . .

Undoubtedly, the news that Vaslav was recuperating became more and more known; therefore it was not so surprising that one day he received a cable with an offer from Mr. Hurok, the theatrical impresario, asking him to come over to New York and appear. My son-in-law, who had just arrived to spend the week-end with us, advised me to cable back accepting the offer, for then we automatically could have escaped from Europe and would have been able to depart at once. But I felt I could not accept a contract for Vaslav and commit him. There was no question at the time that Vaslav should appear in public. Nevertheless, I hoped that the impresario, who was a Russian himself and who had made his name and fortune in America managing Russian dancers in the past, would have vision enough and a humanitarian spirit in helping to get the greatest Russian dancer out of the European inferno. What I did not know at the time was that there was quite a group of dancers who had got together and who worked in silence to keep Nijinsky out of the United States and from public life. Illness had removed the artist with whom they could not compete. They dreaded his coming back.

About this time I received a letter from Lady

Morrell's husband in London, who was looking after Vaslav's interests there. He informed me that owing to the new currency regulations no more funds could be sent out of Great Britain. This was a hard blow. I realized that we could not go to England, being stateless, and if we stayed in Switzerland for some time we would not have enough money. Now it became more important than ever to proceed to the United States.

Vaslav's nurse, Mr. Kempf, who had looked after him so splendidly during the insulin shock treatment and who was on the staff of the State Hospital in Münsingen, volunteered to come up to us when he was off duty at the Asylum. This meant that one day a week and on Sundays he could relieve me. Luckily, Münsingen was only two hours distant and I could accept his proposition. Vaslav was overjoyed, as Kempf was a good and gay person and nursed him well. It was a change for Vaslav, as my company must have become monotonous for him in the long run.

The days Kempf could spend with Vaslav, I used to go down to Bern to attend to all business matters, and above all to further our project to leave for America. Very soon I became friendly with the staff of the American Associated Press, who were most helpful, putting through telephone calls, cables, and advising me.

I asked our old friend Laurence Steinhardt, Ambassador of the United States to the U.S.S.R., to intervene at the State Department and explain the case. I asked him to put the matter up to the President, if necessary. Once in the past the American Government had helped us out of war-ridden Europe, and I was confident that now when Vaslav needed it more than ever permission would be granted.

There was a strange calm on the fronts during this winter. Nobody really knew what would happen, but the populace became nervous and those who were living in the lowlands began to search for homes in the mountains. More and more people arrived in motorbuses, carts, and bicycles, bringing their belongings and household utensils with them. It was a strange sight in Switzerland. The borders were hermetically closed, and rumors were around saying that as soon as spring began the Germans might attack France and invade Switzerland. It would have been wise to stay up in the mountains, but Vaslav became restless and Dr. Hammerli Schindler, the great heart specialist whom I consulted again, felt that the long stay in such a high altitude was not advisable. Kempf had to remain at Münsingen now, to stand by the

Asylum, as, owing to stricter mobilization, practically all male nurses were called in. I began to wonder if it would not be better to go down to Münsingen and stay there in the village inn.

I had to be more economical, too, and since our landlord did not have the graciousness to let us remain in our comfortable quarters but squeezed us into two small back rooms on the top floor, I felt it was wiser to leave. The last stroke was that one day when I had to go down to Bern to extend our permit, the help I engaged for the day to be with Vaslav while I was absent had locked him up and had gone to the bars, where I found him drinking upon my return. Immediately I packed and we left for Münsingen.

To be back there, a stone's throw from the Asylum, was not an ideal place for Vaslav; it brought back sad memories, but I had no choice. At least I had reliable help near in case I had to leave for a few hours. As time passed, I had to concentrate more and more on making some arrangements, so much more since Vaslav was a resident of the Canton of Thurgau, where he had spent the last ten years. Now Thurgau wanted to allow him to return only if a guarantee of five thousand Swiss francs were deposited, plus his maintenance. The Canton of Bern, where Münsingen is located, would not allow him to stay for good for the same financial reasons. I had to engage a law firm to represent him. The alien police were harassing me to leave the country, as I had only a six-month visa which had been extended several times. They made more and more frequent visits, inquiring when I would leave, and I became more unnerved. It was an impossible situation.

My days were spent in navigation between the Political Department, to which the inner security of Switzerland belongs, and the Authorities of the Stateless Subjects, begging them to give us permission to stay. I knew that I could earn money only if I were able to get to the United States; to remain in Switzerland without having there a large amount in Swiss currency at our disposal was hopeless.

Finally, after long weeks of anxiety I got a cable from New York saying that a visa had been granted for Vaslav, with permission for him to stay in the States for one year's medical treatment.

It was about Easter time. I cannot describe the joy I felt. At last we were saved—Vaslav could be looked after properly by Dr. Sakel near New York, and he would be in safety.

My visa was in order. I had obtained it some months before in Bern, and it was valid for one year. The cable which brought me this happy news informed me that Vaslav and I would have to appear before the Consul General, who had his offices in Zurich.

Dr. Müller very helpfully lent Kempf for a few days, and escorted by some of the staff of the Associated Press we left joyfully for Zurich. Having the permission in hand, I thought that within a few days we would be able to leave.

I was quite confident when I entered the Consulate General and presented Vaslav's valid Nansen Passport issued by the Swiss Government. The Consul assured me that he had received instructions from the State Department in Washington to grant the visa. He seemed to be annoyed by the fact that the morning papers had already printed the news all over Switzerland that Nijinsky was to be admitted to the United States. He inquired as to how the news had leaked out, and how it was possible that the Associated Press was informed sooner than he himself. I was unable to give him a reply. In fact, the Associated Press knew the fact before I received the cable. It was only later that we found out the reporters in Washington had got the news sooner than we did.

Instead of granting the visa, the Consul told me to leave the passport with him and to return next day. I thought he merely wanted me to come back to fetch the ready document. My amazement was boundless when he informed me next day that although the permission from Washington had been granted, he would not give Vaslav the visa. As he was Consul he could act independently, having the right of discretion to refuse entry. I asked him point-blank why he wanted to bar Vaslav.

"Mr. Nijinsky is stateless and carries a Nansen Passport," was his answer.

"But the State Department in Washington knows this, and in spite of it they are willing to let my husband in."

"Yes, but in a year's time when his permit is up and the war will still be on in Europe, you will ask for an extension."

"I may, but naturally if it is not extended we would leave the country and would go to Mexico or Canada or any other state, away from war and its horrors. I will immediately secure a visa to one of these countries."

"No," he answered, "I won't give the visa—I don't want to be blamed later by my chiefs."

"But I am sure they will not blame you—they fully realize the situation and have taken every aspect into consideration before they agreed. They know what they are doing in Washington."

But the Consul was unalterable in his decision.

I began to tremble, knowing that this refusal meant to us the shattering of all our hopes, of the possibility of Vaslav's final recovery, and of endless suffering. It was the end.

I was numbed and don't know how I went out of the place. As from a distance, I heard the young attaché's voice, who escorted me to the entrance. At the time, I could not even take in fully the meaning of his words.

"Mrs. Nijinsky, I am so sorry, I am really sorry. I understand how you feel. The Consul's attitude is inexplicable to me. He is in a bad temper. Do appeal to the State Department, to the President. It is an injustice to bar Nijinsky from the United States at the present time."

Upon the advice of my young friends in the Associated Press, we returned to Bern. Here in a small hotel we took lodgings. Here, since we were nearer to all Government offices, I had more hope of obtaining permission for our stay should our American appeal fail, which I had lodged immediately with the American authorities. Cabling back and forth began once more, and I was ready to make any sacrifice to get Vaslav to the United States.

Events followed each other with vertiginous rapidity. The great calm of the winter months gave place to fierce attacks on one front after the other. First Denmark was invaded; soon after Norway was attacked and taken, then Holland and Belgium. The west was aflame; the Swiss feared the worst, and I still had no reply from the United States.

Our way towards the west was almost closed, and I prayed each day that permission would arrive before it was too late.

An old friend of my mother's, who had been living in Switzerland for thirty years, advised me to return to Hungary before it was too late. "You won't be able to keep your husband here unless you can deposit a few years' maintenance in Swiss francs." His opinion was based upon the information his lawyers got from the various governmental departments.

"In Hungary they know who you are—Francis de Pulszky's * granddaughter. Your husband will be received with open arms."

"But I don't want to go there—we have been prisoners of war there."

He replied, "But now Hungary is neutral; it is a quiet and prosperous country; you will be all right there. Your mother and your family will be glad to receive you. I spoke to them, and they assured me of that when I visited them a few months ago in Budapest. Go there before it is too late—you can still go through Italy and Yugoslavia."

I wrote to my mother inquiring, and she replied

* Statesman, founder of the Hungarian democracy.

that Mr. Kanitz told the truth. I felt reassured that if worst came to worst we should have a refuge in a neutral country. My American lawyer wrote me that it might take weeks before an answer to the appeal would be forthcoming. The Associated Press informed me almost hourly of the happenings and advised me also to leave Switzerland, as the German Army was turning towards the Swiss side of the Rhine.

Air-raid alarms began, everybody was scared, and we lost our heads. The American Consul in Bern was sending all American subjects back, and advised me to make use of my American visa before all visitors' visas might be annulled.

I was at a loss. I could escape, but what would happen to Vaslav?

Dr. Müller proposed, "Go and leave him here. After all, if you are not here any more and your husband is left alone, stateless and without funds, the authorities will be obliged to hospitalize him."

"But where and how?"

"Well, they will commit him to one of the State asylums in Canton Bern, third class. He will have a bed and food. And if our country is attacked, we will take the patient to the mountains and the rest is in God's hands. . . ."

For a few hours I thought feverishly: What was

my duty towards Vaslav, what was the right thing to do? To try to force my way to America to work for him there and send him money through the Red Cross, as I was assured might be possible later; to abandon him alone as a third-class patient now that he had partly regained his lucidity; or to stick with him and try to get through with him to Hungary and await the decision of Washington? I finally decided to do the last—whatever happened.

But there was no more time to lose. France was invaded and taken, the Germans were in Paris, Italian war rumors started, and according to the Associated Press the road through Italy and Yugoslavia to Hungary might soon be barred too.

Chapter 4

Hungary

AFTER TWENTY YEARS of absence, on a sweltering day in July, exhausted by a long, tiring trip, we arrived in Budapest, the capital of Hungary, the very place where we first met so many years ago.

Crossing the Danube, we saw basking in the blazing sunshine the outstanding landmarks: the chain of mountains encircling the city, the Royal Palace raised upon the hill which dominates the town, the Parliament, old Buda, the Island of St. Marguerite—sights once so familiar to us.

Slowly the train pulled into the station. I felt we were in the Orient. After the neat, clean Swiss stations it was such a contrast suddenly to be plunged into this old-fashioned, dilapidated terminus, crowded with wildly gesticulating people, peasants wearing national costumes, barefooted children, poorly clad, dirty rabble. Thrown pell-mell on the platform were lying mailbags, trunks, suitcases, huge baskets loaded with vegetables and live poultry. An indescribable hubbub filled the air. Passengers were shouting to each other, while the children's crying mingled with the crowing of the cockerels brought up to the market by the villagers. It was a strange spectacle. We felt lost in these startling surroundings.

I looked around expecting that after this seemingly endless journey, and an absence of two decades, my relatives would naturally be waiting for us, but I looked in vain. There was nobody to welcome us. I sensed instantly that we had made a terrible mistake in returning here. But what to do? It was impossible to turn back. Vaslav, noticing my embarrassment, said smilingly, "Don't worry, they did not receive your message in time."

We drove to the Ritz Hotel and from there I called up my family, only to be informed by the butler that they were out of town. I knew they had left deliberately.

During the next few days, left to ourselves in the hotel, we thought over what we were going to do. It was understood that we should await here the result of our appeal to the United States immigration authorities, and as soon as they overruled the decision of the American Consul General in Zurich barring Vaslav's admittance, we would proceed through

Yugoslavia and Greece to the United States. This was the only open route; towards the west the way was closed by the German Army. Only primitive cargo boats kept up the service between Greece and North America, but what did this matter so long as it was the way to safety and freedom?

At that time Hungary was neutral, and according to what I had heard from the well-informed diplomats and American journalists, it would remain so. Budapest was gay and carefree; one could not feel that a world conflagration was raging around this small country. Just as in Switzerland, so here the blessings and advantages of neutrality manifested themselves. Prosperity reigned, factories worked to full capacity, shops were laden with merchandise, whatever heart and eye could wish for. Hotels, night clubs, and theatres were crowded with foreign diplomats, artists, businessmen, and spies. Hungarian society ladies paraded the streets in the latest French models. The whole manner of life reminded me of that of Zurich during the First World War.

After a few days, my relatives called upon us at the hotel. Our meeting took place in the lobby. My family was accompanied by a friend of my stepfather's as a witness, a clear sign of their antagonistic attitude towards us. Twenty-one years had not changed their feelings. Our meeting was polite but lacked all warmth. It was obvious that we were unwelcome to them in Hungary. In the eyes of the public they did not wish to refuse us hospitality; therefore, they declared to the press and wrote to us that we would be received with open arms.

I explained our situation and our intention only to remain in Hungary for a short time. They smiled sourly. I told them that owing to the insulin shock treatment Vaslav was now, thank God, socially healed and authorized to live at liberty in my custody, but I could see that they disbelieved every word I uttered.

Nevertheless, it was agreed that, as arranged by correspondence, we were to live in their house among the hills of Buda on the outskirts of the town. The very same apartment on the second story of the mansion was again allotted to us which we had occupied during the First World War. It was here that we spent the next two years.

At first we were full of hope. Letters from America were most encouraging, but as time went on I began to lose courage, no matter what my attorney wrote. He claimed that interminable red tape prevented Vaslav's admission to New York, in spite of the visa granted by the State Department.

My family did not make life easy for us, looking at Vaslav with mistrust. Nobody could have been more docile, quiet, and good-natured than he was.

Nevertheless, he could not disarm them. I was deeply worried, realizing the great mistake I had made in bringing him to my family's home, where he had suffered so deeply in the past. It was a great error with far-reaching consequences to place him here in this antagonistic atmosphere, charged with discord and suspicion, especially after the insulin shock treatment. Vaslav needed now to be surrounded with sympathetic, understanding, and kindly people. He was timid, like a child making his first contacts with life and society; he had to readjust himself to reality and his fellow human beings. He had spent twenty-two years in his very own dream world, a universe full of terrifying hallucinations, menacing threats, bottomless torture, insufferable horror. These had alternated with elated, dazzling artistic creations, joy and happiness, when his inspired thoughts took the form of living personages tender and loving, not merely choreographic, fanciful beings but unblemished entities in this place where sound, color, and plastic movements attained perfection and were a reality to him. Now one had to treat him tenderly like a fragile plant and not rebuke him. Instead of loving co-operation, we only met with hardness.

I decided to keep away from my family as much as possible. From now on we lived alone, hardly seeing anybody, taking our meals in our rooms, high above the intriguing, misapprehending members of my family.

The days passed slowly. During the summer we spent most of the time walking in the woods just as during the First World War, and in the winter we stayed at home and played chess or I read to Vaslav. We were like prisoners, day after day locked up in two small rooms. Vaslav was oppressed by the atmosphere of the house. He did not complain, but he was glad every time we went out and met someone who was kind to him and treated him like a normal human being. One day we met M. Pali Strauss, who during our stay in New York in 1916 had spent so much time with us and presented Isadora Duncan to Vaslav. It was indeed a great joy to meet such a loyal friend here after so many years. Pali Strauss was an *homme du monde* of great culture, a connoisseur of art, owning a wonderful collection of pictures.

"You should not have brought Vaslav back to Hungary, the very same place where he had suffered so much as a prisoner of war, where he had to undergo such hardships among your relatives, who did not behave well towards you in the past," he reproached me.

I knew he was right, but the mistake was unfortunately made and there was no way out. Pali Strauss was a shrewd man and a good friend.

"You must come and see me often," he said. "I will try to amuse Vaslav and we must find a way to enable you to leave the country, and above all your relatives' house. Unfortunately, my town house is let to the French Ambassador, so I can't offer it to you. My estates are requisitioned and full of the army, but we will find a place where you can go with Vaslav in the meantime."

To render life more agreeable to Vaslav, he took us for long motor drives to the near-by villages, to gypsy restaurants, to the pictures.

Upon Strauss' advice, I quite frequently dined with Allied diplomats and visited the American Consulate, becoming more and more worried as I realized that our visas had been forgotten at the bottom of a drawer in Washington, while the horizon became darker and darker. It was rumored that Hungary might declare war on Great Britain and the United States. At first, it seemed almost incredible that such a small country should dare to do so, but very soon it became a reality. I tried frantically to induce the departing Consulates to take us with them, but they were only able to leave with their own nationals.

Once more we were closed in, in a country at war. This was a terrible blow to us. Our position deteriorated, as up to now we had been able to receive funds from America, but from this point on we were completely cut off. I still had some cash with me which I was trying to keep for emergencies.

As soon as it became known that America was at war, our relatives held a council to which the family doctor and priest were called in. It was decided that they would ask us to leave. The doctor and the Abbé advised them not to do this, but my stepfather was adamant, so a very near relative of mine came up to our room and asked us to go as soon as possible. I told her firmly that we could not and would not. The ground on which the house was built was bought in my girlhood with my own money inherited from my father, so I decided to stay, not having any other alternative.

After this, life in the house became intolerable. I went around with Vaslav trying to find somewhere else to live, but first I had to get some money. I went to the leading newspapers and asked them whether they would be prepared to publish some of my articles on art. They said they would be delighted if I could prove to the Literary Council that I was a pure Aryan. This I was able to do, so I received permission to write. Following the advice of a friend, I also published Vaslav's diary in Hungarian, and this kept us going for a while.

Spring came. One morning I had to go to town and, entering a shop, I noticed that everybody was greatly

upset and gesticulating wildly, telling some sensational news. What had happened? A lady turned to
me and explained that Count Teleky, the Prime Minister, had died during the night. It was said that he
had committed suicide because he did not want to
declare war on Yugoslavia. But people disbelieved
the suicide theory because he was a devout Catholic,
and he had been to confession the evening before. His
father-confessor said that he had behaved as usual,
and there was no reason to suppose that he contemplated such a desperate and unchristian act. It was
rumored that he was murdered, but by whom? The
question was left unanswered. They only knew that
after having visited his wife, who was in a clinic, he
went to confession, came home, and made preparations to receive some visitors late that night. These
visitors were German officers of high rank who left
after midnight. The next morning, Count Teleky's
valet found his master shot. The matter was hushed
up, and it was rumored that the Count had had a fit
of depression on account of the political situation.

The day he was buried I remember standing on
the balcony in the very same place where we stood
at the beginning of the First World War, looking
down on the ceaselessly marching regiments gar-
landed with flowers and singing. This time the road

was empty. Only a few peasants and passers-by stood around.

Suddenly a shrill howling pierced the silence and became more and more intense. It was terrifying; my heart almost stopped beating. I looked at Vaslav, who seemed unconcerned. I knew he did not realize fully what it meant. He must have thought it was a factory siren, but I knew it was the warning of an approaching air raid. So it had come true. It was a most uncanny sensation. I did not dare to explain to Vaslav, not knowing what his reaction would be. So I just said, "Let us go in now, it is time for lunch."

The raid lasted half an hour while we ate our lunch in silence. I was listening the whole time for the sound of approaching planes, but nothing happened. The whole city and suburbs were petrified and motionless. Our rooms were in a small tower above the house, two stories high—the worst possible place, but we had no shelter so we could do nothing. To my great relief, suddenly the all-clear sounded.

Later in the day we were told by returning neighbors that it had not been a genuine air raid. While the funeral procession was taking place, in which all the senior clergy, magistrates, and members of the Government took part, headed by the Regent himself, two Serbian planes approached the city and, after circling above the hearse, dropped a laurel wreath on it. The purple silk ribbon bore the dedication:

"To the last Hungarian Gentleman. The Yugoslav Nation."

Chapter 5

War with Russia

ONE MORNING while we were driving with Pali Strauss, our car was stopped on the quai of the Danube, which is the main road leading from Vienna to Budapest. Heavy lorries full of German soldiers in field uniforms drove past in an endless stream, followed by thousands and thousands of tanks all heading towards the south.

"This will end badly," said Strauss as we turned in the opposite direction.

Every time Vaslav saw soldiers he became pale and silent. I felt I must get him away from here, somewhere where he would not see them.

Strauss finally found a small convalescent home in Buda which was well kept and into which we moved. Here at least, when I had to go out shopping or on errands, Vaslav was not left alone but had company;

this was the best solution we could find for the moment.

The months passed. The Germans occupied the Balkan Peninsula and the circle was closing in on us.

During the following winter we quite often visited the hospitable home of Countess Dobrojensky, one of Vaslav's great admirers, the widow of a Czech aristocrat but Hungarian by birth, and she frequently asked us to tea in her home, where we spent many happy hours. When Vaslav was present we talked only about art and literature, avoiding war news so as not to upset him.

It was from her that I first learned that on her Czechoslovakian estate there was a soap factory, and the people in the near-by village spread the rumor that the soap was made out of the corpses of the massacred Jews. I did not believe her, it seemed so fantastic. It was she also who told me one day, "My dear Romola, the Germans are exterminating all mental patients, and although nobody could notice any trace of illness in Vaslav now, he might be in danger; we must do something to get him away." But where to?

Although Hungary was at war with Great Britain and the United States, one did not notice any change as yet. The only difference was that the city was crowded with German officers and a few restrictions were introduced. The German High Command made it clear to the Hungarian Government that they considered it outrageous, with Hungary also at war, that the Hungarians should live such luxurious lives while the allied German nation was kept on such short rations.

Vaslav spent his days reading and drawing and took little interest in what was going on in the world, but one day he said, "Femmka,* can't we leave here, can't you do something?"

I made up my mind that I would try. The roads to the west and south were closed, so our friends suggested that we should try the road towards the east, through Russia and China, to the United States.

Among our acquaintances there was Puffy Huszar, a colleague of my mother's, a well-known actor who had lived for years in Hollywood. When he retired he came back to Hungary and bought an estate. Being of Jewish origin, he now realized that his position was unsafe and decided to return to Hollywood. He chose the route via Russia and strongly recommended me to do the same.

"I had no trouble," he said. "I went to the Russian Embassy and they were charming to me. They like artists. I explained my case and had no difficulty in

* Nickname by which Vaslav called me.

getting a transit visa. Why do not you do the same and get out of Europe?"

His idea seemed to me a practicable one, so one morning, without saying anything to Vaslav, I went to the Russian Consulate, which was housed in a private villa. The doorman let me pass and I was shown into a small room where a woman sat at a large desk, dressed like my governess thirty years ago, in a shirt-waist and dark skirt. She was eating an apple and flirting with a young man who stood near, paying little attention to the people waiting around. After a while she called me to her desk and I stated who I was. She looked me up and down, then put her apple on the desk and said, "Wait here; I will see whether the Consul will receive you or not."

I waited and after some time she came back and showed me into another room. This was large and lofty, well furnished, with velvet curtains; the floor was covered with soft carpets. On the walls hung immensely large portraits of Stalin, Molotov, and Voroshilov. The room was empty. I waited and waited but nobody came, so I began to wonder whether I had been forgotten. I looked around and had the feeling I was not alone. Suddenly a door opened and a young man came towards me. He was dressed very simply and looked like a factory inspector.

"Will you come in? I am the Consul."

I introduced myself and told him that now, after twenty-two years of illness, my husband was socially healed, thanks to a new treatment, and that I was anxious not to imperil the improvement we had obtained after so much suffering and hardship. I had tried desperately, since the outbreak of the war, to get him out of Europe to a safe place, and above all to the doctor who had cured him and who was practicing in New York. Could we go east and try to get to the States from there? Would they give us a transit visa?

"Well, I have to ask Moscow for permission; we have to look up all the old records of Nijinsky. It will take about three months. But," he continued, "there is no doubt that he is a Russian. He left our country in 1911 to go on an artistic tour and did not return. He became ill and could not obey the edict of 1923, which commanded all Russian subjects to report to their Consulates. You, of course, are not Russian. Marriage, according to our laws, does not make you one. However, I will see if you can get a transit visa and will let you know."

Then he went on to tell me all that had been done during the past years in Russia in art and in ballet, and showed me illustrated papers from Moscow with pictures of the large new Tchaikovsky Concert Hall, which according to him has the best acoustics in the world.

"Don't forget to tell all this to your husband; show him the photos of the ballet. We know who Nijinsky and Chaliapine are, we have not forgotten them!"

Three months passed. On June 22 we went into the town and Vaslav sat in the car waiting for me. People were discussing some sensational news and newsboys were running around with extra editions shouting, "Germany at war with Russia! The Russian border has been overrun!"

I stood rooted to the spot. I could not move. It could not be, it was too ghastly! Once more we would be prisoners of war.

"Roma,* why are you so silent, what is the matter? What is worrying you?" asked Vaslav.

I remembered the advice Professor Bleuler had given me years ago, that one must tell the truth and tell it gently, when one cannot avoid making certain facts known to a mental patient. So I said, "The German Army has attacked Russia. If Hungary sides with Germany, we must face the fact that perhaps we may be interned again. Don't be frightened, we are together."

* Diminutive of my Christian name.

It was some days later that Mrs. Lily Sacher, a friend of mine, asked us to come up to her flat, as she noticed that Vaslav looked tired. It was a large flat on the third floor with windows overlooking the Danube and the hills of Buda. As we were sitting and talking over what might happen if Hungary went to war against Russia, the air-raid signal sounded.

At first there was a mad rush of people running for shelter. The trolleys and buses stopped, people jumped off and vanished in doorways, the caretakers after a few seconds closed the doors. The whole city became motionless. On the deserted streets policemen in steel helmets scrutinized the sky. We looked at each other, opening the windows. My friend's family, with the other occupants of the building, quickly went down to the cellar.

"Let us stay," said Vaslav; "here we have air."

We did not realize what an air raid might mean. The moments passed which seemed to me like an eternity, but nothing happened. After an hour I became quite at ease and relieved. Vaslav in the meantime was looking at books dealing with Italian masters of the Cinquecento. The all-clear sounded and later we returned home.

In the evening we heard that the warning was given as Kassa, in northern Hungary, was being attacked by Russian planes. This, however, was not true. German planes with Russian markings had made a provocative raid! They attained their aim. The country was at war with Russia.

The Swedish Embassy now took over the Russian interests. I knew I had no more time to lose. I decided to pay a visit to the Embassy and spoke to the Ambassador himself, who was most kind and anxious to help.

"Your Excellency, we are in dreadful trouble. We are here with very little money, practically stranded. Our way to the United States is blocked. My husband is recuperating after twenty-two years of illness, and I have to protect his physical safety, as well as his mental balance, which he has regained by almost a miracle. Everything will be lost if we have to stay here. Please help us to get out of the country!"

"First I have to find out whether you are considered stateless or Russian subjects, then I will get in touch with the Allied Governments and the International Red Cross. Nijinsky, a great artist and a person who has been ill for such a long time, is entitled to protection, and even safe-conduct back to Switzerland if we cannot help otherwise."

But official proceedings were slow, and in the meantime something had to be done. We decided to leave the capital for the present and go to the country. Countess Dobrojensky suggested that we should go to one of her country places in the east of Hungary. This idea was dropped, because we felt that among the peasants, foreigners might be looked upon with hatred and this might provoke their hostile attitude. So it was decided that we should go to one of the innumerable little summer resorts near Lake Balaton. A distant relative, Pavel Vihus, as Vaslav called him, who usually passed the summer by the lake, went to look for a place where we could stay, and within a few days he found the ideal place for us.

It was a small summer settlement on a hill dominating the southern shore of the lake, with charming little bungalows. Well-kept gardens surrounded the cottages and even the surrounding woods were nicely kept. At one end was a hotel; from its large terrace there was an unforgettable view over the lake. On the other side of the settlement there was a picturesque, dusty Hungarian village with its thatched roofs, its deep wells; geese, ducks, and pigs wandered about the dusty road. In the old tavern during the evenings the gypsy band played, while the local peasants sat around drinking and singing.

We rented a small cottage built in the park of a large estate. The owner's big house was at the southern end of the park. Our cottage was near the woods into which a little path led. It was simply furnished but clean. I engaged a Hungarian male nurse to help me attend to Vaslav and keep house. Brindus, the male nurse, an honest Hungarian of peasant origin, was the most devoted person and served Vaslav with affection and loyalty. Although they could not speak to each other, they very soon became friends and got on splendidly.

We settled comfortably, taking our meals either in the hotel or at the peasant tavern. Vaslav was gay and happy now. This place must have reminded him of his own country. At last he was freed from the restraint of the awkward position which weighed upon us so much in Budapest.

We drifted into a peaceful routine. In the mornings we went down to the lake and lay in the sun for hours, bathing from time to time in the tepid, velvety water of the Balaton. It is a unique lake, very beautifully situated, and its water is marvelous, having medicinal and hot springs. Sometimes we took a boat and rowed on the lake, watching the fishermen with their large nets catching the world-famous fish called "fogas."

We explored the neighborhood on foot or in a peasant cart, and sometimes even made excursions to the other side of the lake. There were a few places of interest—the fashionable spa Balaton Füred, with its hotels and sanatoriums; and the lovely Tichany, with its ancient abbey of the Premonstratensian order. The lofty old church is a gem of the baroque style, with two towers dominating the northeastern side of the lake. This building is famous for its echo, which repeats a call twenty times, and which greatly amused Vaslav, who repeatedly called to the echo. Many old legends are told about the Tichany: how a fairy is kept in prison and repeats the calls; how the cattle of the abbey ran into the lake chased by evil spirits— and, in fact, the shells which are thrown up by the lake near Tichany have the form of animal hoofs. We were shown around the church, the spacious library, and the school kept by the monks. The place had now become a haven of refuge under the protectorate of the Vatican and the Swiss Red Cross. Many sick people and refugees asked and received protection there during the war.

Vaslav enjoyed the romantic atmosphere so much that I took him to Badacsony. This is a burnt-out volcano on the northern slope of one of the higher peaks in the chain of hills surrounding the lake. The most exquisite wine is produced there, and wherever one looks the hillside is covered with vineyards. Most of them are on land belonging to Hungary's foremost nobleman, Prince Paul Esterházy.

On top of the hill was a small old estate which once belonged to the great Hungarian poet Kecskemety but is now a prosperous winehouse and restaurant. Here we spent a delightful day, with Vaslav wandering in the vineyards. The view reminded us so much of that in Madeira. How far fate had thrown us since the day *The Avon* stopped at Funchal!

Our life in these simple, enchanting surroundings did Vaslav a world of good, and we enjoyed ourselves like two carefree children. On Sundays we went to the lovely little whitewashed church built on the cliffs, from which we could look over the lake with its deep azure surface. Everything was so peaceful— one felt in a lost Italian village.

Every night I walked down to the hotel at ten o'clock to hear the latest news broadcast from Belgrade. Here we learned of an attempted English landing in Normandy. I also heard what was going on in the Balkan Peninsula and on the Eastern front. More and more I realized that we were walled in by a Germanic world. The broadcast invariably closed with the song "Lili Marlene," which by now was hummed and whistled everywhere and by everybody. On the winding wood path which led from the hotel to our cottage, under the whispering trees I strolled home. The lake was glittering in the moonlight, a soft warm southern breeze ruffled the sheet of water, and on the roadside beautiful flowers were blooming. At one corner stood a statue of Our Lady of Lourdes among the heavy-scented blooms. Here I knelt every evening and prayed that we should be able to leave the country in safety.

In spite of all the anxiety during this summer, we felt happy and content. One almost forgot the ghastly holocaust which raged through Europe.

While bathing in the lake on a sunlit morning, I heard the sensational news that the Regent's eldest son, Stephen Horthy (who was to succeed him), had crashed on the Russian front. It was the 20th of August, St. Stephen's Day, Hungary's patron saint.

Our intention was to stay as long as possible here in the country, but we had to change our plans unexpectedly. A few days later when we were rowing on the lake, suddenly another boat accosted us with two gendarmes in it. They ordered us to land at once, as they wished to talk to us. I could not quite understand the reason and was worried, because ever since the First World War when we were prisoners, Vaslav had had a nervous fear of uniformed persons. Luckily, they spoke Hungarian and therefore he could not understand them.

Their manners were rather rough. They told us that somewhere not very far away a Russian parachutist had landed and got away. They knew we were Russians, so they wanted to know how and why we came here and whether we knew anybody in the neighborhod. I assured them laughingly that we certainly did not land here by parachute, and had no further interest than to spend the summer here quietly. I asked them to come up to the house and look at our papers and the permit from the police in Budapest authorizing us to stay here during the summer.

They read and reread our documents, turned them around a dozen times, shook their heads disapprovingly, and said there was something fishy about the whole matter. They asked us to follow them, but I refused, saying my husband had been ill for so many years that I would not upset him by going with them. I requested that they get in touch with the police in Budapest and find out all about us. Finally, I succeeded in persuading them and they left grumbling.

But Brindus and I decided that the safest way out of all trouble was to return to the capital without delay. Provincial authorities were old-fashioned and out-of-date, and the gendarmes were known to be wild and savage. We were not very far from Lepseny, where the Hungarian oil wells were situated. The country police kept a close watch on all foreigners, everybody was suspicious of them, and endless complications might arise; so with regret we packed hurriedly and returned to Budapest.

Chapter 6

Budapest

IT WAS LATE at night when we arrived in the capital. The whole of the station was covered with heavy black draperies, and the lights were dimmed and also veiled in heavy black gauze. It was a ghastly sight. Pavel and a friend awaited us at the station, and we quickly hurried Vaslav away. "Will-o'-the-Wisp," as we nicknamed Pavel, explained that the casket of the Regent's son was expected, and therefore the whole town was plunged in mourning. That was the reason for the gloom in the station and the black draperies.

Our next task was to find a quiet place to spend the winter. After a long search we found a little house on the top of the Svabenberg, one of the highest hills near Buda, which is all wooded and has many summer houses nestling in its midst. The house belonged to a well-known Hungarian Jewish journalist, who had been sent to the front in the Jewish labor corps which was always sent on ahead of the fighting troops to pick up the mines. His wife was hiding in the town and was glad to rent us the house.

On the ground floor a destitute Polish refugee couple lived. The husband, a scientist, looked very poor and unhappy. When we visited the house, the landlady, who was showing us around, gave them notice.

"They have to get out anyhow; they owe me the rent for months."

Vaslav watched them. The man looked exhausted and infinitely sad, and his wife was in tears. We entered their room, which was used as a living room, bedroom, kitchen, and bathroom in one. There was an indescribable disorder. In the middle of the room there was a large wooden basin in which she washed their laundry, and on a small iron stove she cooked their frugal meal. Vaslav sat down and listened to the scientist, who apologized in Polish.

"Forgive us for this messy place, but I had no time to clean it up. My wife went marketing and today is laundry day. Of course, we will get out in time for you to move into the house."

Vaslav smiled and said gently, "You know, *gaspada*,* my mother was also Polish, she was born in

* *Gaspada* is the Russian for "folks."

Warsaw. It would give me such pleasure to talk to you often. Please do me the favor of staying on. We have rented the house and I have no need for this studio. It would be so nice to have you living down here. We would not be so lonely."

The scientist just stood there stretching his hands towards Vaslav and saying, "God shall reward you for your kindness to us."

Soon we moved into the house and tried to make it cheerful, but this was extremely difficult, as it was built of reinforced concrete and looked like an African blockhouse in the desert, and whatever one did the passages remained icy cold. We had little heating material, so we only succeeded in keeping Vaslav's room warm.

Even now when I think back I have to shudder. It was furnished with ultra-modern furniture; one could not sit on the chairs, they were so uncomfortable, and the couches were extremely hard. Vaslav, as usual, had no words of complaint and was thankful for whatever I was able to offer him.

He spent his days quietly, mostly in the company of Brindus, taking long walks in the forest and, in the afternoon when it grew dark, reading or listening to the radio, while I went around the town trying to sell copies of the numbered edition of Vaslav's diary. This was our only means of livelihood now.

The Literary Council, which had given me permission two years before to write articles, now forbade it, so I could not write any more. I went to see the Secretary General, who said, "I am sorry, I understand your difficult position. We only wished to see in you the wife of a sick artist, the daughter of our great actress, and above all, the granddaughter of our statesman Francis de Pulszky, who so many years ago with Kossuth founded the Hungarian democracy and fought against the Hapsburgs for the liberty of our country. But we were advised, in fact reminded, that you are a Russian subject and belong to the enemy, so now we are obliged to forbid your literary activity, even though it is only connected with the art of dancing."

I was not even surprised. I knew who the kind informer was—the very same person who had already caused us so much trouble in the First World War! He was Oskar Pardany, my stepfather.

It was for me a difficult and humiliating task to go around town and ask people to buy the special edition. I had never sold anything in my life. But we had to live, and Vaslav had to have a warm room and proper food.

Prices went up daily—in fact, hourly. The longer hostilities lasted the less merchandise there was, for now practically everything was sent to Germany. Food also became scarcer.

I decided I would approach the owners of the great industries and the banks. All of them had libraries for their officials and workmen, so they could use the book.

I was rather at a loss, because I had not lived in Hungary since the First World War and then we were interned, so I was out of touch with Hungarian society. My newspaper friends advised me to whom to go. Every time I went into a place I went hot and cold, and wished I could go scrubbing floors instead of begging people to buy a book. Somehow people were kinder than I thought and made it easier for me to sell my merchandise, *Vaslav's Diary*. Very few people refused me; some of them even bought several copies, and most of them had an admiring word for Vaslav's dancing, having seen him in the past.

For some weeks I went on making these rounds, but I sold almost all the copies and exhausted the list of possible buyers. I wondered what I should do next. Naturally, I did not mention this matter to Vaslav, as I was anxious not to upset him.

During my rounds I visited the National Bank of Hungary and asked to see the General Manager, Mr. R. Quand. He was known as the most brilliant young financier in the country, a man of great integrity, and he rose to this high position on account of his outstanding ability.

He received me at once and immediately bought five copies. Then we began to talk about old times when he had seen Vaslav dance; about Karsavina, who had lived in Budapest for some years—how lovely she was, what a superb artist and now what a devoted wife. We wondered how she was and were worried about her, as we knew that London was heavily bombarded by the Germans.

I took an instant liking to Mr. Quand, who proved to be a man of the world and of great culture. It was unmistakable that although he was a good Hungarian, his sympathies were with the Allies, and he did not doubt of their ultimate victory. We became quite good friends and I told him all about our present life, our difficulties and hopes for the future.

That he was kind-hearted was beyond doubt, but what I did not know then was that he was deeply religious and acted as a real Christian ought to act. It was a relief after all those dreary months to talk to a man of such character.

I promised to return because he told me to look upon him as a friend, and to come to him whatever trouble we might be in. I went home gaily as if someone had lifted a great burden from me. I felt we had found a real friend. Vaslav noticed the change in my mood, and I told him about my new acquaintance. He was happy, too, and said he would like to meet him.

Winter came and it was an unusually hard one. There were days when the thermometer sank way below zero, and we heard that in Russia it was even worse, where it dropped to 45 to 50 degrees below zero.

"We can stand it," said Vaslav. "The Russians are used to it, but the others will not be able to."

He very seldom mentioned the war, and we carefully avoided all allusion to it.

Christmas came. I had very little money and was worried as to how we could celebrate a nice Christmas Eve. Brindus must have noticed it.

I told Vaslav that we would not make a lot of fuss as times were difficult, and he smilingly said, "Don't bother, we will be together and have a peaceful evening."

On Christmas Eve I returned home to the Svabenberg on the last funicular, about seven in the evening, and had about half an hour's walk to our house through the wooded slope. It was bitterly cold and the snow was frozen under my feet. The night was calm and clear; thousands and thousands of stars were shining brilliantly above as I raised my eyes. The branches of the towering pine trees bent under the heavy burden of snow. It was a real Christmas night.

The house was lighted and Brindus had made a good fire, so it was pleasantly warm as I entered, even in the passage. As I arrived he greeted me saying, "Will you forgive me? My wife and son arrived. May they stay overnight in the little spare room?"

"Of course, they must stay during the holidays. Ask them to come up."

Vaslav was already playing with Brindus' little son, who was proudly showing him his toys and presents. In the sitting room the little Christmas tree which I had bought the previous evening was already placed in the middle, gaily adorned with candies, nuts, apples, and candles.

On the table we spread a tablecloth, and on this I placed my few modest gifts for Vaslav and Brindus.

They were mostly useful presents—a warm shawl, some fur-lined gloves, warm woolen socks, all hidden treasures which I was able to get only because the owner of the haberdashery used to supply goods to my father many years ago.

Brindus came in and asked me if they might invite us to dinner. His wife, who had traveled for twenty hours and came in this icy midwinter from the eastern part of Hungary, was already busy in the kitchen.

Later in the evening, in the sitting room where the Christmas tree was standing, we laid the table.

First lighting our tree, we called in Vaslav and the little boy. They were both enchanted. Brindus put his presents on the table: a large piece of Hungarian lard, a huge ham, some smoked meat, a bag of white flour—all unobtainable treasures in the city, which his wife had brought with her.

We sat around the table and had an excellent Hungarian dinner with which I served the precious Tokay wine, similar to the one I had offered Vaslav so many years ago during our trip to the Argentine.

In the company of this kind-hearted peasant family, we almost forgot that we were in enemy country surrounded by great danger.

The New Year of 1943 began. I was busy running around to the Swedish Embassy and to the Red Cross, trying to get news and help from abroad, but all was in vain. My friends in England were powerless to get us out. Our money dwindled and there was no hope of earning any more. What could I do? I did not want to say anything to Vaslav; I got more and more worried. Our only distraction was to go to the symphony concert rehearsals in the mornings. Furtwängler was conducting and he very kindly allowed us to listen, but when within two days we heard Beethoven's Fifth and Sixth symphonies eight times, our heads began to go round!

Then Ansermet came to conduct. Years before he was our assistant conductor with the Russian Ballet, a young beginner. We also listened to his concert, and I went up to see him in the hotel to ask him if he could not do something to get Vaslav at least back to Switzerland. I hoped he might, because he was very influential in his native country. But he was busy with his work and social obligations, and I felt that now Vaslav did not mean much to him. But he told me one thing which gave me a shock. He said it was known in Switzerland that on the German border many trains were filled with the inmates of the mental homes, who were sent to different places, and when the trains arrived at their destinations only corpses were in them. The Germans exterminated everybody who had ever suffered or was suffering from a mental illness!

This horrible news petrified me. It was imperative that we should get Vaslav out of Hungary, a country allied to the Germans. What could happen in Germany might happen here, too, one day. When I told the news to Brindus, he became very depressed.

"We could hide the master at my wife's farm," he said, "but sooner or later the gendarmerie would notice. We must think of something else."

I spoke to Countess Dobrojensky, who again offered her castle in the eastern part of Hungary, but there the same danger existed.

Then I consulted our family priest, Abbé Huszar, a lifelong friend and a man of great learning. I knew he would advise me well.

"Well, you will have to do the impossible and get Vaslav back to Switzerland. Try to get him back to the sanatorium where he spent so many years—surely the management of the nursing home where you have spent a fortune will be helpful in such extraordinary circumstances. Transport of sick people is still allowed."

I asked Ansermet to intervene and request Mr. Reinhardt, of Winterthur, a great patron of the arts in Switzerland, to help us. He helped Stravinsky for years, and also Richard Strauss during the war.

Mr. Reinhardt's reply was most disappointing and surprising. He said he only helped artists who were still active.

My other undertaking failed equally. The management of the sanatorium where my husband spent so many years replied that they would accept him only if two years' board (which amounted to twelve thousand Swiss francs) were paid in advance in Swiss currency. This—owing to the currency regulations all over Europe—was a condition which could not possibly be fulfilled.

Receiving the depressing news, I went up to the Swiss Legation in Budapest and asked for an interview with the Chief Passport Officer. It was quite difficult to obtain this. Some junior official came out and asked me to tell him what I wanted, but I insisted on seeing his chief. I was told that he was too busy; nevertheless I said I would stay even if I had to wait hours. He shrugged his shoulders and went in.

After some time the man I wanted to see came out with a young conductor from the Opera House. He was full of attention and polite talk. They chatted a long time about operas and the conductor's coming tour in Switzerland. Finally, the passport officer bade him farewell and returned to his office, ignoring me. But still I was not discouraged. I waited and waited and finally I was shown in.

The Chief Passport Officer hardly listened to me when I explained to him the reason for my visit— that I wanted to get my husband back to a nursing home in Switzerland to save his life. As an artist of world-wide reputation who had lived in Switzerland for over twenty years, after having spent a fortune there in medical fees for nursing homes, I felt he had the right to claim asylum, especially as he had been carrying a Swiss Nansen Passport for over ten years.

He only hemmed and coughed and turned over the leaves of the passport. At last he spoke.

"Well, well, it is difficult. I can't do anything about it."

I got wild! Where was their famous humanity? Where was the right of asylum I had heard about all my life? Where was the spirit of Mr. Dunant * and other noble Swiss who had really helped those in need and misfortune?

"Well, whatever you say I insist that you report the case to Bern—I can't accept your refusal. What do you expect me to do?"

"Just nurse your husband here in Hungary."

"And if the Gestapo kills him, what then?"

He shrugged his shoulders, turning his big cigar round in his lips.

I went out and slammed the door!

Vaslav had no idea of the danger he was in, but neither Brindus nor I had another quiet moment. I went up to the Red Cross and asked them to intervene at Geneva, but of course as it was the Hungarian section of the Red Cross I could not tell them the real reason why I was anxious to get Vaslav out of the country. They promised to get in touch with the International Red Cross and see what they could do.

Time passed—nothing happened.

* Founder of the International Red Cross.

The winter was bitterly cold, one of the hardest in our generation. At the beginning of February, late one night, we heard somebody knocking at the front door. We were already in bed. Brindus got up and went down to see who was there.

"I only hope it is not my call for mobilization!" I was worried. I heard voices, and after some time Brindus came up.

"There is a Hungarian officer downstairs. He asked if you would allow him to stay the night. He has just arrived from Russia and knows nobody in Budapest. He seems very tired, almost exhausted."

"Show him in."

So Brindus brought him up. He was a fair, handsome young man of about twenty-two in a worn-out condition, hardly able to stand on his feet. His uniform was torn, his boots were in shreds. He sat down.

"It is so kind of you to let me in. I am a stranger in the capital, I am from Somogy,* but I must have rest before I continue my trip."

While Brindus went down to the kitchen to prepare some hot food we talked. He continued his story.

"I have just arrived, I have walked two thousand miles, or better to say I ran it with some comrades. We thought we would never get to Hungary. We had to hide from the Germans, otherwise they would

* A Transdanubian province of Hungary.

have sent us back. I would rather shoot myself than return to that inferno!"

"Where have you come from?"

"From Stalingrad. You cannot imagine what it was like. We marched and advanced for weeks; the Russians retreated—we could not see them, they went back so fast—always deeper and deeper towards the east. The Germans were very proud and said, 'You see how they run before the victorious and invincible German Army!' Yes, they retreated, and we found everywhere empty villages and larders, even burnt-out farms and towns. . . . The few peasants who were left behind were hiding and had hardly enough food for themselves. I never trusted this rapid advance, I felt there was something queer about it—and so there was. The Russians, they know their country, they know how inhumanly cold it can be. They don't mind those blizzards which blind one, they don't feel the cold which made us numb and which froze our soldiers, who were falling like flies. Who could resist such a climate? We were not equipped for it, our uniforms were too light, we had no fur-lined overcoats and hoods such as they had. Our boots froze to our feet and we had to cut them off. We realized long ago that it was sheer madness to continue, but what could we do? Our Hungarian regiments were commanded by the Germans.

"Then we approached Stalingrad. We listened in to the O.K.W. bulletins on the radio announcing the imminent fall of this important city. This seemed to us rather a rash statement. Yes, we were near Stalingrad—only a few miles away we could see the outskirts of the city, but we were unable to approach it. Heavy firing went on day and night, and we had only a few planes available. The supply units were unable to reach us for over a week. We had used up all our reserves of ammunition and food. The German officers promised that all these things would be swiftly sent on to us by plane, but these were vain promises. The ever-boastful reports of the High Command spoke of our brilliant advance, but only we knew how few of us really got so far—how many of our brave comrades lost their lives in the snow—how many were left behind on the roadside or the swampy, undermined fields which stretched on for thousands and thousands of miles before us. At each turn a new unknown and uncanny danger lurked. What did they to the rear know of our sufferings and hardships in the piercing, merciless cold wind, of our marches through the blinding blizzards? The marvelous tanks and machines so much heralded in our press were of little use to us here in the deep, bottomless snow into which they sank, so that they were unable to advance and we had to abandon them. At home they did not realize that we were almost starving—that we were lost beyond reach—here in Russia, nearing the Asiatic border. What even we did not realize was that we were surrounded, trapped in the slowly closing steel grip of the Red Army!

"What came afterwards was indescribable. I cannot even today say how and what happened. It seemed as though the ocean suddenly overwhelmed us. At first it was dark night and the firing from the Russian side ceased. This was the first respite for weeks. Everything was so calm, so silent, one could almost hear the snow falling to the ground. We did not dare to move in this weird silence. Suddenly on the horizon we saw the first pale strip of light announcing dawn. Then commenced the horror. . . . Thousands and hundreds of thousands of soldiers came rushing towards us, and it seemed that they were followed by endless thousands more—in neverending columns. We were heavily bombed and machine-gunned, and we saw these endless, enormous masses of humanity pouring towards us with their powerful weapons. For a moment we all stood aghast, and then—first the Italians and then ourselves—we threw down our guns and haversacks and we ran and ran in a mad rush. . . .

"What happened after that I don't know. I was dazed. I only know that I ran until I fell exhausted in a deep faint."

He told us how he succeeded, with the help of the Russian peasants, in escaping and returning to Hungary. It was a most thrilling adventure.

"We have lost the war, there is no doubt about it. Whoever saw what I witnessed at Stalingrad knows it, whatever the Germans say."

And he was right, as the following months and years proved.

Some days later I was called by Mr. Quand to the Hungarian National Bank. I wondered what the reason could be. He received me with his usual affable manner.

"I am very glad to tell you that I have good news for you. I have here sixteen thousand pengös for Mr. Nijinsky's care, so for some time he will be provided for, and your dreadful anxiety on his account will be lessened, I hope."

For the next two years, as though by magic, whenever the money was nearly spent Mr. Quand replenished the deposit.

Now I could concentrate on the matter of our escape.

Spring and summer passed without much change

in our life. No news came from the International Red Cross, or from our friends abroad, and I realized that I could not count on their assistance for our liberation. Brindus feared that he would be called to the colors—and his fear materialized. Much to our distress, he was mobilized.

Chapter 7

The German Invasion

DURING the whole winter I went around and tried to find out what could be done to leave the country. It was rumored that the bulletins of the O.K.W., the German General Staff, were not correct. The wonderful victories they broadcast daily were imaginary, but the office of Dr. Goebbels knew so well how to turn every defeat into a strategic move.

The Germans retreated and conditions became worse in every way. We *felt* the war. Until now it had been mostly through the papers and from the radio that we knew about it—now we began to *see* it. There were fewer and fewer civilians in the city. Transport was becoming scarce; in the offices only a few old and infirm people worked. The situation of the Jews also deteriorated from day to day. They were restricted as to when and where they could go, in which shops they could make their purchases, with whom they could speak. Their public appearance in the theatres or restaurants was forbidden, and in the windows of many shops signs were put up, "We do not serve Jews."

The tolerant and liberal Hungarian nation, under the reign of the late Emperor Francis Joseph I, had given many privileges to the Hungarian Jews. They threw open to them the schools, universities, and many professions. They gave them high positions and titles and allowed them to become members of Parliament. They even approved mixed marriages between the children of the aristocrats and the wealthy, influential Jewish families.

During the last thirty years, it is true, Jews had succeeded in controlling not only large parts of the press, heavy industry, and the banking business but most important commercial concerns in Hungary. Since the First World War and Hungary's independence, a large number of the vast estates had come into Jewish possession.

During the twenty years of Regent Horthy's reign, Jews held an equally important place in Hungary's national life. Nobody believed that the Germans would succeed in discrediting the Jews and undermining their standing here.

But it seemed as though overnight a bitter anti-Semitism had broken out, a bitter hatred against the sons of Israel, and even if they had been baptized for a number of years this did not help them. "Jews are a race, not only a religion," was the phrase which was constantly repeated.

The Regent was a kind old gentleman of the old school. He had been aide-de-camp to His Most Apostolic Majesty of the Austrian-Hungarian Monarchy. Many remembered him as a dashing naval officer in 1910; others as the hero of Otranto, where he was supposed to have scored a naval victory. Still others, with an evil, malicious spirit, said he was to blame for the massacre among the crew of the *Navarre,* the ship he commanded during the naval action. Some important Hungarian politicians could never forgive him for having led the Hungarian troops against their rightful sovereign and anointed King, Charles of Hapsburg. Horthy excused himself by saying that he was first of all a Hungarian, and it was his duty to save his country. But the leading aristocrats, the Esterházys, Festetisches, and Batthyányis (who had given many eminent statesmen to Hungary), felt he went too far by taking the throne from his former master, to whom he had sworn allegiance.

The Princes could not decide who should be elected King of Hungary, and nothing happened, until Horthy, a commoner, occupied the throne as Regent. The malicious inhabitants of Budapest called him the "Admiral without a sea," while society people clamored to obtain an invitation to his court and balls.

Her Imperial and Royal Highness, the Archduchess Augusta (granddaughter of the Emperor Francis Joseph and Empress Elizabeth), and her husband the Archduke Joseph, whose grandfather was the Palatine of Hungary, were the last of the forgotten Hapsburgs who survived the revolution and lived in their former state in their palace in Buda. Whenever the Regent held a reception at the Royal Palace of her august grandfather, the Archduchess would good-humoredly remark, "Today we are greatly honored by being invited to attend the Court."

To which she invariably went. The Archduchess was a wise and great lady, with inborn shrewdness and immense culture.

The sudden change in public opinion was due to the well-organized propaganda of the German Embassy. Admiral Horthy, who had recently celebrated his jubilee as Regent, and with the consent of Parliament had nominated his eldest son as his successor, was now Regent only in name. It was the German Ambassador who ruled the country. People little realized what was going on.

I remember so clearly the momentous historical day of March 19, 1944. It dawned like any other spring morning: it was St. Joseph's Day, which is widely celebrated in Hungary. We were invited to the house of some old friends for lunch, where we arrived after a long stroll in the near-by woods. While we were at lunch the telephone rang, and it was Pavel who had called me up.

"Did you hear the latest news?"

"No," I replied, knowing that some stupendous announcement would be made, as our young friend adored sensations and rather exaggerated all the news.

"The Regent is detained by the Nazis at Headquarters, and the Germans have crossed the border, invading Hungary."

"Nonsense," I replied, "they have the country under their domination already!" Very annoyed, I hung up the receiver.

Our fellow guests inquired, and, hearing the news, doubted its authenticity.

The same day, late in the evening, I suggested to Vaslav that we should go and visit George Chapovalenko. He was of Russian descent, and in his hospitable home we often spent many agreeable hours.

The evening passed gaily and it was rather late when I reminded Vaslav that we must leave or we would miss the last trolley. As we returned home, we saw that thousands and thousands of tanks and motor trucks filled with soldiers in field uniforms bordered the roads. I was surprised and remarked to Abbé Huszar, our family priest, who was with us, "I never knew that the Hungarian Army was so splendidly equipped."

Our amazement next morning was unlimited when we were informed that the army corps which we thought were Hungarians were really Germans— Hungary was an occupied country under ruthless German rule!

Events followed one another with a vertiginous rapidity. German officers took over command, not only of the army and barracks, but also of the Government Administration and civilian life. New orders were given out hourly, and new restrictions were imposed upon the population.

"We will show these irresponsible, light-hearted people what order and efficient organization mean. We will bring German discipline to the Magyar Nation!"

But they made the mistake of their lives. The Hungarians are not a docile race, and with their inborn, fanatic love of independence it was a herculean task for the Germans to convince them that it was in Hungary's interest to fight on foreign territory. The stubborn Hungarian peasants just refused to accept Dr. Goebbels' explanation that they had to defend the country and Hungarian liberty on the shores of the Atlantic or in the steppes of Asiatic Russia.

With a stroke life changed. In no time the grip of the Nazi rule was felt. The carefree life of the capital ceased. Every able-bodied person was mobilized or sent to the factories. The civil servants had to be in their offices early in the morning. The markets were controlled, food and fuel disappeared, interrogations and raids were carried out with the utmost severity. People disappeared or were dragged away from their homes, while the frantic relatives tried to obtain help from the Hungarian police and authorities—but in vain!

When the smartly attired German officers tried to make it clear that the Führer's rule meant freedom to the thousand-year-old Hungarian nation, the peasants shrugged their shoulders and very disrespectfully spat at the officers' feet.

"This is all very well," they said, "but it is far more important that we should be able to bring in our harvest on time; we need our sons at home. The French? Well, they have proved themselves our friends in the past. Our great leader, Rákóczy,* found refuge among them when he had to flee from the Austrians.

* Prince Rákóczy found protection and refuge at the Court of Louis XIV.

"As for the Russians—well, we know them better than you do; we Magyars lived for centuries among them; they are nearer to us than our oppressors the Germans can ever become." This did not sound very encouraging to the officials.

The aristocracy who dreaded the Russians, and the civil servants and Government officials who lived in fear of losing their jobs, were all apparently staunch admirers of the Nazis and stood up for them. The Jews became nervous and retiring.

The whole country had become plunged into an atmosphere of fear. We had all heard what German rule meant to other countries occupied by them. What effect would the invasion have upon our life? This was the thought foremost in our minds. Vaslav did not show any sign of anxiety, but I knew that deep in his heart he dreaded the future.

Within a few days the persecution of the Jews began. They had to wear large yellow stars so that they could be easily distinguished from a distance, and the rest of the population was strictly forbidden to talk to them. We were ashamed ourselves that such inhuman humiliation could be tolerated by us Christians. I tried to keep Vaslav away from the town, as I knew he would not pay any attention to the restrictions in force, and indeed what I had feared very soon happened.

One day we were in the Post Office awaiting our turn, when a Mrs. L. entered with her brother. She was an old school friend of mine and a Jewess. They pretended not to see us and timidly waited in a corner while the people present looked at them with contempt and shrank away as if they had some disgusting contagious disease. It took Vaslav a second to notice Mrs. L. and her brother.

"Oh, hello, how are you? I am so glad to see you," he said and ostentatiously kissed her.

"For God's sake, stop him," said Lily's brother. "We shall all get into trouble."

The people around us became hostile and murmured among themselves. Presently another friend, also a Jewess, timidly approached me and whispered, "You know, Romola, what happened? It is ghastly. I sent a parcel to my Aunt Ella, who is in the Asylum at Steinhof near Vienna, and it was returned to me this morning marked 'Addressee deceased.' You know what that means; those swine have liquidated her!"

All I had heard of the German atrocities towards the sick and helpless came into my mind, and I knew we had no more time to lose. My fears were realized.

Abruptly I turned away from her and began almost to run over the bridge towards the hill at Buda where the Royal Palace stood and the Regent resided. I brushed aside the Alabardos * who stood guard at the gates, and passed them like a whirlwind before they could stop me. Knowing the labyrinth of the innumerable passages and stairs of the palace, I went straight to the wing in which the Court Marshal's office was situated, now better known under the name of the Cabinet Office.

Elegantly dressed grooms, lackeys with silk breeches and patent-leather shoes and powdered wigs were hovering about the passages, but thinking that I was one of the household they let me pass and I entered the office of Mr. Domoter, the First Secretary to the Court Marshal, whom I had known from former times.

Mr. Domoter sat at his desk deep in thought reading a report. He looked up and was astonished to see me there, unannounced—unexpected—panic-stricken and out of breath!

"What wind blows you here? What has happened?"

"I forced my way to you; please help me to see His Excellency at once. I *must* obtain an audience with the Regent; it is a matter of utmost importance to us!"

---

* Alabardos Regiment, the bodyguard of the Hungarian Monarch; for centuries their uniforms were those of medieval times.

He shook his head disapprovingly, but nevertheless he did what I asked and disappeared behind the
heavily gilded white door which still bore the arms
of the Emperor Francis Joseph.

I looked around at the pearl-gray damask-covered
walls and at the exquisite mahogany furniture of the
purest Empire style with which the room was furnished. I saw the heavy crystal chandelier reflected
in the mirror which adorned the wall opposite the
portraits of the proud Austrian Archdukes. Below
the windows, deep down at the bottom of the hill,
agelessly, sluggishly the Danube flowed on, while
once more history was being made on its banks.

Suddenly Mr. Domoter returned.

"His Excellency will see you as soon as the morning conference is terminated."

His Excellency, G. Ambrozy, came towards me
with outstretched arms as I entered the large, lofty
salon, formerly the reception room of the Empress
Elizabeth.

"My dear child, welcome, welcome." He was an
old childhood friend of my father. "How are you
and how is Vaslav?"

"I am here on his behalf, Uncle George. I *must* see
Admiral Horthy! I want to ask him to save us, to
give us safe-conduct to Switzerland—to get us out of
the country. I am desperate. I am terrified by the

Gestapo, it is ghastly, I have already tried through the Swedish and the Swiss Embassies. I moved heaven and earth, all in vain! You know, Uncle George, the Germans exterminate everybody who has ever suffered from a mental illness. You know Vaslav is in danger, you know it! We *must* save him, we *must* get him out of this inferno!"

"My dear Romola, try to be calm and brave, otherwise we will not succeed. Of course we will help you all we can. Let me think. I can arrange an audience with the Regent, but, my dear child, he will only repeat to you what he has so often said these last few days to me, 'I have nothing to say any more, it is Herr Wesenmayer, the German Ambassador, who is ruling Hungary.' Now go home and return here tomorrow at noon. In the meantime, I will see what can be done."

Upon my return home, my sister awaited me with the alarming news that the husband of one of her friends, who was of Jewish origin, had been arrested. During the night the Gestapo entered their house, ransacked everything, and took the husband along with them. Then our charwoman was bursting with distressing rumors. Apparently, the gypsies were also being persecuted.

I realized that this was the beginning of the end. It was a clear April morning when I left for the palace next day to see His Excellency. I took the trolley and was about halfway and nearing the South Terminus when suddenly the sirens began to sound. Soon the second alarm was given and the trolley stopped with a jerk. The passengers jumped off and ran for shelter. I followed the crowd and was swept into a large apartment house, while the janitor pushed us hurriedly down the stairs to the cellar. I felt like a trapped animal among these perfect strangers, deep down under the earth.

The lofty cellar was separated by heavy iron doors, and the place was well lighted. Along the walls wooden benches were placed, and in the corners hurricane lamps, stretchers, first-aid kits, axes, and sacks full of sand were ready for all emergencies.

I felt pretty indifferent. So many times during the last few weeks we had been interrupted in our daily tasks by the alarms, and locked up for hours, but nothing ever happened. It became almost a daily routine. The populace was well aware of the fact that at heart the Regent was for the Allies, and the great majority of the Hungarian nation, too. They felt sure the Allied Command knew this, and that therefore Hungarian territory would not be bombed. Their planes merely flew over Hungary in order to get to Austria and Germany from the North African bases.

It was said that the Hungarian antiaircraft guns never shot at an Allied plane, much to the annoyance of the German Command. We were irritated by what we thought was unnecessary loss of time through these alarms.

The quiet murmur of the people suddenly ceased! A terrific crash occurred and suddenly the ground began to rock under our feet. What happened during the next half hour I can hardly remember, I was so dazed. I prayed and prayed for Vaslav, that God should have mercy upon him. Never in my life did I feel so lonely, knowing him alone and unprotected.

When after hours of waiting I emerged once more into the sunlight unhurt, I found a very different place. The streets were covered with litter, twisted steel, broken glass, plaster—parts of the houses blown away, others in flames. Ambulances were rushing about taking moaning wounded people to hospitals.

I forced my way through to the Royal Palace which was near by, and succeeded in gaining admittance to His Excellency.

First of all I asked him to find out for me what had happened and how Vaslav was. He was able to get through to the convalescent home and announced to me happily that it had not been hit and all was well there.

The result of our conference was that he advised me to take Vaslav out of Budapest and hide him in the country under an assumed name.

"Get some papers of some deceased relative whose age is about the same as Vaslav's (your Abbé can do that for you), and go towards the Austrian border, towards the lion's den. There you will be safer, there the control of the Gestapo is less severe. Don't go towards the east or Yugoslavia; it would be too dangerous. We Hungarians will shut our eyes. Escape!"

With a few lines of written recommendation, and his blessing, he sent me away.

With feverish haste we secured the necessary papers. Vaslav remained calm and serene, but I could hardly look at him, feeling so conscience-stricken for having brought him to Hungary, into this deadly danger.

Chapter 8

Sopron

THE PLACE we chose as a hide-out was Sopron, a little Hungarian border town in the Burgenland on the shores of Neusiedler Lake. The wooded hills which surrounded the small, quaint old town were used for winter sports in better times. Among the pine forests many pretty little bungalows nestled, and well-kept paths led through the chain of mountains which stretched towards Austria.

Pavel was also hiding there, and sent me word that he had found a small inn where the proprietor would be willing to take us. He specialized in hiding people for a good reward! The house was in the forest, and it seemed so peaceful. There was a beautiful view of the lake, and of the town of Sopron lying below in the valley through which ran the main road from Budapest to Vienna.

Sopron itself was a gem of the purest baroque style,

with its quaint palaces, churches, and convents. As far as one could see beyond the lake, the hills to the south were covered with vineyards, all belonging to Prince Esterházy, while the north side, where we were to live, was covered with deep pine forest. "A good place to hide," said our future landlord.

Upon my return to Budapest after arranging things at Sopron, I had to organize Vaslav's departure, which was not a simple matter as he had to travel in comparative quiet. I managed to arrange with the President of the Hungarian Railway, who was an old friend of my mother's family, to reserve a small compartment on the train for us. About six o'clock in the morning I went to the convalescent home to fetch Vaslav. Only the Sister on night duty was up. Vaslav was awaiting me already dressed, and wondering what was happening.

"Vatzinko, don't be frightened, we are leaving here. You are coming with me and we will stay together and I will look after you alone."

Vaslav pressed my hand and smiled, saying, *"Très bien, allons!"*

We sat in the car holding hands silently. Everything went well. We arrived safely at the station and installed ourselves in the compartment, waiting for seven o'clock, when the train was due to start. Unfortunately, we had to wait for the Bucharest train, which was attached to our convoy and which was two hours late, very much to my distress. I was frightened in case we might have another alert during the journey. It usually started about 11 A.M. What I would do with Vaslav if this happened I did not know. I felt inwardly very nervous but tried not to show it. Finally, we said good-by to our friends, and the train left Budapest.

To pass the time I suggested playing cards with Vaslav, and this we did. Later, we went to the restaurant car for lunch and lingered over it as long as possible. I thought that in case of an alarm we had a better chance of getting out quickly. But although the trip seemed endless to me, the day passed without incident. We arrived safely late in the evening—I was more than grateful to fate.

Like two carefree children we settled down and tried to organize our life. We were served by a pretty, gay gypsy girl. Vaslav took a great liking to her and amused himself by making her show him the different gypsy dances. We took long walks and Vaslav enjoyed every flower, every stream, every butterfly; he was happy to have peace around him, the glorious nature, and me. We used to talk for hours, making plans for the future, when once again we should be able to travel freely and make a small home somewhere in the country, a small ranch with our own vegetable and flower garden, our own farm. There we would work peacefully for the art of dancing.

"Vaslav, you will advise us how to do the things we want to do, how to create the Festival Theatre of the Dance, and the High Academy you always wanted to create in Russia. Let us make it international— open to every race and creed."

"Yes," he agreed, "that is what we will do."

I was convinced that once the war was over, great possibilities were open to us. Now that Vaslav was well enough to advise and supervise, I was sure that all the dancers and choreographers from all over the world would surround him. They would collaborate and assist to form an artistic center from which new forms of choreographic art could be created. . . . How little did I know that I was still an incorrigible idealist who believed in humanity!

Sometimes we explored the small town. It had a medieval atmosphere, with its convents, where the monks and nuns still prayed and worked like many others centuries ago in the very same place.

During the week-ends Pavel came to visit us in secret, since he was a political refugee and in constant danger. We discussed the news which he was able to obtain through his small radio set. Like everyone else, he was convinced that sooner or later the Allies would land somewhere on the Balkan Peninsula and advance into Hungary, which would be the day of liberation.

The days and weeks passed quietly for us. I did my best to amuse and interest Vaslav. I translated to him the books I read, and we played chess and cards during the evenings and were happy to be in each other's company once more.

Sometimes an alarm was given. If it caught us in the forest, we just sat down among the trees and watched the mighty airplanes which flew over us in formation in great numbers, shimmering silver in the dazzling sunlight.

One day, in a small shooting lodge which was transformed into a tavern where we were sitting, the landlord called me out onto the terrace where we could see almost to Wiener Neustadt on that brilliant summer day, with the whole valley in bloom below us. Hundreds of brilliant airplanes were flying around chasing each other above the not far distant Austrian border town; one could see, against the azure blue of the sky, people jumping from the planes opening their parachutes, which looked like so many shrimp-colored mushrooms, gracefully descending towards the ground. Here and there sudden flames burst from the planes, and with vertiginous rapidity they crashed to earth. It was an air battle between Americans and Germans, and the Hungarians looked on. I was glad that Vaslav had stayed in and was not aware of what was going on.

As we walked home through the forest, we saw on the ground and hanging on the trees thousands and thousands of silver ribbons like the trimmings on a Christmas tree. Vaslav picked them up and looked at them but we could not explain their meaning. It was only later we were told that they were thrown by the enemy planes and had something to do with radar interference.

It became more and more difficult for me to maintain a quiet atmosphere around Vaslav. We never spoke of the war, but life around us became more restless, and the town as well as the surrounding country became overcrowded with people who arrived from the capital and from all parts of Hungary. Within a few months the town, instead of having thirty thousand inhabitants, had three hundred thousand. They lived everywhere: in tents, in cars, wherever they could find a place.

It was in August that the news came that the Russians had invaded Rumania. Now everybody in Hungary realized that an invasion from the east was imminent.

Events succeeded each other with tremendous rapidity. The Russians advanced, and the population fled towards the west. Very soon many of our acquaintances from Budapest arrived in Sopron. There was indescribable chaos. Some of them obtained permission to cross the border to Austria, and others tried to cross illegally.

The radio was always surrounded and everyone awaited the news. On the 15th of October we heard Admiral Horthy declaring that Hungary had lost the war and must capitulate. During his speech everybody listened motionless, and when it was ended they cryingly embraced one another. They felt that now, the war being over for Hungary, they were saved. Pavel arrived in the evening with all his belongings, and we decided to join forces to organize our further moves. But soon the news came that Horthy had been taken prisoner by the Hungarian Nazi party, and their chief man Szalassy formed a Government under the protection of the Nazis!

We all knew that now the real trouble for us would begin.

We felt that there were too many people around who might recognize us, so after long discussion we decided to find another refuge. Not far away were some small villas, and Pavel found one for us. The landlady, who had once been a member of an opera company in Germany, was glad to get some quiet lodgers, as she was afraid of the hordes of refugees and could not leave her house unoccupied. So we moved into her house, where we were better hidden than at the inn. Next to us lived two elderly ladies, staunch Nazis, interested in horoscopes; they were suspicious and we were in constant fear they might denounce us. But within a few days Pavel succeeded in turning their heads and making them his admirers, which helped us to the extent that they would have told any lie to the Gestapo to protect our little party.

Our lives from now on became less peaceful. Early in the morning while Vaslav was resting we had to clean our rooms and then go marketing. Later, we made expeditions to fetch coal and pick up wood in the forest. We had to find food, which was difficult, prepare our meals, and nurse Vaslav.

The more he realized our difficulties, the more he tried to help us. While Pavel cut the wood, he picked it up and arranged it in a neat heap. When the meals were ready, he helped me to lay the table, and when I went to the peasants to get vegetables or eggs, he accompanied me and carried the basket. He enjoyed our little circle, our primitively organized family life. He was thankful for the smallest attention. It made our task easy knowing that we could supply him with a warm room, a good bed, sufficient well-prepared nourishment, and clean clothes.

I was able to get up at dawn and walk for hours to the coal mines, and to drag back on the little sleigh with Pavel the necessary fuel, which we obtained there from the foreman in exchange for a pair of shoes or a silk blouse for his wife. Gradually, all our wardrobe was drifting to the peasants for food.

Our money was dwindling and I had to have some more. We did not believe that the end of the war and our liberation were so far distant. I did not mention our new difficulties to Vaslav, but decided, with Pavel and a friend, that the only thing to do was to go to Budapest and sell some family heirlooms. Fortunately, they were gold, the only thing which still had some value. It was not an easy decision. It entailed a long, adventurous journey, and it meant leaving Vaslav. He felt rather dependent on me; it was hard on us both.

In Sopron there was a hospital with a department for nervous diseases which took only sixteen patients. It was very simple, almost primitive, but the head doctor seemed to be a reasonable and kind man. I asked him if he would take care of Vaslav during those few days, and he consented. I still had to break the news to Vaslav. He only bowed his head sadly and I saw the tears running down his cheeks.

More and more I came to understand how cruel it is to send anybody mentally ill to a clinic among strangers. Even to us strong and healthy people it is a shock when we have to enter a nursing home. How much more dreadful it must be for a sensitive, timid being, inhibited in expressing himself, to be surrounded by indifferent attendants who are mostly impatient and unkind.

I don't want to remember that ghastly journey under constant air raids, the hectic days in Budapest where I spent most of the time in the shelter, and when there was a respite for a few hours running around trying to sell those heirlooms. But I had to have money for Vaslav; we had to go on living! After ten days I succeeded and left.

I had bidden farewell to my mother and sister, wondering if we should ever meet again. As we steamed out of the burning capital, I did not realize that I was seeing it for the last time.

The return journey to Sopron was a nightmare. I managed to force my way into a train among some nuns who were fleeing from Transylvania. People were lying under the carriages, sitting on top, or hanging on to the steps. Everyone was frantic to get westwards, as the Russians had broken through the lines of defense in the Carpathians, and it was merely a question of time when they would come.

Along the tracks at one important station, long trains of cattle trucks were drawn up. The trucks were sealed and the trains were surrounded by gendarmes, and one could hear the crying and screaming of people. Only a small, square opening served to air the trucks, and at one of these I saw two arms lifting a baby who seemed to gasp for breath.

I asked the nun who was jammed near to me in our carriage what it was.

"They are transporting the Jews to Auschwitz for liquidation," she whispered.

Immediately I arrived, I fetched Vaslav and we went home together.

As we had a radio, we listened in secret to the "Voice of America," and every afternoon friends came to join us. We had quite a strange crowd. One elderly lady who lived at the inn and always wore a shawl over her hair, we called the Great Maza. She was silent and brave, and the whole day long she investigated the various cellars in the neighborhood to see which would make the safest air-raid shelter. There were the Secretary of State and his wife, who had fled because of their anti-Nazi activities, and lived in the next bungalow; and Count B. and his family, who later helped us all out with flour and other commodities brought up from his estate. A Nazi nursing sister, Irene, took a great liking to Pavel, and became very useful in covering us. An old acquaintance from Budapest, Mr. Charles, also came to share our exile and proved rather useful in later weeks.

It was unsafe to take Vaslav into Sopron any more since the new regime had come into power; new restrictions were ordered.

First they put all the Jews into ghettos. Part of the town was closed, the windows of the houses were walled in, and the streets leading to their quarter barred with heavy chains and guarded by soldiers with machine guns to prevent any of the inmates' escaping. It was a ghastly sight.

For about six weeks we had a respite, and were almost lulled into thinking we were safe. Gradually, our walks became excursions as we tried to get familiar with the countryside to find places where we could be even better hidden if it became necessary.

One day we strolled in the direction of Banflava, a small village the other side of the mountains, about an hour's walk through the forest. We had to pass a small cemetery on the slope of the wooded hill. German soldiers were digging mass graves. This unusual activity surprised us, and we glanced in their direction and saw them enveloping corpses in wrapping paper and throwing them into the ditch. They shouted to us to keep silent and to get away. We began to run in the direction of the village.

A winding road led down to the village which was in the valley. On top of the hill, a Carmelite convent and a lovely baroque church were built. We were told that under the convent, deep down in the mountain, there were caves and underground passages which led for miles and miles to another village. They were partly formed by nature, partly excavated by the inhabitants centuries ago when Hungary was under Turkish domination.

We immediately felt this might be a good hiding place, but we had to have permission to get in. Pavel made friends with a peasant woman who had a house near the stairs leading up to the convent and rented there, for a fabulous price, the use of the kitchen and a small covered veranda. We left Pavel there and went to see the Abbess. She received us behind a latticed window, heavily veiled, so that we could not see her face. I explained our request, to allow us, in case of danger, to hide and live in the underground passage. At first she was rather difficult. She said that having the responsibility of the whole convent and all the Sisters, she could not very well risk coming into conflict with the authorities. I begged her, I told her about our predicament, about Vaslav's illness and his great faith in God. Then she seemed to soften. . . .

"Come back later if you see there is real danger."

It was All Saints' Day. To get home we had to cross a small cemetery on the slope of the hill. Our friends carried bouquets of chrysanthemums which they intended to put on some relative's grave. While they were looking for the place, we strolled slowly around, with Vaslav looking at the old tombstones and trying to decipher the faded inscriptions. Suddenly among the many Hungarian names, we found an old broken wooden cross with the inscription:

"Vasily Ivanovitch Gortchakoff 1896–1916."

We looked at each other . . . a young Russian who gave his life in the First World War with the idea of defending his country, Vaslav's country. He was here resting among the enemy, far from his home and his people. On all the other graves there were candles and flowers, according to the old Hungarian custom. This one was bare and neglected. We murmured a short prayer, and slowly Vaslav dropped the chrysanthemums he was carrying in his hands on the grave.

Chapter 9

The Air Raid

WE SOON BECAME quite expert in understanding the code language used by the antiaircraft authorities. When the radio gave the warning, we knew what direction the enemy aircraft had taken and how many were on the way. If they said "Spring 6 Henry, Paul," we knew they were heading towards Czechoslovakia, and when they said "Great Crocodiles, Spinach," it meant Budapest was to be attacked by strong detachments. At first we only laughed about it, but later we became proud of our knowledge. Everybody was far too careless, not realizing the danger of an attack.

The tireless Pavel discovered new ways of supplying us with food. He made the acquaintance of Mrs. Vera Drobnich, a Russian-born lady married to a Hungarian engineer who had lived a long time in Russia. Mrs. Drobnich owned a store and, now that she knew in secret that Vaslav was a countryman of hers, supplied us "under the counter" with all kinds of treasures.

Every day new waves of panic-stricken refugees arrived, bringing more and more alarming news. Many who had pretended to be great Nazi enthusiasts suddenly dropped their disguise and were hoping for a Russian victory. Most of the members of the aristocracy still saw their salvation in a German victory, and insisted on spreading the rumor that a strong German army corps was advancing from the south which would push back the Russians who were nearing Budapest.

One day I was going down once more to get some coal. This time I had to go to the City Hall, where I was to meet the Mayor's wife, who knew my mother and who might get us permission to have more fuel. I raced down in a snowstorm to keep my appointment with her and be back for breakfast. I obtained the authorization quickly, and the moment the official stamped it the sirens went. Everybody tried to get down to the air-raid shelter, but I decided to go to our dressmaker, who lived just across the square. However, the moment I passed the front door a policeman took hold of my arm and pushed me down the stairs towards the shelter. That moment there was a terrific crash, a strange smell of sulphur, and the sound as of thousands and thousands of railway trucks unloading coal. This time the unexpected had happened and we were bombarded! Hundreds of American planes flew in waves over the center of the city. I was relieved that Vaslav and the others were safe at home in our house. The air raid lasted for hours. All the officials of the city were in the cellar, and they had a radio set and got all the reports from the Military Commander concerning the attack. We heard exactly which buildings were hit and could follow every incident of the attack. I could hardly keep still, and took hold of the arm of a Hungarian reporter who sat next to me on a wooden case.

"Just pinch me if you are nervous. I know how you feel," he said.

"I want to leave, I can't stand it," I screamed.

"It will soon be over. The planes are heading north," came the report. "One wave is attacking the station and another wave, the Löver."

This was the place where our house was situated.

"My God, help Vaslav!" I murmured, and everything went black before me.

Late that evening, when I succeeded in getting out of the shelter, I had to cross a sea of bricks, broken glass, and every kind of debris—in fact, a town in ruins—and scramble through deep holes in the ground and ditches. With a superhuman effort I got home, completely exhausted.

Vaslav stood covered with dust among the broken furniture, in the roofless room, surrounded by the others. He just gazed steadfastly and silently at me.

"We thought you were killed," the others screamed. "Thank God you are safe!" And everybody at once tried to explain what had happened.

From that day we were like trapped animals. Day and night we worked to make a roof of old canvas, to fill up the holes where once the windows were. I realized that Vaslav could not stay there, so once more I took him down to the hospital, where at least they had a roof and warm rooms and some food. And what was more important—an air-raid shelter and medical help.

All these years Vaslav had evinced a blind faith in me. He allowed me to make all decisions, and followed me wherever I took him. Sometimes it almost broke my heart to put him in a nursing home, but his safety was essential—I had to save him and I trusted God to guide me.

Our move had been wise. Later that night we learned that the Hungarian Government had fled, with all the civil and military authorities, to Sopron! The large hotel, a stone's throw from us, became the Hungarian Parliament, and the German Embassy took over the inn in which we had passed the summer.

We would have to go away from here, but where

to? Hungary was now only a narrow strip extending from Szombathely to Sopron, which became Hungary's capital. Automatically, the raids of the Gestapo became more frequent. We had not another quiet moment.

Life became increasingly difficult. The gypsy girl came to say good-by, because, after the Jews, the gypsies were rounded up and put into concentration camps. Long columns of barefooted women clad in smart dresses and once expensive fur coats, now hanging in rags, were marching towards Austria. They were driven by officers and sergeants of the Todt Organization,* and when they fell down exhausted by the roadside the soldiers whipped them. They were Jewesses of the smart set. We knew many of them. I was glad Vaslav could not see them; it would have broken his heart.

I talked to the senior psychiatrist at the hospital, and we decided that Vaslav should have a special attendant to be always with him. Luckily, he found a male nurse who was Polish. I don't think he was very honest, but at least the doctor assured me he would be gentle. I had seen so many nursing homes and clinics all over Europe, and even in the smartest and most expensive ones the patients are often roughly treated. They have discipline, give useless treatments,

* A detachment of the German Nazi party and army.

and are something between a school and a prison;
but they don't give what these suffering people need
—home atmosphere, gentleness, and love, to which
they respond readily. But I had to choose between
wounding Vaslav's soul and risking his being killed
by a bomb.

Air raids followed air raids. Between the attacks,
when there was a respite, I ran out into the garden
and looked towards the hospital to see if it had been
hit. I can't describe what I suffered during those
hours; I was seldom nervous for myself, thinking
only of Vaslav's safety.

At night we listened in secret to the B.B.C. broad-
casts to find out how far the Russians had advanced,
but they still stood before Budapest. The frequent
visits of the Gestapo forced Pavel and other political
refugees to hide in bombed cellars. This convinced
me that for Vaslav, the only relatively safe place was
the hospital, where he was unknown to the others.

Youngsters of sixteen were now joining the army.
Day and night, long strings of carts drove past towards Austria. They were piled with furniture, mat-
tresses, household utensils, stoves, cases, cages of poultry. These were followed by horses and cattle. Women
and children were perched on the top of the carts
while the men marched along beside them. In the
night one could see their small hurricane lamps like

many thousands of red points in the darkness. A never-ending string. They were the Swabians who had lived for centuries in Hungary and were now being repatriated in Germany.

All this time, Vaslav remained quiet and made no reference to the air attacks. At the first alarm he was always taken by his attendant to the bunkers. I noticed only that whenever a plane flew over he instinctively bent down. The hospital was not very far from the railway bridge, which was still intact. I was dreadfully worried, but all our acquaintances and the doctor tried to convince me that he was still safer down there than up in the Löver, where practically everything was bombed. Often we spent the air raids in the woods, lying on the snow for hours and hours. I could not take Vaslav there in midwinter.

I often wondered about the famous help of the Red Cross, that great humanitarian international organization who were collecting funds all over the world . . . they who did not extend their help to a sick artist, a genius like Vaslav. There was no human help. God alone could save us.

Spring approached, and with it came the Russian Army. The panic was indescribable. Everybody tried to get a visa for Germany. The German Embassy was mobbed. People who had friends among the Nazis packed and fled by train or car, on horseback

or on foot—in fact, by whatever means they could.
Our little shooting lodge was partially destroyed
in an air raid. A German army detachment was
camped around it, and the partially built Hotel
Cyclamen was full of petrol tanks and rubber tires.

On the 12th of March I was in the attic trying to
hang up our laundry to dry when a tremendous bombardment shook the house. I could hardly get downstairs.

"We are not attacked," shouted our neighbor, a
Hungarian officer, "it is Vienna." That was seventy-
five kilometers away, and still the ground rocked
under our feet.

"The Opera House is burning!" screamed the
staunch Nazi lady who was listening to the radio.

Towards evening it began to snow heavily, and
there was an uncanny stillness. We were sitting at supper when suddenly we heard knocking at the front
door. I went out to see who it was, and as I opened
the door there stood Vaslav in his old gray winter
coat, wearing his little tyrolean hat and carrying a
bundle in which his clothes and belongings were
wrapped. Next to him stood the Polish attendant,
Stan.

"Vatzinko mili moi ya, ochen rada chto ty zdes!"
("Vatza dearest, I am very happy you are here.") I
kissed him and escorted him to the table.

The Air Raid

Stan informed us later, "I had to bring Mr. Nijinsky home, even if the danger of bombardment is greater here. We have received orders to exterminate our mental patients by tomorrow morning!"

Chapter 10

The Siege

SURROUNDED by the fleeing Germans, we were under constant air raids, huddled together. The days and nights passed like a nightmare. But in spite of everything we were happy. Our landlady, Mrs. Wild, became more and more lenient towards us. She suspected by now that we were hiding under false names, but she felt that the Germans were beaten. After each air raid Sister Irene came up to see if we were still alive, and our little circle of friends visited us during the night to find out the latest news. Hungarian soldiers arrived, in rags, starved and exhausted, from the ever-nearing front, begging for food and shelter. Mrs. Drobnich came with baskets full of flour and eggs, whispering that the Russians had broken through the Transdanubian defense line and their heavy guns could already be heard.

Late one afternoon, when supper was just ready to

be served, a dreadful crash occurred. A small but powerful bomb hit our front garden. I dropped a dish and, dragging Vaslav by his hand, took him down to our kitchen in the cellar, where we turned off the lights and sat in darkness while the first Russian bombers circled overhead and dropped their bombs. When the attack was over we were exhausted.

"Don't undress, Vatza, just lie on your bed." The others did not agree with me, wanting to get a rest, but I insisted.

"They will come back. Be ready to go to an air-raid shelter. Let us go now!"

But I was overruled!

It must have been about two o'clock when I heard far-distant firing and strange noises. I woke Vaslav.

"Come, let's go."

We crossed the garden silently and went out into the woods towards the Hotel Cyclamen. The forest was dark, although the night was brilliantly clear, as there was a full moon. Suddenly the sky became as clear as at midday. Small planes were circling overhead, and huge, mysterious machines which looked like organs were shining and illuminating the sky. These were the famous "Stalin organs."

The attack began. We started to run, but it was too late. Frantically I prayed to God, "Don't let my Vatza be killed by his own countrymen!"

"Take cover!" someone screamed. I pushed Vaslav down into a ditch, throwing the plaid rug I was carrying over his head to prevent him from seeing what was going on. Wounded fell right and left; blood streamed. Vaslav pushed the rug back; kneeling with outstretched arms, he looked up at the bright sky with its circling Russian planes.

Sopron was in flames. Half the inhabitants had already gone; the other half were hidden in the forest, in near-by caves. The Germans hurriedly withdrew, and nobody watched us any more. From now on we had only one thought: to survive until the Russian troops arrived. We were told the town would not resist, and the white flag would be raised as soon as the Germans had withdrawn.

With Pavel and Stan, we prepared our rucksacks and started out with Vaslav and the three old ladies towards Banflava to a peasant house. Here we installed our radio set and listened for the announcements of the O.K.W. From these we learned, long before the alarm was given, when the American heavy bombers passed the border. This gave us time to get into the rocky underground passage in the hill. It was a long and winding passage which stretched for miles, forty-five feet below the level of the ground. Electric light was installed, but the rocky walls were damp. Both sides were full of huge wooden cases belonging to some powerful concern which had hidden them there, containing valuable merchandise. I hoped it was not ammunition, and I was assured that it was not!

This passage was linked with the one under the convent, and about eight hundred people had places in it; but as the front moved nearer, more people came and soon we were over two thousand. We had two commanders, one a native of Sopron, the other the nephew of a friend of my mother's, a young man of the Hungarian minor nobility, with his wife and two small children. When he saw us there he found a place far back in the passage, about twenty minutes' walk from the entrance, and had a wooden bench put there for Vaslav. There he could at least sit and sleep and be on a dry spot.

The American bombers invariably arrived about ten o'clock. We figured out that they must leave from some south Italian base at sunrise. They flew over us every day towards Prague or Austria, once in a while bombing Sopron and the neighborhood; but as by now the railway stations, barracks, and ammunition dumps were destroyed, we hoped to be spared.

The cave was overcrowded: peasants, townsfolk, children, old people, officers, and nuns, all packed together. Everybody tried to secure a place where he could at least stretch out. Many perched on the wooden cases, and if anybody tried to get between them, they just pushed and kicked them down. It was absolute chaos.

At first one of the two commanders, a Hungarian major, shouted his orders. He warned us all to keep quiet and obey instructions, and to follow the orders of the doctor who stood beside him. With the help of two civilian officials, he made the crowd understand that only the most rigid discipline could save us. They warned us to preserve the greatest cleanliness, and to help each other, and not to cling to worldly belongings beyond the bare necessities of clothing and food. They began immediately to throw out trunks, carpets, furs, perambulators, etc., which were blocking the passage.

Above the entrance to the cave there was a large peasant house built half into the rock. From above it looked like a simple farmhouse. The house had been taken over lately by the radio officers of a German antiaircraft unit and the S.S., as we learned from one of the nuns. A large room deep in the rocks was occupied by Mrs. Elsa D., a well-known German soprano who scored a great success in the late nineties, and was still a good-looking woman. We knew that she had married a German Jew many years ago, but with great assurance she now introduced him as "my second husband, Count Zichy." Her daughter, a very energetic girl, was a trained hospital nurse, and this was a great asset in these days. Mrs. Elsa was most helpful and allowed us to sit in her kitchen when there was a calm moment between the air raids.

Deep down under the earth around where we were settled was a strange crowd. There was the young wife of our civilian commander with their two charming little sons, both of whom were suffering from measles, as were most of the children in the cave. Next to her, the Countess Szacheny, with her husband and her lover. They were all ardent Nazis, and, in fact, the Count represented the Nazi party in Parliament; but now they kept quieter than a few weeks ago and continuously drank strong spirits.

In one corner there was quite a large family, the wealthy owner of an instrument factory with his mother, his wife and two lovely children, and their servants. They occupied quite a large space and had a number of bags with them. When the commander tried to throw some of them out, the man resisted and they had a regular fight, until Mr. S. took the commander aside, whispered into his ear, and plunging his hand into one of the sacks took out gold bars which he gave him. The sacks contained gold and jewels, and he boasted that this was only a small proportion of his belongings; the rest he had buried in a safe place.

At dawn, when all was calm, we went up to wash ourselves at the near-by fountain and to have a breath of fresh air. The days and nights passed in silence, and we lost all track of time. We didn't care; we all became rather indifferent towards everything. Pavel was lying shivering in the damp at our feet. He had measles and was running a high temperature.

We had to be careful not to drink any but boiled water, for the doctor told me we had a typhoid suspect among us. So from that time I had to fight my way through to Mrs. Elsa's room at the entrance to boil water for Vaslav and us. If we had to go out to get some fresh air when it was dark, Vaslav picked his way carefully among the people so as not to step on them and hurt them.

One morning we noticed a group of people talking excitedly together. They shouted angrily, pointing at us, and we wondered what was the matter. A man came up to me.

"We are told your husband is insane. We don't want him here; he must get out."

Behind him was a menacing group. I looked towards Vaslav. He was sitting pale and tired on his hard wooden bench. They all spoke Hungarian, so he could not understand.

With one jump I sprang towards the man and slapped his face with all my strength.

"You savage, *you* will get out of here, not my husband."

At that moment the commander sprang to my side with a loaded revolver in his hand.

"Quiet! Sick or not sick, this gentleman will stay. He is the calmest, the most obedient among us all. Without a murmur he sits patiently in his corner while most of you are drinking, cursing, and making trouble. Unless you keep quiet, I will put you out."

The man slunk away like a beaten dog, and the crowd dispersed.

Towards evening the children of Mr. S. were crying bitterly, and the mother-in-law was quarrelsome. The children complained of being hungry, but their father refused to give them anything to eat. We were all surprised, as usually they had the best meals—tins of corned beef, dried fruit, biscuits, and even chocolate. But they never offered anybody anything. It was only later that we knew why he refused them.

For days now we had eaten only dry biscuits, and we felt Vaslav was getting weaker, so Pavel and I decided that we must get him some warm food. He volunteered to go home at night and see what had happened to our house and to bring some cooked food. This he did, and next afternoon he was back with some boiled ham, hard-boiled eggs, and noodles wrapped in a cloth. It seemed like a feast to us. He also brought the latest news.

The house had been partly looted by the Germans who had left with the rest. Apparently, columns of refugees were going towards Austria but were being machine-gunned by the Russian planes. The Red Army was only ten miles away, approaching from Esterhaza on the main road to Vienna. Mrs. Elsa came and announced happily that the S.S. officers had left in the night, the radio station in the house was abandoned, and the Swabian population of Banflava was marching towards the frontiers.

Hungarian soldiers and officers came in greater and greater numbers to our shelter, discarding their uniforms and disguising themselves in peasant or other civilian clothes, begging us not to denounce them.

By the evening, the children of Mr. S. turned blue and became unconscious. We took them out into the fresh air and tried to revive them, but our doctor declared they were poisoned and beyond help. Their father admitted having given them poison, because he did not want them to meet the enemy. Some of the people thought his action heroic.

It was Good Friday and a detachment of German soldiers came back. We were distracted! So our liberation was still not as near as we had hoped. I felt that Vaslav, who was absolutely silent all this time, could not stand the strain very much longer.

Next day one of the Carmelite nuns called me to help her to bring in some water from the fountain. The air was strangely calm. We had not had an air raid for several hours, the church door was wide open, the convent seemed peaceful and the village below completely deserted. It was uncanny. Not a breath of air ruffled the trees. Then suddenly, turning towards the forest, we had the feeling that the whole forest moved—just as in *Macbeth*!

"Look, the Germans are back," whispered the nun, looking towards the slope covered by forests in the direction of Austria.

"No, they can't be. The German uniform is steel blue, and those are greenish yellow. They must be Hungarians."

Planes approached, so we went underground.

Later that day an order came through that all wine must be poured away into the streams, but instead of following this very wise order, all those who could get hold of barrels drank and drank until practically everyone was dead drunk.

"The Russians can't be very far," said somebody.

"Let's go home," suggested Stan. "If nobody is there the house will be looted, and Mr. Nijinsky can't stand the air here any longer."

So we decided to return home. It was a clear night. As we emerged from underground, a cold, limpid air hit us. My little family started; we passed the cemetery, then entered the forest where the darkness enshrouded us—while from the horizon the flash of bursting guns inflamed the sky.

Chapter 11

Liberation

IT WAS Easter Sunday. Once installed at home, Vaslav fell asleep. The others tried to clean themselves, while Pavel went to bed with his measles, useless and helpless.

In the valley we could see the fighting troops streaming towards the west like the advance of Genghis Khan. A most gruesome and magnificent sight. Thousands and thousands of tanks, heavy guns, and cavalry, covered by hundreds of planes, rolled along through the green, smiling spring countryside. Peaceful villages nestled among the trees here and there, as the victorious Red Army passed through them with a dizzying rapidity; only trampled fields, flaming villages, and clouds of smoke were left behind.

Within a few hours not only was the town occupied, but also the forest and all the houses were invaded. The Russian soldiers came into the houses in small groups.

Our gates were broken down and three tall young Russians carrying automatic machine guns entered our house.

"*Nemetzki, Nemetzki!*" ("Germans, Germans!"), they shouted loudly.

In a second everybody in the house disappeared panic-stricken behind curtains and beds. Only Vaslav remained quietly lying on his couch while I stood beside him. The Russians shouted at me.

"Nazi?"

Vaslav, unexpectedly shouting still louder, replied in Russian.

"Keep quiet!"

The soldiers stood dumfounded and lowered their automatics.

"A Russian? How does he come here? Is he a prisoner?"

"Yes, he is my husband, an artist." I did not know that I had pronounced a magic word.

Next morning two trembling Hungarians in plain clothes arrived.

"We are detectives and were sent here to fetch you. We are sorry but can't help it. You have to come down to the *Kommandatura*."

Pavel shivered in his bed.

"Don't go, they will kill you."

The three old ladies and the caretaker's wife Bözsi began to cry and said farewell to me. Bözsi volunteered to come with me, but the detectives declined.

"We have strict orders only to bring down the lady, but you can follow," they said turning towards Bözsi. "But you can't go to the building of the *Kommandatura*; even we are not allowed to enter."

Vaslav was still asleep.

"Let me first quickly prepare his breakfast, and then let us hurry—I want to be back before my husband awakes."

The detectives looked at me with astonishment, but gave permission. I could see by their expressions that they did not believe that I would ever return. I quickly prepared something in the kitchen and then rejoined them.

Never in my life did I go so fast down that hill to Sopron. Whatever awaited me, I wanted to have it over quickly. Everything I had read or heard or seen in films in the past about Russia and its regime whirled around and around in my thoughts. I was dazed. The town was completely changed. The streets were full of Russian soldiers, tanks and lorries everywhere, horses grazing in the gardens, doors broken down. Those houses which still had windows had them wide open. Before the hospital, stretchers were laid out with wounded soldiers, and from every house the sound of the radio was pouring out in an indescribable medley, playing Tchaikovsky, Rimsky-Korsakov, and Strauss waltzes. No Hungarians were in sight. Sopron had become a Russian town overnight.

The detectives handed me over to the sentinel in front of the *Kommandatura,* and he called another soldier who told me to follow him. There were soldiers and officers running around, others sliding down the banister. I was taken up to the first floor, where we crossed through many offices full of busy officers, but nobody paid any attention to me. Then I was taken through a room where many strange-looking civilians, all Russians, were sitting writing dispatches. They looked at me very searchingly. I had the feeling of being lost in an unknown world.

Finally, I entered a small room. There was a large desk covered with papers, and a bed on which were hastily thrown parts of a uniform, an astrakhan cap, and a sword. The radio played Balakierev's music for the ballet *Tamar.* I thought what a long way I had gone since that early spring day in 1912 when I first heard this tune at the performance of the Russian ballet.

A tall, handsome officer entered, spotlessly attired. I noticed that he must be of high rank, judging by the heavy gold badges he wore on his shoulder. My escort saluted and left us. The officer sat down and scrutinized me.

"You live in this town—are you a native?" he asked in broken German.

"I was born in Budapest," I replied in Russian. "My parents were Hungarian. We only came here about a year ago to hide, as my husband has been suffering from a mental illness since the First World War, when we were prisoners in Hungary, too."

"Your husband is incapable of work? What was he?"

"He is an artist, a dancer born in Kiev, and was a member of the Opera House in St. Petersburg."

"When did he leave Russia?"

"In 1911. He was sent with the Russian ballet on an artistic tour through Europe and later to America."

"Do you know many people here in this town, any Russians?"

"No, we were hiding. We only came in contact with a few acquaintances from Budapest. I don't know of any Russians." Prince Matscharsky, a White Russian refugee, came to my mind, but I kept silent about him. I hoped for his sake that he was far away by now. His prophecy was coming true; by May the end of the war would be a fact.

"How long have you been married?"

"Since 1913."

He jotted down a few notes on a paper before him. "Your name?"

"Romola Carlovna Nijinskaya."

"What did you say? Nijinskaya?" He closed his eyes for a second and murmured "Nijinskaya . . ." and then suddenly, as though struck by lightning, he straightened up, threw his pencil on the desk, and dashed out of the room.

I waited. An hour must have passed. I still stood there waiting—for what? By now Vaslav must be awake. Was he able to have his breakfast alone? Could he dress? He was so used to me, I got worried. If only one of the old women could help him. What if Russians came to the house?

The door opened suddenly and the officer entered, accompanied by an older one of higher rank. The newcomer sat down at the desk while the younger one pushed a chair towards me saying, *"Sadites poja-lusta."*

I sat down.

"You claim to be the wife of Nijinsky, our great

dancer, who with Chaliapine showed the Western world our art?"

"Yes."

"The man you are hiding is your husband, I understand. He became ill after the first war, and you were prisoners in both wars here in Hungary?"

"Yes."

"Where have you lived since the last war?"

"In Hungary, Austria, France, and Switzerland. We were going from country to country in search of a treatment to restore my husband's health."

"Your husband was unable to work? Who looked after him during these twenty-six years?"

"I did."

"What is your profession?"

"I have none. I was brought up like all other society girls, studying general education, the arts, music."

"So how did you provide for both of you?"

"At first I used the funds my husband gave me which he earned while he was dancing. Later, when I saw that the doctors' fees, treatments, and nursing homes would swallow all our savings, I began to write, lecture, and work for films."

"You mean you had to pay for the nursing homes and doctors?"

"Yes."

"During the twenty-six years, no government paid for him, none of his colleagues provided for his care?"

"No."

The Commandant turned round, gave just one look at his aide-de-camp, and spat on the floor. Pulling out his cigarette case, he offered me a cigarette, "Kuritye." I accepted. He rang a bell and two other officers and a man in plain clothes entered. He turned to me again, ordering, "Tell us where and how you met Comrade Nijinsky."

I obediently began and told them our life story.

When I had ended, the Commandant wrote what looked to me like a letter. He signed it and put many seals on it; then he handed it to me.

"Keep this with you all the time. You will be escorted home. If there is anything you need, come and ask for me." He stood up and bowed. *"Dosviedanye."* ("Good-by.")

Chapter 12

Under Russian Occupation

OUR LIFE was very uncertain. We did not know from one minute to the next what would happen. From hour to hour different orders were posted on the walls of ruined houses; the town looked more and more as though we were in Asia, in Turkestan!

Within a few days the whole countryside was overrun with the Russian Army. Officers lived in all the houses; the soldiers camped in the streets and in the forests. The Löver was a huge Russian camp. The villas had to be evacuated by the civilian population. Only Mrs. Drobnich was left in her home, and we did not receive an order to leave.

During the first days a quiet Russian officer, Mischa, came to live with us with his aide-de-camp. He was silent and secretive.

Constantly small groups of Russian soldiers visited the house. They looked around, sometimes sat down, looked at the pictures and furniture, remarked "Bourgeois," and left again. Most of them asked for wine, which we gave them, but we had to taste it before they touched it. The others requested watches or a phonograph, but after a few days we did not have anything to offer them except wine.

The house next door to us, which was empty, was taken over for an officers' mess. Cattle and horses grazed all around our house. Tents were put up under the trees, and in the evening the soldiers cooked their meals on an open fire. Later on, the soldiers began to sing and play the balalaika, while in the officers' mess they sang and played cards until late into the night. Passers-by were held up by soldiers on the streets and taken away to work. Sometimes they returned, sometimes not.

Mischa disappeared as silently as he had come, leaving five large bags of flour. This was a princely present.

A strange life began for us. At my request, an officer of high rank was billeted on us, Stephan Danilovitch of Moscow, with his aide-de-camp. It seemed that in the Russian Army every lieutenant had his aide-de-camp, this one being a private.

Stephan Danilovitch was a very kind-hearted man; he treated us with the attention of a big brother. At first he tried to be too familiar with me, but when he found out who Vaslav was he began to treat me with respect, saying, "Romola Carlovna, *tee maja sestra*" ("you are my sister"), and gave orders to his private to look after me when he was out.

The head cook of the officers' mess sent us over oil and meat and all kinds of food. The garage was filled with great barrels of wine, and Stephan Danilovitch insisted that we should take our meals with him. I excused Vaslav, saying that he had to be kept quiet and eat alone and earlier. The house was filled with guests, as Stephan Danilovitch never sat down to a meal without having ten to twenty officers at the table. They all ate from one large dish.

Vaslav used to stroll around the garden and lie in his garden chair, watching and wondering what was going on. He never asked any questions, just listened and listened, but his eyes became more and more attentive. They were not so dreamy and distant as they had been during the last twenty-six years. It almost seemed as if he were awakening from a long and deep sleep. Shyly, more and more, he approached the soldiers and sat down among them. It seemed that some inward barrier broke down, and he seemed melted towards the outside world. In the evenings he stood and listened to the plaintive, nostalgic sound of the balalaika for a long time.

It was the first time since 1919 that people had not

stared at him, had not shrunk from him because he had suffered from a mental illness. They spoke to him with the same nonchalant manner as they did to us, and were not frightened. At first I warned them.

"Leave Vaslav Fomitch alone, don't talk to him; he might get annoyed and impatient, he is afraid."

But they just laughed.

"He won't be afraid of us," they said. "Let him do as he wants."

For the first time in many years I felt that we had all treated Vaslav as if he were different from us, and that this might have been a dreadful mistake. Under the suggestions of the psychiatrists, perhaps we unintentionally did the wrong thing in watching him and trying to order him around instead of letting him do freely whatever he wanted. As the days and weeks passed, I noticed that the primitive Russian soldiers had a better method of treating him than we had, with all the doctors and nurses of the last twenty-six years. Slowly Vaslav became more and more easy in his manner and actions, and to our great amazement he began to express himself and ask for things. I could hardly believe it at first.

Today I know . . . if we had never taken him to a nursing home, if I had taken him to his native country at the beginning of his illness, if at that time

Russia had been a country at peace, he would not have become so ill. In our great ignorance of his mental state, we did the worst possible thing. We locked him up and put him into solitary confinement, and slowly we isolated him from the world. I have never forgiven myself for this.

Every morning, Simon the private used to bring large cans of milk for the officers. One day I asked him to let us have some. Vaslav Fomitch had not had any for months and months—might I have some? Stephan Danilovitch heard me and disappeared through the window—his favorite entrance. Within half an hour a soldier arrived with three cows.

"Keep them here for milk for Vaslav Fomitch."

When the rumor spread among the soldiers of the camp who Vaslav was, they entered our garden to gaze at him. Often in the evening they danced their peasant dances, trepak, Cossack, and the Cherkess dances. Vaslav became more and more interested; he clapped his hands and began to encourage them. One evening when the shouting, singing, and dancing was in full swing, he stood up, jumped in the middle of them, and began to whirl and dance.

From that evening onwards, he could do and go anywhere. Respectfully they made way for him, and the soldiers came and brought him all kinds of presents—fruit, food, clothes, whatever they could lay hands on. I noticed the deep respect they had for him and his art.

Often when Stephan Danilovitch's soldiers went to the country with their carts they took us along. We never knew where they intended to go. Once they drove along in search of wine, and we went from tavern to tavern to get the barrels. The innkeepers were only too happy to be left in peace and gave their wine willingly. The soldiers appeared to be indifferent towards the natives as long as they did not suspect them of being Germans—in fact, they became friendly with the Hungarians. For this reason, I was quite amazed when I saw them get in a dreadful rage when we were on one of our wine expeditions. They took hold of a landlord and pushed him around. I tried to quiet them while I told the landlord in Hungarian to try to disappear, which he did. On the way home, I ventured to ask the reason for their sudden anger.

"He was a bourgeois."

"But no, he is a peasant, I know!"

"He couldn't be," Ratislav answered, "he was too fat."

After a time I found the best method with them was never to show any fear. This had a soothing effect even on the wildest of them.

Once Stephan Danilovitch had to go to Wiener Neustadt, and we were alone in the house with Simon, who was asleep. Three gloomy-looking soldiers with loaded guns broke in. They wanted watches and we didn't have any more. One of them, the leader, was furious and called me a Nazi. I answered, "We are not. You are drunk!"

"I don't care."

He pointed his loaded gun at us. We were sure we were going to be shot. The old women screamed, and he made us march into the garden. Instead, he took our small electric flashlights and vanished.

Our house in the evenings was full of young Hungarian girls who had hidden in the attics and cellars, in fear of the officers who wanted to rape them. I succeeded in getting the officers to sit around the table and drink while we talked. I had to tell them about my journeys and about the ballets, and soon the girls were forgotten.

One evening Stephan Danilovitch had to go away again on a trip to the country, as he was in charge of the repairs to the Sopron-Vienna line. Late in the evening three officers arrived. One was a fair, good-looking boy who could have played the part of Lensky in *Eugen Onegin*. The second could have been Vorontzoff to Anna Karenina. Both had excellent manners. The third was handsome, too, but rather rough. He took my room and said, "You will stay here with me."

I shook my head. He got wild and locked the room, putting his gun on the table. The other two tried to quiet him but he would not listen.

"You will do as I order you; we are at war. I shall shoot you otherwise."

Locked in with three men, for one second I felt I was lost.

"Tovaritch, have you a sister or mother?"

"Yes."

"Well, how would you feel if they were treated like this by the Germans?"

"They probably were." But I noticed he became quieter.

"You seem to forget that my husband is a country-man of yours who only brought glory to his native land. He is sick and helpless. I have worked for him, slaved and suffered for twenty-six years. Tovaritch, I appeal to you."

The officer murmured something unintelligible, and turning to his comrades he ordered them to give him some wine. He kicked at the door, which opened, and I left.

We were completely cut off from the outside world, and we wondered what would happen to us. Vaslav was confident as ever. I replaced for him father and mother, and even his own will to decide. With God's mercy we had survived the war with all its horrors, and the German invasion, but what would happen now?

To go back to Budapest, a shattered, ruined town, would be impossible. I could not find work and we would starve. Russia? This would have been the natural place to go. I remembered that the Consul in Budapest had assured me that Vaslav was not a refugee but a child of the people, an honored artist; that the present ruling classes knew well who Gorki, Tolstoi, Pavlova, and Nijinsky were. I was made to understand that Vaslav would get the necessary medical care, he would be provided for all his life, and I could continue to work, write, and lecture on dancing. The dreadful fear of what would happen to Vaslav should I be unable to find work or die would vanish.

This was the nightmare of my life. I remembered all the hardships and suffering we had both gone through during these twenty-six years when I could not earn enough, and the indifference and heartlessness of the people. Vaslav would be cared for and provided for always. It was a wonderful thought. He would get a small place in Yalta or the Caucasus, wherever the doctor thought it would be best for him; I could stay with him and nurse him, I was assured. . . .

But then my grandfather's clear, realistic manner of thinking got hold of me. Who would guarantee this? How could I be sure of what awaited us? I remembered how we were practically chased away from Switzerland, only because we did not have sufficient means to live there, in the middle of the war. It was a difficult decision I had to make.

At the moment, I felt it was better to stay quiet and await developments.

The next few days many things seemed to happen in the world. One evening Stephan Danilovitch came home from work earlier than usual and said, "Today we ceased work in honor of the great President, our friend Roosevelt, who died."

Then came the news: "Vienna *kaput,* Berlin *kaput,*" the Allies were advancing, the German leaders were killed or captured, and Hitler was not to be found.

Late at night on May 5th, I was awakened by Stephan Danilovitch. He said, "Go to Vaslav Fomitch and explain to him why all the war planes are in the air; he might get frightened. We are going to fire all our guns and ammunition. We are celebrating. *Waina Okontechale.*" ("The war is over.")

Chapter 13

The Flight to Vienna

THE FOLLOWING WEEKS we tried to find out what was happening in the world. Jews returning from Dachau and Theresienstadt seemed to be well-informed. They discussed the situation readily with the Hungarians of the town. According to them the whole of eastern Europe was to be occupied by the Russians, who had rapidly brought in their reforms and manner of living. It was clear that under their occupation the countries were to be bolshevized. The western Allies did not seem to care. The Jews claimed that Berlin and Vienna would be ruled by an international organization formed by America, Great Britain, Russia, and France. If we wished to escape we should go to Vienna at once was their advice. Kyra was in Italy, Bronia, Vaslav's sister, in the United States. Surely if we went west we could join them and succeed in making a happy and peaceful home for Vaslav in the United States.

After all the turmoil and hardships he had gone through during the years of war, the company of his beloved sister and daughter was the ideal thing for him. Therefore I decided that we should go west. But how to get to Vienna, how to obtain permission?

We were assured that the territory between Sopron and Vienna and all along the former Austro-Hungarian border was "No Man's Land." There were no guards, no formalities. The railway line was not yet completely restored; very few trains were running. Nobody could tell for sure whether or not they took civilian passengers, but the best information I could obtain about this would come from Stephan Danilovitch, who was the commander of the battalion repairing the railways. Military motor trucks were going back and forth to Vienna, we knew, and the Russian soldiers often gave lifts and even took people to Vienna.

Pavel suggested that we two should first try to get through, investigate the situation, and then, if our plan was feasible, come back to fetch Vaslav. But without the permission of Stephan Danilovitch I did not dare to do it. I knew he was our protector. I felt all along that he would even risk his life to save us. The first moment of sympathy towards us which he had shown when he arrived in Sopron had turned to a deep, fond feeling. He had given many proofs of his devotion during the past few months.

How could I forget the day when he slapped the face of the soldier who took me away for potato peeling, the day when he saved me from being put on trial because of Bözsi, the caretaker's wife, who became too friendly with some of the soldiers and denounced us women in the house, saying that we had made her work too hard in the past?

How can I forget those nights when, at the point of his pistol, he guarded me in his room to prevent my being raped? How can I forget his many attentions and his care of Vaslav, whom he treated like a younger brother?

I waited for an opportunity to break the subject of our plan to him. It came the day when Stephan Danilovitch informed me that, as the stretch of the Hungarian Railway had been repaired, he with his battalion had been ordered to Wiener Neustadt.

"Stephan Danilovitch, please take us along; we will feel so lost and frightened without you. What will become of us?" I saw he was worried. "Can't you take us along with you?" He only shook his head. "Then let us go to Vienna."

"Why to Vienna, to a starving city?"

"We will feel safer there. Please help us."

He hesitated for some moments, then said, "All right, do as you like."

We were overjoyed. I informed Vaslav of our plan and asked for Dr. Varvashovski, who was always helpful in looking after him during our absence.

For several days Pavel and I tried to get on a military truck, but did not succeed. Finally we got on a train and after a long, tiresome journey we arrived in Vienna. A desolate, bomb-shattered city was before us as we stepped out of the dilapidated railway car. The Eastern Terminal was a mass of charred ruins; trolleys did not run yet, so we had to walk to the Ringstrasse, a distance of about twenty minutes. It took us three hours to get there, for we had to jump and crawl through the huge craters caused by the explosions and tumbling houses. Everywhere were burned-out buildings. One could see through them: hanging wires, bric-a-brac of plaster, granite and glass, mingled with broken furniture and the remains of once luxurious interiors were lying around.

In the ruins, the entire city was beflagged with thousands of Red Russian flags. On the large buildings oversized portraits of Marx, Lenin, Stalin, and Voroshilov adorned the walls. Russian soldiers were everywhere, walking around, driving in motorcars, many of which were decorated with expensive oriental rugs, which, if they did not fit the seats, were simply cut in half, much to my great amazement. Horses were grazing in the parks. In the streets and squares, on small mounds of earth, Red flags were flying in the wind.

"What are those?" I asked a passer-by.

"Oh, graves of people who have fallen in the street fights and air raids."

The town was overcrowded with Russian soldiers. All the hotels—the Bristol, the Imperial, the Grand—were occupied by the Russian Army. We did not know where to turn. No shops, no coffeehouses were open. I began to get tired of wandering around and sat down on a bench opposite the old burned-out Bristol Hotel, where once Vaslav and I had lived with Kyra during the First World War. How happy and carefree we were then! Vaslav was in good health, and although we were interned, we had hopes of getting out of Austria. Life was before us and now, after twenty-six years, what had become of us!

A young and distinguished-looking man sat down beside me and began to talk to me.

"Can I help you? I see you are strangers."

"Oh, yes, please tell us where we can find lodgings and food."

He smiled. "If you are lucky and find some former

friends alive you might be able to sleep somewhere. But food—" He waved his hands in despair. "Food is almost unknown to us."

Pavel ventured going round and trying his luck, leaving me in the care of my young companion, who introduced himself as Prince Thurn-Taxis and tried to entertain me with all his adventures during the fight for Vienna.

Late in the evening, when I had almost given up hope, Pavel returned with the joyful news that he had found suitable lodgings at the famous Sacher Hotel, once the well-known meeting place of the archdukes and aristocracy of the monarchy. The hotel had not been requisitioned yet; its entrance was heavily bolted, and the windows were barred by wooden panels. The whole place had the air of an uninhabitable building. It is true that it was partly damaged by the last bombardment. Nevertheless, it looked quite comfortable from the inside. The manager tried to give the impression that the house lacked every comfort as they hoped in this way to be forgotten.

At first when Pavel forced his way into the hotel, the manager turned him away, but when he learned that he was seeking refuge for Vaslav, he consented. But he warned him he would be unable to provide food. Very quickly the manager made arrangements and a princely suite of rooms with bathrooms was made habitable. As if by magic, expensive rugs were laid down, furniture was brought in, exquisite table and bed linen appeared which till then had been carefully hidden.

As the manager informed us, a few old distinguished customers of the hotel were camping there in secret: Prince Auersperg, Count Berchtold, Madame la Baronne Drache, a leader of Viennese society, and Madame Joseph Kainz, the widow of the world-famous Austrian dramatic actor. They had survived the fight and bombardment in the Sacher.

Down in the famous and even now spotlessly clean kitchens of the Sacher, glittering frying pans stood in rows on the shelves. Around a long table in the pastry kitchen sat a group holding council during the evening meal, which consisted of a plate of pea soup.

They welcomed us and became enthusiastic at once when they heard that we were trying to bring Vaslav here, immediately offering their advice as to how to solve the problem of nourishment and informing us as to where to obtain bread and other necessities, of course, everything in the black market, the only place where food was obtainable at fabulous prices: a loaf of bread for 100 marks (about ten dollars), a box of canned cheese for 250 marks and a pound of lard for 1500 schillings. They said that here in Vienna we could eventually meet the western allied troops and make our way towards the west.

As soon as we had made the necessary arrangements in Vienna, we started our return trip to Sopron, to fetch Vaslav, but this was not as easy as we had hoped. Only once a day a train left Vienna going towards Hungary, but this train left only whenever the Russians permitted it. Sometimes it was stationed at Vienna for several days. On the advice of Sacher's wise old head porter, we tried our luck every day at noon at the station, to try to find a place in or on top of the carriage and hope for the best.

The train was supposed to leave at seven in the evening. For ten days we tried to depart. Sometimes we were kicked off the train as soon as we installed ourselves. Sometimes we were not even able to board it. Passengers fought, screamed, pushed each other. The Russian soldiers just looked at them. And then, in the evening, when we were half-starved, exhausted, and expected to leave, the soldiers boarded the train and threw us off. Only once did we succeed in remaining on the train, but by the time we arrived at Wiener Neustadt we were pushed off again. It was three o'clock in the morning during a terrible rainstorm. I was desperate, seeing our home journey unfulfilled. It was by sheer luck that we met at the station a friend of Stephan Danilovitch, who knew us and sent us back to Vienna.

We knew our only way back to Sopron was by motor. We tried everything, begging, bribing, to obtain a car. After innumerable setbacks, with the help of the kind lady Baronne Drache, we got an introduction to the Austrian Red Cross. They were willing to send a car which was to take us down to Sopron and bring Vaslav up to Vienna. After a smooth and hurried trip, we arrived at Sopron in the evening. Vaslav, overjoyed, ran to the car as it turned to the house.

During the whole night we packed and took down our hidden suitcases. In an old laundry bag I put the few valuables which we still possessed and the Nansen Passport given to Vaslav by the Swiss authorities. In the eyes of the Russians this was the worst possible document we could have. It would have been wiser to destroy it, but on the other hand it was the only means of identification we had, so we had to keep it, whatever happened.

Through the assistant commander of Sopron, Vasily Ivanovitch, a bosom friend of Stephan Danilovitch, we obtained marching orders to Vienna and a Russian escort. It was arranged that our car should leave shortly after 5 P.M. and arrive in Vienna while it was still daylight. The seventy-five kilometers

which separated us could easily be done in three
hours. Our car drove on the very same road leading
through the valley upon which two months previously we had seen Marshal Talboukijn's army galloping through. Now it was deserted. Very few houses
stood in the burned-out villages. Dusk fell. We had
already passed the place where once the Austro-
Hungarian border had been. Our driver switched on
the lights and we drove faster, coming to a fork in
the road. The driver hesitated for a second, not knowing which way to turn. Suddenly from the left, huge
light reflectors were pointed on the car and a group
of Russian soldiers shouted: *"Stoit!"* ("Stop!")

They surrounded us. There was a long explanation
by our escort, the showing of our Red Cross papers
and the Russian marching order, but it was to no
avail. The officer tore it out of our escort's hand,
pointed his loaded pistol at the driver, and jumped
into the car, while two other soldiers leaped on the
running board. We were arrested! Resistance would
have been in vain.

Vaslav slept in the corner while I murmured prayers. So this was our end.

I did not dare to speak or to move. With my feet I
kicked the laundry bag under the seat. I knew if they
found the Nansen Passport it would be fatal, as this
would suggest that we were White Russians.

Our car was taken first to the commanding officer's house. He was having a party. Through the open windows we could see the gay gathering of Russian officers drinking and singing, while we waited trembling in the car. Then one of the soldiers returned. The commander could not be bothered with us.

So the others decided to take us to the schoolhouse. I had to wake Vaslav. He was tired and confused, not understanding quite what had happened. But he saw me standing smilingly near him. He sat down and waited patiently. The hours passed. Vaslav, like a big baby, dropped his head and began to sleep. I kept his head on my shoulder.

What would be our fate? What should I do? I prayed and prayed to my little Jesus of Prague, which I always carried with me. He had miraculously saved us so many times. Suddenly I whispered, "*Tovaritsci izvinyitye.* (Comrade, forgive me.) My husband is so ill. He is a countryman of yours, a great dancer. Please let him rest. He will collapse." He shrugged his shoulders. I had a few faded photos of Vaslav in my bag, photos taken in Russia in his youth in dancing costumes. I threw the bag onto the table. The soldiers looked at the photos, turned them round. Then one stood up and gave us the sign to follow him, which we did. It was a clear moonlit night. We marched, the eldest soldier before us, the three others by our side, until we arrived near a small peasant house.

The soldiers shouted. A frightened Austrian peasant couple opened the door. They stood submissively, awaiting orders. These were to keep and feed us until the morning. I quickly threw my coat down, and while the peasant woman bent to pick it up I whispered to her: "There is a bag under the coat. When the soldiers leave, hide it."

One of the soldiers was left behind. He soon began to play cards with our Russian escort and forgot all about us. The woman warmed some milk, which I gave to Vaslav, and then we laid him on the large, soft bed of our landlord. Entirely dressed, I rested on the bed next to him, while a Red Cross representative and his assistant lay at our feet.

During the night we speculated on what we could do, and decided that in case, in the morning, matters became worse, one of the Austrians should try to escape and get word to the commander in Sopron.

Next morning our escort, with marching orders, went up to the Major in charge of the camp, while Vaslav peacefully dressed and partook of his breakfast. He never showed any signs of fear of the Russian soldiers. As the hours passed, I became worried and asked the soldier guarding us to take us along to the commander. Near his house we sat on a stone in the sunshine and waited.

After some time the Major came out of his house shouting and cursing those who had arrested us. Hurriedly our car was pulled up and we were ordered to leave for Vienna.

It all seemed so incredible. As we neared Vienna our Austrian escort whispered the explanation to me. We had been arrested for the sake of our motorcar, which was a good one. They wanted to keep it, but seeing who we were and that we had a special recommendation to the Commander-in-Chief in Vienna, they did not dare to touch us.

As we drove up before the Sacher, a joyful crowd greeted us, headed by Baroness Drache.

It took hours before they got the story of our dangerous adventure. We settled down happily in our cool, shady suite of rooms. It was June. Vienna, in spite of the war damages and occupation, was at its best. Life began to stir among the Viennese. The Russian commander ordered the shops to be opened although the merchants protested, saying that they had nothing to sell. It is to the credit of the Austrian artists that the theatres which were not destroyed through the bombardments soon opened.

The Opera Mouse opened at the Theater an der

Wien. The famous Burgtheater started its performances at the Ronacher. Costumes and scenery were gathered together. Scores of operas were loaned by various musicians to enable the orchestras to play. Almost everything was missing or destroyed. At one of the first performances of *Lohengrin,* we saw Elsa in a Biedermeier dress wearing modern shoes and a medieval headdress. But they all sang and played beautifully. I knew it would give great pleasure to Vaslav to attend these performances. So very soon we got into the habit of being present at the opera and concerts. Sometimes we even walked for an hour to get to the Volksoper, as no cars were available. The streets were still covered with litter, so we chose the near-by Imperial Gardens for our walks. We only had to cross the Mozart Platz and, through a side entrance which connected the Albertina, Palace of the Archduke Albrecht, with the Hofburg, we could enter this delightful secluded park. For long hours we sat and read while Pavel was running around to obtain food.

Very soon many artists came to visit us and we were surrounded by quite a sociable crowd.

In the little group living at the Sacher there was a Polish Baron and his wife Xenia. She was a very capable woman who spoke many languages and did a lot of business on the black market. She seemed to be very friendly with the Russians, much to the disgust of the other Austrians. She not only had a pull with the Russians but also was friendly with Mr. Collignon, who apparently represented France in Austria. It was rumored that during the war Mr. Collignon had worked for the Allies in Vienna. Under the Nazi rule, among many other occupations he was employed as a stagehand at the Opera House. As soon as Vienna capitulated, he took charge of the magnificent palace of the French Embassy. He seemed to be all-powerful. He intended to send back by motor truck all those French war prisoners who came into Vienna. There were many who had escaped from Germany, where they had to work as slave laborers. Collignon was supposed to repatriate them to France. Baroness Xenia assured us it could be arranged that for five thousand schillings for each person, we could be sent to Paris too. We paid her the required amount and hoped to be off soon, although the trip seemed fantastic and, according to many people, impracticable. We had successfully passed all the medical examinations and had our repatriation papers.

Our departure was promised from one week to the other. Several times we had already packed our baggage just to learn a few hours before we were to leave that the journey was postponed. Then at last the 25th of July was set as the date for our departure to France. Pavel went ahead, as we did not want Vaslav to stand around in the crowd.

Pavel returned late at night saying that the trucks were overcrowded, our place had been taken by others, and all he got was a promise that we would get on the next transport. But there was no such thing, as even this one was turned back by the Russians at the demarcation line.

Much to the horror of the little group of camping aristocrats, one afternoon a Russian Colonel walked into our hotel. He sat down in the lobby and found the place to his liking. The trembling manager had to show him around, and within a few hours the place was occupied by Russian officers of high rank. The aristocrats vanished. Madame Kainz, as the widow of a great artist, and we were allowed to stay on. Baroness Xenia too. The bar and drawing rooms were opened, and endless banquets and feasts were held. Food was brought in by the carload. All the bathtubs were filled to overflowing with tomatoes, cucumbers, and fruit. The kitchen was overloaded with fish and meat. We had no worry about getting nourishment. I just had to stand in the row of the privates in the kitchen at meal hours, and the chef served me plentifully.

The Flight to Vienna

So once more we were in the midst of the Russian Army. No more Austrians or civilians were permitted to enter the premises. We could meet them only in their own homes or in the park. Among them was Josef Gregor, the great historian of theatrical art. He kindly invited me to the Hofmuseum, to the Archives, where I began to work on a new book, the biography of Fanny Elssler, the great Viennese dancer of the early nineteenth century. Vaslav was greatly interested in my work and helped me with valuable suggestions. Opposite the Imperial Archives on the Joseph Platz was the palace in which the British Embassy once had resided. The palace was deserted. Only a huge British flag with the well-known royal arms covered the first-floor entrance to the offices. I wandered around and called, "Is anybody here?" After a few seconds the flag was drawn aside and a small white-haired lady peeped out. It was Blanche, an English lady who for thirty years had served the Embassy loyally. She remained in Vienna during the war and had hidden all documents which could not be taken out in time. She was so fragile and so lonely in this vast, lofty sixteenth-century palace. She called me in. We sat down when I had introduced myself, and I told her our story. She was very interested, and asked me to visit her again. It was from her that we first learned that the Allied troops were standing only about a hundred kilometers away near Linz waiting for orders to enter the town.

The heat was unbearable. Even the sidewalks began to melt. Our lobby in the Sacher, constructed of marble, was cool. It must have been here that I contracted pneumonia. One morning I could not get up and, as I learned later, I was dangerously ill. Vaslav became restless as soon as he saw something was the matter with me. He crawled on my bed, watching me intently, and was not to be induced to leave.

For three days I lay helpless with a high temperature. Baroness Drache forced her way up to us and brought me a couple of cooked tomatoes which she had picked herself in the gardens of her estate, Schloss Inzensdorf, twenty kilometers away. This wonderful, kind, great lady was brave enough to undertake such a long trip, which she had to make partly by foot, to bring in supplies for her friends.

Somehow nature and the will to live pulled me through, and soon I took up the daily routine. Vaslav was overjoyed and exuberant. More than ever he became close to me. All the long years we had spent together I had felt like a shadow following a miraculous being, but now I knew I was part of him, and whatever happened we could not exist apart. At the beginning of our life together, he had been my husband, my brother, my guide, my truest friend, but since his reawakening I was not only his wife and companion but his mother and life itself to him.

Our surroundings had changed in a kaleidoscopic fashion these past years. We had lived among so many different races, such different mentalities and social orders, we had gone through such unspeakable dangers and hardships, we had come so close to death, to the fundamental problems of human life, that all values changed for us and these experiences fused us into one indivisible being. Nothing mattered any more. We had no wish but to stay like this forever.

Chapter 14

Life under the International Command

AROUND NOON, we few civilians living at the Sacher met in one of the small drawing rooms on the ground floor. Here we sat around and partook of our meals. The Russians left us alone and did not pay much attention, so more and more friends, among them Austrians, sneaked in to visit us. News was exchanged. Food which we received from the kitchen was shared with them, and many pleasant hours were spent together. Many people arrived from Hungary, Czechoslovakia, and Poland. Very soon this gathering became like the ones customarily seen at the old Sacher Hotel. Mostly they were aristocrats, who of course never mentioned their titles, and members of the clergy and artists. They all had one idea: to go west —but how far nobody knew.

One day early in the autumn, as we were lunching,

the young Austrian waiter shouted "Jesu Maria" and dropped the dish he carried. We all looked up, startled by the exclamation. There, before us, stood a group of officers in shorts, very smartly attired in British and French uniforms. We could hardly believe our eyes.

They all talked at once, embraced some of our Austrian friends, and in a few moments we learned that they were old acquaintances, some of them Austrian-born, who had joined the Allied armies. Others were British and French who had been in Vienna many times before the war.

They had just marched into Vienna. The Allied troops were pouring in. It was late in the day when the telephone rang in our suite. The Austrian porter spoke:

"Madame, will you please come down? The Provost Marshal of the American Military Police, Colonel Yarborough, is here with his aide-de-camp. He wishes to speak to you."

I wondered what he wanted and nervously flew down the stairs. By this time I had had enough of meeting officers of high rank. It was always the portent of something disagreeable. As I entered the lobby, I saw an extremely handsome, fair young man. He jumped up as I approached and introduced himself and his escort.

"We just arrived and I learned that you are here with your husband."

"Yes, and what do you wish?" I asked wonderingly, hesitatingly.

"Oh, I read your book about your husband some years ago when I was stationed in Manila. If I can be of any help to you, please call on me. We are at the Auersperg Palais. Please do not hesitate. . . ."

During the next few days life in Vienna changed rapidly. The city was divided into zones. On the border of each zone tall billboards warned the passers-by in four languages that they were entering the Russian, French, American, or British Zone. The Russian women soldiers, with their multicolored little flags with which they regulated traffic, disappeared and their places were taken by the military policemen of the respective zones. They were also circulating on motor bicycles, trying to prevent the Russians from driving on the sidewalks, which they did with great pleasure.

Instead of the carloads of dried peas with which the Viennese population was fed up till now, different sorts of bread and food were brought in and divided. Endless red tape was introduced, with dozens of ration cards, a system which meant hours of standing around the offices without much result.

The shops and coffeehouses opened timidly, and the inhabitants began to circulate in the town more freely. The most important buildings had been allotted to the Four Powers. The Russians kept the Hofburg, while the British installed themselves in the Palace of Schönbrunn, leaving to the Americans and French less imposing palaces. The hotels also were divided among them, and the Russians kept the Grand and Imperial. The Bristol became American, while the Sacher was to be British. District 1 became international, ruled by the Four Powers together. It was decided that each month in turn one of the Allies would preside over the Allied Council and rule the city. Each week the four commanders met to agree upon current affairs.

The town was to be cleaned up, the little graves unearthed, and the victims buried in the cemeteries. It was about time, for during the heat of the summer the corpses began to decay, and as they were hardly under the ground, it infected the air. The horses had to leave the parks and were sent to stables. Tumbling houses were either torn down or blasted.

In the evenings the jeeps of the International Military Police patrolled the streets. The American, with his steel helmet, sat side by side with the high astrakhan-capped Russian, while the Briton with his little beret and the Frenchman with his kepi took back seats. The long, endless column of the marching troops singing melancholy Slav songs of the steppes ceased.

During the mornings tremendous activity reigned at the Russelpark near the world-famous Karlskirche in the inner part of the city. Here, next to each other, the French, the Russians, the Americans, Austrians and Balkan refugees were buying and selling all kinds of goods—expensive jewelry, heirlooms of great families, masterpieces looted from the museums, flashlights, foods, dresses, pell-mell with American cigarettes, drugs, and wrist watches—and more wrist watches. It was like a World's Fair, with gesticulating, shouting people. Once in a while the American Military Police appeared and surrounded the place, trying to prevent this illegal market.

Orders and restrictions came out day after day. Very soon the Russians packed up and left the Sacher, only one Colonel refusing to go. He was told that the British Army had requisitioned the hotel. But the Colonel remained.

A detachment of British officers came in, inspected the place, and made arrangements to disinfect the building. Everybody, the Austrian staff included, was ordered to leave within a few days.

The Russian Colonel barricaded himself in his apartment and declared he would stay. At first the

British pleaded with him, but without result. Then, as they intervened at the Russian Command, the Colonel was ordered to leave by his superiors, but he still remained, until one evening a British Major with four soldiers came in to put him out. It was quite a fight between them which ended in the bar, when all had a number of drinks. They walked out arm in arm and locked the entrance behind the back of the Russian Colonel.

We, too, were ordered by the British to leave. It was a tremendous blow. We wondered where to go. The situation was quite desperate, as the private buildings were mostly without windows, hot water, or gas, and in many places, without electricity. There were no hotels, no nursing homes open. The winters, as I knew from my experience in Central Europe, were cold, so we could not camp with Vaslav in some deserted apartment in town.

When the British Town Major in command flatly refused to grant permission, I decided to appeal to the British commander. After many formalities I succeeded in being received by Major Lord Inchcape, who was attached to the Command. He was a very amiable young gentleman who listened patiently to my request and promised to bring it to the attention of the commander but without giving me any hope. "The hotel is requisitioned. Only members of the

British Army can be billeted there," I pleaded. "Just tell your commander we have survived the war, the German occupation, the Russian invasion. We have nowhere to go. There is no place in Vienna with light and heat. All I can do if you turn us out is to sit in the ruins of the Opera House." I was half crying, half joking, but he smiled and said, "I will, of course, explain the extraordinary circumstances and will let you know."

Our other friends had to move out. Mrs. Kainz was in despair. She was almost eighty years old and rather helpless. Being an artist's widow was no longer any help to her. We were in the presence of strict military rules, where nothing else counted. Of course we did not say anything to Vaslav about the impending difficulties. Some days later Major Lord Inchcape paid a visit to us and brought the decision of the commander. He was willing to allow us three to stay at the Sacher until we were able to obtain permission to leave Austria. But we were not allowed to receive any civilian visitors on the premises.

This quite exceptional, kind gesture towards Vaslav made us deeply grateful. Now we were under the protection and on the territory of the United Kingdom.

But as soon as the Russians left the place, food disappeared too. We had the utmost difficulty in buying nourishment on the black market, and the following weeks were the worst of the whole war. For some time we were able to obtain potatoes and nothing else —then, for days and days, only dried peas and lentils. Our diet was monotonous beyond words, and at the end Vaslav was unable to swallow it. Pavel ran around to obtain something. He bartered with the Russian soldiers. He made the acquaintance of Madame Eisenmenger, the companion of Frau Schratt, the famous Austrian actress, once friend and companion of the Emperor. Madame Schratt had been dead for some years, but in her palace the household was still kept up, and many of her former friends took refuge there and lived as paying guests. Her precious furniture and belongings were sold one by one to obtain food and fuel, and Madame Eisenmenger was able to get some fruit, vegetables, and sometimes meat from former gardeners and merchants of the Imperial Court. She sold those among the former circle of the *Gnädige Frau,* as her former mistress was known all over Austria. She was herself a great admirer of artists, and hearing that Vaslav was in need of food, she shared whatever she was able to obtain with him.

Then the kind Miss Blanche advised me to see the various representatives of the Red Cross, so I made the rounds once a month. The British, the American, the Danish, and the Swiss Red Cross each gave a parcel for Vaslav.

The autumn passed and I noticed that Vaslav became thinner and paler. The doctors I consulted were of the opinion that the badly balanced diet of canned food was detrimental to his health and that I must obtain for him natural, fresh nourishment at any price. One could not go on like this year after year.

I was at my wit's end when by chance Brigadier General Churchill, nephew of Winston, arrived one day at the hotel. I did not know him, but he had heard about our being there. He introduced himself to me and I told him about our plight. He promised to intervene.

Colonel Gordon Smith had at the time an important post at the British Headquarters. He was a great balletomane and had witnessed the performances of the Russian Ballet in London and Paris between 1909 and 1914. He, too, had heard of our predicament. So he came to see me. I told him that I had gone down to the Captain who managed the hotel some time ago and had asked him for just one hot meal a day for Mr. Nijinsky, but he had refused, saying, "The food belongs to the army, and I cannot give you, a foreigner and civilian, anything." What could I answer to this?

Colonel Gordon Smith seemed displeased and

asked me to follow him to the Captain's office. Seeing his superior, the Captain immediately stood at attention. "Now, Captain X," said the Colonel, "what ridiculous talk. The British Army can spare one hot meal a day for a sick man, so see to it that Mr. Nijinsky gets it."

The Captain took the order literally and withheld breakfast and dinner, but sent up luncheon for Vaslav. At last some hot food. . . . We were isolated at this time. Nobody could come to see us except members of the Allied armies.

Through their visits Vaslav's life became more interesting. We were taken around for drives to the Wiener Wald and Schönbrunn, which gave him a great deal of pleasure. The following winter passed quite pleasantly. The concert and operatic season was in full swing and we attended many performances, among which perhaps the ballet and dramatic productions which were held in the Redoutensaal, the large ballroom of the Imperial family at the old Hofburg, were the most delightful.

The great art collections of the Viennese museums and the Albertina were found and exhibited at the Hofburg too, so one winter morning when a great snowstorm caught us while wandering around the Imperial Gardens I suggested to Vaslav that we go there.

It must have reminded him of his youthful visits when he danced at the Hermitage Theatre and Peterhof. As soon as he entered the palace, with electric rapid steps as if he were at home, he ran up the stairs. He recognized almost every picture, naming them. Oh, a Velásquez, the Madonna with the Cherries, a Raphael, and so on. It surprised me, as for twenty-six years he had not been inside an art gallery. Among our many rounds, visiting old Vienna and its lovely churches, the Sunday visits pleased Vaslav most.

At the imperial chapel, at eleven o'clock, High Mass was held. In this dark, gloomy chapel, adorned with masterpieces, the high clergy celebrated the Mass exactly as it was done during the time of Empress Maria Theresa. The many glittering candles, the heavy sixteenth-century silk brocade worn by the priests, the profusion of flowers on the altar, made an unforgettable impression. The music played by the organist of St. Stephen's Cathedral accompanied by the Viennese Philharmonic; the soloists were members of the Opera, while the Viennese Choirboys accompanied them. Each Sunday we heard a Mass by Handel, Haydn, Mozart, or Schubert.

Vaslav sat quietly on the balcony reserved for the Allied High Command. His face bore an expression of ecstasy. He was at ease and completely happy in this, his element, art and beauty.

be traced to the Russian Ballet. Who could ever equal those dancers who appeared then, in the masterpieces of Petipa, Fokine, and my husband, the originators of the romantic and impressionist school of choreography? Who could equal Pavlova's lightness, her unique points and arabesque? Who could ever equal the pure technique, the dramatic expression of Karsavina? Who could ever match the appearance of Nijinsky, *"Le Dieu de la Danse"*? Who could fly and float through space as he did? Who could achieve the heights of purity and tragic force, his grace, while always being complete master of his art? But the outbreak of the First World War, followed by the Revolution, brought an end to the Russian Ballet.

Diaghileff's own company, which he formed after 1914, was a private enterprise of young, not highly trained artists. Once in a while a real dancer, driven by the Revolution, joined his troupe, which had become a private company and made most interesting experiments with young French and Spanish painters and musicians. But it lacked the real, great dancers, and after all this is the paramount factor in a ballet company. Pavlova's death, Nijinsky's illness, Karsavina's marriage robbed the world of its greatest dancers. I was convinced that performances like theirs could not be repeated. I was wrong. As one ballet followed the other, we could hardly believe our eyes, and unheard-of enchantment unfolded before us.

As was done for the Russian Ballet in 1909, the settings, the costumes were all created by outstanding painters. The classical repertory was danced in perfect style, in dramatic expression, and the technique was like that of the performances at the Mariinsky Theatre during the time of the Tsars. And the dancers—what artists! Vaslav and I looked at each other. Then he drew his chair nearer the stage and forgot everything around him, gazing at Galina Sergeievna Ulanova, who looked as fresh as a rosebud in a June dawn. As soon as she dances, a metamorphosis takes place. At one moment she is Winged Victory, a fairy queen from a childhood dream, then again a Marquise of Fragonard. With each part she has a different body, a new personality. Her slender form seems to grow and shrink before one's eyes. The ease of her movements, her delicacy, her precise austerity give her dancing a religious tone.

In the next ballet she was utterly different. We could hardly believe that it was the same pure-looking girl when she adopted the provoking poses of a seductress. Vaslav, enthralled by her dancing, spontaneously broke into applause.

Ulanova seemed a reincarnation of Taglioni with her superb ethereal motion, of Elssler with her as-eyes, and unheard-of enchantment unfolded before us.

As was done for the Russian Ballet in 1909, the settings, the costumes were all created by outstanding painters. The classical repertory was danced in perfect style, in dramatic expression, and the technique was like that of the performances at the Mariinsky Theatre during the time of the Tsars. And the dancers—what artists! Vaslav and I looked at each other. Then he drew his chair nearer the stage and forgot everything around him, gazing at Galina Sergeievna Ulanova, who looked as fresh as a rosebud in a June dawn. As soon as she dances, a metamorphosis takes place. At one moment she is Winged Victory, a fairy queen from a childhood dream, then again a Marquise of Fragonard. With each part she has a different body, a new personality. Her slender form seems to grow and shrink before one's eyes. The ease of her movements, her delicacy, her precise austerity give her dancing a religious tone.

In the next ballet she was utterly different. We could hardly believe that it was the same pure-looking girl when she adopted the provoking poses of a seductress. Vaslav, enthralled by her dancing, spontaneously broke into applause.

Ulanova seemed a reincarnation of Taglioni with her superb ethereal motion, of Elssler with her as-be traced to the Russian Ballet. Who could ever equal those dancers who appeared then, in the masterpieces of Petipa, Fokine, and my husband, the originators of the romantic and impressionist school of choreography? Who could equal Pavlova's lightness, her unique points and arabesque? Who could ever equal the pure technique, the dramatic expression of Karsavina? Who could ever match the appearance of Nijinsky, *"Le Dieu de la Danse"*? Who could fly and float through space as he did? Who could achieve the heights of purity and tragic force, his grace, while always being complete master of his art? But the outbreak of the First World War, followed by the Revolution, brought an end to the Russian Ballet.

Diaghileff's own company, which he formed after 1914, was a private enterprise of young, not highly trained artists. Once in a while a real dancer, driven by the Revolution, joined his troupe, which had become a private company and made most interesting experiments with young French and Spanish painters and musicians. But it lacked the real, great dancers, and after all this is the paramount factor in a ballet company. Pavlova's death, Nijinsky's illness, Karsavina's marriage robbed the world of its greatest dancers. I was convinced that performances like theirs could not be repeated. I was wrong. As one ballet followed the other, we could hardly believe our

Very soon after the Allied troops occupied Vienna I got busy contacting our friends and lawyers abroad in an effort to obtain visas. I tried Switzerland, France, Great Britain, and America in turn. Having formerly been a resident of London, I obtained repatriation papers from the British. But what about Vaslav? His case was more difficult.

The Swiss promised only a transit visa, if we had a final one. Our friend Laurence Steinhardt, who has been United States Ambassador in various countries during the past decades, to whom I had written, asked the American authorities to do all they could to get us out of Austria to the United States. So once more endless visits to the different offices and correspondence began.

Chapter 15

Encounter with the Soviet Ballet

ONE DAY, when I returned home, I found in our sitting room a young Russian officer with impeccable manners, speaking French and German fluently and without any accent. He was a member of the Russian Political Police. He had come to inquire about Vaslav, his health and his plans. If he needed anything —food or medicine—it would give him great pleasure to give it.

Together with Pavel, we felt rather embarrassed. The officer hinted that it would be desirable if we moved to one of their hotels where Vaslav could obtain all he needed and the best medical care. During our conversation I told him how happy Vaslav was, seeing the ballet performances in Vienna.

"Ah, so Vaslav Fomitch is still interested in his

art. You know at home we have a marvelous treatment invented by Professor Bogomoletz. If he came home I am sure he would get well. He could go to Livadia or to the Caucasus to recuperate. You would have your own home. He would have all the medical attention . . . a private attendant."

I thanked him, but did not commit myself.

He departed, expressing the wish to see Vaslav personally, which I said I could arrange.

The following week we received an invitation to attend a performance at the Ronacher Theatre given for the Russian *Kommandatura*.

An invitation by any of the Allied Command to a civilian in Vienna was at that time an order. It was especially requested that Vaslav should attend. During my conversation with the Russian officer I had mentioned the wonderful performance at the Viennese State Opera House of *Pique Dame* with Madame Hongen and Mr. Schoeffler. So I thought perhaps this opera would be given.

Upon our arrival at the Ronacher Theatre we were led to a box near the stage. The house was crowded by members of the Russian Army. Only a few Austrian artists were in the stalls, including Madame Wiesenthal, the famous Viennese dancer, the directors of the Opera and Burgtheater. The program of the performance was not announced.

Before the curtain was raised our young Russian officer came in. He bowed before Vaslav and said in Russian, "This performance is given as a surprise for you. We hope you will approve and enjoy it."

As the overture opened, we sat up. It was Tchaikovsky's *Nutcracker* suite. A memorable evening began. We had never anticipated that from the ruins of Vienna would arise such an amazing expression of the art of the dance. Only twice before had I seen dancing of such perfection and inspiration. When I had gone to see a small group of dancers in Budapest as a child, members from the Mariinsky Theatre of St. Petersburg had captivated the audience with their grace and beauty. Olga Preobrajenskaya, the dashing Legat brothers, and Maria Petipa were the stars of that unforgettable evening. The perfect dramatic expression, their technique and pure classicism could not be surpassed. They resurrected the majesty, the splendor of Louis XV, in their interpretations of gavottes and minuets. For me this was the first revelation of the choreographic art.

The arrival of the Imperial Russian Ballet in Paris marked the second time I encountered perfect dancing. The troupe, all members of the Mariinsky Theatre too, permanently changed the concepts of the world of dancing, music, painting, and scenic art. I believe the source of inspiration of modern art can tonishing vivacity and precision, of the matchless arabesques and lightness of Pavlova, of Karsavina's admirable technique and dramatic expression. All the great women dancers of the past were embodied in her form. Her Giselle, her Juliet in *Romeo and Juliet,* cannot be equaled. Undoubtedly she is the greatest dancer of our day.

In the next ballet *divertissement,* Madame Kapustina and Boris Borisoff, the two leading character dancers of Russia, appeared. The nonchalance and ease with which they mastered folk dances was amazing. The essence of Poland's soul was personified when they danced the mazurka, with style and abandon. No one who saw it will ever forget the fierce temperament, the fiery color of Kapustina's gypsy dance. It filled us all with nostalgia for the vast steppes, the feeling inspired by the sight of swarthy gypsies around a campfire just after night has fallen.

Kapustina, black eyes flashing, her slim body in a crimson skirt and wide leather belt studded with gold, glittering golden earrings and gleaming bracelets, moved like a panther, whirled, then slowly abated the fury of her dance to a striking climax.

Vladimir Preobrajensky partnered Ulanova. He is a superb dancer trained in the best tradition of the classical style of the Imperial School—or the Soviet Academy of Choreographic Art, as the institution is called now. He reminded us of the best qualities in the dancing of Mordkin at the height of his career. And as for Chibukiani, Sergeiev—what a perfection of elevation! Worthy followers of my husband.

The art of the ballet luckily is not dead. There are still great dancers in this world. I had almost forgotten what dancing was like, since the last World War.

Vaslav did not pay any attention to us. He only gazed and gazed at the stage and after each ballet applauded through the intermissions, just as a young, enthusiastic student would have done. The audience imitated him and cheered.

The performance was concluded by Fokine's *Sylphides,* which Vaslav had created with Karsavina. As they started to dance the variations, Vaslav clutched his hand and followed each step, accompanying their dance with a perceptible movement of his body. A storm of enthusiasm broke loose.

It was next day that we visited Galina Sergeievna Ulanova at the Grand Hotel. We were civilians, and even members of the Allied Forces were not admitted. As we passed between the two soldiers guarding the entrance with submachine guns, I was struck by the strangeness of the world I was entering. Officers of high rank, soldiers, mingled with the artists waiting in the hall. They greeted us with tears in their eyes, their arms full of red roses for the *"Spectre de la Rose."* They crowded around my husband to assure him that they venerated and cherished him still. One could see they all were happy to have Vaslav among them and felt towards him as though he were a divinity.

We followed Galina Sergeievna into her apartment. There she told us how, as a child, she had been taught by her parents, classmates of Vaslav, to revere his art; how the tradition was still being upheld in the Soviet Ballet School, and the same method taught as in the past; how the statues and paintings of great dancers and choreographers—Camargo, Salle, Taglioni, Noverre, Vestris, Vaslav, Pavlova—still adorn the walls and fill the halls as a source of inspiration for the students to respect and honor; how the methods of Petipa, Johannsen, Legat, Cecchetti are taught; how the ideas of Fokine and Nijinsky are kept alive. She told us all about how their present repertory was formed, of all the great ballets of the classical romantic and modern school, their new creations of the ballet, *The Spring,* after Pushkin's story "The Prisoner of the Caucasus," *The Golden Century,* by Shostakovitch, and of her favorite ballet, Prokofiev's *Romeo and Juliet,* with choreography by Levrovsky, the leading choreographer of the Kirov Theatre, the former Mariinsky.

She spoke with great enthusiasm about her other

colleagues, Smjonova, Lepishinskaya, Messerer. She informed us that they were filming each ballet so as to keep intact the choreography and to be able to hand it down to the following generations correctly, and not merely by hearsay, as it had been done until now, and how these films are shown, during the rehearsals and training, in slow motion to enable the dancers to detect their mistakes and to correct them. She further recounted that just as in the past, the top students who pass the final examinations with distinction become members of the Leningrad and Moscow Opera Houses, while the others get engagements throughout the Soviet Union. Each town of over twenty thousand inhabitants has its own ballet company and schools run on the same lines as those in Leningrad.

Galina was charming, a kind, unspoiled child, a great artist with a soul. After talking to her, it seemed as though no changes had taken place since our youth, as though we had been transported into the atmosphere of real art, the great, the golden period of the ballet.

Chapter 16

The American Zone

DURING the following winter and spring, Major Lord Inchcape came to see us from time to time, inquiring when we would be able to leave. Although he had always been more tactful, I understood that his superiors were anxious that we civilians should leave the premises. I felt rather embarrassed, not wishing to abuse the hospitality extended by the British Army. But to obtain an exit permit from Austria and visas for abroad was beyond my control.

Vaslav never asked where and why we were going, never showed any interest in any business matter. In fact, he had taken for granted whatever happened, ever since the day he was first taken to an asylum in 1919. He knew I was there to look after him, and whatever I offered, luxury or poverty, he shared it with contentment.

At the time very few exit permits were given. The

members of the occupation forces were under their
respective military rules and left Austria only on
leave or when they were withdrawn. For ordinary
mortals it was quite exceptional to leave the country.
They were only permitted to go on important governmental missions. The exit permit was issued by the
Allied Council and had to be countersigned jointly
by all the Four Powers. It was unthinkable for us to
submit such a demand. Those who were competent
in the matter felt that the Russian Command would
never allow us to leave, and in fact they wondered
that up till now we had not been sent back to Russia.

I felt it would be beneficial for Vaslav if he could
join Kyra. She had lived in Italy since 1939 and was
now in Florence. Many British and American officers
coming from there had recently brought us news
about her. Knowing that Vaslav was longing to see
her, I tried to obtain a pass through the British
authorities. They were occupying a part of Italy, but
as Vienna was an "international island" in a Russian
ocean, my plan was not feasible. Colonel Yarborough,
true to his word, had been helpful to us ever since
his arrival. He gave us military passes, many useful
gifts, and protection in every way. It was a tremendous relief to know that we had behind us an influential military person to whom we could turn in any
need.

Colonel Yarborough was universally respected and loved in Vienna. He was kind and just to everybody, and to us he was a real guardian angel. So whenever anything troubled me I used to go up to his office at the American Military Police headquarters in the Auersperg Palais.

I went to him to ask his advice as to what we could do to relieve the British of our presence. He very charmingly offered the suggestion that we go to the American Zone, saying that he would supply the necessary passes and transport. He suggested that first I go and select a suitable place for Vaslav. Many estates and castles belonging to foreign citizens were under the custody of the American authorities, and as he said, I could choose among them. He at once telephoned to Salzburg to Captain Taylor, the Chief of the Security Office, who assured him that a list of places which I could inspect at once would be awaiting me.

After Easter, Colonel Yarborough sent me to Salzburg, in his own official car, escorted by his security officers, who were on official business. The car passed the demarcation line without stopping, the Russian guards saluting, allowing us to pass the dividing bridge on the Enns.

For the first time in years I was in an almost free atmosphere. Once more I felt like a person who had a right to say and do as she wanted. The few days I passed in Salzburg as guest of the security officers at their hotel in the Gabelbrau were delightful. They did everything in their power to spoil me and make life agreeable. I went round the Salzburg area and visited many enchanting places around the lovely lakes of Attersee and Wolfgangsee and in the mountainous country. After looking over so many castles I finally chose a castle near the Grossglockner, one of the most beautiful spots in Europe. It was halfway between Kitzbühel and Zell am See. The castle, built in the eleventh century, had many wings. Some had been added later. It perched high up on the cliffs in a secluded spot, surrounded by the Alps dominating the Salzach Valley. The river, with its foaming, bottomless green water, rushed from the glacier towards Salzburg. Deep down the glen snuggled a small village on the banks of the rushing stream winding through the valley.

It was difficult to approach the castle, which towered over the steep cliffs nestling in the green, dark forest with the magnificent view of the Alps. I knew Vaslav would love to live there. It was medieval and romantic, with its drawbridge, dungeons, towers and ramparts, private chapel, banquet hall, and torture chamber, in which in past centuries witches and prisoners were held. The interior of one wing of the castle was transformed into a quite up-to-date residence. Each bedroom had its private bathroom and electricity. The rooms, with lovely painted Renaissance ceilings, looked like heaven to me, especially as in this wing even central heating had been installed. I told the escorting officer that to live here would be too good to be true.

Upon my return, Colonel Yarborough assured me that we should not lack anything and informed the British that soon we would leave for the American Zone. How we would get through there I did not know, but I knew we were in the best of hands and whatever Colonel Yarborough arranged would be the right thing. We did not mention our plan to leave Vienna to anybody. One July morning a large American military car drove up to the Sacher and our luggage was put in.

Vaslav was not in the mood to go out that morning. I waited around with the Americans until we could induce Vaslav to come for a motor drive. Finally he agreed. We drove fast towards Melk and Linz, passing the Russian guards on the road without stopping until we came to the demarcation line, which is the Enns River.

Before we reached it, my heart began to beat furiously, but outwardly I remained calm. I knew that within the next few moments our fate would be de-

cided and it depended upon the Russian officer and
the two guards who lingered at their post near the
bridge. We stopped. The officer looked into the car
and saw us civilians. He asked me who we were.
Where were our passes? I was petrified. I clutched
Vaslav's hand, hoping that he would not answer. If
he said one Russian word I knew he would be turned
back. But he did not pay any attention to the guards.
He was looking at the river, the country around. I
began to talk quickly in German to the cook and
housekeeper whom I had engaged in Vienna and
took along, hoping the guards would think I was
Austrian. Our driver, an American soldier, spoke
Russian fluently. He was working for the American
Intelligence Service. He knew the Russian ways well
and for this reason had been chosen for this task to
take us over to the American Zone. What he answered
I did not know, as they were standing at some distance from our car. I saw him showing some American passes issued by the American Military Police.
The officer listened attentively; then he looked into
the car again and I heard our driver saying, "The
man in the car is insane. We are taking him to an
asylum." The officer waved his hand and the soldiers
opened the gate. We were on the bridge, and within
a few moments on American territory.

After a few days' rest in Salzburg we were taken

up to the castle duly escorted by members of the Security Police. The mayor of the little community was commanded by the Chief of the American Occupation Forces to extend all assistance to us, to see that we lived undisturbed. An awe-inspiring document was placed on the entrance door forbidding anybody to enter without special permission.

Within a few days we were comfortably installed in the south wing of the castle. Vaslav's apartment was on the ground floor. He could walk out of the hall directly to the inner courtyard. His rooms overlooked the chain of Alps and the long valley of the Salzach. It was incredibly beautiful.

The routine of our household was quickly organized, since I had brought along a cook and a housekeeper, and very soon the peasant women, hearing that we had arrived, timidly offered their services. Everybody was anxious to serve in the castle. They knew we were under American protectorate and also that we possessed many treasures in the form of medical supplies, chocolate, sugar, coffee, and all the commodities which they badly lacked. They did not want any salary—only food and clothing.

On the advice of an American officer, I engaged for Vaslav a White Russian officer who had been at one of their camps. Feodor was an elderly man who had left Russia at the outbreak of the Revolution and after many adventures had arrived in France, where he had lived for many years. The Germans took him for forced labor to Hamburg, where he passed the second war, finally to land at the end in one of the American military camps in Bavaria. The Security Police guaranteed his honesty. So I engaged him as a valet. He was lazy and scheming. His entire day was spent in trying to work out plans to organize a revolution in Russia. We only laughed at him. But he spoke Russian and was useful as a valet.

Vaslav was full of fun and happiness. His joy was boundless at the sight of this enchanting place. Like happy children, we ran around the park, the woods, and explored the castle with its dungeons, ramparts, and towers. It had such a romantic atmosphere. Often we went to our little chapel, which we restored and put in order very soon. I even asked the village priest to come and celebrate divine services on Sundays. After that the priest was invited to stay for lunch, joined by a former owner of the castle, who lived in the neighborhood. The castle had belonged to a long-extinct family of Tyrolean Counts who for three hundred years were the landlords and owners of the entire county. After the fourteenth century it became the property of the Archbishopric of Salzburg. The Archbishop resided there in the summer and the

place under his rule was the seat of the Church
authorities. Here the peasants who did not pay their
taxes were imprisoned. The heretics were tortured
and the witches were either thrown down the sword
tower or burned.

While Vaslav loved to walk around the ramparts
to watch the magnificent sunset from the largest
tower, Feodor investigated the cellars, torture chambers, and secret passages. Soon he found one leading
underground, deep down towards the small hamlets
on the opposite side of the valley.

The castle, which in Napoleonic times became the
property of the Count Larisch, finally came to the
last owner, a Herr Philippe, who often visited us
now. He helped us with advice if the fireplace
smoked and informed us where the pumps were
which brought the water up from the spring deep
down under the castle. It was he who told us the
legend that a gold treasure of enormous value was
buried somewhere in or about the castle. This news,
told in Feodor's presence, finished his services. In no
time he vanished. Whenever he was needed the entire staff continuously searched for him.

Feodor made finding the treasure his lifework. All
dreams about starting a Russian revolution were forgotten, and, armed with axes and shovels, he disap-

peared underground. Vaslav thought it great fun, this treasure-hunting, and enjoyed the expeditions like a young boy.

Very soon it became known in the American Zone that we were residing in the castle. Many officers of the American Occupation Forces with their wives asked permission to come to visit us. As the castle was about three hours by motor from Salzburg, I invited them to stay overnight. So very soon we had quite a crowd. The Americans were joined by the French and British from all over the Tyrol and Salzburg, and we had visitors even from Vienna.

During this year we made many agreeable friends. They used to come up in their cars followed by jeeps loaded with all kinds of food and drink. We were provided for, for years to come. Among our many visiting friends, we were most happy to welcome a British lady, Mrs. Marguerite Power, who was attached to the British Element of Vienna. We could never forget her. During the first days of the Occupation in Vienna she had looked us up, bringing the first tea we had had for years. She was not only kind and helpful, but a real authority on the ballet, which is her great hobby. Marguerite became one of our dearest and most loyal friends.

We used to take our guests around to the valleys and hidden mountain lakes. Some climbed the lofty peaks, some motored with us. There was fishing in the Salzach, and there were many gold and emerald mines to be visited. Life became quite gay. I was always busy receiving the guests and preparing the rooms, and much to Vaslav's enjoyment I ran around from the kitchen to the larder, carrying a huge bunch of keys, giving orders, making arrangements while the staff and the peasant girls helped me. It often happened that the departing guests' motors were still in the courtyard while the expected ones arrived. We had a full house.

After so many years of hardships, I felt the change was quite beneficial to Vaslav. He loved to have many gay people around him and could listen to their talk for hours when we were sitting around the fireplace in one of the drawing rooms. He played table tennis with them, and was quite proud when he succeeded in beating his opponents. He applauded them when, after supper, they danced in the huge bar. Our place soon became like a fashionable hotel in full season and not a long-forgotten castle of medieval knights.

We celebrated Christmas quite as in the good old days. A huge, richly decorated Christmas tree, reaching to the ceiling of the banquet hall, was erected. We put tables under it, a large one for the staff, one table for each guest, and another for the natives of the village. All were loaded with presents. Everybody was content and happy, for during the past years none of us had known what Christmas was and meant.

On New Year's Eve we asked the priest to have a midnight Mass. During the afternoon, with Vaslav and the help of our guests, we decorated the chapel. At night, when we all passed through the rampart leading to the chapel, we were greatly impressed. The illuminated castle against the moonlit, lofty, mighty peaks of the Alps made an unforgettable impression. Under the star-studded winter sky, the dark green pine trees bending heavily under their enormous burden of snow, our procession walking through the arcaded passages, candles in our hands, looked very much like Elsa's wedding procession in *Lohengrin*.

As one season followed another, we became so used to this romantic life, so fond of the place, that we had almost forgotten the past. Once more Vaslav was free to go around whenever he liked. For hours he sat in the park or in the courtyard, and we were not obliged to follow or watch him. This was the best thing that could happen to him. For years in the nursing home, he had been watched day and night. Through this constant observation he became very dependent on his companions. Later, during the war, I had to be with him constantly, trying to avert all disagreeable incidents or dangers. So now I was anxious that he should become more and more independent, and therefore I let him alone. After a few months my method brought its result. Vaslav, who during the last twenty-seven years had lost the habit of expressing his desires, now very definitely began to say what he wanted or did not want. He also began to go out alone in the park and even opened the castle gate and sneaked out like a naughty boy. As soon as the gatekeeper or a strolling peasant lad reported this to us, we raced after him, to the forest or the pastures. On the main road leading to Kitzbühel and Zell many military motors raced by and we were afraid to let Vaslav stroll alone. So I pleaded with him not to leave the castle grounds unaccompanied, and he afterwards docilely walked around the court.

About this time I invited Kyra to come and visit us and arranged through the French and American authorities the necessary passes for her. We motored up to Innsbruck and the Brenner Pass to meet her. We were snowed in by a heavy blizzard for two days in the mountain inn waiting for her in vain. On none of the incoming trains could we find her.

Late in the winter I had the opportunity, through the courtesy of the French authorities and commander, to get a pass to Paris. It was the first time since the beginning of the war that I was permitted to leave Austria. The reason for which I undertook this trip was to try to obtain the necessary visas for Vaslav and to prepare a place where he could go to live. To my utter amazement, I did not find Paris as I had expected, as it was after the First World War. It was a depressing place at the time; and although Paris had not lost anything of its charm and the Parisians were as wonderful as ever, I noticed that the country had gone through an ordeal and great privations and at the time it was not the land where a person needing care and peace should settle. So after making preliminary arrangements for Vaslav's trip, I returned to Austria. During the journey I paid a short visit to Switzerland and to our family doctor in Zurich, Professor Dr. Rohr, who had attended Vaslav in the past. I reported to him all that had happened to us and especially about Vaslav's physical health. I told him that the village doctor noticed that his blood pressure was too high. Professor Rohr prescribed a diet and told me to bring Vaslav along as soon as possible for a real check-up. So, as soon as I returned home I got busy obtaining permission for the trip. But this involved so many new demands that I had to contemplate another trip to Bern and Paris.

As soon as I was back, the usual visiting crowd began to come. Among our friends were many refugees from Hungary who had lived in Salzburg. Count Teleky, a lifelong friend, came with his sister and brother-in-law, who was of Russian descent. Members of the Swiss Consulate also visited us, and I tried to get Vaslav permission to stay a few days in Zurich. But the endless red tape worked very slowly. While we waited for some news, I went down to Salzburg. It was here that I again met a charming Hungarian young lady, a friend of ours, Marian Boldog. She was also a refugee from the south of Hungary. She had been through the whole tribulation of the war and had fled from the invading forces through Sopron to Salzburg. Here she had made the acquaintance of a young American GI, Rex Luna, who was in charge of provisions at the Gabelbrau when I arrived there with Vaslav. He was very kind and saw to it that Vaslav had all he needed. I could not forget this, and when I heard from them that finally they had obtained permission to marry I proposed that their wedding should be held in our castle.

The village priest was summoned. The young peasant children were dressed up in their national costumes. The chapel was decorated with alproses. The American guests came in great numbers, and the castle, as in medieval times, hummed with activity and gaiety. The unusual activity in the courtyard and banquet hall amused Vaslav, who happily mingled with the guests and helped in the preparation of the festivities. For three days we celebrated the romantic wedding, as it had been the custom in every self-respecting castle in past centuries. But to remain here in Austria eternally was not our aim, even though life had been made as pleasant as possible for us. At the time nobody was certain what would happen. Peace treaties seemed remote and nobody expected peaceful conditions.

So once more, during the early summer of 1947, I went to Switzerland and France, and this time also to England, to obtain visas for Vaslav. With the help of the French commander in Austria and Sir Alfred Duff Cooper, the British Ambassador in Paris, this time I succeeded. The British Government gave Vaslav permission to stay in England indefinitely. So at last his way back to the west was open. After a warm, sunny autumn, we closed the castle, "Nash Zamok" (our castle), as Vatza used to call it. The following November, when the first snow fell, we said good-by to this enchanting place, where we had spent such a romantic interlude.

Chapter 17

Great Britain

WE BOARDED the Arlberg Express at Kitzbühel,
which was French territory. Our exit passes were
signed by the French commander, as we intended to
go via Switzerland to France. Through this subterfuge it was possible for us to leave Austria without
the Allied exit permit, as General Béthouard was
omnipotent on French territory.

The train coming from Vienna was delayed. We
waited at the small, snowed-in station. A few French
officers lingered around. Pavel attended to everything, the stamping of the passes, tickets and luggage, while I asked Vaslav to wait in the motorcar
which was pulled up near the platform.

It was clear winter weather, and although at last
the day had dawned for which I had been hoping and
praying for so many years, my heart was sad. Every
time we had to move I felt depressed. When are we

going to have peace at last, a real home? We had been wishing for one for a lifetime. Vaslav's illness in 1919 had shattered all our life. Ten years ago it seemed as though we would succeed, and then the Second World War threw us back. But we were saved during the air raids. We were not crippled. And so I thought I had no right to be dissatisfied. Vaslav was on the way to mental recovery, and I was quite proud to show him to the Swiss doctors. I was sure they would be delighted to see the improvement.

During my stay in England, it was arranged with an old childhood acquaintance of mine, a film magnate, that we should make a picture of one of my stories, and he signed me up. He also promised that he would see to it that Vaslav and I could proceed to the United States. "Don't worry, just come to England. I will see to everything once you are here." I knew that there were quite a number of Vaslav's colleagues in London, including Karsavina and Madame Legat, and I hoped to form a small artistic circle in our home which would give Vaslav much pleasure and stimulate interest in him.

Now, Vaslav looked anxiously out of the car. As always, he was pleased to travel. He loved journeys, but he was also subconsciously frightened at every change, not being quite sure what would happen to him. I felt and knew this. So I waited with him at the car, and when I had to go to the customs, I came back every few minutes to assure him that all was well and soon we would be leaving.

Vaslav was only relieved when we were finally settled in our compartment. It was a pleasant trip and all went well except when we stopped at St. Anton am Arlberg. A band was waiting at the station to welcome a few Austrian soldiers, natives of St. Anton, who had just returned from Russia, having been prisoners there. The indescribable noise which the band and the receiving committee made frightened Vaslav, and he regained his composure only when the train pulled out.

We arrived in Zurich late at night and went straight to the Hirschlanden Clinic, where Professor Rohr had a suite reserved for us. Here we wanted to make a thorough check-up on Vaslav's physical condition. The very competent male nurse I had engaged to accompany us to England unfortunately had taken a day off on the very day when the examinations were to be made. Professor Rohr, who was anxious not to annoy Vaslav too much, did not make a blood test. His report was good in general, although he noticed, too, that Vaslav's blood pressure for his age was too high and prescribed a strict diet and medicine. In 1935 in Kreuzlingen, it had already been noticed by a German heart specialist that Vaslav showed signs of the beginning of arteriosclerosis, but the doctors who had attended him since then doubted the correctness of this diagnosis.

Now, after nine years, we had proof that the insulin shock was successful, as Vaslav had remained *sociable* all these years and his mental condition had improved steadily. The doctors admired his wonderful musculature and felt it amazing that in spite of the fact that he had not practiced for so many years he was still so athletic and fit. They recommended a quiet life without worry or distractions and the effort to continue to interest him and lead him back to a normal life as we had done in the past seven years.

There was a strike on the French railways and we were not quite sure if we could get through, so we decided to go straight through Basle to London.

The French and British immigration and customs authorities, with the utmost courtesy, allowed Vaslav to go through. The sea was stormy, and much to Vaslav's amusement, we all lay in our cabins quite seasick while he nursed us, which was quite a change, and much fun for him.

We arrived in Dover late at night, and as we motored up to London through the deep fog, a feeling of depression took hold of me.

For a few days we remained in London. Vaslav was thrilled at the sight of the town where he had had so many triumphs. Time did not mean as much to him as it did to us. And although, once in a while, when he wanted to tease me, he called me *"Staria Kukelka"* ("Old Doll"), I do not think he was quite aware of the fact that two decades had passed since he had been in England. He only knew that his recollections of his former stay in England were good, and therefore he was exceedingly pleased to be back.

During the following three years the English authorities were kind and thoughtful, and Vaslav at last found a real asylum and complete freedom. Nobody ever worried him. The people who came in contact with him treated him with the same courtesy that they would have if he had never been mentally ill, and he responded with normal behavior. During his entire stay in England he never became excited or upset, as he had done once in a while in the past.

We decided to live in the country and went first to a place near London—about twenty miles away. Here a well-known shooting lodge, built in the time of Queen Elizabeth, had been transformed into a smart country hotel. I knew the place and remembered that the few week-ends I had passed there had been agreeable. So we went to stay there.

This old house in Tudor style pleased Vaslav, but the attendant and I were not so happy. Although we had four rooms, we were not as free as we would have been in a private home. We were meeting strangers constantly, and the food seemed to us most unsuitable for someone who had to be on a diet.

So I went house-hunting once more. We passed a dreary winter playing chess and cards, taking walks and visiting the near-by cinemas, which Vaslav enjoyed immensely. He was greatly impressed by technicolor, which he saw here for the first time. *The Ideal Husband,* with Paulette Goddard, delighted him.

I extended invitations to Karsavina, Madame Legat, and a few others to come and visit us. Madame Legat came at once. She was as kind and friendly as she had been in the old days. Nadia Legat, the widow of our dear *Maestro,* Vaslav's beloved teacher, understood the situation at once. She encouraged Vaslav to be his old self, and talked to him in Russian of his youthful days in the Imperial School and at the Mariinsky. She found the way to his heart. Of all those who came in contact with Vaslav she was the one who came the nearest to him these last few years. She sized up his feelings, his timidity, and knew very well how to handle him. For Nadia, Vaslav had never been ill. She felt that he was a genius, far ahead of us, on a different level of mentality, and that there was fundamentally nothing wrong with him. I am sure that she was right.

Nadia visited us frequently. Vaslav welcomed her visits, as at last, after twenty-eight years, there was somebody who was competent in the art of choreography, an artist to whom he could talk. I am sure that during all those years Vaslav must have missed his fellow artists. Nadia always knew how to interest him, and when she expressed the desire for Vaslav to dance and admired his wonderful thighs and feet, Vatza just laughed and said, "Oh, I have lost the habit."

When spring came we moved to a charming English country house which I had found near Sunningdale in Windsor Great Park. Here very soon we began to lead the life of an English family. Our days passed calmly and uneventfully. Vaslav spent his days taking long walks in the forest or sitting in the garden. We motored around and took occasional excursions to Windsor Castle and other places of interest, and we usually stopped in the quaint English inns for tea.

During the past years of Vaslav's illness I had deliberately kept him in ignorance of every disagreeable and painful occurrence. Although I am a truthful person—perhaps too frank—I never told him that his mother and Diaghileff had died years before. Vaslav never asked, but it was my belief that he was inhibited about inquiring about persons or matters which touched him deeply. So once in a while I told him a merciful story, saying, "Babucha [Grandmother] sends you her love. She has written me asking how you are. She can't come to see you because she is too old, but we will go and visit her one day."

I also spoke often of Bronia and Kyra, explaining their continuous absence by the fact that they were too busy, on account of their careers. Vaslav smiled, pretending to believe, but I felt that he knew the unpalatable truth. I hoped that in the near future Bronia would come to Europe to visit us. I made efforts to get Kyra to England, but I am sure she never realized what her visit would have meant to her father. I placed her photo on the table near the armchair where Vaslav used to sit in the drawing room. The first few months he admired it, and then, later, when her visit did not materialize, he would brush it aside or turn it over as soon as he came into the room. He resented her absence.

Vaslav soon became a familiar figure in the neighborhood. As the English are usually discreet, nobody bothered or stared at him; but when they saw him smile, they greeted him and were friendly. The children would stop, and so did Vaslav, and he began to play with them.

Mr. Wollheim, Diaghileff's manager, who had known Vaslav since his first visit to London, asked us to visit the ballet performances which were given during the season. So did Sir Charles Cochrane. We dropped into the habit of motoring up to London to attend the various shows and ballets.

The press photographers, who frequently asked us to be allowed to take photos, had luck with Vatza. As he was used to being photographed, he invariably good-humoredly acquiesced to their demand.

We went to see Ram Gopal, the great Indian dancer, perform with his company. Very few people ever understood his great art so well as Vaslav did. He was extremely interested in every movement, in every phase of his dancing, and as he came into our box during intermission to have tea with us, Vaslav greeted him as an old friend. There was a strong secret link between the two, a spiritual and artistic understanding.

As the season went on, Carmen Amaya and her company of Spanish dancers came, so I proposed to Vaslav that we should go. I knew that when we were in Spain Vaslav attended many performances of native dancers and was a great admirer of Pastora Imperio. Amaya's company was quite interesting, but it was Lussilo's dancing which delighted Vaslav, and he applauded him enthusiastically.

For a few months we had to interrupt our theatrical visits. A series of unfortunate events happened to

us. I have never been superstitious but almost became
so then. One summer day the horseshoe which hung
over the entrance fell down. I did not like it, as subconsciously I had a foreboding of some misfortune.
The staff laughed and I tried to assure myself that it
was just stupid nonsense, but shortly after I fell headlong down the stairs and tore a ligament. I was
laid up and Vaslav, as always when I became ill, was
restless and nervous and dissatisfied. He took my foot
in his hand tenderly and was full of attention when
he came to sit near me. For eight months I was crippled and unable to walk. I was hardly beginning to
go around on crutches when the attendant gave notice.
This was a dreadful blow to me, as Vaslav liked him
and he had proved to be the right person and took
wonderful care of him. But no amount of pleading
helped, and he left.

It was impossible to find a trained male nurse in
London. The one who came from Switzerland to replace the old one was so incompetent and annoyed
Vaslav so much that I had to let him go. So once
more I had to be the constant attendant. With my
bad leg, it was very difficult, especially since I could
not accompany Vaslav on long walks. During our
stay in England we had two family doctors in constant attendance: Dr. Csato, a Hungarian, and Dr.
Wilson, who lived near us. They came regularly to

examine Vaslav and to look out for his blood pressure, which had become almost normal for a while. We were also in constant touch with Professor Rohr. They all assured me that everything about him seemed all right.

On top of all the misfortune which had befallen us, my contact with the film company suddenly ceased. The picture they contemplated did not materialize and I was put off their payroll. This was a considerable blow to us. Vaslav, of course, did not know this and I did not tell him. I had to keep running the household in the manner which he had been used to, which meant a great expense, but I wanted him to have the same standard of living which he had been used to when he had danced.

I have had to endure a great many criticisms in my life—even hostility. A little group of Diaghileff's former friends first spread the rumor which became almost a legend and has been repeated to this day. They criticized my literary activities and the fact that I was lecturing, and they resented the fact that I did not disappear with Vaslav into oblivion and accused me of exploiting his name in order to make money. If my efforts and work can be called "exploiting," then they were right. I took up the fight, and although I had never been trained to work in my youth I began to earn money as well as I could. But I was obliged to do it for my husband. In spite of all the hostility and criticism of the dancers and some balletomanes, I am happy I did it. It was my duty to my husband and a tribute to a genius.

I found out very soon that the hostility was not only aimed at me. Unbelievable as it may seem, there was and is a small group of ballet experts who made it their business to belittle Vaslav as an artist. They have never seen him dance. They never knew the real Russian ballet. All their knowledge about choreographic art is from hearsay and from books, although they are today considered leading authorities on ballet in England and the United States. They have surrounded themselves with dancers who still resent my husband's genius. They either write about him belittlingly or purposely omit his name from the ballet books, as though Nijinsky had never existed. Although a dancer's fame is ephemeral and he is unable to leave proofs of his gifts to future generations, and in spite of all these malicious people, Vaslav's greatness cannot be undone. I was embittered by the attitude of the dancers, and with the exception of Madame Legat, they had not behaved towards Vaslav as he deserved. But when I went into Vaslav's sitting room and he looked up from his drawings, which he had started to do again, and smiled at me with such charm and tenderness, I forgot everybody and everything. He radiated such naïve purity, he was so candid, that one felt purified. The bitterness caused by the calumnies, the corrupt and ungrateful world, dissolved in his ever-forgiving presence.

Vaslav had a soul so great, so pure, that the manifestation of his spirit could only be approached humbly by us human beings. He had showered much beauty upon the world through his art and dancing in the past, and since his illness his very being had uplifted all those who came in contact with him.

It gave me the most perfect happiness to sit quietly in the same room with him. One felt protected, content, in his presence, he emanated so much tenderness and goodness.

Often I worried about what would become of him should something happen to me, and I decided it was time that I bought a house to make a permanent home where he could remain, as I did not wish that any relative ever should send him back to a nursing home. Quite alone at the time, I could not carry out my project, and therefore I spoke to a few persons in the ballet world. I encountered the utmost hostility, and there were even people who exploited my husband's name for their commercial shows.

Vaslav's former attendant decided to return during the summer, and once more the long walks which Vatza had enjoyed so much were undertaken. When they crossed the garden, Vatza would look up and wave to me at my window. I had noticed that lately, while walking, he had been holding his hand over the back of his hip. I mentioned this to the attendant. He had noticed it too. We told this to the doctors, who thought it must be either a habit from his dancing days or a neurological pain.

I often asked Vaslav if he felt all right. He invariably said, *"Da, da, ya choustoui haraso."* ("Yes, yes, I am all right.") He never complained about himself, and only once in a while, when he was very silent, he said, "My head aches."

During the autumn Vaslav sat for a young Polish sculptor who made his bust, and also, much to his interest, took a cast of his feet. Then one day Madame Legat phoned and asked us to come to her school so Vaslav could become the godfather of the little daughter of a young dancer—which he did. We went to the christening. Vaslav, greatly impressed by the Russian Orthodox service, which he had attended so many times in the Imperial School, went through the whole service most patiently, while he played with the little baby. After the service the pupils of the dancing school performed for him, and he encouraged them in their work.

Vatza was always patient and helpful to children and young dancers who showed talent and an earnest

desire to work hard and devote themselves to the art
of dancing, but he was a strict master when he noticed
that dancing was a mere pretext to attain other aims
—fame, money, or a career through the stage. To him
dancing was sacred, and therefore he discouraged
dilettantism.

One day I took him along to the performance of a
ballet company that had been much heralded, wonderfully publicized, and ably managed by an excellent lady business organizer. The company sadly
lacked male dancers; the *corps de ballet* had not had
proper training, each one dancing for himself to a
different tempo. One hardly could take them seriously. As soon as the curtain was raised and *Swan Lake*
began, Vaslav, sat back, shook his head, and said,
"Nye haraso, nye haraso." ("No, no, not good.") It
was heartbreaking to see that in spite of the tremendous interest which had manifested itself in ballet
during the last twenty years all over the world, in
spite of the many young dancers who shoved ability,
there was a tremendous decline in choreographic art.
This is probably due to the fact that nowhere on the
European or the American continent is there a school
similar to the Imperial School of Dancing. The many
excellent dancing teachers cannot train great dancers
in their private schools; neither can they develop
their pupils at these schools—pupils who have outside

interests and concentrate on obtaining a contract quickly somewhere.

The many ballet companies all over the world unfortunately do not have a very high standard, and the talented dancers who join them sooner or later are spoiled by overwork and the scarcity of eminent choreographers.

As time passed by, I began to realize that our trip to the United States was more remote than ever, although during the years we spent in Great Britain I had left nothing undone to obtain it. Now it depended on whether I would be able to obtain an affidavit for Vaslav from somebody residing in the United States. I had written to former friends and world-famous conductors and artists in the United States, who in the past had worked with Vatza or were friends, but none of them was helpful. I realized also that Vaslav needed a change of climate as well as a more varied diet; owing to the food restrictions in England, it was almost impossible to look after him as one should. So I decided to take him on a vacation to the mountains of Switzerland later in the year.

Chapter 18

Last Days

THE AUTUMN was warm and full of sunshine—a real Indian summer. We picnicked a great deal in Windsor Great Park, and with house guests who frequently came to spend week-ends with us we used to go to pick the berries and sweet chestnuts in the woods. Vaslav liked those gay gatherings and followed us to the kitchen when we were making the jams and chestnut creams. If he was very pleased with the dishes we prepared, he rewarded us with a little minuet or a czardas, and as we applauded him he pirouetted away giggling. All these last years he would call me "Kukla" (Doll), and when he was very satisfied with me he said "Kukelka" (Little Doll). Whenever anything troubled him he came straight to me.

One morning in the late sunny autumn, he was sitting in the garden basking in the sunshine and listening to a concert which was being broadcast on his little portable radio, while I was in the sitting room working on one of my books. Suddenly he ran to me. He had an attack of hiccups. I gave him some water to drink, asking him to swallow it in small gulps nine times, as I had seen it done during my childhood in Hungary. But the attack did not stop. I called up our private physician, Dr. Wilson. He was out. I immediately called up two other physicians in London, who advised me what drug to give him and said that the attack was of no importance, that it was simply an irritation of the diaphragm.

But during the following days the attack returned and I phoned Professor Rohr in Zurich for advice. He told me to have a check-up by a prominent physician in London and to send him the result of his analysis.

I knew that Professor J. Plesch, formerly a great authority in Berlin, who had been practicing in London for the last twenty years, still lived here, although he had retired from practice. Professor Plesch was a great patron of art and admired and loved artists, so I called him up and asked him if he would see Vaslav. Immediately he consented, and we motored to town to see him.

Professor Plesch was the first person who enlightened me by saying that "High blood pressure is not a disease in itself, but a symptom, and it is essential that we should find out the underlying cause, as one has to try to cure this." He ordered several laboratory tests, but I informed him they had been made regularly and showed him the analyses. He looked at Vaslav again and said, "Well, I don't think the kidneys are quite in order. We must put him on a still stricter diet, and after six weeks I will see again."

Around the middle of December I was advised that my mother, who was eighty-nine years old, had suddenly become ill, and I was called by wire to Hungary. For a few days I hesitated as to whether I should fly to her or not. But upon my inquiries of competent officials, I was advised that although I could go, nobody was able to guarantee my exit from Hungary. Of course, under the circumstances I could not go and leave Vaslav. On Christmas Day I received the news that my mother had died. It was a dreadful shock to me. Although for many years I did not live near her and there had been misunderstanding between us in the past, she was my mother, and I simply could not grasp the fact that she who had always been, had suddenly ceased to exist.

The new year again brought complications, as the lease on the house expired at the end of January. We tried to find another place somewhere in the country and even went as far as Sussex and Kent.

When the end of January approached I was really

worried. I could not take Vaslav to a hotel, as it would have been impossible to keep him on a diet there. A nursing home was equally unfeasible, for this would have been a psychological shock to him, which we must avoid. He loved his home, "Dom Nash Dom" ("home, our home"), as he used to say. I begged the owner of the place to renew our lease for three months, to give me time to find something suitable, but he was immovable, in spite of the fact that I explained to him that Vaslav must have special care which we could give him only in a private home.

On January 30th I still did not know where to go, and while we were packing, Vaslav melancholically said, *"Kak Cigansky"* ("like gypsies"). Yes, indeed, we were like the gypsies, wandering from one country to the other, from one place to the other. In the end I took Vaslav with the attendant for a few days to the same country hotel where we had lived at first. Then, as though out of the blue, a perfect stranger, Major Wright, who had heard of our predicament through some estate agent, called me up, saying, "I have a house near the sea, not far from Arundel. It has central heating. It is small, but very pleasant in the spring. I would be glad to lend it to Mr. Nijinsky." I gratefully accepted his offer.

We motored down in a dreadful gale, the wind

howling. It was an atrocious drive. When we moved, as always, Vaslav was puzzled and nervous. After a few days, somehow we settled down, and when the sun began to shine and the first crocuses began to bloom, we were more cheerful. I noticed that Vaslav's face was flushed once in a while. The attendant said he was sunburnt because he had been walking near the sea without a hat. Unfortunately, Professor Plesch became ill and could not receive us. His secretary advised me to get somebody else, and informed me that Professor Rohr had replied to them after receiving the analysis, recommending a Swiss medicament and that we should continue the diet prescribed by Professor Plesch.

So I was calmed. I knew that they were great authorities in their field. Vaslav had seemed very quiet and silent lately. To amuse and distract him, we continued our visits to the places of interest around the country and used to stroll in the park of Arundel Castle. Vaslav did not seem to enjoy his walks and would sit down quickly when we reached a bank.

One morning the telephone rang. Serge Lifar, *maître de ballet* of the Paris Opéra, spoke from Paris, and asked me whether Vaslav would come to Paris in the spring to attend a gala ballet performance which the Opéra intended to give for the purpose of raising funds for a new grave and monument for August Vestris, the celebrated dancer of the eighteenth century.

Vaslav immediately consented, as Lifar said that his presence would help the cause enormously. But when Serge mentioned the aim of the performance I had an uneasy feeling.

Some days later he phoned again that the performance would be set early in June. This suited us, as I wanted to go with Vaslav to Paris in May on our way to the mountains in Switzerland. Here in England he was so isolated, the artists neglected him. I was sure that in Paris the dancers would be different.

We had always liked Lifar, with his spontaneous temperament. One could feel that he was a real artist and friend. Serioja also mentioned that on April 2nd he would arrive from Paris with the ballet of the Opéra to give a performance on television, asking Vaslav to attend it. I promised he would.

I went up to London to attend to some business, and as usual I phoned home once or twice every day to find out how Vaslav felt and if he wished anything. The attendant informed me that Vaslav had had a slight indisposition of no importance, but they would come up Sunday. I told him to call in a doctor, but he said it was not necessary.

Sunday morning I went to the airport to receive

Lifar and after lunch to Waterloo Station to receive
Vaslav. He waved to me gaily as he saw me on the
platform.

Later in the afternoon Serge came up to the hotel
where we were staying. He brought a friend along
and we passed a very gay and pleasant afternoon.
Vaslav was delighted to have with him a fellow artist
and countryman. The French gentleman who had accompanied Seroja saw Vaslav for the first time.
When I escorted them to the elevator, he said to me,
"I am so amazed at how fit Vaslav looks. He is quite
a young man, and so sociable. It is really wonderful."

The British Broadcasting Corporation also invited
us to attend the rehearsal of the television show in the
afternoon of the following day.

In the morning Vatza complained of a headache,
but said he would like to go out. Our first visit was
to the Wallace Collection. Vatza went from picture
to picture and stood for a long time before the picture
of the ballerina Camargo by Lancret.

At lunch in a restaurant Vaslav was very gay and
signed a few photographs which were brought to him
to autograph.

We spent the entire afternoon at the Alexandra
Palace watching the rehearsal of the Paris Opéra
ballet for television. It immensely interested Vaslav,
who adored mechanical inventions and was thrilled

by this new invention. Near Vaslav's feet the chief engineer had placed a television set where he could watch the performance at the same time that he watched the dancing on the stage.

Anna Viroubova, whom we had already seen in the original version of *Les Sylphides* some months ago, now being a member of the Paris Opéra, danced. Her dancing enchanted Vaslav, who smiled to her all the time.

The rehearsal was interrupted by the tea which Mr. Norman Collins, manager of the television, offered us. Serge and a few high officials of the company were present, and Vaslav seemed cheerful and happy.

When we returned home that evening, Vatza retired at once and had a light supper. I chatted with the attendant, as we noticed that he closed his eyes and did not wish to talk to us. Suddenly I noticed that he clutched his hands, and then with the fingers of one hand he tapped on the other some dancing movements as he used to do many years ago when he was composing and concentrating on a new bit of choreography. "How strange," was my impression. Then suddenly with his left arm he began to make *porte de bras* around his head as he used to do while dancing *Le Spectre de la Rose*.

The attendant just nodded and said that Mr. Nijinsky had been very deeply impressed, no doubt, by this afternoon's performance. "I think it is better if we leave him quiet."

We were supposed to return home the next day, but I felt it would be advisable to see our own physician first. I called him around ten o'clock. He said he would come as soon as he was finished with his office hours. I asked him to come at once. Vaslav had no temperature, but he refused to eat and lay limply on his bed. His pulse was slightly faster than usual. I began to telephone around to my acquaintances in an effort to find a reliable doctor. It was already about three in the afternoon. Finally a very good Hungarian doctor was recommended to me. He had been practicing in Germany and London lately. I called him and asked him to come at once. As soon as I hung up the receiver, Dr. Csato, our family doctor, arrived. He examined Vaslav and said there was nothing serious.

"But, Doctor, see how apathetic he is—and unable to keep any food."

"Oh, that is nothing unusual." And prescribing a house remedy, he left, assuring me that I was overanxious.

He had hardly left us when the other doctor arrived. His diagnosis was utterly different. He was alarmed by Vaslav's high blood pressure and took a blood test. He told me that until he got the report from the tests, he would be unable to begin any treatment, as he might give the wrong medicine. He was not sure what had caused Vaslav's condition and said, "If he is suffering from arteriosclerosis, then he will need just a few injections. But if this is not the case, and he is suffering from the kidneys, we will be facing a far more difficult task."

I begged him to do something at once, but he said he could not. I began to lose faith in all these doctors and phoned to Zurich, but Professor Rohr did not answer. I wired him. The hours passed. Vaslav was lying listlessly while I frantically telephoned around for medical help.

The next afternoon the other doctor returned and said the report was worse than he had anticipated. We decided that Vaslav should be taken to a clinic the next day where treatment would be given. The doctor told me that he had to find a place for him, as clinics and hospitals were overcrowded, and gave instructions that we should dress Vatza the next morning and take him by taxi. He wished to avoid an ambulance so as not to alarm Vatza.

I received the answer from Zurich that Professor Rohr had left some days ago for his Easter vacation for an unknown destination. As I had the utmost confidence in him, I tried the Swiss broadcasting station and asked them to broadcast the announcement that Professor Rohr was requested to fly to Vaslav. But my call was in vain.

It still did not penetrate into my brain that Vaslav's life might be in danger. Tremblingly I went up to his room. He was sitting up in his bed, for the first time in two days, and looking at the illustrated papers, smilingly and quite interested. The attendant and I were much relieved. But the night was bad and Vaslav was restless in the morning. His face became quite pinched and flushed and he did not respond to any of our questioning. He seemed dazed. We were unspeakably worried and summoned an ambulance. Never will I forget it, as we took him to the clinic wrapped up in blankets looking like a new-born baby, listless and helpless.

It was Thursday morning. Doctors came and began to treat him. They brought streptomycin and told me that Vaslav was in a coma, but if they succeeded in pulling him out within twenty-four hours he would be saved. What happened then I cannot remember. I was dazed myself. The doctor told me I was free to call any other physician to consult, which we did. The next physician said Vaslav was beyond human help. His kidneys were gone.

I tried Zurich again to obtain some other authority. I stood by Vatza's bed while the attendant held his left hand, which was bandaged and through which food and medicines were constantly administered intravenously. But he was quite unconscious. His eyes were closed all the time.

During the night a priest came. I don't know who called him. While the house physician, who was very helpful, took me to the other room, the priest administered the last sacraments. I was kneeling down and did not understand anything of what was going on around me. I heard the priest saying, "Pray with me for your husband." The words hardly penetrated to my brain. I did what I was told like an automaton. Vaslav moaned constantly and with his free hand he was wiping his face. The night passed. I was trembling. The anguish I felt was inexpressible.

Good Friday dawned. Vaslav's face had become more normal. He did not pant any more. The doctors said he was better. The streptomycin had begun to act. He was coming out of the coma and understood what was going on around him. We all should be careful what we said. The doctor even said he would again take up the fight against the illness, as there was hope.

Later Vatza again began making movements with

his arms as in *Le Spectre de la Rose*. Then suddenly he said, "Mamasha" ("Mother"). I don't know whether he was calling his mother or me. And then he stretched out his right hand to me for me to kiss it. I bent down and kissed it.

During the night Vaslav seemed better, and in the morning he was conscious. He opened his eyes. They were clear and lovely. He looked at me with a tender, loving gaze.

The nurses were all hopeful. He had his breakfast and seemed to have passed the crisis.

Later, after Vaslav had taken breakfast, the head nurse assured me that all was now well. The other nurses, too, were hopeful and, the crisis apparently passed, the doctors had gone, although only over my protests. Then, suddenly, another nurse dashed into the room saying that Vaslav's attendant wanted me.

When I came into Vatza's room, he was sitting up in the arms of the attendant, who was shouting desperately, "Look, look!"

I saw immediately that something was wrong. I ordered the nurses to give him an injection, some oxygen. Vatza sighed just once. The sun beamed through the window. The nurses stood by helpless, while the attendant laid Vatza back. His eyes, his mouth closed. He seemed to stretch, while in my mind thoughts and feelings were racing: "You were privileged among so many millions of women to share his life, to serve him. God gave him to you. He has taken him back."

New York, 1952.

Index

Index

Index

Index

Index

Index

A Note about the Author

A good deal about the author—her life and her character —is very self-evident in the pages of this book and in Nijinsky, *the biography of her husband that she published in 1934. It was the endless and unself-conscious devotion shown in this biography that inspired the late Otto H. Kahn to call her "the most loyal woman but the greatest fool that ever lived."*

On the paternal side, Mme. Nijinsky comes from a line of distinguished Hungarian patriots and scholars. Her mother, Emilie de P. Markus, was the foremost tragedienne of the Hungarian stage. Romola herself was educated at the State School of Budapest and the Sorbonne in Paris. She was trained as an actress by Réjane, Le Bargy, and Lucien Guitry, of the Comédie Française, and in ballet by Cecchetti, of the Imperial School of St. Petersburg, and by her husband, Vaslav Nijinsky.

She is a well-known lecturer on the dance, and is at present engaged in writing a history of the subject in terms of the greatest dancers and choreographers of the past. She makes her home in New York City.

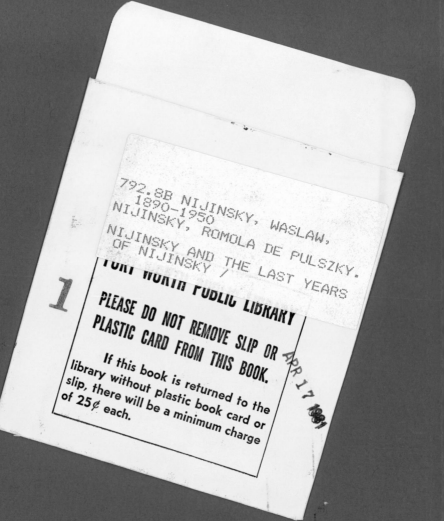